MAGILL'S
LITERARY ANNUAL

1982

# MAGILL'S LITERARY ANNUAL

## 1982

*Essay-Reviews of 200 Outstanding Books
Published in the United States during 1981*

---

*With an Annotated Categories Index*

Volume Two
Los-Z

*Edited by*
FRANK N. MAGILL

**SALEM PRESS**
**Englewood Cliffs**

LIBRARY OF CONGRESS CATALOG CARD NO. 77-99209

ISBN 0-89356-282-3

First Printing

PRINTED IN THE UNITED STATES OF AMERICA

# LOST IN AMERICA

*Author:* Isaac Bashevis Singer (1904-    )
Translated from the Yiddish by Joseph Singer
*Publisher:* Doubleday & Company (Garden City, New York). Illustrated. 259 pp.
$17.95
*Type of work:* Autobiography
*Time:* The 1930's
*Locale:* Poland and America

*The third volume in the author's ongoing "spiritual autobiography"*

The mere existence of Isaac Bashevis Singer's *Lost in America*—in English translation, in a large printing—confirms one of the great hidden laws of twentieth century literature. This law can best be stated with recourse to the Gospels: "For whosoever will save his life shall lose it: but whosoever will lose his life for my sake, the same shall save it." It applies to many writers who otherwise have little in common: to Franz Kafka, whose parables and enigmatic tales were virtually all unpublished when he died, who asked his best friend Max Brod to burn all his manuscripts; to James Joyce, who followed *Ulysses* (1922), a book which asked its readers to learn to read in an entirely new way, with seventeen years spent composing *Finnegans Wake* (1939); to Aleksandr Solzhenitsyn, who, under a death-sentence from cancer after years in labor camps, in exile in Asian Russia, wrote his manuscripts in a microscopic script and hid them every night. It applies also to Isaac Bashevis Singer, who chose to imprison himself in a dying language, to write about a culture that no longer exists. All of these writers have been read by millions and will continue to be read for generations to come.

*Lost in America* is the third volume in Singer's ongoing "spiritual autobiography," following *A Little Boy in Search of God* (1976) and *A Young Man in Search of Love* (1978). Like all of Singer's works, it is translated from the Yiddish; like the two preceding volumes in the series, it is a beautifully produced book, elegantly bound, printed on fine heavy paper, and marvelously illustrated with paintings and drawings by Raphael Soyer, including a number of color plates. The illustrations alone are worth the price of the book.

Singer's autobiography does not conform to the usual expectations of the genre. In an author's note prefacing *Lost in America*, he says that the series "does not pretend to be completely autobiographical." Many of the people he describes are still living; he has omitted important events and distorted dates, places, and other facts. He then issues a cryptic summary: "I consider this work no more than fiction set against a background of truth. I would call the whole work: contributions to an autobiography I never intend to write." The storyteller escapes.

*Lost in America* presupposes a knowledge of at least the previous volume in the series, *A Young Man in Search of Love*. Singer has been writing this idiosyncratic autobiography in serial form, and the division into separate volumes is rather arbitrary. *Lost in America* begins in Warsaw, right where *A Young Man in Search of Love* left off. Indeed, the book is almost half over before Singer even arrives in America.

"At the onset of the 1930's," Singer begins, "my disillusionment with myself had reached a stage in which I had lost all hope. If truth be told, I had had little of it to lose." Against the backdrop of Adolf Hitler's ominous presence, he quickly sketches a situation familiar to readers of his novels. He is desperately short of money. His applications for a visa and a passport—needed for emigration to America—have met with complications. Nothing, however, is as complicated as his romantic entanglements. He is living in a hovel in the country with Lena, a Communist just out of prison—although he despises Communism. In Warsaw he has an apartment; in Warsaw he visits Stefa, with whom he has an ongoing affair, conducted with the tacit approval of her rich, peculiar husband. The same night in Warsaw he visits his cousin Esther.

The reader will immediatly recognize elements from *The Magician of Lublin* (1960), *Enemies* (1972), *Shosha* (1978), and other novels and stories of Singer's. One of the fascinations of *Lost in America* is this awareness of the "raw material" which has been transformed by art, although Singer has forestalled any neat conclusions with his author's note.

The "plot" of this memoir continues along familiar lines, as autobiography mirrors the fiction which originally mirrored the life. "I felt that a man cannot go through life directly but must muddle through, sneak by, smuggle himself through it," Singer writes, and indeed he muddles through. His voyage to America; his acclimation to the new land; his serialization of a new novel; his recruitment by an artsy Yiddishist summer colony: all are fraught with troubles, some comical and some nightmarish, and complicated by further romantic entanglements. The volume ends with his intense awareness of estrangement, summed up in the book's last sentence: "I am lost in America, lost forever."

From first sentence to last sentence there seems to run a curve of despair, yet there is a kind of subplot running through the book which counters this despair. Singer himself, in an interview published as *Isaac Bashevis Singer on Literature and Life* (1979), provides the best account of this subplot:

> If I were to become for a moment a critic of my own writing, I would say that it always stresses the power of the spirit over the body in one way or another. I don't feel that life is nothing but a kind of chemical or physical accident, but there is always a plan behind it. I believe in Providence. I believe in spiritual powers, good and evil.

Again and again in *Lost in America* there is evidence of Singer's spiritual orientation and of his belief in Providence. The financial crisis with which the book begins is resolved when two checks arrive—one from Paris, one from

America—just in the nick of time. Coincidence? Singer clearly does not think so.

This episode sets a pattern which is repeated throughout the book. In order to obtain passport and visa, Singer must lie to the American consul. He says that he has been invited to America to speak about literature. He answers questions falsely, yet, as he observes, "all the lies I told the consul that day came true years later." There is a suggestion that Singer muddles through, despite his weakness and his sins, because he has faith, because he knows he is merely a man, because—as he puts it—"I made my accounting with the divine or Satanic forces, not with the human."

Many readers will find Singer's spiritual orientation absurd and even embarrassing, but no reader of Singer should fail to acknowledge it. When Singer says that he believes in "spiritual powers," he means just what he says. Unfortunately, many critics do not observe this elementary respect for the text; beginning with their own discomfort with any notion of "spiritual powers," they confidently explain away every trace of the supernatural in Singer's work. His imps and demons, for example, are "wonderful devices," merely "symbolic equivalents or coordinates to human conduct." The result is ersatz Singer, not the real and quite wonderful thing.

Although he will soon mark his eightieth birthday, Singer's hand has lost none of its cunning. *Lost in America* has the hypnotic, compulsive readability of his best fiction. Perhaps his caustic judgments passed on most of modern literature and his contempt for "commentary" are due in part to a justifiable resentment, for despite the Nobel Prize he has not received the recognition he deserves. He shares that relative neglect with Georges Simenon, another prodigy. Their sheer genius, their narrative gift, is not fashionable, and to protest their neglect one need not endorse Singer's wholesale assault on twentieth century literature. Whatever the critics have said, or not said, Singer—like Simenon—has found readers aplenty.

*John Wilson*


## Sources for Further Study

*Library Journal*. June 15, 1981, p. 1308.
*The New York Times Book Review*. LXXXVI, June 21, 1981, p. 7.
*The New Yorker*. LVII, August 17, 1981, p. 106.
*Quill & Quire*. XLVII, August, 1981, p. 31.
*Saturday Review*. VIII, June, 1981, p. 50.
*Time*. CXVII, June 15, 1981, p. 80.

# LOUIS D. BRANDEIS AND THE PROGRESSIVE TRADITION

*Author:* Melvin I. Urofsky (1939-    )
Edited by Oscar Handlin
*Publisher:* Little, Brown and Company (Boston). 183 pp. $14.95
*Type of work:* Biography
*Time:* 1856-1941
*Locale:* The United States

*A brief biography of Louis D. Brandeis emphasizing his lifelong advocacy of political progressivism*

> *Principal personages:*
> LOUIS DEMBITZ BRANDEIS, Associate Justice of the United States who helped formulate the New Freedom
> WOODROW WILSON, twenty-eighth President of the United States, 1913-1921
> WILLIAM HOWARD TAFT, twenty-seventh President of the United States, 1909-1913
> THEODORE ROOSEVELT, twenty-sixth President of the United States, 1901-1909, who led the Progressive Party
> FELIX FRANKFURTER, Associate Justice of the United States, 1939-1962
> CHAIM WEIZMANN, a principal modern proponet of Zionism and First President of the State of Israel

Melvin Urofsky's *Louis D. Brandeis and the Progressive Tradition* is a rather brief, interestingly written volume in the Little, Brown and Company series known as the Library of American Biography. The series attempts to provide compact, well-written, solid, biographies to supplement survey courses in American history. The Urofsky book accomplishes these objectives quite competently. The problem, however, is simply that the Library of American Biography as a whole and the Urofsky book in particular follow standard biographies of the subject, utilize conventional sources, and almost preclude new or innovative interpretations. This may be seen in a comparison of *Louis D. Brandeis and the Progressive Tradition* with another biography published a few months later, *The Brandeis/Frankfurter Connection* (1982, Oxford University Press) by Bruce Allen Murphy.

The Urofsky book is a conventional biography that covers the entire life of L. D. Brandeis. Born in 1856, Brandeis died just prior to American entry into World War II in 1941. Given a life that spanned a considerable period of American history, a period that encompassed much change in American life and society, Brandeis "clung to a belief in essential, immutable values" and "his vision of what constituted a good society remained intact." Urofsky's portrait of Brandeis stresses his consistency over a long lifetime of political and legal activity. According to Urofsky, Brandeis' "life and work displayed the highest ideals and most effective practices of the progressive tradition."

This commitment to progressive and liberal values was clear even at the outset of Brandeis' career. Establishing himself in a successful legal practice following his studies at Harvard Law School, Brandeis wholeheartedly accepted the values and traditions of Boston's Brahmin class. He also favored free competition and individual responsibility. As a lawyer, he threw himself into his work with intelligence, enthusiasm, competence, and attention to detail. He soon built his practice into one of the largest in all of New England. He also became involved with and supportive of the public welfare and interest.

As a self-appointed advocate of the public, Brandeis not only pointed out problems but also proposed solutions. Frequently he was significantly involved in educating the public. He shared with the progressives a desire to limit the power of large and potentially monopolistic corporations. Brandeis sought to regulate or control large corporations in order to restore the type of free competition that characterized the American economy of the pre-Civil War period.

One example of this interest in curtailing the power of corporations was Brandeis' participation in Boston's Public Franchise League, a citizen lobby that effectively prevented the Boston Elevated Railway Company from receiving special favors from the City of Boston. Brandeis wrote a major report in 1902 that eventually brought the Massachusetts State Legislature to accept the public interest over that of the company. This was Brandeis' first effort at lobbying in behalf of the public. From this point Brandeis went on to make a reputation for himself as a public advocate. Brandeis was not just an advocate of one side, however; he also favored competence and efficiency in companies and occasionally provided them with analyses of their operation that improved their efficiency and permitted a reduction of cost for the public.

In his efforts to improve corporate efficiency and provide protection for the public, Brandeis learned the value of public opinion and the techniques or methods of manipulating public opinion through lobbying. These methods were employed in one of Brandeis' major accomplishments. The insurance companies so fully controlled the price of life insurance and kept that price so high that industrial workers could not afford life insurance. To meet this need, Brandeis developed the idea of life insurance sold at savings banks. This insurance could be afforded by workers and Brandeis was able to win acceptance of the idea in the Massachusetts Legislature, which approved it in 1907 over the protests of the insurance companies.

Having established his desire to assert the public interest against monopolistic corporations, Brandeis continued this commitment in a variety of ways. In the late nineteenth and early twentieth centuries the Supreme Court and the legal system were characterized by *laissez-faire*, ignoring the public and invariably supporting business. National attention was directed to Brandeis in his brilliant arguments against *laissez-faire* before the Supreme Court in 1908 in the case *Muller* v. *Oregon*. In this case Brandeis' brief spent only two pages on the legal question—whether the State of Oregon had the legal right to establish a maximum hour law for women—and focused, instead, on the effects on the health and morals of working women of not mandating a maximum hours law. Citing study after study, Brandeis made clear the responsibility of the Supreme Court and the legal profession not only to consider the law but also to be concerned about the consequences of the law. This case profoundly changed the perspectives of the nation's courts and lawyers and identified Brandeis as America's foremost advocate for the public.

In pursuing the public interest, Brandeis became involved in the Ballinger-Pinchot controversy during the William Howard Taft Administration. In Urofsky's view, Brandeis, as the attorney for Lewis Glavis, "directed the progressive side," or the Pinchot side. Urofsky totally misconstrues the respective positions of Pinchot and Ballinger, identifying the views of Pinchot with those of John Muir and the preservationists and assigning the views of conservationists, such as Pinchot, exclusively to Ballinger and his supporters. Brandeis and Pinchot lost the case, but both continued a public attack on the Taft Administration that eventually forced the resignation of Ballinger and that set the stage for the election campaign of 1912.

The election, involving Taft, Theodore Roosevelt, and Woodrow Wilson, was one of the most exciting in all of American history. Taft represented political conservatism, Roosevelt advocated "the New Nationalism," and Wilson campaigned in behalf of "the New Freedom." Brandeis was the author of "the New Freedom." He and Wilson both believed that early nineteenth century free competition should be reestablished by limiting the monopolistic practices of big business. Prodded by Brandeis, Wilson hoped to "so restrict the wrong use of competition that the right use of competition" would "destroy monopoly." Urofsky's analysis of the respective views of Wilson and Roosevelt is rather simplistic, overstated, and speculative. For example, he argues that "Carried to extremes, one program could lead to anarchy, the other to fascism," as if Wilson and Roosevelt, two competent and responsible politicians, dared contemplate carrying their respective political platforms to extremes. Urofsky's analysis of the reasons for Wilson's election victory is immoderate and speculative; he insists that the electorate chose Wilson not only for his economic but also for his psychological and moral alternatives.

Once in office, Wilson and his adviser, Brandeis, sought implementation of "the New Freedom" through (1) tariff reduction; (2) strengthening antitrust laws; and (3) modification of the monetary system. Urofsky's analysis of "the New Freedom" does not advance much beyond Arthur S. Link's _Woodrow Wilson and the Progressive Era_ (1963). These policies resulted in a substantive reduction of the tariff, the establishment of the Federal Reserve System, and two significant antitrust steps: (1) the Clayton Act and (2) the establishment of the Federal Trade Commission. Throughout Urofsky's treatment of the Wilson policies there is an inaccurate description of the position of the business community that ignores the work of Gabriel Kalko in *The Triumph of Conservatism* (1963). Ignored as well is the progressive program that was forced on Wilson in the latter half of his first administration.

While Brandeis was deeply involved in policymaking in the first Wilson Administration, he was also becoming increasingly involved in Zionism. Much of Urofsky's description of Brandeis and Zionism derives from his fine work, *American Zionism from Herzel to the Holocaust* (1975). If *Louis D. Brandeis and the Progressive Tradition* reveals Urofsky's lack of expertise on the politics of the period, it also reveals his formidable knowledge of American Zionism. On this subject, the biography is excellent.

Urofsky's description of the fight leading to the appointment of Brandeis to the Supreme Court in 1916 is rather good. He includes the elements of the popular perception of Brandeis as a Progressive, the Brandeis brief in the *Muller* v. *Oregon* decision, and anti-Semitism as the major reasons for opposition to Brandeis. Despite the controversy, Wilson, Brandeis, and their supporters eventually prevailed and Brandeis became a justice of the Supreme Court.

From his appointment to the Bench, Brandeis attempted to avoid any embarrassment to the Supreme Court and therefore reduced his public appearances as an advocate of Progressivism or anything else. He continued, however, to support Progressivism behind the scenes, and this is precisely why the recent book by Bruce A. Murphy, *The Brandeis/Frankfurter Connection*, is so interesting. Murphy documents that Frankfurter remained in Brandeis' pay from 1916 through 1938. In return, Frankfurter's students at Harvard did research that Brandeis suggested, some of Brandeis' unsigned letters ended up as articles in *The New Republic*, and Brandeis' ideas and suggestions in behalf of Progressivism went far beyond the shelter of the court. Murphy asserts that Brandeis also offered specific advice and suggestions to the administration of Franklin D. Roosevelt. This behind-the-scenes activity is not adequately covered in the Urofsky biography.

Urofsky's account of Brandeis in the 1920's focuses on his increasing involvement in the court and in matters relating to Zionism. His description of the conflict which matched Brandeis, assimilated Jewry, and the American Zionist against the European Zionists and the immigrants to America is a dramatic, well-told, and accurate story. The opposition between Brandeis and his followers on the one hand, and Chaim Weizmann and his followers on the other, split Zionism and led to ineffective action in the 1930's, when cooperation might have averted the Holocaust. The tragedy that Urofsky documents was one of political manipulation and divisiveness at a time when unity was required. Urofsky sides with Brandeis and his followers on the ground that they stood for organizational ability, fiscal integrity, and honesty. Fiscal integrity and organizational ability were not enough, however; the new Jewish immigrants required an emotional content, a devotion to Israel and to Jewish peoplehood that neither Brandeis nor his followers could provide or even comprehend. Thus, the masses of American Zionists eventually turned from Brandeis to Chaim Weizmann. Sadly, each side had deficiencies that the other side could but would not fill and the result was contention and hostility rather than cooperation.

Urofsky's description of Brandeis in the 1930's also focuses primarily on the court and on cases in which Brandeis reflected progressivist or Zionist views. Brandeis' role in Zionism in this period consisted primarily of giving advice. Frankfurter's relationship to Brandeis in the 1930's is briefly sketched. The major event of the 1930's was the Great Depression. Urofsky briefly describes the response of Roosevelt to the Depression and the establishment of the various programs of the New Deal, depicting Brandeis as a supporter of the New Deal and some of its programs. The advisory relationship that Murphy describes between Brandeis and Roosevelt is not clear in Urofsky's account. Urofsky attempts to justify Brandeis' opposition to New Deal programs in the *Schechter* case, in the *Panama Oil* case, and in the *Radford* case in 1935 and 1936. These and other decisions destroyed the NRA, the AAA, and the Frazier-Lemke Act. The court destroyed other New Deal Programs as well, and by 1936, the Roosevelt Administration was forced to begin rebuilding the New Deal. Roosevelt's court-packing effort did not win the support of Congress and the public, but frightened the court into a more liberal view, and Roosevelt was soon able to appoint new Justices who supported his policies. In 1939 Brandeis resigned from the court and two years later died.

Urofsky concludes his book in the belief that Brandeis' life manifested a consistent advocacy of Progressivism. Although Urofsky's thesis is well-argued, his case is weakened by a faulty understanding of the events surrounding his subject. While his knowledge of American Zionism and Brandeis' involvement in it is of the highest quality—he is the expert in the field—his understanding of early twentieth century environmentalism and conservationism is badly flawed. His knowledge of the views of the business community omits any understanding of the work of Gabriel Kolko and Robert Wiebe. His comprehension of the New Nationalism and the New Freedom is derivative and follows the work of Arthur Link. On some points, Urofsky is unnecessarily intemperate and raises rather speculative issues. Altogether, the Urofsky biography is a well-written, general biography that follows standard views of Brandeis, covers little new ground, and contains a number of significant flaws, omissions, and errors. The book is recommended with reservations. It may suffice for students of survey classes; it can hardly be recommended for scholars of the period.

*Saul Lerner*

## Sources for Further Study

*American Historical Review.* LXXXVI, October, 1981, p. 942.
*Choice.* XVIII, April, 1981, p. 1158.
*History: Reviews of New Books.* IX, July, 1981, p. 183.
*Library Journal.* CV, December 15, 1981, p. 2566.
*National Review.* XXXII, December 12, 1980, p. 42.
*The New Yorker.* LVI, February 2, 1981, p. 101.
*School Library Journal.* XXVII, May, 1981, p. 93.

# LOVE AND RESPONSIBILITY

*Author:* Karol Wojtyla (Pope John Paul II, 1920-    )
Translated from the Polish by H. T. Willetts
*Publisher:* Farrar, Straus and Giroux (New York). 319 pp. $15.00
*Type of work:* Theological ethics

*An argument for sexual behavior to be faithful to its created purpose and to the nature of human beings*

The initial reaction of a non-Catholic to John Paul II's treatment of sex is likely to be: "How can he say anything credible about it if he is celibate?" The author (then Bishop Wojtyla: he wrote the book eighteen years before becoming Pope) anticipated this question in the Preface to *Love and Responsibility*. What a priest may lack in immediate experience, he argues, he makes up for in breadth of secondhand experience and scholarship. A scholar need not be a soldier to write about war, nor must a scientist be an astronaut to write about space. Indeed, the priest is in an opportune position to write an ethics of sex: purposefully detached, he can describe, without the fog of immediate self-interest, the character of sexual relations, and he can prescribe, because of his immersion in a tradition rich with values, that behavior which is best for those who choose not to be celibate. To ignore this book because of John Paul II's celibacy, then, is to act on thoughtless bias. It is also unfortunate, because despite some weaknesses, the book is often insightful, challenging, and even inspirational.

Like all mainline Catholic moral philosophy following Thomas Aquinas, *Love and Responsibility* is based on natural theology. Put simply, natural theology says that people behave morally when they act in accord with the natural order. That which is natural, though, is not simply that which is physical or biological, but rather that which follows God's activity in creation. The order of nature, writes John Paul II,

> is generally confused with the "biological order" and so deprived of all importance. It is much easier to understand the power of the natural order (and its constitutive significance for morality, and for the development of the human personality) if we see behind it the personal authority of the Creator.

To understand John Paul II's moral reasoning, then, it is necessary to understand that the natural is evident in but not reducible to the environment. The natural is God's revelation through nature in accordance with sacred scripture, the historical Church, and reason.

From this base in natural theology, John Paul II identifies personhood as the beginning and end of all moral behavior. Human beings are different from all other animals because of their rationality, their unique inner life. Human reasoning capabilities allow them to transcend urges and instincts; that is, they have a free will, and with this freedom comes responsibility. Unlike animals which must obey their instincts, humans can will their behavior. Because they have the power of choice, their actions can be good or evil. Good deeds occur when people choose to behave in accordance with the created order.

Behavior toward humans is good when they are treated as *persons* rather than as objects. Using people as the means to an end denies them their intelligence and creativity; it usurps their freedom. God did not create people as a means even toward His ends. Instead, He endowed people with the ability to determine their own ends. Treating others as persons rather than as the means to an end is to allow them to work toward their own personal goals.

To treat others as persons is to love them. Love means consciously seeking a good together with others, never putting oneself above others or the mutual good. On the contrary, the person acting in love may subordinate himself or herself in service of the good or of others. Love as a virtue is the ultimate good toward which people should strive; experienced love is a process, and as such never *is*, but rather is always *becoming*.

Moral sexual behavior can only occur when the natural purpose for sex fuses with the personalistic norm, according to which people are never to be used as the means toward an end. John Paul II argues,

> In the sexual relationship between man and woman *two orders meet: the order of nature*, which has as its object reproduction, and *the personal order*, which finds its expression in the love of persons and aims at the fullest realization of that love.

According to John Paul II, the natural purpose of sex is procreation, so the possibility of childbearing must always be present in the sexual act. This simple maxim precludes two types of behavior. Sex not between a man and a woman, whether homosexual relations or masturbation, is wrong because God designed human sexual organs for union between genders for the purpose of procreation. Artifical means of birth control are likewise misdirected, because they too do not follow the natural order. Sexual partners must always be willing, if they are physically capable, to produce and rear offspring. The only forms of birth control that should be exercised are those that nature herself provides: abstention in relations outside of marriage, since the partners are unwilling to rear children, and rhythm, since it follows the fertility cycle that the female body goes through naturally. Contraceptive devices unnaturally prevent the created goal of sex, and premature withdrawal stops the natural climax of the sexual act.

Following the order of nature is but one criterion of good sexual behavior; sex must also adhere to the personal order, which forbids using persons as a means to an end. To use, says John Paul II, is not to love, because using means treating a person as an object. Using occurs whenever enjoyment is the sole or primary intent of the sex act, as in sexual relations outside of marriage and sex without the possibility of procreation. In fact, all unnatural sexual behavior can be traced back to seeking pleasure rather than the person as the highest good. Distortions occur when sex becomes an experience that should be sought for its pleasure rather than an experience that happens to give pleasure.

Love, says John Paul II, "is always a sort of interpersonal synthesis or synchronization of attraction, desire and goodwill." A man and a woman who are attracted to each other should seek the truth about each other first, to really get to know one another, and then seek the truth about their feelings. This principle is in keeping with the personalistic norm. All too often, however, this order is reversed, so that the partners focus more on their feelings than on each other's character. This reversal—seeing a person through the lens of emotion rather than reason—often leads to idealization, because one person identifies the other by emotion rather than by character. Such idealization is risky. If someone has invested deep feelings in a person with whom she is incompatible, she will feel cheated once she sees her partner as he really is. Sentiment can thus lead to hatred. For genuine love to flourish, each partner must seek knowledge more than feelings.

Knowledge of and feelings for the other are necessary but insufficient conditions for sexual intercourse, however. Desire and goodwill must also be present. Desire is natural because humans are incomplete without the companionship of others. Goodwill complements desire, because while desire longs for another person, goodwill longs for that person's good.

The combination of attraction, desire, and goodwill is marriage, the permanent bond between a man and a woman. Intercourse is proper here because only in marriage is the likelihood of using precluded. Only in marriage have two people chosen to dedicate their entire lives to each other. In marriage, which is marked by the shared goal of family, cohabitation becomes socially legitimate and there is always a possibility of parenthood. Marriage partners should not have intercourse only to procreate, though, for that would be using each other as a means to an end. Rather, sexual union must signal interpersonal communion. The husband and wife naturally complement each other, and sex, as an act of love, signifies and communicates that unity.

*Love and Responsibility* clearly errs in the last chapter on sexology. In it, John Paul II claims that contraceptives are physically harmful, a statement that is at best an exaggeration. Birth control pills, IUD's, and diaphragms have drawbacks, many of which are statistically minimal, but condoms, for example, are physically safe. He also claims that climax should always be reached by both partners, an enjoyable experience to be sure, and one to be sought, but one that is not always possible. John Paul II damages his credibility most, however, by insisting that males are inherently more aggressive than females. "For the purposes of the sexual act," he claims, it is enough for her to be passive and unresisting, so much so that it may even take place without her volition while she is in a state in which she has no awareness at all of what is happening—for instance while she is asleep, or unconscious.

John Paul II minimizes female aggressiveness and appears to be unaware of lubrication, the female counterpart of the male erection.

Such exaggerations, while damaging to the author's authority, leave his thesis unscathed. The thesis, however, is questionable on other grounds. If the purpose of sexual intercourse is procreation, then why does the sexual urge persist in women after menopause, when they cannot conceive? Why do women, when they are infertile, still desire sex? Why are men and women who are sterile motivated toward sex? Why may women desire sex during early stages of pregnancy? If the aim of sex is primarily procreation, then nature, it would seem, would not give the desire to those who, for reasons permanent or temporary, cannot produce children. It would appear that the sex drive is naturally oriented first toward pleasure and climax, and then toward procreation, rather than toward procreation with pleasure as an inevitable byproduct, as John Paul II maintains.

Similarly, John Paul II's advocacy of sex during the woman's infertile period tends to undercut his argument that sex without the possibility of parenthood is reciprocal using. If nature has provided a means for birth control that humans are not to augment artificially, then why is it all right to supplement the body's healing process artificially? John Paul II's case would be much stronger if he had differentiated between temporary and permanent means of birth control. The possibility of procreation exists, albeit to a small degree, when temporary artificial means are used and normally when their use is suspended, but the possibility is usually precluded in sterilization. John Paul II's argument would be consistent if he allowed certain temporary means of artificial birth control but forbade sterilization.

Following John Paul II's guidance would obviously lead to the treatment of people as persons rather than objects, but it seems likely that there are other ways to treat people as persons as well. If the sex drive toward climax is actually primary and conception is only secondary, then person-oriented sex would seek interpersonal bonding as its primary aim and procreation as a possible secondary aim. Parenthood would become more conscientiously planned and less incidental, and the children, from the beginning, would almost always be wanted and cared for to the best of the parents' abilities. John Paul II obviously disagrees:

> If the earth is threatened with overpopulation, if the economists complain of the "over-production of people" to the point that production of the means of subsistence cannot keep up with it, we ought to aim at limiting the use of the sexual urge, having in mind its objective purpose.

There seems to be no point in "limiting the use of the sexual urge," however, if its central function is to provide interpersonal bonding and pleasure rather than to produce children.

To construct a sexual ethics based on natural theology, as John Paul II has tried to do, requires a clear integration of physiology, revelation, and reason. Revelation, according to Christianity, is historical and accessible through the Bible and church tradition. Because revelation is historical, it must be understood in historical terms. To apply biblical teachings and the teachings of the later church without explaining their social and cultural setting is to be unfaithful to historical revelation. Reason must be faithful to biblical and ecclesiastical tradition, historically understood, and to what is known to be physiologically accurate. The integration of physiology, revelation, and reason would indicate that intercourse leads to unity through sexual pleasure, that there should be mutual meaning generated through intercourse. This meaning can be the enhancement of love between the partners or through participation in procreation.

In *Love and Responsibility*, John Paul II has clearly explained the Roman Catholic position on sexual behavior. In so doing, he has presented an argument for personhood that the religious and nonreligious alike would do well to heed. At the same time, however, he has put forth a debatable position about the nature of sex, an argument not likely to win followers, but one that will hopefully expand and inform the ceaseless dialogue on sexual morality.

*John P. Ferré*

### Sources for Further Study

*Booklist*. LXXVII, June 1, 1981, p. 1280.
*Choice*. XIX, November, 1981, p. 392.
*Kirkus Reviews*. XLIX, June 1, 1981, p. 730.
*Library Journal*. CVI, June 1, 1981, p. 1231.
*The New York Times Book Review*. LXXXVI, September 20, 1981, p. 13.
*U.S. Catholic*. XLVI, November, 1981, p. 48.

# THE LOVE HUNTER

*Author:* Jon Hassler (1933-    )
*Publisher:* William Morrow and Company (New York). 311 pp. $12.95
*Type of work:* Novel
*Time:* The present
*Locale:* Rookery, Minnesota, and a remote area of Manitoba, Canada

*A narrative involving a love triangle wherein friendship is tested against experience and love against time and morality*

> *Principal characters:*
> CHRISTOPHER MACKENSIES, a divorced middle-aged man; student counselor at Rookery State College
> LARRY QUINN, Christopher's close friend, a former teacher of history at Rookery State College who is dying of multiple sclerosis
> RACHEL QUINN, Larry's wife, who must work to support her dying husband and teenage son; also director of the Rookery Community Playhouse

Jon Hassler's third novel, *The Love Hunter*, is an attempt to explore the moral dilemma that Christopher MacKensies finds himself facing. Chris's best friend, Larry Quinn, who has been a strong and vigorous man, is entering into the last stage of a degenerative disease. No longer able to walk or support himself and racked by pain, he has become deeply depressed. Once an idealist, he has become bitter; a firmly rational man, he is driven by pain to fits of irrationality. Sometimes, because of his dependence on others, he becomes petulant and trying. Believing that Larry would prefer death to the grim future that the disease makes inevitable, Chris considers the idea of a mercy killing, but the moral issue of justification is clouded by the fact that Chris has fallen in love with Larry's wife, Rachel, and she has confessed her love for Chris. At the same time, she loves her husband, and she tells Chris that they cannot be lovers as long as Larry is alive.

Chris is unable to distinguish his own need for Rachel and his desire to release Larry from the inexorable progress of disease. Once, when Larry becomes so irrational as to require hospitalization, Rachel turns to Chris for comfort, and for the first and only time she goes to bed with him. This experience drives Chris into making a decision. Larry must die, and Chris begins to plan the murder. Uncertain from the start that he will be capable of carrying out the plan, he nevertheless proceeds to set it in motion. The novel revolves around the working out of this plan and Chris's doubts and justifications.

The situation Hassler sets up promises much, not only in the way of suspense and in the opportunity to examine the dimensions of human emotions and need where people are forced to operate within the strictures of moral behavior, but also in the illumination of the darker regions of the human psyche. Unfortunately, the novel provides neither suspense nor illumination.

From the beginning, the story is implausible as Hassler fails to provide his hero with a believable plan for a murder that will appear to be accidental.

In the beginning of the friendship, when they were young high school teachers in Owl Brook, Chris and Larry had been hunting companions, and during the season had spent long hours together every week on the lake in a duck blind. Even after they had separated, each to move to a different graduate school, they held a yearly reunion in order to hunt together. After graduate school, both men had come to the state college in Rookery, where only Larry's illness had interrupted their shared pursuit of game.

Because of their shared hunting experiences and because of a dream in which Chris sees himself pushing and holding Larry's head down under the green algae-laden waters of the lake, Chris makes a plan to take Larry on a hunting trip which will provide Chris with the opportunity to drown Larry. Instead of a nearby lake or even a place familiar to them, Chris proposes a hunting camp in a remote and rugged spot in the Canadian wilderness. Chris's action lacks credibility, but even more implausible is Larry's response. Nowhere does Hassler explain what possible arguments could have been used to persuade a man racked by pain, unable to stand or walk, incontinent, and without a healthy muscle left in his body, to undertake a three-hundred-mile ride to the wilds of a primitive hunting lodge to wade through marshes and reeds in order to shoot ducks. The only clue the author offers is Chris's rationalization that Larry could only be hunting death. Nor does Hassler explain why Rachel, said to be an intelligent and sensitive woman who loves and cares for her husband, allows him to undertake such an arduous trip, which would take him out of reach of medical attention. Nor is it credible that a man of any intelligence at all would choose a place of unfamiliar terrain and uncertain conditions, a place he has never been, as the scene for the staging of a murder that must appear to result from an accident.

As improbable as the plot is, an even greater deficiency is Hassler's failure to give credibility or depth to his characters. While they are ordinary, normal people living conventional lives, any individual life examined closely reveals the strange and deep complexities that give value to and illuminate a real work of art as opposed to the work of a technician; and while stereotypes serve well the purposes of satire, which this novel comes close to being, or the function of today's morality plays, soap operas, which enable an audience to participate on a quick and easy level in the struggle between good and evil, what Hassler creates is something of an unfortunate and uncomfortable cross between the two.

On the one hand, Hassler says that Chris is pierced to the heart by sorrow and pity when he looks at Larry. On the other hand, what Hassler shows of Chris's interaction with Larry is something entirely different. Chris is inconsiderate and unheeding of the sick man's very simple needs. At one point, for example, he will not stop on the highway for Larry, although Chris knows

Larry's problems with incontinence. At another point, Chris is shown being callous in response to Larry's need for reassurance, thus driving Larry into a fit of anger and frustration in which he picks up the first thing he can find and slams it across the room. The heirloom vase that Larry breaks belongs to Rachel, but Chris does and says nothing until Rachel reacts. As head of the College's student counseling services, Chris is supposed to be a leader in his field, but even here, in interaction with students, he is shown to be indifferent, callous, and superficial. At one point when his telephone conversation with Rachel is interrupted by a female student, Chris becomes so angry that he pushes the girl out of the door and slams it after her. The student problems that Chris deals with are trivial, dull, or funny; nowhere does he exhibit the least degree of professionalism or expertise that would be expected from a man who has risen to the top of his profession.

Even in the early days of their youth, what is demonstrated is Chris's envy of and competition with Larry. During the hunting season, Chris sees himself as competing with Rachel for Larry. Only after Larry goes back to graduate school does Chris decide to do so; and because Larry is an inspired teacher and Chris not so good, he decides to become a counselor instead. Larry's marriage is happy; his son is a born-again Christian. Chris is never happy in his marriage; his son takes up with a rock group and his daughter is on drugs. Eventually, Chris's wife and children drift out of his life, and it is only after Larry's illness has made him both physically and psychologically vulnerable that Chris begins his conquest of Rachel.

A question arises as to the author's design when he demonstrates the utterly selfish behavior of a character and at the same time asks the reader to accept that he is motivated by love. Even that intent is left open to speculation, for Chris is never tested. Whether he is capable of murder is left undecided, for, at the crucial moment, the author lets a storm intervene. Larry and Chris, with a drunken guide, are in a small boat and are in immediate danger of drowning. Nearby, also on the lake, is a young boy in a small boat. At the crucial moment, Larry takes control of the boat and the situation, managing to get everyone safely to shore. Only Chris is injured, when he is struck accidentally in the mouth. Exhilarated by the events and hailed as a hero, Larry is returned home to Rachel to live the few remaining months of his life in relative happiness. Chris loses a tooth and must be content to sit by and wish for Larry's death.

Rachel is the only major female character in the book, although there are many who are introduced—only to disappear. She is represented as a paragon of all wifely virtues. Beautiful, wise, and witty, tender and caring, she is also capable of working to support her family. She is the town's leading actress and director of the community playhouse. She even jogs every day. Asked by Chris how she manages all of this activity and, at the same time, deals with a husband who has grown increasingly despondent and a teenage son who is often in conflict with his father, Rachel replies: "Oh, I make popcorn." Indeed, she seems as real as those all too pervasive females who dish out the correct cereal, keep clothes April fresh, always carry in their purses a tube of the right cavity-fighting toothpaste, a bottle of aspirin with the most effective pain-killing ingredients, and sometimes a can of coffee with the richest taste. Actress she is—not only in the arena of Rookery, but also in the drama of real life. When Larry dies, she rushes to the telephone to call Chris who is, as it were, waiting in the wings. "Chris," she cries, "I've lost my leading man."

The juxtaposition of the trivial and the trite with the grim circumstances of Larry's disease and death serves to produce doubt in a reader's mind. Does the author mean to say that Chris and Rachel are less than humane? Does Hassler imply that Larry, described as a "brilliant scholar" whose life work is the logging history of Minnesota, an inspired and inspiring teacher, a loving husband and father, a man possessed of all the virtues of vigor and skill, must be wasted away as painfully as possible in order that those other two paragons Chris and Rachel, may wed and bed? Not even all the poetry which the three read aloud to one another and quote at length or all the classical music which they discuss gives a clue that these are real people, nor do the quotations or the lengthy discussions become a convincing device for providing insight into the moral dilemma which is ostensibly the center of the novel.

Hassler's use of images which might shed some light as to what he had in mind leads only to the same confusion. The most obvious imagery is that of birds and the theater. The title of the novel, the duck hunt where the men are described in the act of killing, and the name of the town where they first meet, suggest predators and predation. "Rookery" is literally a feeding place of crows, scavenger birds; but it also carries the meaning in its verbal form of lying, stealing, and cheating. Those images in conjunction with various other contradictions ought to cast the story into a satiric mode. Such is not the case, however, even when incidents apparently insist on irony. This phenomenon is best illustrated in the theater imagery. Rachel's training and experience in the theater is limited to the Rookery Playhouse. This fact is juxtaposed with Chris's notion that she is a great and rising star of the theater, which gives him cause for doubt. The trouble with loving an actress, he believes, is that he has no way of distinguishing real emotions from playacting ones. In a seeming contradiction at the end of the book, with Larry dead and Rachel available, Chris sees himself as a bit player with stage fright, afraid of embracing life, but with Rachel's help, he believes, he will be able to emerge upon the stage. What happens will depend upon her, what role she chooses to play, and what role she chooses for him, and in what play. The tone is serious; the character is in a moment of self-examination. Whether Hassler intended satirical commentary, sentimental charade, or serious treatment of a moral dilemma, as indicated in the blurb on the novel's dust jacket, is hard to decide.

Also bothersome is the number of apparently pointless anecdotes and extraneous characters, most of whom are treated in a derogatory manner (stupid, pathetic, or abrasive female students; women named Poo Poo or wearing t-shirts with provocative invitations; crude male hunters who tell vulgar stories; community actors and actresses portrayed as comic and ridiculous), the author's habit of presenting exposition by means of parenthetical phrases; and the now clichéd effort to call on the male mystique of the hunting ritual to endow a narrative with sacred message.

*Mary Rohrberger*

## Sources for Further Study

*Best Sellers*. XLI, September, 1981, p. 205.
*Booklist*. LXXVIII, September 1, 1981, p. 28.
*Kirkus Reviews*. XLIX, April 15, 1981, p. 520.
*Library Journal*. CVI, May 15, 1981, p. 1098.
*The New York Times Book Review*. LXXXVI, August 16, 1981, p. 9.
*Publishers Weekly*. CCXIX, May 8, 1981, p. 248.

# LOVE IN BLOOMSBURY
## Memories

*Author:* Frances Partridge (1900-    )
*Publisher:* Little, Brown and Company (Boston). Illustrated. 244 pp. $14.95
*Type of work:* Autobiography
*Time:* 1900-1932
*Locale:* England

*A book of memories by a woman on the fringes of Bloomsbury, chronicling her childhood and education and emphasizing her friendships and social relations with many of the members of the Bloomsbury group*

> *Principal personages:*
> FRANCES PARTRIDGE (NÉE MARSHALL), a Bloomsburyite
> RALPH PARTRIDGE, her lover and eventual husband
> DORA CARRINGTON, the wife of Ralph
> LYTTON STRACHEY, a biographer and essayist, beloved of Dora

It is to be hoped that readers do not come to this book with false expectations, but they might well be forgiven if they do, because the combination of the words *love* and *Bloomsbury* might easily be taken to promise a gallery of titillating revelations of kinky practices. Indeed, if one were to be told beforehand of the basic situation of these memoirs, one could certainly be forgiven for thinking of empurpled hedonism and dissipation; for this book is about a woman who lives with a man who is married to a bisexual who is passionately devoted to a male homosexual whose lovers have included the man with whom the first woman is living. It must be said at the outset, however, that such expectations will not be fulfilled. No closets are opened here, no confidences divulged, no secrets laid bare.

The book is, in fact, a modest, straightforward, often engaging memoir of a young woman's Edwardian childhood and of her life in Bloomsbury in the 1920's and early 1930's. Frances Partridge (née Marshall), now in her eighties, looks back over the first thirty-two years of her life: the liaisons of Bloomsbury are mentioned, the personal relationships named, but they are presented here as a part of the landscape, as facts with which one lived. One of the lessons of the book might well be how ordinary many rather strange and unconventional things looked to those on the inside. The book emphasizes friends and social relationships; and among other things it is not, is any sort of analysis or criticism of the intellectual or artistic accomplishments of the Bloomsbury group. Bloomsbury, like Watergate, continues to spawn an unending succession of books, of attack and defense, of justification and reminiscence. There is little that is new about Bloomsbury here, but this should not be taken as a criticism of the work, because it does not presume to tell new things. Its great virtue is that it gives the actual feel of what it was like to live and move on a daily basis among such people and in such an atmosphere.

Frances Marshall was born in 1900, the youngest of six children of William and Margaret Marshall. Her father was an architect whose roots were in the Lake District, while her mother came of Irish stock, was mildly musical and a staunch suffragette. In typical Edwardian fashion the father was a large and dominant man who supported a London house in Bedford Square and a country home at Hindhead. Frances grew up surrounded by the inevitable nanny and governesses, William Morris wallpaper, and advanced thinking. The Marshall family, as she explains, "stood for love of Nature . . . for Words-worthian poetry and its pantheistic outlook; for eugenics, agnosticism, and the march of science; for class distinctions courteously observed." Frances herself decided at the age of twelve that she did not believe in God. The young Frances was early attracted by picture books, often taken to museums, and acquired a facility in drawing and painting which was stimulated by her sister Ray, a professional artist.

In reading the pages which detail the Marshalls' life before World War I, one cannot help but be reminded of George Bernard Shaw's *Heartbreak House* (1919) and the portrait there of cultured, leisured Europe, full of advanced ideas. In similar fashion, as Frances is graduated from Newnham, one is inevitably reminded of Shaw's Vivie Warren, a product of the same institution. Her father's heroes were Charles Darwin, John Ruskin, Alfred, Lord Tennyson, and Leslie Stephen, all of whom he personally knew. The Marshalls were on visiting and dining terms with such as the Asquiths and Ricardos, Arthur Conan Doyle, William Beveridge, assorted Stracheys, and Logan Pearsall Smith. As a small child Frances even met Henry James. In spite of ordinary childhood problems such as fear of the dark and a persistent curiosity about sex, Frances probably had as good a preparation as possible for her later life in Bloomsbury.

Boarding school, Bedales, came when Frances was fifteen; she entered Cambridge at eighteen, as the war was drawing to a close; at twenty-one she completed her formal education, suffered the loss of her father, and moved to London to seek her way in the world. The scenes at Bedales and at Cambridge evoke a lost world and serve to remind one how really recent is the acceptance of formal higher education for women. Even against the background of the war and after the obligatory first few weeks of discomfort and discontent, partly occasioned by cold showers and pre-breakfast runs, Frances was very happy at Bedales. There a passion for dancing began which was carried over to her University years. When she entered Cambridge, her father invested two thousand pounds for her and required her to live off the proceeds from then on. Serious subjects mingled with the frivolous at Cambridge, where Frances took her degree in the rather unusual combination of English and Moral Sciences. The sketches of some of her new friends and her teachers are delightful, especially that of Pernel Strachey, sister of Lytton and Principal of Peile Hall at Newnham.

In 1921, after her husband's death, Mrs. Marshall removed to a house in

Brunswick Square in Bloomsbury. Frances lived with her mother, and after a brief spell of administering intelligence tests to nine-year-olds, got a job as general dogsbody and accountant at the bookshop of Francis Birrell and David Garnett, who later married her sister Ray. It was an archetypal Bloomsbury setting and occupation, and Frances seems to have been the only one who could keep the accounts straight. In the course of all this she managed to meet and become friends with Lytton Strachey, Roger Fry, Desmond and Molly McCarthy, Virginia Woolf, Duncan Grant, and others. A number of the scenes in the rather unbusinesslike bookshop are engaging, as are the brief pen-portraits of many of the Bloomsburyites. They are presented affectionately, not as objects of study, and it is easy to see how they became a part of the familiar furniture of Frances Marshall's world.

In 1923, a series of events began which were to change Frances' personal life. In that year she met Ralph Partridge, who was an intimate friend of Lytton Strachey and the husband of Dora Carrington. Ralph, who died in 1960 and who appears to have been a bit of a hearty in the midst of all the aesthetes, became with Strachey the coowner of Ham Spray house in Wiltshire, a setting for much of the activity in the second part of the book. (After the deaths of Strachey and Carrington, Ralph and Frances, who eventually married, took up residence at Ham Spray.) Dora Carrington lived with Strachey at Ham Spray and devoted herself to him, though she was not averse to accepting lovers of either sex. The growing romance, then, of Ralph and Frances threatened to disturb the order of affairs at Ham Spray. In 1925, Ralph and Frances toured Spain together and in May, 1926, after assuring, and being assured by, Strachey and Carrington that their living together need not upset the arrangements at Ham Spray, they set up housekeeping together. Whatever the complications of social life in such a setting, it is clear that the love of Ralph and Frances was true and permanent. Thus it is that the *love* of the title probably refers most of all to this love.

Part I of the book closes with the almost obligatory denunciation of convention, which the author regards as a means of avoiding thinking out one's own values. She does however admit the actual power of social conventions and her own confusion at her ambiguous situation. She rather curiously says that one drawback to her situation was that it prevented her having a child. It is a little difficult to understand why, if all the other conventions meant so little, this one should have concerned her.

The second half of the work is somewhat different from the first, having less narrative drive and being more composed of anecdotes and excerpts from diaries and letters. One dominant impression of this part, which concentrates on the Bloomsbury experience, is talk. How those Bloomsburyites could talk and loved to talk! Many of them, indeed, were better talkers than anything else. Many had trouble managing their personal lives or finances, had trouble bringing works of art or scholarship to completion, but they were all very witty, outspoken, and clever. At times their portraits here remind one of Evelyn Waugh's Bright Young Things of the Twenties (though even Waugh never thought of a Hermaphrodite Party!), and it must be admitted that some of them, however charming and however much they reveled in the unconventionality of Bloomsbury, were of much less importance than they or their friends thought them to be. A word which is frequently repeated in this book as a term of praise for various friends is *clever*. Much could be and apparently was forgiven by Frances and by Bloomsbury if one were clever. It did not seem to matter much that the cleverness sometimes masked ineptitude, shallowness, triviality, and selfishness.

The major set piece of Part II as well as its climax is the drawn-out decription of the agonies, distortions, and general upset occasioned by the illness and death of Lytton Strachey and the subsequent suicide of Dora Carrington. In both of these Ralph and Frances were deeply involved. Strachey became ill at Ham Spray in the latter part of 1931. Nurses arrived, specialists traveled down from London, various diagnoses were proposed, and various treatments given. Ralph and Frances were frequently in attendance and when separated wrote each other lugubrious letters detailing the progress of the case. The traffic grew as supporters of those supporting the principals arrived at Ham Spray and nearby inns; many were in tears. As the Press kept watch, Strachey died on January 21, 1932, of, as the autopsy later showed, an undiagnosed stomach cancer.

The feverish attention now shifted to Carrington, whose whole emotional life had been tied to that of Strachey and who had several times threatened suicide. The traffic between London and Ham Spray remained heavy as plans were made, friends called in, schedules juggled, and expedients proposed to raise Carrington from her stricken grief and to leave her alone as little as possible. In any event she managed to shoot herself on March 11. These double deaths were no doubt horrific for those involved, but at times the descriptions and the toings-and-froings become overheated. Phrases like "a tremendous comfort," "unspeakable horrors," "haunted by strange unmerited guilt," "the poor creature," and even that old standby "the fatal day" give the events at times the air of Victorian melodrama. Even Frances herself admits to a vein of hysteria in the whole affair.

In addition to the coming of age of Frances and the Bloomsbury experiences, there are three other themes in the book worthy of mention. The first is the explanation and defense of the character and actions of Ralph Partridge, and in this the work is clearly a true love story. The book closes, by the author's deliberate design, with the dying fall and the quiet resolution of four love letters exchanged between Ralph and Frances.

The second theme is the love of nature, which is seen from the opening chapter and runs right through the whole work. Frances' response to natural scenes is simple and direct. From visits to Ireland and the Lake Country during her formative years to walks in the countryside to tours of France and Spain, the thread is clear. (It is amazing how much the Bloomsburyites liked to walk in the country—almost as much as they liked to talk, especially when they could combine, as they often did, the two.)

The third theme is perhaps the key to the work and its appeal—friendship. In the course of the book one meets many of the friends of Frances Partridge. She clearly has a great capacity for friendship, and her loyalties are strong. Friendship, as she maintains, "fertilizes the soil of one's life." In this book she introduces many people, presenting them not as objects for scholarly analysis, nor as strange or amusing or horrifying characers, nor as a collection of names to be dropped, but as *friends*. In a sense the whole book is a paean to friendship.

*Gordon N. Bergquist*

### Sources for Further Study

*Booklist*. LXXVIII, September 1, 1981, p. 19.
*Library Journal*. CVI, August, 1981, p. 1544.
*Listener*. CV, January 29, 1981, p. 149.
*The New York Times Book Review*. LXXXVI, September 27, 1981, p. 14.
*Newsweek*. XCVIII, October 5, 1981, p. 81.
*Observer*. July 19, 1981, p. 29.
*Spectator*. CCXLVI, February 21, 1981, p. 18.
*Times Literary Supplement*. February 13, 1981, p. 156.

# LUCK'S SHINING CHILD
## A Miscellany of Poems & Verses

*Author:* George Garrett (1929-    )
*Publisher:* Palaemon Press (Winston-Salem, North Carolina). 62 pp. $20.00
*Type of work:* Poetry

*In his first full-length collection of poems since* For a Bitter Season *(1967), George Garrett reminds readers that he is a poet of unique gifts and accomplishments*

Though George Garrett's first book, a collection of poems, appeared twenty-five years ago, and though he has published four full-length collections of poetry since then, it still seems at times necessary to recall, in view of his much larger reputation as a novelist, that his poetry is among the real treasures of contemporary literature. Stuart Wright, who produces elegant books under the Palaemon Press imprint, has provided a reminder in his splendid setting of these forty poems; this book is almost as much a pleasure to handle as it is to read.

Reading it, one is struck by a curious mixture of surprise and familiar delight. In nearly all of his writing, Garrett has been faithful to the themes of love and its delights and terrors, and of the frailty of human aspiration, not only in the face of certain mortality, but also in the eyes of God. Here, these themes reassert themselves, but the poems are fresh and new; they are not repetitious of earlier successes. As usual, the diction is often so colloquial as to lull the reader toward a suspicion that the poet's language is offhand. Garrett seems to have learned much about the uses of conversational diction from the Elizabethans. He is, of course, the author of two novels set in that period; and the epigraphs to this book and to its five sections are taken from Sir Thomas Wyatt, Giles Fletcher, Sir Walter Raleigh, and Francis Bacon. Even the modern epigraph, on the task of the translator, is taken from C. S. Lewis' *English Literature in the Sixteenth Century* (1954). Nearly twenty years ago, in creative writing classes at the University of Virginia, it was Garrett's custom to use the poems of Raleigh as examples of flexibility in tone and diction.

Garrett's poems are often so conversational as to include factual errors, by way of drawing the reader into them, to engage him in something like a dialogue, so that at the conclusion the reader has the feeling that he has participated in arriving at it. "Another Hat Poem," for example, begins in an offhand way to say that the speaker has been trying out different voices and different hats. Then: "I have been taking off countless hats/ like the boy in the (James Thurber?) story. And never keeping any one on for long." One is pressed to think of the right James Thurber story; meanwhile, the Dr. Seuss story of Bartholomew Cubbins asserts itself in the reader's memory, and he addresses the question mark, "Well, possibly. Anyway, proceed." Three more stanzas of explanation, and the poem ends: "Meantime better to be alive and foolish than bald as an apple, silent as a stone—one more hatless skull with a fixed grin." The grammar and meter gives the lines a sharp edge of truth; the poem is slight and amusing in certain ways, but it winds up reminding itself and its readers that all humans are foolish, and lucky to be so; we all come to that spondaic fixed grin.

The arrangement of poems in *Luck's Shining Child* is similarly witty and deceptive; there is a lively tension between the section titles and the poems in the sections—as well as between certain poems and their titles. The first and last of the sections are called "My Self" and "My Self (Again)." Here, then, according to the conventions of the day, one will find those poems which explore the inner life of the poet, that give voice to his joys and complaints. These poems are not confessional in the usual sense, however; though they often begin with some detail of the speaker's life, they enlarge quickly, placing the self in perspective of the larger world.

The title poem, for example, opens the collection, and is for several stanzas a funny portrait of a man so broke he has the soles of his shoes repaired one at a time. His students try to imagine him as a symbol of various dualities, but the truth is that he is broke:

> What I am trying not to do
> is imagine how it will be in my coffin,
> heels down, soles up,
>
> all rouged and grinning above my polished shoes,
> one or the other a respectable brother
> and one or the other
>
> that wild prodigal whom I love
> as much or more than his sleek companion,
> luck's shining child.

Here again, rhythm and grammar are apparently at odds; by all rules of sentence structure, "luck's shining child" is the newly repaired shoe, the "sleek companion"; and surely this is what is meant, primarily. The placement of the phrase at the end of the poem, however, and the careful arrangement of line-breaks in this stanza make it possible at least to wonder for a moment whether that "wild prodigal whom I love" is luck's shining child as well. As Garrett has said in an earlier poem, good luck sometimes seems worse than any wound; this poem puts the question on the knife-edge once again.

"Main Currents of American Political Thought" is a title which at once seems, at the head of a poem, to warn the reader away from seriousness; yet five of the poem's six stanzas offer a moving evocation of a life which has vanished—the gracious certainty of the life Grandfather lived, which led him to say once that free public schools and the petit jury would keep the democratic spirit of this country alive. The reader half expects some reversal of

what has seemed a conservative outlook, but the concluding stanza contains
a two-part surprise:

> What became of all that energy and swagger?
> At ninety you went out and campaigned for Adlai Stevenson
> in South Carolina. Half that age and I have to force
> myself to vote, choosing among scoundrels.

The idea of a ninety-year-old South Carolinian campaigning for Stevenson
runs counter to most stereotypes of American politics; it seems that this very
unpredictability is among the things being mourned in this poem.

The second section of *Luck's Shining Child* is called "Maine Weathers,"
and takes its epigraph from a remarkable description of Russian winter by
Giles Fletcher, who says, among other things, "that water dropped downe or
cast up into the ayre, congealeth into Ise before it come to the ground." These
eight poems all take as points of departure various phenomena of the weather
in Maine, but they all come closer than anything in the "Self" sections to
revealing the inner weather out of which the poems came. "Mundane Meta-
morphosis," for example, begins with a description of the speaker, waking
to find himself dull and heavy as lead, to raise the windowshade upon a
brilliant day; he imagines Columbus being lifted from despair by discovery,

> Or stout Balboa rusty as an old woodstove
> inching his bulky self up to another limb
> sweat dripping beneath his dented helmet
> then inching his dented helmet above another
> whose leaves sigh with his weight and weariness
>
> To see suddenly and always the blue eye of God
> which greets his gasp with an enormous wink
> The river is burning and the gulls cry doom
> but the man of lead now smiles to discover
> that even his teeth are rich with silver and gold.

Quite aside from the fine ending, which has the ambiguity displayed in previous examples, it is an uplifting experience to encounter at last a wonderful
line containing "stout Balboa," who has become English literature's leading
symbol of the primacy of poetic effect over historical accuracy. The insistent
avoidance of romance in that stanza, the portrayal of the great voyager as a
kind of Don Quixote, is consistent with Garrett's concern always to try and
render history as it must have felt, and not as readers have learned to visualize
it through the illustrations of Howard Pyle, whose *Men of Iron* rarely showed
a speck of rust.

Most of the poems in this section are similarly concerned with drawing a
mood from weather, and then make it clear that it is the mood that determines
the way the weather is perceived. Nature does not rejoice or grieve, but only

seems to; human beings are transient and frail. Yet their glory is that they have the words for these things.

Section III, "A Few Translations," addresses by implication the themes of naming and of speech. "The business of the translator," says C. S. Lewis in the passage chosen for the epigraph, "is to write down what he thinks the original meant." These few translations from Italian and German poetry are first of all remarkable for their success as poems; they are thoroughly natural and moving in English. Comparison with some of the originals reveals Garrett's willingness to make small rearrangements in the order of the images, so that, though his translations might not always serve as dependable "trots" on pages facing the originals, they successfully find the poetic means of conveying what the original conveys. One small illustration should suffice; "La Capra" (The Goat), by Umberto Saba (1883-1957), begins "Ho parlato a una capra." Literally, this might be rendered "I have talked to a goat." The next three lines describe the goat, tied to a post, bleating in the rain. The poem concludes with the poet's recognition of universal grief in the voice of that goat. So Garrett's first line, "One time I talked to a goat," is not recklessly conversational after all, but carefully interpretive of the tendency in Romance languages to use the continuous past, especially in conversation, even when the past perfect is more nearly what is meant. Garrett's line gets the conversational tone and the suggestion that the conversation took place in a more remote past than is conveyed by the present perfect tense in English.

Garrett is not a prolific translator; he appears only to have made occasional translations when he came upon a poem in another language and recognized in it something with which he wanted to work. The result is that the translations have received the same attention and care that have been given to the other poems.

The fourth section of *Luck's Shining Child* is called "Love and Other Fooleries," and is composed mainly of moving love poems addressed to a woman with whom the speaker has lived a long time. A few are amused reactions to lustful notions aroused either by his wife or by the sight of some other woman, fleetingly glimpsed. Garrett has always written about women with extraordinary perception and economy, sometimes adopting swashbuckling personae. In this group of poems he drops most of the masks, as he says he will do in the first poem of the section, "Feeling Good, Feeling Fine." The central metaphor of the poem is that of the soldier, back from hard duty, singing in the shower: "I hang my dogtags and towel on a nail/ to lightheaded, lighthearted, stand/ in rosy steam and sing your name." Shedding the dogtags is, for the soldier, a gesture almost of rebellion, certainly of momentary freedom; and that is what is being referred to at the end of the poem, which has earned the old quotation: "The letter kills, the spirit giveth life."

Returning ostensibly to the Self in the final section, Garrett ends this book in a brilliant display of variety—of form, tone, attitude. Among the best are

"For an Actress" and two fine evocations of the literary life, "Out on the Circuit" and "Envoy." "Out on the Circuit" has its humorous moments, its ruthless depiction of the speaker as he awakens in some Howard Johnson's with a monstrous hangover; but the poem is equally ruthless in its recognition of the way the professional responds to the challenge, and to the knowledge that his check is in his inside coat pocket:

> I raise my glass to share a toast with the stranger in
>     the mirror,
> to rejoice together in the inexhaustible resources of
>     self-deception,
> beyond the deepest dreams of decent salesmen and cost
>     accountants.
> See how my hands are steady. Now I know how it is to
>     live forever.

In the presence of a new book by a living poet, many readers indulge themselves in habits developed over several years of being in the business themselves: watching for new techniques, stanza forms, metaphors, seeing how it is done. In the presence of these poems, it is more tempting, and more appropriate, to be carried into informed reverie by the mastery and wisdom they exhibit, and to be grateful for the craft and generosity that have produced them.

*Henry Taylor*

### Sources for Further Study

No listing.

# LUCY
## The Beginnings of Humankind

*Author:* Donald C. Johanson (1943-    ) and Maitland A. Edey (1910-    )
*Publisher:* Simon and Schuster (New York). Illustrated. 409 pp. $16.95
*Type of work:* Science
*Time:* 1974 to the present
*Locale:* East Africa

*A work of popular science which tells of the discovery of Lucy, a 3.5 million-year-old fossil ancestor of humankind, providing by the way a history of paleoanthropology and an explanation of its current techniques and its day-to-day problems*

> *Principal personages:*
> DONALD C. JOHANSON, a young paleoanthropologist who discovers Lucy
> EUGÈNE DUBOIS, the discoverer of the Java Man
> RAYMOND DART, the discoverer of the Taung Baby
> LOUIS LEAKEY,
> MARY, his wife, and
> RICHARD, their son, a famous family of paleoanthropologists

In Ethiopia, just north of Addis Ababa in the Afar triangle, a woman named Lucy died, probably either of accidental drowning or of a severe illness. She was in her mid- or late twenties. She had walked erect, just as modern humans do. Her brain, however, was not much bigger than that of a chimpanzee, and she was not a user of tools. Her apelike face was not much more than three feet from the ground. She died in 3,500,000 B.C. It is possible to read about Lucy—she was named after the Beatles' song—because in 1974 her fossilized skeletal remains were discovered by Donald C. Johanson and an associate.

How was Lucy found? By accident, certainly, for Johanson and his associate practically stumbled over her one November day, but if finds in paleoanthropology—the study of humankind's ancestors—are largely accidental, they are nevertheless accidents that occur within a highly planned environment. As in archaeology, digs are carefully mapped and gridded and all finds are diligently marked within these maps and grids. Moreover, the modern paleoanthropological dig is a multidisciplinary enterprise which relies on the services of geologists and of specialists in the evolution of creatures other than man. These expensive, sometimes multinational and unwieldy teams of scientists must be financed and administered. Finally, a suitable site must be selected; Afar was suitable because the dryness of the climate encouraged the preservation of fossils and the geology, although complex, made accurate dating at least possible.

It may seem preposterous that an erect-walking human ancestor existed nearly four million years ago, but the date is airtight, confirmed by five separate methods, each supportive of the others. In geological dating, the age of fossil-bearing rocks is deduced from purely geological principles. Potassium-argon and fission-track dating are measurements of the radioactive decay in these rocks. Paleomagnetism relies on the fact that over millions of years there are occasional measurable reversals in the earth's magnetic poles and that these are reflected in its rocks. Finally, biostratography correlates hominid forms with other fossils, such as those of the pig, the dating of which is more nearly certain. On the basis of these five methods scientists agree that Lucy is 3.5 million years old.

She was also bipedal—that is, she walked erect, unlike apes and monkeys. Monkeys do not walk at all and chimpanzees and gorillas are knuckle walkers. According to one theory, man's ancestors became bipedal because they needed their hands for tool use. A very plausible idea, but one that cannot be sustained in the light of the evidence Lucy provides. Lucy was bipedal, but she was not human; no tools were found with her or with similar hominids—they seem to be a human invention. In any case, her small brain made serious tool use out of the question.

It is easier, as it turns out, to undermine the tool-use theory than to construct a new theory that the evidence of Lucy will support. In the book, however, some measure of support is given to a very speculative idea which relates bipedalism to the survival of the species. According to this speculation, all species tend to survive either by giving birth to an enormous number of young to whom they give little or no care (like the oyster), or by giving birth to a few young whose care then becomes their intelligent concern, as in the case of the gorilla. The oyster relies on chance, the gorilla on intelligent care. The gorilla strategy—which is also that of humankind and its ancestors—has this danger, however. Too few offspring may be born and the species, like the modern-day gorilla, may become extinct or nearly extinct despite the quality of infant care. One way to avoid this pitfall is to increase the possibility of pregnancy in the species. This is, in fact, the solution inherent in the human menstrual cycle, unique among living things. The survival of the human species, then, depended on maximizing the number of offspring without at the same time reducing the amount of intelligent infant care. This survival strategy led to a cluster of adaptive traits, such as pair bonding and social structures. Within this cluster, bipedalism makes sense: it allows the female to develop the careful mothering so necessary to the long infancy of the human child.

Whatever the truth about the origin of Lucy's bipedalism, that bipedalism is clear evidence of her hominid status. A second compelling proof of this status comes from the structure and arrangement of her teeth. Since most fossil remains are of jaws and teeth, it is on these that paleoanthropologists must generally rely if they are to decide whether a particular questionable fossil is more apelike or more human. Fortunately, there are many clear dental differences between human beings and apes. In chimpanzees, for example, male and female canines are different; in humans they are alike.

Chimpanzee canines are pointed; human canines are relatively blunt. Using these and other analogous ape-human comparisons, Johanson was able to place Lucy squarely between apes and humans. Neither one nor the other, she was a hominid, an ancestor of humankind.

The discovery of Lucy—bipedal, hominid—led necessarily to a radical restructuring of the human family tree. The most widely accepted tree in the 1960's and 1970's made a nonhuman, *Australopithecus africanus*, the common ancestor of two branches: one was nonhuman and consisted only of *A. robustus*; the other, human branch consisted of *Homo habilis*, *H. erectus*, and *H. sapiens*. In Johanson's family tree, on the other hand, Lucy, a nonhuman (officially named *Australopithecus afarensis*), is the common ancestor from which two branches descend—the nonhuman one of *africanus* and *robustus*, and the human one mentioned above. The discovery of Lucy has also pushed back human evolution a million years.

*Lucy* is not only about the discovery and significance of an important fossil, however; it is also about paleoanthropology itself, its human details, its history, and its techniques. Reading the book one gets the feel of living in the Afar region with its blazing heat, its discomfort, its monotonous food, its lack of bathing facilities. One also gets glimpses which show why intelligent, ambitious men connive to get to Afar to endure that life: the thrill of discovering human fossil remains and of knowing one's career is assured and that fame is just around the corner.

In addition to paleoanthropology's human details, *Lucy* introduces a number of the people who, beginning in the late nineteenth century, have turned this pursuit from a game of amateurs into a science: Eugène Dubois, the Dutch scientist who found the Java Man in 1893; Raymond Dart, who uncovered the Taung Baby in 1924, and, most important perhaps, the three famous Leakeys—Louis, his wife Mary, and his son Richard, the last two of whom quarreled with Johanson's interpretation of Lucy. From the stories of these men and women, one learns both how young paleoanthropology is and how far it has come in less than a century.

The key to the transformation of paleoanthropology into a science is in its use of improved technologies, especially those which have vastly improved the accuracy of fossil dating. *Lucy* explains these technologies in detail and with the greatest clarity. This workmanlike prose is the contribution, one assumes, of Maitland A. Edey, an experienced scientific journalist; clarity is always his foremost concern. The text is complemented throughout by appropriate photographs and drawings.

*Lucy* can be fairly compared in quality only with James Watson's fine book *The Double Helix* (1968), another scientific autobiography. *Lucy* compares favorably, but one might wish that, like *The Double Helix*, Johanson's book omitted one of its persistent devices—the conversation that probably never happened.

"You mean, all the potassium-40 in the world is gradually decaying and turning into argon gas?" I asked.

"That's right. There's less and less of it. And more and more argon every day."

"Where does all that argon go?"

"Ultimately into the atmosphere."

Despite this fault, *Lucy* remains a fine book for the general reader.

*Alan G. Gross*

## Sources for Further Study

*Archeology*. XXXIV, July, 1981, p. 74.

*Choice*. XL, October, 1981, p. 278.

*Christian Science Monitor*. LXXIII, April 8, 1981, p. 15.

*Chronicle of Higher Education*. XXII, May 26, 1981, p. 15.

*Humanist*. XLI, July, 1981, p. 53.

*Library Journal*. CVI, February 1, 1981, p. 354.

*National Review*. XXXIII, June 26, 1981, p. 737.

*The New York Times Book Review*. LXXXVI, February 22, 1981, p. 1.

*The New Yorker*. LVII, March 9, 1981, p. 132.

*Saturday Review*. VIII, February, 1981, p. 67.

# MATTHEW ARNOLD
## A Life

*Author:* Park Honan (1928-    )
*Publisher:* McGraw-Hill Book Company (New York). Illustrated. 496 pp. $19.95
*Type of work:* Literary biography

*A thoroughly researched and definitive biography of the great nineteenth century poet and critic*

> Principal personages:
> MATTHEW ARNOLD, poet and critic
> DR. THOMAS ARNOLD, his father and Headmaster of Rugby School
> FRANCES LUCY WIGHTMAN, Matthew's wife
> ARTHUR HUGH CLOUGH, a poet and a close friend of Matthew's

In 1939, Lionel Trilling began his famous critical biography of Matthew Arnold by saying that he had consulted almost no unpublished material and by warning readers that whatever biographical material he used was incidental to his critical purpose. Park Honan, in this new, extensively researched and documented biography, has taken just the opposite approach and might very well have begun his book by warning readers that whatever critical comments he makes are incidental to his biographical purpose. Honan says in his Preface that he was only a student when he first read Trilling's study and that although the book challenged him, it did not take him close to Arnold's life. In an effort to make up for that deficiency, Honan spent ten years in researching and writing *Matthew Arnold: A Life*, a definitive biography for the Arnold specialist and the general reader alike. Trying to find every known fact about Arnold, he pored over diaries, letters, and journals, largely unpublished, to accumulate a mass of biographical data, three-quarters of which has never before appeared in a study of Arnold.

Certainly no one can doubt the claim that this is the fullest account of Arnold's life to date. Moreover, no one can doubt, after consulting the more than fifty pages of notes and citations, that this biography is both thoroughly researched and authoritative. It is surely clear after reading this book that one knows more about Matthew the man than ever before; however, as to whether one knows more about Matthew Arnold the poet or Matthew Arnold the critic, or even Matthew Arnold the intellectual spokesman of his age— that is another question, which involves one's fundamental expectations of a literary biography.

Biographical literary criticism, that is, the use of a man's life as a way of understanding his art, is a risky business and may involve the biographical critic in speculations both fanciful and farfetched. Most readers, however, come to a biography of a literary figure with the expectation of seeing at least some relationship between the man and his art. Although Honan notes in his Preface that he respects the distinction between life and art, he says that he has tried to show how Arnold defined himself in his work. Indeed, the most disappointing aspect of this massive biography is that Honan has respected the distinction between life and art too much. On the one hand, there is such a slavish regard for documentation and detail that the vitality of Arnold's life does not come through for the general reader. What is presented is Arnold as the subject of a biography, not Arnold the re-created and rendered figure of real experience.

On the other hand, the problem with this biography for the Arnold specialist is that although Honan's book tells a great deal about Arnold's life, it has too little to say about what generated his art and dominated his thought. Park Honan is, by training and experience, a critic. His early book, *Browning's Characters*, was one of a half dozen books published in the early 1960's that started a revival of interest in Victorian writers. It was a book that helped to show that the Victorians were the true harbingers, both in thought and artistic technique, of the modernist method and point of view. In that light, the relative lack of critical analysis in Honan's biography of Arnold is all the more disappointing, especially since his subject was the primary proponent of the critical spirit in the nineteenth century and one of the great critical minds of the last hundred years.

The most important early influence in the development of Matthew Arnold was that of his father, the great Dr. Thomas Arnold, Headmaster of Rugby School, and the most important problem young Matt faced was establishing his own identity as distinct from that of his father. His first reaction was a kind of rebellion, for the young Arnold was a lazy late-bloomer, although he was the eldest son and his father's fondest hope. In his earliest years Arnold picked up the family nickname of "Crabby," not for his disposition but because of the crablike crawl he developed as an infant; he wore leg braces until he was four. Arnold's father was disappointed but somewhat indulgent concerning his son's lackluster school performance. In one letter to the young Matt, the father, after learning that "Crabby" has received "unsatisfactory" twice in one week, chides: "it makes me sadly afraid that my boy Matt is an idle Boy, who thinks that God sent him into the world to play and eat and drink."

In spite of the inauspicious beginnings of his academic career, and much to the astonishment of everyone in his family, Arnold won a Balliol College Scholarship and went to Oxford in 1841. Oxford, Honan says, was treated by Arnold as if it were a country house. On one memorable occasion, Arnold, after being scolded by a passing clergyman for capering naked on the banks of a river, haughtily replied, "Is it possible that you see anything indelicate in the human form divine?" While at Oxford, Arnold applied himself more than previously, but his former neglect of his Latin and Greek studies proved too much to overcome; his father was not alive to see Arnold earn only a second-class degree. Still, Arnold, in another surprise, won a fellowship to

Oriel College and began the intense reading in German Romanticism—Johann Wolfang von Goethe, Friedrich von Schiller, Immanuel Kant, and Friedrich von Schelling—that was to affect his poetry later on. In fact, it was during this period that the basic conflict that plagued Arnold's art began to manifest itself. In one of the few places that Honan deals with the division in Arnold that often devastated his poetry, he notes that Arnold was rational and intuitive by turns: "The lyricist struggled with the moralist." As a result of his reading of Aristotle and Samuel Taylor Coleridge, Arnold felt that poetry must be more than beauty, but his extreme reaction to this view and his fear that romantic passion would endanger his self-possession resulted in what many critics rightly recognize as the damaging preponderance of discursive argument in his poetry.

In 1849, at the age of twenty-six, Arnold published *The Strayed Reveller and Other Poems* under the disguised authorship of "A." Honan calls the book the best first collection by an Englishman from Arnold's time to the present "for sheer lyrical beauty." As if this claim were not vast and unjustified enough, Honan further asserts that "The Strayed Reveller" itself has only been equalled in intensity in the twentieth century by T. S. Eliot. Honan does little more than offer summaries of such poems as "The Strayed Reveller" and "Resignation" to justify such extravagant claims. It is ironic that whereas Arnold wrote his sister after the publication of this first collection of poems that he was much against the modern habit of using poetry as a channel for thinking out loud instead of making something, it is precisely "thinking out loud" or intellectualizing that characterizes much of Arnold's poetry. In later years, Arnold remarked that although he had perhaps less intellectual vigor than Robert Browning and less poetical sentiment than Alfred, Lord Tennyson, he had more of a fusion of the two than either. That fusion, however, according to most critical opinion, was not often achieved. It is unfortunate that Honan's biography does not sufficiently deal with this central tension in Arnold's poetry—the tension between detachment and involvement that plagues many of his poetic personae. Of course, Honan can justify his approach by arguing that he must not hypothesize what cannot directly be supported by primary biographical materials; however, it is hard to believe that such a dominant poetic dichotomy played so small a part in Arnold's life.

Another problem of Honan's biography resulting from the focus almost solely on direct documented biographical data is that only half way through the text does one finally reach the publication of Arnold's greatest poem, *Empedocles on Etna* (1852); within one hundred pages of the conclusion of the book, Arnold has only just been appointed to the Poetry Chair at Oxford. The ten years he held that Chair and began publishing his lectures and essays—those crucial ten years between 1857 and 1867 when he became the leading critic of the Victorian Age—get a comparatively brief treatment; less space is spent on the development of Arnold's thought than on his experiences as

Inspector of Schools. The shift Arnold made from his earlier view that poetry must make something to the view that poetry can only subsist by its contents, can only be valuable insofar as it teaches and integrates religion, is no more accounted for than the fact that Arnold became easier and more natural in his behavior after his marriage to Frances Lucy Wightman, because, as Honan surmises, she must have ridiculed his "affected wincing, grimacing, and smirking."

Arnold's relationship with his sister Jane, model for Fausta in "Resignation" and often addressed as "K," is indeed fully documented here, as is the further effect Frances ("Fanny") had on Arnold by leading him to appreciate opera, painting, sculpture, and modern novels. His erratic, Hamlet/Horatio friendship with Arthur Hugh Clough, who accused him, rightly it seems, of egotism, pride, and coldness, is also detailed. It was to Clough that Arnold wrote after deciding to spend less time on poetry, telling him that his respect for reason was steadily increasing. Arnold's American lecture tour, much of it disastrous because his voice simply did not carry strongly enough to hold the attention of his audiences, is also fully detailed.

For a biography of a great literary voice and a great thinker, however, such details of personal attitudes and alliances do not compensate for the lack of effort to integrate that voice and thought with the man himself. Surely such personal poems as "The Buried Life," "Dover Beach," and "The Scholar Gipsy" deserve more than summaries and surface generalizations. Surely such important ideas as "most of what now passes for religion and philosophy will be replaced by poetry" deserve more scrupulous attention than Honan gives them. In particular, the reader deserves better than Honan's passing comparisons between Arnold and various twentieth century figures. In one outlandish comparison, Honan notes Arnold's view that the critic must respect the "extremely elusive nature of art" and suggests that such a view anticipates Roland Barthes. Honan then cites a passage suggesting that literature is onion-like, with no kernel, just infinite envelopes. For the reader unfamiliar with the poststructuralist implications of such a description, the context for the quotation is so ambiguous that one might think it is from Arnold himself. However, a check of one of the hundreds of Honan's end-notes informs the reader that the quotation is not only not from Arnold, but also that it is not from Barthes either; rather, it is a quotation from Jonathan Culler's description of a Barthian view in his book *Structuralist Poetics* (1975). Arnold's view of the elusiveness of poetry is no more like the view of Barthes than his poem "The Strayed Reveller" is like the poetry of T. S. Eliot.

Much of this criticism of Park Honan's *Matthew Arnold: A Life* is based on the assumption that a biography of an influential thinker and poet should deal with that person's art and thought if it is to be of value to specialists in the field, or that it should be an enlivened, if not lively, narrative account of a human life, if it is to appeal to the general reader. None of this is to suggest that Honan's book is incomplete, incompetent, or inaccurate. Honan has indeed produced a likeness, but like so many bourgeois portraits of the Victorian period, it just is not satisfying as a picture.

*Charles May*

## Sources for Further Study

*Contemporary Review*. CCXXXIX, October, 1981, p. 220.
*The Economist*. CCLXXX, September 5, 1981, p. 95.
*Library Journal*. CVI, July, 1981, p. 1423.
*New Statesman*. CII, August 28, 1981, p. 18.
*The New York Review of Books*. XXVIII, December 17, 1981, p. 18.
*The New York Times Book Review*. LXXXVI, August 9, 1981, p. 9.
*Newsweek*. XCVIII, September 7, 1981, p. 75.
*Spectator*. CCXLVII, September 12, 1981, p. 18.
*Times Literary Supplement*. August 28, 1981, p. 971.
*Wilson Quarterly*. VI, Winter, 1981, p. 159.

# THE MEETING AT TELGTE

*Author:* Günter Grass (1927-    )
Translated from the German by Ralph Manheim
Afterword by Leonard Forster
*Publisher:* Harcourt Brace Jovanovich (New York). 147 pp. $9.95
*Type of work:* Novel
*Time:* 1647
*Locale:* Telgte, Westphalia

*An arrrangements committee bungles a major writers' and literary scholars' conference*

Principal characters:
> CRISTOFFEL GELNHAUSEN (GRIMMELSHAUSEN), author of *Simplicissimus the Vagabond*
> SIMON DACH, a Königsberg poet and professor
> LIBUSCHKA, a landlady, Grimmelshausen's "Courage"
> AUGUST BUCHNER, a Wittenberg professor of poetry
> DANIEL VON CZEPKO UND REIGERSFELD, a Silesian religious poet
> PAUL GERHARDT, a Lutheran pastor and hymn-writer
> GEORG GREFLINGER, a Hamburg newspaper publisher
> FRIEDRICH VON LOGAU, a Silesian epigrammist
> JOHANN SCHEFFLER, a Silesian poet
> HEINRICH SCHÜTZ, a religious and operatic composer
> GEORG RUDOLF WECKHERLIN, a poet and diplomat
> "I," the narrator

At a recent writers' conference, a literary agent was asked about the gap between copies of a book sold and copies actually read. The agent replied that he did not know and did not care. In the case of *The Meeting at Telgte*, readers encountering Günter Grass for the first time (and some readers of his previous big books) are likely to feel put upon, and this little book will make a quick trip from coffee table to attic.

The potential readership of Grass's new novel is broader than one might expect from the subject matter: a fictional conference of the actual leading German writers of 1647. Those familiar with this period in German history and literature will receive the maximum value from this book. The information in the Afterword and other appendices will refresh memories but will not provide remedial education.

Most helpfully, the Afterword puts this novel in the context of Grass's life and work. This 1674 conference exists in parallel with a real conference in 1947 convened by Hans Werner Richter. The question of what German writers could do for a troubled Germany was more positively answered in 1947 and launched Grass's own career.

The broadest base of readers who will understand and be entertained by this novel consists of writers and scholars who will experience a peculiar *déja vu*. If it is Grass's joke that writers and scholars are the same through the ages, it is also true that Germany has so insidiously shaped learned societies throughout the Western world, especially literary societies, that the agenda, paper topics, and problems of Grass's imaginary conference in 1647 are strikingly similar to those of the annual Modern Language Association convention and practically any regional or local gathering of English teachers on "creative writers."

The initial problem of the conference is raising travel expenses. Comic relief is provided by the bungling of the "arrangements committee." The conference begins with tributes to departed colleagues and papers on linguistics and rhetoric. The first day ends with the more staid types going to bed early, a few seeking sex, the majority spending the night with drink, bawdy wit, and gossip. Events in the real world become matters for assimilation into scholarly consideration. The relations between music and literature are explored and dull details about travel to and from the conference fill the leisure time. Various manifestos on politics and literature are debated. "Natural art" and artificial art are compared. The arrangers come into ethical conflict with the fund raisers over the big banquet. The conference site burns to the ground. This is the agenda.

Dialogue is almost completely nonexistent. The unnamed narrator records the events of the novel in the manner of a secretary taking minutes at a meeting. In place of coaxing travel expenses and time off from department chairpersons, the conferencegoers of 1647 must obtain patronage. Similarly, in place of big-city muggers, some conferencegoers are attacked by highway robbers.

Simon Dach's symbolic notion to convene the writer's meeting at the site of ongoing political-military peace conferences proves impractical. The military has commandeered the site and the landlord refuses to give a refund. Enter Christoffel Gelnhausen (Grimmelshausen), a soldier-author who claims both the practical knowledge to facilitate the conference and the sensitivity to appreciate it. He kindly offers to take over the practical side of the arrangements, leaving Dach and his colleagues their proper role as impractical intellectuals. Under his guidance, the conference moves to Telgte.

The usual tributes are made to deceased colleagues: well-intentioned, pompous, meaningless to those who do not know the deceased, offensive to those who do and disagree with the chairperson's assessment. Controversial papers are presented on the linguistically proper meter in poetry and rhetorically proper characters in drama. While the elders seek bed and the youngsters seek sex, the middle-aged seek drink and conversation. (Meanwhile, Phillip von Zesen finds bodies floating in a stream and is too overcome by the literary possibilities to be frightened.)

In the drunken byplay between Gelnhausen and Libuschka, the landlady, the biggest ongoing irony of the novel is established: Gelnhausen, of later fame as Grimmelshausen, as the humble butt of his "betters."

An informal seminar on sex around the world at the top and bottom of the social scale extends into the early morning. The arrival of Heinrich Schütz generates controversy on the issue of church music *versus* "good" music, after Schütz has told the group more about his uneventful travels than they want to know.

Shaped poetry is read aloud and, of course, the shapes are not communicated. A lengthy play is read aloud by its author until the audience begins to fall asleep. A debate ensues between those who misinterpret the play because they slept through part of it and those who remained awake. More poetry is read and one listener complains that he cannot comment without seeing and reflecting on the poems at his leisure. Complaints about the food interweave with abortive attempts to present political manifestos. Johann Rist asks the group to bear with him as he reads from a rough draft. More poems are read, including a dog's monologue.

Gelnhausen enlivens the proceedings with a feast, and only after the conference has gorged itself does the nonpartaking Schütz make Gelnhausen admit the obvious: the wine is sacramental, the decorations also from a church, and the food from a murdered farmer. Gelnhausen claims that he merely murdered and robbed the original robbers and murderers. The intellectuals do not know how to handle Gelnhausen. They are guilty of "lusts that swelled their sentence structure" and feel a "universal guilt that amounted to a universal acquittal."

With Gelnhausen's conduct no longer an issue, the group delves into art and pornography as represented by a new "Abélard and Héloïse." Is it a fit subject? Must it be so graphic? Finally, Dach's own presentation, a poem on the destruction of a cucumber bower, is a paean to the good old fat days as contrasted with the accidental emblem of the conference: a thistle. The political disarray of the final attempts to write a manifesto find their objective correlative in a fire which destroys the draft manifesto and the conference site.

These issues are indeed ageless. Which is worse, writers and scholars each in their own ivory tower or coming together for a Tower of Babel exercise in noncommunication? Grass provides a partial antidote. Surely, if veterans of conferences can see themselves and the humor of their pomposity and muddled sense of purpose as people and artists and scholars, there is some hope of redemption and actual accomplishment.

*T. G. Shults*

## Sources for Further Study

*The Atlantic Monthly*. CCXLVII, June, 1981, p. 101.
*Christian Science Monitor*. LXXIII, May 11, 1981 p. B2.

*Library Journal.* CVI, March 15, 1981, p. 680.
*New Leader.* LXIV, May 18, 1981, p. 5.
*The New York Review of Books.* XXVIII, June 11, 1981, p. 35.
*The New York Times Book Review.* LXXXVI, May 17, 1981, p. 7.
*The New Yorker.* LVII, August 3, 1981, p. 91.
*Saturday Review.* VIII, May, 1981, p. 71.
*Time.* CXVII, May 18, 1981, p. 87.
*Times Literary Supplement.* June 26, 1981, p. 717.

# THE MISMEASURE OF MAN

*Author:* Stephen Jay Gould (1942-    )
*Publisher:* W. W. Norton and Company (New York). 352 pages. $14.95
*Type of work:* Science
*Time:* The nineteenth and twentieth centuries

*A thoroughgoing debunking of the errors of craniometry and intelligence testing as aspects of biological determinism and its social prejudices*

Stephen Jay Gould is the author of *Ever Since Darwin* (1977), *Ontogeny and Phylogeny* (1977), and *The Panda's Thumb* (1980). In 1980 he won the National Magazine Award for Essays and Criticism, and in 1981 both the American Book Award for Science and the National Book Critics Circle Award for Non-Fiction. He teaches geology, biology, and history of science at Harvard University. By way of summarizing Gould's credentials, *Newsweek* (March 29, 1982) called him America's foremost writer and thinker on evolution.

*The Mismeasure of Man* merits the accolades it has received (including the National Book Critics Circle Award) for its treatment of the controversies which perennially surround the testing and measurement of man's intelligence—and thus his "nature." *The Mismeasure of Man* deserves reading and pondering for its scope, for its honesty of approach, and for what it exposes as prejudice and even deliberate deception, but it also deserves reading as a testimonial to the author's effort to see things as they really are, without the racist and sexist assumptions which have distorted so much human thought.

In the midst of his technical and highly statistical summaries, Gould interjects anecdotes and observations about his own life, about his son's learning disability, and about his wife, his colleagues, and his students at Harvard. *The Mismeasure of Man* is objective and impersonal where it needs to be but personal and human in overall tone and attitude. Gould's shifts in diction, from formal and technical scientific language to informal and even colloquial phrases and asides, make *The Mismeasure of Man* all the more accessible to the ordinary reader.

Gould's persona, then, in this book as in much of his other writing—including his monthly column for *Natural History* magazine—is that of an eminently qualified expert at the top of his field who deems it important also to be a popularizer, one who thinks it matters for the non-scientist to be informed about his or her evolving nature as a member of *Homo sapiens*. Gould chooses a quotation from Charles Darwin to serve as the epigraph and keynote for his book: "If the misery of our poor be caused not by the laws of nature, but by our institutions, great is our sin." It is as something of a clear-eyed, revisionist crusader, then, intent upon righting past and present miseries of certain "downtrodden" classes of society—as a result of scientific, pseudoscientific, and personal biases—that Gould takes stock and asks for a reckoning.

He is a scientist utilizing the ideals of scientific methodology to rectify science's own miscalculations, to correct some of his partners' own damaging errors. At the same time, Gould is affirming science's ability to seek out revised versions of the truth. He devotes one short but significant chapter to the justification of his debunking attack on his scientific predecessors who wound up mismeasuring man's intelligence, advancing three guiding principles which vindicate and direct his critique of biological determinism.

First, the author sees science advancing by means of the replacement of ideas, not by the addition of them. Second, scientific debunking must truly increase knowledge and not merely replace one social prejudice for another one. An ailment such as pellagra, for example, can only be cured if it can be proved to be the result of a vitamin deficiency and not a genetic disorder inherent in poor people. Finally, as an evolutionary biologist, Gould believes that Darwin's central truth is the evolutionary unity of humans with all other organisms. Thus, man's narcissism and arrogance is much out of place. *Homo sapiens* is a unique species but so is each other species—and to acknowledge the uniqueness of all life should in no way demean humans.

It should also be remembered that it is cultural evolution and not biological evolution which is changing at breakneck speed. One generation can pass along information about television and computers and bombs in a very rapid and direct way because it operates in the "Lamarckian" mode of acquired characteristics. The gene-coded advancements, seldom reversible, of biological evolution move slowly and indirectly. Biological determinism fails to recognize these differences between cultural and biological evolution and makes distinctions among groups of people—distinctions, for example, of degrees and kinds of intelligence—mistaking the products of cultural change for those of Darwinian or biological change. Therefore, Gould asserts that the biological uniqueness of *Homo sapiens* should lead to the rejection and not the endorsement of the arguments and explanations of biological determinism.

It is in this latter way in particular that Gould's arguments come in conflict with those of sociobiology, which attempt to account for the origin and maintenance of genetic and adaptive behavior. To Gould, adaptation in the human species is a given, but it cannot invariably be traced to genetic influences. Biological models and analogies can be useful in studying the adaptive processes of organisms without linking them to genetic programming, but sociobiologists, Gould believes, too often mistake analogy for fact. Sociobiologists, he thinks, seek the genetic basis of human behavior at the wrong level insofar as an exception or instance of some deep-structured rule of human behavior does not codify as "innate" that particular trait or rule. The search among specified traits of behavior for the genetic basis of human nature is a kind of biological determinism, and Gould is more interested in biological potential.

Apart from his conclusion, and another chapter which establishes the broader historical and methodological context for his discussion, Gould presents his case in five long, complex but provocative chapters. The first deals with American craniometry before Darwin, focusing on the scientific racism of Louis Agassiz as a theorist of polygeny, and Samuel George Morton as the empiricist practitioner. It is here that Gould first explores the scientific assumptions elaborately but speciously advanced concerning the reputed inferiority of blacks and Indians. An ensuing chapter deals with Paul Broca's research at the height of the popularity of craniology. Broca, along with Francis Galton, speculated about the brain sizes and shapes and the characters of both eminent men and criminals. Their research, including arguments against the superiority of women, won them a "school" of believers. Gould then turns to the measurement of body types and Cesare Lombroso's far-fetched but catchy theory of *l'uomo delinquene*—the criminal man—one of the most influential theories of criminal anthropology. Lombroso regarded criminals as evolutionary throwbacks, atavists who could be recognized on sight as "born criminals" by their visage and anatomy.

With this groundwork in the acceptance of craniometry and the measurement of bodies, Gould then investigates the related subject of mental testing. One chapter concerns the work of Alfred Binet in IQ testing and the subsequent erroneous applications of his work by H. H. Goddard, who coined the term "moron" and resorted to trick photographs to prove his point; Lewis M. Terman, who began testing for IQ on masses of people and advanced some categorical assertions which he only reluctantly recanted; and of R. M. Yerkes and his grand scheme of utilizing soldiers to establish once and for all absolute degrees of intelligence—only to overlook obvious variables of the environment's impact on his subjects. A final chapter deals with the faked statistical evidence of Sir Cyril Burt and his staunch belief in the innateness and hereditarianism of intelligence—so biased a belief that even his collaborators were imaginary.

All in all, Gould unveils an amazing number of logical and procedural fallacies, a startling number of instances of outright prejudice and bigotry among allegedly objective researchers; and once again dramatizes how professional ambitions can skew data and results. Most of the instances of mismeasurement which Gould recounts can be regarded as nothing less than outrageous and, insofar as theory touched actual lives, regrettable, monumental mistakes.

The familiar notion here is that human beings have always sought to classify and rank one another, find out and somehow label those more beautiful, more talented, and more intelligent. It is one thing to intuit such distinctions, such favorites, and act on one's intuitions. It is quite another to attempt formally and "scientifically," to identify those individuals who are smart and those who are not. Any such attempt is intrinsically a social and political enterprise; depending on who is in power to do the measuring and make the judgments, the results can be quite sinister. Gould attempts in *The Mismeasure of Man* to point out the scientific vulnerability and the overriding politics of all arguments for biological determinism.

During the nineteenth century it was the "science" of craniometry which sought to put people in their places. In the twentieth century, intelligence testing has taken center stage, proceeding too often as if intelligence were a single, inherited, quantifiable component—*ipso facto* of more significance than other aspects of personality.

Writing as both a scientist and a historian, Stephen Jay Gould takes a decidedly unconventional approach. His work is impeccably argued yet refreshingly humane, even if not very "scientific." Certainly future generations will benefit from Gould's detective work in *The Mismeasure of Man*. It is unfortunate that the scientists about whose work this book is written and their subjects and societies cannot do the same.

*Robert Gish*

## Sources for Further Study

*Booklist*. LXXVIII, September 1, 1981, p. 2.
*Library Journal*. CVI, October 15, 1981, p. 2012.
*The New Republic*. CLXXXV, November 11, 1981, p. 28.
*The New York Review of Books*. XXVIII, October 22, 1981, p. 12.
*The New York Times Book Review*. LXXXVI, November 1, 1981, p. 11.
*Newsweek*. XCVIII, November 9, 1981, p. 106.
*Saturday Review*. VIII, October, 1981, p. 74.

# MONTY
## The Making of a General, 1887-1942

*Author:* Nigel Hamilton (1944-    )
*Publisher:* McGraw-Hill Book Company (New York). Illustrated. 871 pp. $22.95
*Type of work:* Biography
*Time:* 1887-1942
*Locale:* England, Ireland, India, France, Palestine, and Egypt

*The first part of a projected two-volume biography of Field Marshal Sir Bernard Law Montgomery, Britain's foremost military commander of World War II, covering his ancestry through his victory over Rommel's Afrika Korps at El Alamein*

> *Principal personages:*
> FIELD MARSHAL SIR BERNARD LAW MONTGOMERY, Commander of the British Eighth Army
> BISHOP HENRY HUTCHINSON MONTGOMERY, his father
> LADY MAUD MONTGOMERY, his mother
> FIELD MARSHAL ALAN BROOKE (VISCOUNT), Chief of the British Imperial General Staff
> FIELD MARSHAL EARL ALEXANDER, British Commander in Chief in the Middle East
> FIELD MARSHAL SIR CLAUDE AUCHINLECK, Alexander's predecessor as Commander in Chief in the Middle East
> SIR WINSTON CHURCHILL, British Prime Minister, 1940-1945
> MAJOR GENERAL SIR FRANCIS DE GUINGARD, Chief of Staff of the British Eighth Army
> SIR BASIL H. LIDDELL HART, British military writer
> FIELD MARSHAL ERWIN ROMMEL, Commander of the German Afrika Corps

General Bernard Law Montgomery may well have been the most successful British field commander of the twentieth century, as his biographer Nigel Hamilton asserts, but he was also the most controversial, largely because of his ruthless determination to succeed. In this weighty tome, Hamilton minutely examines Monty's life from birth to victory in the Battle of El Alamein, where General Montgomery defeated the German Afrika Korps under the legendary Rommel. Hamilton promises another volume—presumably equally huge—covering Monty's subsequent career, including his command of British forces in the invasion of Europe, the defeat of Nazi Germany, his rule as Chief of the Imperial General Staff and Britain's premier soldier, and his years of retirement, assiduously nurturing his fame. Since the present volume begins with Monty's supposed ancestry going back to the time of William the Conqueror, the sequel necessarily will cover a briefer time span.

This is both an "official" biography, in the sense that Monty provided the materials and blessed and in fact initiated the enterprise, and a labor of love, as the author explains in an "Author's Note." Monty took him under his wing as a youth and during the last twenty years of his life treated him almost as his own son. Hamilton candidly remarks that in undertaking this biography he was repaying a debt of gratitude, although he hastens to add that his intention was neither to whitewash nor flatter his subject. He has succeeded to a degree in both respects, more especially in the first: while Hamilton is careful not to gloss over Monty's faults—he was increasingly, after his service with the British Expeditionary Force during World War I, vain, opinionated, callous towards his peers and sometimes insubordinate towards his superiors, and often "breathtakingly mean" towards critics and those whom he felt did not measure up to his standard of military professionalism—it appears that, except in a few instances, notably the 1942 Dieppe raid and the operation at Arnhem in 1944, Monty was almost always right and the very model of a professional general officer.

Monty himself no doubt would have approved of Hamilton's biography as a shield against the sniping of his critics, both brother officers, British and American, who served with him, and historians. Russell Weigley, for example, in *Eisenhower's Lieutenants* (1981) reports that American generals Dwight D. Eisenhower, Omar Bradley, and George Patton were all dismayed, or worse, at Montgomery's failure to close the Argentan-Falaise gap in France in 1944. He quotes General Bradley's aide to the effect that the Bradley headquarters refrained from criticizing Monty because of his enormous prestige in Britain and his "almost professional papal immunity." A meticulous planner, Montgomery probably included Hamilton's work as a foundation stone of the monument to his everlasting fame.

Hamilton's father, Sir Denis Hamilton, was an old friend and admirer from Eighth Army days; in addition, he was Monty's literary adviser and, in 1962, editor of the *Sunday Times* and Editorial Director of Thomson Newspapers. In that year, Monty proposed to Sir Denis that Thomson Newspapers acquire his private papers and diaries. Those included papers dealing with his World War II service from his assumption of command of the Eighth Army in 1942, his tenure as Chief of the Imperial General Staff, his chairmanship of the Western Union Defence establishment, and his stint as Deputy Supreme Allied Commander of the North Atlantic Treaty Organization—some forty-four volumes in all. As he wrote to Sir Denis: "I imagine that when I am dead, somebody will want to write the full story of my military life in high command. It would be impossible to do this without my diaries and private papers." In a review of Hamilton's book in the *Times Literary Supplement*, Michael Carver wrote that Thomson Newspapers, in return for the copyright to the Montgomery Papers, paid the Field Marshal an annuity; that immediately after Dunkirk in 1940 Monty began to keep official papers and to keep a diary, contrary to military regulations; that while Chief of the Imperial General Staff he removed many historically important documents from the War Office, some of which he destroyed, including those linking him with the disastrous Dieppe raid. Hamilton assures the reader that the Montgomery Papers "will ultimately be preserved in one of the major national archives, together with the tape-recorded interviews and research material relating to this biography."

Except for the detail, sometimes numbing and often repetitious—Hamilton repeatedly quotes at length from Monty's lecture notes and orders to his commands—much of what is new in the book concerns Monty's early life and his family relationships. Monty's grandfather, Robert Montgomery, had been Commissioner of Lahore in the new Indian province of Punjab when the Sepoy Mutiny of 1857 broke out. For skillfully disarming the Sepoy regiments of Lahore he received the thanks of Parliament and, in 1865, returned to England as Sir Robert, bringing with him his four sons by his second marriage, of whom the second was Henry. Henry Montgomery was sent to school in England at the age of eight and was seventeen when his father came home from India. Thereafter, he attended Cambridge University, having along the way acquired a missionary fervor which carried him to ordination in holy orders and, in 1876, to assignment as curate in the Westminster parish of the brilliant, eccentric Frederic William Farrar, whom Hamilton calls one of the luminaries, if not geniuses, of Victorian England. Farrar, later to become Dean of Canterbury but never a Bishop, was an intellectual and an educational reformer; his young curate was a practical, methodical man who believed that even parish work could be managed scientifically. Although his future grandson, Bernard, later disdained his Farrar blood, Hamilton suggests that Monty inherited many traits from his maternal grandfather. What was most important, however, was that Henry Montgomery fell in love with Farrar's third daughter, Maud, then fourteen years old. Two years later, the young curate, aged thirty-three, married Maud.

According to Hamilton, Maud exercised a powerful, lifelong influence on Bernard, the fourth of her five children. Like her husband immersed in the work of the parish, she had little time for her children and managed them and her household by imposing a rigid discipline. Quick to punish transgressions, Maud tyrannized not only the children but also her husband who, ironically, seemed content to let his young wife manage even the family accounts. Bernard was by all accounts the black sheep of the family and often felt the pain of his mother's disapproval. Feeling himself unloved, Bernard rebelled against Maud's tyranny, and the conflict of wills, Hamilton believes, scarred Bernard for life. The effects of this unhappy relationship account for a kind of schizophrenia in Monty's later conduct: a capacity for genuine affection and generosity, on the one hand, and a mean, intolerant abusiveness on the other.

Henry Montgomery was consecrated a missionary bishop and sent, with his family, to Tasmania in 1889, remaining until 1901. Back in England, the fourteen-year-old Bernard was sent to St. Paul's School, where at last he had a chance to assert himself. He immediately joined the army class and, upon graduation, entered Sandhurst, but in neither school did he distinguish himself. Yet when he joined the Royal Warwickshire regiment in 1908 and was posted to India he developed an obsessive seriousness about his military career, in which he henceforth exhibited his father's meticulous sense of order and his mother's iron will. He soon became known in the army for his clear, concise exposition of military problems and for his insistence on rigorous training. He was always weak on strategy, as Hamilton several times notes, but his reputation as a master of tactics earned him, first, assignment to a staff college, and later to a series of instructorships. In fact, he might have spent his career as a training officer and teacher, assuming that the growing number of brother officers who found him opinionated, conceited, and overtalkative—always "babbling"—did not arrange to cut it short, if war had not intervened.

There is general agreement that Monty's record in World War I (the Great War) was brilliant. His bravery under fire was already legendary among the Royal Warwickshires when he was severely wounded at the First Battle of Ypres in 1914, winning the Distinguished Service Order. Fate gave his career another nudge when he returned to duty; he was assigned as brigade-major to a brigade training school in England under a commander who was happy to let the twenty-seven-year-old captain put his ideas into practice. Thereafter, he was assigned to a series of division and corps staff positions which gave him experience in the handling of increasingly larger military formations— opportunities which, at his age and rank, he would never have gained in times of peace. He was appalled at the frightful slaughter of the First Battle of the Somme—the British sustained fifty-seven thousand casualties on the single day, July 1, 1916—but surprisingly, in view of his constant criticisms of senior commanders throughout the rest of his career, he apparently failed to express condemnation of Field Marshal Sir Douglas Haig. Nor does Hamilton, who usually but not always seconds Monty's judgments. His experiences on the Western Front, however, no doubt did mark a turning point in Monty's career: his self-confidence was greatly enlarged and his impatience with others, including superiors, who failed to meet his own standards of military profes- sionalism was accentuated; and he became more obstinate than before on the necessity of rigorous and realistic training. In view of his often touchy relations with American commanders a quarter of a century later, Monty's reaction to the entry of the United States into the war in 1917 is interesting: he was glad that America had finally declared war because America would send food and money!

Until he was thirty-seven, Monty had led an ascetic life of total preoccu- pation with the army, and then he fell in love with a girl of seventeen, who eventually rejected him. Hamilton sees the mother-son relationship behind Monty's indifference to female companionship, and the example of his revered father as playing a part in his infatuation with Betty Anderson. His pursuit of Miss Anderson led to his meeting Betty Carver, a widow his own age with two young sons. They were married and lived happily for ten years, until Betty died of complications from an insect bite received while vacationing at a seaside resort with their nine-year-old son (Betty's sons were both by then officers in the Royal Engineers). Monty and Betty complemented each other: she appreciated his passion for order and efficiency, while her artistic nature and lively, inquiring mind drew him out of the shell of repressed love. The harsher traits of Monty's character were submerged during those years, but Betty's death shattered him and he plunged back into his profession with more single-mindedness and self-righteousness than ever.

Monty was by then a Brigadier, but in October, 1938, he was promoted to Major General and given the Eighth Division in Palestine, with the mission of quelling an Arab insurrection and maintaining order. He had no illusions concerning the problem—he had served there several years earlier and had also commanded British forces in Ireland during the "Troubles"—but he welcomed the chance to command a division and to get out of England. After he returned to take command of the Third Division in December, 1939, following the outbreak of World War II, Monty could say that he had enjoyed the war "out there" and that the Arabs were not at all anti-British!

The war that he had been predicting for more than a decade had finally broken out. Long before, he had, with rare prescience, remarked that another war with Germany would be a "good thing . . . it would be much better to have it now & get done with it. A modern war would not last very long, & would be such an awful affair there would be no more war for 50 years." Monty took the Third Division to France and was at Louvain, in Belgium, when the German onslaught came in the spring of 1940. He withdrew his division to the French border in good order, but there followed the collapse of the French on the right and the confusion leading to the British evacuation at Dunkirk. During this hectic period, Monty performed brilliantly and his division proved the value of his brand of training. His corps commander, General Sir Alan Brooke, was impressed, and thereafter, as an area commander in England and then as Chief of the Imperial General Staff, he usually supported Monty, eventually winning for him command of the Eighth Army in Africa.

Although the British had succeeded in evacuating the bulk of their expeditionary force from France, Monty decried any celebration. To him, it was a humiliating defeat and he concentrated on preparing to avenge it. As corps commander under General Sir Claude Auchinleck, he scrapped his superior's strategy of beach defense against an expected German invasion in favor of a concentration of mobile forces for counterattack. His relations with "the Auk" were insubordinate and chilly, and even Hamilton admits that his denigration of Auchinleck was unfair. He was saved from the consequences of his behavior, however, by the mediation of Viscount Alan Brooke and by his transfer to the Eighth Army command, succeeding Auchinleck, who meanwhile had been made Commander in Chief in the Middle East as well as Army commander.

Perhaps Monty's greatest accomplishment after arrival in Africa was to dispel the mood of defeatism in British command circles in Egypt and bring order to a chaotic situation. Hamilton describes Monty's handling of the Battle of Alma Halfa, the prelude to El Alamein, and the preparations for El Alamein. As to El Alamein itself, Monty was able to demonstrate the correctness of his view concerning the "encounter" battle. Monty had for years maintained that the army should seek to engage the enemy on ground of its own choosing and launch a mass attack combining all arms, armor, infantry, artillery, and air support at a weak point in the enemy's defenses. This theory was in conflict with the "indirect approach" long preached by his old friend and former military commentator for the *Times* of London, Sir Basil Liddell Hart. The narrow front at El Alamein, in fact, dictated Monty's tactics, but even Hamilton admits that they were not faultless. Monty's victory over Rommel, however, with the Stalingrad campaign in Russia, marked a turning point in the war and established his fame.

Monty's fame is sufficiently well-grounded without Hamilton's hyperbole. That aside, his book is by far the most thorough biography to date of the hero of El Alamein. It is an indispensable source for students of World War II, and they will await with anticipation Hamilton's next volume.

*Albert H. Bowman*

### Sources for Further Study

*Business Week*. September 28, 1981, p. 15.
*The Economist*. CCLXXIX, June 13, 1981, p. 91.
*Library Journal*. CVI, September 15, 1981, p. 1725.
*Listener*. CV, June 18, 1981, p. 780.
*National Review*. XXXIII, August 21, 1981, p. 965.
*New Statesman*. CI, June 12, 1981, p. 17.
*The New York Times Book Review*. LXXXVI, October 4, 1981, p. 14.
*Newsweek*. XCVIII, September 14, 1981, p. 82.
*Punch*. CCLXXX, June 24, 1981, p. 1023.
*Times Literary Supplement*. June 12, 1981, p. 657.

# MORNINGS ON HORSEBACK

*Author:* David McCullough (1933-     )
*Publisher:* Simon and Schuster (New York). Illustrated. 445 pp. $19.95
*Type of work:* Biography
*Time:* 1869-1886
*Locale:* The United States

*A biography of the young Theodore Roosevelt and his family*

> *Principal personages:*
> THEODORE ROOSEVELT, the future President of the United States and scion of a wealthy New York family
> MITTIE BULLOCK ROOSEVELT, his mother, a celebrated Southern beauty
> ELLIOT ROOSEVELT, his brother, a tragic victim of alcoholism
> ALICE LEE, his first wife

David McCullough has established himself as a gifted and productive historian. His earlier books include the widely acclaimed *The Johnstown Flood* (1968) and *The Great Bridge* (1972), the story of the building of the Brooklyn Bridge. These were followed by the epic *Path Between the Seas* (1977), on the development of the Panama Canal, which won a number of awards including the National Book Award for History and the Francis Parkman Prize. These volumes exhibited unusually creative use of source materials; remarkable insight into personalities, institutions, and technological developments; and the style of a master craftsman. With *Mornings On Horseback*, his first attempt at biography, McCullough maintains the standards of his earlier works and advances the craft of biography to new levels.

*Mornings On Horseback* re-creates the family and social environment that shaped the personality, outlook, and self-image of the young Theodore Roosevelt. It is the story of a rather remarkable child who overcame nearly fatal attacks of asthma and won his struggle to manhood because of the nurturing affect of his family and the rarefied culture of New York. The biography does for Theodore Roosevelt what *Sunrise at Campobello* (1958) did for Franklin Delano Roosevelt: it illustrates the transformation of the inner man through his battle against ill-health and other tragic personal circumstances.

Like *The Path Between the Seas*, this book offers all the elements of a great novel; it is an enthralling story filled with penetrating character studies and vividly crafted *mise-en-scènes*. The study is also a brilliant example of social and political history which destroys several myths about the young Roosevelt and breaks new ground. For example, for the first time Roosevelt's generally poor health and asthmatic condition are closely examined. McCullough draws upon information gleaned from private Roosevelt family papers and upon present-day medical knowledge of the affliction and its psychosomatic aspects.

The author displays an extraordinary talent for character development. Roosevelt's father, the first Theodore Roosevelt, emerges as a forceful family leader, a talented businessman, a selfless and socially sensitive community leader—the very exemplum of a wealthy aristocratic gentleman. In this figure of boundless energy and urbane sophistication, the frail, small namesake found a loving father and a role model. McCullough presents Roosevelt's mother, Mittie Bullock Roosevelt, in every shade of her complex, enviable personality. A Southerner and celebrated beauty, she consistently exhibited unsurpassed devotion to the varied and special needs of her family. In her, "Teedie" (as Roosevelt was known as a child) had an affectionate and supportive parent who instilled in her sickly child the moral and physical courage to overcome his physical shortcomings. Other family members grace the book: the adoring sisters Anna and Corinne and the affectionate but star-crossed brother Elliot (father of Eleanor Roosevelt) who succumbed to alcoholism. Finally, there is the tender and beautiful Alice Lee, Roosevelt's first love who died so tragically young. The biography achieves its remarkable power by capturing this diverse and intensely human assemblage of Roosevelts in vivid detail.

Drawing upon a variety of sources, McCullough illustrates how the asthmatic attacks of Roosevelt's youth profoundly shaped his personality. The nocturnal episodes were shattering, numbing experiences for both the victim and his parents. On many occasions, the protective parents tended a child "battling for breath, tugging, straining, elbows planted on his knees, shoulders hunched high, his head thrown back, eyes popping." On a child as acutely sensitive and intelligent as "Teedie," the affliction had a profound impact that shaped personality, outlook, and self-regard. Yet these attacks made him the absolute center of attention, and, like many other asthmatics, Roosevelt developed a penchant for commanding center stage. Also, he was often able to take the inevitable reverses of childhood and adulthood with notable stoicism. "Teedie" thus became tenacious, independent, aggressive, and a seeker of fame. In some powerful way, an obsession with the outdoors and a vigorous approach to life were the products of Roosevelt's childhood disease.

One is touched by the scrawny youth with sticklike arms and legs undertaking daily workouts at a gymnasium. He remained embarrassingly undersized and underweight and rarely ventured far beyond his family circle until he went to college. His days were also filled with dozens of books on manly adventures (such as Daniel Defoe's *Robinson Crusoe*, 1719) that added to his admiration for and desire to emulate the brave and strong. World-traveled, adept at languages, and exposed to the outdoors, Roosevelt took full advantage of the opportunities offered by his family's wealth and social station. He rapidly developed a fondness for taxidermy and the allurements of the American West.

At the age of seventeen, the five-foot, eight-inch, 125-pound boy went off to Cambridge, Massachusetts, to become a "Harvard man." The limits of his social world, defined by Oyster Bay and New York City, were soon expanded.

His health improved almost miraculously as a young man (now known as "Teddy"), and he invested his prodigious energies in classwork and extracurricular activities. His grades were excellent even though he carried as many as nine academic subjects. He was also a figure of incessant activity outside the classroom. He rowed the Charles River in a one-man shell, took boxing lessons, enrolled in a dancing class, and went on long hikes. He joined the Rifle Club, Art Club, and Glee Club, and still found time to be an officer in the Natural History Society and help publish an undergraduate magazine. Yet, despite his good scholastic record, he did not display a keen intellectual curiosity or excitement. College merely provided an outlet for his boundless energy.

The image of the young Roosevelt which emerges from the book is that of a somewhat pampered, snobbish aristocrat. While at college, he had a comfortably furnished apartment, a manservant to black his boots and care for other personal needs, and a woman to do his laundry. Although bookish, he seemed to care little for politics or national affairs. His name and background gave him an advantage he could exploit. Roosevelt mixed easily and naturally with the school's young Brahmins and their respective families, and he became a subject of great sympathy when his father died. As a student, his circumstances were always comfortable; the annual income from his inheritance was three thousand dollars greater than the salary of the college president.

Alice Lee, Roosevelt's first wife, was clearly the great love of the young man's life. This "rare and radiant maiden," as he called her, was extraordinarily attractive, slender, graceful, and had honey-blond hair. McCullough does a masterful job of describing their courtship. One sees the love-consumed youth engaging in an eager, restless, passionate pursuit of this beauty. The author also deftly shows how Alice won the hearts of Teddy's family and, after their marriage in 1880, lived in close harmony with the remainder of the clan. She became one of them and unselfishly shared Roosevelt with his adoring widowed mother and sisters.

These almost idyllic circumstances were shattered in early 1884. On February 14, Roosevelt's mother died of typhoid fever, and eleven hours later Alice succumbed to Bright's disease, having given birth to her first child two days earlier. Disease had again struck the tragedy-prone family. During this same period, Roosevelt's brother Elliot began to display an alarming disposition for strong drink and the pleasures of the flesh. Elliot was a charming, generous, and gregarious person, glamorous as Theodore was not. Because of his own afflictions, Roosevelt was able to steel himself against tragedy, but he deeply felt such losses. On the day of Alice's death, he made the following entry in his diary: "The light has gone out of my life."

Despite personal tragedies, Roosevelt won his spurs as a politician in the early 1880's. At the tender age of twenty-three he sought and won election to the New York Assembly. Despite his age, the youngest member of the body plunged ahead, deferring to no one and making his presence felt. He was a spectacle of political aggressiveness who soon won the attention of the press. Despite a trivial, patronizing maiden speech, Roosevelt left no doubt that he would leave his mark on Albany. Initially a high-principled, blue-blooded amateur, Roosevelt soon displayed a great deal of political acumen. He was his party's nominee for Assembly speaker at the age of twenty-four and was seldom still or out of sight. Roosevelt was a leader in Civil Service reform and led the battle for labor reform in the cigar industry. He did not regard politics as a gentleman's diversion; Roosevelt would not shrink from a tooth-and-claw political fight and took on professional politicos in a fearless and forthright manner. Thus, by the age of twenty-five Roosevelt was clearly exhibiting all the talents of a natural politician. He had a genius for gaining the limelight with his gestures and theatrics, and exhibited the undefinable quality of "presence" in his undersized and overdressed way. Press reports on his activities were filled with adjectives such as a "fearless," "courageous," "manly," "tireless," "plucky," and "brilliant."

Roosevelt was no less committed to living the life of a "ranchman." He found great appeal in the freedom of the open-air existence and invested heavily in a Dakota Bad Lands ranch during the cattle boom of the early 1880's. The eastern aristocrat spent a fortune on buckskin clothing, expensive bridles and saddles, and engraved knives and guns to look and act the part of his version of the gentleman cowboy. He was fearless in his opposition to rivals and an aggressive investor, but fell victim to a savage winter that wiped out most of his stock. After a few years, he ended his Western adventure and sold his holdings.

The book concludes with Roosevelt's quixotic campaign for mayor of New York in 1886. Despite his third-place finish behind Abram Hewitt and Henry George, he was able to state that "At least I have a better party standing than ever before." Thus, at the age of twenty-eight the former sickly youth, who had suffered agonizing personal losses in his young adulthood, was whole in body and spirit and poised to achieve greatness. With verve and trenchant insights, David McCullough presents the forces and persons that shaped the character and personality of the man who became the nation's youngest president.

*Michael C. Robinson*

## Sources for Further Study

*Business Week*. August 3, 1981, p. 9.
*Choice*. XIX, October, 1981, p. 300.

*Library Journal*. CVI, May 15, 1981, p. 1069.
*National Review*. XXXIII, September 18, 1981, p. 1095.
*The New Republic*. CLXXXV, July 4, 1981, p. 34.
*The New York Review of Books*. XXVIII, August 13, 1981, p. 19.
*The New York Times Book Review*. LXXXVI, July 26, 1981, p. 3.
*Newsweek*. XCVII, June 22, 1981, p. 76.
*Saturday Review*. VIII, June, 1981, p. 48.
*Time*. CXVIII, July 20, 1981, p. 74.

# MOUNTBATTEN

*Author:* Richard Hough (1922-    )
*Publisher:* Random House (New York). Illustrated. 302 pp. $16.95
*Type of work:* Biography
*Time:* 1900-1979
*Locale:* Great Britain, India, Southeast Asia, the United States, Ireland, and various other locales

*A balanced study of the life of Lord Louis Mountbatten, naval hero, statesman, and relative and adviser to the British royal family*

>  *Principal personages:*
>  LOUIS, EARL MOUNTBATTEN of BURMA
>  EDWINA, COUNTESS MOUNTBATTEN of BURMA, his wife
>  PRINCESS VICTORIA, MARCHIONESS of MILFORD HAVEN, his mother
>  PRINCE PHILIP, DUKE of EDINBURGH, Mountbatten's nephew and the husband of Queen Elizabeth II
>  SIR WINSTON CHURCHILL, British Prime Minister, 1940-1945, 1951-1955; a close friend and associate of Mountbatten
>  JAWAHARLAL NEHRU, Leader of the Indian Congress Party; first Prime Minister of an independent India, 1950-1966

On August 27, 1979, the world was shocked to hear the news of the assassination of Lord Louis Mountbatten by the Provisional Irish Republican Army. He, along with one of his two grandsons, a young neighbor boy, and a Lady Brabourne, had been killed when a gelignite bomb exploded the family's small boat, *Shadow V.* They had died during a morning sail near the family retreat, Classiebawn Castle, County Sligo, in the Republic of Ireland not far from the Ulster border. Without doubt, Lord Mountbatten was the intended victim, since he, next to the immediate members of the royal family, had become the personification of the United Kingdom. The I.R.A. was clearly aware of the impact the assassination would have, not only on Britons but also on people throughout the world, especially in the United States, Canada, India, and Southeast Asia, who, since World War II, had come to respect and revere this most prescient and accessible of men. The Queen, Prince Philip, and Prince Charles had also lost a deeply loved and highly regarded family member and adviser. The loss was especially great to Prince Philip and Prince Charles since Mountbatten had played the role of uncle and surrogate father to the former and that of great-uncle, godfather, and surrogate grandfather to the latter. Mountbatten's state funeral, which he had personally planned to the last detail, was the largest and grandest Britain had witnessed since that of Winston Churchill. To the strains of "The Sailor's Hymn" in Westminster Abbey, the world bade farewell to Louis, First Earl Mountbatten of Burma, Chief of Combined Operations and Supreme Allied Commander, Southeast Asia, last Viceroy of India, First Sea Lord and Admiral of the Fleet, a man who for more than forty years had played a vital role in world affairs.

Until recently, Mountbatten had not been the subject of a biography covering his entire life. Various aspects of his career had been treated, but the only work approaching biography until the publication of the present volume was John Terraine's *The Life and Times of Lord Mountbatten*, first published in 1968 and reissued in 1980 with a postscript following Mountbatten's death. Terraine's book, based on a twelve-part television series in which Mountbatten actively participated, is not truly a biography, but a compilation of Mountbatten's own observations about himself and others given continuity with transitional passages by Terraine. Mountbatten did not wish a full-scale biography published during his lifetime because he feared no one would believe it. Vanity was one of the distinctive features of Mountbatten's personality. Stating on occasion, perhaps jocularly, that he had always been right, he asserted that a biography in which he personally participated in writing would not be believed. He did, however, indirectly assist in the writing of this biography. In 1971, Richard Hough first met Mountbatten to discuss eighteenth century naval history, a subject on which the author was working at the time. Indeed, Hough has established his reputation as a naval historian and novelist, and is the author of *The Potemkin Mutiny* (1960), *Captain Bligh and Mr. Christian* (1973), and *The Last Voyage of Captain James Cook* (1979). Mountbatten later invited Hough to write a dual biography of his father and mother, *Louis and Victoria* (published in the United States as *The Mountbattens* (1975). In the preparation of *Louis and Victoria*, Hough acquired manuscript material from Mountbatten, gained access to the Royal Archives, Windsor, and secured interviews with Mountbatten's family, friends, shipmates, and former colleagues. He was also in close contact with Mountbatten throughout the 1970's and had lengthy conversations with him. The book under review, therefore, is largely an outgrowth of earlier research and interviews with established contacts, and much of it had been completed at the time of Mountbatten's death, enabling Hough to publish his biography in Britain on the first anniversary of the assassination of this authentic twentieth century hero.

Lord Mountbatten led a life rich in association with major historical personages and in high adventure. Born on January 25, 1900, he was the son of Prince Louis of Battenburg, who briefly headed the British navy early in World War I, and Princess Victoria of Hesse, later the Marchioness of Milford Haven, the favorite granddaughter of Queen Victoria. Christened Albert Victor Nicholas Louis Francis, he became familiarly known throughout his childhood and youth as Dickie. His childhood was passed in association with the royal families of Hanover, Hesse (his father and mother were members of the house of Hesse), and Romanov. Especially memorable were his summer holidays at Heiligenberg with his aunt and uncle, Empress Alexandra and Nicholas II of Russia, and their children. Indeed, he claimed to have fallen in love with his female Romanov cousins and had intended to marry the ill-fated Maria. During his youth and throughout much of his life, Mountbatten was deeply influenced by his exceptional mother, Princess Victoria, who, a socialist "by instinct and conviction," trained her son to work amicably and effectively with those of conflicting political convictions. His mother took charge of his education during his youth and, along with Mountbatten's wife, Edwina, guided him throughout the remainder of her long life. His father, who had adopted Britain as his native country and through concerted effort had risen to the apex of the Royal Navy as First Sea Lord, remained a somewhat distant figure for the young boy but was nevertheless a figure of near idolatry and was to instill in his son the all-consuming ambition that was to direct his life.

The halcyon days of the young Battenberg's childhood ended with World War I. The hysterical fringe of the British public who regarded anything German as suspect successfully lobbied for Prince Louis of Battenberg's resignation as commander of the Royal Navy, an event which broke his heart and was to influence his son deeply. Dickie's goal became to succeed his father as First Sea Lord and in so doing to rehabilitate and enhance fully his family's name and honor. Indeed, it was at the same time that the British royal family changed the family surname to Windsor and the Battenbergs Anglicized their surname to Mountbatten. Lord Mountbatten was to become obsessive about the rehabilitation of his family name and honor. He encouraged his nephew, Prince Philip, to assume the name, and his lengthy campaign was eventually successful in the addition of his surname to that of Windsor for the children of Prince Philip and Queen Elizabeth.

Mountbatten's father's example and his own inclination led him to a naval career. During World War I he saw naval action in the North Sea, attaining the rank of sub-lieutenant. Following the war, Mountbatten attended Christ's College, Cambridge, and engaged in a whirlwind of social activities in Cambridge, London, and in the great houses of England. In 1921, he accompanied his cousin, the Prince of Wales (later Edward VIII), on a forty-thousand mile tour on the battle cruiser *Renown*. During this trip a close friendship was cemented between the young men which survived the later abdication crisis. Shortly before the beginning of the tour in October, 1921, Mountbatten established the most significant bond of his life. In July, 1921 he met Edwina Ashley, the granddaughter and sole heiress of Sir Ernest Cassel, an enormously rich international banker. Edwina had the brains, beauty and youth which complemented Mountbatten's aristocratic mien, decisiveness, ambition, and competitiveness. She and Mountbatten's mother shared a variety of interests; each enjoyed a superior intelligence and pragmatic outlook, and, although born into families with a conservative outlook, they shared broadly socialistic views about domestic and world problems. Flat broke (her grandfather had died leaving her as sole heiress, but with the stipulation that she was to receive only three hundred pounds a year until she was twenty-one or until she married), she borrowed one hundred pounds from a relative, booked passage on the cheapest ship she could find, and sailed to India, under conditions of great discomfort and privation, to see Mountbatten, with whom she had corresponded throughout his tour with the Prince of Wales. Arriving in Bombay, she traveled by land to Delhi, where the young couple became engaged. They were married on July 18, 1922, almost exactly a year after their initial meeting.

The effect of the marriage on Mountbatten was threefold. Not only did it make him supremely happy, but also he acquired through marriage a personal fortune that allowed him to indulge his expensive tastes and gave him the free time and financial security to advance his career. Most important, he acquired a partner who offered him indispensable aid and advice in the various assignments he later accepted and enhanced his reputation as well as her own through her untiring services to humanitarian causes, especially during World War II and as the last Vicereine of India. Although their marriage was unusual by conventional standards (Edwina had numerous extramarital affairs, most notably with Jawaharlal Nehru, to which Mountbatten inexplicably did not object), Edwina had an obsessive drive that helped to associate the Mountbatten name with broadly socialistic causes. She traveled constantly, often under great pain and to near total exhaustion, and in her travels developed a sincere empathy with the problems of the world's poor. Although the rigors of travel and service led to her early death, she helped to establish in post-independent India an especially high regard for herself and her husband and a respect for Britain that would not have been a legacy to that troubled land had it not been for her genuine and demonstrated compassion.

Mountbatten became a figure of international prominence during World War II. His wartime exploits became widely known primarily because of his friend Noel Coward's internationally acclaimed film *In Which We Serve*, which, though fictional, was based upon Mountbatten's command of the destroyer *Kelly*. Although bravado led Mountbatten on occasion to act carelessly and lose several vessels, he nevertheless was greatly admired by most of those who served under him. His most important contribution to the Allied war effort was his service as Supreme Allied Commander in southeast Asia, which culminated in his acceptance of the formal Japanese surrender at Singapore on September 5, 1945. Mountbatten's experiences in southeast Asia bred in him a lifelong hatred of the Japanese. Indeed the Japanese were the only major nation intentionally omitted from the invitation list for Mountbatten's funeral, drafted by Mountbatten himself.

In March, 1947, Mountbatten undertook what he personally regarded as his greatest achievement: his service as the last Viceroy of India for the purpose of effecting a transfer of power from Britain to an independent Indian government. Although Mountbatten was politically identified with Winston Churchill, it was Churchill's Labour Party successor as prime minister,

Clement Atlee, who convinced Mountbatten to assume this thankless task, despite Churchill's disapproval. Mountbatten accepted it only with the understanding that he would enjoy plenipotentiary powers in dealing with the Congress Party, led by Nehru; its rival Moslem league, led by Mohammed Ali Jinnah; and the scores of princes and maharajahs bound to Britain by treaties. Originally setting a deadline of fourteen months for completing the negotiations necessary for independence, Mountbatten succeeded in working out a transferal of power in less than five. On August 15, 1947, India became an independent nation, which Mountbatten served briefly as Governor-General. The cost of independence, however, was high. It had been achieved quickly by accession to Jinnah's demand for the partition of India and the creation of an independent Moslem nation, Pakistan. The immediate tragedy was the uprooting of thousands of people on both sides of the border and the exhaustion, starvation, and massacre that followed. The long-term effect was, of course, the creation of an Indian-Pakistani enmity which continues to plague the region. Although Mountbatten and others have regarded his work in India as his greatest, Hough looks upon it as his most disastrous failure. Feeling that Mountbatten was duped by the intransigent Jinnah, he concludes that

> Mountbatten should never have been given the job, which for reasons of duty he inevitably accepted. His German mind and naval upbringing made him constitutionally ill equipped for the slow, patient negotiations with the Oriental mind, navigating amid the intricacies of political and inter-religious, inter-racial shoals and currents.

On Independence Day, Hough asserts, Mountbatten's pleasure and pride should have been tempered by "a touch of humility and even shame . . . So much of what he accomplished in his life he could be justly proud of. But not of those months in India. Churchill's word 'scuttle' for the transfer of power was . . . an exaggeration. But not much of an exaggeration."

Following several years of service in the Royal Navy and a series of promotions, Mountbatten finally attained the summit of his career in April, 1955, with his appointment as First Sea Lord, and shortly after as Admiral of the Fleet. Finally he had attained the rank for which he had worked since his youth. The family name had been fully vindicated. In his new role Mountbatten thoroughly modernized the Royal Navy. By the time his term of office expired in 1958, the navy "was a very different service, fined down, fast and twice as professional, . . . with nuclear power, missiles, computers and commando carriers all in use or on order." After serving as Chief of U.K. Defence Staff and Chairman of Chiefs of Staff Committee, he retired in 1965. The remaining years of his life were devoted to membership in various diverse organizations, appearances at official functions, the preparation of the television series on his career, serving as an adviser to various members of the royal family, and time with his daughters and their families (Edwina died in

1960 while visiting Borneo).

Richard Hough has performed a commendable job in chronicling Mountbatten's life. He knows his subject thoroughly. He has produced a thoroughly researched, well-illustrated, lucidly written book rich in anecdote and important information. Indeed, this is much more than a biography. It is, to some extent, a history of many of the most important events and personalities of the first half of the twentieth century. Most important, Hough has not been intellectually seduced by his subject. Although he does not deny Mountbatten his heroic stature, he concludes "that his inspiration to achievement was greater than his actual achievement." Especially repugnant to Hough was Mountbatten's often irritating vanity and his pride of achievement in India. This is a balanced, highly readable account of a major performer during a turbulent era.

*J. Stewart Alverson*

**Sources for Further Study**

*Choice*. XIX, September, 1981, p. 144.
*The Economist*. CCLXXVI, August 30, 1980, p. 75.
*Library Journal*. CVI, February 15, 1981, p. 445.
*National Review*. XXXIII, June 26, 1981, p. 733.
*The New York Times Book Review*. LXXXVI, July 26, 1981, p. 11.
*The New Yorker*. LVII, August 31, 1981, p. 98.
*Observer*. August 31, 1980, p. 29.
*Quill & Quire*. XLVI, November, 1980, p. 47.
*Saturday Review*. VIII, April, 1981, p. 81.

# NEW RULES
## Searching for Self-Fulfillment in a World Turned Upside Down

*Author:* Daniel Yankelovich (1924-    )
*Publisher:* Random House (New York). 279 pp. $15.95
*Type of work:* Sociology

*A well-conceived work that deals with the social and ethical future of the United States*

Using analogies from geological tectonic plate theory, Daniel Yankelovich suggests that society and culture in the United States are undergoing vast transformations, especially with respect to personal ethics, and that there is "evidence of startling cultural changes." His contention is that what is taking shape is nothing less than the search for a new American ethic. To support his contentions concerning "new rules," he employs a multifaceted methodology: he draws upon life histories, a number of national surveys, census data, and one national survey of fifteen hundred persons done especially for *New Rules*.

*New Rules* is arranged in four sections which are well-served by a fine-print fourteen-page index. Part One deals with what Yankelovich regards as the search for self-fulfillment. Part Two deals with characteristics of that search and how it finds itself in "violent" collision with traditional rules of an older ethic. Part Three deals with new economic patterns which must be dealt with in any consideration of ethics. The final part deals with what Yankelovich thinks is the newly emerging ethic of commitment.

Yankelovich, who is himself in the opinion survey business, has, he thinks, detected in his working materials evidence of vast contemporary cultural changes: the "typical" American family of breadwinning husband and housewife with one or more children is no longer typical (in fact, they constitute only fifteen percent of all American households); millions of women no longer regard having children as self-fulfilling; more women than men are enrolled in institutions of higher learning; and there is a decline of competitiveness, a decline in the importance given to status as defined by wealth, and an increase in the number of younger persons who lack life-goals. With such a ferment, it is not surprising that Yankelovich can claim that there is a decisive break with the past, a break that, moreover, will affect not only cultural lifestyles but also the political and economic systems in America. Most prominent in this contemporary cultural mix is the so-called "search for self-fulfillment."

The search for self-fulfillment abandons many of the rules of the ethic that predominated in American life since the 1700's, particularly the older norm of self-denial and deferred gratification. Yankelovich's tables show (if correct) that only twenty percent of the American adult working population still follow the ethics of self-denial. Many fewer people are willing to work at a job merely because it is a job and many have taken jobs with lower pay and less responsibility or monotony instead of higher-paying jobs for which they are well qualified. Yankelovich identifies that fraction of the American adult population who are involved in the search for self-fulfillment (however defined) as constituting some eighty percent of the total. If this is true, then he is perhaps correct in claiming that this "search" is the leading edge of a "genuine cultural revolution," confined to the young in the 1960's but now spreading into the larger society, albeit not without modification (especially the rejection of the antimaterialism of the 1960's). The immediate consequences of this ongoing cultural revolution, Yankelovich argues, are unrealistic demands on social institutions and a battle of moral norms as the search for self-fulfillment comes up against the older ethic of self-denial. His forecast is that from now to the turn of the century there will be turmoil in American culture—demands translated into political terms (and sometimes in single-issue politics) added to the resurgence of religion and the appearance of new religious movements. It is interesting to note that Yankelovich's analysis is exactly opposite to that of Gerard K. O'Neill's recent futurist book *2081* (1981). O'Neill thinks that any revolutionary change will be produced not in the realms of politics, culture, or religion but will be solely technological. Yankelovich has little to say of technology in *New Rules*.

Yankelovich found that the most fruitful survey question was "What are the people pursuing their self-fulfillment actually looking for, and how are they going about finding it?" He thinks that the searchers for self-fulfillment are seeking to elevate the "sacred/expressive" aspects of their lives and to downgrade the influence of impersonal, manipulative forces. "Sacred" as used here does not have the traditional religious connotations but rather is another name for "intrinsically valuable" or "valuable in its own right," implying a distinction between "intrinsic" and "instrumental" values: self-fulfillers are attempting to maximize those aspects of their lives that are valuable in their own right and to de-emphasize the instrumental facets of their lives which are not intrinsically valuable but valuable only as a means to an end. If Yankelovich's analysis is correct, then it can be understood why someone would take a low-paying but rewarding job instead of a high-paying job that would involve drudgery or danger. An earlier generation would not have morally approved of such a choice and, in fact, would have looked with disapproval upon someone who did not take the opportunity to gain money and status.

The "expressive" side of the search for self-fulfillment is opposed to instrumentalism as well. Expressive aspects of a person's life are the locus of creativity and are valuable in their own right. Yankelovich thinks that for seekers of self-fulfillment there is a "moral intuition" that the sacred/expressive aspects of life are life's root meaning. In turn, life's root meaning as *self-fulfilled* is realized in the search for community, community which an otherwise affluent industrial society has failed to provide. Yankelovich, while not using the terminology, is making use of the old *Gesellschaft/Gemeinschaft* distinction. The implication is that at an earlier time human life was on a human scale and that there then existed a warm feeling of community; this has been replaced by an industrial, high technology, impersonal, instrumental society. If Yankelovich is correct, it is not surprising that the search for self-fulfillment *as currently conceived* by the seekers has failed and landed the seekers in predicaments and contradictions.

Yankelovich believes that the strategies employed by the seekers are defective in both economic and psychological senses: economic, in the assumption that economic security is somehow a right; psychological, in that in attempting to expand the sacred/expressive aspects of their lives the seekers achieve instead a restriction of their lives. This paradox results from attempting to modify under incorrect assumptions the nature of the "giving/getting compact." Nevertheless, Yankelovich sees millions of people trying the defective strategies of self-fulfillment. They are actually trying to replace the older ethic of self-denial with an ethic of moral duty to self. Their large numbers constitute a "psychoculture" of shared cultural meanings. This psychoculture is in direct conflict with contemporary economic reality, for the once-dynamic economy is no longer so and may be structurally different from the economy of the postwar quarter-century which created so much in the way of affluence in goods and services and which promised to fulfill Jean Baptiste Say's law of an ever-growing economy.

Yankelovich thinks he has detected two forms of what he calls the self-fulfillment predicament—a strong and a weak form. He notes a triple bind in the strong form: possessed of an abundance of choices the strong formers do not have a concomitant knowledge of how to make the right choices and, indeed, have a feeling that free choices actually threaten their freedom. The second bind is that a stagnant economy makes it difficult to achieve self-fulfillment ends. And, the third bind is that created by the seekers having defined themselves, their lives, and their self-fulfillment in terms derived from "self-psychology," most recently known as the "human potential movement." Yankelovich is surely on to something here. The proliferation of psychology cults of self-fulfillment has been, since the late 1960's, a feature of the American cultural landscape and has affected millions of Americans—"Do your own thing!" If those who are caught in the strong form of the self-fulfillment predicament are indeed defining or describing themselves in such terms and if such terms are defective, it should come as no surprise that the search for self-fulfillment has largely failed. The victims of the strong form predicament number seventeen percent of working Americans or about seventeen million people. Yankelovich sees that the declining relevance of the old self-denial ethic lies at the heart of the triple bind and, further, that the conflict between self-denial and self-improvement lies at the heart of the cultural revolution he sees taking place.

Those who find themselves in the weak form of the self-fulfillment predicament are the great majority, falling between the seventeen percent of strong formers on one end of the spectrum and the twenty percent who follow the old self-denial ethic on the other. They have stable commitments, inner lives rarely subject to upheaval, a moderate commitment to the old self-denial rules, and, while subject to the same pressures affecting the strong formers, are not dominated by those pressures. These weak formers may quit jobs because of their unwillingness to hold on *merely* for economic security or respectability. As Yankelovich maintains, they may be conventional in their values in many respects but have absorbed some of the self-fulfillment ethos.

In Part Three of *New Rules*, Yankelovich addresses what he feels are the new economic realities and makes some forecasts on the basis of his analysis. Americans, he holds, are hopeful and fearful at the same time about economic matters. There has been a shift from economic optimism to a mood of gloom with an accompanying mistrust of institutions and a less hopeful attitude about what the future will bring; simultaneously, there is a hopeful awareness of the possibility of new ways of expressive fulfillment. The "psychology of affluence" has run up against harsh new economic realities. Yankelovich forecasts that Americans will show an adaptiveness as reality breaks through. He finds in his surveys three predominant views of the economic future, all of which he thinks are incorrect: complete economic collapse; return to economic growth in the postwar pattern; and the continuation of the psychology of virtually unlimited affluence. He forecasts that the future economy will be *sui generis*—possessed of its own unique properties (which he does not attempt to sketch out). The economy will have to change, he thinks, because of the current and continuing claims against the standard of living to which Americans have become accustomed. He identifies three such claims; the first is the price of energy, particularly petroleum. He forecasts that as oil approaches forty dollars a barrel alternative energy forms will become attractive, but OPEC hires economists and will surely keep the price, if possible, just below the level at which it will become attractive to invest in other forms of energy such as coal, oil shale, tar sands, solar, biomass, and so on. The second claim upon affluence is the entitlement programs of the past fifteen years, which involve transfers of wealth, particularly those programs which are indexed to inflation; the third is the decline in American industrial productivity because of corporate greed. Yankelovich and coauthor Bernard Lefkowitz in an article in *National Forum* (LII, Spring, 1982) add to the above the demand for environmental protection. It escapes understanding why the enormous demands of national defense spending are not mentioned in either *New Rules* or the article.

Yankelovich forecasts that, as a result of these pressures, there will be first, an unavoidable short-term reduction in the American standard of living; second, a developing conflict between those who are indexed to inflation and those who are not; and third, conflicts between working and nonworking parts of the population manifested as a have/have-not confrontation. Thus, the decade of the 1980's will have its unique features emerging from the clash between a constrained economy and the psychology of affluence. Out of these troublesome times, however, Yankelovich thinks there will emerge a new ethic of commitment, the outlines of which are just now beginning to become clear.

With the old rules of self-denial clearly unacceptable to millions and with the manifest failure of the self-fulfillment ethic as it was conceived in faulty psychology, a third ethic is necessitated—a true cultural revolution which first went astray in the predicaments generated by the attempt at self-fulfillment *independent of cultural context*. The new ethic supposedly will see the re-attainment of community and a more realistic concept of self-fulfillment within the shared meanings of a psychoculture. The personal freedom to achieve the sacred/expressive aspects of one's life *can* coexist with the imper-sonal forces of modern technology. The new ethic of commitment is to involve two sorts of commitments: closer, deeper personal relationships and emphasis on the sacred/expressive aspects of life. Yankelovich has in his surveys been measuring yearly the "search for community" social trend; since 1973, the proportion of Americans engaged in such searching jumped from about one-third to about one-half at the beginning of the 1980's.

There are to be two steps to the commitment ethic. The first is the realization that the self is both personal and cultural, is more than just the sum of one's wants, and that deep, lasting commitments are necessary for genuine self-fulfillment. The second is the necessity for "clear signals" from the larger society and its leaders concerning the new rules of the giving/getting contract. Yankelovich forecasts that the changeover will take several decades. The 1980's are forecast to be times of conflict and economic stress, but by the end of the decade the adaptation process to the new ethic should be manifest, thus foretelling the future.

Issues polling, upon which Yankelovich has relied heavily, is quite different from the sort of thing done when one polls preferences between two political candidates. For issues, there is likely to be a *range* of opinion along a con-tinuum, as Yankelovich has indicated for the spectrum going from the tra-ditional ethic to the weak form of self-fulfillment predicament to the strong form. With this range, interpretation becomes absolutely critical. It is not a question of whether the fifteen hundred persons surveyed especially for *New Rules* constitute a truly random sample of adult working Americans—they probably do. The question is whether they gave answers in which they really believed, whether they really understood the questions, whether the questions were properly worded, and whether the interpretation of answers justifies the assessments of the contemporary scene and the forecasts of the future made in *New Rules*. A picture contrary to that of *New Rules* emerges from Stephen

Rosen's 1976 book *Future Facts*. Also relying on the opinion survey technique it was "found" that the young adult cohort of the population in 1976 would be the numerically dominant group in the 1975-1990 period. If one makes the assumption that their values will dominate American culture in proportion to their numbers, a picture of the future emerges which is quite different from Yankelovich's. Rosen's study suggests that values on the upswing include "salvation," "cheerful," "clean," "a comfortable life," and—the most sharply rising of all—"national security." Declining values include "equality," "wisdom," "loving," and "sense of accomplishment." The decline in "sense of accomplishment" as a value would seem to contradict the idea of "self-fulfillment" and the decline in "loving" would seem to belie the claim that a new ethic of commitment is emerging or has been emerging in the period from 1973 to the early 1980's. One can only throw up one's hands. Sociocultural forecasting is the most difficult kind, far surpassing in difficulty scientific prediction and technological forecasting.

Yankelovich's analysis tacitly assumes that a number of other trends with which social and cultural and ethical ones interact will remain the same or not change in any qualitative manner (these are what technology assessors call "state-of-society assumptions"). Hence, the future would be surprise-free for *all* interacting trends, including the so-called new ethic of commitment. Uncertainty is only to be found in the economy. Qualitative change and discontinuity, however, have always been part of human history; the self-fulfillment ethic identified in *New Rules* is an example of a sea change from the older ethic of self-denial. Is it not possible that changes in the international system will have effects on American values? Will technology bring about drastically changed life-styles? Current defense spending and militarization suggest a possible movement to a garrison state with renewed cold war sentiment. Could an ethic of commitment survive and flourish under authoritarian or semiauthoritarian conditions? Government and other large institutions intrude, with the help of technology, into ever more intimate and smaller corners of people's lives. They resent this, as has been shown in Yankelovich's book, but can they do anything about it? Mistrusting and resenting large institutions, especially government, is one thing, but getting them off one's back is quite another.

What can one finally say about such a book as *New Rules*? There is definitely some truth in it, particularly in the analysis of the ethic of self-fulfillment, but, as always when looking to the future, the picture becomes murky. One can hope that Yankelovich is engaging in genuine exploratory trend extrapolation with respect to the ethic of commitment and is not forecasting by inadvertent self-fulfilling prophecy the kind of future he would like to see.

*Robert L. Hoffman*

## Sources for Further Study

*Christian Century*. XCVIII, October 14, 1981, p. 1036.
*Christian Science Monitor*. LXXIII, August 26, 1981, p. 17.
*Commentary*. LXXII, October, 1981, p. 78.
*Library Journal*. CVI, July, 1981, p. 1403.
*The New Republic*. CLXXXV, September 9, 1981, p. 28.
*The New York Times Book Review*. LXXXVI, July 12, 1981, p. 1.
*Newsweek*. XCVIII, August 10, 1981, p. 65.
*Saturday Review*. VIII, June, 1981, p. 59.
*Time*. CXVIII, August 3, 1981, p. 18.

# NIGHTINGALE FEVER
## Russian Poets in Revolution

*Author:* Ronald Hingley
*Publisher:* Alfred A. Knopf (New York). 269 pp. $14.50
*Type of work:* Literary biography and criticism
*Time:* 1889-1966
*Locale:* The Soviet Union

*A composite critical biography of four masterful twentieth century Soviet poets—Anna Akhmatova, Osip Mandelstam, Boris Pasternak, and Marina Tŝvetaeva—set against the historical background of pre-Bolshevik Russia and the Soviet Union until the middle 1960's*

Ronald Hingley's insightful study of four of the greatest twentieth century Soviet poets—Anna Andreevna Akhmatova (1889-1966), Osip Yemilyevich Mandelstam (1891-1938), Boris Leonidovich Pasternak (1890-1960), and Marina Ivanovna Éfron Tŝvetaeva (1892-1941)—mixes in just measure biography, criticism, and historical reconstruction. In treating his subjects, Hingley, a professor of Russian literature at Oxford University and a noted translator and critic, examines the four lives and a composite sociobiography, showing how their relationships as friends or lovers, as artistic rivals or supporters, always as embattled dissidents within a hostile environment, united them at last in their tragic destinies.

As a thematic key to the poet's struggle, Hingley chooses as his title and his epigraph a phrase from Mandelstam: "and there is no hope/ For heart still flushed/ With Nightingale Fever." Composed in 1918, a few months after the Bolshevik Revolution, these lines are prophetic of the disaster that was to overtake all four gifted poets. By "nightingale fever," Mandelstam meant Philomela's self-destructive impulse to sing, to use the powers of one's art in the face of certain ruin. Like the fabled nightingale of the Greeks, Mandelstam and his three contemporaries were obsessively driven to sing, urged by the "fever" of their art. Hingley shows how the poets deliberately placed their lives in jeopardy, not because they were counterrevolutionary enemies of the Soviet authorities, but because the very act of singing—of writing poetry—was necessary to their existence.

To examine the four poets in a context of political upheaval, Hingley fashions a composite biography, skillfully counterpointing their relationship against a background of twentieth century Russian history. His method has both advantages and disadvantages. A chief limitation, of course, is his need to fragment the story of each poet's life into arbitrary periods. Certainly a continuous narrative is easier for most readers to grasp than one that intricately weaves into its pattern other lives. Nevertheless, Hingley is able to enrich his study of individual poets by demonstrating their collective fate. Indeed, the four masters were united by common aspirations and suffering, no matter how different their temperaments. As they matured, artistically and emotionally, they continued to influence one another. Even after the deaths of Mandelstam and Tsvetaeva—the former in a concentration camp and the latter a suicide following years of struggle and exile—the surviving poets commemorated through their lives and work a bond of fidelity to their fallen comrades.

Hingley traces three stages in the careers of each poet: "Peace and War" (1889-1921), a time mostly of pre-Bolshevik education, early writings, and first adjustment to the Revolution of 1917; "Between Convulsions" (1921-1930), a difficult period of struggle with the Soviet cultural dictators, usually without much success, to maintain artistic integrity; and finally, "Terror and Beyond" (1930-1966), the dénouement of Stalinist tyranny, culminating in the purges of 1937-1939 and their aftermath, followed by the post-Stalin years up until the mid-1960's.

During the early years of the century, all four poets shared similar socio-cultural backgrounds: all arose from the middle or upper-middle classes rather than the proletariat; all were well-educated; all achieved precocious success within the advanced literary circles of their day. In spite of the fact that, as a group, the poets were members of a privileged class of pre-Revolution society, they were liberals who either ignored Czarist institutions or wrote from the bias of Western rather than Slavic civilization. Of the four, two were nonobservant Jews—Mandelstam and Pasternak—and consequently were not entirely accepted as equals within the social structure. Nevertheless, they were generally admired by the literary class, spoke French and German fluently, and, like the two women, traveled to Western Europe, sometimes for long excursions. Similarly, Akhmatova and Tsvetaeva as cultivated intellectuals had considerable freedom to move in the circles of artists; both enjoyed the upper-class education of foreign governesses and tutors; both published verse in their youth; and both were grounded in classical civilization that included some training in Latin and Greek. All four poets spent their childhood and youth in metropolitan centers: Pasternak and Tsvetaeva in Moscow, and Akhmatova and Mandelstam in or near St. Petersburg (Leningrad). By 1917 all four poets had established their names as promising talents, and two of them—Akhmatova and Mandelstam—had already moved toward the center of attention among intellectuals.

Soon, however, the poets were to contend with political pressures more repressive than the Czar's ever were. In the delicate balancing act of accommodating to the Party line on the one hand and, on the other, of keeping their integrity as artists, the poets generally tilted toward freedom. Fully aware that they could not long survive in a police state by flaunting authority, they nevertheless continued to write, to publish, or, when they could not publish, to read aloud their poetry. As Hingley points out, the bulk of their poetry coul not, by any reasonable standard, be considered seditious to the

Party, but the Party functionaries treated the poets as suspect, not so much for what they wrote as for what they neglected to write. Refusing to exalt Stalin or to compose pretentious drivel about collectivism, they isolated themselves from the officially sanctioned versifiers. Because of this isolation, they sealed their fate. Of the four poets, only Pasternak continued to remain in Party favor during the dangerous middle years of the 1930's, an accident of caprice owing to Stalin's admiration of that poet's courage—or perhaps his misunderstanding of Pasternak's verse as supportive of the regime. The other poets, also afflicted with "nightingale fever," moved more rapidly to their public disgrace.

With the Stalinist purges of the late 1930's, each of the poets suffered great hardships: Mandelstam, after serving a sentence of internal exile, was arrested and sent to a labor camp in Siberia and died, according to the best available reports, on December 27, 1938, at Vladivostok, at a transit-point for Kolyma; Akhmatova's son Lyov Gumilyov was arrested in 1938; and on August 31, 1941, Tsvetaeva, after "measuring" herself for death for a year, committed suicide by hanging. Even Pasternak, who had managed throughout much of this time to count on Stalin's protection, undermined that flimsy basis of support by declaiming his verse in public with outspoken courage. During the brief political thaw following Stalin's death, he published his prose masterpiece *Doctor Zhivago*, for which he was awarded in October, 1958 the Nobel Prize in Literature. The Party pressured him to refuse the award by threatening to exile him from his homeland should he journey to Stockholm. Fearing that the secret police would persecute his beloved Olga Ivinskaya, he wrote to *Pravda* a letter offering his public apology for *Doctor Zhivago*. Yet Khrushchev would not forgive him: Pasternak's great offense in writing the book, as Hingley points out, was to show "that human beings should *live*, and not (as Soviet and other politicians would make them) *prepare for life*."

For Hingley, the great legacy of all four poets is precisely their gift of life, of creating in their verse a fuller appreciation of what life—ecstatic or tragic—means for its own sake. That gift endures, although the "nightingales" suffered much pain for the joy of their singing. Hingley points out that the gift of their song sustained many of their contemporaries who also had to endure terrible years of oppression. In prison camps they recited from memory the lines of Akhmatova, Mandelstam, Pasternak, and Tsvetaeva. In her touching memoir *Within the Whirlwind* (1981), Eugenia Ginzburg recounts the story of how important these poets were to her in the camps of Siberia, how she remained sane and even hopeful in spite of her privations simply by recalling their beloved verses. For a whole generation of Soviet dissidents, the four great poets spoke the thoughts and stirred the emotions they dared not voice or reveal in public. More so than in the West, Russians of the twentieth century have trusted in their major poets, have been sustained and strengthened by their songs.

In order to convey to a wider Western audience some of the impact these poets had upon their native readers, Hingley has the difficult task of surveying the whole Soviet cultural and political scene. He cannot take for granted a Western intellectual's familiarity with the dominant literary conventions that influenced modern Russian poetry, nor can he assume that the reader is familiar with the works of poets such as Aleksandr Blok, Nikolai Gumilyov, or Vladimir Mayakovsky, who affected in ways either personal or aesthetic his four subjects. He must explain, at least in outline, the particular Russian direction of literary movements such as Acmeism, futurism, and symbolism. Finally, he cannot show direct parallels to the major Western schools of twentieth century poetry, as the four Russians were, for the most part, indifferent to or ignorant of Ezra Pound, T. S. Eliot, William Butler Yeats, Rainer Maria Rilke, and Paul Válery. Instead, their roots were in Greek classicism or in nineteenth century Romantic Russian and European poetry.

Hingley understands these roots well. Historian, editor, critic, and translator (all the translations from the Russian are his own), he is perhaps uniquely qualified to place the poets in their proper milieu. To this task he brings not only an infectious enthusiasm for the poet's work but also a compassionate understanding of their lives. Through his book, once again Western readers may hear the tormented "nightingales" sing of life, of courage, of the joys and sorrows that are part of being human.

*Leslie Mittleman*

### Sources for Further Study

*The Kirkus Reviews.* XLIX, Septemper 1, 1981, p. 1132.
*Library Journal.* CVI, September 1, 1981, p. 1632.
*The New York Times Book Review.* LXXXVI, December 20, 1981, p. 6.
*Publishers Weekly.* CCXX, October 23, 1981, p. 56.

# NISA
## The Life and Words of a !Kung Woman

*Author:* Marjorie Shostak (1945-    )
*Publisher:* Harvard University Press (Cambridge, Massachusetts). 402 pp. $20.00
*Type of work:* Anthropology/memoir
*Time:* c. 1920-1974
*Locale:* Botswana

*A first person account of life in one of the oldest African cultures, with commentary by an anthropologist*

The !Kung San, more widely known as Bushmen, who live in and around the Kalihari desert in Angola, Botswana, and Namibia, are among the last survivors of the hunters and gatherers whose way of life sustained the human race for tens of thousands of years. Now, as growing populations move with agriculture and modern technology into the lands the !Kung depend upon for their livelihood, their culture seems doomed to extinction. Within another generation a book like this one will be impossible to write. *Nisa*, therefore, is much more than only another volume of popularized anthropology; it is an irreplaceable record of a society that has an important place in human history.

Author Marjorie Shostak, an anthropologist associated with Harvard University, has based her work on her belief that there are many elements linking modern society and the ostensibly primitive !Kung. In recounting the story of one woman's life, and in addressing this story to the general reader rather than to specialists in her field, she is affirming the universality of human experience. She notes in her Introduction that when she went to northwest Botswana in 1969, she hoped to find the answers to two questions: "What was it like being a woman in a culture so outwardly different from my own? What were the universals, if any, and how much would I be able to identify with?" Her book provides clear and detailed answers to both questions.

A part of the fascination of this book for some readers will be Shostak's account of how her research evolved. She spent twenty months among the !Kung on her first visit in 1969 and 1970, observing the culture, living and working with the people, and learning the language and its complicated clicks (represented in English by such symbols as the exclamation point). Once she could speak fluently enough to communicate, she set up a series of interviews with nine women ranging in age from fourteen to seventy-five. These interviews provided her with an accurate picture of the typical !Kung woman's life, and they are the primary sources for the ethnographic discussions that make up about half of each chapter in the book.

Although she had in effect fulfilled at least one of her goals, Shostak was still dissatisfied with her results as she approached the end of her stay. After a year and a half she had failed to achieve any real intimacy with her subjects, and she had been unable to obtain a truly vital account of one individual's experiences. Just a few weeks before she was scheduled to leave, she decided to try once more to achieve deeper communication with one of her subjects, the woman she here calls Nisa. Her initial reaction to Nisa had been negative. The African woman appeared loud, demanding, and none-too-subtle in her constant allusions to the generosity of other anthropologists, who had given her tobacco, food, and clothing. However, Shostak had recognized in Nisa's early interviews both gifts as a storyteller and a willingness to share her experiences. She decided to try once more. The two women carried on a number of conversations during Shostak's final weeks in Africa in 1970 and renewed their friendship on her second field trip four years later. This book is the result.

In her Introduction, fifteen chapters, and Epilogue, Shostak interweaves Nisa's vivid first-person narrative with commentary that sets her experiences in context. The restrained, objective tone of Shostak's explanations of the !Kung culture provides an effective contrast to the often highly colored, almost lurid episodes in Nisa's monologue.

The typical !Kung community is small, family-centered, and, in spite of the striking amount of violence in Nisa's story, generally peace-loving. While this society is not completely egalitarian, men and women share many responsibilities, especially those connected with child-rearing. Both groups spend much of their time accumulating food essential for the survival of the group. The women, occasionally accompanied by the men, are responsible for gathering the roots and nuts that form the staples of their diet, while the men hunt the more greatly prized meat. These activities leave them ample time for playing with children, talking endlessly, participating in ritual ceremonies, and, if the evidence of Shostak's interviews is accurate, engaging in enough romantic intrigues to satisfy the most avid soap opera fan.

The !Kung move frequently to find new sources of food and water; they have few possessions, and they can quickly construct the grass huts in which they live. Their stability comes from family ties. Brothers and sisters maintain lifelong connections, grandparents and aunts help with child care, and the different generations provide education and support to one another. They pass down the skills most crucial to their survival—the ability to track animals, to recognize the footprints of their companions, to find rich food sources in the most barren-looking land, and to minister to the sick with the appropriate herbs. Although illness and death are everpresent threats, their way of life seems appealing and extraordinarily efficient.

Both the pleasures and the sorrows of !Kung life are illuminated in Nisa's words, skillfully translated by Shostak to communicate both the intensity of the experiences and the picturesqueness of the language. There is childlike simplicity in some of Nisa's phrases, yet her reactions to her encounters with birth, death, love, and separation are those of an adult, and it is in them that

Shostak found those universals for which she was searching.

The earlier chapters convey a sense of the lively, spirited, sometimes self-willed child Nisa must have been. Her first memories, from the early 1920's, are of her weaning, which she bitterly resented, and of the birth of her younger brother. Since the !Kung child is nursed until the mother becomes pregnant again, usually in three to four years, the two events were closely linked. Nisa describes herself filled with resentment at being deprived of her nourishment and security: "I was always crying. I *wanted* to nurse! Once . . . I was especially full of tears. I cried all the time." Her mother responded to her feelings in an extraordinary way. When her labor began, she took Nisa with her to a large tree not far from the village and there, with the child watching, gave birth to a baby boy. She then sent Nisa back to get her "digging stick," telling her that she intended to bury the baby and allow her daughter to nurse again. When Nisa protested that she wanted to keep her brother, her mother reluctantly agreed. As Nisa tells the story, she seems convinced that the boy owed his life to her; Shostak is uncertain whether the story should be taken at face value or as an example of an unusual method of dealing with sibling rivalry.

Nisa's distress at being weaned was not really resolved for years. The remainder of the section entitled "Earliest Memories" recounts her constant battle with her parents over food. She stole it, cried at the sight of it, and hoarded it, and she was regularly beaten by her parents for doing so. Her grandmother eventually took her for an extended visit in another village, then returned her to her parents with strict orders to feed her well and stop hitting her. The satisfaction the child felt is still evident in her reflections many years later: "O, but my heart was happy! Grandmother was scolding Mother! I held so much happiness in my heart that I laughed and laughed."

Many of Nisa's childhood memories are ones shared by contemporary Western children—fights with siblings and friends, distress at breaking valuable objects (in her case, ostrich egg water containers), delight at splashing around in the rain. No American child, however, could experience the joy she felt in catching and killing a baby kudu and proudly bringing its meat back to the village. As a preadolescent, she had few responsibilities, but in observing and helping her elders, she was receiving an education in the skills she would need for survival.

For girls, adulthood arrives with the birth of the first child. Growing up seems to have been an unusually painful process for Nisa. Following their tribal custom, her parents arranged a marriage for her when she was about twelve. (A son-in-law was a desirable addition to any family, for he was another male to assist in the hunting.) The parents of the couple built them a hut, and the bride was ceremonially carried to it and set inside. She reacted as the child she still was: "I cried and cried and cried. Later I ran back to my parents' hut, lay down beside my little brother, and slept, a deep sleep like death." Her family then provided a young married woman to serve as chaperone for the couple. Nisa, reared in a culture in which children early observed their parents' sexual activity, realized almost at once that her husband and the chaperone had become lovers, and her parents quickly ended the first of her tribal marriages. The second lasted a little longer, but Nisa persisted in running almost nightly to her mother. This union ended when her husband refused to share his meat with her and her father, a serious offense among a people for whom gift-giving is an important symbol of relationship.

After refusing to be co-wife of a young man named Kantla, Nisa met Tashay, who became her first real mate. Once again she ran home frequently when they were first married, but as she matured physically she began to accept the relationship as inevitable, if not entirely satisfactory. At one time Tashay brought home a second wife, a young girl Nisa resented and fought. Once, she says, she tried to stab her rival with a knife. Eventually, "I chased her away and she went back to her parents." Later Tashay left for several months to work for a neighboring tribe and, as Nisa put it, "I learned about having lovers."

Nisa's narrative is filled with extramarital intrigues. It is not clear how typical her experience has been, but Shostak reports that much of the women's conversation is connected with sexual relations. When she learned to participate in their humorous treatment of the subject, she was more readily accepted as one of them. She notes that although polygamy is accepted, monogamy is more common, with divorce being easy and not unusual. Nisa's account suggests that husbands were considered entitled to beat their unfaithful wives and their lovers, yet she shows little guilt and considerable satisfaction in her many love affairs, even when they brought physical assaults on her.

Immature as Nisa was in her attitude toward marriage as a young bride, when the time came to accept adulthood at the birth of her first child, she showed the fortitude her society expected of all women. Like her mother, when she felt her labor begin, she left her village and sat down beside a tree to await the birth, stifling all impulses to cry out in pain—that would have disgraced her in the eyes of her husband's people, with whom she was living at the time. Only after she had delivered the infant and walked back to her hut did she receive help from an older woman. The significance of this episode in the life of the !Kung woman is indicated by Shostak's decision to begin her work with Nisa's description of the childbirth scene and to repeat the same passage later in its proper chronological place.

The chapter following "First Birth" is poignantly entitled "Motherhood and Loss." As in most primitive societies, the greatest enemy was disease, and Nisa suffered more than most from her people's short life expectancy. Her husband Tashay died as a young man, just weeks after her fourth child, her only son, was born. Two of her daughters died in early childhood, the son in his mid-teens. She experienced further tragedy when her one surviving daughter, a beautiful young girl, newly married, was killed by her husband. Nisa's comments on these events reveal both her pain and her courage:

> The death of any of your family is hard, but if others are alive, after a while your heart stops hurting. But when each one dies until, finally, they are all dead, your pain continues month after month after month. You look at other people who are surrounded by their families and you ask yourself why your whole family had to die. Your heart pains and you cry and can't stop. You cry and don't eat; you become thin, thin to death. Only some far distant moon, when that strikes, do you feel like a person again.

By the time Nisa was in her thirties, her people were in closer touch with other ethnic groups. She and Besa, the man she married after Tashay's death, both worked for Europeans in a Bantu community for a time. Although she eventually separated from Besa and returned to a !Kung village, her life, like the lives of all her people, has been increasingly affected by outside forces— even by the anthropologists studying them. Shostak and her husband probably saved Nisa from more devastating personal loss when they provided lifesaving medicine for her present husband, Bo, and the young niece whom she is rearing. (This child is the daughter of the brother for whose life she pleaded at his birth.)

Nisa's life today remains rooted in the traditions of her people—their legends, their trancelike healing rituals she can practice as a post-menopausal woman, their belief in gods who regularly intervene in their lives—but she is also a part of a world that includes farming, trade, money, alcohol, even warfare. Fighting has not been part of the !Kung life for many generations, but the men are currently being recruited by the South Africans as trackers and scouts for their guerrilla warfare against Namibian militants. Nisa faces her changing culture philosophically: "I lived and lived and now I am old. As I am today, I know about many things, the things people long ago spoke in front of me and the things I have seen."

Shostak's book conveys throughout the deep affection and understanding she developed both for the woman she came to address as her aunt and for the !Kung as a whole. She has provided for the reader what she says Nisa's story was for her: "a great gift—a window on a complex world that is quickly passing."

*Elizabeth Johnston Lipscomb*

## Sources for Further Study

*The Atlantic Monthly*. CCXLVIII, December, 1981, p. 92.
*Kirkus Reviews*. XLIX, October 1, 1981, p. 1282.
*Library Journal*. CVI, December 15, 1981, p. 2404.

*Nation*. CCXXXIV, January 2, 1982, p. 21.
*The New York Review of Books*. XXVIII, December 17, 1981, p. 67.
*The New York Times Book Review*. LXXXVI, November 8, 1981, p. 9.
*Publishers Weekly*. CCXX, September 25, 1981, p. 81.

# NUCLEAR STRATEGY IN A DYNAMIC WORLD
## American Policy in the 1980's

*Author:* Donald M. Snow (1943-    )
*Publisher:* University of Alabama Press (University). 284 pp. $25.00
*Type of work:* Military strategy
*Time:* 1945 to the present
*Locale:* The United States

*A systematic analysis of the conditions and problems concerning the formation of American nuclear strategy in a changing global environment*

An impressive number of books on nuclear issues have appeared recently and many more are reportedly coming out this year, a clear reflection of the growing debate over nuclear strategy. Interest in the strategic posture of the superpowers is no longer confined to the relatively small community of policy-makers and military and academic experts in the field. A larger sector of the general public has become more fully aware of the indescribable horror of a nuclear holocaust. Also, many people are apparently disconcerted over the Reagan Administration's military buildup program, the tough confrontation talk, and statements about "limited" nuclear war. Donald M. Snow's book provides a comprehensive treatment of the problems relating to nuclear strategy. It is a timely and welcome work, for it makes this technically and theoretically complex subject matter more widely accessible.

Deterrence, that "elusive art," underlies United States strategic force planning. The incredibly powerful American nuclear forces are intended to deter a nuclear attack on the United States and its allies by threatening catastrophic retaliation in return. Strategic nuclear weapons, along with American and allied theater nuclear weapons and conventional forces, are also to deter nonnuclear attacks, especially a large-scale attack on Western European NATO allies. Imperative to successful deterrence is the mounting of a *credible* retaliatory threat; however, what might be considered sufficient force to deter attack may not be seen the same way by the adversary. For this reason, the United States has insisted upon "essential equivalence" with the Soviet Union in strategic nuclear forces. This means that the strategic nuclear forces of the two superpowers are to be equal and that Soviet advantages in some categories are offset by American advantages in others.

The key to a stable nuclear deterrence system is the maintenance of Mutual Assured Destruction (MAD). In implementing MAD, the United States relies on an incremental force configuration of three elements, the "Triad," consisting of land-based Intercontinental Ballistic Missiles (ICBMs), Submarine Launched Ballistic Missiles (SLBMs), and strategic bombers. The resultant strength, diversity, and survivability is to ensure that the adversary does not have any incentive to launch a first strike. According to the Pentagon, the

United States refrains from deploying the kind of forces that would directly threaten the Soviet capability to retaliate. Although that claim is arguable, the United States primarily seeks to remove incentives to strike first and to sustain relative stability for the deterrence system. From the American perspective, a commensurate Soviet restraint has been notably lacking of late.

The deterrence system's capacity to deter is undermined by the dynamism of the arms race, subject to quantum leaps in capability. Both sides relentlessly develop their war-fighting nuclear technology. New delivery systems, more accurate warheads, improved guidance systems, better data processing and advanced targeting capabilities follow one another in never-ending spirals. Other developments are in the offing, which render deterrence more fragile than ever. These include charged particle beams, hunter-killer satellites, and submarine detection technology, potentially affecting the survivability of the nuclear submarine fleet. Deterrence is the product of capability and credibility. To achieve it, the volatile and destabilizing arms race has to be brought under control.

Experts and theoreticians are attempting to come to grips with the problem, but their task is all the more difficult because of uncertainty regarding the problem's theoretical formulation, not to mention the disagreements regarding basic concepts. In the course of his analysis, Snow refers to two prominent conceptual devices dealing with nuclear strategy matters. One of these is the action-reaction phenomenon approach. Within its context, for example, the American deployment of Multiple Independently Targetable Reentry Vehicles (MIRVs) was a response to Soviet efforts to develop the Anti-Ballistic Missile (ABM) system. MIRVs, however, constituted a potent new offensive weapon system in Soviet eyes and spurred an arms buildup on their part, leading to the current quantitative imbalance.

The other approach comes from game theory. Specifically applicable to the strategic arms race is the Prisoners' Dilemma analogy, named for the scenario typically justifying the selection of payoffs in situations involving independent choice in a combination of conflict and cooperation. In the scenario two men are in the custody of police, suspected of serious crimes. They are held incommunicado and are cross-examined separately. It has been made clear to them that if they both remain silent and admit to nothing, they will get off with a relatively minor charge. If one of them turns state's evidence and the other remains silent, the first will go free while the second will receive a severe sentence. If both "rat," they will both get a fairly stiff sentence. Strategy one, to cooperate, would be mutually advantageous; strategy two, however, to double-cross, entails a higher individual payoff. Moreover, neither player trusts the other and does not want to be the "sucker." As it turns out, the players in such a game most often choose the second option, guided by self-interest and mistrust; the higher the stakes, the more likely will individual rational choice dictate a noncooperative, double-crossing action.

Fortunately, national governments, unlike the two prisoners, can and do communicate. Therefore, they can commit themselves to pursue strategies of joint cooperation. Formal agreements, such as those resulting from the strategic arms limitations talks (SALT), can create such a commitment, which requires satisfactory verification methods enabling each party to detect betrayal before it becomes effective. Under prevailing conditions a situation of strategic parity offers a reasonably good solution. Strategic "bean counting" is consequently a most serious enterprise. Compared are arsenals, numbers of warheads, raw megatonnage, megaton equivalents, and "kill-factors." According to official figures, the American ICBM force is composed of fifty-four Titan and one thousand Minuteman missiles, of which 550 are MIRVed Minuteman III's. These land-based missiles are seen as increasingly vulnerable to attack, as missile accuracy is constantly being improved. The so-called MX mobile ICBM program is a hedge against this growing vulnerability. The SLBM force is composed of forty-one nuclear submarines equipped with a total of 160 Polaris and 496 Poseidon missiles, the latter carrying up to fourteen MIRV warheads. The Poseidon submarines are being replaced by the much larger Trident submarines, each carrying twenty-four missiles and designed to give the United States a survivable sea-based strategic deterrent through the 1990's.

The third element of the American strategic forces are the 350 heavy bombers, the B-52's. Although aging, these huge planes are still considered to be highly effective. The decision has been made to equip a portion of them with modern air-launched Cruise missiles to penetrate the Soviet defenses. The Soviet strategic forces have expanded enormously in the last several years. In contrast to the United States, the Soviets have placed greater emphasis on land-based missiles and have a numerical superiority of ICBMs, said to total fourteen hundred, but the Soviet SLBM force also continues to expand. According to United States government figures, they now have about 950 SLBMs. Their current bomber force is less than half the size of that of the United States. A new plane, the Backfire bomber, with characteristics and capabilities between heavy and medium bombers, is being deployed at a steady pace.

In general, there still is effective strategic parity between the two super-powers, but the Soviet Union is expanding its forces at a faster rate than the United States at this time, giving particular urgency to an understanding of Soviet strategic views. Snow addresses the question of why the Soviets tried to exploit the period of détente to surpass the United States in strategic capabilities. He notes that the American and the Soviet views of deterrence strategy are not mirror images. An important difference is the Soviet view of deterrence and a *war-winning* capacity as complementary, not opposing, concepts. This posture, perhaps unintentionally, tends to reinforce the American perception of Soviet bellicosity. Nevertheless, the Soviets continue to compete unfavorably at the qualitative level. Snow concurs with assessments of the Soviet Union as having a more limited scientific and technological base and a bureaucratic style that does not promote dramatic technological breakthroughs.

For the deterrence system to function, it must be stable. This does not require a precise equality of forces, but rather their relative invulnerability. If talks should commence between the superpowers, they should aim at reducing the Soviet threat to American land-based missiles and avoid any additional American threat to those of the Soviet Union. An offer to abandon the MX missile for appropriate concessions by the Soviets might be a fruitful point of departure. The unratified SALT II treaty is not as flawed as the Reagan Administration has made it out to be, according to many analysts. No more favorable and mutually acceptable formulas have as yet been advanced than those contained in that treaty. At present the sad fact is that there are no restraints on further massive buildups by the Soviet Union. The generally accepted estimate of the number of warheads in American possession is thirty thousand. Of these, about ten thousand are considered to be of strategic caliber. The Soviet Union will soon have an equal number of strategic warheads. An exchange of only a fraction of these weapons could kill most of the urban population and destroy most of the the industry of both sides. In fact, each superpower holds the entire population of the other as hostage. This mode of mutual deterrence is obviously not a good foundation for world peace, but are there alternatives? Doctrines have been advanced that would retain the use of nuclear weapons on the battlefield or in a controlled, selective strategic war, in which the bulk of the civilian population could be spared. Also proposed have been more strictly defense-oriented strategic postures, attempting to defend more directly the civilian population through impenetrable air and missile defense systems over urban centers. Alas, a deterrence system based on the MAD concept is the prospect for the foreseeable future. Strategic doctrine must face those inescapable realities and must concentrate on making the system more stable to reduce the threat to humankind.

Although public pressure for a freeze on nuclear weapons is mounting, a halt-in-place stance at this time does have its pitfalls. As the Reagan Administration has pointed out, effective deterrence at this stage requires the capacity to destroy the other side after absorbing a first strike. This capacity may indeed be somewhat impaired and tempt the Soviet Union into a first strike posture. It may be wise, however, to heed the proposal made by several influential former participants in nuclear strategy formulation, calling for a renunciation of the "first-use" position in case of a Soviet attack in Europe with conventional forces. With its nuclear strategy, the United States must ensure that the nuclear threshold is not crossed. The kind of systematic study of the problem presented by Snow can be of much help in this effort. It also has considerable utility as a reference tool with its extensive documentation and helpful glossary.

*Manfred Grote*

## Sources for Further Study

*Choice.* XVIII, July, 1981, p. 1607.
*Library Journal.* CVI, May 1, 1981, p. 979.

# THE OFFICERS' WIVES

*Author:* Thomas Fleming (1927-    )
*Publisher:* Doubleday & Company (Garden City, New York). 714 pp., $15.95
*Type of work:* Novel
*Time:* 1950 to the present
*Locale:* West Point and American military bases in Europe, Hawaii, and the Far East

*A panoramic view of the effects of policies and politics of the American Army between 1950 and the late 1970's on the personal lives of career officers and their wives*

> *Principal characters:*
> PETER MACARTHUR BURKE, an army officer who has been involved in corrupt New Jersey politics
> JOANNA, his wife, daughter of a German-American heiress
> ADAM THAYER, another army officer, descendant in fact and mind of the Puritan founders of America
> HONOR, his wife, extremely beautiful and fun-loving
> GEORGE ROSSER, another army officer who wonders whether he might not be better suited to civilian life
> AMY, his wife, an ambitious but reckless woman
> SAM PERKINS, also an army officer, an intelligent and peace-loving man
> RUTH, his wife, a woman who hates the Army and officers in particular

When Ernest Hemingway, in *A Farewell to Arms* (1929), had Frederic Henry state "I was always embarrassed by the words sacred, glorious, sacrifice and the expression in vain," most writers and readers felt that a new era had come for the novel of men at war. Hemingway's chief literary rival at the time, Erich Remarque and his book *All Quiet on the Western Front* (1929), was making the same point. For later generations, there have been books such as Norman Mailer's *The Naked and the Dead* (1948), Joseph Heller's *Catch-22* (1961), and Thomas Pynchon's *Gravity's Rainbow* (1973), each more insistently reinforcing the empty rhetoric of war-makers and the absurd pointlessness of the bitter sacrifices involved. Thomas Fleming, a man of great knowledge of military history and no novice at novel-writing, seems, in general, to have ignored his literary forebears in writing *The Officers' Wives* in 1981. So do most of his characters, for of the major ones, especially throughout the debacles of Korea and Vietnam, only two ever question the relevance of those "abstract nouns," and of them, only one questions the way the Army is applying them, not their existence as a true ideal for every officer and soldier to realize in his vocation. The wives' function is primarily to help them achieve these goals, as well as to improve their husbands' chances for promotion.

If Fleming's attitude toward heroism and other traditional military values undermines the credibility of his novel, an equally serious problem is structural: in spite of Fleming's grasp of history and the military, and his mastery in interweaving intricate plot lines, the counter-theme of the male-female "war" threatens to dominate the novel, pushing it toward soap opera.

No one who has been even briefly connected with the military will doubt the author's expertise after his brief descriptions of American bases such as Ft. Ripley, Ft. Staunton, and Ft. Leavenworth. Only the name, the size, the climate, and the terrain change, not the separation of ranks: the rows of barracks; the married enlisted men's quarters crowded with minority groups; the almost all-white population of the officers quarters, very small, almost lacking in privacy, overflowing with young children in the junior officers section; the separate senior officers quarters, growing in size and elegance appropriate to rank—all orderly and clean, at least on the outside. Fleming describes the Officers Club, the dances and parties where the men gravitate to one end of the room for "army talk" while the wives are left together to chat about "women's things"; the Officers' Wives Club and its endless committees, coffees (sherry is served), luncheons (cocktails are served), the bridge lunches or afternoons, the "official" officers' wives book; the endless lines at the base hospital, the competent doctors who soon become bored dealing primarily with pregnancies, deliveries, and childhood diseases; the overflowing commissary on pay day.

Fleming is convincing in his evocation of the life-style and physical presence of Mautbrunnen, and Donaulinger, Germany; of Ankara, Turkey; of Yokoshima, Japan; the Hawaiian beaches and Schofield; and Bangkok, Thailand—all have an authentic ring. Occasionally, the settings become symbolic of interior states of mind: the city of Boston as opposed to Ft. Staunton as Joanna has her first anxiety attack; the omnipresent ice coating all of Ft. Leavenworth while Joanna's marriage and her attachment to the Army "team" freeze over. The darkness, chaos, and evil of the night in Korea when Honor is raped (a bit of heavy-handed symbolism, especially since it almost happens again when Adam is in Vietnam) become rapidly symbolic of the chaotic evil of the entire Korean situation.

The historical background which surrounds and gives meaning to these locales reminds the reader of the dangerous potential for crises beginning in small, distant nations to become full-fledged wars, as physically and morally debilitating as Vietnam. The atomic bombs of today, the military tactic of overwhelming force seems no longer viable in such situations, as Fleming has Adam Thayer conclude in his fictional doctoral dissertation, an idea fought about in the Pentagon, but ignored by politicians and military leaders in general for almost twenty years. Thayer's concepts, as the brighter men realize, could give the Army a new focus and purpose. In real life, however, as in this novel, few officers are as reckless with their potential for promotion as Adam Thayer. Even his best friends, who understand what is happening and believe his policy on coercive wars to be correct, will not offend their superiors by publicly saying what they privately believe.

Officers are all too mindful of the risks of speaking out; confrontations such as Arnold Coulter's with Douglas MacArthur and, later, Adam Thayer's with Willard Eberle, can destroy a potentially successful career. Military life is full of such small pitfalls: failure to participate in actual battles can delay promotion, as George Rosser knows, although he finally has his chance in Vietnam; participating in battle can mean capture, such as Arnold Coulter's almost four-year absence in World War II, which keeps him from ever becoming a general in spite of his expertise. Participating in battle can also mean death, as "Lover" McKenzie, Johnny Stapleton, and eventually, Pete Burke learn; for the survivors who show courage and leadership without losing too many men, it can mean early promotions and medals, along with physical and/or psychological wounds, as with Pete Burke, but if too many are killed, it can lead to exile and early retirement, such as followed Rosser's commander at Donaulinger. If duty tours at the Pentagon are ignored for service in battle or personal reasons, one's career can be stalled well under the General level, as happens later to Pete Burke and to Hank O'Connell. Only the very few survive to become generals: George Rosser, who thought of quitting for more money several times, who is not certain that it was worth it all (and he is unaware of *all* it took on his wife's part); and Sam Perkins, who is able to survive wounds, the emotional loss of his family, and the emotional wounds of colleagues, to become whole again, a man whose quiet leadership and effective negotiating are glimpsed at crucial moments throughout. Then there are the generals, Eberle for example, who get there through clever unscrupulous political use of others, whose only vows are to and for themselves.

Other questions raised—such as the correct balance of civilian politics and aims with the military's, the omnipresence and oversimplification of the media, and potential strife among the many branches of the Army itself—are not answered, nor are the problems surrounding fraternization of officers with enlisted men, integration of minority groups at any rank level, and the financial and mental stress of military families, followed up in any serious way. Yet these are among the very problems which must be faced and solved to insure America's survival as a world force respected for its integrity in the use of its military power.

Amidst the complexity of these problems Fleming focuses on a more personal issue and value—married life, an important contemporary theme but one which should not be allowed to engulf the book, as it does for the casual reader. Although broken marriages, sexual problems, and divorce are often used as symbolic of the times, they cannot sum up all of the moral and political problems that are central to *The Officers' Wives*. Each of the four marriages of the West Point roommates, class of 1950, suffers from military life, either strained, torn asunder, or held together in an empty façade. As the couples cross and recross the United States, Asia, Europe, the reader becomes more and more involved in their sexual problems and experiences, which are almost incestuous, to the detriment of Fleming's other, more significant themes. Although each marriage crisis has military career pressure as a common ingredient, each is believable within the depth and range of individual character development: each of the women discovers another self within that needs expression beyond the bounds of her stereotyped roles, while the men, recognizing, as do the wives, how much control the force of history has over their lives and how little control they, themselves have, move toward other comforts. The theme of war is introduced by explicit wording into the marriages of Joanna and Pete Burke, and of Honor and Adam Thayer. Before the novel begins, both men are dead and their wives, through anguish, anger, suffering, loss, and isolation, have come to a relatively serene acceptance of their past and their present selves, their "separate peaces." Joanna, in addition, has been awarded Major General Sam Perkins as a second husband, having elected to rejoin the fellowship not of the brave but of the suffering, which act as healers rather than destroyers.

At the conclusion of the novel, all the major officers' wives—Amy, Honor, and Joanna—are reunited for Adam Thayer's funeral to recognize that Adam was a "war casualty" just as surely as Pete Burke, the two men who from the first embodied, almost symbolically, the best of the military and American traditions—one the descendant of New England Puritans who perceived his role as a questioner and shaper of the integrity of America's world role; the other, a traditional conservative Irish-American who acted within the established vision of America's force as a defender of freedom throughout the world; both uncompromising and fully dedicated to duty, honor, and country but often in dissent about the practical implementation and implications of such ideals. The wives, as suggested in an early brief foreshadowing incident when Joanna meets a General's wife, agree that they represent the "walking wounded." Joanna, the primary consciousness and conscience of the novel, recognizes that to "Duty, Honor, Country," another, perhaps most significant, element must be added—love: "Old love for the dead. New love for the living." She learns that these two opposing truths are not contradictory, just as she earlier learned that the force of history was a living presence, affecting individuals' lives and careers.

To say that Thomas Fleming's best-selling *The Officers' Wives* is an often cumbersome soap opera, complete with heavy-handed symbolism, stereotyped minor characters, and a rather contrived happy ending, and to maintain, on the other hand, that it is a book filled with well-developed major characters and substantial insight into the philosophical, political, and military problems of postwar America, is to recognize that "opposite truths can coexist." Despite its obvious commercial ambitions, Fleming's novel deserves such an even-handed judgment.

*Ann E. Reynolds*

**Sources for Further Study**

*The Atlantic Monthly*. CCXLVII, April, 1981, p. 122.
*Best Sellers*. XLI, May, 1981, p. 45.
*Book World*. XI, March 29, 1981, p. 4.
*Booklist*. LXXVII, February 1, 1981, p. 730.
*Harper's Magazine*. CCLXII, April, 1981, p. 96.
*Library Journal*. CVI, February 15, 1981, p. 469.
*The New York Times Book Review*. LXXXVI, April 12, 1981, p. 14.
*Quill & Quire*. XLVII, June, 1981, p. 39.

# THE OHIO GANG
## The World of Warren G. Harding

*Author:* Charles L. Mee, Jr. (1938-    )
*Publisher:* M. Evans and Company (New York). 248 pp. $14.95
*Type of work:* History
*Time:* 1865-1923
*Locale:* The United States

*"An historical entertainment" based upon the political life of Warren G. Harding and his Ohio cronies*

Principal personages:
WARREN G. HARDING, twenty-ninth president of the United States, 1921-1923
FLORENCE "DUCHESS" HARDING, his wife
NAN BRITTON, his mistress
HARRY M. DAUGHERTY, Attorney General of the United States, 1921-1924
GASTON B. MEANS, "Special Employee" of the Bureau of Investigation

Although Charles L. Mee, Jr., warns the reader from the beginning that his book is "an historical entertainment," it takes some time to grasp fully the approach he has taken in his tale of "the Ohio Gang," an infamous group of late nineteenth century and early twentieth century politicians.

Frequently referred to by historians and political commentators, "the Ohio Gang"—sometimes called "the Ohio Dynasty," because of the number of presidents the state produced—is by itself a study in the potential evils of the democratic process. From Ohio came seven of the twelve presidents between the Civil War and World War I and more federal jobholders and cabinet members than from any other state. The national party of power in those years was the Republican Party; as an emotional backlash from the Civil War and because of carpetbagger politics in the South, the Democrats, the party associated most closely with the Confederacy, had only two of their members elected president between Abraham Lincoln's death and Warren G. Harding's election: Grover Cleveland and Woodrow Wilson. A third Democrat, Andrew Johnson, succeeded to the presidency upon Lincoln's death.

Every Republican president in those years came from Ohio, except Chester A. Arthur and Theodore Roosevelt, from New York; ironically, both of these non-Ohio politicians became president only upon the assassination of their Ohio predecessors, James Garfield and William McKinley. It is plain that this group of politicians, then, exercised almost unbelievable power in Washington and, indirectly, in the nation and the world.

In Warren G. Harding's Administration, major office holders from Ohio included Harry M. Daugherty, Attorney General, whose chief qualification was his successful management of Harding's nomination campaign; Ed

Scobey, former Sheriff of Pickaway County, Ohio, who became Director of the United States Mint; Gaston B. Means, "Special Employee" of the Bureau of Investigation (the forerunner of the FBI and also run by an Ohio appointee), and Dick Crissinger, Comptroller of the Currency and eventually governor of the Federal Reserve System, whose chief qualification for appointment had been his position as head of a small bank in Marion, Ohio. Appropriately, Marion was the town where Harding published a newspaper.

As a publisher, Harding was given ample opportunity to practice his favorite pastime, what he called *bloviating*, defined by Mee as liking "to talk, to pass the time of day, to exchange pleasantries, to idle away the hours discussing politics." That newspaper, the *Marion Star*, can serve as an early indicator of Harding's approach to politics and to life in general. Originally there were three owners, Harding, Jack Warwick, and Johnnie Sickle. Harding was always known for his ability to "go along" with most things and most people, especially when such nonchalance would be beneficial to his ambitions. Thus he allowed a disagreement with Sickle to smolder until Sickle gave up and moved away; Warwick's portion of the paper came as a result of a poker game—another of Harding's favorite pastimes.

The newspaper's editorial policy, as described by Warwick, was one of out-and-out boosterism. "We exploited railroads that never got beyond the blueprint and we saw smoke rolling out of the chimneys of factories before the excavations were made for the foundations." Such a policy of fabrication of dreams and nonentities would serve Harding well when he campaigned for president on a promise of a "return to normalcy," described by Mee and other historians as "a return to an age that never was."

As an easygoing sort, Harding was a favorite of the party bosses, especially in a state such as Ohio, famous for its bosses who rewarded the faithful—and Harding was faithful, having served as candidate for various county and state offices for more than ten years in elections when it was known before the ballots were counted that a Republican would never win.

One reward came when Harding was given the nomination for lieutenant governor in 1903, along with Myron Herrick as governor; they won and Harding began to see the advantages of cooperation. He wanted the nomination for governor later for himself, but when Herrick said he desired renomination and the bosses agreed, Harding amiably withdrew his request. For such obedience, he was given the opportunity to deliver the nominating speech in 1912 for William Howard Taft, a speech full of allusions and platitudes, a speech which brought boos from the progressive elements of the party. Just as the boos were not enough to prevent Taft's nomination, Taft, himself, was not enough to win the election, but Harding had played the game. His next reward was the nomination for the United States Senate, a position he won in 1914.

As Senator, he introduced no legislation which "might be construed to be either important or controversial." That is, he practiced the adage, "Don't rock the boat," and practiced it well. His reward for six years of mediocrity was the Republican nomination for president, not because of his policies or proposals or successful political record. He was nominated because he was not likely to do anything which would prove uncomfortable to the well-oiled machine. As Senator Frank Bandegee of Connecticut explained the choice of Harding to a reporter: "There ain't any first-rater this year . . . We got a lot of second-raters and Warren Harding is the best of the second-raters." More fainthearted praise hardly seems possible.

What strikes the reader is how closely Warren G. Harding resembles George Babbitt, Sinclair Lewis' fictional glad-hander. Babbitt, too, was full of accommodation and boosterism, hot air and platitudes. Harding, the real-life character, however, is another case of fact outdoing fiction.

All these anecdotes are humorous, without doubt, and Mee does call his book an "entertainment," but Harding's nomination and election can be attributed not only to party politics and "the smoke-filled room" (a phrase which came from that 1920 Republican convention) but also to fear and disillusionment in the United States at that time. The war had ended in an armistice, an accommodation. Millions of American men had been drafted into the Army in a great show of American power and ability as a world leader. Most of these soldiers never were shipped to Europe, much less took part in the great chance for glory and conquest many still thought war would be.

Woodrow Wilson's plan for an organization of all major world powers which would eliminate the need for additional wars, that is, the League of Nations, could not pass the Congress. Americans had shifted from a concern for world peace and the establishment of their nation as a world power to a growing position of antiinvolvement with other nations. Immigrants began to suffer local and national abuse. The Ku Klux Klan became a national force on a platform of bigotry, based upon hatred of blacks, Jews, Catholics, and foreigners. The Espionage Act had attempted to squelch negative debate and discussion about the war, and the focus of the government agents even following the end of the war often was upon the foreign-born, especially if they also happened to be Socialists. Such persons were not necessarily wrong or anti-American in their views, but they were vocal, and their suppression was a visible sign that America was for "Americans."

Unfortunately, just being an American was not enough, finally. The International Workers of the World, also called the IWW or "Wobblies," some from old-line "American" stock, called for radical changes in the political system and, perhaps even more important, in the economic system. Bombs sent by political radicals and addressed to public leaders began to appear in post offices. Free enterprise itself was called into question, yet "the American way" had been built on a belief in rugged individualism and free enterprise.

Fear was everywhere.

Thus, Harding's calm, quiet, front-porch campaign for president, based upon that promise of a "return to normalcy" which could be interpreted by each voter as he or she wanted or needed to interpret it, seemed to offer the most appealing solution to the nation's problems—whether political, social, or economic.

Political analysts often explain the results of elections on the theory that the public voted not for the winner but against the loser. Certainly this principle can be applied in the case of Warren G. Harding's victory.

It is Mee's analysis of this part of the era of "the Ohio Gang," however, that keeps his book from becoming a mournful, dull liturgy of the failures and foibles of the American culture. He takes a position from the beginning which says to the reader that the whole story will finally become ludicrous without any attempts by the author to impose his interpretations and viewpoints upon the material. Ultimately, Harding's role in the story becomes farcical.

In order to concoct his "historical entertainment," Mee uses approaches often denied the totally objective scholar. As "facts," he presents direct quotations of alleged conversations and first-person descriptions of events with only one other witness, who, by the time the comments or descriptions were made public, was conveniently dead. The statements are taken directly from the memoirs of the various parties involved.

For example, when Mee wants to discuss Nan Britton—Harding's mistress—and her meetings with the President in the White House, the documentary evidence comes from Britton's own published story of her affair. Did the President and his mistress meet clandestinely in a closet just off the President's office? Probably only two people know the answer to that question, and one of them never commented publicly, but the silence of one party does not require the other party to be equally silent, and Mee quotes Nan Britton: "In the darkness of a space not more than five feet square, the President of the United States and his adoring sweetheart made love."

Did this and the other meetings described by Britton ever take place? Historical evidence, documented fact, indicates some such meetings probably did occur, but allowing Britton to tell the story as she remembers it, makes the events even more absurd than would the sworn testimony of an investigator giving the number, dates, and locations of the trysts. (Mee does allow one such investigator to talk, the one used by Mrs. Harding to gather the evidence against the President. At least, that is what the investigator says, but he is the same person who later claimed Mrs. Harding poisoned the President, a reference Mee relegates to a note on sources at the end of the book.)

After a while, the direct quotations taken at face value lend a certain tone to the book, a satirical tone enhanced by the author's penchant for effective punch lines. For example, during Wilson's Administration, thirteen thousand post office jobs had been removed from patronage and placed into Civil Service categories; Harding returned the jobs to the patronage ranks to be administered by his Postmaster General, Will Hays (whose greatest fame was to come later in the 1930's as head of the Hollywood film censorship office). Newspaper editorial writers were appalled at Harding's blatant political action, but Hays saved the day, in Mee's terms, "according to the usages of honest corruption" by giving the jobs to loyal Republicans who gave "almost a day's work for a day's pay." The editorialists were appeased, and, in fact, again in Mee's terms, "praised Hays for not practicing politics with the Post Office."

Such satirical twists appear, also, in Mee's chapter titles, with one building upon another: Chapter XXI, "Bribery," Chapter XXII, "Corruption," Chapter XXIII, "Bribery and Corruption," Chapter XXVI, "Bribery and Corruption and Sex and Suicide." Many of these chapters are only a page or two long and are devoted to a single fascinating anecdote.

In the "Epilogue," Mee says his book is intended as "a consideration, an essay, with a little of the old soft shoe . . . a fable," which is a tale told to point a moral.

If there is a moral to this tale, it is that any boy—even the least capable—*can* grow up to be President of the United States.

*John C. Carlisle*

### Sources for Further Study

*Best Sellers*. XLI, September, 1981, p. 226.
*Booklist*. LXXVII, July 1, 1981, p. 1386.
*Business Week*. August 17, 1981, p. 8.
*Library Journal*. CVI, July, 1981, p. 1412.
*The New Republic*. CLXXXV, September 9, 1981, p. 34.
*Time*. CXVIII, July 27, 1981, p. 80.

# OLD GLORY
## An American Voyage

*Author:* Jonathan Raban (1942-    )
*Publisher:* Simon and Schuster (New York). 409 pp. $16.95
*Type of work:* Travelog, autobiography, social history
*Time:* The fall and early winter, 1979
*Locale:* The Mississippi River and adjacent towns

*A record of the author's journey, in a sixteen-foot boat, down the Mississippi River from Minneapolis to New Orleans*

Travel literature is a rich and varied literary form; in part this is because of the correspondences which exist between reading and traveling. When Emily Dickinson cast her famous metaphor comparing frigates to books she was more than a little bit accurate. If reading is a kind of journey then so is writing, and no other kind of writing points this up in quite the same way that travel writing does.

It is perhaps too much of a generalization to say that, at heart, all life and all literature are based in travel. The case could, however, be made for such an assertion. From the darkness of the birth canal to the narrow-walled grave, from the first page to the last, numerous journeys are started and ended. Oftentimes vicarious journeys must suffice, voyages only imagined, dreamed. Rarely do the journeys of literature cross over into the journeys of life. When they do, the event is likely to be momentous, with a significance both individual and universal. Such is the case of *Old Glory: An American Voyage*.

The Mississippi River has itself long been a kind of metaphor for America, coursing as it does the heartland of the country, receiving many other noble rivers in its own progress to the Gulf of Mexico. Minneapolis, St. Louis, Memphis, New Orleans, even such smaller cities as LaCrosse, Dubuque, Quincy, Natchez, Baton Rouge (not to mention countless other places)—all of these river towns (aside from the industry and commerce associated with shipment of goods along the length of the river) connote in their North/South axis much of America's history and image, from early nationhood through the Civil War to recent civil rights struggles. Furthermore, St. Louis, as the historical gateway to the West, and Nauvoo, as the departure point for the Mormon march to Salt Lake City, both point to the importance of the Mississippi River as another axis, another topographical and migratory orientation: East/West.

Perhaps the Mississippi can most fittingly be thought of in terms of the "Old Glory" metaphor which Jonathan Raban develops throughout the eleven chapters of his book. At its most obvious, Raban's title refers to the American flags which he sees on the masts and decks of barges, tows, flatboats, yachts, skiffs, and on town flagpoles. Beyond that, however, Raban's book is about the wonder of place, people, and idea; about the process and history (another kind of journey), of America itself—and most especially of the Mississippi River as its representation.

Integral to America's essence is its European and in particular its British beginning, and the somewhat ironic edge to Raban's title derives from his perspective as an Englishman. At the start America represented to European immigrants a glorious promised land, and much of America's early literature, whether in diaries and journals or travelers' letters home, is a recounting of American voyages. So Raban's subtitle reverberates back across the Atlantic with echoes of, among others, Hector St. Jean de Crevecoeur and his glorification of American enterprise and settlement. Raban's travelog arcs back also to Mark Twain's seminal dramatization of a boy's life on the Mississippi, *The Adventures of Huckleberry Finn* (1884).

The America which Raban first dreamed as a seven-year-old child in England was, although separated by an ocean and a century, one and the same with Twain's, for in reading about Huckleberry Finn's exploits, Raban in his own boyhood envisioned a similar trip. At the age of thirty-seven, after deciding against both teaching and marriage, in the autumn of a year (1979) filled with news of greater moment—the Pope's visit to the United States, Ronald Reagan's challenge of Jimmy Carter for the presidency, the American hostage crisis in Iran—Raban atavistically simulates Huck's river ride, not on a raft to Cairo with Jim but rather alone on a sixteen-foot, aluminum-shelled, blunt-backed, "customized" boat equipped with a small outboard motor, a swivel chair, a carpentered chart stand, a candy-striped canopy and playfully dubbed by its creator, Herb Heichert, "Raban's Nest." Although not outfitted to order, the impertinence of Raban's boat matches his own temerity as a solitary middle-aged boy challenging the aged but ageless delights and dangers of the Mississippi.

As the conventions of travel literature go, trips are made for both practical and impractical reasons, for enjoyment and pleasure—to see and to know different, often exotic places and people; and in the process, though it is not usually stated as an end in itself, to learn something more about oneself, one's own personal motives and beliefs. Traveling is living. So it is in *Old Glory*, where Raban as a Britisher abroad passes through the lives, jobs, and entertainments—the homes, offices, factories, bars, churches, picnics, and political rallies—of northern, midwestern, and southern Americans. He learns much about these individuals and about American class structure and values, but he learns even more, by way of implicit and explicit comparison and contrast, about himself. Although he retains his articulate, urbane, high-brow identity as a cultured tourist, as a stranger afloat on a relatively provincial inland America, he is always empathetic even when at obvious odds with some of the life-styles and attitudes he encounters.

One quality which generally endears Raban to the people he meets and to the American reader looking on, is his humanness and (despite the solitude and loneliness which tend to dominate the trip on and off the river) his gregariousness—due partially to the publicity given the whole trip, which elevates Raban into something of a celebrity. In all of these ways, *Old Glory* transcends the travelog at its most rudimentary and becomes late twentieth century social history in tandem with autobiographical soul-search.

There are several "structures" and themes in *Old Glory*—each reinforcing the other and the extended metaphor of the title. Fundamentally, the notion of a Britisher touring and re-creating one of America's most recognized nineteenth century myths, that of rafting down the Mississippi, is paralleled by time on the river, usually alone, and time off the river: in the river towns, with lonely moments in hotels and restaurants, but invariably with other people. Raban journeys from London to New York (where he keeps a checking account to finance the material needs of the trip as they arise) to the headwaters of the Mississippi in the twin cities of Minneapolis/St. Paul; he locates the river (more or less ignored by the residents, he feels) and a boat, he gathers his supplies (which include indispensable charts and books brought with him); then he sets off on the voyage proper, after a short shakedown run in his boat, really learning how to handle it and respond to the changing moods of the river and the weather as he goes.

Dividing the journey into two large segments and various smaller ones, Raban stops in strategic towns in nine states: Minnesota, Wisconsin, Iowa, Illinois, Missouri, Tennessee, Arkansas, Mississippi, and Louisiana. Passage through the twenty-five locks above St. Louis represents the first phase of the voyage, and the less-controlled, widening river below St. Louis represents the second. It is on this leg of the voyage that Raban is finally convinced to buy a marine radio to communicate with other boats, a decision which undoubtedly saves his life.

Since the trip is of interest to the media he is at times recognized, because of advance publicity, and he does have a sketchy itinerary, which includes interviewing prominent and representative citizens and civic leaders—and being interviewed as well. At each stop he also reviews past and present political and economic national history as it affects that locality. Generally, however, the voyage is a serendipitous series of chance meetings, friendships, and "dates"—including one personal and rather prolonged romantic affair with a St. Louis woman named Sally. It is from this live-in interlude and its threatened permanent commitments that he runs away to the growing wildness of the river, making in effect a second start. In varying degrees of involvement with all the people's lives he crosses, Raban is cast in the role of the inquisitive voyeur whose main compulsion is to move on, to beat the fall of night and the encroaching winter and reach his destination, the mouth of the Mississippi.

The need to make it, to accomplish the goal of traveling the length of the river and say, "I did it," soon fades, however, into the realization that the true prize of the whole effort resides in being on such a river ride, in just doing it. This theme is implicit throughout *Old Glory* insofar as Raban is retrospectively reliving his trip in the process of writing about it. Notes were taken on the actual trip down river, but the writing of the book, a second journey, took place some months later back in England. The trip, however, is revealed in all of its immediacy, in its own present, at once in time and outside of it. Even though the travelog aspect of *Old Glory* does end in New Orleans some five or so months after Raban cast off from Minneapolis, the final pages of the book are expansive, with Raban still on the broadening water—like the authentic, seasoned river "captain" and voyager he has become—in league with his river friend, Captain Bob Kelley, Huck Finn, and maybe even Odysseus.

Just as plot is a function of character in fictional narative, so in *Old Glory* it is futile to separate river time from shore time, Raban alone from Raban with the people he meets on and off the river, the narrative of river and writer. The reader finishes his voyage with Raban and the book knowing the author in a more intimate way than the people he met knew him. One can only speculate what those individuals and their towns thought of the book when the print version of their lives was recognized. Judging popularity by sales, *Old Glory* was bought with all the interest attendant to exposé or *roman à clef*. Of course, not everyone Raban portrays is identified by full name or in some cases even real name, but everyone and everything, most especially the riverscape, are distinct and memorable. Even the most ordinary people come to flesh and blood life if only fleetingly. In some measure this is attributable to the author's ear for speech, idiom and dialect, regional twangs and drawls.

Aside from the pleasures of Raban's own persona, his own felicitous way with words, *Old Glory* is a triumph of local color and ambience. There is no doubt that Raban was there, in America, on the spot—and that he saw it and heard it for what it is. What the indigenous population might take for granted, not even notice, Raban dramatizes with verve, so that the commonplaces of conversation become unique in their own glorious way.

In addition to his good ear for American speech, Raban's characterizations, of himself and others, are buoyed by his sense of humor, his ability to not take himself too seriously and to satirize himself when he does. Self-parody is not the extent of Raban's humorous jabs, however; many of the people he meets fall victim to his satire, but Raban is far from acerbic and condescending. He may be appalled by red-necks and racial prejudice, most notably by the segregation he finds in some of the towns along the way; by violence, hooliganism, and fear for personal safety in certain parts of St. Louis or in the backwaters of Louisiana; he may wince at the emptiness of the lives of rich and poor, white and blue-collar workers; but he is always respectful of those he meets (notably the boatmen and lock operators)—and of the river which could end his water voyage and his life in a second's lack of attention.

Thus *Old Glory* is not a splendidly clean and perfect flag which Raban flies as his symbol of America. Rather it is a frayed, soiled, and weather-beaten one flying all the more gloriously for what it has seen and been through. Huck's river, after all, was not all idyllic perfection.

Call it travelog, autobiography, social history, new journalism, epic, whatever—*Old Glory: An American Voyage* is a rich and wonderful excursion into the heart not just of the United States but into the nature of man and the large and small voyages of life.

*Robert Gish*

### Sources for Further Study

*Christian Science Monitor*. LXXIII, November 9, 1981, p. B4.
*The Economist*. CLXXXI, October 24, 1981, p. 93.
*Library Journal*. CVI, September 15, 1981, p. 1733.
*Nation*. CCXXXIII, September 26, 1981, p. 280.
*The New Republic*. CLXXXV, October 28, 1981, p. 39.
*The New York Review of Books*. XXVIII, November 19, 1981, p. 10.
*The New York Times Book Review*. LXXXVI, September 6, 1981, p. 1.
*Newsweek*. XCVIII, October 5, 1981, p. 83.
*Saturday Review*. X, September, 1981, p. 57.
*Times Literary Supplement*. October 23, 1981, p. 1227.

# ON HEROES AND TOMBS

*Author:* Ernesto Sábato (1911-      )
Translated from the Spanish by Helen R. Lane
*Publisher:* David R. Godine (Boston). 496 pp. $17.95
*Type of work:* Novel
*Time:* c. 1955
*Locale:* Argentina

*A novel of contemporary Argentina which interprets the twentieth century predicament through evocations of nineteenth century conflicts*

> Principal characters:
> ALEJANDRA, a young woman in Buenos Aires
> MARTÍN, a young man in love with Alejandra
> BRUNO, the confidant of Martín
> FERNANDO, the father of Alejandra

Ernesto Sábato first published *On Heroes and Tombs* in 1961, in Spanish, thirteen years after the widely acclaimed appearance of his short novel *El túnel* secured for him a place in the canon of contemporary Latin American literature. After twenty years of problems with translators and publishing houses, this English version of *Sobre héroes y tumbas* appears, with alterations and annotations by the author. Helen R. Lane has created a skilled, very readable translation of a linguistically complex novel. The novel is also complex in other ways—aesthetically and ideologically—to such an extent that it may seem too esoteric and disparate for the average serious reader of fiction. Not until the final pages does this long work seem to have a coherent structure, and even then, there is less cohesion than readers usually expect in a novel.

*On Heroes and Tombs* has an obsessive air about it, which Sábato admits in his preliminary note. He indicates that the novel is a particular type of fictional narrative "whereby the author endeavors to free himself of an obsession that is not clear even to himself." Responsible literary criticism consists, in part, of maintaining a skeptical attitude toward the comments that authors make on their own work. This authorial pronouncement, however, confirms the impression created by a first reading of this fictional text. There is an obsession here, and it is not at all clear. The result is an impressive display of verbal imagery, a dazzling consort of unusual characters and events, and a denouement that leaves the intricate maze intact and the obsession unresolved.

The text is in four parts. In "The Dragon and the Princess" and "Invisible Faces," the omniscient narrator traces the relationship of two young people, Alejandra and Martín, and the young man's mentor and confidant, Bruno. The third part, "Report on the Blind," is a strange dissertation on a mysterious cult of blind people conspiring to control society, written by Fernando, Alejandra's father. According to the Foreword of the novel, this report was found in Fernando's apartment after the police discovered his body and that of his daughter in the burned ruins of her apartment. The fourth part, "An Unknown God," is a narrative of Martín's attempts to understand, with Bruno's help, his relationship with Alejandra. In this last part, the perspective of the narrator becomes clearer. The novel is narrated by an unnamed person who obtained his information from Bruno, who participated in some of the action narrated and learned the other details of the events from Martín years after the death of Alejandra. The narrator acts as an organizing consciousness of all this material—the episodes of the current history of Alejandra and Martín, Martín's recollections of the events years later, Fernando's psychotic report on the blind cult, and the interpolated passages of the history of Alejandra's ancestors fighting in the Civil War of the early nineteenth century.

As the narrator slowly reveals a panoramic collage of details and events, it becomes clear that the only thread of continuity to this world is an unrelenting obsession to understand the meaning of existence. This explains the curious episode in which Bruno and Martín encounter on the street Argentina's most famous writer, Jorge Luis Borges. The meeting stimulates a discussion of Borges' work that leads to no conclusive statement and that seems to bear no relationship to the principal developments of the narrative. There is, however, a parallel between the work of Borges and the ontological emphasis of the experience narrated in Sábato's novel. Life is a labyrinth, an intricate maze of questions for which there is no answer. As one of the characters says about Borges' philosophical statements, that is a simplistic and puerile analysis of human existence, yet it is also accurate. Human experience is a mysterious labyrinth if one tries to find a systematic rationale for it, which is precisely what Martín tries to do. Bruno also tries, as he dissects the experience of Martín. Finally, the narrator tries to unravel the maze as he reconstructs the events in order to find some meaning in the existence of these people. Fernando's report is another attempt to solve the mystery of existence. He finds an answer, in the midst of his hallucinations. He interprets everything as the result of a conspiracy of the blind.

Alejandra is the focus of the novel. Martín and Bruno and the narrator all indicate that to understand Alejandra is to understand Argentina. She is a decantation of Argentine history, descendant of Unitarists, but partisan to the Federalists. Her flesh is something more than flesh, "something more complex, more subtle, more mysterious, . . . already a *memory*, and therefore something that would resist death and corruption." Bruno suggests that memory is the thing that resists time and destruction, the memory of the past, which forms an eternal continuity of existence. In Alejandra are concentrated the civil strife surrounding the fight for independence from Spain in the early 1800's, the wave of European immigrants to Argentina, the Communists, anarchists, and Perónists in the twentieth century, the pimps and whores. Alejandra is, for Martín, his native land, the symbol of warmth and mother, yet a synthesis of "everything that was chaotic and contentious, perverse and dissolute, equivocal and opaque."

In her relationship with Martín, Alejandra reconstructs her past. She recounts all that she can remember in a fierce search for something absolute, something that will join together all the disparate elements of her experience. Martín sees her as the key to the ultimate truth of his own existence. The scene in which he first makes love to her is symbolic of his desperate attempt to understand her and to unlock the mystery of life. She is, however, as elusive as the "mirages of an oasis in the implacable, endless desert."

Martín's frustration leads him to believe that there is no meaning to anything. Bruno tries to help him, reciting Buddhist poetry about the transmigration of souls, all the while thinking how difficult and delicate everything is. Life is a march toward nothingness, and to give life meaning, a man may gather up a mongrel dog, care for him, and thereby become the very meaning of the dog's existence. Man, however, unlike the dog, is rational. The haunting question of purpose will not go away.

The "Report on the Blind," written by Fernando shortly before his death, narrates an intricate story of intrigue and deception. Fernando, who enjoyed at the age of twelve putting out the eyes of animals and birds and playing hide-and-seek games in the dark, becomes aware of a plot to murder him because of his role in the blinding of his accomplice in crime, Celestino Iglesias. Fernando's document reveals a world of blind people who have developed a network of communication that pervades society and enables them to take their revenge on the sighted. For Fernando, to understand this conspiracy of the blind is to reach the ultimate truth of existence. His surveillance of Iglesias, who must pass through a ceremony of induction into the world of the blind, leads him into a mysterious labyrinth of rooms, tunnels, and sewers beneath the streets of Buenos Aires. In a hallucinatory state, he is led into an enormous cavern in which he experiences a cosmic union with the Phosphorescent Eye, "the beginning and end of his existence." He then finds himself in a room with the Blind Woman, the incarnation of all the ideology of the Blind Sect, and experiences another cosmic union, copulation with this mythical creature who represents for Fernando the culmination of the long quest that he had "slowly, patiently, and delibertely pursued, to the very end, over the space of many years."

When Fernando awakes from his hallucination, he knows that he is going to his death. It is inevitable, for he has willed it by his pursuit of the ultimate truth. The Foreword to the novel reports that Fernando's document brings into question the circumstances of the death of Alejandra and Fernando. Perhaps she was not suffering an attack of insanity when she shot her father and set the fire in which she died. The novel does not provide an explanation to the crime, nor does it obviously justify the fact that fully one-fourth of the narrative consists of this report, which seems to have little relationship to the story of Martín, Bruno, and Alejandra.

Fernando's "Report on the Blind" is, in fact, a search for the meaning of existence which parallels the attempts of Martín, Bruno, and the narrator to understand Alejandra, thereby finding ultimate truth. This search for truth also appears in the passages scattered through the text which evoke the history of Alejandra's ancestors, Celedonio Olmos and Bonifacio Acevedo, fleeing to Bolivia with the rotting body of General Lavalle. The final pages of the novel present another version of that search, as Martín travels toward Patagonia with the truck driver Bucich, and finally experiences a feeling of peace under the vast, open skies of the desolate south.

Throughout the novel, there are moments that evoke other seemingly unrelated incidents of the narrative. Fernando's encounter with the Blind Woman waiting for him in the labyrinth recalls Martín's sudden confrontation with Alejandra's great-aunt Escolástica on the stairs of her home. The mummified head of Acevedo kept by Escolástica evokes memories of Lavalle's head, carried to Bolivia by the defeated Unitarist forces. The memories of maimed children fleeing the seige of Barcelona evoke the flight of the Unitarist soldiers, the panic of the residents of Buenos Aires seeking refuge from terrorist bombs, and the flight of Fernando through the labyrinth of the sewers.

All these correspondences create a sense of continuity in the narrative, which suggests that everything is related, that there is a totality that, captured and organized in some meaningful way, would explain existence. That explanation of the human condition is, in fact, achieved in the novel. Fernando's "Report on the Blind" is an unravelling of the mystery of why things happen as they do and what they mean. Fernando justifies everything by interpreting it as a plot directed by an elusive sect. His report, of course, is the product of an irrational mind in a hallucinatory state. It becomes, then, an ironic commentary on the ultimate truth sought by the other characters of the novel. The irony is enhanced by the police report in the Foreword, which suggests that Fernando's report explains something about the death of Alejandra.

The narrative complexity of the novel is a reflection of its ideological complexity. The relationships between the multitude of characters and events are not easily determined, and become only partially clarified by the end of the work. Only in the "Report on the Blind" does a "well-ordered plan" emerge, and that report is the product of a deranged mind. Only in fleeting moments do the characters find meaning in their lives—a man caring for a mongrel dog or the soldiers struggling to save their leader's body from desecration by the enemy.

Sábato's novel is a stylistic tour de force, but it does not have the narrative power of the work of some of his Latin American contemporaries. Carlos Fuentes' *Terra Nostra* (1976), for example, displays a similar array of stylistic and linguistic complexities. Fuentes also has a strong sense of what makes a novel work. Sábato, in his novel, does not. Perhaps his work is the result of so intimate an obsession that he is unable to communicate that personal experience in narrative form. The novel does, in fact, suggest the impossibility of resolving that conflict of human rationality and human existence. Had Sábato better understood the nature of his obsession, his novel surely would have communicated more clearly his ontological concerns.

*Gilbert Smith*

## Sources for Further Study

*Library Journal.* CVI, June 15, 1981, p. 1324.
*The New Republic.* CLXXXV, September 23, 1981, p. 25.
*The New York Review of Books.* XXVIII, October 22, 1981, p. 54.
*The New York Times Book Review.* LXXXVI, July 26, 1981, p. 1.
*Newsweek.* XCVIII, September 21, 1981, p. 103.
*Saturday Review* VIII, June, 1981, p. 55.
*Time.* CXVIII, August 17, 1981, p. 78.

# ON THE STROLL

*Author:* Alix Kates Shulman (1932-    )
*Publisher:* Alfred A. Knopf (New York). 301 pp. $12.95
*Type of work:* Novel
*Time:* The present
*Locale:* Midtown New York

A pimp, a runaway, and a shopping-bag lady narrate their encounters with one
another

> *Principal characters:*
> PRINCE, a small-time pimp
> ROBIN WARD, a runaway
> OWL, a shopping-bag lady

The streets surrounding The Port Authority Bus Terminal in midtown New York are known by the prostitutes who frequent them as "the stroll," hence the title of Alix Kates Shulman's third novel. *On the Stroll* begins and ends at The Port Authority, making the reader aware that Shulman is using the ancient and honorable literary motif of life as a journey to underscore one of her novel's most significant themes: especially in this neighborhood, everyone is a transient. Shulman's other thematic interests—in power relationships between women and men, in the search for love and truth—are equally ancient and honorable. In less skilled hands than hers, such material might be trite, but Shulman's wit, her sharp eye, and her transparent, colloquial style infuse these familiar themes with vitality and contemporaneity. The crime-ridden setting of *On the Stroll* is the perfect milieu for this gifted novelist's perceptive sociological observations and for her portrayals of three characters—a pimp, a runaway, and a shopping-bag lady—whose actions and motives, at first remote and objectionable, quickly become as comprehensible as the reader's own.

It is obvious that Shulman writes from direct observation of street life and also from extensive reading and interviews. Her handling of detail is convincing in part because her acknowledgments include references to The Port Authority Youth Service Division, the West 42nd Street Project, and the book *Black Players* (1973), by Christina and Richard Milner. By drawing on these resources, Shulman informs her readers while she entertains them with the rituals and patterns of street subculture. One learns, for example, that a pimp uses affection to attract a potential prostitute, but that it is the prostitute who claims the pimp by giving him all her funds, called "choosing money." This transaction symbolizes the complicated financial and emotional arrangements between the two. The prostitute must make her "trap" each night, and the pimp may charge her for clothes, food, and mistakes. The pimp's dependence on the prostitute for money is balanced by her dependence on him for love. Without allowing himself to be touched emotionally—"a blow to the heart kills"—the pimp must manipulate the prostitute's emotions so that she is both afraid of him and reliant on him for comfort, security, and love. All the intricate elaborations of the pimping code are thus aimed at control. As Prince puts it,

> The one thing a player could never afford to compromise, not even for a minute, was his position of power. If, for instance, a man let a woman begin to dominate him, his manhood would soon be threatened; he had to regain the upper hand quickly or else, according to the pimping code, the woman would take over and make a trick out of him.

Prince, who is only twenty-five but already worried about getting old, is a hard-working student of the code. Beginning each day with pushups and deep knee bends, he aspires to match the successes of Bluejay and Sweet Rudy, his mentors at pimping and three-card monte. With his nervous stomach and catlike fastidiousness—he is constantly bathing, getting his clothes pressed, and having his nails manicured—this "Prince among men" is the 42nd Street counterpart of the young executive on the make. His history of personal failure motivates him to maintain the tastefully decorated apartment, the fancy car, and the colorful wardrobe which are both the fruits of his labor and the tools of his trade. Obsessed by the belief that men must control women, Prince is deeply appreciative of the "childlike docility" of the sixteen-year-old runaway whom he catches at The Port Authority in the novel's opening pages. He understands her need to trust him and to be cherished by him, and he carefully manipulates that need, timing his responses so as to create and maintain a profitable dependence.

Shulman's objective treatment of Prince's commitment to the pimping code generates understanding of, if not sympathy for, this conscientious young Filipino-American who wants only what many young men want: success, wheels, and a compliant woman. It is not so much Prince himself that Shulman implicitly asks her readers to condemn, but rather the social system which produces pimps and prostitutes, the system which has valued male dominance and female submission and which trades on human sexuality. The notion that all men are tricks, all women whores, and the parallel Shulman suggests between prostitution and other female-male relationships, including marriage, makes her reader aware of the feminist consciousness which links this novel to Shulman's other work.

*On the Stroll* is not a polemic, but Shulman's interest in women's issues may account for the fact that the novel's two female characters, Robin and Owl, are far more sympathetically treated and more fully realized than Prince is drawn. In flight from a raging, abusive father and in symbolic pursuit of a maternal figure on whom she can rely, as she has not been able to rely on her own alcoholic mother, Robin Ward arrives at The Port Authority curious, wary, and ready to conquer the Big Apple, perhaps as an actress or a flight attendant. Although at sixteen she has already experienced casual sex, Robin is an innocent; she has felt desire only once before Prince makes love to her.

After a week of his coddling, Robin finds herself on the street, a "baby-pro" who must make her trap each evening before she can come home to the sympathy, massages, and hot baths which Prince provides to keep her going. From Prince, Robin learns to value her body; he sees to it that she takes her daily contraceptive, bathes regularly, and has a monthly medical checkup. His support is emotional as well as physical. Prince understands Robin's psychological needs better than she does herself. He knows, for instance, how much she fears and loves her father, how much she needs her mother, how seriously he must take her habit of running away from difficult situations, and how responsive he must be to her craving for affection.

Robin's naïveté is an invitation not only to Prince, but also to Owl, the bag lady who is this novel's finest and most unforgettable character. Reminiscent of Doris Lessing's Hetty in the story "An Old Woman and Her Cat," Owl is mentally unstable but clever enough to know that on the street there is safety in being thought crazy and filthy. When she first sees Robin at The Port Authority, she thinks the fragile, blonde sixteen-year-old is her own daughter Milly, with whom she longs to be reconciled. Owl's past is contained in the shopping bags she carries with her, one for each phase of her exciting and dangerous life. By nature a transient as well as a collector, Owl is given to mystical visions, in bus stations and airports, of the unity of all things and all people. These glimpses of reality allow her to indulge herself in the "most extravagant feelings, the pure contemplation of life and death" and to arrive at conclusions about truth. While these conclusions are merely a bag lady's ruminations, they are at the same time the simple yet profound discoveries that every person makes in the course of a life's journey: the young become old, nothing changes, nothing lasts.

Despite her penchant for mysticism, Owl is practical. She lives on almost no money and still has resources left over to feed abandoned cats and starving birds. In this feeding, as in her collecting, her method is to "adopt . . . a discard, redeeming it through love." As she arranges and rearranges her collections, preparing to be reunited with Milly, Owl, herself a discard, affirms the dignity and value of her crazy, generous life. The contents of her shopping bags reveal that her fierce independence arises from a troubled childhood, a stint as a WAC during World War II, the treachery of a husband who had her committed to a mental hospital, the painful losses of her children. Knowing that death is near, Owl wants to find her daughter, to share with the younger woman the contents of the bags so that Owl's rich life will not be lost forever.

Owl's search for a daughter and Robin's yearning for a mother finally bring the two characters together in a moving conclusion for which Shulman has most artfully prepared through repetitions of imagery involving birds, feathers, and flight. Owl is a protector of fledglings, Robin imagines herself "nestling beneath the soft maternal wing," and the novel's epigraph, from

Mother Goose, is "Birds of a feather flock together." For a short time, at the novel's end, Owl and Robin do flock together, and their convergence, along with the similarities between them that Shulman has so subtly laid down, suggests that in the brief passing of a life, a trusting, innocent Robin must and will become a streetwise, scavenging Owl if she is to survive. When Owl gives Robin her passport, the parallelism between the two transient characters is completed; Shulman then extends the parallel to include the reader as well: the passport photo, Robin realizes, "might be a picture of anyone." The bird and flight imagery with which Shulman links Owl and Robin is the most pervasive of several clusters of detail which make reading *On the Stroll* an extremely satisfying experience. Shulman also develops Robin's association with the seashore and Owl's fascination with fire so as to contrast the two women, while at the same time drawing them together.

By narrating the story through the points of view of all three of her main characters, Shulman allows the reader to see them intimately, as well as from a distance. Transitions from one point of view to another are accomplished with grace; Shulman is adept at the cinematic narrative techniques of montage and shifting, techniques which are ideal vehicles for her characters' kaleidoscopic movements within the ten-block area which is the novel's setting. Shulman endows this small space with all the filth and squalor and perversion it possesses in life, but she enriches it, too, with Prince, Robin, and especially Owl, three characters whose preoccupations are those of all humans: comfort, truth, love, growing up, growing old. Perhaps the stroll, sociologically unique and exotic as it seems, is not such a remote place after all.

*Carolyn Wilkerson Bell*

### Sources for Further Study

*Kirkus Reviews*. XLIX, July 15, 1981, p. 900.
*Library Journal*. CVI, August, 1981, p. 1568.
*Ms*. X, January, 1982, p. 41.
*The New York Times Book Review*. LXXXVI, September 27, 1981, p. 12.
*Publishers Weekly*. CCXX, July 31, 1981, p. 48.
*Saturday Review*. VIII, September, 1981, p. 60.
*Village Voice Literary Supplement*. October, 1981, p. 5.

# THE ONLY LAND THEY KNEW
## The Tragic Story of the American Indians in the Old South

*Author:* J. Leitch Wright, Jr. (1929-    )
*Publisher:* The Free Press (New York). 372 pp. $16.95
*Type of work:* History
*Time:* The sixteenth century to 1830
*Locale:* The American South

*A history of the Indians who lived in the southern part of the United States*

The story of the Indians in the Old South is a dramatic and tragic one. The white man was a constant challenge to the Indian's survival. As the English population grew, that of the Indian declined. Indian wars followed one after another with terrible repetition until some coastal tribes became extinct.

When the English arrived in Virginia in 1607, they had with them a fully developed mythology about the native societies. This mythology began to develop in English literature in the 1550's, before any important meeting between native and white occurred, and was predicated upon two viewpoints. The first was based on the belief that the natives were ignoble savages, indeed children of the devil. The portrait drawn of them emphasized their nakedness, promiscuity, lack of order and discipline, and violent nature. In contrast, the Englishman represented culture, civility, and character. The belief in this irrevocable difference created the tendency toward violence that broke out soon after the first settlers arrived and continued into the nineteenth century.

On the other hand, the Indian was also seen as a noble savage, free from the sins and wars of Europe. His independence, bravery, and stoicism were admired, yet he was still a savage.

Whichever view was accepted by the English, the mythology created by the white man developed with little accurate information and continued for hundreds of years. The concepts were difficult to change, even after greater contacts between whites and natives produced more facts about Indian society.

Attempts to bring the natives to Christianity failed and, because of this failure, Europeans blamed the natives. That the savage was supposedly unteachable helped justify the exploitation that represented native-white relationships, and led to the numerous violent confrontations which began in 1622.

There is also evidence that the whites landed among a people who already knew and detested them. There is information that the Southern Indians had several chances to develop views about the whites, both from information told them and through direct contact. The first direct contacts probably took place in the early sixteenth century, when Giovanni de Verrazzano sailed into Chesapeake Bay. By the end of that century, a Spanish expedition under Pedro Menéndez de Avilés had unleashed terrible attacks upon the Indians. Thus, the Indians knew something of Europeans years before the Jamestown settlers arrived in 1607.

Nevertheless, when the settlers arrived at Jamestown, they were welcomed by the Indians. This was probably because Powhatan, their chief, wished to gain greater control over other tribes. It was thereby necessary to aid the first settlers, for they could become important allies in his political plans.

At the time Jamestown was established, Indian culture was going through a period of expansion, and the English appeared to offer no serious challenge to Powhatan's Confederation. The Indian population was large and powerful, numbering perhaps ten thousand people. They lived in a well-ordered society and were ruled by a complex system of government. This political sophistication can be noted in the chain of command, which extended through the Confederacy, with Powhatan at its head.

As Wright points out, however, while the Indians aided the first settlers, the whites attempted to place the Indians under their control and demanded an annual tribute. Captain John Smith, the leader of the settlers, believed that the Indians should become servants of the whites. Because of this attitude and the fact that the Indians were dying of the white man's diseases, the relationship was becoming more difficult, and it appeared that Jamestown might suffer the tragic fate of Walter Ralegh's Lost Roanoke Colony. It was during this tense period that John Smith supposedly almost lost his life to an Indian tomahawk, only to be saved by Powhatan's daughter, Pocahontas. Relations were further improved in 1614 when she married John Rolfe. For almost a decade there was peace. Then in 1622 the Virginia tribes under a new chief attacked the whites, killing almost four hundred settlers. English reprisals were swift and deadly. For almost twenty years, there was peace, until the last major Indian uprising occurred in 1644, when Indians killed five hundred whites and Virginians killed more than a thousand Indians.

In 1646, the Confederacy yielded most of its land, and beginning in 1665, its chiefs were selected by the royal governor of Virginia. By the eighteenth century, all semblance of the once powerful Confederacy had disappeared. Today only a few thousand Powhatans survive.

The Indians of the South were a linguistic mixture of Muskhogean, Siouian, and Algonkian. With the founding of Jamestown, these tribes felt the pressure of an expanding British presence. The westward thrust of white agricultural settlements placed increasing pressure on the tribes, causing their displacement and ultimate extinction. Among the tribes that faced this threat were the Tuscaroras, Shawnees, and Susquehannas.

The Carolinas were founded on the fur trade. Its traders traveled as far west as the Mississippi River. There they encountered the Yamasees, Catawbas, and Creeks, whom they corrupted and often destroyed. Georgia, founded in 1733 by James Oglethorpe, rounded out the Southern Colonies, and soon its fur traders were encroaching upon the land of the Cherokees and later confronted the western tribes, such as the Choctaws and Chickasaws.

In an excellent chapter, "Goose Creek Men," Wright deals with the Carolina Indians and the fur traders. The traders' first economic concern was trade in deerskins, for which there was considerable demand in Great Britain, but growing more important as time passed was the trade in Indian slaves, who were usually shipped to the Caribbean islands. Charleston, founded in 1670, became the center of this trade. Indians equipped by white merchants with guns and horses were sent to the west to shoot deer and capture Indians.

Much of this violence was directed at the Spanish missions in Florida. Missionaries were burned slowly at the stake, their missions destroyed, and their native charges were marched hundreds of miles to the slave market in Charleston for sale. An especially bloody raid was launched by the Carolina traders in 1704, during which hundreds of Spaniards and Indians were slaughtered, thirteen missions burned, and four hundred slaves captured. In these tragic caravans of the seventeenth and eighteenth centuries, hundreds of Indians were marched to death or lifelong servitude in the islands. This removal antedated the Trail of Tears by almost two centuries.

According to J. Leitch Wright, Jr., fur traders generally were rascals who spread terror wherever they traded, but the Carolina traders were especially reprehensible, worse than most traders on the frontier. They exploited, cheated, and enslaved Indians throughout the South. Two tribes were so mistreated that they launched revolts that almost destroyed the Carolina settlements.

In 1711, the Tuscaroras exploded with pent-up fury against the Carolina traders. Incidents between the Indians and the white settlers had increased by the early eighteenth century. Like the Virginia Indians, the Tuscaroras carefully organized their attack on the whites. One of the first whites to die was the naturalist and historian John Lawson, who was roasted over a fire by the Indians. In two years' time, hundreds of whites were killed, until the Carolina militia, supported by the Yamasee Indians, defeated the Tuscaroras, killing or enslaving nearly seven hundred. Those Indians who survived the devastation fled northward to their kinsmen, the Iroquois in New York.

A short time later, the Yamasees rebelled against the whites because of exploitation and continued mistreatment. As Wright notes, this was more than merely the Yamasees against the whites, for a number of tribes, including the Catawbas, Cherokees, and Lower Creeks, joined the Yamasees. The war almost destroyed the Carolina colony. Almost all the traders were killed and about two hundred settlers were massacred by the Indians. The fear of the British was intensified when it was believed that the Spanish in Florida were behind this Indian uprising. The revolt was put down brutally by the whites and, by the 1760's, only twenty Yamasees were still alive out of a population that had earlier numbered nearly six thousand.

The Indian policy of Carolina was the prevailing policy in the South. Developed by the proprietors of Carolina, this policy was opportunistic and oppressive for the natives. Rules were drawn up that required fur traders to have licenses in order to trade with the Indians for furs and slaves. An attempt was made by the colony to stop the enslavement of friendly Carolina Indians, but this attempt failed. Treaties were required when dealing with the important western tribes, but even though there were a number of restrictions placed on Indian trade, such as the banning of the use of rum, traders broke the rules constantly.

As Wright demonstrates, the British, unlike the Spanish, were little concerned with converting the Indians of the South to Christianity, even though the Virginia Company charter mentioned that one of the major reasons for establishing settlements in the New World was to bring Christian life to the natives. The King of England pushed for the expansion of the Christian religion to the heathen. Some Indian children were taken from their families and placed with Christian families. Indian schools were opened in Virginia and a few natives were transported to England for their education. The Indians in the South did not, however, turn to Christianity in large numbers. They were angered by the fact that their children were taken from them. The natives were devoted to their religion and the actions of the Christian missionaries to convert them sometimes caused conflict.

The missionary attempt to remove Indian children from their families helped cause the Indian War of 1622 in Virginia. Though these bloody wars weakened the desire of whites to convert the Indians, the attempts at Christianization continued into the eighteenth century. The College of William and Mary had some Indian students; fourteen attended in 1712, twenty a few years later, but by 1754 there were only eight. Housed in Brafferton Hall, they were segregated from the white students. Yet despite some success, the Indian school did not succeed. Another attempt to found an Indian school on the southwestern frontier at Christanna also failed.

The Moravians were deeply involved with bringing Christianity to the Indians. German missionary Christian Priber lived with the Indians to learn their ways in order to convert them to Christianity, but Priber was arrested by British officials and accused of being a French spy. He died a short time later in jail.

The workers for the Society for the Propagation of the Gospel in Foreign Parts converted a few Southern Indians, but by the 1760's their interest in the Indians had waned. Other organizations made halfhearted efforts into the nineteenth century to Christianize the natives, but most Indians continued to reject the white man's religion.

Wright devotes a chapter, "Br'er Rabbit at the Square Ground," to the important relationships between blacks and Indians. After Africans appeared in the South, they often lived and ate like Indians. Indeed, much of the black "soul food" can be traced to the Southern Indians, and a great amount of black folk medicine, such as the use of sumac, sassafras, and ginseng, can be traced to Indian origins.

Because Wright attempts to cover so much ground, he must compress a number of important events in a few sentences. Land rights, trade difficulties, and the many wars are often given but a few lines. Though there are a few generalizations about Southern Indian life, much of his work is based on anecdotal accounts. Wright has written an imposing study, admirably assembled, and well-documented from primary sources. He has added an entertaining and important account to the history of the American Indian.

*Richard A. Van Orman*

**Sources for Further Study**

*Choice.* XIX, October, 1981, p. 301.
*Journal of American History.* LXVIII, December, 1981, p. 636.
*Library Journal.* CVI, March 15, 1981, p. 660.
*Southern Living.* XVI, November, 1981, p. 196.

# ONLY THE DREAMER CAN CHANGE THE DREAM
## Selected Poems

*Author:* John Logan (1923-    )
*Publisher:* The Ecco Press (New York). 209 pp. $14.95
*Type of work:* Poetry

*Selected poems from five volumes appearing between 1955 and 1973*

These selected poems are arranged in five sections bearing the titles of five collections published by John Logan between 1955 and 1973: *Cycle for Mother Cabrini* (1955); *Ghosts of the Heart* (1960); *Spring of the Thief* (1963); *The Zig-Zag Walk* (1969); and *The Anonymous Lover* (1973), from which the title poem is taken. Poems from Logan's two collections published since 1973—*The House That Jack Built* (1974), and *Poems in Progress* (1975)—are included in *The Bridge of Change: Poems 1974-1980*, also published in 1981.

Logan's poems are frequently philosophical and bookish, specifically pre-occupied with the sruggle between body and soul. The opening poem, "Pagan Saturday," draws the distinction between spirit and flesh. On a hike with other students, the speaker experiences a moment of spiritual intensity: "sudden/ As fear light as laughter I felt/ A creature flare with beauty/ At the back of my eye." This experience is different from a simple lyric sense of physical well-being or exhilaration. The speaker is aware that "my limbs and body/ Sang on me sometimes—/ But this was brighter than my arms."

"A Dialogue with La Mettrie," prefaced by a passage from the eighteenth century materialist's book, *Man a Machine* (1798), deals more explicitly with the question of man's essential nature. Paraphrasing Julien Offray de La Mettrie, Logan speaks of "the delicate moral/ Hum in the anxious matter" and concludes: "Man is a machine./ And there is no other thing/ Underneath. Except I believe/ Ambiguity, with its hope/ Or its ancient agony." Logan's search is for a way to refute La Mettrie's mechanical view of man, a way to account for "this arch of feeling." He wishes to be "cut free/ Of the grieved matter of La Mettrie."

Death offers freedom from the flesh. In "Cycle for Mother Cabrini" Logan is grateful that the body is

> subject to laws
> Of decay. . . .
> For flesh is my failing:
> That it shall fall is my
> Salvation
> That it shall not
> Conquer is my blind hope.
> That it shall rise again
> Commanding, is my fear.
> That it shall rise changed
> Is my faith.

The interplay of theme and image that unifies this collection can be located in this stated position in the 1955 poem. It is the interplay between the physical and spiritual, the failures of the flesh, the hope of overcoming the merely physical and mechanical aspect of man's nature, the hope of spiritual change that concern the poet in succeeding sections of the collection.

In "Eight Poems on Portraits of the Foot" it is the wish, Logan says, "for some genuine change other than our death/ that lets us feel (with fingers of the mind)/ how much the foot desires to be a hand." In "Three Moves," external changes serves only to remind him of the difference between physical and spiritual change. "Three moves in six months and I remain/ the same." A friend inquires about his soul and the speaker realizes: "I hadn't thought about it for a while,/ and was ashamed to say I didn't know." Some ducks at his third residence within a six-month period become a symbol for the speaker's inability to undergo spiritual change; or, at least, he contrasts his unachieved human potential for such spiritual change with the inability of animals to achieve it: "these foolish ducks lack a sense of guilt,/ and so all their multi-thousand-mile range/ is too short for the hope of change." What the experience of this spiritual change might be like is indicated in "Two Preludes for La Push," in which natural settings serve as analogs of spiritual meanings, somewhat after the manner of Thomas Merton: "In a hush/ of holy fog. . . ./ the white, furious waves mash and rush. . . . These waves/ are sudden, violent, unpredictable as grace."

The most effective poems in the collection discover scenes and situations that serve as adequate symbols for the crass and sometimes bestial nature of man when he is bereft of any spiritual dimension or possiblity. "The Thirty-three Ring Circus" consists of thirty-three verse paragraphs full of vivid details sharply observed. The thirty-first paragraph is representative: "By a dead bon-/ fire lies the charred/ button-down/ shoe of a clown." A trip to the zoo provides Logan with one of his most effective renderings of the human condition as he sees it. "The Zoo" concludes:

> This Primate House echoes
> with our mixed cries;
> it reeks with our ambiguous breath.
> Each one caged as an oracle
> I feel each upright animal
> can tell
> how much my life is a human life,
> how much an animal death.

Despite the sustained concern for man's spiritual aspect, and for states of spiritual and emotional intensity, the description of these experiences is often frustratingly vague. Even the report of physical sensations occasioned by close proximity to a girl degenerates, after an initial simile, into an enumeration of parts of the body: "I felt a soft caving in my stomach/ As at the top of the highest slide/ When I had been a child. . . ." When the speaker's hands again touch the girl's: "It was then some bright thing came in my eyes,/ Starting at the back of them and then flowing/ suddenly through my head and down my arms/ And stomach and my bare legs . . ." ("The Picnic"). On the other hand, purely external objects and actions are frequently rendered with vivid force: "There is a high/ Hill of sand behind the sea and the kids/ Were dropping from the top of it like schools/ Of fish over falls . . ." ("Shore Scene").

However fervently hoped for, the genuine spiritual change never comes. Instead, the speaker is aware that "The name of God is changing in our time" ("Spring of the Thief"). Instead of undergoing a change, the speaker admits to a death in life in "Poem, Slow to Come, on the Death of Cummings": "Your death fulfills and it is strong./ I wish I had not died when I was so young." Flying to Detroit on an Easter weekend, he addresses the felt presence of his ninety-year-old grandmother ("Grandmother in the Aeroplane") and announces: "Everything has died. . . . I want to stay up here forever,/ Grandmother. For I am tired of the fogged earth/ down there/ with its esoteric itch of flesh."

Logan least effectively engages his central theme of the struggle between flesh and spirit when he is bookish and learned, and when his images, instead of having the authority of direct experience, are merely decorative. In "Lines to His Son on Reaching Adolescence," the speaker admonishes the son: "But for both our sakes I ask you, wrestle/ Manfully against the ancient curse of snakes." This allusion to the Genesis story is superseded by a reference to Greek drama and to the Psalms, and there are subsequent references to Laocoön, William Shakespeare's Polonius, and St. Augustine. The likely effect of the poem would be to bewilder an adolescent, or send him scurrying for a reference book.

These frequent literary allusions raise the problem of decorum. The elevated tone of the allusions does not comport well with the rather mundane situation which is frequently the poem's occasion. In this connection "A Trip to Four or Five Towns," dedicated to James Wright, is especially illustrative of how any incident, however slight, is likely to remind Logan of something literary. A friend who "took a leak in a telephone booth" reminds Logan of "E. E. Cummings on the Paris lawn": "'Reprieve le pisseur Américain!'" Half a dozen lines later, when a womanizing acquaintance is attacked by a jealous boyfriend, Logan is reminded of Orpheus: "I saw the blood of a poet/ flow on the sidewalk. . . . I thought/ of the torn limbs of Orpheus/ scattered on the grass on the hills of Thrace." Aside from the doubt that this low life is deserving of such elevated allusions, there remains the question of whether the allusions even accurately render the experience.

The many literary allusions are but a part of a sometimes suffocating bookishness. There are many poems to poets, saints, and martyrs (who appear to be interchangeable). There are theological references, bits of church history and literary history. The poems bear apparatus fore and aft. Titles occasionally belabor the occasion, as in "Lines Against a Loved American Poet After Hearing an Irish One's Nickname." Titles are followed by subtitles: "The Death of Southwell. A Verse Melodrama with Homilies on Light and Sin." Often poems bear a dedication and an epigraph (sometimes two epigraphs). Notes at the end of poems frequently provide the exact date and place of composition. Other end-notes, as if they were some sort of credential, reflect much learning. "The Lives of the Poet," dedicated to Wallace Fowlie and bearing two epigraphs, has an end-note: "After Fowlie and Aeschylus and after a remark of Maritain's on Wilde."

Despite such trappings—a dedication to Paul Carroll, two epigraphs, one from Karl Marx, one from Heinrich Heine, and an end-note—and despite the error in Heine's dates—Heine was born in 1797—Logan's "A Century Piece for Poor Heine 1800-1856" commemorates Heine's life with great force and energy. "He tried to kiss his father's/ Hand but his pink/ Finger was stiff as sticks/ And suddenly all of him shifts—/ A glorious tree of frost!/ Unburdened of the sullied flesh." In the life of Heine, as in "The Thirty-three Ring Circus" and "The Zoo," Logan finds an adequate vehicle for his own concern with the struggle between flesh and spirit.

Rarely, but memorably, Logan's lyric impulse frees itself from bookishness, philosophical musings, and ideation, and pays genuine and spontaneous homage in songs of the limbs and body. "Suzanne" and "Love Poem," two of Logan's most successful lyrics, contain not a single bibilical or classical allusion. Instead, his eye is on the beloved object and, as is often the case in such descriptions, there is a tendency to enumerate, as in "Suzanne": "the way you turn/ your blonde head./ The way you curve your slim hand/ toward your breast." In "Love Poem" the enumeration is a way of evoking the absent lover, of possessing by naming: "the lost, beautiful slopes and fallings of your face,/ the black, rich leaf of each eyelash. . . ./ I want to smell the dark/ herb gardens of your hair—touch the thin shock/ that drifts over your high brow when/ you rinse it clean. . . ." Flesh is not always Logan's failing. Here he succeeds memorably. These lyrics are more genuinely psalmlike than others that merely allude to or directly borrow the language of the psalms.

*Jim W. Miller*

**Sources for Further Study**

*Book World.* XI, August 2, 1981, p. 6.
*Booklist.* LXXVII, May 15, 1981, p. 1239.

*Georgia Review*. XXXV, Winter, 1981, p. 892.
*Library Journal*. CVI, May 15, 1981, p. 1082.
*The New York Times Book Review*. LXXXVI, June 21, 1981, p. 15.

# THE ORIGINS OF HISTORY

*Author:* Herbert Butterfield (1900-1979)
Edited, with an Introduction, by Alan Watson
*Publisher:* Basic Books (New York). 252 pp. $20.95
*Type of work:* History
*Time:* Approximately 2000 B.C. to about A.D. 1850
*Locale:* The Middle East, China, and Europe

*An investigation of the earliest origins of history, including the annals of the pre-classical empire, the Hebrew scriptures, Greek and Chinese historiography, the development of historical criticism, and the secularization of history*

Sir Herbert Butterfield was a man who cared deeply about history, a man who spent his life reflecting on and writing about past events, people, and ideas that interested him. Much of his writing focused on European politics and diplomacy, but he also explored broad topics such as Christianity, war, universal education and their impact upon history. In addition, Butterfield had a continuing interest in historiography, the "history of history," and this led him to publish such well-received studies as *The Englishman and His History* (1944), *Man on His Past* (1955), and *The Whig Interpretation of History* (1963).

In the last decade or so of his life, he began to ask even more fundamental questions about the origins of history. How and why did people begin to conceive of a past that lay beyond human memory? What were the roles of chance and divine intervention in these early histories? How did people move toward explanations of cause and effect that were independent of God or providence? Invited to give the Gifford Lectures at the University of Glasgow during the 1960's, Butterfield used the occasion to examine why people in some regions became interested in history and how they gradually developed a concept of the past. Although at first he had intended to publish these lectures, he soon realized that he must explore the subject more fully to do justice to the breadth of his themes, and he spent the next dozen years or so working on this topic along with several other projects. After his death, Butterfield's wife turned the historiographical material over to his friend and fellow scholar, Alan Watson, to edit and publish.

In Watson's graceful Introduction to *The Origins of History*, he shares some of the conversation and correspondence he had with Butterfield about this book. When Watson received the manuscript materials, he found that five of the eight chapters of the book had been extensively revised and required very little editing. The last three chapters dealing with the Christian attitude toward history, the development of historical criticism, and the secularization of history were not in such finished form. Nevertheless, Watson assures his readers that the writing is essentially Butterfield's, that the extensive bibliography was compiled from Butterfield's own card index, and that all the original notes and manuscripts have been deposited along with the author's other papers at the Cambridge University Library. Although Watson believes that Butterfield at one time had planned a separate chapter on Islamic history, the editor has left the much briefer treatment Butterfield wrote in its original place in the book. In fact, there is no doubt that the book is overwhelmingly Butterfield's creation and that the editor has merely exercised a light, sensitive, helping hand on the material. Indeed, the only editorial shortcoming is the failure to provide any footnotes, even for direct quotations.

Butterfield's basic assumption throughout this book is that Western civilization is not only scientific in character but also remarkably historically minded. Why, he asks, did some civilizations, such as that of ancient India, fail to develop significant traditions of historical scholarship while others, in Europe and China, did form such traditions? His answer is that some basic views of life, inextricably related to religious beliefs, act to deny the significance of history. It is this insight which sends Butterfield on a fascinating journey back through thousands of years and a variety of cultures in search of the beginnings of history.

In the very earliest stages, before there was any systematic notion of the remote past, the author notes, there was still an interest in storytelling. People not only remembered and told about their own experiences, but also heard tales of the past from parents, grandparents, and elders of their communities. Stories of gods, buildings, and events as well as traditions were handed down through the generations in this manner. Eventually the most enduring of these stories, such as that of Gilgamesh, became epics. Butterfield does not believe, however, that the epic played a very significant role in the development of history. He points out that while in Mesopotamia it seems to have spurred an interest in the past, both China and Egypt lacked national epics and still produced a rich array of historical literature.

Nor can lists and records be shown to have greatly encouraged the development of history, the author argues. They represented a kind of craze, he thinks, a mania for enumerating both unique and mundane events that appeared in Egypt and Mesopotamia around 2000 B.C. and in Greece much later. While lists, particularly those that strung together previous lists, gave people a sense of the length of the past and suggested ways of subdividing that past, they were not themselves the products of a genuine interest in the past. Disputes and wars, the author believes, were far more important. In affairs such as border controversies the past was an important tool for justifying claims, while wars had to be explained both to the gods and the people.

It is in Mesopotamia that Butterfield first finds the emergence of a world view really favorable to the development of history. A sense of insecurity, a vision of the cataclysmic character of earthly life, and a dependence on the erratic flooding patterns of the Euphrates combined to convince people that the state must be highly developed if they were to survive. Even then misfortunes occurred and destiny seemed, ultimately, beyond human control. The past came to be seen as cyclical, alternating periods of blessing and of curse. Finally the Sumerians developed the rationale that these must represent a judgment on human conduct; history and destiny were related because sin was punished. In Butterfield's opinion, it was this reflection about and interpretation of the past that spread throughout all Western Asia and eventually became a theme in the most ancient Hebrew scriptures.

Butterfield believes the essential contribution of the millennium between the Mesopotamian cyclical interpretation and the historiography of the Old Testament was the development of the narrative treatment of historical events. Monarchs stimulated the production of a great deal of official history about contemporary events, intended primarily to commemorate or justify their reigns. In ancient Egypt the Pharaohs wished to be remembered after death, while the Hittites used a more nearly factual and objective history to explain government policy. The Assyrian annals also furthered the development of the narrative historical tradition.

In this early historiography, however, Butterfield finds the most striking originality in the Hebrew scriptures. These seminomadic primitive people would seem unlikely to be obsessed by history, yet their central religious belief in the covenant that made them God's chosen people, along with the trauma of the exodus and the existence of a promised land, led them to think in terms of a linear (rather than cyclical) history directly related to their destiny. In addition, their history was dynamic and collective, the history of a people and a nation. In a careful analysis of parts of the Old Testament, Butterfield attempts to demonstrate that, unlike previous histories, the historiography of Israel was enriched and deepened by interpretation and reinterpretation.

In contrast, Butterfield suggests that in spite of the claim that Herodotus was "the father of history," the Greeks failed to achieve the same level of historical mindedness. Separated from their pre-Homeric past, unable to read the Linear B of the Mycenean civilization, Greeks believed the past extended back only a few hundred years. This foreshortened view of history persisted until the fifth century B.C., when the Greeks came into contact with the Egyptians. Yet Butterfield argues that neither this new knowledge nor the existence of a national epic (the *Iliad*, c. 800 B.C.) nor the development of a kind of "scientific" history in Ionia and Athens were sufficient to counteract the central tendency of Greeks toward philosophy rather than history. Butterfield's examination of Chinese historiography is used as a further basis for comparison, for in the pre-Confucian era China developed a narrative, although ritualized, historical tradition. The teachings of Confucius raised the status of history even more, at the same time giving history both a secular and moralizing tone. While many historians would disagree with Butterfield's ranking of the Judaic, Chinese, and Greek contributions to historiography, his arguments are both stimulating and provocative.

Butterfield uses a neoidealistic approach to the study of history: observation and reflection lead (by a somewhat mystical process) to the discovery of patterns, connections, and truths about the past. He once told Alan Watson that the belief in Christ and His Spiritual Kingdom gave the observer of mundane events a neutral detachment and elasticity of mind toward worldly matters. It is not surprising, then, that for the author the emergence and spread of Christianity are the most significant events in early historiography. While the first Christians believed the end of the world was imminent and therefore concentrated on saving souls, other Christians soon turned their attention to the collection of the stories and sayings of Jesus and then connected their own faith with Judaism by accepting the Old Testament. In Butterfield's view, this development was both momentous and fortunate, for he believes that at that very moment the Jews were turning away from history toward law in reaction to their many disappointments. Thus it was the Christians who carried forward the development of history, primarily through the conversion of Constantine and the writings of Augustine.

Butterfield's thoughts about the rise of historical criticism are much less fully developed than his ideas about the earlier periods of historiography. He generalizes vaguely that historical criticism tended to be related to clashes between vested interests, yet notes that the sixteenth century controversy over which nations could claim to be descended from the ancient Trojans provoked a high level of critical endeavor that was contrary to all vested interests. The Reformation, of course, raised other issues directly related to history and stimulated the use of manuscript sources and archives. It was the seventeenth century classical scholars and theologians, according to Butterfield, who finally moved historical criticism beyond the merely negative stage of simply rejecting some authors as unreliable. New techniques for analyzing new kinds of evidence were developed, he asserts, but he leaves both the chronology and the nature of these new techniques unclear.

Butterfield's treatment of the secularization of history also raises questions of both clarity and logic. He argues that the mere technique of collecting and reporting the facts was one factor in the continuing secularization of history. Indeed, here he seems to suggest that only when factual explanations appeared inadequate did early historians resort to divine intervention. Yet he has already demonstrated that early history was firmly grounded in religious beliefs, and has characterized the attempt to ascribe a degree of rationality to the gods as the first search for general laws. His discussion of Islamic history in this context does nothing to clarify his argument. Furthermore, according to the author, Greek secular history came about because their religion (unlike Judaism) was insufficient to explain worldly events and thus the Greeks searched for political causes for the rise and fall of their city states. After the Christians made the Old Testament a part of their own past, history became the unfolding of God's plan; although the sacred and the secular were separated during the Renaissance, they continued to exist side by side until the victory of the Scientific Revolution and the development of a secular idea of progress in the eighteenth century. Butterfield ends, rather than concludes, his study with a very brief treatment of the rise of philosophies of history and the clash between what he terms the "universal" history of G. F. W. Hegel and the "academic" history of Leopold von Ranke.

Perhaps if Sir Herbert Butterfield's health had not failed so rapidly toward the end of his life, he would have reworked his last two chapters and removed these ambiguities. As it is, the process seems to have been aborted: the text includes the necessary observations and reflections but the organizing patterns have not fully emerged. Nevertheless, even Butterfield's unfinished thoughts, expressed as they are in his flowing narrative style, are of interest to all serious students of historiography.

*Susan Becker*

## Sources for Further Study

*Choice*. XIX, December 1981, p. 543.
*Contemporary Review*. CCXXXIX, September, 1981, p. 162.
*Encounter*. LVII, December, 1981, p. 58.
*Guardian Weekly*. CXXV, July 5, 1981, p. 22.
*History Today*. XXXI, November, 1981, p. 55.
*Illustrated London News*. CCLXIX, August, 1981, p. 76.
*Library Journal*. CVI, December 1, 1981, p. 2311.
*National Review*. XXXIII, November 27, 1981, p. 1434.
*Spectator*. CCXLVII, August 1, 1981, p. 19.
*Times Literary Supplement*. August 7, 1981, p. 897.

# PALM SUNDAY
## An Autobiographical Collage

*Author:* Kurt Vonnegut (1922-    )
*Publisher:* Delecorte Press (New York). 330 pp. $13.95
*Type of work:* Autobiographical collage

*A pastiche of speeches, letters, fiction, articles, an account of Vonnegut's ancestry, and even a musical comedy, woven together by the Vonnegut voice, this volume forms a kind of autobiography presenting the life and opinions of Kurt Vonnegut in his own words*

A native of Indianapolis, Kurt Vonnegut grew up in the heart of "middle America" and has been characterized as "good old Dad from Indiana." Age fifty-six when *Palm Sunday* was published, he is looking back on a long life and looking around at the life that is the lot of Americans. He finds the values of middle American ways a distortion of life as it should be lived. In this respect, he is a descendent of Henry David Thoreau; and perhaps for that reason and the fact that his writing is always engaging and even humorous, he has served as a culture hero for the young from the early 1960's when his work was widely read among college students. In an interview, he has said that he writes out of wanting his readers "to stop hating and start thinking." He thinks the planet is in danger and wants to create "an image of life that is beautiful and surprising and deep." His contribution to American life has been to entertain his readers with a simple-sounding yet wise and ironic voice that highlights the blunders and major blemishes of our culture. His views, if adopted, would supply his readers with a humane and enduring vision of life for an uncertain future. This is why his mordant wit is popular. At root, his effect is positive.

Vonnegut says he has a "stubborn simplicity." Simple he might seem, but he is preoccupied with helping people survive with dignity and sanity in a world that often seems hell-bent on destroying itself—with inventions, with money, with anti-Communist wrath, with atomic science, or with unreasoned violence—and even hiding from the harsh facts of life through the use of needlessly polite language. He has observed that "it is dangerous to believe that there are enormous new truths, dangerous to imagine that we can stand outside the universe. So I argue for the ordinariness of life, the familiarity of love." This is not "simple"; rather, heroic. These themes—and others, such as the blight of loneliness among Americans—preoccupy him in *Palm Sunday* as well as his other work. *Slaughterhouse-Five* (1969), his best and most famous work, is never so direct and forthright as the Vonnegut readers will find *Palm Sunday*.

This book, a collage of nineteen sections consisting of autobiographical material readers have seen for the first time, a story ("The Big Space Fuck") and a musical comedy (*The Chemistry Professor*, an updating of *Dr. Jekyll and Mr. Hyde*), and numerous essays, letters, and speeches, is a bit "clumsy" and "raw," as Vonnegut admits in his Introduction; but for the millions who find his kind of simplicity wise and entertaining, the book is a mine of gems. He reminds the reader that he is among "America's last generation of novelists"—along with J. D. Salinger, Edward Lewis Wallant, and James Jones. He is "angered and sickened and saddened" that his *Slaughterhouse-Five* was burned in a furnace by order of a school board in North Dakota, in 1973, and that books by Bernard Malamud, James Dickey, and Joseph Heller, among others, are regularly thrown out of public school libraries by school board members, who "commonly say that they have not actually read the books, but that they have it on good authority that the books are bad for children." For a novelist who wants to create "an image of life that is beautiful and surprising and deep," to improve the quality of American life, such behavior by adults is "disgusting." Vonnegut puts it simply in a letter to the Drake, North Dakota, School Board Chairman: "The news from Drake indicates to me that books and writers are very unreal to you people."

As Vonnegut points out, probably in vain, his books ". . . beg that people be kinder and more responsible than they often are." He also points out that the coarse language of some of his characters comes from the coarse language that people use in real life—"especially soldiers and hardworking men speak coarsely, and even our most sheltered children know that." The words "didn't damage us when we were young. It was evil deeds and lying that hurt us." These sentiments are among his most repeated themes. He likes to remind the citizens of communities where books are banned that they are members of American civilization and that the public outcry against them indicates that "your fellow Americans" feel they have "behaved in . . . an uncivilized way." Stated most boldly, Vonnegut says, "If you are an American, you must allow all ideas to circulate freely in your community, not merely your own." He is right; but his books are still being banned here and there by "good citizens" who still do not read or understand well what they do read.

If anyone can defend the use of obscenity, when used wisely and deliberately in literature, Vonnegut can. He is truly impatient with the book "banners," for he intends to say only this to them: "'Have somebody read the First Amendment to the United States Constitution out loud to you, you . . . fool!" Vonnegut is quite careful where he places his coarse language. In a chapter on "Obscenity," he argues that the "nice manners" of social class victimize their users. Because people of "class" protect themselves by manners, they lack the "simple and practical vocabularies" for "their excretory and reproductive systems" and for "treachery and hypocrisy." "Good manners had made them defenseless against predatory members of their own class." He tells how his parents were victimized financially by friends of theirs in this way. And Queen Victoria? She had "created arbitrary rules," manners, at the "outermost edge to warn her of the approach of anyone so crude" as to bring to her attention the suffering of the Irish and other cruelties in everyday life. "If she would not even acknowledge that human beings sometimes farted, how could she be expected to hear without swooning of these other things." She had, he argues, persuaded her polite society that they could be self-governing "only after they had stopped thinking about all the things that human beings can't help thinking about all the time," such as sex, violence, indignities, suffering, and the like. This is classic Vonnegut thinking, probably persuasive to those who already have a "simple and practical" vocabulary to use when needed. Others will go on to protect themselves from the vile and base by erasing it from their vocabulary.

Another of his central ideas has received much deserved attention, but no resolution. When Sargent Shriver was running for vice-president with George McGovern when campaign ideas were scarce, Shriver asked Vonnegut for one. As Vonnegut pointed out, the number one American killer was not cardiovascular disease, but loneliness. He came up with the slogan that appeared on buttons and bumpers and flags and billboards: "Lonesome No More!" Though he is probably in some way right, his idea that McGovern-Sargent could swamp the Republicans "if they would promise to cure that disease" did not receive the serious attention it deserves. Vonnegut says "The nuclear family doesn't provide nearly enough companionship." He wants Americans to "return to extended families as quickly as we can" so we will be "lonesome no more." To him, "people are in fact crying out not so much for money as for relief from loneliness."

He treats the subject of divorce, observing that those who divorce "very likely wrangle and wail and weep formlessly about money and sex, about treachery, about outgrowing one another, about how close love is to hate, and so on." He suggests that, when marital mates become incompatible, that they express their regrets, after they have tried to make the marriage work, and say "Too bad. Good-bye." As for incompatible parents and children, the alienated one could "bug out of his own house for months, and still be among relatives." No one need search for "friendly strangers" in such places as massage parlors, bus stations, bars, or even churches. They would, in an era of the extended family, have "scores of other homes to go to in search of love and understanding." If one thinks long about such a radical idea—and its present gradual evolution into reality—the notion is "beautiful and surprising and deep," precisely that for which Vonnegut says he is striving. Regardless of those who have set their minds against such a humane and loving idea, it is circulating and doing some good for the sanity of millions. Vonnegut's simple psychology of the family is very much a major implication in the research on loneliness and aloneness in today's culture. If people were to "stop hating and start" loving more, the murders, drugs, suicides, runaways, and zany religious cults might not steal so many away from the planet. His suggestion is not *the* solution to loneliness, but it is a real solution for many companionless Americans.

In a section called "The Sexual Revolution" (which contains all manner of comment apart from revolutions, sexual or not), Vonnegut uses the occasion of his own divorce from a wife of twenty-five years to explain the plight of "an American father." She had, with their two daughters, gotten caught up in the "born-again Christians" phenomenon, "working white magic through rituals and prayers." He is probably right when he says that wagging tongues, when the departed father is not around, probably tell tales "of booze and wicked women." "Closer to the truth," he says, is the story of the man's "cold sober flight into unpopulated nothingness." While booze and women, good and bad, may come along in time, he argues that "nothingness is the first seductress." He quotes the lyrics from the Statler Brothers' "Flowers on the Wall" to illustrate his point for middle-class divorcées. The song is about "the end of a man's usefulness." The man in the poem is counting flowers on the wall; in other words, he "has no appreciable utility anymore."

From this autobiographical point, he moves to a principle, "the most universal revolutionary wish," which is "to be honored by angels for something other than beauty or usefulness." Then, perhaps so his readers do not think him entirely sexist in his explanation of the American fathers' departure from middle-class "hearths," he points out that the current women's liberation movement, in the broadest sense, "is a wish by women to be liked for something other than their reproductive abilities." This statement is an oversimplification, of course, but there is a kernel of truth and a bushel of humor in his explanation of the rejection of the Equal Rights Amendment by male state legislators. He says the truth is that they are saying "'We're sorry, girls, but your reproductive abilities are about all we can really like you for.'" This is the "Serious Humor" that is his trademark. Lonesomeness, for Vonnegut, may not derive so much from merely being alone, but from the nothingness, the uselessness men and women come to feel in their lives with one another. His "sexual revolution" chapter turns out to be a plea for the abandoning of sexual shame and for discovering and appreciating the many sides of the selves within each person. In that way, no one will lack the essential companionship and intimacy for leading a fulfilled life.

Vonnegut joins Henry David Thoreau as a popular cult hero of undergraduates. As Ralph Waldo Emerson said of Thoreau at his funeral, he was "an architect of the noblest society"; and so is Vonnegut. Both are valuable for their confrontation with "the essential facts of life." Vonnegut has published some of life's "meanness" to the world, and though he has not retreated from society, he has created a Walden of the mind, a mental garden of simplicity and wisdom that reminds his readers of a better world they could be making. The wonder is that so radical and all-American an author as Vonnegut has become so popular. He is, after all, a freethinker, as he says, in the tradition of Bertrand Russell, Ralph Ingersoll, Clarence Darrow, H. L.

Mencken, and his great-grandfather Clemens Vonnegut. He may not be so insistent that his readers think as he does, so much as he hopes they will rethink the shoddy premises of a faltering civilization. Somehow, he is able to think, as Thoreau was, free from the constraints of popular attitudes and mores. Certainly, his ideas are more profound and less applicable than they first seem to be—much like those of Thoreau. Their value, as with all idealists, is that they can remove themselves from conventional thinking to see the possibilities that may lie in the unforseeable future.

The details of so many matters he mentions do not come to life in this book. Readers do not, for example, learn about who his first wife and his two daughters are, nor do they learn about any of the 372 "friends" he has who are great people. (He offers the list in irony.) If he says, "We thought we could do without tribes and clans. Well, we can't," then his readers are left to find which road will lead to the nirvana of the extended family, no censorship, and a lonesome-no-more existence. Along the way, will the problems of housing, the fragmentation of the cities by casual overdevelopment, the difficulty with mass transit progress, the economy, the need for nuclear power, and perhaps the greedy nature of man somehow disappear if one runs headlong in the directions Vonnegut suggests? The complex problems of modern morality and urban civilization do not lend themselves to simple solutions, even the ones Vonnegut offers. Yet, this is an individual who has not let the railroads of success, marriage, or conventional thinking ride on him. He is Man Thinking, that ideal proposed in Emerson's famous essay, "The American Scholar." As such, Vonnegut is a precious national resource, for he merely offers his ideas in their simplicity, leaving it up to readers to recognize their truth and to find their own ways to apply them.

*Palm Sunday* is thus didactic in the best sense of the word. Vonnegut is Emerson's scholar in an age when few are available. This book should be in the firehouses, the hospitals, the living rooms, or the universities of the country, not to be taken literally or followed blindly but to stir readers to think of the bases of their lives. As a Man Thinking, Vonnegut does not "defer to the popular cry"; he is, as Emerson says he must be, "free and brave." Whether one agrees or disagrees with his judgments, America needs a Vonnegut to show the ways to improve the collective mind.

*Gary L. Harmon*

## Sources for Further Study

*The Atlantic Monthly*. CCXLVII, April, 1981, p. 124.
*Business Week*. XI, March 8, 1981, p. 6.
*Choice*. XIX, September, 1981, p. 84.

*Library Journal*. CVI, February 15, 1981, p. 454.
*Nation*. CCXXXII, March 21, 1981, p. 346.
*National Review*. XXXIII, May 1, 1981, p. 499.
*The New York Times Book Review*. LXXXVI, March 15, 1981, p. 3.
*Saturday Review*. VIII, March, 1981, p. 77.
*Times Literary Supplement*. June 19, 1981, p. 692.
*Virginia Quarterly Review*. LVII, Summer, 1981, p. 98.

# PARIS IN THE THIRD REICH
## A History of the German Occupation, 1940-1944

*Author:* David Pryce-Jones (1936-    )
*Publisher:* Holt, Rinehart and Winston (New York). Illustrated. 294 pp. $25.00
*Type of work:* History
*Time:* 1940-1944
*Locale:* Paris

*A thoroughly researched, highly detailed, and richly illustrated account of the German occupation of Paris, emphasizing French acquiescence to or collaboration with the German authorities*

> *Principal personages:*
> PIERRE LAVAL, President of France, 1935-1936; and Minister of Foreign Affairs, 1934-1936
> MARSHAL HENRI PHILIPPE PÉTAIN, Premier of Unoccupied France
> PAUL REYNAUD, Premier of France
> ADOLF HITLER, Chancellor and Führer of Germany, 1933-1945
> STANDARTENFÜHRER HELMUT KNOCHEN, Commander of the SD in Paris, responsible for external security
> GENERAL HEINRICH VON STÜLPNAGEL, replaced his cousin, General Otto von Stülpnagel as German Military Governor

The German occupation of Paris, which began in June, 1940, and ended in August, 1944, is an event that has fascinated historians because of the insight it offers in understanding human nature under extreme stress. Several books have appeared since the war concentrating on the German occupation and the collaboration of the Vichy government, of which the most important are Henry Amoroux's *La Vie des Français sous l'occupation* and *La Grande Histoire des Français sous l'occupation*, and Robert Aron's *Histoire de Vichy* and *Histoire de l'occupation*. These works and others have demonstrated that the claim by thousands of Parisians immediately following the war that they had participated in the resistance is unfounded. Indeed, the two basic human drives of survival and ambition led most Parisians either to acquiescence to German authority or to open collaboration with the Germans and their goals. Many, especially the native Fascist parties jockeying for power, were even more enthusiastic than the occupying forces themselves in realizing Nazi objectives. Unfortunately the general reader outside France has had little opportunity to learn about the occupation because most accounts have not been translated from the French. An exception to this is Marcel Ophüls' documentary film masterpiece, *The Sorrow and the Pity*, an ambitious undertaking similar in structure to the book under review. The length of the film (it runs almost four-and-a-half hours) and its lack of broad commercial appeal, however, limit its showings to large cities and major university communities. This void has fortunately been filled with the publication of David Pryce-Jones's *Paris in the Third Reich: A History of the German Occupation, 1940-1944*, with Michael Rand as Picture Editor.

David Pryce-Jones is a young historian and novelist of great productivity. He has written two books on the Middle East, *Next Generation: Travels in Israel* (1964) and *The Face of Defeat* (1973); a book on the Hungarian Revolution; a biography of Unity Mitford; and seven novels. Although his purpose for writing *Paris in the Third Reich* is never explicitly stated, it appears to be threefold. A primary reason is the obvious: to provide a balanced account of what happened in Paris during this four-year period and how the French and Germans responded. Second, by including an epilogue on the 1979 trial for war crimes of three Germans involved in the deportation of French Jews to Auschwitz, Pryce-Jones argues forcefully for the moral necessity of attempting, perhaps futilely, to expose and bring to justice those who committed horrendous crimes against their fellowmen in the name of bureaucratic efficiency. A third reason, a personal one, is related to the author's own experiences during the period of the occupation. In May, 1940, Pryce-Jones was at the home of his mother's family about thirty kilometers north of Paris. The family fled to the south and the child spent some memorable time in the Vichy zone. Thus he has retained a lifelong fascination with events that transpired during those impressionable childhood years.

*Paris in the Third Reich* is not Pryce-Jones's achievement alone. Of near equal importance is that of the picture editor, Michael Rand, for the volume contains more than a hundred contemporary photographs, many in color, which re-create almost every aspect of Parisian life during this period. The photographs are the work of two men, Roger Schall and André Zucca. Before World War II Schall was a fashion photographer and a frequent contributor to many German and French fashion periodicals. In 1938, he traveled to Nuremberg to cover the Nazi Party rally for *Paris-Match*. When the Germans occupied Paris, he was immediately contacted and given free-lance assignments in black and white, mainly in the fields of fashion and entertainment. Shortly after the Liberation he published a selection of his wartime photographs in *A Paris sous la botte des Nazis*. Schall, now retired, continues to live in Paris. André Zucca worked for *Paris-Soir* and *Paris-Match* before the war. With the occupation, the Germans took over the *Paris-Match* printing works and began the publication of their own magazine, *Signal*. Zucca was hired to work for this publication. A friend of several Nazi sympathizers or collaborators, Zucca went into hiding after the departure of the Germans because of his fear of reprisals. He died in 1973. Zucca was best-known for his color photographs, many of which have not been published previously. The photographs of Schall and Zucca, expertly chosen and arranged by Michael Rand, immeasurably enhance the text and are most evocative to those familiar with Paris.

*Paris in the Third Reich* is divided into three parts of unequal length. Approximately two-thirds of the book is given to the twelve-chapter section entitled "The Occupation," which contains Pryce-Jones's description of conditions in Paris between 1940 and 1944. Most of the remaining third of the book is devoted to interviews with some of the Germans and French survivors of the occupation which corroborate the author's argument that life in Paris remained surprisingly normal throughout most of the occupation. The text concludes with a brief epilogue. To aid the reader in following the complex course of events and the large cast of characters in Paris during this period, a glossary precedes the text. In it is included a list of the abbreviations widely used by the author and of the main personnel in the major German organizations operating in Paris. To assist the scholar in further study of the problem of the occupation, a brief bibliographical essay and a lengthy section of footnotes are also included.

One of the most remarkable features of the German occupation of Paris, which began on June 13, 1940, was the ease with which it was accomplished. When the blitzkrieg in the West had begun only a month earlier, hardly anyone believed that continental Europe's major city was within a few weeks of the loss of its independence. The German advance was so rapid that resistance melted away and flight from Paris and northern France became epidemic. Those who remained were soon faced with the decision of how they would respond to occupation. The French government had already fled from the capital to Bordeaux on June 10. From there the Premier, Paul Reynaud, planned to move the seat of government to colonial North Africa and to continue the war from there. Reynaud, however, soon found himself in a minority within his own cabinet and was forced to resign, at the same time acquiescing to Marshal Henri Philippe Pétain's demand that the government sue for an armistice. Pétain was appointed premier and immediately sued for peace. The octogenarian Marshal was then invested as head of state of the new Vichy government with Pierre Laval as his premier. Both have, since the war, had passionate defenders and detractors. Those who support them maintain that they subjected France to the humiliation of nonresistance and occupation and patterned their own regime at Vichy after the German model as a means of saving France from the devastation undergone by Poland, where the Nazi advance was resisted. Pryce-Jones, as well as other detractors, regards Pétain and Laval as enemies of French republicanism and as political opportunists. "The men who built and supported the Vichy regime," Pryce-Jones asserts,

> were those who most naturally should have resisted the Germans, since for years they had been claiming to possess the monopoly of patriotism and nationalism. Instead, patriotism and nationalism had come to be harnessed to surrender to the Germans. . . . What the [Vichy] regime really represented was the complete desertion of national and traditional values.

Indeed the Vichy regime, recognized by the Germans as the legitimate native French government with technical control over the unoccupied area of southern France and with representation in Paris, became little more than the impotent smoke screen for the implementation of Nazi policies in France and the basis for the German claim of the legitimacy of its occupation force. The government, and especially Pétain, who had come to represent the virtues of old France, lost almost all independence originally granted it, and was used by the Nazis for fostering in France the goals of totalitarianism and the liquidation of Jews and as a major source for the resources and manpower needed to fuel the Nazi war machine. What is most amazing and unfortunately revealing about French character during the war is that Pétain was wildly cheered in Paris less than four months before the liberation in August, 1944. Indeed, popular allegiance could be shifted almost instantaneously. Those who had cheered Pétain hailed the entrance into Paris in August, 1944, of his most ardent foe, General Charles de Gaulle.

Although sixteen Parisians committed suicide rather than submit to the humiliation of occupation, there was otherwise no meaningful resistance to the German entry into Paris. The city which was "far and away the greatest of Hitler's prizes, smoothly but assuredly assumed its place in the Reich that was intended to last a thousand years." Within a matter of days museums, post offices, banks, and the metro were back in service. Restaurants and nightclubs welcomed the German conquerors, who often acted and were treated like tourists. The curfew was quickly extended, educational institutions reopened, and Paris quickly regained much of its traditional atmosphere of *joie de vivre*. Most Parisians exhibited an understandable "eagerness to oblige," but many, in their desire to improve their status at the expense of patriotism, went further, and the initial ingratiation moved swiftly toward collaboration. An observation of Otto Abetz, German Ambassador from 1940 to 1944, is most cogent:

> "I have been receiving parliamentarians, municipal councillors, *préfets*, magistrates. Out of fifty of these dignitaries, forty-nine have asked me for special permissions of one sort or another, or for gasoline coupons—and the fiftieth spoke of France."

With French assistance the Germans quickly asserted their control over the media, the police, and the transportation system. The press, in particular, felt the heavy hand of German interference. Innocuous publications dealing with such topics as sports, car racing, and women's romances remained free of German control. Others, however, were placed in the hands of French collaborators who were required to write or accept material for publication that was laudatory of Nazi goals or achievements or inoffensively fictional. Some writers and publishers took their jobs seriously and attempted to ground their pro-Nazi arguments in their interpretations of current events and history. Most disgustingly, however, the Nazi Party representative in Paris encouraged and subsidized a French gutter press that was virulently anti-Semitic. The most ignominious of the lot was *Au Pilori*, which was based on its German counterpart, *Der Stürmer*. In articles devoid of news, the contributors to this organ revived nineteenth century racism and hatred. Advocating "'the arrest and deportation of *all* Jews without exception,'" *Au Pilori* and similar organs prepared Frenchmen for the most tragic chapter in the history of the occupation: the arrest and deportation to death camps of French and non-French Jews. Most distressingly, the French government lent support to *Au Pilori* in the form of regular advertisements for the national lottery.

Without question the most reprehensible feature of the German occupation was the persecution, arrest, internment, and transportation of Jews to the death camp at Auschwitz, and active French participation in or acquiescence to this brutality is especially repugnant. The campaign against the Jews began with the attempt to excite anti-Semitic sentiment among Parisians and took the form of an anti-Jewish exhibit which opened at the Palais Berlitz in early September, 1941. In October, 1941, Standartenführer Helmut Knochen, the Commander of the SD in Paris, which was responsible for external security, ordered the destruction by explosives of seven synagogues. Soon after, Knochen engineered the resignation of the German Military Governor, General Otto von Stülpnagel, who favored a policy of relative leniency as a means of undermining resistance. He was replaced by his more tractable cousin, General Heinrich von Stülpnagel, and by March, 1942, the Final Solution was under way.

The first trainload of Jews departed Paris for Auschwitz on March 27, 1942. Although a small number of Jews were granted *dérogations*, or exceptions, to arrest and deportation, the vast majority quickly felt the force of German (and French) brutality. Within a brief period tens of thousands of *délations* (denunciations) passed into the offices of the German authorities and the French police. This was followed on July 16, 1942, by "La Grande Raffle" (the Great Raid) during which some fifteen thousand Jews were arrested, temporarily housed under terrible conditions in an indoor sports arena, and finally transferred to the internment camp at Drancy, from which they were transported to Auschwitz.

The first Jews arrested were either foreign refugees or stateless or naturalized French. Many of them left behind children who had been born in France. The question of their fate immediately arose. The Vichy government, through its representative in Paris, Laval, took no interest in the plight of these unfortunate children. Some four thousand children were rounded up, all under twelve years of age, incarcerated at Drancy, and eventually taken to Auschwitz. This was without doubt the most pitiable episode during the occupation, and the greatest indictment was that the German authorities used compliant Frenchmen to do their work, thus giving the policy of the Final Solution a legitimacy with Frenchmen as a whole. "It is impossible," Pryce-Jones asserts, "to credit the ignorance claimed after the war by the senior French officials and policemen who worked alongside [the German authorities] day after day in close cooperation and partnership."

Pryce-Jones chronicles not only the outward normalcy of Parisian life, given the exigencies of war, but also traces the change in attitudes as the war progressed and as it became apparent that those who collaborated or acquiesced were going to be on the losing side. The level of tension increased as collaborators had to make choices about the best means of avoiding or escaping the retribution from their fellow nationals which would inevitably follow the defeat of the Germans. For the most culpable, such as Laval and Pétain, few options were left. Although Laval, ever the political chameleon, tried to revive the Third Republic which he had been instrumental in destroying, he failed and was ultimately returned to France, tried, and executed in 1945. Pétain who, by the end of the occupation, had become only a figurehead in his own government, supplanted by collaborators and Fascists "in all but name," escaped with his life but spent the remainder of it in prison. Others were less fortunate than Pétain. Indeed, "what the French did to themselves after the occupation was in some ways more painful than what Germans had done to them during it." The number of Frenchmen killed by fellow Frenchmen following the Liberation "equalled or even exceeded the number of those sent to their death by the Germans as hostages, deportees, and slave laborers." With liberation the myth of the resistance was born. Suddenly many who had acquiesced or collaborated and escaped detection or punishment claimed that they had always sided with the forces of resistance. Historians have succeeded, however, in dispelling this myth.

This is an important book which demands the attention not only of the historian but also of the psychologist and sociologist. With restrained eloquence Pryce-Jones has demonstrated the fickleness of human nature under stress and the fragility of institutions and basic morality. His study is a testimony to the tragic fact that the effective occupation force is one which does not crush but corrupts.

*J. Stewart Alverson*

### Sources for Further Study

*The Economist.* CCLXXXI, October 17, 1981, p. 114.
*Human Events.* XLI, September 26, 1981, p. 11.
*Library Journal.* CVI, September 15, 1981, p. 1731.
*Listener.* CVI, October 8, 1981, p. 407.
*The New Republic.* CLXXXV, October 21, 1981, p. 30.
*New Statesman.* CII, October 23, 1981, p. 19.
*The New York Times Book Review.* LXXXVI, September 27, 1981, p. 20.
*The New Yorker.* LVII, January 25, 1982, p. 96.
*Observer.* October 11, 1981, p. 33.
*Times Literary Supplement.* November 6, 1981, p. 96.

# PEACE BREAKS OUT

*Author:* John Knowles (1926-    )
*Publisher:* Holt, Rinehart and Winston (New York). 193 pp. $10.95
*Type of work:* Novel
*Time:* 1945, shortly after World War II
*Locale:* Devon School, New Hampshire

*A short, moral tale centered on the conflicts developing between the students in a New England prep school in 1945, as they and the rest of the nation seek to find a basis for life in the postwar world*

*Principal characters:*
PETE HALLAM, a former Devon student, World War II veteran, now a Devon teacher
ERIC HOCHSCHWENDER, a student and activist
WEXFORD, a student, editor of the school paper, activist
COTTY DONALDSON, a student, football captain, senior class president
NICK BLACKBURN, a student
TUG BLACKBURN, a student, Nick's brother
JOAN HALLAM, Pete Hallam's ex-wife
ROSCOE LATCH, a Latin teacher
DEBORAH LATCH, Roscoe's wife

The title of John Knowles's most recent novel is taken from Bertolt Brecht's Mother Courage, when the camp follower and opportunist exclaims in horror when she hears that "peace has broken out" just when she has bought supplies that she intends to sell to the soldiers at enormous profit. Peace, elusive as it sometimes seems, and desirable as most people claim it is, can be a mixed blessing. At the very least, it can be a time of turmoil and conflict, a period during which individuals find it difficult to adjust to the new situation in which they suddenly are thrust. Just as war can demand difficult adjustments, so peace can be a time of trauma. This pain and confusion can be part of the lives even of people who were not directly involved in the conflict. In *Peace Breaks Out*, John Knowles constructs a moral tale out of the difficulties that a group of prep schoolboys encounter as they face the postwar world.

When Pete Hallam, Devon, Class of '37, returns to his old prep school after being mustered out of the service in 1945, he is looking for peace and quiet, for a place in which he can rest and collect himself after the years of horror that he has experienced on the European battlefront. The reality that he encounters, however, is not as tranquil as he expected. The violence of individual emotions and beliefs can sometimes upset a life almost as much as the violence of physical conflict.

Knowles's short novel illustrates better than many history books the continuum of history. Although historians and teachers may try to construct hard and fast lines around events in history, in actuality the lines are decidedly blurry. When one looks at the sequence of events that make up history, one sees that the edges run together much like the edges in a watercolor drawing. Although peace is officially declared and the troops are returning home, the line cannot so easily be drawn cutting off the passions of the war from the concerns of the peacetime populace. This is especially true of the young people whose intellectual awareness ripened during the conflict. They cannot help but see the world in terms of sharp, contradictory definitions, and they are uncomfortable if anyone tells them that definitions might actually be ambiguous, that shades of gray do indeed exist.

Pete Hallam, after surviving the horrors of war, with minor physical and mental wounds, is grateful to return to a place such as Devon, which he regards as a paradise, a world untouched by the cruelty and violence that he has endured for so many years. Emotionally and morally exhausted, he is eager to find a place to rest. As he says to himself, he is tired of G.I. talk, tired of ruined villages, tired of destroyed human lives, tired of the residue of war. Soon, however, he sees that Devon and its students are not untouched by the war. Perhaps they were too young to have actually been enlisted in the Army, but they were mature enough to observe and to feel the violence that was consuming much of the rest of the world. As Roscoe Latch, Pete's former Latin techer, points out, these boys are "aware." It is too late to protect them from the realities of the world. They know that life on earth is not innocent.

The postwar concern with right and wrong, the intense fear of *new* enemies, already is visible at Devon School, as Pete Hallam undertakes his duties as teacher and coach. The incipient paranoia that eventually culminated in the Joseph McCarthy era, is budding even in this small New England prep school. The boys are intelligent enough and aware enough to be influenced by the concerns that are floating through the rest of the country. The father of one of the boys is in President Truman's cabinet; other parents are successful businessmen, industrialists, movers and shakers, individuals who either are involved in determining public opinion or who react violently to it.

Several of the students, including Wexford, the editor of the school paper, are concerned with the moral position of the United States, now that the long war is over. After all, the very fact that brings joy to Pete Hallam may be a source of guilt to others. America was not physically touched by the war. True, many United States citizens suffered and died in the course of the war; the country at large made sacrifices, endured rationing and other hardships of varying intensity. No American city was bombed, however. Nazi troops did not march down American streets. While other countries may have achieved some kind of catharsis through the violence of the war, the United States—Wexford feels—remains corrupt and decadent, unpurified. The rich became richer—he has only to look at his own father to confirm this—and the country is, by and large, no worse off than it was before. In fact, it may be better off. The paradox is deeply troubling to him.

John Knowles always has been essentially a moral writer. His novels, beginning with *A Separate Peace* (1960), have embraced moral questions. Although using the backdrop of the larger world, he has focused intently on the microcosm to represent the larger, fundamental issues that confront men and women. Relentlessly, he shows how there can be no escape from the basic moral questions. No one can hide—as Pete Hallam cannot hide—from the concerns that haunt the rest of the human race. Pete Hallam must confront—in the actions of these boys he finds himself trying to influence—the continuing human struggle to find a moral meaning to existence on earth. The irony is that one man's moral truth is another man's heresy. Perhaps, Hallam thinks, the only answer—and that by default—is the brute strength that eventually determines the victor or the defeated. America was stronger; does that necessarily mean that America was the more virtuous? He believes very much that the cause of the Allies was honorable, but when confronted with the smaller, vicious battles of his students, he is no longer sure about who was right or wrong. Even America can produce neo-Nazis. Even America can allow the innocent to suffer. There is no paradise.

The other students are overwhelmed when confronted by the antagonistic forces of Eric Hochschwender's blatant Nazism and Wexford's moral righteousness. Both of them proclaim that America is still poisoned, that the great war they all have endured did not end in a clean peace. In fact, Wexford insists, America is more corrupt than ever; because the country did not *physically* suffer, its vices were not bled or scraped away. The adolescent logic may be faulty, but the passion behind it is difficult to battle.

Just as McCarthy would soon be looking for internal dangers to the American way of life, so Wexford is already looking for an internal menace to the "Devon Spirit." "Americans haven't really been . . . tested," he states, and so the corrupters still exist, ready to attack the freedom that the rest of the population takes for granted. Who are those corrupters? Perhaps only individuals who disagree, those people who undermine one's power and influence, the individuals who challenge the status quo.

At the same time, the question of the basic American principle of freedom of speech becomes important here, because Eric Hochschwender very loudly proclaims his own racist beliefs while seeking the protection of the United States Constitution. If America is secure in its freedom, if it is actually based on the principles that it announces so loudly, then Hochschwender or anyone else should be allowed to say anything. The institutions that hold up America should not be so fragile that the ravings of one eccentric student will bring them down. This is the issue that Knowles raises in *Peace Breaks Out*. It is not a minor issue, and it is one that will continue to be relevant for a long time.

It is significant that the student Nick Blackburn, at one point in the novel, is shown reading Nathaniel Hawthorne's *The Scarlet Letter* (1850). That nineteenth century novel of the power of intolerance and the repercussions of actions based on hatred and intolerance has a great deal to teach the students at Devon School, but they are too caught up in their own times to see the relevance of past eras to their own, and are too engrossed with their own passions and sensibilities to take a lesson from the passions or moral conflicts of fictional characters of the past. With the superiority of the young and the righteousness all too often characteristic of Americans, they barge blindly ahead, not stopping to think about who might suffer as a result of their stubborn arrogance.

As have so many Americans since the founding fathers, these intelligent—if only partially educated—boys are eager to scorn the "latest rotten European 'isms." Their parents by and large agree with them. Of course, the most potent European "ism" to be guarded against—from their affluent point of view—is socialism, but Fascism, Communism, or any other "ism" is just as much to be guarded against: a symbolic evil, representing an alien world, "un-Americanism." The fathers might talk of taxes and the destruction of "Rugged Individualism," but to the boys the menace is only the shadowy, vague menace of those who are "different."

In the end, of course, the innocent suffer as a result of the intolerance of a few individuals. As in any moral tale, the plot becomes schematic and somewhat predictable. Much of the strength of *A Separate Peace* came from the fact that it was understated, set against a background of implied violence. The horror was—until the very end—psychic and emotional, and the lesson to be learned was not underlined in red ink. The story in *A Separate Peace* was as spare in its telling as the message was restrained. In *Peace Breaks Out* these virtues have been replaced by a more obvious, flat-footed style, and a much more blatant message. Although Knowles's intentions remain of the highest order, the quality of his art has suffered.

Nevertheless, the novel contains many good scenes and moments of finely rendered truth. When he is observing young men together, confronting their own vulnerability and moral limitations, Knowles is as good as any writer working today. It is when he is forced to invent, when he leaves behind his closely observed reality and ventures into more rarefied territory that he loses control. *Peace Breaks Out* could have been a novel as fine as *A Separate Peace*, a classic in modern American literature. Instead, it must be relegated to a lower rank, to that shelf reserved for well-crafted failures, books that suffer from their own excess of good intentions. Whatever reservations one might have about it, *Peace Breaks Out* remains a worthy effort by one of America's most interesting and skillful novelists. The regret is that it is not what it might have been, or what Knowles might have achieved.

*Bruce D. Reeves*

## Sources for Further Study

*Christian Century.* XCVIII, October 7, 1981, p. 1002.
*English Journal.* LXX, September, 1981, p. 75.
*Horn Book Magazine.* LVII, August, 1981, p. 461.
*Library Journal.* CVI, January 15, 1981, p. 165.
*The New York Times Book Review.* LXXXVI, March 22, 1981, p. 3.
*Newsweek.* XCVII, April 20, 1981, p. 92.
*Saturday Review.* VIII, March, 1981, p. 72.
*School Library Journal.* XXVII, February, 1981, p. 80.
*Time.* CXVII, April 6, 1981, p. 80.
*Wilson Library Bulletin.* LV, June, 1981, p. 773.

# THE PERSISTENCE OF THE OLD REGIME
## Europe to the Great War

*Author:* Arno J. Mayer (1926-    )
*Publisher:* Pantheon Books (New York). 368 pages. $16.95
*Type of work:* History
*Time:* 1848-1914
*Locale:* Europe

*A study of the continuing political dominance and cultural preeminence of royalty and the noble classes during an era of increasing liberalism and democracy in the nations of Europe*

> *Principal personages:*
> HERBERT HENRY ASQUITH, British Prime Minister, 1908-1916
> ARCHDUKE FRANCIS FERDINAND, heir to the crown of Austria-Hungary
> WASSILY KANDINSKY, a Russian-German artist
> NICHOLAS II, Czar of Russia, 1894-1917
> FRIEDRICH NIETZSCHE, a German philosopher
> RICHARD STRAUSS, a musical composer
> RICHARD WAGNER, a musical composer
> WILLIAM II, German Emperor, 1888-1918

In the Introduction to *The Persistence of the Old Regime*, Mayer gives three premises upon which his study was based. His major premise is that historians have overemphasized the forces of industrialism, cultural modernism, liberalism, and the rise of the middle class in their analyses of European history during the later nineteenth and early twentieth centuries. This, Mayer thinks, distorts the realities of European society in that era. He proposes, therefore, to counteract that widespread distortion of interpretation by showing that the preindustrial, premodern, nonliberal elements of European society were not decaying during the nineteenth century but were still vital, persistent, and indeed, still constituted the very essence and foundation of the political and civil structure of the major states of Europe. A second premise Mayer postulates is that the Great War of 1914-1918 was largely a result of the "remobilization" of Europe's ruling classes: a culminating expression of their ancient feudal standards and their way of life. Mayer's third premise is that World War II should be considered as an outgrowth or continuation of World War I. After 1919, the ruling classes had again recovered sufficiently to try to "resist the course of history" by aggravating the economic crisis of the 1920's and 1930's, sponsoring Fascism, and thus contributing to the new outbreak of war in 1939.

Mayer frankly states that he is not attempting to offer a balanced interpretation of European history between 1848 and 1914. It is his purpose to counteract the chronic overstatements of liberal historians concerning the putative decline of the old regime, and so he concentrates on the continuing strengths and pervasiveness of the ruling classes, even at the risk of skewing historic reality in the opposite direction. Furthermore, he reveals his own ideological orientation when he declares in the Preface: "I conceive of this book as a Marxist history from the top down, not the bottom up, with the focus on the upper rather than the lower classes."

The foundations of the Old Regime were laid in the sixteenth to eighteenth centuries, but it was suffused with elements of feudalism which went back to a much earlier era. Economically, the Old Regime was based on land and peasant labor dominated by hereditary and privileged noble landholders. Monarchy was the standard form of government of the Old Regime. The hereditary monarchs ruled with varying degrees of absolutism while utilizing and depending on the support and services of the landed nobilities. Religious institutions formed a third major component of the Old Regime. Rooted in landholding, closely tied to the crown and the landed nobilities, and preserving much of their feudal legacy, the Roman Catholic and Eastern Orthodox institutionalized churches served as pillars of the Old Regime.

Historians have customarily regarded the eighteenth century as marking the height of the Old Regime, and seen its downfall as dating from August, 1789, when the nobility of France voluntarily surrendered their feudal rights and privileges. Equally well known to historians is the resurgence of the Old Regime in the midyears of the nineteenth century, but that resurgence has been of less interest to most historians than the gains made by the forces of progress and change.

From his reading of nineteenth century history, Mayer seeks to show that by the mid-nineteenth century, the European aristocracy had regained its dominance over the military forces and the bureaucracies in the nations of Europe, and had again infused those services with the time-honored precepts, protocols, and standards of the noble classes. The nobles had also regained their lands, their wealth, and social status in the nations of Europe.

There were, to be sure, variations in the resurgence of the aristocracy from nation to nation: greater east of the Elbe, less in Western Europe. Even in England, however, where supposedly the bourgeoisie were ascendent, Mayer finds that the aristocracy were, in truth, the ruling class, right up to 1914. He admits that the English House of Commons, elected by an expanding male franchise in the later nineteenth century, did increasingly impose limitations on the monarchy, and that the economy of England was steadily industrialized with commensurate growth of the power and influence of the middle classes, but still the English aristocracy retained much of its traditional authority. The English continued to "love a lord" and to show respect and deference to the nobility. There was, Mayer concludes, never any movement in England to remove those feudal elements of the Old Regime: the crown, the royal courts, the House of Lords, or the public service nobility. Those continued to dominate much of political life, and the landed interest remained strong in the economic life of England.

Furthermore, an "active symbiosis" of the nobility and the bourgeoisie evolved. The bourgeoisie adopted the cultural norms, the symbols, traditions, and customs of the old elites. The middle class built country houses like those stately homes of the aristocrats. They sent their children to aristocratic schools, married into the aristocracy, and "excelled in emulation" of their social betters.

An example of this would be Herbert Henry Asquith, the first English prime minister to come out of a nonlanded family since Benjamin Disraeli. Although nominally a Liberal spokesman for the middle classes, Asquith was infected with a desire to emulate the aristocracy. He, like so many other of the middle class, became an enthusiastic supporter of aristocratic standards in the arts and in manners, and kept his distance from the contemporary currents of artistic and cultural modernism which the aristocracy disliked. While the nobility frequently opposed him politically, and frustrated or delayed his efforts at political reform, Asquith did not retaliate by tampering with the aristocratic possession of the highest offices in the diplomatic corps, the state, or the imperial bureaucracy.

It is to the matter of the emergence of modernist, or avant-garde artistic expression that Mayer devotes one of his longest chapters in the book. He speaks of "official high culture" standards in the arts of bulwarks against which the modernist waves beat in vain. The official high culture dictated the revival and reproduction of the venerable styles from the past: the electic revival in architecture, the Pre-Raphaelites in painting, religious works, historical epics, popular fables. These were familiar, and liked by the aristocracy, and so they formed the accepted and official artistic milieu.

Two musical composers upon which Mayer focuses are Richard Wagner and Richard Strauss. Wagner was a genuine stylistic innovator in the field of grand opera but, in content, his works were imbued with elitism and feudalism, stressing heroism, emotionalism, romanticism, and kingship. Catering to the wealthy educated aristocracy, Wagner's great opera house at Bayreuth became (in the words of the novelist Thomas Mann) a "musical Lourdes . . . a miraculous grotto for the voracious credulity of a decadent world."

Richard Strauss in his earlier compositions, such as *Elektra* and *Salome*, sought through vocal dissonance and psychological extremism to provide musical counterparts to the current Expressionistic style of painting. These avant-garde efforts met with such hostile receptions—*Salome* was banned in England—that Strauss capitulated and returned to the familiar conservative, superficial romantic presentations that the aristocracy liked with *Der Rosencavalier* (The Red Knight).

Nonobjective, avant-garde painting had perhaps its chief exponent in Wassily Kandinsky, who, although he abandoned traditional line and form, drew his inspiration from a distant, idealized past, and from the folk art and primitive art of the contemporary world. That Russian-German artist was, like many of the old aristocracy, repelled by the defilement of European society by industrialism and commercialism. His aim was to attain an intellectual expression of mystical or spiritual sensibilities, to be "like the disciples of early Christianity who found the strength for inner stillness amid the roaring noise of their time." Kandinsky believed that the masses were too dishonest and greedy to appreciate his works; that only the elite educated aristocracy could understand his "pure ideas."

Sharing a distaste for the masses and their thrust for power was a galaxy of so-called Social Darwinist writers. These contended that men were naturally unequal; therefore, social organization must always of necessity be structured hierarchically. Large segments of people must be kept subordinate, even uneducated, if high culture and learning were to thrive. Such views also constituted the essence of the writings of Friedrich Nietszche, the chief exponent of elitism in the nineteenth century. To Nietzsche, as to the Social Darwinists, the world is in a state of permanent struggle, not merely for survival, but for domination, exploitation, and subjugation of man by man. This Will to Power, as Nietszche saw it, should not be thought of as a merely physical strength or money power; rather, the highest expression of the power drive would be found in artists, philosophers, and intellectuals. These are the true aristocracy, and the rest of mankind should be subordinated so the "best people" may be free to preserve and pursue high culture.

These views were, of course, further undergirding for the claimed superiority of the aristocracy. They, and the intelligentsia, by the later nineteenth century saw all about them evidences of cultural decay and social and economic leveling which, they feared, would ultimately bring the end of high culture. Accordingly, they adhered more strongly to their traditions as a bulwark against the unwashed multitudes.

Mayer cites three royal figures as the epitomes of the resurgent ultraconservative elitism of the later nineteenth century and early twentieth century. Nicholas II, Emperor and Autocrat of All the Russias and the largest landholder in his realm, had received from his predecessors the motto "Autocracy, Orthodoxy, Nationality," all three of which he constantly sought to preserve and defend. Men of common birth were raised to noble rank by the emperor, and they became especially ardent champions of the old regime in Russia, resisting liberal or democratic ideas that might dilute the autocracy. Supported by the Church and the ultraconservatives, the prestige of the autocratic "Little Father" remained intact until the outbreak of World War I.

A second example of ultraconservative royalty was William II, ruler of Europe's mightiest nation, the German Empire. Like his cousin, Nicholas II, William was the largest landowner of his empire and the leading upholder of the traditional status quo. That "supreme and swaggering war lord" was also Europe's leading antimodernist in the arts. During his reign Germany became filled with replicas of classical artwork and heroic statuary whose purpose was to uplift the German people morally and spiritually by forcefully portraying virtue, beauty, honor.

The most extreme—almost a caricature—of ultraconservatism among the royalty of Europe was Archduke Francis Ferdinand, heir to the crown of Austria-Hungary. Mayer gives a long list of the Archduke's attitudes and proclivities: haughty, arrogant, proud, absolutist, fervent Catholic, antidemocratic, anticapitalist, antilibertarian, antisocialist, anti-Semite, anti-Slav, antimodernist. The army was his chief preoccupation and yet he was totally uninterested in new weapons and tactics, believing that the cavalry was still queen of battles.

It would, of course, be that very ultraconservative Francis Ferdinand whose assassination at Sarajevo in 1914 triggered the outbreak of World War I. The terrorist bullets that cut down the archduke were also directed at the ruling classes of Europe and their institutions, but that larger target was too diffused, too pervasive, and too entrenched to be brought down by a few terrorists. It took two world wars and enormous economic changes to finally bring down the Old Regime.

As the study of a large topic, *The Persistence of the Old Regime* has both strengths and weaknesses. Its chief value lies in the extensive delineation and illumination of its major thesis: the perseverance of the influence and standards of the European aristocracy. That thesis is not novel or original, but few historians have concentrated so thoroughly on the topic as Mayer does here, and he has seemingly researched extensively—his bibliography of works studied covers some sixteen pages.

On the other hand, the sources he uses are all secondary or tertiary materials, which, to the professional historian, do not provide the reliability and authenticity of primary sources. Added to that, Mayer gives no footnotes or documentation of the sources for his quotations or factual material, a practice probably intended to increase the book's appeal to the general reader but at the expense of the scholarly reader.

Indeed, it is hard to say what type of readership this book is directed, since it falls between popular history and a scholarly monograph. Futhermore, it is intentionally unbalanced in its presentation, ideologically slanted, and, worst of all, floridly overwritten.

*James W. Pringle*

### Sources for Further Study

*Choice.* XVIII, June, 1981, p. 1472.
*Critic.* XXXIX, July, 1981, p. 5.
*The Economist.* CCLXXX, August 29, 1981, p. 82.

*History: Reviews of New Books*. IX, August, 1981, p. 217.
*Library Journal*. CVI, February 15, 1981, p. 450.
*The New Republic*. CLXXXIV, April 11, 1981, p. 33.
*The New York Review of Books*. XXVIII, April 2, 1981, p. 19.
*Virginia Quarterly Review*. LVII, Autumn, 1981, p. 119.

# PERSONAL IMPRESSIONS

*Author:* Isaiah Berlin (1909-    )
Edited by Henry Hardy, with an Introduction by Noel Annan
*Publisher:* The Viking Press (New York). 219 pp. $13.95
*Type of work:* Essays

*A collection of tributes to and memories of a diverse gallery of distinguished persons*

This is the fourth volume of Sir Isaiah Berlin's collected essays, all carefully edited by Henry Hardy. His mastery of Russian intellectual history is shown by *Russian Thinkers* (1978), while his more general command of speculative philosophy dominates *Concepts and Categories* (1979) and *Against the Current* (1980). The present work consists of tributes to and memories of a diverse gallery of distinguished persons. It can be classified under three basic headings: men in public life (Winston Churchill, Franklin D. Roosevelt, Chaim Weizmann, Albert Einstein in his views toward Israel); academicians at or visitors to Oxford (L. B. Namier, Felix Frankfurter, Richard Pares, Hubert Henderson, J. L. Austin, J. P. Plamenatz, Maurice Bowra, Auberon Herbert) and writers (Aldous Huxley, and most vividly Boris Pasternak and Anna Akhmatova).

First, a summary of Berlin's impressive credentials: he is a polymathic thinker who taught social and political theory at Oxford from 1938 to 1967, then became President of Wolfson College there until 1975. He is President of the British Academy, and holds honorary degrees from and fellowships in universities of the United States, Israel, England, Scotland, and Wales. He may well be the greatest living exponent in the English-speaking world of the history of ideas.

In this collection, he is more relaxed and personal than when analyzing the concepts of Giambathsta Vico, Johann Gottfried Herder, Karl Marx, Aleksandr Herzen, or Mikhail Bakunin. With the exception of Roosevelt, Berlin is here describing intimates who have filled his own horizon. His tone is always appreciative and often empathic; his outlook is elegantly cosmopolitan and international; his generosity of feeling is notable: perhaps his only flaw is a disinclination to be severe with his subjects' shortcomings. He has a passion to praise, to admire heroes. Though his special love is for the life of the mind as led at Oxford, he can understand people quite different from himself in temperament and interests. He both professes and practices pluralism, mistrusting totalitarians and technocrats, advocating liberty, variety, honesty, and above all humanistic sympathy. His portraits are rendered in lively, precise, evocative prose.

In his essay on Franklin D. Roosevelt, Berlin concedes a few weaknesses—opportunism, occasional cynicism, mental laziness—but then sketches a glowing portrait of him that establishes criteria for the kind of person he most admires:

he was large-hearted and possessed horizons, imaginative sweep, understanding of the time in which he lived and of the direction of the great new forces at work in the twentieth century . . . he was in favour of life and movement, the promotion of the most generous possible fulfillment of the largest possible number of human wishes, and not in favour of caution and retrenchment and sitting still. Above all, he was absolutely fearless.

Churchill is compared and usually contrasted to Roosevelt: he was a great nineteenth century conservative with an eighteenth century prose style patterned after Edward Gibbon and Dr. Samuel Johnson, whereas Roosevelt was a twentieth century innovator who welcomed the future. Though both men are celebrated as lovers of life, Roosevelt is seen as far more optimistic, empirical, buoyant, improvisatory, while Churchill is more introverted, tradition-bound, romantic, broodingly aware of darkness as well as light. Berlin praises his countryman as a mythical hero who saved Britain in 1940 "not by catching the mood of his surroundings . . . but by being stubbornly impervious to it."

Berlin's passionate Zionism colors his eloquent profile of Chaim Weizmann, who was to become Israel's first President. He regards Weizmann as not only a great man but also a genius, the most gifted representative of a bourgeois Jewry semi-emancipated from the pietism of their ancestors, devoted to their families, socially realistic, stoic in the face of persecution, determined to achieve a democratic homeland in Palestine. Berlin loves Weizmann's imperturbable self-confidence, authority, charm, dignity, control, and refusal to indulge in self-pity or pathos. A lifelong Anglophile, Weizmann had to endure the slings and arrows of the pro-Arab British Foreign Office, particularly the "brutal ill-humor" of Ernest Bevin; he was also reviled for his gentlemanly ways by East European Jews of more militant persuasion; Britain's betrayal of the Balfour Declaration after World War II, wounded him in an irrecoverable manner. However, his consolation was of historic proportions:

He knew well that his achievement was without parallel. He knew that, unlike any man in modern history, he had created a nation and a state out of flotsam and jetsam of the diaspora, and had lived to see it develop an independent, unpredictable life of its own.

Albert Einstein had his differences with Weizmann and other Israeli statesmen, but remained a staunch Zionist. Berlin stresses the scientist's sad awareness of Judaism's rootlessness in the gentile-dominated communities of the West—hence the need of a national home that would restore Jews to psychic and social health. Paradoxically, Berlin demonstrates that Einstein, stressing man's needs for social ties, was himself a homeless, lonely individual who found intimate relationships extremely difficult.

Berlin is understandably more anecdotal and conversational in his portraits of Oxford colleagues. Here he is literally, emotionally, intellectually at home, rendering impressions that are fondly personal in line with the title of this book. He is warm toward all his subjects, bringing them alive with polished ease.

The most difficult candidate for Berlin's understanding and appreciation is the great historian Lewis Namier, notorious for his arrogance, intolerance, and quarrelsome nature. Berlin shows compassion for Namier's difficult family history and first marriage; respects his superb mind; sympathizes with his failure to obtain a Chair at Oxford; and insists that Namier's books elevated the standards of English historical scholarship for at least a generation. He stresses the contrast between Namier's brilliant intellectual gifts on the one hand, and his self-destructive bitterness and solitude on the other. Once, after Berlin had sent Namier an off-print of one of his lectures, Namier replied with this note: "You must indeed be a very clever man to understand what you write." Instead of taking offense, Berlin was delighted by the response, and relished reading it to his visitors.

Namier's approach to history was the opposite of Berlin's: he investigated individual lives in the most minute, *pointillist* detail, and was reluctant to undertake the wide syntheses and eclectic judgments that Berlin prefers. Berlin illuminates the origin of Namier's outlook by tracing it to the antimetaphysical, antiimpressionist positivism of Ernst Mach, Adolph Loos, Sigmund Freud, and the Vienna Circle of philosophers. He salutes his tortured, embattled colleague for his moral and intellectual integrity, his devotion to the highest scholarly standards, his unwillingness to curry favor with or appease any of his powerful enemies.

The longest, most personal and most moving essay is a fifty-two page account devoted largely to Berlin's meetings with the great poets Pasternak and Akhmatova in 1945 and 1956. Berlin sets the scene for the encounters by indicating his own love for the literature of his native Russia, which he left in 1919 as a ten-year-old lad. He paints a harrowing picture of the isolation, desolation, and persecution of Russian intellectuals and artists under the Soviet regime. The Great Purge of 1937-1938 particularly resulted in wild, indiscriminate, often anti-Semitic arrests and imprisonments of an extraordinarily talented group: Vladimir Mayakovsky committed suicide in despair; Osip Mandelstam, Vsevolod Meyerhold, Isaac Babel, and Boris Pilnyak were all killed in concentration camps; the poet Marina Tsvetaeva returned to the Soviet Union from France in 1939, ended her live in 1941. Informers, false witnesses, and forced confessions of implausible espionage abounded. At the beginning of World War II, "Russian literature, art and thought emerged like an area that had been subjected to a terrible bombardment, with some splendid buildings still relatively intact, but standing bare and solitary in a landscape of ruined and deserted streets." Pasternak and Akhmatova were probably the most splendid buildings left standing, though in a condition of anguish, living a form of internal exile.

In 1945, Berlin was attached to the British embassy in Moscow. He had

known Boris Pasternak's sisters in Oxford, and this gave him the pretext he
needed to see the writer in Peredelkino, an artist's village in the suburbs.
Berlin's memoir of their meetings is unforgettably vivid:

> He was once described by his friend the poetess Marina Tsvetaeva as looking like an Arab
> and his horse: he had a dark, melancholy, expressive, very *racé* face, now familiar from
> many photographs and his father's paintings; he spoke slowly, in a low tenor monotone,
> with a continuous, even sound, something between a humming and a drone, which those
> who met him almost always remarked; each vowel was elongated as if in some plaintive,
> lyrical aria in an opera by Tchaikovsky, but with more concentrated force and tension.

Pasternak spent much of his time rendering William Shakespeare into Russian, and was steeped in traditional Western literature and philosophy. He
particularly admired Marcel Proust and James Joyce among the moderns. He
showed his sense of intellectual isolation by telling Berlin: "We are like people
in Pompeii . . . buried by ashes in mid-sentence." In 1945, he had not heard
of Jean-Paul Sartre or Albert Camus; by 1956 he had read two of Sartre's
plays, but Camus had not been permitted publication in the Soviet Union,
being condemned as "reactionary and pro-Facist."

Berlin visited Pasternak frequently; they became intimates. The poet was
a confirmed Slavophile, in the tradition of Mikhail Lermontov, Lev Tolstoy
and Feodor Dostoevski, with a passionate attachment to the Russian soil.
Berlin believes this obsession might account for Pasternak's denial of his
Jewish origins. "He was unwilling to discuss the subject—he was not embar-
rassd by it, but he disliked it: he wished the Jews to assimilate, to disappear
as a people."

Many of their talks were, of course, devoted to discussing the victims of
Stalin's reign of terror. Berlin recounts a remarkable anecdote: in the late
1930's Pasternak received a phone call from Stalin himself, asking him whether
he had been present when his fellow-poet Mandelstam had recited a lampoon
about the dictator. Pasternak evaded a direct reply, instead urging Stalin to
grant him an audience, so they could "speak about matters of supreme
importance." Stalin repeated his question; Pasternak his answer. Then Stalin
replied, "'If I were Mandel'shtam's friend I should have known better how
to defend him'"—and put down the receiver. The episode preyed on Pasternak's mind for many years as he harrowed himself with self-accusations—
*would* another response by him have been more effective in saving his condemned fellow poet?

By 1956, when Pasternak and Berlin met again, "his estrangement from
his country's political order was complete. He could not speak of it . . .
without a shudder." He had completed *Dr. Zhivago* (1957); unable to get it
published in Russia, he risked imprisonment by assigning world rights of
distribution to an Italian publisher. He called the book "my last word, and
most important word, to the world." He wanted it to "travel over the entire

world, to 'lay waste with fire' (he quoted from Pushkin's famous poem *The Prophet*) 'the hearts of men.'"

Though Pasternak and Anna Akhmatova were good friends, they often disagreed in their literary judgments. Pasternak loved Tolstoy, but despised Dostoevski: "His novels are a dreadful mess, a mixture of chauvinism and hysterical religion." He also admired Anton Chekhov but was bored by Franz Kafka and Ernest Hemingway. Her preferences opposed his in all these instances. She was particularly negative about Chekhov: "his universe was uniformly drab; the sun never shone, no swords flashed, everything was covered by a horrible grey mist—Chekhov's world was a sea of mud with wretched human creatures caught in it helplessly."

Anna Akhmatova lived in Leningrad, and Berlin also looked her up in 1945; she was then an old, stately lady living in a single, poorly furnished room on the top floor of a magnificent late baroque building. In 1937-1938, both her second husband and son had been imprisoned—as well as Mandelstam, who had loved her and dedicated one of his most beautiful poems to her. Her first husband, the distinguished poet Lev Gumilev, had been executed some years earlier. She recited some of her greatest poems to Berlin; on their first meeting they talked through the night and until noon the next day. Like Pasternak, she preferred persecution and death in her own country to freedom and tranquillity abroad.

In January, 1946, Berlin left Russia. When he paid a farewell call to Akhmatova, she gave him a collection of her verse with a new poem inscribed on the flyleaf. It had been inspired by his long-lasting first visit, and was dedicated to him. Sadly, when the official edition was published later, the dedication to Berlin had to be omitted out of regard for Akhmatova's safety.

In 1956, when Berlin returned to Russia, she was unable to receive him: her son had been rearrested in 1946, and she was subject to furious attacks by Party hacks. In 1965, Akhmatova was allowed to receive an honorary degree at Oxford. She told Berlin then that the paranoid Stalin had been enraged by his 1945-1946 calls on her—Berlin worked for a foreign government, after all, and "all members of foreign embassies or missions were spies to Stalin." The day Berlin had left the Soviet Union (January 6, 1946), uniformed police were placed outside the entrance to her staircase, and a microphone was screwed into the ceiling of her room to terrorize her. Akhmatova went so far as to insist, in 1965, that "the mere fact of our meeting, had started the cold war and thereby changed the history of mankind." Thus does paranoia beget paranoia.

With all her sufferings, Akhmatova insisted on conducting herself like a royal princess, detesting people's pity, insisting to Berlin that her pride and dignity mattered more than others' compassion. She died soon after her Oxford visit. Concludes Berlin: "The widespread worship of her memory in the Soviet Union today, both as an artist and as an unsurrendering human being, has . . . no parallel." He adds that his friendship with Pasternak and Akhmatova "affected me profoundly and permanently changed my outlook." His homage to these great personages is a splendid climax to a collection of gracefully composed and luminously evocative essays. The tribute Berlin pays Felix Frankfurter when he came to Oxford fits the author with equal justice: "He liked whatever could be liked, omnivorously, and he greatly disliked having to dislike."

*Gerhard Brand*

### Sources for Further Study

*Christian Science Monitor*. LXXIII, March 9, 1981, p. B2.
*The Economist*. CCLXXVII, November 22, 1980, p. 116.
*History Today*. XXXI, January, 1981, p. 56.
*Library Journal*. CV, December 15, 1980, p. 2565.
*The New Republic*. CLXXXIV, January 31, 1981, p. 35.
*The New York Review of Books*. XXVIII, February 5, 1981, p. 4.
*The New York Times Book Review*. LXXXVI, February 8, 1981, p. 1.
*Newsweek*. LVI, February 9, 1981, p. 123.
*Saturday Review*. VIII, January, 1981, p. 75.
*Times Literary Supplement*. December 26, 1980, p. 1459.

# PHILOSOPHICAL EXPLANATIONS

*Author:* Robert Nozick (1938-    )
*Publisher:* The Belknap Press of Harvard University Press (Cambridge, Massachusetts). 764 pp. $25.00
*Type of work:* Philosophical essay

*An original and provocative exploration of epistemology and ethics*

This ambitious and lengthy work, alternating between high seriousness and brilliant levity, shuns what Robert Nozick calls "local vices" and celebrates "global virtues." With tough-mindedness, joy, and wit Nozick insists on the humanizing power of philosophical inquiry. An accomplished professor of philosophy at Harvard with a reputation for controversy—his *Anarchy, State and Utopia* (1974), which won a National Book Award, attacked social and political liberalism—Nozick's purpose in *Philosophical Explanations* is to pull philosophy out of the doldrums and reestablish its centrality for the life of the mind.

Respectful of science's narrow perspectives and tolerant of the reductive approaches of the social sciences, Nozick nevertheless feels that man must strive for "non-reductionist explanations" of the great problems of human existence. He uses "Explanations" in the title of his book to dramatize his avoidance of the limiting restrictions of "proofs." Leave proofs, he implies, to the logicians, scientists, psychologists, and anthropologists; "explanations" are closely connected to the actual experience of reality and although tentative often feed "understanding" more effectively than overly prescribed proofs which sacrifice understanding to theory. "Do I love truth less or love understanding more?," Nozick asks himself. Unsure, he covers his tracks by using this book to "fill the basket of philosophical views" on a variety of fundamental philosophical issues: "Does life have meaning? Are there objective eternal truths? Do we have free will? What is the nature of our identity as selves? Must our knowledge and understanding stay within fixed limits?"

To describe Nozick as "covering his tracks" is no idle colloquialism. "Tracking" is his avowed method for tracing the way the mind connects evidence to proof based on belief. He calls these "tracking conditions . . . subjunctive conditions" and in a brilliant chapter entitled "Knowledge and Skepticism" works out a carefully detailed argument, replete with symbolic logic and witty examples, to "explain" his idea of the way the mind "explains" truths to itself. Unable to refute the skeptic's "worries," Nozick sidesteps skepticism, which is overly focused on untracked facts, and stresses the "transitive" nature of the "tracking" mind.

In an early chapter, "The Identity of the Self," Nozick spells out the "closest continuer schema" for documenting the self's ability to deal with the process of changing identities. A conflation of the "closest continuer schema" and "tracking conditions" defines the heart of Nozick's approach throughout the length of his tome. It is an approach that encourages the general reader to follow Nozick through some intricate chapters studded with complex formulae far beyond the layman's understanding. Nozick seems to pull the reader along as he covers his *own* professional tracks; he does this in the ethical sense of the "pulling" or exemplary spirit discussed in his chapter on "Foundations of Ethics." One of the chief delights of this impressive book is the way it gives the student-reader the courage of his own questions and strengthens him in the hope that philosophy *can* be understood. The following passage demonstrates Nozick's trust in "tracking," even when it takes the form of a student's uninformed "gliding":

> My departmental colleagues are meticulous intellects who instill in students the importance of mastering all the details whereof they speak; while I think it important for students also to learn how (and when) to "fake" things, to glide over topics with a plausible patina, trusting (fallible) intuitions that something like what they say, something of that sort, can be worked out—preferably by someone else. I agree, of course, that sometimes gliding over the details shields one from seeing that one's general conception just cannot be worked out, and a very different one is needed. . . . On the other hand, often the details merely reinforce a picture, adding nothing of real philosophical interest. What then can one do but follow one's hunches?

The above calls attention to the essential quality of Nozick's book that has earned for him both praise and derision: its creative impressionism. Not only does his book invite the reader to "glide," but also Nozick himself often seems to soar above all the thorny issues he is raising; he does so with a trust in his own creative thinking that defies not only the restrictions of knowledge theory but also some of the oldest warnings of rationality, metaphysics, and what some have called the tragic sense of life.

Yet, in fairness to the author, one must remember that at the beginning of his work he insisted that his thinking be judged on the collective premises of an explanatory approach. What gives Nozick the confidence of his individualism ("Could I not rather be a star or the Messiah or God?") is *not* a naïve solipsism or egotism; on the contrary, his discovery, through the "tracking condition" of the explanatory power of the idea of "organic unity," subsumes self to "global virtue." To respond to the world is to discover its underlying unity: "Ethical action and more generally responsiveness to value is part of an even more general category that includes knowledge as well: responsive connection to the world . . . establishes a tight organic unity between us and the world."

Whereas traditional ethics and value theory stress rational principle as the guiding norm—Immanuel Kant's Categorial Imperative is the stellar example—Nozick calls *value* the result of a kind of "probability." Value flourishes when a person who is "making free decisions . . . ends up tracking bestness." Bestness, as a norm, is arrived at through what Nozick calls a form of "evolutionary selectiveness." Nozick makes sure that one cannot easily dismiss these ideas as determinism. He insists that "organicism" precludes any simple categorization of "determined or indetermined" forces; whatever gets one "tracking bestness" is in the service of a pursuit of value.

Nozick's equation of "value" with "organic unities" leads him to renewed conviction of the sanctity of the self. It was the self "tracking" its perceptions that enabled Nozick to combat skepticism, and it is the "pull" of the "value seeking I" in others that encourages Nozick's belief in the value of his own "being as I." Reality enables the self to become the greatest possible organic unity. A person, says Nozick, "must harmonize his own value and spiritual improvement while advancing the value and spiritual improvement of others."

Ultimately, the discovery of self leads to the richest enlightenment philosophy provides: insights into the "Meaning of Life." Why do people fear death more than they mourn their absence from the past that predates their birth? Why is immortality a future-directed fantasy? Because, suggests Nozick, people crave unlimited "possibilities." People cringe at death not because it cheats them of the future as time, but because "it limits the possibilities" that they can realize. Possibility captivates the imagination because it constantly expands and broadens capacities for increasing the "measure of the degree of organic unity . . . life brings to the realm of value." Because the "Humanities" pursue value more assiduously than other forms of knowing, Nozick gives them the highest marks for explaining the meaning of life. With the concept of "empathetic understanding," which echoes the doctrine of sympathetic imagination espoused by many Romantic poets and thinkers, Nozick brings together in the most impressive "organic unity" of his entire treatise the poles of his argument: Knowledge and Value.

Critics have accused Nozick of cosmic generalization—"global vices," as it were. They have also questioned the originality of his enterprise: philosophy has always done more explaining than proving. While all these criticisms are not without foundation, Nozick's conviction that "reductionism" in thinking is not always worth the verifiable "truths" it settles for cannot be dismissed. This, it would seem, is a point more than worth making in a world increasingly more fragmented by perceptions (such as Deconstructionist literary criticism) that feed on the destruction of hard-won organic unities in culture and society as well as in epistemology, ethics, and the arts.

*Peter Brier*

### Sources for Further Study

*American Spectator.* XV, January, 1982, p. 32.
*Book World.* XI, October 18, 1981, p. 10.

*Commonweal.* CIX, January 15, 1982, p. 24.
*Library Journal.* CVI, November 1, 1981, p. 2142.
*The New Republic.* CLXXXV, October 7, 1981, p. 32.
*The New York Review of Books.* XXIX, February 18, 1982, p. 32.
*The New York Times Book Review.* LXXXVI, September 20, 1981, p. 7.
*Village Voice Literary Supplement.* October, 1981, p. 13.

# PIONEER WOMEN
## Voices from the Kansas Frontier

*Author:* Joanna L. Stratton (1954-    )
Introduction by Arthur M. Schlesinger, Jr.
*Publisher:* Simon and Schuster (New York). Illustrated. 319 pp. $16.95
*Type of work:* History
*Time:* 1850-1912
*Locale:* Kansas

*An account of the lives of the women who settled Kansas, described chiefly in their own words*

Historian Arthur M. Schlesinger, Jr., observes in his Preface to this book, "Women have constituted the most spectacular casualty of traditional history." Because their activities have generally been confined to the private rather than the public sphere, their contributions have often been dismissed as negligible. One woman who was determined to rectify this neglect of the achievements of her sex was Lilla Day Monroe, the first woman licensed to practice law before the Kansas Supreme Court. During the 1920's, she collected more than eight hundred accounts of life on the Kansas frontier written by women settlers and their descendents. She planned to publish the narratives as a tribute to the pioneer women's "hardihood, perseverance, devotion, and ingenuity in making the best of everything," but she died with her project incomplete. Monroe's manuscripts remained in her daughter's attic until 1975, when her great-granddaughter, Joanna Stratton, then an undergraduate at Harvard, rediscovered them and began the process of weaving them together into a coherent whole.

Stratton's rich assortment of primary sources offered her several options. She could follow Lilla Day Monroe's original plan and publish an anthology; she could use the narratives as the basis for a chronological survey of women's role in the settlement of the state; or she could select and order her materials to illustrate many different aspects of the lives of her writers. The third option is the one she chose. She incorporates excerpts from dozens of the narratives to describe the arrival of the early settlers, the major obstacles that faced them, the patterns of family and community life, and their involvement in the larger conflicts of the nation—the Civil War and the temperance and suffrage movements.

Stratton's decision to blend her primary sources into her own survey of life on the frontier gives her book considerable appeal for a wide nonspecialist audience. Her approach is limiting in some ways, however. First, because most of the excerpts are little more than a page long, the reader has little opportunity to develop a sense of the individual voices and personalities of the writers. Second, without a clear chronological framework, it is difficult to visualize how families moved from the very primitive conditions described in the first chapters to the comparative comfort of town life pictured later. Stratton acknowledges the limitations of her method in her Foreword, describing her book as "a personal account of the pioneer experience, described by those for whom 'history' was nothing more than daily life." What emerges from this work is not a set of portraits of striking individuals, but rather a composite picture of representative pioneer women, strong, courageous, resourceful, and compassionate.

The pioneer women needed strength and courage to face the conditions that met them when they left their homes in the East. One of the early immigrants, Carrie Sterns Smith, left a wry account of sharing a stagecoach, first with a dirty, nauseated child, then with a pungent bundle of freshly-tanned leather. She finally took refuge on the outside seat with the driver. Mrs. Henry Inman set out more luxuriously on the Union Pacific Railroad but found herself stranded in a blizzard for two days with a carload of men. Many other settlers arrived in the prairie schooners, covered wagons large enough to carry their household goods. Illness and accident marred their journeys, too. One poignant passage recounts the death of a young girl after she was kicked by a wagon horse as she returned from an evening stroll to her family's campsite.

If the women reached their destinations safely, they faced another challenge—to make a pleasant home out of the log cabin, dugout, or sod house provided for them. There were drawbacks to each of these structures. The log cabins, even with newspapers covering the walls, offered little resistance to winter winds. The dugouts hollowed out of hillsides were subject to flooding in heavy rains, and their dirt roofs were not deterrent to snakes. The sod houses, with two-foot earthen walls, provided effective insulation against the parching heat and bitter cold of the Kansas climate but also left settlers at the mercy of the rains. Yet, while more than one woman is described as weeping at the first sight of her new home, most seem to have succeeded in creating a measure of comfort with their modest possessions. Emma Hill wrote of her cabin, "It had a dirt floor and a dirt roof, but I tacked muslin overhead and put down lots of hay and spread rag carpet on the floor. I put the tool chest, the trunks, the goods box made into a cupboard and the beds all around the wall to hold down the carpet . . . we were real cozy and comfortable."

Nature provided the greatest difficulties for the pioneers. It seems almost unbelievable that any family was able to survive, much less prosper, in the succession of blizzards, droughts, floods, prairie fires, and plagues of insects described so vividly by the women and girls who endured them. The women took their places beside the men as they struggled along ropes in deep snowdrifts to feed the livestock, beat out spreading fires with wet grain sacks, and labored unsuccessfully to shield their garden vegetables from a "storm of grasshoppers."

The pioneers frequently had to struggle against man as well as nature. Indians posed a constant threat. While some were friendly if unnerving in their predilection for wandering into homes uninvited and exploring every nook and cranny, others stole, kidnaped, and murdered settlers. Even more widespread brutality grew out of the conflict between pro-slavery and anti-slavery forces in the years immediately before and during the Civil War. The horror of this period is clearly conveyed in the recollections of three women who lived through it. John Brown's niece, Emma Adair, wrote of the raid in which Brown's son and numerous others were killed and the town of Osawatomie almost totally destroyed. Ann Julia Soule and Lavina Gates Chapman witnessed and later described the burning of the town of Lawrence, another abolitionist stronghold, and the massacre of most of its male inhabitants by the forces of the notorious William Quantrill, a Confederate sympathizer.

Even in those rare periods without crises of natural or human origin, the pioneer woman had to exercise skill and fortitude if her family was to survive. Stratton includes many passages describing daily activities: growing and preserving food; gathering wood or buffalo chips for fuel; weaving and dying fabrics for clothing; making soap and hauling water for doing laundry. With professional medical help hundreds of miles away from most settlements, women learned to deliver babies, treat attacks of malaria, stitch wounds, even reattach scalps of Indian victims from time to time. Amy Loucks, who had learned medical skills from her physician brother and her own reading, treated ailments and injuries in the area around Lakin in the 1880's. Her son later described some of her activities:

> One time a posse summoned her to treat a badly wounded prisoner. With a small vial of carbolic acid as an antiseptic, a knitting needle as a probe and a pair of common pincers, she removed the bullet and saved the man's life. At another time, with a razor as a lance and her embroidery scissors, she once removed three fingers from the crushed hand of a railroad brakeman.

Over and over again the writers refer to the dependence of the settlers on each other for both practical help and emotional support. It is to this community of spirit that the women refer when they comment that difficult as life was on the frontier, "there were also compensations for the brave, joyous, determined pioneer." They learned through poverty and scarcity to appreciate the simplest objects—the dried fruit and the rag doll in the Christmas stocking, the fireworks on the Fourth of July, the white flour for special baking. Far from cities, they created their own amusements, and Stratton quotes a number of accounts of festive meals, dances, picnics, and evenings spent reading aloud or singing around a precious piano imported from the East.

Even in the earliest days of the settlement of the state, women's responsibilities extended beyond their homes and families. As Stratton points out, school systems did not develop until late in the nineteenth century, and before then, each community had to find and support its own teachers. Since these teachers often received little compensation beyond room and board in the home of a pupil, the positions were apt to go to young women, some of them no more than fifteen or sixteen. Their supplies consisted of whatever materials they could collect:

> There were histories from Illinois, spellers and writing books from Iowa, readers from St. Louis city schools, and even some old blue-backed spellers. . . . True, there was not a suspension globe for explaining mathematical geography, but an apple and a ball did very well.

The clarity and freshness of the memoirs quoted throughout the book suggest that the schools did their jobs well in spite of their limited resources and inexperienced instructors.

The church, too, depended upon the energies of women for many of its activities. Early congregations, generally Protestant and often interdenominational, met in homes, schoolrooms, stores, or even railroad depots. They were usually served by circuit-riding ministers whose visits called for a flurry of cleaning, and the baking of golden-brown bread, marble cake, gingerbread, and pies of half a dozen varieties. In addition to cleaning and cooking before services, women taught Sunday School, provided music, looked after the needy, and raised money for buildings. Not all of their efforts were equally constructive; Stratton quotes a remarkable passage written by a staunch Presbyterian who was adamantly opposed to raising funds for her new church building with a dance. She prayed that the structure would be blown down before it could be so desecrated, and she saw her prayer answered by windstorms, not once but twice.

It was natural that women so accustomed to taking active roles in their homes and their communities should become leaders in public movements. In Kansas, as in the eastern states, the temperance issue early aroused wide support among them, for it was perceived as a moral cause that directly affected the stability of home and family. Through the efforts of a strong Woman's Christian Temperance Union and other groups, Kansas passed a prohibition amendment, the first in the country, in 1880.

Kansas women were early involved in the movement for women's suffrage as well. Lucy Stone, Henry Blackwell, Susan B. Anthony, and Elizabeth Cady Stanton campaigned extensively in the state for the women's suffrage amendment that was presented in 1867 along with one guaranteeing the vote to black men. The exhilaration and exhaustion of working for this temporarily unsuccessful cause are evident in a long selection written by the Reverend Olympia Brown, an ordained minister of the Universalist Church, who traveled by horse and buggy around the state into areas where "to lose our way became almost a daily experience." Although the amendment was defeated, suffrage activity was revived in the 1880's, and in 1887 women were granted the right to vote and hold office in municipalities. By 1900, at least fifteen women had served as mayors. In 1912, Kansas became the eighth state to ratify a women's suffrage amendment—testimony to the initiative and capabilities of the women whose contributions to the state are so graphically demonstrated in this book.

Perhaps it is a mark of the success of Stratton's work that she leaves her reader wanting to know much more about these women whose words she quotes. What happened to young Lillie Marcks, who watched in horror as grasshoppers smothered the fires set to destroy them? To Mrs. A. S. Lecleve, who put her two small children in the care of the family dog and then delivered her third baby unassisted? To Ann Julia Soule, the schoolteacher who hid with her family on an island during the Osawatomie raid? How did families make the transition from dugout to frame house, from near starvation to small town society? This book and others like it make clear the need for a generation of social historians to analyze and evaluate the contributions of women to the development of the United States.

*Elizabeth Johnston Lipscomb*

## Sources for Further Study

*American West*. XVIII, July, 1981, p. 64.
*The Atlantic Monthly*. CCXLVII, April, 1981, p. 126.
*Choice*. XVIII, June, 1981, p. 1478.
*Christian Science Monitor*. LXXIII, April 15, 1981, p. 17.
*Library Journal*. CVI, March 1, 1981, p. 557.
*The New York Times Book Review*. LXXXVI, March 8, 1981, p. 7.
*The New Yorker*. LVII, May 4, 1981, p. 169.
*Newsweek*. XCVII, March 16, 1981, p. 88.
*Virginia Quarterly Review*. LVII, Summer, 1981, p. 88.

# PRACTICING HISTORY
## Selected Essays

*Author:* Barbara W. Tuchman (1912-    )
*Publisher:* Alfred A. Knopf (New York). 306 pp. $16.50
*Type of work:* Essays
*Time:* 1936-1981
*Locale:* The United States, Europe, Israel, Japan, and China

*A collection of essays spanning the career of Barbara Tuchman and attempting to focus on the topic of "practicing history"*

One of the most distinguished writers and historians in contemporary America is Barbara W. Tuchman. Who can forget the fast-paced mystery-storylike *The Zimmerman Telegram* (1958), with its complex description of the events leading to United States entry into World War I? *The Proud Tower* (1966) described an era of plenitude, Western society at the height of cultural and intellectual development, a generation in the midst of affluence and dedicated to a belief in progress. All of this was to be destroyed by the tragedy that befell the West and undermined its value system in World War I. The scope and nature of that tragedy were described with much of the intricacy and power of Leo Tolstoy's *War and Peace* (1865-1869) in Tuchman's *The Guns of August* (1962). Moving to biography, Tuchman's *Stilwell and the American Experience in China* (1971) portrayed General Joseph Stilwell and the context in which he functioned—the Sino-American relationship. *The Distant Mirror* (1978) sought to reflect contemporary life in the complex cultural matrix of the high Middle Ages. It succeeded magnificently both in conveying portraits, colors, and flavors of that time and in suggesting the correspondence with the twentieth century promised by the title. Any one of these works would have made a reputation for a historian. To have written all of them means that Tuchman is definitely an outstanding historian.

Celebrity as a writer and scholar imposes certain responsibilities and obligations both on writers and on their publishers. Tuchman's publisher evidently has concluded that her public requires a larger measure of information about the author than has been made available through her historical volumes. Rather than mandating a new publication, Alfred A. Knopf decided to patch together a collection of Tuchman's journalistic essays from 1936 to 1981, with no representative writings from the 1940's or the early 1950's. The result is a book entitled *Practicing History*.

The essays that make up *Practicing History* no doubt accomplish what the publisher intended—they give insight into a side of Tuchman that her historical volumes do not convey. These essays, rather than being scholarly papers designed for inclusion in the dusty, dull journals that only academic historians cherish and bother to read, were designed for such semipopular publications as *The Nation, The New York Times Book Review, The Atlantic Monthly,*

*Newsday*, *The New York Times*, *Harper's Magazine*, and others. Some of the essays were addresses given at commencements or other fairly significant occasions. These essays, designed for a literate, thoughtful, reasonably well-read audience, reveal literacy, reflection, a catholicity of interests, and breadth, rather than profoundity or concern about the technical and historiographical problems of the professional historian. For this reason the essays manifest good writing style, well-turned phrases, wit, and charm. Many are a delight to dip into and the reader goes away refreshed from interaction with a mind that is as bright and pleasantly entertaining as an after-dinner chat. This is, in fact, the purpose of most of the essays and speeches that make up *Practicing History*. They *are* designed to be pleasantly entertaining for the literate and they succeed admirably in this objective.

Beautifully conveying a public side of Barbara Tuchman, these essays are not intended to reveal anything more than they do. Yet, in addressing the very important, the awesome problem and responsibility of *Practicing History*, one might hope, one might seek, one might appropriately expect. . . . What of the innermost heart of the historian—the deep recesses of her historical soul, her commitment to her profession, and her philosophy of the meaning and nature of history? Directions are suggested, hints offered, the surface is skimmed, but this fulfillment remains incomplete. It is perhaps unfair to want more than an author and a publisher attempt, but despite many fine qualities, *Practicing History* leaves the reader somewhat unsatisfied and with many questions that the author has not answered.

What the author has done is much to be commended. *Practicing History* is divided into three parts: "The Craft," "The Yield," and "Learning from History." These sections are not chronologically organized. Something should therefore be said of Tuchman's career. Having been graduated from college in 1933, she accepted a volunteer post for the American Council of the Institute of Pacific Relations, an organization of countries bordering on the Pacific Ocean. Headquartered in Tokyo, Tuchman traveled to Europe in 1935 and published for a fee her first article in *Pacific Affairs*. Her experience in Tokyo eventuated in a 1936 article in *Foreign Affairs*. In that same year, she went to work for *The Nation*, which her father had purchased. Tuchman's career having been launched, she represented *The Nation* as a reporter during the Spanish Civil War and remained in Europe after 1937. Returning to the United States in 1938, the news of the defeat of the Spanish Republic, Tuchman says, "cracked [her] heart," "replaced [her] illusions with recognition of *realpolitik*," and "was the beginning of adulthood."

Marrying in 1940, Tuchman bore a child in 1941 and took a position with the Office of War Information in 1943. In that capacity, she began an interest in General Stilwell that led to her study of *Stilwell and the American Experience in China* (1971). The major events of the 1950's were the birth of two additional children and the production of two books, *Bible and Sword* (1956)

and *The Zimmerman Telegram* (1958). The 1960's brought extended journalistic efforts, the publication of *The Guns of August* (1962) and *The Proud
Tower* (1966), and much public recognition as a fine historian. That recognition grew in the 1970's with the publication of the Stilwell book (1971) and
*A Distant Mirror: The Calamitous 14th Century* (1978). Always a journalist
and historian, Tuchman has remained acutely aware of the need to write for
a popular audience and has been one of the profession s most skillful practitioners of the art of good writing. Although Tuchman, herself, questions
whether she has produced a philosophy—"I am rather afraid of philosophies"—she has remained deeply wedded to the importance of writing.

While avoiding philosophy, practicing writing over a lifetime has, in her
view, conveyed "certain principles and guidelines" relating to history. These
"principles and guidelines" represent the foci of the essays that make up
*Practicing History*. Tuchman believes that accident plays an enormous part
in history. She speaks of human conduct "as a steady stream running through
endless fields of changing circumstances." She discusses "good and bad always
co-existing and inextricably mixed in periods as in people." She raises the
spectre "of cross-currents and counter-currents usually present to contradict
too-easy generalizations." Given these views, which could generate flights of
speculation, Tuchman insists that evidence should precede theses, that chronology yields cause and effect and *"wie es eigentlich gewesen,"* and that historians should attempt to avoid their own biases, prejudices, and frames of
reference. Advocating such principles, like supporting virtue, belabors the
obvious. All of these principles, as well as the philosophical view that, in the
words of Sir Charles Oman, the great military historian, "The human record
is illogical . . . and history is a series of happenings with no inevitability about
it," may be seen in Tuchman's 1963 Phi Beta Kappa address at Radcliffe
College. In that essay, Tuchman articulated a view that she has consistently
practiced in her books: "To write history so as to enthrall the reader and
make the subject as captivating and exciting to him as it is to me has been
my goal. . . ."

These principles were reiterated in a series of essays entitled, "When Does
History Happen?" (1964), "History by the Ounce" (1965), "The Historian as
Artist" (1966), "The Historian's Opportunity" (1967), "Problems in Writing
the Biography of General Stilwell" (1971), "The Houses of Research" (1972),
and "Biography as a Prism of History" (1978). These essays are pleasant to
read and consider, but they do not develop their themes significantly. The
essays are literate, well-written, nicely designed for the popular audiences to
which they were directed, and highly repetitious.

A series of essays reflecting Tuchman's views on a variety of important
issues that have arisen during her lifetime are much more varied and interesting for the reader of *Practicing History* than the essays on practicing history.
The only problem here is that these issues mostly reflect Tuchman the jour-

nalist and not Tuchman the historian. Since about two-thirds of *Practicing History* is made up of essays of this sort, the title of the book is misleading, if not inappropriate. Moreover, these writings are not illustrative of Tuchman's historical "principles and guidelines." Once the reader becomes aware of this fact, the reader may forget the principles and read these essays for insight into the opinions of Tuchman the journalist.

Tuchman's 1936 article on "Japan: A Clinical Note," correctly observed that Americans must become sensitive to Japanese views and concerns. These include the concept of "face," the ability to avoid Western consistencies, the fear of inequality, sensitivity to racism, and the use of different tactics from those employed in the West. Tuchman conveyed an understanding of some intellectual and psychological qualities in the Japanese that Western diplomats should consider.

Tuchman's essay of 1937, "What Madrid Reads," was an interesting analysis of the intellectual currents abroad in Madrid in the midst of the Spanish Civil War. She conveyed a fascinating portrait of the way that intellectual life persisted in spite of the ideological differences of the opposing sides in the Civil War and was, in fact, more important than the war: "A year of siege and shells has shattered the surface of life, but underneath the old wheels are still turning."

In "Israel: Land of Unlimited Possibilities" (1967), Tuchman wrote a lengthy and detailed description and analysis of the problems and potential of Israel after almost twenty years of its national existence. Impressed as she was with Israel's potential, Tuchman described the emergence of a new society in Israel. In "Israel's Swift Sword" (1967), Tuchman provided a detailed description of the Israeli Defense Forces. That description provided an explanation of Israel's military victory in the Six-Day War of 1967.

Tuchman's review in 1979 of Henry A. Kissinger's *Kissinger: Self-Portrait* commented on Kissinger's creative approach to Middle-Eastern Diplomacy. Kissinger, however, was severely taken to task for his policies in regard to Vietnam. Tuchman concluded that "The four years of additional death and devastation were a waste." That Kissinger did not recognize this meant, for Tuchman, a lack of comprehension. This interpretation of Kissinger is consistent with Tuchman's essay "Vietnam: When, Why, and How to Get Out" (1968). In this essay, written during the last year of the Johnson Administration and before Kissinger had taken office, Tuchman argued that the United States should simply declare its objectives met in Vietnam and leave. The American involvement should "be closed down." Two additional essays on Vietnam indicate Tuchman's concern with and involvement in this issue.

The only other issue on which Tuchman reacted significantly, as she did on Vietnam, was Watergate. Four articles were written on the presidency from February, 1973, through September, 1974. Reflecting on the problems of the presidency as demonstrated in the Watergate events, Tuchman, in "Should

We Abolish the Presidency," "A Fear of the Remedy," "A Letter to the House of Representatives," and "Defusing the Presidency," concluded that the presidency of the United States should be abolished and a cabinet system of government should be created to replace it. Only then could the potential abuses of this branch of government be avoided.

The opinions of Tuchman on Vietnam and the presidency are interesting, but they are not historical narrative, have nothing to do with the problem of *Practicing History*, and have little to do even with the journalistic reporting that is well illustrated in the articles on Japan, Spain, and Israel.

It is clear from an analysis of Barbara Tuchman's *Practicing History* that the essays which make up the book fall into three categories: (1) discussions of the "principles and guidelines" of historical writing; (2) journalistic description; and (3) opinions on current events. While the journalistic descriptions and opinions might help the reader to understand a complex woman, they contribute nothing to the problem of writing history. The "principles and guidelines," although embodied in interesting essays, are so general and repetitious that they contribute little to an understanding of the writing of history. How then is one to view *Practicing History*? The literate, pleasant essays that make up this book provide insight into the writing, thinking, and opinions of Barbara Tuchman and not into the art of *Practicing History*. They should be read, but—lacking historical substance—they represent a curious contrast to the important volumes on which Tuchman's reputation as a historian is built.

*Saul Lerner*

### Sources for Further Study

*The Atlantic Monthly*. CCXLVIII, October, 1981, p. 106.
*Business Week*. October 26, 1981, p. 10.
*Christian Century*. XCVIII, November 11, 1981, p. 1169.
*Christian Science Monitor*. LXXIII, October 14, 1981, p. B3.
*Library Journal*. CVI, August, 1981, p. 1539.
*The New Republic*. CLXXXV, October 21, 1981, p. 37.
*The New York Times Book Review*. LXXXVI, September 27, 1981, p. 7.
*Smithsonian*. XII, December, 1981, p. 192.
*Village Voice*. XXVI, September 30, 1981, p. 39.
*The Wall Street Journal*. CXCVIII, October 26, 1981, p. 26.

# THE PRESENCE OF FORD MADOX FORD
## A Memorial Volume of Essays, Poems, and Memoirs

*Editor:* Sondra J. Stang
*Publisher:* University of Pennsylvania Press (Philadelphia). 245 pp. $20.00
*Type of work:* Critical essays and memoirs

*Selected critical essays and memoirs treating Ford Madox Ford (1873-1939), with several brief, previously unpublished writings by Ford including a tale, a sonnet, letters, and an essay on women's suffrage*

To do justice by Ford Madox Ford—that has been a chief obligation of literary critics since 1939, when the author died largely ignored by scholars and the reading public alike. As early as 1939, Granville Hicks in *Bookman* had described Ford as "a neglected contemporary." For the next two decades his reputation as a major figure among twentieth century English novelists languished, except for an occasional reevaluation in the journals. Not until 1951, with the impetus of Mark Schorer's perceptive Introduction to *The Good Soldier* in a paperback reprint, would Ford's position among his distinguished contemporaries move forward, perhaps slightly back of the front-line of James Joyce, D. H. Lawrence, and Joseph Conrad, but certainly to the fore of other English writers whose reputations had been established before the 1930's. To compensate for his long period of neglect, critics by the score—Richard A. Cassell, John A. Meixner, Paul Wiley, Kenneth Young, to mention several prominent names—have since examined in meticulous detail the complexities of Ford's fiction, and several fine biographies, most notably Arthur Mizener's and Frank MacShane's, have attempted to adjust in a proper perspective the difficult psychological questions concerning Ford's life. Through this considerable critical industry on a twentieth century writer one central theme may be understood: to separate from his perceived psychological and moral limitations as a human being Ford's genius as a man of letters.

In *The Presence of Ford Madox Ford*, Sondra J. Stang has addressed this problem directly. Most of the critical essays that she has collected for the volume and, above all, the memoirs she has commissioned from intimates of Ford, attempt to capture the elusive "presence" of the man. The most valuable of these pieces, brief appreciations by Jenny Bradley, Caroline Gordon, Julia M. Loewe, Robert Lowell, Mary McIntosh, Wally Tworkov, and Janice Biala, examine Ford's character from a variety of subjective points of view, so that a reader's impressions of the writer are bound to be influenced favorably.

Why should any present-day admirer of Ford, the author of masterworks such as *The Good Soldier* (1915) and the four-volume *Parade's End* (1924-1928), the editor of *Transatlantic Review*, the discoverer and promoter of many literary talents, need to recapture the artist's presence? Or put another way: what aspects of his presence have not already been defined by Ford's autobiography *It Was the Nightingale* (1933) or by the more recent exhaustive biographies?

The answer to the first question is that justice to Ford demands a closer look at the writer's alleged psychological deficiencies. By his contemporaries, Ford was often perceived as a superior artist but a dangerous friend: a liar, backbiter, megalomaniac, betrayer. These charges are serious, mostly false, and terribly demeaning. In a more relaxed age of literary nitpicking, other prominent Edwardian writers squabbled publicly with certain of their contemporaries. Somerset Maugham travestied Hugh Walpole (*Cakes and Ale*, 1930); Frank Harris, Arnold Bennett, and George Moore wrote and spoke unkindly about fellow writers. The tone of their quoted remarks or published memoirs was generally peevish rather than truly malicious, gossipy instead of mean-spirited. Compared to these and other indiscreet Edwardians, Ford perhaps stood out as especially offensive because his pronouncements were often theatrical; he loved an audience, loved to play the role of literary master hectoring dim-witted neophytes, and above all he loved to turn a clever or memorable phrase.

Unfortunately for the writer's reputation, some of his offensive phrases were too well remembered, were passed around in literary circles to end up slightly altered with a seemingly malicious sting. So it was that Ford, in his real nature generous to friends, especially to writers down in their luck, was calumniated as a spiteful, envious, bumptious cad. Worse, his predilection for telling stories in a theatrical, amusingly embellished fashion earned him the reputation of a liar. It was this charge that stuck for the next generation, one far less relaxed, of writers such as Ezra Pound and Ernest Hemingway, who regarded Ford as a poseur or a bumpkin. Added to Ford's indiscretions in speaking with candor but not always good common sense about fellow writers, his physical unattractiveness marked him quite undeservedly as an object of ridicule. In time, the image of his comical-disgusting mannerisms tended to blur a true picture of his presence familiar to friends and loved ones. It is this presence, in justice to Ford and in respect of the sense of fair play, that Stang offers the reader.

Unlike many other memorial volumes that provide appreciative rather than genuinely critical essays, Stang's collection of tributes, for the most part, adds in significant ways to a contemporary understanding of Ford. To be sure, the two introductory essays by Graham Greene, as well as poems by Richard Howard ("Homage") and Howard Nemerov ("Remembering Ford Madox Ford and *Parade's End*"), are merely commemorative. Similarly, Allan Tate's fine piece, "Ford Madox Ford," is a composite of several short essays written on several occasions and reconstructed as an appreciation. The other essays, however, were commissioned especially for the volume or, in the separate case of David Dow Harvey's contribution, "Ford and the Critics," had been composed earlier but had never previously been published. Among the more impressive essays are Denis Donoghue's "Listening to the Saddest Story," Roger Sale's "Ford's Coming of Age: *The Good Soldier* and *Parade's End*," and William Gass's "The Neglect of *The Fifth Queen*."

In addition to these critical studies, Stang has also collected several previously unpublished writings by Ford. Appended to Alison Lurie's essay on Ford's fairy tales for children is a brief story, "The Other," reprinted from a typed manuscript of the Ford holdings at Cornell University. Less interesting is one of his impromptu sonnets, quoted in Mary McIntosh's memoir. Edward Naumburg, Jr., also contributes several unpublished items, letters to and from Ford, as well as an early version of a chapter from *Some Do Not* (1924). Finally, Naumburg includes in his essay, "A Collector Looks at Ford Again," a 1912 contribution to a symposium on women's suffrage, a brief piece never before noted by Ford's bibliographers.

In the second, perhaps more useful part of the book, Stang has collected a group of new or previously unpublished memoirs by individuals who knew Ford at different periods of his life. Among the contributors are Ford's daughter, Julia Madox Loewe; Janice Biala, the companion of his later years; Caroline Gordon, who first met Ford when she was twenty-seven years old; Robert Lowell, who met Ford in 1937 and had sharp and affectionate recollections of the novelist's facility in public speaking; Mary McIntosh, who knew Ford well in the 1930's and described him as "probably the most generous person I have ever known, with the greatest of all generosities, the giving of himself"; and Wally Tworkov, who was eighteen when he first met Biala and Ford in 1934, and remembered the master's consideration for other, lesser writers. Tworkov quotes Ford as describing himself: "I am an old man mad about writing."

Only one memoir is bound to disappoint admirers of Ford. Jean Rhys, listed among the contributors in this section of the volume, actually declines to speak at length about Ford because, as she explains in a letter to the editor (1978), she is writing an autobiography that will express a full account of him. Nevertheless, she mentions Ford's "great generosity to young writers." To compensate for the brevity of these remarks, most readers will appreciate the historically significant and fuller memoirs by Janice Biala. In 1961 she prepared tapes for a broadcast of WBAI in New York City, "Memories of Ford Madox Ford"; and in 1979 she consented to be interviewed in Paris. Without sentimentality, Biala summarizes Ford's life as "a battlefield . . . he died a lonely and terrible death." Yet as an intimate of Ford for nine years, her judgments are especially trustworthy when she reports on "his gaiety, his confidence, his optimism, his wild sense of humor."

Assembling the materials for this volume, Stang has obviously enjoyed her dedication to the task. In addition to writing a helpful introduction, she provides a Foreword by William Trevor and an Afterword by Edward Crankshaw. Frank MacShane's affectionate essay, "Two Such Silver Currents," may be considered another postscript. Stang also includes a chronological list of Ford's books, a compilation of his books still in print, and a fascinating group of photographs showing the master at different stages of his life. Taken as a whole, *The Presence of Ford Madox Ford* offers impressive, often touching new information about the writer. Previously, Ford biographers have gone far to reconstruct his character from spiteful gossip and envy, but the evidence from this volume supports a much more favorable assessment of the man as sane-tempered, kindly, playful, conscientious, sensitive, and loyal. Those who knew him best, loved him. For them his presence endures. Stang and her contributors have helped to capture for modern readers of Ford the essence of his life as an artist.

*Leslie Mittleman*

### Sources for Further Study

*The New York Times Book Review.* LXXXVI, May 17, 1981, p. 11.
*Times Literary Supplement.* December 25, 1981, p. 1504.

# RABBIT IS RICH

*Author:* John Updike (1932-    )
*Publisher:* Alfred A. Knopf (New York). 467 pp. $15.00
*Type of work:* Novel
*Time:* 1977
*Locale:* Brewer, Pennsylvania

*The third novel in the chronicles of Harry (Rabbit) Angstrom, this book explores the conflicts—both internal and social—that Harry faces now that he has reached middle age*

Principal characters:
> HARRY (RABBIT) ANGSTROM, a middle-aged Toyota agency owner and manager
> JANICE ANGSTROM, his wife
> NELSON ANGSTROM, his son
> BESSIE SPRINGER, Janice's mother
> CHARLIE STAVROS, Harry's sales manager at the Toyota agency
> MELANIE, Nelson's girl friend from California
> RONNIE HARRISON, Harry's friend
> RUTH BYER, Harry's former mistress

To make the everyday lives of ordinary people interesting requires a special talent and skill. A temptation for a novelist when writing about the mundane affairs of ordinary existence is to color the action, trying to make it appear more dramatic than it actually is. Writers often prefer to portray extreme situations and to focus on the crises and dramatic encounters in life, rather than revealing the hidden emotions behind the apparently even surfaces of most lives. John Updike always has been especially effective when prying beneath this veneer and exposing the frustrations and pains all people carry beneath their social masks. In *Rabbit Is Rich*, his third book in the chronicles of the life and times of Rabbit Angstrom, he is near the top of his form.

*Rabbit, Run*'s (1960) gangling basketball hero unable to cope with real life, who became a middle-class man grasping for his soul in *Rabbit Redux* (1971) a decade later, now is an overweight, middle-aged Toyota dealer, financially successful, but still seeking the peace and satisfaction that American life is supposed to provide but which always seem to be withheld. Not a complicated man, he is willing to settle back and accept the material success that life finally has blessed him with, but events conspire to keep him from enjoying his complacency. With this book, Rabbit Angstrom's place in literary history as an American Everyman is secure.

America is suffering from double-digit inflation; the energy crisis is mounting; Skylab may fall on his head and kill him in his sleep—anything can happen—but basically Rabbit is an optimist. He wants to believe in the future, both his own future and his son's future. He finds it difficult to accept the gloomy prophecies of the pontificators around him. Despite the newspapers and television, despite the pressures of trying to survive in an often violent and frightening world, Rabbit has been able to isolate himself from much of what goes on in this world. Only when his son, Nelson, returns to Brewer and the family circle does Rabbit discover to what degree he has managed to insulate himself.

*Rabbit Is Rich* is, more than anything else, a novel of father and son, a novel of the perennial generational conflict that is always with us. Each generation reacts against the world in its own way, and that way more often than not is incomprehensible to the generations that preceded it. One generation's revolution may turn out to be the conservatism or passivity of another generation. Instinctively resisting the ties of family and responsibility, Rabbit found it very difficult to settle down when he was young. He craved freedom, adventure, change. Only after two decades of confusion and struggle has he finally been able to find satisfaction in the middle-class comforts and security that he has been told repeatedly he ought to cherish and accept as his destiny. His son, now a young man, sees the world from the opposite point of view. Nelson matured during the chaotic, turbulent 1960's and 1970's, and now is quite ready to settle down, assume a position in the small-business community, and grow fat and contented just as generations before him have. Rabbit cannot understand how a young man such as Nelson can be ready to give up the freedom and lack of responsibilities of young manhood in order to embrace a premature middle age.

On no level do Nelson and Rabbit agree. When Nelson returns to Brewer after dropping out of Kent State College and spending time in a Colorado commune, Rabbit is curious about his son, more than anything else, but soon he is appalled by the limp, complacent figure that he sees his son has become. Ripe for a mid-life crisis, Rabbit is catapulted into a bout of genuine self-analysis and personal confrontation by this prolonged, painful battle with his son.

Rabbit Angstrom, from his first appearance in 1960, has been a fundamentally decent, somewhat limited man who feels yearnings that he cannot wholly explain. Part of his agony is a deeply felt hunger for a meaning to his existence. Although no philosopher, Rabbit has an existential need for a reason to his life. He tries to find this meaning in marriage, in parenthood, in materialism, as he once—briefly—found it in basketball and in the well-being of a perfectly-tuned, athletic young body, but every reason that he grasps now crumbles in his fist. He survives by virtue of his own, inherent, good nature, but he will die with that gnawing in his gut still unsatisfied.

The action of the novel is neither unusual nor thrilling; the characters are not bizarre or remarkable. Through the skillful weaving of incident and revelation of character, Updike manages to present in *Rabbit Is Rich* nothing less than the "state of the union" of America in 1979. Within the apparently casual style and structure of the book—as chatty and apparently haphazard as everyday life—are collected the acutely perceived and accurately rendered details that can expose an entire civilization.

No one in this book is evil or deliberately menacing; no one sets out to hurt anybody else. Yet, old wounds are reopened and new injuries are inflicted. The reader cares about these unremarkable individuals and their pains, because in their precisely rendered individuality they assume an appealing universality.

When Nelson Angstrom appears on Rabbit's doorstep with his vegetarian girl friend, he has no intention of precipitating a conflict with his father, but what happens is inevitable. The two men can never hope to communicate; their perceptions of the world are too different for them to be able to find a common ground on which to begin. Nelson and Melanie automatically criticize their elders for their middle-class life of consumption and materialism, without stopping to consider if they are fundamentally any different. Each generation confronts the other dogmatically, certain that it must have the true answers.

None of these people are intellectuals. They pick up slogans, catch-phrases, ideas that are in the air, and accept them or challenge them without examining them. Melanie and Nelson are sincere when they express disgust with American middle-class materialism, but they cannot see that, in their own ways, they are quite as materialistic as the individuals they are so easily condemning.

From his own point of view, Rabbit cannot understand why his son is running. He, twenty years ago, ran, too, but in a different direction. Where he ran away from both home and responsibilities, Nelson now is running back home, seeking borders, fences, reponsibilities, all of the limitations that spell out security. At the same time, Rabbit is shocked by the selfishness of the younger generation, as represented in his son. Nelson cannot see why Rabbit should not fire his long-time sales manager, Charlie Stavros, and replace him with Nelson. Despite their complaints, life has been easy for Nelson and his generation. They have not faced the material disadvantages of a depression or world war; if they have gone hungry, it was from choice, a statement against or for a system of beliefs. Reared for the most part by indulgent parents, they are accustomed to receiving whatever they need or want without working for it. Rabbit now looks at this grown man who is the product of his own carelessness and is unsure how to cope with him. All he knows is that his son is not the man that he would have liked him to be.

The statement that John Updike makes with *Rabbit Is Rich* is both sobering and touching. By not pointing fingers or assigning blame, he emphasizes the pitiful quality in his characters, people who are not important enough or extreme enough to be tragic. One cannot look up to them or seek to emulate them; all one can do is see one's own flaws magnified sufficiently to become grotesque. While one does care about Rabbit and his family, one also finds them slightly boring. These are people one would avoid in real life, just as one tries to avoid the drunk with his endless stories of a failed love-life or disastrous business dealings.

*Rabbit Is Rich* does not contain the atmosphere of dread, the sense of despair, that dignified the plight and the hero in *Rabbit, Run*. The ordinariness of life is not raised to the level of intensity that Updike achieved in the earlier novel. The pain in that first novel of the series was almost unendurable. With *Rabbit Is Rich* the pain becomes dull and nagging, a mediocre sort of agony, worthy of only mediocre souls. Even the sexy parts of *Rabbit Is Rich* seem washed out and tired compared to similar passages in the first book. Rabbit Angstrom once had a soul that was in danger, but which was worth fighting to save; now, his soul has been sold, bit by bit, until what remains is compromised and indifferent, its struggles far less than earth-shaking. The awe one once felt for Rabbit has become a quiet nodding of the head: Yes, one says, as one reads about his plight in this current book, this is how it is—isn't that too bad? Impressive, in a way, but not the reaction caused by a masterpiece.

The weakening of power reflected in this book can probably be attributed to its style. Updike's prose here is more casual than in most of his books, sometimes almost pedestrian, and the dialogue is less tight and sharp than the dialogue he has created in the past. The writing often seems slightly blurred, as if he were rushing to cram as much into it as possible, just to make certain that he did not leave out anything that might conceivably be important.

Less perfectly structured than *Rabbit, Run*, *Rabbit Is Rich* achieves much of its power through a piling up of detail in the manner of John O'Hara. The earlier book was both more simple in its structure and more selective and poetic in its style. *Rabbit, Run* ascended to an almost tragic note, but *Rabbit Is Rich* concludes with a feeling of well-fed satisfaction. The questions that Rabbit asks are more or less answered; and, if some of them are not answered, they are evaded sufficiently to allow him to get on with his life. After all, he only lives once and he might as well make his peace with the imperfections of existence and make the best of his situation. While this attitude may be pragmatic, it is not the message of first-rate literature. The final taste that this book leaves one with—and this is in spite of some very real virtues—is both bland and bitter, rather like a custard that has gone off.

If John Updike decides, after another decade, to update his chronicles of Rabbit Angstrom, continuing his portrait of life in America during the second half of the twentieth century, he would do well to tighten his grip on his subject matter. Even a flabby character, if worth writing about at all, deserves a taut portrayal. Rabbit may, in the end, be a truly tragic American hero, a figure not much less appealing and important than Willy Loman, but Updike must make up his mind that his hero, for all of his flaws, is a man with a soul worth losing—or saving. Compromise simply defeats both hero and author.

*Bruce D. Reeves*

## Sources for Further Study

*The Atlantic Monthly*. CCXLVIII, October, 1981, p.94.
*Commentary*. LXXII, October, 1981, p. 72.
*Commonweal*. CVIII, November 6, 1981, p. 624.
*Library Journal*. CVI, July, 1981, p. 1445.
*Nation*. CCXXXIII, November 7, 1981, p. 477.
*The New Republic*. CLXXXV, September 30, 1981, p. 30.
*The New York Review of Books*. XXVIII, November 19, 1981, p. 3.
*The New York Times Book Review*. LXXXVI, September 27, 1981, p. 1.
*The New Yorker*. LVII, November 9, 1981, p. 201.
*Psychology Today*. XV, October, 1981, p. 110.

# THE RED COAL

*Author:* Gerald Stern (1925-    )
*Publisher:* Houghton Mifflin Company (Boston). 87 pp. $12.95
*Type of work:* Poetry

*In these eighty-six poems, Gerald Stern retains the mood of celebration which marked* Lucky Life *(the 1977 Lamont Poetry Selection), but the poems look back more frequently and they look more closely at the darker side of experience*

*Lucky Life* and *The Red Coal* confirm that Gerald Stern ranks among the dozen or so most important American poets at work today. Stern's voice, consistent but varied, bears repetition, for his poems achieve intensity without self-consciousness, generality without moralizing. He shares the anagogical vision of such writers as Joseph Conrad and Flannery O'Connor, for whom objects and images, the things of the world, are significant in themselves, not because the writer has contrived to render them symbolically. Nothing Stern observes appears trivial, for the poems are meditations upon his experience, not raw reportage.

Stern's meditations in *The Red Coal* arise from a love affair with the world as enormous as Walt Whitman's but less self-congratulatory. The "I" of Stern's poems neither seems to insist upon itself nor to get lost in swirling catalogs, possibly because Stern's poems effectively integrate the perceiver in the drama of his perception. Invariably, Stern is *in* his poems, even when the first-person pronoun does not appear. The poet does not use his experience to make poems so much as he dwells upon his experience to see what he may learn from it about the business of living and dying.

For Gerald Stern, what the world judges success came late; hence, his two major books reflect a maturing and distilling process. The poems lack the anger, despair, and ecstasy characteristic of youth; they give instead reflection and the kind of cautious introspection of a man who long ago learned that telling everything obscures what matters. Stern no more wishes to impress with a tour de force performance than he wishes to titillate with confession or awe with erudition. With such a poet, one can no more point to mistakes of judgment, lapses of power, than one can plot stages of development. One can only enjoy and single out the best poems for praise.

Stern's title poem recalls his friendship with fellow poet Jack Gilbert (*Views of Jeopardy*, 1962), particularly their stay in Paris in 1950. Gilbert might well have been thinking of a poet such as Stern in the final lines of a poem called "The Abnormal Is Not Courage," for he speaks of "The beauty/ That is of many days. Steady and clear." Courage, he says, "is the normal excellence, of long accomplishment."

Several of Stern's poems celebrate past periods in the poet's life, but perhaps none so tellingly as "The Red Coal," which looks back to the spring of 1950 when Stern walked "with Jack Gilbert down the wide sidewalks" of Paris, "thinking of Hart Crane and Apollinaire." The poem tells that Stern saved a photograph "of the two of us" from a time "before the burning coal entered my life" and "put it beside the one of Pound and Williams" because he "wanted to see what coals had done/ to their lives too." Now, apparently, "the coal has taken over" and "we are at its mercy." What Stern and his friend Gilbert needed was knowledge, "and now," Stern writes, "we have that knowledge. We have that knowledge." Still, the knowledge brings no joy but tears, and the tears are "what we bring back to the/ darkness . . ./ what, all along, the red coal had/ in store for us. . . ."

Like most of Stern's poems, "The Red Coal" involves continuity, for Stern places himself and Gilbert in a succession of modern poets—Guillaume Apollinaire and Hart Crane, Ezra Pound and William Carlos Williams, the circumstances of whose lives enrich the poem. Apollinaire and Crane died young, the one a victim of World War I, the other a suicide. Perhaps no two persons did so much to shape the literary sensibilities of the present as Pound and Williams, whom Stern imagines as aging men "looking into the sun,/ 40,000 wrinkles between them,/ the suffering finally taking over their lives." Although Stern recognizes that the tears "are what we bring back to the darkness," he continues to think life is lucky. He remarks how lucky he and Gilbert were to live in New York, and he thinks "how we carry the future with us."

That theme, too, seems central to Stern, whose poems regularly imply the extent to which the past still lives. If the red coal signifies a burning out, that burning arises from living meaningfully and it leaves traces for the future. Just as Stern ended *Lucky Life* with a poem called "Something New," thus suggesting that the end of the book was also a beginning, so *The Red Coal* ends with a poem which emphasizes the on-goingness of life. "Here I am Walking" is one of the poems in *The Red Coal* which involves looking back, taking stock. "This is something different," Stern writes, "than it was even five years ago"—the time *Lucky Life* appeared. "I have a second past to rake over," he continues, ". . . another 2,000 miles of seashore/ to account for," an allusion to images in the earlier book. Stern ends the poem and the book with the prediction that he will be just where he was twenty-five years ago, doing various things including "breathing in salt" and "living in dreams,/ finding a way to change, or sweeten my clumsy life." The idea may not be new, but few poets have expressed it at once so familiarly and so evocatively. Life changes, but not from failure to success; rather, as circumstances change, the essentials recur and demand that people sweeten their clumsy lives.

Stern's opening poem "The Faces I Love" pairs with the concluding poem to sum up the book's fundamental meanings. At first glance, "The Faces I Love" seems a poem of resignation, of ending, for it opens "Once and for all I will lie down here like a dead man," but, by the opening line of stanza three, the poem's meaning takes a brighter turn: "In the end my stillness will save me." The apparent gains of stillness are small ("I will have my own chair"), but they allow the poet to examine himself and "to look back in amazement at what I did/ and cry aloud for two more years, for four more years." Stillness enables the poet to remember the faces, recall the names, "to put them back together—/ the names I can't forget, the faces I love."

"The Faces I Love" demonstrates Stern's ability without loss of poetic intensity to incorporate and summarize the texture of contemporary life in a short poem. When he lies down like a dead man, he says he will let the Socialists "walk over my face," the Fascists "crawl through my veins," the Krishnas "poison me with their terrible saffron." The poem invigorates the abstract by associating it with palpable concretions, as when Stern says he will let "dishonor rise from me like steam." In the midst of what appears nightmarish, Stern writes that the leopard "will walk away from me in boredom/ and trot after something living. . . ." The leopard's boredom and its trotting lift it from the realm of symbol and make it terribly real. Other mundane images serve the same purpose: in the end, rather than gaining abstract salvation, the poet will have his own chair. He will "pull down the blinds" and watch his "nose and mouth/ in the blistered glass." Thus, the poet surprises the reader with juxtapositions of the physical and the spiritual in preparation for the task of putting back together "the names I can't forget, the faces I love."

Stern is able to write deeply personal poems precisely because he recognizes the line between the confessional and the general. One does not feel that Stern is compelled to tell his secrets, or that he seeks to disguise the personal by imposing literary tricks. Instead, one feels that his imagination clothes the initial poetic impulse in the dramatic concretions of shared experience. Quick turns of thought, intrusions of startling imagery, then, do not call attention to themselves; instead, they delight, and, in doing so, they add up to a fuller understanding of a situation or frame of mind. The poems permit ready generalization, and they lose nothing because their meanings are clear, even obvious.

Some poems ("Rotten Angel" and "The Shirt Poem," for example) begin with surprise. Few adjectives sit so ill, at first glance, with *angel* as *rotten*, but reading the poem proves it the perfect word, for Stern again yokes the spiritual with the purely physical in a poem expressing his desire to be connected "with life as long as possible . . . to disappear slowly,/ as gruesome as that sounds." The poem's opening line thrusts the reader into Stern's special real/unreal world: "My friend, still of this world, follow me to the bottom of the river/ tripping over roots and cutting themselves on the dry grass." The friends drink beer and cry; they are "a little bored" by Stern's death "and a little tired of the flies and sad ritual." The desire in "Rotten Angel" to disintegrate slowly is to allow time for those "who want to see me in my own light/ and get an idea of how I made my own connections" to do so. The poem ends with a wonderful catalog of experiences those friends might see, culminating with a very physical "angel" gasping and dipping his head in the water "to escape the gnats/ swarming after him in the dirty sunlight/ a million miles from his New York and his Baltimore and his Boston."

The opening of "The Shirt Poem" is equally surreal: the shirts are "screaming from their hangers, crying for blood and money." Later, the "shirts are howling and snapping." The shirts, not seen for ten years, grieve the loss of "the dream of brotherhood" and "the affectionate meeting/ of thinkers and workers inside a rented hall." The poem is an elegy of lost idealism, recollected not in tranquillity but in guilt "for the rich life" Stern now lives and for the sins of the nation summed up in "the enormous budget and the bureaucracy and the/ permanent army."

Whimsically and savagely, Stern frees the shirts from their dark closet to stand as witnesses, and he asks that his poem be given to Rabbi Kook, who sang songs "against death in all three languages" and to Sigismundo Malatesta "who believed in/ the perfect world and lived in it . . . always seeing the heart/ and what it wanted, the beautiful cramped heart." Stern says he is writing about the past "because there was/ still affection left then, and other sorrows."

"The Shirt Poem" and others in *The Red Coal* distinguish Stern from many of his contemporaries, for whom the well-made poem has become an end in itself. Not content to "make poems," Stern writes with passion about what matters most. In "A Hundred Years From Now," he imagines himself trying to explain the spirit of America "behind our banality, or devotion/ to the ugly and our suicidal urges." He affirms that "the eternal is also here,/ only the way to it is brutal." He ends a truly remarkable poem, "Your Animal," with the statement "—It is my poem against the starving heart./ It is my victory over meanness." A poem such as "These Birds," in which all but two lines open with the words "as if," invites the reader to consider the difference between a fully human life and the kind most people live—and that without ever turning away from the announced subject of "These Birds."

Technically, Gerald Stern remains as impeccable as he was in *Lucky Life*, but the gains of time, the deepening of his confidence, have allowed him to risk even more in *The Red Coal*, giving readers a set of poems at once emotional and restrained. The best poems in *The Red Coal* deserve ranking with the work of writers such as Robert Penn Warren, whose seasoned poems belong not to an age but to the ages. A single poem, "The War Against the Jews," is adequate to warrant including Stern among the august, for it demonstrates both his engagement and his objectivity. With pain but without rancor, Stern invokes (without naming it) the Nazi war machine through observation of wooden figures "going to their death." The toys move beneath an "iron clock," at once part of the toyland scene and suggestive of time's inexorable finality. One wooden figure, "carved while he still could remember his mother's garden," summons up the pathos of the wasted youth of Germany without denying the dehumanizing effect of their mission on the soldiers. The personal and the mythic combine to accommodate the horrors of the holocaust as part of this century's lived experience. The poet "would give anything" to break into the scene he describes and to scream, "Stop! It's a dream! It's a dream!"

Stern would appeal to victims and to victimizers: "Go back to your shuls. Go back to your mother's garden. O wooden figures, go back, go back," but there is no going back. What is past is carried along toward the future, these poems assert, and, with that wisdom, the poems also provide sufficient hope to continue growing somewhere.

*Leon V. Driskell*

### Sources for Further Study

*Book World*. XI, July 5, 1981, p. 10.
*Booklist*. LXXVII, April 15, 1981, p. 1135.
*Georgia Review*. XXXV, Winter, 1981, p. 874.
*Library Journal*. CVI, March 15, 1981, p. 664.
*The New York Times Book Review*. LXXXVI, May 10, 1981, p. 12.
*Poet Lore*. LXXVI, Autumn, 1981, p. 179.

# REINHARD HEYDRICH
## A Biography

*Author:* Günther Deschner (1941-  )
Translated from the German by Sandra Bance, Brenda Woods, and David Ball
*Publisher:* Stein and Day (New York). Illustrated. 351 pp. $18.95
*Type of work:* Biography
*Time:* 1904-1942
*Locale:* Germany

*The life story of a major figure in Nazi Germany, head of the Gestapo, the SS Security Service, and the chief executive officer for the "final solution to the Jewish question"*

> *Principal personages:*
> REINHARD HEYDRICH, second in command of Hitler's SS
> LINA VON OSTEN HEYDRICH, his wife
> HEINRICH HIMMLER, Reichsführer of the SS
> ADOLF HITLER, Chancellor and Führer of Germany, 1933-1945

When Reinhard Heydrich was assassinated on May 27, 1942, by agents of the Czech government in exile, Günther Deschner was only a year old. As a child too young to remember such events, he grew up and was educated in postwar, American-dominated West Germany. He earned the Ph.D. and went from success to success in the world of West German publishing and journalism. His biography of one of the most powerful and most feared members of the Nazi hierarchy was published in West Germany in 1977 and appears here in an English translation without any additions or revisions for the American reader. It is significant not only for the information it offers on the history of the Third Reich, but also as one example of the way in which popular historians in postwar West Germany are dealing with their country's past.

Deschner's approach is evident from his opening sentence: None of the major figures of the Third Reich, he writes, was "more enigmatic" or "more controversial" than Heydrich. He was a "historical giant" whose career paralleled the rise of Hitler's empire to brief hegemony. As head of the SS intelligence service (called the SD) and of the German secret state police (called the Gestapo) he literally had the power of life and death over millions. Adolf Eichmann transported Europe's Jews to their deaths at his order. Czechoslovakia was pacified under this "protection." He was a skilled amateur violinist and a model husband and father, whose widow is still loyal to his memory. He was called "Hitler's most evil henchman" by the British, and Hitler himself called him the "man with the iron heart." Yet the Czech press under the Prague Protectorate of 1942, the author pointedly notes, hailed him as the "darling of the Czech workers." This "conflict of opinions," writes Deschner, presents a difficult challenge for a historian. Deschner's overall thesis—the key to solving the enigma he poses—is that Heydrich was simply "a technocrat *par excellence*," a man without any basic ideology. He was scornful of the "old fighters" of the Nazi Party and even of the "dogmas and phantasies" of his immediate superior in the hierarchy, Heinrich Himmler. He was driven not by the hates and desires of the true believer, but by the restless urge of a perfectionist of power. He emerges, concludes Deschner, as "one of those technocratic geniuses" whose goodness or evil depends on the nature of the tasks put before them.

Deschner does not avoid mention of the terrible actions taken at Heydrich's commands. He admits that Heydrich was "partially responsible" for the killings during the purge of June, 1934, "the night of the long knives," as well as for the large-scale detentions in concentration camps of Germans suspected of anti-Nazi opinions and activities during the mid-1930's. He recognizes Heydrich's role in the faked "Polish attack" on Germany territory used to justify the start of World War II. He briefly and dispassionately describes the mass shootings of Jews and other individuals carried out by Heydrich's *Einsatzgruppen* in 1941. He reports the Wannsee Conference of January, 1942, at which the "final solution of the Jewish problem" was laid out by Heydrich before the top echelons of the German government. He recounts the draconian measures taken by Heydrich to emasculate Czech resistance when he was sent to Prague to pacify the "Protectorate of Bohemia and Moravia" in late 1941. The facts of the Nazi crimes and Heydrich's part in them are clearly stated. Deschner is not part of that perversely dedicated group of self-styled revisionists which is attempting to prove that the Holocaust never took place. Indeed, though he is critical of the Nuremberg Trials in general, he agrees that had Heydrich survived to stand trial there, he would certainly have deserved to have been convicted and executed.

Nevertheless, the reader is led again and again to an implied conclusion that Heydrich was really not such a bad fellow after all. He was forced out of his naval career with little justification on a matter of personal honor, and he was more or less "trapped" into his job with the SS intelligence service by chance and by his own ambition. If he had any real political hates, they were directed against the Roman Catholic Church (though he had been reared a Catholic) because of its "quasi-totalitarian" claims and its "Jesuitism." Anti-Semitism was far less important to him. In his own view, the Jews deserved to be expelled from Europe, but genocide was not his chosen instrument; forced emigration from Europe was his preference, and mass murder was only undertaken when emigration was rendered impossible by the exigencies of war. The policy did not "win from him any degree of approval." When given the chance to take control of Bohemia, he was pleased to get a "fresh start" so that he would no longer have to serve in the unpleasant role of "dustbin" for the Reich.

In Prague, Heydrich could play his role as an enlightened technocrat, parceling out harsh but evenhanded justice, even while giving material concessions and demonstrative recognition to those Czech workers who willingly accepted his leadership. He would be "the Führer's Wallenstein," re-creating the role of the great general of the Thirty Years War. He was assassinated just as his administrative policies in Bohemia were beginning to bear fruit. His assassins did not even represent the indigenous Czech underground, Deschner argues: they were agents parachuted in from London as a provocation to the leaders of the Reich. Thus the "martyr of Prague," too proud to travel under heavy guard like the "Party grandpas," met his end. The retaliatory shootings and the destruction of the town of Lidice were unjustified, Deschner admits, since there was no credible evidence of the involvement of that town in the assassination, but Alexander the Great, after all, had behaved with equal ruthlessness toward Thebes when it had revolted against his role. Thus Heydrich's policy of renouncing "blind terror" in favor of "graduated, selective intimidation" was abandoned just when it had begun to succeed. The Czechs could not directly retaliate while German power remained intact, but after 1945 they exploded, creating what Deschner calls "a blood bath among Bohemian Germans."

This biography is more complete, better documented, and more attractively presented than the other English language works devoted to Heydrich, those by Charles Wighton (1962) and by G. S. Graber (1980). For example, Deschner quite properly corrects the widespread misapprehension that Heydrich had Jews in his family tree, basing his account on the well-documented work by the Israeli historian, Shlomo Aronson (1971). Still, Deschner's book is fatally flawed. First, the English language edition has numerous minor translation errors, and it ignores the major questions raised about Heydrich and his role by David Irving and other authors in the four years between the German and English editions.

Second, and more important, the general approach of the author will leave serious scholars with many questions unanswered and it may well mislead the casual reader about the nature of Heydrich and the operations he headed. To be specific: Deschner uncritically accepts the reminiscences of Lina von Osten Heydrich, Reinhard's widow, about the private life and political attitudes of his subject. Readers may be amused at the anecdote of the SA (Brownshirt) leader Ernst Röhm lighting his cigar with an exploding trick match during the early days of Heydrich's service with the SS, and be touched by the domesticity of the rough and ready Brownshirt leader standing as the godfather of the Heydrichs' first son, but nowhere does Deschner examine in detail the role of Heydrich in the 1934 plots against Röhm which led to the cold-blooded shooting of Röhm and hundreds of other German political leaders as old scores were settled and Himmler's and Heydrich's SS solidified its control over the state. Readers are urged to be sympathetic with the hardworking young administrator, who was forced to contend with increasing burdens of office as his power increased, but nowhere does Deschner examine the role Heydrich played in developing the policy goals he sought to imple-

ment, such as the annhilation of European Jewry. Argumentation and documents published by David Irving in 1977 strongly suggest that Heydrich was
far more than a bureaucratic instrument of policies made by others. Deschner,
to be sure, did not have Irving's book before him when he wrote, but the
same documents were available on microfilm to both men, and they were in
personal contact with each other as Deschner's acknowledgments show; one
is led to the conclusion that either Deschner was relatively uninterested in
this matter, or that his research was inadequate to his task.

Deschner's thesis that Heydrich was a technocrat without ideology is partly
correct: the man seems to have been devoted to an ambitious pursuit of
excellence in all that he did, and in more normal times he might well have
spent his ruthless energy and ability on more constructive tasks, perhaps as
a police officer or a corporate executive, and died a generally unlamented
but locally prominent person. Yet the contention that he was without ideology
is hardly convincing. Much of his energy, even as late as December, 1940,
was taken up defending himself against "the slander" that he was of partially
Jewish ancestry. Deschner admits that he had "a complex" on the subject,
yet fails to draw the conclusion that this "complex" was related to his intense
desire to destroy European Jewry. Instead, Deschner concludes that he was
"caught in the trap of the Jewish question" and that "he suffered unspeakably
because of it."

Deschner's contention that Heydrich is controversial makes sense only if
one is willing to take the assertions of the Nazi-controlled Czech press and
Heydrich's apparently unreconstructed widow at face value. Otherwise the
record of injustice, death, and destruction which flowed from his deeds is
about as clear as it can be. It is true that Heydrich was a complex individual,
capable of artistic sensitivity as a violinist, of loyalty to his family, and of feats
of administrative excellence. Like many other Nazis, great and small, he had
numerous private virtues; any biography should no doubt point these out. It
is seriously misleading, however, to dwell upon them while virtually ignoring
the multitude of sufferings which were caused by his policies. The reader of
this biography gets no view of the sufferings of the concentration and death
camps, but is treated to a chapter on Heydrich's sportsmanship as a fencer.
The selection of photographs, with Reinhard in immaculate uniform or
relaxing with his comrades or his family, reinforces this oddly unbalanced
picture.

It is unjust to blame the West Germans of today for the sins of their fathers;
few of them in the 1980's are old enough to have held positions of power or
authority in the Third Reich. Yet the shadow of the Nazi past necessarily
looms behind them. Some react with a radical pacifism exhibited in the many
variations of the "ban the bomb" demonstrations. Others retreat into the
apolitical delights of today's affluence or the hedonistic subculture of sex and
drugs. A very few emerge as defenders of the national socialist past. Dr.

Günther Deschner, one must conclude from his study of Reinhard Heydrich, would fit into none of those categories. He seems to be honestly striving to come to grips with his country's history, searching for some kind of balance which would approach the unbiased truth. It is regrettable that he fails, particularly since a number of other West German authors, such as Karl Dietrich Bracher, Ralf Dahrendorf, and Heinz Höhne, have shown that such balance is indeed attainable.

It seems odd to assert that such a despicable individual as Reinhard Heydrich deserves a better biography, but if *he* does not deserve it, the reading public definitely does.

*Gordon R. Mork*

### Sources for Further Study

*Library Journal*. CVI, December 15, 1981, p. 2386.
*Publishers Weekly*. CCXX, November 13, 1981, p. 79.

# REINHART'S WOMEN

*Author:* Thomas Berger (1924-    )
*Publisher:* Delacorte Press/Seymour Lawrence (New York). 295 pp. $13.95
*Type of work:* Novel
*Time:* The present
*Locale:* A small city in Ohio

*The fourth novel about Carlo Reinhart, a perennial failure who finally finds success*

Principal characters:
> CARLO REINHART, a middle-aged cooking enthusiast
> WINONA REINHART, his daughter
> BLAINE REINHART, his son
> GENEVIEVE REINHART, his ex-wife
> GRACE GREENWOOD, Winona's lover
> EDIE MULHOUSE, Carlo's neighbor
> HELEN CLAYTON, his coworker
> RAYMOND MAINWARING (BROTHER VALENTINE), a commune leader
> MERCER REINHART, Blaine's wife
> TOBY and PARKER, their sons

Carlo Reinhart is one of the most likable characters in American fiction, a naïve, idealistic, lovable loser. Because Thomas Berger is perhaps the least sentimental of major American novelists, Reinhart is never too good, is always completely believable as a middle-aged, Middle American failure who sees almost everything about his past as superior to almost everything in his present. Although Reinhart may find traditional values in places where they may occur only superficially, such as in 1940's war movies, he is far from being a rigid traditionalist. When his beloved daughter Winona is discovered to be a lesbian, Reinhart is not taken aback, although "abnormal" sex has always been repugnant to him. Reinhart realizes he lives in a changing world, and *Reinhart's Women*, the fourth Reinhart novel, shows how he is unable and, eventually, unwilling to insulate himself from this world.

Berger first presented Reinhart in *Crazy in Berlin* (1958) as a naïve young soldier dealing with black marketeers and spies in occupied Berlin. (Throughout *Reinhart's Women*, he refers to his army days as the happiest of his life.) In *Reinhart in Love* (1962), he settles down in postwar America to marry and start a family, only to become the innocent accomplice in the real-estate swindles of his employer. Reinhart has failed as businessman, husband, and father in *Vital Parts* (1970) and also fails to fit in with the rebellious spirit of the 1960's.

*Vital Parts* ends with Reinhart's fat, complacent teenage daughter saving him from death with her uncritical love. *Reinhart's Women* opens a decade later with the new slender Winona a beautiful model and the sole support of her fifty-four-year-old father, who has given up trying to succeed in business to keep house for her. Reinhart's only interests are Winona's happiness and his cooking; he has become a self-taught gourmet chef. He is completely happy with this arrangement and expects it to continue until Winona, twenty-five, finally marries. The change comes more suddenly and in an entirely different form than he has expected when Grace Greenwood, the fortyish business executive he has met in a supermarket, whom he is beginning to look upon as his first girl friend in the ten years since his divorce, turns out to be his daughter's lover.

In *Vital Parts*, Blaine Reinhart was a long-haired revolutionary. Now, he has gone to the other extreme: "his son condemned nothing done for a financial advantage, nor did Blaine recognize as serious any motive that did not have monetary gains as its goal." He and his father cannot communicate regardless of the roles they are playing. Blaine is afraid that Carlo will become his burden or go on welfare now that Winona is going to live with Grace, and he tries to unload him on Paradise Farm, a religious commune in which he has invested. The commune is presided over by Raymond Mainwaring, the son of Reinhart's late friend Splendor Mainwaring. Raymond was Captain Storm, a black militant, in *Vital Parts* but now calls himself Brother Valentine. Reinhart does not intend to become a burden to Blaine or anyone else, since Grace Greenwood has offered him a job demonstrating her company's gourmet foods in supermarkets.

Reinhart's new career is just starting when numerous complications develop. Genevieve, his neurotic ex-wife, shows up to ask him to take her back. When he refuses, she cracks up, accuses him of having an affair with Helen Clayton, the coworker he has just met, and has to be hospitalized. Blaine's wife Mercer leaves him and moves in with Reinhart, bringing along her two small sons, Toby and Parker. Reinhart does have an affair with Helen, an apparent nymphomaniac, and finds himself strangely drawn to his neighbor Edie Mulhouse, a tall, plain young woman a year younger than Winona. After he is a hit on a local television show, he is asked to appear in a regular segment, "Chef Carlo Cooks." The novel ends with most of its plot lines unresolved. Reinhart is about to begin a television career and a romance with Edie and tentatively plans to buy an out-of-the-way restaurant and run it with Edie and Raymond, whose commune Blaine has sold to Arabs. The conclusion leaves the impression that Berger plans further Reinhart novels.

*Reinhart's Women* is a quieter, more relaxed novel than its three predecessors, reflecting its hero's relative tranquillity. It lacks the black humor and wild satire of the earlier books and is written in a more subtle style with fewer of the puns Berger so dearly loves. It is still, however, a comic novel, and much of it is very funny, especially the treatment of television banalities when Reinhart appears on the *Eye Opener Show* and his conversations with his greedy grandsons. Six-year-old Toby asks, "Do you go to bars and take dope and have sex with hookers?" Berger's satirical portraits of Blaine and Mercer as insensitive, self-absorbed materialists is painfully accurate. They are worthy representatives of what Reinhart calls "the most boring era in the history of the race."

Another satirical target, as it is in Berger's *Regiment of Women* (1973), is the changing roles of men and women. His hero does not resent those changes: "Reinhart had had nothing to fear from female 'liberation': under the old system women had either disregarded him or run him ragged." In fact, the system frees Reinhart to find himself. Partly because he has never liked business anyway, he sees nothing wrong with being his reasonably well-to-do daughter's housekeeper. Not only is he a better mother to Winona than Genevieve had been, he is also a better cook than his ex-wife, his mother, or any woman he has known. Cooking is the first thing at which he has excelled. He defines his new self to Blaine:

> without benefit of a movement, I am liberated from all sorts of restraints, including those I have imposed on myself. It was ridiculous that I lived half a century trying to measure up to the principles of other people.

Like the young people of the 1960's, however, Reinhart has dropped out, turned his back on a world he feels has rejected him. Reinhart's kitchen has become his refuge from this crazy world: "Whatever the state of the world outside, everything made sense when Reinhart was with his pots and pans." In the kitchen, he can attain a harmony denied him in the outside world because "food is kinder than people."

Food cannot be all there is to life, however, as Reinhart discovers when his relatives' problems force him to leave his kitchen. The world may be chaotic, but Reinhart has an obligation to confront this chaos. He finds that good people such as Edie, Helen, and Grace do exist. He learns that he can feel pity for Genevieve and compassion for Blaine and Mercer, that few people are totally bad. He does not have to forgive Winona and Grace's love but merely accepts it, loving his daughter as much as when he seemed to be the only person in her life. He seems to have learned to love almost as uncritically as Winona did as a fat teenager. Realizing that he is not eternally damned to being betrayed by love, Reinhart finally becomes a lovable winner.

*Reinhart's Women* could have had a bit more satire and humor and fewer cooking details. While it pales beside Berger's masterpiece, *Little Big Man* (1964), one of the most entertaining and insightful novels of the postwar period, it is superior to his previous book, *Neighbors* (1980), whose satire is rather obscure in comparison. Berger's oeuvre is one of the most consistently interesting and diverse of any contemporary American novelist and one of the most unjustly neglected. Reinhart explains to Helen Clayton,

> Cooking is a craft, or perhaps a performing art, but the product that is created is made to be consumed in a unique way: it is taken internally and, if digested, becomes part of the flesh of a living creature. In a sense then, cookery is the *only* truly creative art. But

you do need people to eat the resulting product.

Berger's unique art deserves more consumers as well.

*Michael Adams*


## Sources for Further Study

*Best Sellers*. XLI, November, 1981, p. 284.
*Booklist*. LXXVII, July 1, 1981, p. 1369.
*Commentary*. LXXII, October, 1981, p. 74.
*Library Journal*. CVI, September 1, 1981, p. 1645.
*The New York Times Book Review*. LXXXVI, September 27, 1981, p. 9.
*Saturday Review*. VIII, September, 1981, p. 60.
*Time*. CXVIII, October 12, 1981, p. 109.

# REVOLUTIONARY EMPIRE
## The Rise of the English-Speaking Empires
## from the Fifteenth Century to the 1780's

*Author:* Angus Calder (1942-     )
*Publisher:* E. P. Dutton (New York). 916 pp. $36.00
*Type of work:* History
*Time:* The fifteenth to eighteenth centuries
*Locale:* England and its colonies

*A panoramic survey of the first centuries of British colonialism*

Angus Calder has written the first book of a planned three-volume series which promises to become the standard survey of the first three centuries of English, later British (after the Union of England and Scotland) expansion overseas. It covers a period whose beginning was marked by the establishment of the first English settler colonies and which ended with the independence of the North American colonies and the acquisition of the first major non-settler colony in Bengal. The nature of English expansion changed greatly during these three centuries. While the first century witnessed a number of daring ventures, often by men who, like Sir Walter Raleigh, were backed by powerful courtiers, it produced few concrete results. By the second century of expansion a powerful class of settlers began to develop, particularly in the West Indies, who began to influence domestic English politics, and, by the end of the third century, expansion had been adopted as the official policy of monarchy and bureaucracy.

*Revolutionary Empire*, which took ten years to write, is a self-conscious attempt to refurbish an older tradition of academic history writing which emphasized narration—the telling of a story—rather than analysis. The author has refurbished this tradition by imbuing his narrative with a sensitivity to the theoretical issues and debates which have agitated his contemporaries in the historical profession, particularly those with an economic orientation. He insists that "man lives by stories as well as by bread," and the telling of a story is the main function of his book. This orientation will prove frustrating to those more analytically inclined readers, who will no doubt find Calder's recitation of events tedious. Those who appreciate his attempt to revive the narrative tradition, but who have been influenced by the analytical approach of present-day historical writing, may also be critical of the work, and wish that he had made the connection between particular stories and his overall structure clearer. Though a book of this nature might have found an audience among the "educated reading public," its length, academic prose style, and exhorbitant price may alienate this group as well.

The narrative tradition from which Calder draws portrayed history as the product of the heroic deeds of a relatively small group of exceptional people. Contemporary historical writing tends to emphasize the social and economic determinants of human actions. Calder's approach lies somewhere between these two extremes. While he discusses at some length the activities of a number of participants in the expansion of Britain overseas and, refreshingly, still believes that the actions of individuals do help determine the outcome of historical events, he insists that the "greatness" of these individuals was the product of historical forces largely beyond their ken. He uses their stories primarily to illuminate the relationship between individual choice and historical forces. To the extent that his story is an epic, he says, it is not that of human heroes. Rather, its main characters are "Spices," "Tobacco," "Sugar," "Tea," and "Cotton." It is these "characters" which provide the main links between individuals and events described in the book.

*Revolutionary Empire* will be a daunting work for many. It is densely written, filled with an enormous amount of detail, with much of which even professional historians will be only vaguely familiar. If Calder sometimes seems misguided in his interpretation of particular events, or occasionally gets his facts wrong, his work must be judged, nevertheless, by how well it accomplishes its stated goal. That goal is synthesis, to tie together seemingly disparate events and, in particular, to show the linkages between what was happening in England and in the rest of the British Isles and the world. Generally speaking, Calder achieves this goal. His book contains many digressions, however, such as his discussion of the sectarian battles which shook New England in the seventeenth century, whose importance and relationship to the developing story is not always immediately apparent. Moreover, his discussions of several important themes, such as the disintegration of the clan system in Scotland and Ireland, seem overly long and detailed.

The "revolution" to which Calder refers in the title had three aspects. It was, first of all, an Industrial Revolution which transformed the English landscape and social structure. Without the empire this revolution would have occurred much more slowly, if at all, for the colonies provided a crucial outlet for inexpensive manufactured goods during the early stages of industrialization. Calder points out that the plantations which grew up in the New World, especially the sugar plantations, also provided a model for the division of labor that became the characteristic feature of the nineteenth century factory. Economic growth, in turn, resulted in the increasing power of mercantile and, later, manufacturing interests. This phenomenon is what is generally called the "rise of the middle class." The challenge to the British monarchy which this led to had reverberations across the Atlantic, as English-speaking colonists brought about the second revolution to which Calder refers—the American Revolution. The break with feudal, hierarchical tradition which occurred in North America and which established a model equally as important as the Industrial Revolution could only have occurred, Calder suggests, in a colonial society. The third and final world-transforming revolution he discusses is the conquest of Bengal by a relatively small group of employees of the East India

Company. The revolution in Bengal was related to the previous two revolutions, as both of these were related to the existence of English colonies, for the growing economic disparity between France and Great Britain and their rivalry in North America added fuel to the conflict over dynastic succession in Europe to produce a worldwide conflict that exposed the weakness of the native rulers in India. Once exposed, this weakness led to the gradual conquest of most of the Indian subcontinent.

This summary does not do justice to the subtlety of Calder's argument, but does suggest how he attempts to relate events on a global scale. While many previous writers on the subject of empire have either attributed the whole of modern British history to the existence of colonialism, or, on the other extreme, viewed colonial expansion as a self-perpetuating force, Calder emphasizes how events and trends constantly influenced one another. Though this approach may be less satisfying to those who prefer their history to be drawn in bold strokes, it does seem to capture the historical "reality," if such a term may still be used, better than more simple approaches.

One of Calder's main contributions, apart from his linking together of events over the entire area subject to British influence, is to emphasize the importance of the "Celtic fringe" of England—primarily Scotland and Ireland—in promoting English expansion overseas and economic growth. His discussion of the rivalries and alliances among the clans in these areas will frustrate all but the most diligent reader, but he feels, quite rightly, that an understanding of the relationship between the English and the inhabitants of these areas is fundamental to an understanding of the growth of the English, later the British, empire. He points out that many of the early leaders of the colonialist movement had their first experience of colonization in Ireland, and that the emigration of Scotsmen to Ulster was closely linked in men's minds with the movement of the English to the New World. Later racist attitudes towards indigenous peoples encountered in colonization efforts around the world first appeared in English attitudes towards the Irish.

Scotland, where the author lives and teaches, looms large in his analysis. Calder tries to rectify the Anglocentric approach to the history of Great Britain, which basically ignores Scotland's contribution to British history. He points out that many of those who left the British Isles during the early period of colonization were men set adrift by the breakup of the Scottish clans as English influence spread north. Scottish rivalry with England was also one of the main stimulants of substantial investment in colonial ventures by Scotsmen, who sought to overcome their nation's economic disadvantage by besting the English at their own game. He draws attention to the fact that it was a revolution in Scotland that made possible the overthrow of Charles I. Not the least of Scotland's contributions to the growth of the British Isles to world dominance was a consequence of the Union of the England and Scotland in 1707, which produced the largest free trade area in Europe at the time and further stimulated the growth of the British economy.

Why, exactly, did Great Britain rise to its position as the foremost colonialist power? Calder suggests that it was the unique combination in England of the land hunger which had produced Spain's tremendous expansion overseas with the commercial drive which had characterized Portugal's that led to both the Industrial Revolution and the rise of the "English-speaking" empires. This unique combination, in turn, was partially the result of the fluidity of the English social structure, which both allowed worthy members of the middle class to enter the gentry and allowed the gentry and aristocracy to invest in commercial ventures without sacrificing their status.

*Revolutionary Empire* is a rich and rewarding book, despite the obstacles placed in the reader's path. It is clearly the work of a man in love with, if not obsessed by, his subject. The author manages to convey his love of the subject to the reader, and for this he should be commended, but he might have done well to convey this love somewhat more succinctly.

*Rand Edwards*


## Sources for Further Study

*Choice*. XIX, September, 1981, p. 142.
*The Economist*. CCLXXIX, June 13, 1981, p. 94.
*History Today*. XXXI, September, 1981, p. 56.
*Library Journal*. CVI, June 1, 1981, p. 1218.
*New Statesman*. CI, May 22, 1981, p. 19.
*The New York Review of Books*. XXVIII, December 17, 1981, p. 60.
*Observer*. April 12, 1981, p. 28.
*Punch*. CCLXXX, April 15, 1981, p. 604.
*Spectator*. CCXLVI, May 16, 1981, p. 21.
*Times Literary Supplement*. July 24, 1981, p. 853.

# REVOLUTIONARY RUSSIA, 1917

*Author:* John M. Thompson (1926-    )
*Publisher:* Charles Scribner's Sons (New York). 224 pp. $14.95
*Type of work:* History
*Time:* 1917
*Locale:* Russia

*A brief account of the series of upheavals that led to the triumph of Communism in Russia*

*Principal personages:*
VLADIMIR ILICH LENIN, the leader of the Bolsheviks
NICHOLAS II, the last Czar of Russia, 1894-1917
ALEXANDER KERENSKY, the chief figure in the short-lived Provisional Government
LAVR KORNILOV, Russian military leader and counterrevolutionary - chieftain
LEON TROTSKY, one of the chief lieutenants of Lenin

In Russia, the year 1917 witnessed, in rapid succession, the overthrow of the centuries-old monarchy of the Romanov Czars, a brief experiment in political democracy under the Provisional Government, and the seizure of power by Lenin's Bolsheviks. John M. Thompson, a former professor of history and an expert on Russia's turbulent past, has provided the general reader with an excellent brief overview, arranged in strictly chronological fashion, of the momentous events of that year, one that is both readable and scholarly. Although Thompson's work is not always as dramatic, as anecdotal, or as colorfully written as the works on the revolution recently published by the journalist Harrison Salisbury (*Black Night, White Snow*, 1978; *Russia in Revolution, 1900-1930*, 1978), Thompson's is in many ways a better and more satisfying book than those written by Salisbury: it explains more carefully and in somewhat greater detail why things happened the way they did.

Ever since the triumph of the Bolsheviks occurred, there have been debates about why events turned out the way they did. One such dispute has been the eternal argument between inevitabilism and a stress on the role of free will. Was the fall of the Czar in 1917 inevitable, or could prudent reforms have saved the Romanov dynasty even at the eleventh hour? Was the failure of Russia's liberal experiment of 1917 inevitable? Most important, could anyone or anything have prevented the triumph of the Bolsheviks, or was their victory predestined by some iron law of history?

Another argument concerns the nature of the revolution itself. Almost all students of the period, with the exception of perhaps a few embittered monarchists, agree that the fall of Czarism was the result of widespread dissatisfaction with the Romanov regime, and that, in a sense, the people, or at least the people of Petrograd, really did overthrow the monarchy in a spontaneous burst of rebellion. What, however, of the Bolshevik takeover later in the year? Was it, too, the expression of a powerful wave of popular clamor for drastic social and political change? Or was it, as the American historian Robert V. Daniels has suggested in his book, *Red October* (1967), simply a military coup carried out by a ruthless minority, one that had no real base of popular support?

Thompson straddles the issue of inevitability of the February Revolution. Although asserting that Czarism was not inherently doomed to die, he does concede that the presence of the weak and foolish Nicholas II on the Imperial throne and the shattering effects of modernization on traditional Russian society made its death a real possibility even before the outbreak of World War I. The massive suffering inflicted by World War I on the Russian people and the inability of the Czarist government either to win the war or to end it made the fall of Czarism much more likely than it would have been otherwise; however, Thompson shies away from any acceptance of the notion of inevitability. The author treats in greater detail the issue of the inevitability of the October Revolution, but comes to a somewhat more definite conclusion. Thompson strongly suggests that an anarchical streak in the Russian national character doomed the liberal experiment almost from the beginning. After the overthrow of the Czar, he implies, the only likely alternative to Bolshevism was some kind of right-wing military dictatorship. Yet, while believing that the failure of Russia's liberal experiment was inevitable, he just as clearly does not believe that the Bolshevik seizure of power was inevitable. The political situation was, he argues, extremely fluid for many months after the overthrow of the Czar. For a short time following the bloody and aimless riots of July, 1917, in Petrograd, the author points out, the popularity of the Bolshevik leader, Vladimir I. Lenin, accused by his foes of being a German agent, fell very low indeed. What revived Lenin's chances dramatically, Thompson shows, was the so-called Kornilov Affair of September, 1917.

It is in his discussion of the Kornilov Affair that the author begins to deal carefully with the issue of the degree of popular support enjoyed by the Bolsheviks at the time of their seizure of power. The bungled attempt of General Lavr Kornilov to seize Petrograd and install himself as dictator, Thompson makes clear, permitted the Bolsheviks, for the first time, to pose as defenders of revolutionary ideals. By opposing Kornilov's coup, Alexander Kerensky, the youthful Prime Minister, earned the lasting contempt and distrust of Conservative military officers and politicians. Since Kerensky had originally appointed Kornilov Commander in Chief, and since it was rumored that only personal pride and the desire to remain prime minister had prevented his cooperation with Kornilov's coup, the Prime Minister also became an object of suspicion for the masses of workers and soldiers of Petrograd. The discrediting of Kerensky and the capture by the Bolsheviks of the mantle of loyalty to revolutionary ideals go far, the author implies, to explain why a coup by a minority evoked, at first, so little resistance and such a large amount of, if not active support, then at least passive acquiescence.

Thompson does not deny the importance of individual personalities in the success of the Bolshevik Revolution. The author stresses the role of the strong willed Lenin in prodding a by no means tightly disciplined Bolshevik party into deciding in favor of revolt. Similarly, the author pays due regard to the role of the energetic and persuasive Leon Trotsky in organizing and managing the revolt and cloaking it with the legitimacy of the Military Revolutionary Committee set up by that highly respected quasigovernmental organ of workers and soldiers opinion, the Petrograd Soviet.

At the same time, however, the author does deny that the Bolshevik Revolution was merely a military coup by a minority devoid of all popular support. The author does not think of the Bolsheviks as democrats: their suppression of the Constituent Assembly in January, 1918 and their eventual establishment of a one-party regime, indicates to the author that these men had nothing but contempt for democratic procedures. He does, however, believe that during the crucial period from September through December, 1917, the Bolsheviks' proclaimed goals of peace and of land to the peasants made them far more in tune with the wishes of the Russian masses than any other political grouping. Consequently, the Bolsheviks were able to ride to power "on a wave of popular radicalism." Furthermore, the author points out, Lenin once in power did keep some of his promises: land was given to the peasants and peace, although humiliating, was achieved with Germany by the Treaty of Brest-Letovsk in March, 1918. Although the Bolsheviks had betrayed democracy in the Western sense of the word, they had, Thompson makes clear, succeeded quite well through their exploitation of the deep-rooted hatred of the masses for the old ruling class, capturing for themselves the mystique of the revolution which so many Russians held dear.

Throughout 1917, Russian after Russian proclaimed his loyalty to "the revolution" often without ever taking the trouble to define what he meant by that glorious word. For there were, Thompson demonstrates, many revolutions taking place in the Russia of 1917. In the Russian Army, soldiers revolted against the authority of the old officer class. In the major cities, workers rebelled against the authority of the managers. Throughout the length and breadth of rural Russia, peasants seized the broad acres of the landed gentry. On the periphery of the Russian Empire, in places such as the Ukraine, Finland, and the Baltic states, minority nationalities demanded their right, first to autonomy within the Russian Empire, and then to independence. The whole revolutionary year, the author argues, can be seen as representing the strivings of the millions of people in the Russian Empire for a better life.

What about the losers of that revolutionary year, the Provisional Government that Lenin so easily overthrew, the liberals and the moderate Socialists who had so fervently dreamed of a free Russia, and whose hopes were so cruelly dashed with the Bolsheviks' forcible dissolution of the Constituent

Assembly in January, 1918? Thompson certainly does not share the contempt shown by Lenin and his Bolshevik followers for Russia's political moderates. True, the author does fault Kerensky for his vanity and impulsiveness. Yet, for Thompson the moderates are not figures of ridicule; instead, they are good men who were tragically flawed. That very adherence to principle that, in a sense so ennobled them, was also what kept them from doing what needed to be done if they were to stay in power. Because of their principles, they could not meet the demands of the war-weary for peace at almost any price with Germany, of the peasants for land, or of the rebellious nationalities for self-rule; their refusal to do these things, however, played into the hands of the Bolsheviks. In his assessment of the losers as well as the winners of the revolutionary year 1917, Thompson takes great care to be fair, balanced, and judicious.

One of the few aspects of this book to which exception might be taken is the choice of chronology. The author concentrates his attention on the period from the fall of the Czar, in March, 1917, until the Bolsheviks' signing of the Treaty of Brest-Letovsk in March, 1918. In doing so, he deviates from the practice of such early students of the revolution as William Henry Chamberlin, who saw 1921, the date in which all challenges to Lenin's Bolshevik regime, whether reactionary, liberal, or radical, were finally repressed, bringing several years of civil war to an end, as marking the end of the Russian Revolution. Thompson's approach has the advantage of compression and conciseness; it has the disadvantage, however, of not telling the reader very much about how the Bolsheviks managed to hang on to power as well as about how they seized power. Why were their many enemies, from the counterrevolutionary Whites to the Socialist Revolutionaries, unable to defeat them? Why did not the victorious Allies of World War I intervene more vigorously, in the aftermath of the Armistice, to stamp out the Bolshevik regime in Russia? The author does begin to answer these questions; his brief attempt to do so, however, succeeds only in whetting the reader's appetite for a more detailed explanation.

Although the author's choice of dates might not satisfy everyone, there is not doubt that this book is a solid introduction to a complex historical problem. Although Thompson does occasionally make use of such contemporary sources as collections of private papers, he makes no pretense whatsoever of writing an original piece of scholarly research; instead, his goal is to make the fruits of recent scholarship available to a wider public. When he cites from any source, whether primary or secondary, he places the references at the bottom of the page, making them convenient for the reader to consult. Thompson's book is full of aids to the general reader. The maps, the list of key dates at the back of the book, and the contemporary photographic illustrations are all very helpful to those who are not professional historians. Two tables enable the readers to see at a glance both the complex relationship between the Provisional Government and the Petrograd Soviet and the changing aspirations of important social groups in Russia during the course of the revolutionary year. The explanation of the difference between the Russian and Western calendars of the time, which makes clear why the February Revolution took place in March and the October Revolution in November, is especially useful. The bibliographical essay provides an excellent guide to further reading.

*Paul D. Mageli*

## Sources for Further Study

*Booklist*. LXXVIII, November 1, 1981, p. 368.
*Library Journal*. CVI, September 15, 1981, p. 1732.

# RHINE MAIDENS

*Author:* Carolyn See (1934-    )
*Publisher:* Coward, McCann & Geoghegan (New York). 272 pp. $13.95
*Type of work:* Novel
*Time:* The present
*Locale:* Southern California

A comic novel that observes the frustrations and triumphs of women struggling with the loss of love

> Principal characters:
> GRACE JACKSON, a feisty, complaining sixty-three-year-old woman
> GARNET EVANS, her daughter, a Brentwood matron
> IAN EVANS, Garnet's husband, a television producer

The image of Rhine maidens originates in Wagnerian opera. Maidens on the Rhine sing of the power of love. Men come along, scorn love, and steal the maidens' treasure. And as men had power over the Rhine maidens, so do they over the women in Carolyn See's new novel.

*Rhine Maidens* is an unconventional story about women who have lived their lives through their men. It explores how two women, mother and daughter, respond to the loss of love in their lives. At once hilarious and despairing, *Rhine Maidens* also captures the tacky, seedy, and glamorous modern-day Los Angeles and offers many amusing observations about life in general through the two main characters.

Grace Jackson, once a beautiful ambitious girl, is a demanding old woman in the present frame of the novel. Her first husband left her for a younger woman, a male suitor who bored her committed suicide because of her, and a second husband, an unfortunate drunk, died after a brief, unhappy marriage with her. Grace spends her time lamenting her lost youth and all the disappointments in her life, waiting for something else to go wrong. She misses the glamour of her youth. To Grace, the good life was perfect little black sandals, a paycheck for $27.50, and carrying the right newspaper while shopping downtown. Presently, all she knows how to do is laugh at people.

Grace's daughter, Garnet, is a spectacularly unremarkable Brentwood matron who is living the American dream. Thirty-nine years old, she has a successful television-producer husband, a tastefully furnished home, and two uninteresting children. She lives the rich full life of the West Los Angeles housewife: she shops, she goes to lunch in restaurants, she plays bridge, she takes extension courses at the University of California at Los Angeles (UCLA) in an attempt to learn "what life is all about." She is also the type of woman who takes the labels off two hundred cans for her son's school drive, forgetting that she will not know what is in them. She belongs to sufficiently vague and universal causes such as the World Hunger Project and Mothers for Peace, and she does not buy silk because the Cambodians suffer so much.

Garnet sees all of West Los Angeles filled with women who have beautiful homes, a husband, kids, and an opportunity to go back to school. They have that and nothing more—but they are safe. That was Garnet's reason for getting married, and it was the safest thing she could do. With all she possesses though, Garnet senses that there is something to life that she is missing. She feels locked inside and all of life is "out there." One of her observations is that "they don't teach Happiness I and II at UCLA—not even through Extension."

Carolyn See, an astute observer of the Southern California scene, avoids the obvious clichés and draws a portrait of middle-class suburbia that is chillingly familiar. The situations in which she sets her characters are peculiar to Los Angeles, but the comedy and pathos that are inherent in them speak to everyone.

The plot centers around a visit Grace pays to Garnet and her family. The perennial mother-daughter conflict is explored as Grace and Garnet irritate each other throughout the novel. Grace takes out her frustrations on Garnet and manages to criticize everything Garnet does or likes. Garnet resents her mother's condemnation of her middle-class life but nevertheless tries very hard to please her mother. The story is narrated alternately by Grace and then Garnet as they comment on the same events with wildly differing viewpoints.

Garnet's first attempt to draw Grace into her social circle begins with an invitation to attend her ladies' book discussion club. Grace notices that all the women have "crazy little eyes" and that they spend most of their time talking about nothing. Garnet's attempt to treat her mother to a pleasant luncheon turns into a disaster as Grace makes a scene in the restaurant. While they are in the restaurant, Grace notices that Garnet's husband is also there, but with another woman. Of course, Grace is not surprised to discover the fact. She had decided long before that all men are louts and infidelity is everywhere. What she does not understand, however, is why Garnet has not seen the signs of a soon-to-be marriage on the rocks. "She always was a little slow on the uptake," muses Grace.

In a scene that captures all the silliness and sadness of the EST-like motivational seminars, Garnet persuades Grace to attend a money awareness weekend with her. The group leaders dress like dollar bills and to Grace's dismay, they also sing and dance.

The situations in which Garnet and Grace find themselves are somewhat absurd, as are the characters themselves at times, but they are believable and readers find themselves caring about what happens to these ladies, although it is evident that a large part of their dissatisfaction is of their own making. All of the characters in *Rhine Maidens*, if they do not openly complain, at least sense that there is something missing from their lives. They all have different ways of responding to this sense of loss. Grace has given up any further search for happiness, convinced that it was the men in her life who gave it all to her and then took it all away. Garnet feels that life is just beyond her reach and that "everyone loses everything" anyway. Grace's first husband thought maybe changing wives would have improved his life's situation; Grace's second husband tried to find happiness through alcohol; and Garnet's husband looks for it in the attentions of another woman.

The problems set up in the novel are resolved to varying degrees at its conclusion. Yet the conclusion is too pat for what has already been seen of Grace. Unlike Garnet, no substantial changes are seen in Grace, and the reader is left wondering if Grace will ever let go of her anger and disappointments and get on with life.

See's snappy and clever writing style makes *Rhine Maidens* a delight to read. While she entertains, she provides many wise insights into people's attitudes about themselves. Most important, she teaches that safety is not to be won easily.

*Susan D'Antuono*

## Sources for Further Study

*Best Sellers*. XLI, October, 1981, p. 250.
*Kirkus Reviews*. XLIX, July 15, 1981, p. 899.
*Library Journal*. CVI, October 15, 1981, p. 2050.
*The New York Times Book Review*. LXXXVI, October 18, 1981, p. 15.
*Newsweek*. XCVIII, October 5, 1981, p. 81.
*Publishers Weekly*. CCXX, August 7, 1981, p. 66.

# THE RISE AND FALL OF ALEXANDER HAMILTON

*Author:* Robert A. Hendrickson (1923-    )
*Publisher:* Van Nostrand Reinhold Company (New York). 800 pp. $24.95
*Type of work:* Biography
*Time:* 1757-1804
*Locale:* The northeastern United States

*A biographical study of Alexander Hamilton which attempts to explain why this talented man fell short of true greatness*

> Principal personages:
>> ALEXANDER HAMILTON, American Revolutionary leader; and first United States Secretary of the Treasury, 1789-1795
>> GEORGE WASHINGTON, Commander of the Continental Army; and first President of the United States, 1789-1797
>> ELIZABETH SCHUYLER HAMILTON, Hamilton's wife
>> AARON BURR, a political rival of Hamilton who kills him in a duel

This biography of Alexander Hamilton (1757-1804) is written by one of "Hamilton's own," a man whose career and interests parallel those of his subject. Robert A. Hendrickson (like Hamilton) was not born in New York City but came to make his mark there; he is a recognized war veteran (World War II), a lawyer, and an expert on fiscal and monetary affairs. *The Rise and Fall of Alexander Hamilton* is drawn from the same author's two-volume work entitled *Hamilton* (1976). Hendrickson is a lively writer, a bit melodramatic but at his best engaging, bold, and graceful.

For all these reasons, one is all the more disappointed in the author's seeming inability to "get inside" Alexander Hamilton, to give readers the benefit of his unique vantage point on this man who must be considered one of the most interesting of the Founding Fathers. Hendrickson's portrait is a strange mixture of admiration and puckish disapproval, the former for Hamilton's courage, powerful mind, and bold actions, the latter for the personal weaknesses of a man whose gargantuan appetites would have shocked all but the most sympathetic and understanding.

Like other biographers of Hamilton, Hendrickson makes much of Hamilton's illegitimate birth and difficult childhood in the West Indies. From this environment came a clever boy, one who knew how to manipulate his "betters" to his own end, one eager to grasp his "main chance." Coming to the atttention of wealthy patrons, he was offered the opportunity to go to New York City to attend King's College (now Columbia University) to study medicine. Hamilton jumped at the chance to escape his situation in the West Indies and to leave his past behind him. He arrived in New York in 1773 and was drawn immediately into the maelstrom which became the American Revolution. Throwing himself on the side of rebellion, Hamilton (barely out of his teens) came to the attention of General George Washington, soon becoming one of his *aides-de-camp* (his "beardless boys").

The American Revolution was one of the anvils on which Hamilton was forged. In spite of Washington's mistakes and the jealousy, opposition, and treason of others (the treason of Benedict Arnold as well as the disaffection among Washington's officers are particularly well-told), Hamilton remained loyal to the General. Hence the "bastard brat of a Scotch pedlar" earned the support of Washington, a kind of legitimacy, and the military glory which he craved.

His connections also earned him entrance into the parlors of the Schuyler family, where he courted Elizabeth ("Betsy") Schuyler, daughter of one of the most powerful men in New York. As Hendrickson amply demonstrates, Hamilton had a charm which few women could refuse. Elizabeth could hardly resist his ardent advances. It was a marriage vow which Elizabeth never broke, though she must have come to know that her husband (according to Hendrickson) was very nearly insatiable, even to the point of pursuing (possibly successfully) his own sister-in-law. Throughout the book, Hendrickson appears to be both titillated and repulsed by his subject's sexual appetites.

Once having gained entrance into New York's elite, Hamilton was without peer. As a lawyer, he defended Tories seeking to recover property after the Revolution. He became involved in public affairs as the new nation struggled to find a proper and stable government. He was a leader in the fight for the ratification of the Constitution.

Although he was not Washington's first choice, Hamilton was a perfect person to become the first Secretary of the Treasury. The new nation needed his boldness of vision, the power of his oratory and writing, his influence with President Washington. If Hamilton made mistakes (and he made many, including his trusting of William Duer and his political insensitivity to the rising opposition), they came from his vision of what the new republic could be . . . and was not.

Apparently Hamilton had a sexual drive that surpassed his contemporaries or was unable to resist female advances. Hendrickson spends a disproportionate amount of time either describing or analyzing Hamilton's infidelities. The "Reynolds Affair" is a major episode in this book, given disproportionate treatment. Hendrickson sees this episode as tawdry, a man lured into a sexual trap by a woman and her devious husband. In this treatment (which takes up a fair amount of the book), Hamilton is seen as being ensnared by the wiles of an experienced woman. Yet Hamilton had been lured from the path of marital fidelity before. Indeed, to blackmailers, he was a perfect target.

The rest of the book views Hamilton in opposition to the trends of the times. In his craving for acceptance into the elite, he had underestimated the democratic upsurge of the Jeffersonians. Hamilton fought a desperate but losing battle against these forces. In the end, he would die, once again, in opposition.

Earlier biographers have not ignored the strange counterpoint of Hamilton and Aaron Burr. Hendrickson makes much of this, beginning his book with the duel and virtually ending it there. It seems as if the two were some sort of cosmic enemies, symbols of what was and what was to be. Hamilton was the adopted aristocrat who saw the people as a "headless beast" and believed mankind must be *led* to the right way. Burr probably had no more faith in human beings than Hamilton did, but he was obliged politically to champion the rights of the "headless beast." Ultimately, both lost.

Hendrickson's portrait of Hamilton emphasizes the contradictory nature of his subject, and in the end, the reader is confused. Alexander Hamilton was a great thinker, a man who saw a vision of the republic which in some ways became reality, yet his personal life prevented him from achieving true greatness. The author has presented two Hamiltons which remain distinct rather than an integrated life of a complex personality.

*William Bruce Wheeler*

## Sources for Further Study

*Library Journal.* CVI, October 15, 1981, p. 2020.

# THE ROAD TO CONFRONTATION
## American Policy Toward China and Korea, 1947-1950

*Author:* William Whitney Stueck, Jr. (1945-    )
*Publisher:* The University of North Carolina Press (Chapel Hill). 326 pp. $20.00
*Type of work:* History
*Time:* 1947-1950
*Locale:* The United States, China, and Korea

*A detailed examination of the making of American East Asian policy from 1947 to the entrance of China in the Korean War in the fall of 1950*

> *Principal personages:*
> HARRY S TRUMAN, thirty-third President of the United States, 1945-1953
> GENERAL GEORGE MARSHALL, United States Secretary of State, 1947-1949
> DEAN ACHESON, United States Secretary of State, 1949-1953
> JOHN LEIGHTON STUART, United States Ambassador to China, 1946-1949
> LOUIS JOHNSON, United States Secretary of Defense, 1949-1950
> GENERAL DOUGLES A. MACARTHUR, Commander in Chief of the United States forces in the Far East
> MAO ZEDONG, Chairman of the Chinese Communist Party, 1949-1976
> CHIANG KAI-SHEK, leader of the Nationalist Party in China
> SYNGMAN RHEE, President of the Republic of South Korea, 1948-1960

Reading William Stueck's excellent account of the making of foreign policy more than three decades ago provides a chilling sense of déjà vu: the assumptions, the problems, the fallacies that dominate American foreign policy today are basically the same as those of the late 1940's. The title refers to the American confrontation with China in Korea in the fall of 1950, and Stueck scrupulously details the chain of events and the perceptions and misperceptions of the participants along that road.

At its base, foreign policy is built on assumptions—about the forces at work in the world, about national mission, about international reaction and response. Making extensive use of recently declassified documents and many interviews, Stueck reveals clearly the assumptions of American policymakers that led to tragedy. Emerging from World War II with a sense that collective action might have prevented that disaster, policymakers tried to fit the postwar world into the prewar mold: aggression, especially *Red* aggression, must be stopped. Furthermore, the United States should play a central role in seeing that world peace is maintained. Stueck's major contribution to an understanding of postwar foreign policy—and it is his thesis—is to illustrate that American policy in the late 1940's became in the main a "quest for credibility" in its role as world policeman. Foreign policy elites became obsessed with the fear that a show of weakness might undermine American credibility around the world.

The world must be policed, of course, from "the universal danger of Communist expansion," and it was in China and Korea (and later Vietnam) that American credibility was put to the test against the presumed Communist aggression. Stueck shows how this concern for credibility pushed American policy in China and Korea in different directions. In the Chinese Civil War (1947-1949) it led officials to lessen United States involvement for fear that its resources might be spread too thin and that substantial prestige might be wasted in Chiang Kai-shek's apparently losing effort. In Korea, on the other hand, the United States had already made extensive commitments: after the establishment of Syngman Rhee's government in 1948, withdrawing would simply have meant loss of credibility with consequent severe political repercussions. The United States had to react forcefully in June, 1950, when North Korea invaded the South, in order to assert its credibility. Stueck suggests as well that the shift from containment to liberation in the fall of 1950 centered on the issue of credibility: a strong object lesson showing that aggression might have negative consequences—the unification of Korea by United Nation forces—would make the United States role more credible than if it merely contained the Communist threat at the thirty-eighth parallel.

Behind the quest for credibility in East Asia lay some serious problems. In the first place, there was a strong strain of cultural arrogance. With a few exceptions, most policymakers believed that Europe—the West—had priority over Asia. Cultural chauvinists, such as Ambassador John Leighton Stuart, approached China paternalistically and through American standards and values. Thus they failed repeatedly to understand events and their significance: they underestimated the ability of the Communists to unite the nation; they failed to understand the force of nationalism which stirred anti-American hatred and which ultimately propelled China into the Korean War; they continually overestimated inherent Communist hostility to the United States, thus missing several potential chances at *rapprochement* with the Chinese leaders. Furthermore, there was little knowledge of Korea in Washington. Dismissed at the end of World War II as a country whose people displayed "political immaturity," Korea had low priority in diplomatic assignments. Dean Acheson emerges almost a paradigm of this arrogance, a man who had "not much respect for Asians." As for arrogance, he clearly met his match in Douglas MacArthur, whose insistence that he understood "the Oriental mind" hid a serious lack of understanding of Asian culture and peoples. It was particularly galling for such policymakers to have to deal with Asians such as Chiang Kai-shek and Syngman Rhee, both strong-willed nationalists who increasingly resented American pressure.

A second serious psychic flaw was a paranoiac sense of insecurity. The monolithic threat of international Communism became an overwhelming concern not only abroad but also at home. The concern in the last years of the

1940's for governmental security from Communist agents blossomed into the McCarthy era with its "Communists-in-government" issue, which Stueck sees as a clear danger to the execution of President Harry Truman's foreign policy. When cultural arrogance mixed with the marked national insecurity, the results were serious errors of perception, failures to assess United States goals and needs realistically, and a persistent insensitivity to the needs and desires of other nations. It is the mixture which Graham Greene has called "innocence" which, he says in *The Quiet American* (1956), makes Americans the most dangerous people in the world.

Besides Stueck's excellent insights and observations on the underpinnings of American foreign policy since World War II, he contributes greatly to an understanding of the American foreign-policymaking establishment in this period—its elites and its institutions. As in recent administrations, there was considerable debate and confusion over the direction and meaning of foreign policy between the Departments of State and Defense. During the Chinese Civil War, the State Department clashed repeatedly with the Joint Chiefs of Staff on the extent of American involvement. Stueck argues that the State Department was the source and perpetuator of the credibility "line" in foreign policy while the Defense establishment based its policy recommendations chiefly on military considerations. In 1945, for example, the Korean peninsula was seen chiefly by the military as a "possible launching pad for the Soviet domination of Japan and China"—a view that the government adopted. By 1949, however, Stueck contends, Korea's primary importance was as "a symbol of American reliability worldwide." The author argues that American moves in Taiwan in 1950 to bolster Chiang Kai-shek were motivated primarily by the Pentagon's insistence of the island's military importance in the Western Pacific chain of defense; American efforts at the same time to strengthen the hands of the French against the Viet Minh were motivated largely by the concern with credibility. In any case, Stueck clearly illustrates the poor coordination between State and Defense which continually clogged the making of a consistent policy.

In addition to the government's executive branch, the Congress also played important roles in the making of East Asian policy. The economic problems of 1946 to 1948 promoted a high degree of budget consciousness. Administration requests for increased assistance to China or Korea were met by Congressmen intent upon holding down government expenditures. Stueck suggests that Korea policy sometimes became a "juggling act" between conflicting governmental pressures; congressional debate on Korea became a vehicle for enunciating domestic political concerns and desires and for venting complaints about the administration's policy. The China Lobby, spearheaded by missionaries infatuated with Chiang Kai-shek's Christianity, had a significant impact on Congressional attitudes, exerting continual pressure for a policy more supportive of the Nationalists. In 1948 a similar lobby developed for the government of Syngman Rhee in the Republic of Korea. Seriously hampering the making of policy, these anti-Communist pressure groups merged into the McCarthyite fervor.

For Stueck, understanding policy is more than uncovering general assumptions or analyzing institutions: individuals make policy and different individuals make a difference in policy and its execution. United States policymaking in East Asia was marked by men with dominating personalities and (in some cases) remarkable idiosyncrasies: the already-mentioned arrogance of Acheson and MacArthur, the strong-willed nature of Defense Secretary Louis Johnson, the military predilections of Dean Rusk, and the ludicrousness of Patrick Hurley, are only a few examples. For each of the many participants in policymaking, Stueck provides illuminating vignettes. In at least one case, the decision to invade North Korea, Stueck contends that different personalities in control at State and Defense (specifically Walton Butterworth at State and Louis Johnson at Defense instead of Dean Rusk and George Marshall) may well have led to a different policy.

Stueck's analysis is generally cogent and insightful. In a sophisticated manner he suggests various policy alternatives, describing possible outcomes if those options had been utilized. In the hands of a less-skilled analyst, such a technique might turn into a condemnatory exercise. Stueck succeeds, however, and it adds greatly to the value of his work. He provides at several points comparisons between American policy and roles in Korea, China, and Vietnam: these passages are excellent and to the point.

Stueck's analysis is weakest in his handling of the situation from the Chinese and especially Korean points of view. Stueck apparently does not read Chinese, Korean, or Russian: there are no foreign language sources listed in his bibliography. Admittedly, except perhaps for the Korean situation, scholars do not have access to those sources. Some of Stueck's generalizations, however, are not supportable given the relationships between China and Russia. He gives the Soviet Union vastly more power over China than historical sources warrant, contending that Russia had the potential "to play the Chinese card" almost at will. He argues that China's Korean intervention undermined the Sino-Soviet alliance by bolstering Mao Zedong's prestige and thereby encouraging the Chinese leader to challenge Moscow. Stueck has not paid much attention to the historical relationships between Mao and Moscow nor to the development of the Chinese Revolution. In the light of the historical antagonism between Mao and the Soviet Union, Stueck's analysis here seems too facile. Again, how can Stueck know that "ultimately American efforts to bolster South Korea were only successful enough to push the regime in Pyongyang over the brink from subversive activities to open military attack"? Without access to North Korean records, the author cannot be sure of his assertion.

On the whole, however, Stueck's analysis is convincing and even-handed.

As a good historian, he lets the chips fall where they may. He describes the report of a son of a Chinese missionary to Congress that Chiang Kai-shek was "an Eastern leader who . . . will . . . stand like a rock for the traditional values of Christendom and for those moral concepts at the heart of Christian democracy." Stueck's assessment of this analysis might well serve as description of much American postwar foreign policy: "romantic nonsense."

*R. Keith Schoppa*

### Sources for Further Study

*American Historical Review*. LXXXVI, October, 1981, p. 951.
*Choice*. XVIII, June, 1981, p. 1478.
*Current History*. LXXX, September, 1981, p. 272.
*Journal of American History*. LXVIII, September, 1981, p. 439.
*Library Journal*. CVI, February 15, 1981, p. 458.
*Reviews in American History*. IX, December, 1981, p. 549.

# THE ROAD TO NUREMBERG

*Author:* Bradley F. Smith (1910-    )
*Publisher:* Basic Books (New York). 303 pp. $14.95
*Type of work:* History
*Time:* 1944-1945
*Locale:* The United States and England

*A narrative and analysis of how the American Government developed the plan for the Nuremberg trial of the major Nazi war criminals*

> Principal personages:
> FRANKLIN DELANO ROOSEVELT, thirty-second President of the United States, 1933-1945
> HENRY J. MORGENTHAU, JR., United States Secretary of the Treasury, 1934-1945
> HENRY STIMSON, United States Secretary of War, 1940-1945
> WINSTON L.S. CHURCHILL, British Prime Minister, 1940-1945
> JOHN A. SIMON, British Lord Chancellor, 1940-1945

In 1942, as the Nazi killing machines began in earnest to undertake the "final solution" to the so-called Jewish Question, information on the mass murders began to filter back to government authorities in London and Washington. At first the stories seemed too horrible to be believed. The Nazi record of aggressive warfare had, of course, been clear since the attack on Poland in 1939. The brutality with which the German armies apparently disregarded the standard laws and usages of warfare among civilized countries was also becoming clear, but the crime which would become known as genocide still seemed literally incredible. In December, 1942, after months of attempted verification, delays, and negotiations within the Allied camp, the British and American governments issued a joint statement denouncing the Nazi mass murders and declaring that the perpetrators would not "escape retribution." In November, 1943, Secretary of State Cordell Hull, British Foreign Secretary Anthony Eden, and Soviet Foreign Minister V. M. Molotov issued the Moscow Declaration outlining the Allied policy toward Nazi war criminals: major war criminals at the top of the hierarchy would be "punished by the joint decision of the governments of the allies," while lesser offenders would be turned over to liberated countries for trial and punishment under local laws.

Yet these statements left many questions unanswered: exactly what were the definitions of the crimes involved? Were they traditional violations of the codes of war, such as shooting prisoners and noncombatants, or did they extend into new areas, such as the conspiracy to launch wars of aggression and commit genocide? Which individuals would be held accountable at the highest level? Only the top political leaders? Or would military and industrial leaders be charged as well? Would there be an actual trial, or would a set list of offenders simply be assumed guilty and dealt with through administrative procedures: summary execution? If there were to be some kind of trial, what would it be like? Could it be designed to demonstrate both the absolute power and the absolute justice of the victorious Allies?

These are the questions which were debated vigorously within the American government and military hierarchy in late 1944 and early 1945: these debates form the major substance of Bradley Smith's book here under review. Smith, an academic historian whose book *Reaching Judgment at Nuremberg* (see *Magill's Literary Annual*, 1978) took readers into the judges' private chambers as they decided the fate of the top Nazis on trial, has now turned his considerable skills to the background of the trials. Some of the information he recounts here has been in print for a generation, but much of it is newly unearthed from American archives through his efforts. A companion volume of documents, *The American Road to Nuremberg: The Documentary Record* (Hoover Institution Press, 1981) will be of aid to future scholars of the questions he addresses.

Some readers may be disappointed by *The Road to Nuremberg*. The book deals almost exclusively with the American side of the issue; the British get some coverage, the Russians and French virtually none. The period from August, 1944, to June, 1945, is covered in bureaucratic detail, but the international aspects of "the road" from June to August, 1945, are given very short shrift. Questions such as "Why at Nuremberg rather than at Berlin?" are not covered at all.

Nevertheless the book is a significant contribution to an understanding of American policy toward Germany as the war ended. President Franklin D. Roosevelt, whom one might have expected to have played a central role in policy formation, emerges as an elusive and indecisive leader. At the Quebec Conference in September, 1944, Roosevelt seemed to stand firmly with Winston Churchill and his Lord Chancellor, Sir John A. Simon, who held that the Nazis whose guilt was patently obvious should be shot without any form of trial at all. At that meeting Henry Morgenthau, Jr., deeply angered by the increasing evidence of Nazi atrocities, also favored summary execution. Lord Simon and Prime Minister Churchill had long argued privately for such a course, since it would avoid lengthy legal proceedings. In 1815, they pointed out, Napoleon had also been dealt with by a purely political decision, in his case lifelong imprisonment on a faraway isle. Simon, Churchill, and apparently Roosevelt too, agreed that the Moscow Declaration had implied that a "political" rather than a judicial procedure was the most appropriate one for the leading Nazis. Such a drastic policy seemed consistent with the Morgenthau Plan for the economic deindustrialization of Germany, also apparently agreed upon at the same meeting, but the story of the Road to Nuremberg had barely begun.

It is surprising, perhaps, that the chief objections to summary execution came from the higher echelons of the United States War Department. Henry

Stimson, Secretary of War, a redoubtable Republican who lent important breadth to Roosevelt's war cabinet, was by no means pro-German, but he did have the perspective to see that a Carthaginian peace would not serve the long-run interests of the United States or of the world. He was a lawyer by trade who had made his early reputation "busting" trusts with conspiracy trials under Teddy Roosevelt. Now he reached the conclusion that the same conspiracy law theories could be adopted to try leading Nazi individuals and organizations. The record of their crimes would be spread out for all the world to see, while the justice of the Allied cause would be far better demonstrated than by summary firing squads. By the same token, once the basic case had been proven against the Nazi leadership organizations at the top, theoretically any member of those organizations could be relatively easily brought to justice in subsidiary proceedings. Thus a far greater sweep could be made through German society than by Churchill's firing squads, cleansing it of major and minor offenders and putting the country more firmly on the road to democracy. Stimson also opposed Morgenthau's drastic economic plan to deindustrialize Germany, because he believed Germany's recovery was essential to the long run well-being of the free world.

After the Quebec meeting, Roosevelt and Churchill soon saw the potential hazards of the Morgenthau Plan, and it was quietly scuttled. This change of heart opened up the way for Stimson's approach to the handling of war crimes, and thus a lengthy tale of bureaucratic maneuvering began.

It would be easy to caricature the contest as one between Roosevelt's political crony, Morgenthau, enraged at Germany for its genocidal policy against his fellow Jews, and the aloof, far-sighted, and slightly anti-Semitic Stimson fighting for an abstract concept of justice under law. Smith realizes, however, that such a version would do serious violence to the facts. First of all, though Morgenthau indeed advocated a very tough policy against the Germans, he was by no means the only one opposed to a major war crimes trial. Indeed, whenever any specific suggestion for a trial arose, numerous objections of both a legal and a practical nature came forth from all sides. Draft after draft was written, dismissed, modified, and written again. Many of the objections raised at that time have continued to concern legal scholars and historians (including Smith) to this day. On the other hand, several proponents of the trial scheme were prominent American Jews, such as Supreme Court Justice Felix Frankfurter. Doubtless many Americans, both great and small, had their share of ethnic prejudices during World War II, but the issues concerning policies toward a defeated Germany did not divide them clearly along ethnic lines.

After having been politically embarrassed by the Morgenthau Plan in 1944, Roosevelt refused to be pinned down on exact policies for postwar Germany. Much to the frustration of both the Morgenthau and the Stimson camps, the President played the role of an "artful dodger" on the war crimes trial issue right up until the Yalta Conference early in 1945. Proponents of the Stimson approach hammered out a "consensus document" which met some of the major political and practical objections and secured the signatures of three prominent cabinet members: Stimson, Attorney General Francis Biddle (who later would become an American judge at Nuremberg), and Secretary of State Edward Stettinius. Roosevelt had indicated his apparent agreement with its basic approach in conferences with his chief aide on the question, Judge Samuel Rosenman, and with Stimson, but he neither put his support in writing nor specifically advocated the plan at the Yalta Conference. In fairness, one must recall that Roosevelt was extremely unwell and that he had a multitude of more immediately pressing matters on his mind. Nevertheless, one must conclude that Roosevelt did not exercise any significant leadership role on the American road to Nuremberg.

After Roosevelt's death events moved very quickly. Harry Truman was briefed on the war crimes trial memorandum signed by Stimson, Stettinius, and Biddle back in January, and he adopted it as American policy. He then— through mechanisms even Smith has been unable to pin down— settled on Supreme Court Justice Robert H. Jackson as the United States chief counsel. During these same April days the German concentration camps at Dachau, Belsen, and Buchenwald were liberated by American and British troops. Public opinion was outraged by the gory reports and ugly pictures of Nazi inhumanity, and demanded that those responsible be brought to justice. As Smith correctly points out, the depravity of the liberated camps led to some American errors in understanding of the Nazi system: the emaciated human skeletons at Dachau or Belsen were not "typical victims" of planned extermination policies such as those implemented at Treblinka or Auschwitz. Nevertheless, public opinion firmed up in support of a trial system which would both expose the fullness of the criminal conspiracy and lead to justly severe punishments.

Britain still argued for summary hearings and executions for the top Nazi leadership. The Soviet Union, on the other hand, supported the concept of a trial, doubtless having in mind the Moscow purge trials of the 1930's as a model. In spite of some efforts by Morgenthau to bring the French to an anti-trial position, Charles de Gaulle let the United States War Department know that he would support a trial. The climactic meeting took place at the United Nations' conference in San Francisco in early May. By then Justice Jackson had made his influence felt in newly redrafted American proposals (detailed by Smith). Despite a last-minute attempt by Morgenthau to undermine the pro-trial position, Jackson and the American trial advocates prevailed. Additional drafts and additional negotiations among the Allies eventuated in the London Charter of August, 1945, which set forth the trial procedures. Although important changes in technical detail took place during those intervening months, the major concept which had originated with Stimson and his

War Department lawyer-officers in 1944 carried the day. International law would be expanded in significant ways beyond the traditional concept of war crimes. Specific individuals in the political, military, and diplomatic hierarchy would be held responsible for conspiracy to launch aggressive war. The charge for "crimes against humanity" would be added to traditional war crimes to cover the genocidal mass murders of civilians whatever their countries of origin. Organizations as well as individuals would be on trial, with the implication that any member of the organization could be held responsible for crimes of the common enterprise in subsidiary proceedings. Defendants were given opportunity for legal defense, but severe limitations were placed on the procedures to eliminate undue delay and guarantee that the guilty would not escape because of legal technicalities.

Smith believes that the trial itself and its outcome are sufficiently well-known so that he may be excused from describing them; however, an extra ten or fifteen pages of summary would doubtless have been useful for the average reader, who might feel himself left high and dry when the major narrative ends in June, 1945. Smith simply assumes that everyone knows what happened at the trials and goes on to consider broader questions in his conclusion. He is critical of the American trial plan, in retrospect, noting that it never solved the basic dilemma: to guarantee punishment of the criminals while preserving the majesty of an impartial court. Nor did the new ground broken for international law "produce a world in which aggression and atrocities ceased to exist, or one in which they were controlled through a system of international courts," as Stimson, Jackson, and the other proponents of the trial had hoped. Perhaps, he suggests, the Americans had planned too much and expected too much. In retrospect, it is probably true that one should be neither surprised nor chagrined that the International Military Tribunal was flawed; rather one should be surprised and pleased that it worked out as well as it did.

*Gordon R. Mork*

### Sources for Further Study

*Book World*. XI, May 24, 1981, p. 6.
*Choice*. XIX, September, 1981, p. 146.
*Kirkus Reviews*. XLIX, February 1, 1981, p. 204.
*Library Journal*. CVI, March 15, 1981, p. 660.
*New Statesman*. CII, October 9, 1981, p. 18.
*The New York Review of Books*. XXIX, February 18, 1982, p. 30.
*Publishers Weekly*. CCXIX, February 20, 1981, p. 84.

# ROMMEL'S WAR IN AFRICA

*Author:* Wolf Heckmann (1929-    )
Translated from the German by Stephen Seago
Foreword by General Sir John Hackett
*Publisher:* Doubleday & Company (Garden City, New York). Illustrated. 366 pp.
$14.95
*Type of work:* Military history
*Time:* 1940-1944
*Locale:* North Africa

*An account of the North African campaigns of Field Marshal Erwin Rommel during World War II, related through the experiences of participants of all ranks*

> *Principal personages:*
> FIELD MARSHAL ERWIN ROMMEL, Commander of Afrika Korps, later Panzerarmee Afrika
> GENERAL SIR CLAUDE AUCHINLECK, British Commander in Chief in the Middle East
> LIEUTENANT COLONEL FRITZ BAYERLEIN, Chief of Staff of the Afrika Korps
> GENERAL LUDWIG CRÜWELL, Commander of the Afrika Korps, 1941-1942
> ADOLF HITLER, Chancellor and Führer of Germany, 1933-1945
> FIELD MARSHAL SIR BERNARD LAW MONTGOMERY, Commander of the British Eighth Army
> LIEUTENANT GENERAL WALTHER K. NEHRING, Commander of the Afrika Korps, 1942
> GENERAL ENNO VON RINTELEN, German military attaché to Rome
> GENERAL SIR ARCHIBALD P. WAVELL, Commander in Chief in the Middle East
> GENERAL SIEGFRIED WESTPHAL, G1 Operations, Panzerarmee Afrika

This book has been expertly translated from the third corrected German edition, published in 1976. For the English edition, General Sir John Hackett, the author of *The Third World War* (1982), has contributed an appreciative and thoughtful Foreword. Heckmann, a sixteen-year-old Wehrmacht veteran at war's end, is a journalist whose twenty-six-year career included chief editorial posts in Munich and Hamburg. Since 1972 he has been a free-lance writer.

In his Preface to this edition, Heckmann notes two themes of the book: the first "was the fact that the war in Africa was a decisive dress rehearsal for the Allies which influenced the future of the fighting in Europe to an extent it is hardly possible to estimate"; and second, "Erwin Rommel became possibly the most overrated commander of an army in world history." In the first instance, he shows convincingly that the British had bungled badly in devising armored tactics and in designing and deploying tanks and antitank weapons. The British repeatedly misused their tanks by launching frontal attacks by scattered formations which, moreover, were composed of thin-skinned machines with armament far inferior to that of the Germans. Heckmann repeatedly compares desert tank warfare to naval battles on the high seas, where he says that concentration, movement, and armament are everything. It was not until the decisive Battle of El Alamein that the British Eighth Army had tanks (American-made Grants and Shermans) that could stand up to the German Mark III's and IV's and a general (Field Marshal Bernard Montgomery) who knew how to use them. Heckmann is especially enlightening on the detailed characteristics of the weapons available to both sides. Not surprisingly, he gives superior German arms, in particular the adaptable eighty-eight, much of the credit for General Rommel's spectacular victories of 1941 and the first half of 1942, but Rommel was mightily assisted, he points out, by British blunders, including the unreasonable demands of Prime Minister Winston Churchill.

Heckmann is not unappreciative of Rommel's great abilities; he only seeks to deflate the Rommel legend and reduce the general to true, human dimensions. After all, he notes, the leaders of the chorus of praise for Rommel were Churchill and Montgomery, his eventual desert nemesis, whose own accomplishments thus were magnified. In addition, officers who served under Rommel had an interest in perpetuating the legend of the immaculate warrior, particularly because his pressured suicide over his marginal implication in the Hitler assassination plot had made him something of a martyr and a "good German" to the Allies. Coincidentally, the memoir Rommel wrote of his African campaigns, *Krieg ohne Haβ* (1950, "War Without Hate"; translated into English as *The Rommel Papers*, 1953), did not detract from the legend.

As Heckmann reminds his readers, Rommel was Hitler's favorite general—he even had private access to the Führer, much to the annoyance of the professionals of the High Command of the Wehrmacht—and he resembled Hitler in his thirst for glory and in his addiction to illusions. Rommel is quoted more than once predicting his conquest of Suez, with its great British military base, and then the oil fields of the Persian Gulf. On one occasion, he would imagine leading his Panzerarmee into India to link up with Germany's Japanese ally; on another, his troops would storm over the Caucasus to administer the coup de grace to the "subhuman" Russian enemy. Almost recklessly indifferent to danger, Rommel exuded self-confidence, and because of those qualities, and his record of success, his men idolized him. Rommel met his match in Montgomery, however, who arrived in Egypt in August, 1942, and whose ego was even greater than Rommel's. Heckmann repeats a delicious story:

> When Monty heard of his appointment, so the story goes, he mused aloud gloomily about the tricks his trade could play on a man. "That's the way it goes with us professional soldiers. You work your way up the ladder, make a name for yourself—but one decisive

defeat is enough to lay your career in ruins."
Someone interposed: "Come, the Eighth Army's position is not all that hopeless. I
wouldn't paint quite such a black picture as that." Montgomery woke from his reverie:
"What do you mean? I was talking about Rommel."

Such was Rommel's fame during the years of uninterrupted German victories that the war, at least in Africa, had become personalized. Later, in
Tunisia and in Normandy, United States General George S. Patton sought
Rommel as his personal antagonist, in competition with Montgomery. There
is perhaps some irony in the fact that Montgomery used Rommel's favorite
tactic, a wide left hook around the German flank, at El Alamein in October,
1942.

The debate concerning Rommel promises to be a very long one. David
Irving, in his book, *The Trail of the Fox* (1977), calls Rommel a twentieth
century Hannibal, citing similarities in the tactics and other circumstances of
the two men. Irving is not uncritical of Rommel, however, especially of his
tendency toward self-pity when things went wrong, but most British and
American writers have been even less critical. Heckmann's own judgment
appears to have been summed up in a private letter written in 1959 by Major
General Heinrich Kirchheim to another veteran of Rommel's African war.

Concerning Rommel, my attitude is this: Propaganda—first by Goebbels, then by Montgomery, and finally, after he had taken poison, the propaganda of all the former enemy
powers—made of him the symbol of all that is best in soldiering. His qualities as a leader
were glorified, as were his qualities of character—in particular his chivalry, goodness, and
modesty! The idea was that any official criticism of this by now mythical character would
damage the image of the German soldier.

General Hackett finds this too harsh. Admitting that the Rommel legend has
been inflated, he believes that Rommel's reputation will eventually rest somewhere between the views at the two extremes.

The real value of Heckmann's book lies in its portrayal of war in the desert
as experienced by those on both sides who fought and died. He interviewed
hundreds of survivors (more than fifteen hundred, according to the dust jacket
blurb), from generals to privates, and he presents the war "from the bottom
up." Gleanings from those interviews are liberally sprinkled throughout the
text, supplying it with immediacy and power. Heckmann conveys the sights,
sounds, and smells of battle to an unusual degree: tanks nosing over the crest
of a ridge, the bark of the tank guns, the burning smell of cordite, and the
constant confusion of fluid combat.

The book is therefore a succession of vignettes of war in an inhospitable,
parched climate. Thirst was a principal affliction, but lice and an assortment
of desert creatures were constant companions. Death and maiming occurred
all around: "A splinter tore his belly open, he stepped into his own entrails
as he ran, and he died in the most dreadful pain." A doctor reached an

eighteen-year-old boy who, incredibly, was still conscious after being struck by artillery fire:

"Well now, where's it hurting you, young man?" asked the doctor. "Oh, everywhere, actually, I can't really tell anymore." He had three severe skull injuries, through which the brain was visible; one eye had been torn from its socket; there was an enormous hole under one shoulder blade, which went deep into the lung; one elbow joint was shot to pieces; and barely a finger was left on one of his hands.

The desert war was "clean" only in the sense that it was fought mostly in a sea of sand and rock, without cities and towns and civilian populations to be destroyed, too. That, presumably, was the war without hate.

The vivid battle scenes are held together by the rush of events and by the author's focus on Rommel. Heckmann's interviews are supported by extensive research in military archives in Britain and in Germany and in the memoirs and private papers of numerous veterans. The interviews comprise a unique resource to be mined by other writers, as David Irving has in *The Trail of the Fox*. Heckmann's illustrations include pictures of many of the various types of tanks and antitank weapons used in the desert war, as well as pictures of veterans of assorted ranks, as they appeared then and thirty-odd years later. Two pictures are particularly suggestive: one is of General Sir John Hackett, then NATO Commander of Northern Army Group, conferring with his superior, General Peter Graf Kielmansegg, Commander of Central Europe; the other, of a regimental reunion of Eighth Army veterans with their invited guest, a German who as a young gunner in Africa had earned the Knight's Cross for destroying nine of that regiment's tanks in one engagement.

*Rommel's War in Africa* is a brilliant re-creation of a part of the larger war, in which tactics and armaments were tested and gradually improved for the greater battles which lay ahead. The book ends with El Alamein, which, almost simultaneously with Stalingrad, marked the turning of the tide. In that view, the African campaign was decisive, and Rommel was Germany's last heroic commander.

*Albert H. Bowman*

**Sources for Further Study**

*Booklist*. LXXVII, April 15, 1981, p. 1136.
*Choice*. XVIII, May, 1981, p. 1320.
*Guardian Weekly*. CXXIV, June 28, 1981, p. 22.
*Human Events*. XXXIX, December 29, 1979, p. 17.
*Library Journal*. CV, December 15, 1980, p. 2568.
*The New Yorker*. LVII, March 9, 1981, p. 134.
*Observer*. August 9, 1981, p. 23.

# RUMOR VERIFIED
## Poems 1979-1980

*Author:* Robert Penn Warren (1905-    )
*Publisher:* Random House (New York). 97 pp. $9.95; paperback $5.95
*Type of work:* Poetry

*This, Warren's third book of poems during a four-year period of remarkable productivity, continues his fusion of fiction and recollection, meditation and speculation*

The existence of some of these poems is briefly mentioned in Robert Penn Warren's "Afterthought" to *Being Here* (1980), in which he makes a few remarks concerning the structure of that book, and the necessity of leaving out of it "certain poems composed during the general period." The structure of this new book is not quite as unified, perhaps, as that of *Being Here*; and the subtitles of the two books contain a subtle acknowledgment of that fact. *Being Here* is subtitled "Poetry 1977-1980," and *Rumor Verified* is subtitled "Poems 1979-1980." The first suggests something less miscellaneous; and one need only recall *Or Else: Poem/Poems 1968-1974* to be reassured that Warren is aware of such small distinctions.

As it turns out, this book is not as strong as its immediate predecessors. It was possible to say of Warren's 1978 collection, *Now and Then*, that it contained more of the year's best poems than any other single collection. *Rumor Verified* contains several very fine poems, and the book as a whole might arouse the envy of many a lesser poet; but by the standards which Warren has established for himself, this book is somewhat disappointing.

As it happens, a more recent poem than any of these is powerfully suggestive of the reasons for this book's failure to come up to the extremely high standard of *Now and Then*. It is called "Rumor at Twilight," and it appeared in *The New Yorker* (July 19, 1982). In three stanzas of nine lines each, it recounts a few moments of after-dinner meditation, or rumination, on what seems to be a well-kept lawn. As is so often the case in Warren's recent poems, the speaker uses the second person:

> In a dark cave
> Back on your land, like dark fruits, bats hang. Droppings
> Of generations, soft underfoot, would carpet the gravel—
> That is, if you came there. As you never do. Have you ever
> Felt, between thumb and forefinger, the texture
> Of the bat's wing? Their hour soon comes.

The mastery of this passage is undeniable: there is not a moment's confusion between the *you* who is intended to stand for the speaker, and the *you* who is asked the question about feeling the texture of a bat's wing; the second *you* is the reader, addressed directly in a manner familiar to readers of Warren's recent poetry. The dual meaning of the final sentence above is also under firm control: the bats will soon be out, and they, like everything else alive, will die.

The second stanza describes a person who has, apparently, a good life—respectful children, a kind wife, no financial worries—"just nags." Fireflies suggest those moments of memory "when, in darkness, your head/ Dents the dark pillow, eyes wide, ceilingward./ Can you really reconstruct your mother's smile?" Again, this is splendidly realized. Its only weakness is that it begins to sound like language which Warren has previously used. The image of the man staring ceilingward, in search of the past and its meaning, recurs often in Warren's poems.

The final stanza, however, contains most of this poem's evidence that perhaps too many of Warren's poems are made in the same way:

> You stand in the dark, heart even now filling, and think of
> A boy who, drunk with the perfume of hedge blossoms
> And massive moonrise, stood
> In a long lane and cried out,
> In a rage of joy, to seize, and squeeze significance
> From whatever life is—whatever. Above,
> High over your maples, the moon now presides. The first bat
> Mathematically zigzags the stars. You fling down
> The cigarette butt. Set heel on it. It is time to go in.

Considered in isolation, this is moving and powerful. Why should one take it to task? The problem is that, though it is given to few people to write like this, Warren has written some version of this stanza so many times that one begins to wish he would take up other subjects and images than those of the elusiveness of memory and significance, and other words than *drunk*, *rage*, *joy*, and so on. In short, there is nothing at all wrong with this poem except that Warren has written it too many times before. The question whether this is an unfair reaction belongs to a discussion of literary theory, but it needs to be kept in mind during a reading of *Rumor Verified*. Just how impatient may one be with poems which are better than most poets can produce, but not as good as others by the same poet? The question is slightly more complex, of course, in that it is now possible for many poets to imitate the mannerisms and extravagances that characterize Warren's weaker poems, however powerfully many of those same devices work in his best ones.

On the other hand, it is interesting to notice that many of the best poems in *Rumor Verified* are different in tone and kind from the best poems in *Now and Then*. In the earlier book, long poems based on recollection, such as "Red-Tail Hawk and Pyre of Youth" and "American Portrait: Old Style," gave the book its center of power. In *Being Here*, a concluding poem provided a surprise by returning to a more traditional structure based on four-line alternately rhymed stanzas. Similar short lyrics are more plentiful in *Rumor*

*Verified*, and are each distinctive, fully achieved poems.

"Basic Syllogism," for example, gives a formal, lyric framework to a subject which Warren has often explored; the compression makes familiar gestures seem fresh, and the poem ends with a sound of permanence. In the first stanza, the eye of a man half-asleep "receives/ News that the afternoon blazes bright." Then,

> It blazes in traumatic splendor—
> A world ablaze but not consumed,
> As if combustion had no end, or
> Beginning, and from its ash resumed
>
> The crackling rush of youthful flare.

Here Warren employs his familiar device of using rhymes that draw attention to themselves, as if it were important for the reader to recall that this is a poem, after all; but the technique is muted, so that *traumatic* strikes more forcefully than the rhyme between *splendor* and *end, or*. The final stanza takes up explicitly the sun's basic syllogism, confronting a question as old as poetry, but posed in anything but shopworn language: "I lie, and think how flesh and bone,/ And even the soul, in its own turn,/ Like faggots bound, on what hearthstone,/ In their combustion, flameless, burn." This is the kind of thing that very few poets have the depth of knowledge to carry off. The balance here between subject and individual voice, between words such as *flesh, bone, soul*, and *faggots*, and the distinctive sentence-sound upon which they are strung, is masterfully risky.

Similarly, "Vermont Ballad: Change of Season" takes up the inward grayness brought about in an elderly man by the grayness of the landscape. Then the question:

> But who is master here?
> The turn of the season, or I?
> What lies in the turn of the season to fear?
>
> If I set muzzle to forehead
> And pull the trigger, I'll see
> The world in a last flood of vital red—.

That kind of end, in other words, is not gray; so the speaker goes to the window and stares until he sees

> A man with no name, in the gloom,
> On an errand I cannot guess.
> No sportsman—no! Just a man in his doom.
>
> In this section such a man is not an uncommon sight.
> In rain or snow, you pass, and he says: "Kinda rough tonight."

The thought of a bullet in the head is not thus trivialized; doom is doom, however it presents itself.

Perhaps more typical of Warren's other rhymed poetry, in that its lines are longer, and its rhymes often more self-conscious, is a nevertheless moving poem, "Redwing Blackbirds," third in a sequence of four called "Glimpses of Seasons." The poem recalls, first, a remembered descent of a flock of these birds, then a later recollection of that sight, in the midst of sleep in winter. The vision passes, and the speaker wonders if he will live to see the redwings next year: "If not, some man else may pause, awaiting that rusty, musical cry,/ And catch—how gallant—the flash of epaulets scarlet against blue sky."

In these poems, Warren continues to extend the limits of his art, though he may fairly be accused of working with tired frameworks and phrases in other poems. Even in those modes, in this book once in a while will flash the kind of phrasing and immediacy for which he is famous. The opening poem of the collection, "Chthonian Revelation: A Myth," recounts a mysterious and wordless tryst in a cave on the Mediterranean, following which the two lovers leave the cave and swim toward the headland: "At arch-height of every stroke, at each fingertip, hangs/ One drop, and the drops—one by one—are/ About to fall, each a perfect universe defined/ By its single, minuscule, radiant, enshrinèd star."

As Randall Jarrell put it, a poet is someone who, in a lifetime of standing out in thunderstorms, manages to be struck by lightning a few times. A dozen or two dozen times, he continues, and the poet is a great one. Warren has not been struck many times in this volume, perhaps, but he is still at work in the storm, not content always to work from memory within a sheltered place.

*Henry Taylor*

### Sources for Further Study

*The Atlantic Monthly.* CCXLVIII, December, 1981, p. 88.
*Book World.* XI, October 4, 1981, p. 4.
*Christian Century.* XCVIII, October 28, 1981, p. 1106.
*Christian Science Monitor.* LXXIV, December 14, 1981, p. B2.
*Library Journal.* CVI, August, 1981, p. 1548.
*New Leader.* LXIV, December 14, 1981, p. 17.
*The New York Times Book Review.* LXXXVI, November 8, 1981, p. 13.
*Southern Living.* XVI, December, 1981, p. 120.

# RUSSIA IN THE AGE OF CATHERINE THE GREAT

*Author:* Isabel de Madariaga (1919-    )
*Publisher:* Yale University Press (New Haven, Connecticut). 698 pp. $40.00
*Type of work:* History
*Time:* 1762-1796
*Locale:* Russia

*A full-scale scholarly history of Russia under the rule of Catherine II that deals on a systematic basis with all facets of historical change during her reign*

> *Principal personages:*
> CATHERINE II, Empress of Russia, 1762-1796
> PETER III, her husband; Czar of Russia, 1762
> STANISLAS PONIATOWSKI, an early lover of Catherine; King of Poland, 1764-1795
> CHARLES-LOUIS DE SECONDAT, BARON DE MONTESQUIEU, a French essayist and political thinker
> CESARE BECCARIA, an Italian jurist and social thinker
> EMELIAN PUGACHEV, pretended Czar; leader of Cossack and peasant insurrection
> NIKITA PANIN, a Russian statesman; senior member of the College of Foreign Affairs
> GRIGORII POTEMKIN, a lover of Catherine; Russian statesman and general; governor-general of south Russian provinces
> A. V. SUVOROV, a Russian commander and field marshal

The reign of Catherine II (1762-1796) and the development of Russian government and society under her rule have been explored many times by scholars and by popular writers. On the one hand, there are numerous biographical studies, produced particularly for the casual reader, that deal specifically with the Empress' personal life, and the various lovers and courtiers whose place in Russian politics often enough derived from their relations with Catherine. Such works by and large have stressed Catherine's romantic concerns, and have depicted her many love affairs. For their part, researchers and professional historians generally have dealt with specific questions of foreign policy, political and economic change, and educational and cultural developments to provide monographs that, taken together, have expanded and enhanced knowledge of this portion of Russian history.

Hitherto there have been few efforts at a full-scale history on a broader thematic basis; among Russian writers, only one work, by the Estonian-Russian scholar Alexander Brückner in 1883, has dealt with the entire span of Catherine's reign. Soviet specialists have not supplied a balanced or sustained overview of the period of Catherine's rule, with the single exception of a textbook compiled in 1956 by a panel of historians, much as many Soviet writers in a narrower light have investigated issues and areas that previously had not been considered. Isabel de Madariaga's work is the first scholarly study in English to deal on a broad basis with the substantive questions of historial change in Catherine's Russia. By presenting a clear and well-rounded account of this period, she considers in turn the major areas, domestic and foreign, where Catherine's manner of rule was significant for the evolution of Russian society and government.

Catherine came to the throne in 1762, as the result of a coup d'état against her estranged husband, the strange and erratic Peter III. The author points to those areas where early in her reign Catherine's style of government combined distinctive features of liberalism and absolutism. For the Baltic provinces she suggested the curtailment of local privileges; in 1764 she carried out the abolition of the semiindependent office of the Cossack hetman in the Ukraine. Some of the previously semiautonomous Cossack lands were summarily attached to border provinces administered directly as part of the Russian empire. Many of the practical questions of government Catherine considered were posed within the context of Russia's social structure, which de Madariaga depicts in some detail. The hierarchy of hereditary and service nobility; the peasantry, divided into private serfs, church and court peasants, and those bound to the state; the urban estates and the Orthodox Church all held particular and in some cases conflicting interests.

In an extraordinary expression of the liberal bent of her early years, Catherine took the initiative in 1767 to summon a legislative commission drawn from all the provinces of the country. The nobility, clergy, townspeople, and peasants were represented by a fixed electoral schema. While in Russia this assembly was unprecedented in the extent to which it allowed broad participation in the open deliberation of questions of public policy, Catherine's instruction to the delegates struck an extraordinary tone of lofty idealism. She delivered a lengthy discourse on the framework of natural law within which the sovereign will could be exercised, and stated that the privileges and obligations of all subjects should be respected as set by their respective social stations. More remarkable, in an age when even in the West crime and punishment still were brutally handled, Catherine proposed that judicial inquiries should be conducted without any form of duress. Such precepts, in the main borrowed from Enlightenment thinkers such as Baron de Montesquieu and Cesare Beccaria, had never before been espoused by any European monarch. When the hundreds of delegates met in Moscow from 1767 to 1769, there were serious and protracted debates on the rights of the nobility, and at times as well on the status of the peasantry. Although the legislative commission did not produce a new code of laws, it is likely, as de Madariaga suggests, that Catherine hoped not merely to establish a philosophical basis for her government, but also in a more practical light to win acceptance from the several social estates for her rule as Empress.

Catherine's first ventures in foreign policy were rather forceful and grasping. Russian troops were maintained in Poland, and in 1764, to ensure the election of a king beholden to Russia, they assisted in the enthronement of Stanislas

Poniatowski, one of Catherine's former lovers. Further pressures for a formal alliance with Russia and against the privileged position of the Orthodox Church provoked widespread resistance in Poland; when in 1768 Orthodox Cossack irregulars violated Ottoman territory, war with the Turks broke out. While Catherine and her advisers had not been entirely prepared for this eventuality, Russian armies were able to achieve signal victories in the field. By 1770 they had overrun the Romanian principalities and, in their first expedition into the Mediterranean, Russian naval forces destroyed the Ottoman fleet off the coast of Anatolia. Moreover, fending off Austria's threats of intervention, Catherine and her ministers were able to achieve agreement with the Habsburgs and Prussia for the first partition of Poland (1772). In subsequent operations against the Ottomans, Russia forced the conclusion of peace by which it obtained territories on and access to the Black Sea.

Scattered peasant revolts had taken place from the beginning of Catherine's reign. During the Ottoman war, serious agitation spread among the more unruly Cossacks of the Yaik valley, west of the Urals. In 1773 the false czar Emelian Pugachev raised thousands of rebel soldiers and led his men across an area more than three hundred miles from his headquarters. In savage assaults on landowners and government officials, Pugachev and his followers left a trail of devastation and bloody retribution that marked the most serious rising of this sort to occur in Russia. Government forces were kept at bay for two years and could restore order only after prolonged fighting.

This ordeal brought home to Catherine the need for more systematic and closer measures of administrative control. She turned away from her long-time mentor and political adviser Nikita Panin and relied increasingly on new favorites. During the middle years of her reign, Catherine carried out a number of important reforms, and de Madariaga presents a clear and detailed overview of an area with which Soviet and Western historians have not dealt in depth. In 1775 Catherine issued sweeping directives for the reform of local government: territorial jurisdiction was assigned on a definitive basis, while police, judicial, and financial procedure were more precisely delineated. The Empress also urged that wherever possible schools and hospitals be constructed. In 1785 she drafted charters that specifically defined forms of urban self-government and the rights of the nobility. At the same time, in accordance with those features of absolutism that were a recurrent feature of Catherine's reign, she also imposed uniform administrative practices in frontier regions. The poll tax was introduced throughout the Russian Ukraine, and Catherine summarily abrogated the nobiliary constitution of Livonia. In keeping with her efforts at the integration of border provinces, Catherine entrusted the most celebrated and devoted of her lovers, Prince Grigorii Potemkin, with the colonization and development of the Crimea and other southern provinces conquered from the Turks.

Some of the characteristic features of Catherine's foreign policy were demonstrated once more during the crises of the later portion of her reign. Somewhat unexpectedly, Russia again became involved in a war with the Ottoman Empire (1787-1792), which for a time was joined by Sweden (1788-1790). Russian armies prevailed on both fronts, and forces under the great marshal A. V. Suvorov soundly defeated the Ottomans and compelled the cession of border areas. Moreover, Catherine reacted sharply and with some anxiety to the outbreak of the French Revolution, and was particularly fearful of possible repercussions in Poland. Russian troops were introduced, ostensibly to maintain order, and negotiations were initiated with Prussia and Austria for common action against radical organizations in the neighboring kingdom. While Russian armies brought much of the country under control in bitter, brutal fighting, in her last diplomatic initiative Catherine presided over the final partitions of Poland (1793, 1795) that eliminated it as a sovereign state.

Social and intellectual developments are considered in the remaining portions of de Madariaga's work, to provide a broader evocation of Catherine's Russia. The author supplies a summary account of the country's difficult and uneven industrial growth, and of the fiscal complications encountered when the government introduced paper money. Increased expenditure on civilian concerns such as the improvement of administration and the expansion of the educational system contributed to higher standards of public life. Catherine herself was a patron of the arts and encouraged both architecture and publishing enterprises; during the early years of her rule she was also rather tolerant of political and moral speculation. Literary works, including the first Russian dramas, were composed, and systematic historical works began to be written for the first time. Classical European literature and works of leading Enlightenment thinkers were made available to the reading public in Russia. Widened horizons of this sort brought Russia more closely into contact with Western Europe; with some means of independent expression, and with the growth of publishing activity, the Russian intelligentsia took form during this period. During her later years, Catherine became increasingly suspicious of Freemasons and, after the outbreak of the French Revolution, she ordered the suppression of works she considered inflammatory or subversive. On the other hand, although thenceforth the rift between Russian intellectuals and the government widened, new vistas in the nation's cultural life had been opened, foreshadowing the great literary and artistic efflorescence of the nineteenth century.

Thus while in several senses Catherine's reign was significant for the national development of Russia, de Madariaga concludes that her greatness must be measured against the more enduring consequences of her rule. The expansion of Russia's power and influence was accomplished in an awkward and authoritarian manner that amounted at times to the imposition of the Empress' will upon weaker neighboring states. Her foreign policy, while repeatedly successful, was grounded largely in the strength of Russian armies and the skill of their commanders. On the domestic level, administrative procedures were refined and closer coordination was established for the various branches of government, but many abuses remained, and Catherine did little to reverse the process of enserfment that overshadowed the social life of much of the country. In a more positive light, however, Russia drew much closer to Europe in norms and outlook. Catherine's legislation instilled a sense of honor and dignity; during her reign, government increasingly was left to civilians. Catherine tempered the forms of compulsion by which previous rulers had governed Russia, and indeed in dealing with opposition she was notably more restrained and moderate than her predecessors.

In this sense, the gulf between Russia and the West narrowed, to a greater extent than before or after Catherine. In these ways, therefore, Catherine's reign marked a crucial period in the emergence of Russia as a great power and as a nation.

*John R. Broadus*

## Sources for Further Study

*Choice*. XVIII, June, 1981, p. 1469.
*Christian Science Monitor*. LXXIII, May 20, 1981, p. 17.
*Encounter*. CCLXXIX, April 25, 1981, p. 115.
*History: Reviews of New Books*. IX, September, 1981, p. 240.
*The New York Review of Books*. XXVIII, May 28, 1981, p. 38.
*The New York Times Book Review*. LXXXVI, April 19, 1981, p. 10.
*The New Yorker*. LVII, May 11, 1981, p. 153.
*Times Literary Supplement*. July 17, 1981, p. 807.
*Virginia Quarterly Review*. LVII, Summer, 1981, p. 86.
*Wilson Quarterly*. V, Autumn, 1981, p. 154.

# RUSSIAN JOURNAL

*Author:* Andrea Lee (1953-    )
*Publisher:* Random House (New York). 239 pp. $13.50
*Type of work:* Travel account
*Time:* 1978-1979
*Locale:* Russia

*A series of sketches of everyday life in contemporary Russia; a talented young writer's first book*

"The teller of stories," says Fernando Savater, "has always just arrived from a long journey during which he has experienced both marvels and terrors." Andrea Lee's *Russian Journal* is a traveler's tale, with an intrinsic appeal that has not changed since the beginnings of literature: 2,500 years ago, a Greek traveler reported that in Egypt men urinated in a squatting position, rather than standing up.

In the era of the global village, Russia is still *terra incognita.* In 1971, Hedrick Smith went to Russia for a three-year stint as *The New York Times* Bureau Chief in Moscow. He used the time to travel as widely as the prestige of his position would permit, and thus was able to write the most comprehensive account of contemporary Russia now available, *The Russians* (1976). Yet he frankly admitted that vast sections of the country—and particularly the countryside—were closed to him, and that much of what he *was* permitted to see was clearly doctored.

Because Russia, seen from the West, is still mysterious, new books appear every year offering glimpses of everyday life there. Most of these "Russia-books" are quite ephemeral, repeating one another shamelessly, but there have been some of more lasting achievement: among these are Laurens Van der Post's *A View of All the Russias* (1964) and Mihajlo Mihajlov's *Moscow Summer* (1965). Now Andrea Lee's *Russian Journal* must be added to this select company.

Andrea Lee was twenty-five, a Harvard graduate student in English ("thinking of becoming a writer," the blurb says), when she went to Russia in 1978 with her husband, Tom, a Harvard doctoral candidate in Russian history. They were to spend eight months in Moscow, at Moscow State University, and two months—sandwiched in the middle of their stay—in Leningrad.

In Andrea Lee's hands, the marvels and terrors of the archetypal traveler's tale undergo a sea-change. The marvels become incongruities. There is a towering incongruity in her very first sentence: the main dormitory of Moscow State University, the Lees's residence during most of their time in Russia, is a titanic illustration of "Stalin Gothic," with a "daft excess of decoration that is a strange twentieth-century mixture of Babylonian, Corinthian, and Slavic. . . ."

The Lees's escort (and *stukach*, official stool pigeon) upon arrival in Moscow is Grigorii, a journalism student already well on his way to becoming a perfect Party man. Soon he is lecturing the Lees on American history, and in particular on "the Great Barbecue—the turning point of the Reconstruction period. Don't tell me you haven't heard of it!" Yet this Party *kandidat*, when not denouncing America, is smacking his lips over the underwear ads in Andrea Lee's copies of *Vogue*, and playing incessantly his "incredibly grainy third-hand recording" of Donna Summer's "Love to Love You, Baby."

Instead of terrors there are menacing undertones, an oppressive atmosphere. One Russian friend of the Lees was denounced to the KGB by the parents of his divorced wife . . . simply because they coveted his Moscow apartment. "Seryozha's life was not shattered," Lee says—"it had only been disrupted in a particularly degrading way." Another friend, Volodya, tells them how he was arrested in the 1960's with a circle of dissident young men like himself, workers revolutionized by Russian literature. After a week in Lubyanka prison he was released, told to stay out of politics and away from his former friends if he did not want to go to the camps. Volodya agreed: "They had beaten me on the head in prison, and that did something to me." Now he is forty, with a loving wife and an apartment that is his castle. On Sundays he and his wife, Anna, invite the Lees over for magnificent meals. Volodya plays his favorite Frank Sinatra song, "That's Life," on his black-market West German stereo:

> Leaning back in his chair with a grin on his broad face as lordly and expansive as that of an old Russian *barin* surveying his fief, Volodya, who knows no English, sang along phonetically with the song: "'I've been a poet, a pauper, . . . a pawn and a king. . . .'"

Lee is at her best in scenes such as that: unpretentious, cleanly rendered scenes of quirky individuality. There is virtually nothing in her book—no element of the Russian scene—that was not covered in Hedrick Smith's *The Russians* (1975), but in Smith's massive, thematically organized survey there are few extended scenes. Stories have to be kept short, subordinate to the point at hand. Lee's approach allows more latitude; she accumulates a richness of random, novelistic detail. She disclaims any intention to "explain the character of a political system, or a people. Each entry presents a small piece of Russian reality as seen by an American whose vision, if not refined by study, was at least not much distorted by prejudice for or against Communism."

Lee's *Russian Journal* consists of thirty-six sections, each headed by a date and title ("The Banya"; "Valerii"; "The Blues Abroad"; "May Day"). Until a few years ago, the publisher would have provided—as a matter of course—a table of contents listing these sections. Lacking any such listing (there is no index, either), the reader who wants to look again at a particular section is forced to hunt for it—or improvise his own table of contents as he goes.

The word "journal" in the title is a bit misleading, as are Lee's references to "entries." "Journal" suggests a calculated surrender to chaotic particulars: the writer will set down what the days offer, day by day. Journal entries are often brief, aphoristic, or crammed with detail; rarely are they neatly structured. Lee, perhaps wisely, did not attempt this demanding "formless" form. Although she tried to retain some of the immediacy of a true journal (emphasized by dating each section), there are no "entries" as such in her book, with the exception of one section entitled "Teaching," a running account of the clandestine English class she gave for a small group of Jews who were about to emigrate. Rather, the book consists of well-shaped scenes or episodes, about half of which—as she explains in her Foreword—were written in Russia, and half "composed later, in America, from notes and fragments jotted down at the time."

The thirty-six self-contained sections which make up *Russian Journal* do not add up to a conclusion or a judgment concerning "life in the Soviet Union today." Such conclusions are welcome when solidly supported, as in Hedrick Smith's *The Russians*, but it is one of the strengths of *Russian Journal* that Lee has disdained the half-baked, superficial, and cliché-ridden judgments with which so many travelers to Russia have burdened their books.

Lee has forsaken broad conclusions, as well as the pleasures of a continuous narrative, offering instead an unpredictable succession of disconnected sketches: a vivid, ironic section on Russian hippies—"They are *hippi* (for them, the word is a collective plural and is pronounced 'heepee')"—is followed by a brief and eerie section on Stalin's birthplace, the town of Gori in Georgia, site of the only remaining Stalin museum in the Soviet Union.

*Russian Journal* is the first book of a talented young writer. As such, it would have profited from more thorough editing. To cite only one example, an editor should have pointed out the very frequent appearance of adverbs of the Tom Swift variety, which are used sparingly in good contemporary prose: "Seryozha said ironically"; "said Volodya impatiently"; "he said indifferently"; "I said vaguely"; "said Nadia timidly"; and so on. The emotions labeled by such adverbs should, in most cases, be evident from dialogue and action; this labeling has a distinct and unwanted period flavor. There are a number of small stylistic problems such as this throughout the book, all of which could have been—and should have been—easily resolved by editing.

A more serious flaw is the almost total absence of literature and the wider life of the mind and spirit from Lee's small pieces of Russian reality. Lee devotes considerable attention to rock music; literature is relegated to a few passing references, such as her description of Mikhail Bulgakov's *The Master and Margarita* (1967) as "a modern classic novel disapproved of by the government." Her best friend in Russia, Rima, is a poet, yet her poetry receives just two dismissive sentences. It is difficult to understand this indifference, given Lee's background and given the extraordinary importance of literature—and poetry in particular—in Russia. Lee's manner seems to veer at times toward the cool, affectless world of Ann Beattie's *New Yorker* stories, where everyone speaks the language of pop culture.

Nevertheless, *Russian Journal* is a promising debut, and a small, valuable addition to the store of knowledge about tortured, alluring, mysterious Russia.

*John Wilson*

### Sources for Further Study

*Best Sellers*. XLI, January, 1982, p. 386.
*Library Journal*. CVI, October 1, 1981, p. 1920.
*The New Republic*. CLXXXVI, February 24, 1982, p. 36.
*The New York Review of Books*. XXVIII, November 5, 1981, p. 56.
*The New York Times Book Review*. LXXXVI, October 25, 1981, p. 11.
*Newsweek*. XCVIII, October 19, 1981, p. 102.

# RUSSIA'S FAILED REVOLUTIONS
## From the Decembrists to the Dissidents

*Author:* Adam B. Ulam (1922-    )
*Publisher:* Basic Books (New York). 453 pp. $18.95
*Type of work:* History
*Time:* 1815 to the present
*Locale:* Russia

*A chronicle of the valiant but unsuccessful struggles for political and intellectual freedom in Russia, from the Decembrist movement to dissent in the Soviet Union today*

> *Principal personages:*
> PAUL PESTEL, a prominent activist of the Decembrist movement
> NICHOLAS CHERNYSHEVSKY, a revolutionary writer and activist
> GEORGE PLEKHANOV, founder of Russian Marxism
> ALEXANDER KERENSKY, head of the Provisional Government, 1917
> VLADIMIR ILICH LENIN, leader of the Bolshevik Revolution
> JOSEPH STALIN, Dictator of the Soviet Union, 1924-1953

Nineteenth and twentieth century Russian history, so filled with ironies and tragic paradoxes, has been covered in countless books. Yet, it continues to be a fascinating and intriguing subject matter, as previously neglected material is being presented and a more revealing light is cast on the period. Adam B. Ulam, Gurney Professor of History and Political Science and Director of the Russian Research Center at Harvard University, respected author of several major works on Soviet Russia, addresses anew the baffling question of why the many liberal reform and revolutionary movements have been unsuccessful. His *Russia's Failed Revolutions* is an engrossing account of Russian history since 1815, and it goes a long way toward explaining why Russia has remained a repressive society with a highly authoritarian regime. Ulam contends that the inability of liberal democratic revolutionaries to make the requisite adaptation to nationalism was a crucial failure. Strong nationalistic impulses originally helped spawn oppositionist movements, yet in the end those very forces were effectively exploited by the authoritarian state to preserve itself. Thus, nationalism, rather than serving as a liberating force, bolstered the denial of freedom in Russia.

The story begins with the Decembrists, those "hesitant rebels"—mostly noble officers of the Imperial Army—who staged the abortive revolt of December 14, 1825. Their movement originated in the immediate post-Napoleonic period with the founding of the Union of Salvation, a secret society modeled after a Masonic lodge. Its members, although educated in the rationalist spirit of the eighteenth century, were also under the spell of the great romantic poets Lord Byron and Friedrich von Schiller. The stated goals of the movement included the reduction of illiteracy, the abolition of serfdom, and the establishment of a constitutional government. The latter is particularly noteworthy in view of the fact that in preceding times only conspiracies to commit regicide had occurred, amounting to not much more than the somewhat futile replacement of one autocrat with another. With the Decembrists, for the first time a group organized to overthrow the institution of the autocracy itself. Unfortunately, the rebels went about their business in an irresolute and amateurish manner. Moreover, men such as Paul Pestel, one of the society's leading intellectuals, were contentious and divisive. Bridging the gap between subversive talk and revolutionary action was a very considerable problem. The government, apparently quite well-informed of their activities, was not particularly alarmed. The sudden death of Alexander I and the succession crisis afforded an opportunity that could not be evaded. The rebels made their move, but, as Ulam describes it, it was as if their plan was programmed for disaster.

Nicholas I was determined to preserve the status quo. His reign of thirty years was a time of unrelieved oppression. A secret police apparatus came into being, the Third Section of the Czar's personal chancellery, which kept track of subversive ideas and organizations. A powerful instrument of the ruler, the Third Section was the prototype of similar, ever more efficient, institutions flourishing down to the KGB of today. Nevertheless, there were formidable disruptive forces at work which not even Nicholas I could fully subdue. They made certain reforms inescapable. Change was forced more directly by the impact of the disastrous Crimean War. The Russian surrender after the fall of the Crimean fortress Sevastopol in 1855 was a severe blow to the mystique of the regime.

Nicholas died that year, and his son Alexander II was determined to rule differently, to break with the past. The subsequent period of the 1860's and 1870's was one of social turbulence and revolutionary ferment, sustained by dedicated but largely ineffectual revolutionary students. The monarch wanted to be an agent of social change. He decided upon the most extensive and complex piece of social legislation of the nineteenth century: the emancipation of the serfs. It is hard to imagine, but up to that time Russia had been, in effect, a nation of slaves. Upon emancipation in 1861 there were approximately forty-three million serfs; together with their families they amounted to about four-fifths of the population. For a short time the Czar enjoyed the acclaim of the whole society as an agent of freedom; it was the high-water mark of the autocracy. Even such well-known advocates of revolutionary change as Alexander Herzen and Nicholas Chernyshevsky eulogized the autocrat in their respective publications. Soon, however, the radical intellectuals came to reject the "phony" emancipation. The peasants' lot had not improved materially. Indeed, in most cases they had less land for their own use than before.

A new revolutionary organization known as "The People's Will" stressed political agitation. Alas, to shake the peasants' uncritical faith in the Czar proved an all-but-impossible task. An active nucleus of the organization methodically resorted to assassinations and terrorist action. Following several earlier attempts on his life, Alexander II was killed by a bomb explosion in 1881. Alexander III not only refused to consider the revolutionaries' offer to call a halt to terrorism in return for the etablishment of a national assembly, but also he canceled whatever modest beginnings toward representative government had been made. His reign was severely reactionary and repressive; it put an end to all serious reforms from above and set Russia on the road to disaster.

The country experienced rapid industrialization, entailing a dramatic growth of the urban working class. It was a propitious time for the introduction of democratic socialist concepts and Marxism, effectively undertaken by George Plekhanov. Numerous groups of workers and intellectuals sprang to life, one of these being joined by Vladimir Ilich Ulyanov, alias Lenin. The last Czar, Nicholas II, assumed the throne in 1894. He ruled the doomed regime with unusual ineptitude and insensitivity. Modest expectations regarding representative government were turned away as "senseless dreams." A growing radicalization infected all sections of Russian society, as strikes and riots became more frequent. Ironically, the Czar's own secret police had initiated unionization in various cities in an effort to control this development and keep the radical organizations out. Ulam aptly compares this situation to the tale of the sorcerer and his apprentice.

Compounding the problem was the Czar's adventurism abroad. The difficulties with Japan over areas of China led to the calamitous war in 1904. Russia suffered a series of crushing defeats, contributing to the widening of civil disorder. The turbulence reached the point of upheaval in January, 1905, that "Bloody Sunday," when more than a hundred demonstrators were shot as they approached the Winter Palace in St. Petersburg. This outrage was the spark which ignited the flame of open revolution. Soon half a million workers were on strike and terrorist activities were commonplace. Facing a frontal assault, the autocracy reacted with uncharacteristic vigor and gained another lease on life. Martial law was imposed on the capital. The energetic and able Sergei Witte was appointed Prime Minister. The Czar was persuaded to issue the October Manifesto, envisioning certain constitutional limitations on government and a representative assembly. The first Duma was convened in 1906. The process of selection for membership in this bicameral assembly was mostly rigged. The members had no actual lawmaking capacity, and the Czar's ministers had virtually no responsibility to it. Yet, it proved unexpectedly assertive and critical of the government, leading to its inevitable dissolution by the Czar. The life of the second Duma was even shorter, lasting only from February to June, 1907. For the time being the autocracy had conquered the revolution. Many of the revolutionary elite had fled abroad, were imprisoned, or sent to Siberia.

Meanwhile, the St. Petersburg Soviet of Workers' Deputies emerged as a powerful political organ. It came to share with the government a kind of dual authority in the capital and was the progenitor of the soviet, the institution that was to give the new Russia its name. Successive Dumas, powerless as they were, nevertheless functioned as a public forum, openly criticizing the government and exposing the court's affairs. "Dark forces," most notably in the person of the sordid charlatan Grigori Rasputin, were perceived as influencing the Czar and quickened the erosion of the dynasty's status.

A sharp upturn in industrial strikes and revolutionary agitation was experienced by 1912. Ulam believes that Russia had ceased being an autocracy without becoming a constitutional state. Thus, when World War I came, it was seen in the most diverse political quarters as an answer to prayer. At first, the patriotic fervor muted political antagonisms, but the devastating military defeats brought mob violence at home and hastened the autocracy's demise. The Czar's own generals recognized the impossibility of a continuation of his reign. At last, in March, 1917, Nicholas II was induced to abdicate, permitting a peaceful transfer of power to a committee of the fourth Duma.

The acknowledged leader of the liberal revolution was Alexander Kerensky, Vice-Chairman of the now Petrograd Soviet and the Provisional Government's Minister of Justice and, from July, 1917, to its end, the Prime Minister. For a brief time Russia became the "freest country in the world," in the words of Lenin, the mastermind of the Bolshevik takeover of power in October, 1917. The difficulties encountered by the new government were staggering, as it sought to sustain the war effort while being challenged by extremist forces on the Right and on the Left. Russia was under a bizarre system of dual power. The Provisional Government and the Petrograd Soviet functioned like two half-governments. It was an untenable arrangement which allowed anarchy to prevail.

Lenin's return to Petrograd, made possible by assistance from the Imperial German government, was genuinely a "turning point in history." He came in time to prevent the impending *rapprochement* of the Bolsheviks and the Mensheviks and committed his followers to the destruction of the liberal democratic regime. Lenin's popular slogan "all power to the soviets" brilliantly served his purposes; it meant, in effect, no central authority at all. When the Red Guards of the Bolsheviks took over strategic points of Petrograd on October 25, 1917, they were not seriously challenged. Lenin's party gained control of the city and formed the Bolshevik (Communist) regime.

According to Ulam, if events were called by their right name, these momentous events of October, 1917, would be referred to not as a revolution, but rather as the beginning of a counterrevolution. Within the next three years, practically all the goals that the revolutionary movements and parties had striven for and partially put into effect were destroyed. The Soviet, so important as tool and symbol, ceased being a vital force in politics on any level in Russia after the Communists gained power. In its struggle to survive and rebuild the Russian state and empire, the Communist regime used the nationalist theme much as earlier regimes had when they were seriously challenged. The same may be said regarding its use of the autocratic principle. The Communists' decision to move the seat of government from Petrograd back to Moscow had a symbolic meaning. According to Ulam, they were fleeing from the revolution.

The book concludes on the note that extreme authoritarianism was inescapable for the Soviet state, although it is possible that a leader other than Joseph Stalin would not have resorted to such horrendous terror. Under Stalin, terror became an essential ingredient of the official ideology. Terror was used not only to make people obey, but also to make them believe. In the final chapter Ulam comments on how Stalin succeeded in making a whole nation his accomplice, giving Stalinism its enduring impact. Stalin sought to destroy the Russian revolutionary tradition, to make dissent unimaginable, and he nearly succeeded. Even after some years of de-Stalinization, the current generation of Russian dissidents faces all but insurmountable difficulties.

Ulam's central thesis—that nationalism has been the main force in Russia sustaining illiberal, authoritarian systems—though persuasive, is not entirely convincing. Additional important factors must have played a role in determining the character of Russian society.

Nevertheless, *Russia's Failed Revolutions* is an absorbing and scholarly work, containing new insights on recent Russian history. It is highly valuable also for presenting interesting new vignettes of the more notable activists and revolutionaries; much information is drawn from their own largely forgotten writings. Ulam's book should be read side-by-side with two important studies which also appeared in 1981, covering some of the same ground from different perspectives: Alexander Yanov's *The Origins of Autocracy* and Anton Antonov-Ovseyenko's *The Time of Stalin*.

*Manfred Grote*

### Sources for Further Study

*Choice*. XVIII, June 8, 1981, p. 1473.
*Christian Science Monitor*. LXXIII, April 8, 1981, p. 15.
*Current History*. LXXX, October, 1981, p. 334.
*History Today*. XXXI, September, 1981, p. 55.
*Library Journal*. CVI, February 1, 1981, p. 354.
*National Review*. XXXIII, May 15, 1981, p. 564.
*The New York Times Book Review*. LXXXVI, March 22, 1981, p. 12.
*Quill & Quire*. XLVII, June, 1981, p. 39.
*Times Literary Supplement*. October 2, 1981, p. 1132.
*Virginia Quarterly Review*. LVII, Summer, 1981, p. 90.

# THE SAGE OF MONTICELLO
## Jefferson and His Time, Volume VI

*Author:* Dumas Malone (1892-    )
*Publisher:* Little, Brown and Company (Boston). 516 pp. $19.95
*Type of work:* Biography
*Time:* 1809-1826
*Locale:* Virginia

*A narrative of the life of Thomas Jefferson after he retired from the presidency and returned to his native Virginia*

> *Principal personages:*
> THOMAS JEFFERSON, former President of the United States
> JAMES MADISON, fourth President of the United States, 1809-1817; a friend of Jefferson
> JOHN ADAMS, second President of the United States, 1797-1801; reunited friend of Jefferson
> MARTHA JEFFERSON RANDOLPH and
> MARIA JEFFERSON EPPES, Jefferson's daughters

With this final volume, historian Dumas Malone completes one of the most ambitious projects ever undertaken by a scholar-historian in this century: a six-volume biography of Thomas Jefferson, one of the most interesting, complex, accomplished, and energetic of the Founding Fathers, a man who gave his name to the age in which he lived and which he dominated. Reviews of earlier volumes have called the project "ambitious," "magisterial," and "monumental." Now finished, *Jefferson and His Time* (6 volumes, 1948-1981) lives up to all its praise.

Some years ago, Malone was asked how any biographer could possibly capture the multisided and always elusive Jefferson. After all, the man had done so much, had had so many interests and experiences, and had encouraged his powerful mind to roam so widely. Among other things, Jefferson could be called an agronomist, an architect, a politician and statesman, a musician, a scientist, a philosopher, a businessman, an intellectual and social commentator, an educator, and many more deserved titles. How could any one biographer snare this man? Malone's reply, typically modest and self-deprecating, was, "I try not to get lost on the side roads or pathways, but stick to the main highway."

What is the "main highway" to Malone? In his introduction to the first volume of this biography (published in 1948), Malone offered readers the "road map" he would follow for the next thirty-three years:

He [Jefferson] was confident that time was fighting for his ideas, and that human progress was certain, if only tyranny and artificial obstructions were removed. . . . If he must be given a single designation, he was a liberal. Liberty was his chief concern, and his major emphasis was on the freedom of the spirit and the mind.

Through the first five volumes, Malone keeps to his central theme as he follows his subject through his development and his many public offices, climaxing with Jefferson's presidency of 1801-1809 (volumes 4 and 5).

The sixth volume, entitled *The Sage of Monticello*, examines the last seventeen years of Jefferson's life. After four decades in the public spotlight, Jefferson was an *observer* of national events, on the sideline, where (if one is to believe Jefferson himself) he would have always preferred to have been. He turned his attention to improving Monticello (with special care given to his gardens), basking in the affections of friends, neighbors, and grandchildren, and trying to put his financial affairs in order and extricate himself from debt.

Yet Jefferson in retirement remained a keen observer of national and international affairs. Though he tried desperately during his presidency to avoid war with England, by 1810 his patience seems to have been exhausted, and when war finally did come in 1812 Jefferson understood that the British had left Americans only the two options of submission or war. Not disposed to criticize or oppose his friend, coworker, and presidential successor James Madison, Jefferson supported the war and allowed his anti-British feelings free rein. Indeed, when the war ended without resolving what he considered to have been the major outstanding issues between the two nations (especially the impressment of American seamen), Jefferson showed considerable irritation.

While perhaps not as intellectually flexible as in his younger years, Jefferson seemed to recognize that postwar America required new answers to its problems. To be sure, he never abandoned his opposition to a public debt (his own debts were causing him greater and greater strain) or to a national bank, but he did understand that his previous opposition to native manufacturing and tariffs were outdated after the War of 1812 and needed to be revised. Never enthusiastic about either manufacturing or tariffs, however, Jefferson accepted them as a "necessary evil."

In the last decade or so of his life, Jefferson's need to dominate those around him seems to have increased. Though Malone does not say so, perhaps this inclination was caused by Jefferson's realization that he had so little time left (he was seventy-two years old at the end of the War of 1812, though generally in good health) to do all the things he wanted to do. He meddled in the lives of his grandchildren, but certainly out of love and concern rather than malice. Yet perhaps the greatest example of Jefferson's will (to say nothing of his willfulness) is his almost single-handed effort to found the University of Virginia, a project which he undertook in 1779 and never abandoned even after the founding in 1819. To Malone it is a story of triumph, a victory which to the author confirms his conclusion that in his later years Jefferson "rendered his most memorable public services as an advocate of enlightenment." The "sage of Monticello" constantly pressured the state legislature, dominated the board, designed the buildings, selected the faculty, set up the administration and the curriculum, and chose books for the library. Indeed, no institution of higher learning owes more to one individual.

Yet the battle to found the "academical village" was constant and wearing, and in the end Jefferson came away with less than he wanted. The niggardly state legislative made funding a problem: faculty appointments (especially that of the controversial Thomas Cooper—who ultimately did not come) were difficult; the architecture (now much admired) was the subject of much discussion. If Jefferson did not win all his points, he won enough so that the University of Virginia became a new educational model for a new nation, a place where, as William Howard Taft once remarked, Jefferson was still spoken of "as though he were in the next room."

Malone weaves other important threads into the fabric of Jefferson's later years, all told before but now seen in the larger context of the man's life: the renewal of his friendship with John Adams; the selling of his personal library to the government, to become the nucleus of the Library of Congress; the increasing distress over the slavery crisis. Yet through it all, Malone never loses the central theme, never strays far from his self-created highway. And at the end of this enormously ambitious project he can declare (as he did at the beginning of it) that

> [T]o those who exalt force and condone deception he [Jefferson] will always be a visionary, to be ignored or silenced. But to all who cherish freedom and abhor tyranny in any form he is an abiding symbol of the hope that springs eternal.

In the years since Dumas Malone began his multivolume work, other biographies of Jefferson have appeared, some of which emphasize points with which Malone does not deal in depth or points with which he disagrees. Some of these other works add to a fuller understanding of Jefferson. In the end, however, Malone's contribution towers over all of them. If no biography of any man or woman is definitive, Malone's *Jefferson and His Time* is as close as one is likely to get.

*William Bruce Wheeler*

### Sources for Further Study

*The Atlantic Monthly*. CCXLVIII, August, 1981, p. 83.
*Christian Century*. XCVIII, October 28, 1981, p. 1106.
*Christian Science Monitor*. LXXIII, August 10, 1981, p. B1.
*Library Journal*. CVI, June 15, 1981, p. 1301.
*The New Republic*. CLXXXV, August 1, 1981, p. 32.
*The New York Review of Books*. XXVIII, August 13, 1981, p. 4.

*The New York Times Book Review.* LXXXVI, July 5, 1981, p. 1.
*The New Yorker.* LVII, July 20, 1981, p. 110.
*Newsweek.* XCVIII, July 27, 1981, p. 65.
*Time.* CXVIII, July 27, 1981, p. 80.

# SAKI
## A Life of Hector Hugh Munro

*Author:* A. J. Langguth (1933-     )
*Publisher:* Simon and Schuster (New York). Illustrated. 366 pp. $14.95
*Type of work:* Literary biography
*Time:* 1870-1916
*Locale:* England, the Balkans, Russia, and Paris

*The first full-length biography of Hector Hugh Munro reveals many hitherto unknown facts about the life and character of an artist of the British short story*

> *Principal personages:*
> CHARLES AUGUSTUS MUNRO, a British police officer in Burma
> MARY FRANCES MUNRO, his wife
> LUCY JONES MUNRO, his mother
> CHARLES ARTHUR,
> ETHEL, and
> HECTOR HUGH, his children
> CHARLOTTE ("AUNT TOM") and
> AUGUSTA MUNRO, his spinster sisters
> A. ROTHAY (ROY) REYNOLDS, a journalist friend of Hector Hugh
> JOHN LANE, Hector Hugh's publisher

Up to now, little has been known about Hector Hugh Munro except that he used the pen name "Saki"; that he wrote a number of witty short stories, two novels, several plays, and a history of Russia; and that he was killed in World War I. His friend Rothay Reynolds published "A Memoir of H. H. Munro" in Saki's *The Toys of Peace* (1919), and Munro's sister Ethel furnished a brief "Biography of Saki" for a posthumous collection of his work entitled *The Square Egg and Other Sketches* (1924). A. J. Langguth's *Saki* is the first full-length biography of the man who, during his brief writing career, published a succession of bright, satirical, and sometimes perfectly crafted short stories that have entertained and amused readers in many countries for well over a half-century.

Hector Munro was the third child of Charles Augustus Munro, a British police officer in Burma, and his wife Mary Frances. The children were all born in Burma. Pregnant with her fourth child, Mrs. Munro was brought with the children to live with her husband's family in England until the child arrived. Frightened by the charge of a runaway cow on a country lane, Mrs. Munro died after a miscarriage. Since the widowed father had to return to Burma, the children—Charles, Ethel, and Hector—were left with their Munro grandmother and her two dominating and mutually antagonistic spinster daughters, Charlotte ("Aunt Tom") and Augusta. This situation would years later provide incidents, characters, and themes for a number of Hector Munro's short stories as well as this epitaph for Augusta by Ethel: "A woman of ungovernable temper, of fierce likes and dislikes, imperious, a moral coward, possessing no brains worth speaking of, and a primitive disposition. Naturally the last person who should have been in charge of children." Because of Hector's delicate health as a child, he escaped such beatings as were generously administered to Charles. Mischievous and sly as a small boy, Hector as he grew older and even as a man sometimes indulged in practical jokes whose flavor often resembled that which spices his stories.

Hector followed his father and his brother Charles into the Burma military police, but after seven bouts of fever he returned to England and settled in London to write. His first book scarcely anticipates the later writing which would bring him fame. *The Rise of the Russian Empire* (1900), influenced by Edward Gibbon's *The History of the Decline and Fall of the Roman Empire* (1776-1788), romantically pictures a Russia that Munro was not to see until as a foreign correspondent he lived in St. Petersburg (now Leningrad) in 1904. The reviews of his history disappointed Munro. Wisely, as it turned out, he shifted his writing to political satire and parody, in which he collaborated with a popular cartoonist, Carruthers Gould. Parodies of Lewis Carrol's *Alice's Adventures in Wonderland* (1865) and Edward Fitzgerald's *Rubáiyát of Omar Khayyám* (1859), published in *Westminster Gazette*, drew attention to the writer who signed himself "Saki" (the wine bearer in the *Rubáiyát of Omar Khayyám*).

Langguth comments on Munro's choice of the name by which he would be remembered. "He was young and merry and bright," says Langguth, but he was also

> old and sad and cruel. It was Hector who would write the best of the stories; it was Munro who would go off to war. But the name of Saki could stand for both of them—for Hector when he passed on his joyous errand among the guests, for Munro when he sought the cup [of death] at the river-brink. In Omar Khayyam, Hector Munro found an ambiguous pseudonym more appropriate than he could know.

In keeping with this view of Munro, Langguth refers to him as Hector until the more serious and seemingly fatalistic side of his nature begins to predominate. From 1913 to the end he is usually called Munro.

The publication in 1902 of *Alice in Westminster* (with Carruthers Gould's cartoons) was both a critical and a popular success. Munro's conservative political views influenced his acceptance of an offer from the Tory *Morning Post* to write as a foreign correspondent, and during the next six years he sent news articles to London from the Balkans, Russia, and Paris.

Munro had begun his writing career by imitating Gibbon. He had parodied Lewis Carroll and the Edward Fitzgerald translation of the *Rubaiyat*, and in 1902 he published several parodies of Rudyard Kipling's *Just So Stories* (1902). In September, 1901, though, Munro introduced to readers a character of his own invention, a young dandy and social butterfly named Reginald who was to become the protagonist of a series of fifteen stories collected and published in book form under the title *Reginald*. The popularity of Reginald as a character led to the publisher's entitling Munro's next book *Reginald in Russia* (1910) despite the fact that Reginald appeared only in the title story.

The Reginald stories, as many of their titles suggest, usually depend less upon plot or other narrative characteristics than upon Reginald himself and his opinions or observations, which are by turns impudent, rude, sardonic, and irreverent. The satire is often directed at British stuffiness and pretense.

The two Reginald books were published by Methuen & Company. The first received several favorable reviews; little attention was paid to the second. Neither volume brought much money to Munro, and he switched to John Lane, who published all six of his remaining books, including the two posthumous ones, *The Toys of Peace* and *The Square Egg and Other Sketches*.

*The Chronicles of Clovis* (1911) had only a modest sale, but the volume of twenty-eight stories contained several which were later to be anthologized as classics of modern British short fiction. In "Tobermory" a talking cat wreaks havoc by revealing secrets about men and women at a house party in a fashionable home. "Mrs. Packletide's Tiger" employs a blackmail scheme by which Louisa Mebbin gains a pleasant cottage in Dorking through a threat to tell the true story of Mrs. Packletide's attempt to outshine Loona Bimberton socially.

Langguth points out that the blackmail or exposure theme appears in several Munro stories. Munro knew that he himself could have been the object of exposure threats if anyone had been tempted to try. Briefly supplying some information about her brother to an American correspondent in 1952, Ethel declared: "One subject he never wrote on, was sex, and I am certain if he had he would have made fun of it. The best way to treat it." There was a reason why he might have chosen not to write about sex: he was homosexual. He could create young men like Reginald in the early stories and Clovis Sangrail in later ones, whose mannerisms and waspish tongues might, for many readers of later generations anyway, suggest possible irregular sexual proclivities. He did not need to court trouble for himself, however, by treating a theme that might have drawn too much attention to his own proclivities.

Langguth reports that word had quietly spread about Munro's interest in young men. John Lane published Munro's books and also those of Oscar Wilde—whose love affair with young Lord Alfred Douglas had led to Wilde's disgrace and a prison term. Lane knew more about Munro's sexuality than he wanted the general public to know. According to Langguth, "When anyone raised the topic around Lane, he put his hands over his ears and pretended not to hear."

If Ethel divined any special significance in her brother's frequent references to young men in his letters to her from several countries during his years as a foreign correspondent, she apparently paid little attention. It is possible, though, that some of the many letters she destroyed might have revealed more about his sexual preferences than he would have wanted known. In her

"Biography of Saki," when she quotes an excerpt from one letter she remarks that it was written "when he was chumming with a friend, one Tocke." Writing of his stay in St. Petersburg, she again mentions "a friend who was chumming with him." She does not specify the degree of "chumminess," but Langguth says that it sometimes included live-in arrangements.

To Langguth, Munro's bringing Turkish baths into several stories suggests "unmistakable first-hand knowledge." He may at times have gone to such baths seeking male partners. Langguth also reads a possible sexual meaning into some cryptic squiggles in the margin of a number of pages in Munro's diary, and he suspects that a lover is being protected by a nickname in the dedication of *The Chronicles of Clovis*: "To the Lynx Kitten, with His Reluctantly Given Consent, This Book is Affectionately Dedicated. H. H. M." Apparently, until the appearance of Langguth's biography, Munro's sexual inclinations, though known by numerous friends and acquaintances, were kept discreetly hidden from the public.

With a collection of clever parodies and three books of short stories that displayed his wit and verbal adroitness, Munro had demonstrated by 1911 that he was a master of the brief literary narrative. Then, like many another short story writer before and since, he was pressured into writing a novel. The result was *The Unbearable Bassington* (1912), which Langguth calls only a "half-success." At least Munro showed in it that he was more than a mere comic writer.

This novel was followed in 1913 by *When William Came*, a brief novel picturing an England that has been defeated by Kaiser William's Germany in a war which was won through a superiority in ground and air forces. The novel is chiefly memorable for its prophecy of the catastrophic and, for most people, unexpected war which began in 1914.

It is for his stories that Munro is read and remembered today; his fourth collection, *Beasts and Super-Beasts* (1914)—its title a take-off of George Bernard Shaw's *Man and Superman* (1903)—contains among its thirty-six tales several that show him in top form. "The Open Window," probably the most frequently reprinted of Saki's writings, is an artful blend of humor and a ghost-story theme. In "The Schartz-Metterklume Method," mischievous Lady Carlotta, seizing a sudden opportunity to impersonate a governess, employs engaging inventiveness as she entertains herself in carrying out Mrs. Quabarl's instruction to teach four young boys and girls so as to make them *"interested in what they learn."* "The Lumber-Room" gives Munro one of several literary opportunities, long delayed, to get revenge on his Aunt Augusta for her treatment of the Munro children. Several stories carry over from *The Chronicles of Clovis* variations on the werewolf theme and a curious streak of cruelty which today might pique the interest of a psychiatrist.

When war came in 1914, Munro was angered by the agitations of British pacifists, and in an article in *Outlook* he wrote, "If these men are on the side of the angels, may I always have a smell of brimstone about me." The article, Langguth says, reveals "the moralist hidden within the satirist. Once freed, this scourge and scold could never be cajoled into taking up again with raillery and innuendo."

Munro enlisted in the cavalry but transferred to the Royal Fusiliers. He rejected offers of a commission as an officer and opportunities to serve as a German interpreter. He was excited by the prospect of direct conflict. He rose from private to corporal and, though he was in his forties, he retained good health despite the rigors of trench life.

He would probably have relished the sudden drama which ended his life in November, 1916. His company had been sent out of the trenches in early morning darkness. During a lull in the roar of guns, a soldier lighted a cigarette. Munro said, "Put that bloody cigarette out." Hearing the words, a sniper fired and the British Saki quaffed at last the "darker Drink" from the goblet offered by the Persian wine bearer whose name he bore. He was forty-six. Many years later Ethel Munro wrote a correspondent, "I am thankful that Saki did not live to be old; he hated the thought of old age. . . ."

If, as a result of Langguth's revealing and appreciative biography, Munro's collected stories enjoy a revival, it will be one they richly deserve. Although they present characters, scenes, and action belonging to Edwardian England, the best of them display a nimble wit, high spirit, and a linguistic virtuosity that are timeless.

*Henderson Kincheloe*

**Sources for Further Study**

*The Atlantic Monthly*. CCXLVIII, August, 1981, p. 87.
*Harper's Magazine*. CCLXIII, August, 1981, p. 76.
*Library Journal*. CVI, July, 1981, p. 1424.
*National Review*. XXXIII, July 10, 1981, p. 788.
*The New Republic*. CLXXXV, September 23, 1981, p. 38.
*The New York Review of Books*. XXVIII, October 8, 1981, p. 33.
*The New York Times Book Review*. LXXXVI, August 16, 1981, p. 12.
*Saturday Review*. VIII, July, 1981, p. 80.
*Time*. CXVIII, September 7, 1981, p. 67.
*Times Literary Supplement*. November 6, 1981, p. 1293.

# SAM SHEPARD
## Seven Plays

*Author:* Sam Shepard (1943-     )
*Publisher:* Bantam Books (New York). 288 pp. $3.95
*Type of work:* Drama
*The collected plays: La Turista*, 1967; *The Tooth of the Crime*, 1972; *The Curse of the Starving Class*, 1978; *Buried Child*, 1978; *Tongues*, 1978; *True West*, 1980; *Savage/ Love*, 1981

*Seven plays, produced from 1967 to 1981, that demonstrate the full range, power, and lyrical intensity of one of America's most impressive, provocative, and enigmatic dramatists*

The publicity blurb on the cover of the Bantam edition of *Sam Shepard: Seven Plays* calls him "America's most brilliant and irreverent young playwright." This statement, although a typical advertising cliché, is worth examining, both for what it says and what it implies. "Most brilliant"?—perhaps, though the primary appeal of Sam Shepard's plays is visceral, not intellectual; "irreverent"?—certainly, though the "irreverence" is hardly the simple cynicism of a Kurt Vonnegut or Thomas Pynchon; "young"?—while thirty-eight is not exactly doddering (Shepard was born November 5, 1943), it is not what is usually thought of as "young" in an American artist—particularly one who has been writing for almost two decades! The implication of the phrase is that Shepard is a new discovery, a relative beginner who has just caught the attention of the public. That implication says more about the state and recent history of American theater than it does about Sam Shepard.

Shepard's first plays appeared in the mid-1960's, and he quickly established himself as one of the central figures in the New York "Off-Off Broadway" movement, a burst of noncommercial, experimental theatrical activity that aimed at nothing less than a thorough rejuvenation and transformation of the American theater. In this it was a dramatic counterpart to the wider social, political, and cultural agitation that characterized America in the late 1960's and early 1970's. As the "greening of America" never quite happened, however, so the "New American Drama" never crystallized. While Off-Off Broadway is still alive, it can no longer be considered a "movement"; it has become simply a relatively noncommercial, experimental regional theater. Of the dramatists who made up the core of the OOB movement, only two have achieved national reputations that seem likely to last, Lanford Wilson and Sam Shepard, and both needed a decade and a half to do so.

It was not until *Buried Child* received the Pulitzer Prize for drama in 1979 that Shepard's name became generally known, perhaps helped by his emeregnce as a first-rate film actor in *Days of Heaven, Resurrection*, and *Raggedy Man. Sam Shepard: Seven Plays* is a recognition of that new reputation. It shows his development in five representative plays, from his first full-length effort, *La Turista* (1967) to one of his most recent, *True West* (1980). The other two "plays," *Savage/Love* and *Tongues*, are actually semi-improvisational "theater pieces" put together in collaboration with Open Theater director Joseph Chaikin, and are, while interesting, not especially germane to Shepard's development.

Perhaps it is unfair to ascribe Shepard's struggle for recognition to simple neglect; he is a most difficult playwright. From the beginning of his career Shepard's audiences and critics have been impressed by the power of his plays and, at the same time, frustrated by their inability to articulate the sources of that power or even understand with any precision their own reactions to the works. Even the most problematical of modern playwrights—Samuel Beckett, Eugene Ionesco, Jean Genet, Harold Pinter, Bertolt Brecht, Edward Albee, to name the most obvious—can eventually be pigeonholed as either some kind of "realist" or as a practitioner of one of the many "nonrealistic" approaches to theater that have proliferated in the modern drama ("symbolism," "surrealism," "expressionism," "Absurdism," "theatricalism," "Epic Theater," and so on). Shepard fits into none of these categories. His plots seem erratic, arbitrary, fragmentary, and frequently fantastic, yet they also seem to be heightened versions of the real, immediate world. His characters are bizarre, obsessive, and insane; their identities constantly shift or dissolve altogether, yet they are not symbols or ciphers or abstractions: they are real human beings. Shepard's plays deal with many of the fundamental questions of our time and culture—identity, meaning, death, the "American Dream," success and failure, love, family, roots—yet there is not one Shepard play whose "theme" can be abstracted and contained in a single phrase.

Perhaps it is not even correct to call Shepard's works, especially the earlier efforts, "plays" at all: "theatrical rituals" would probably be more accurate, with equal emphasis on both words. They are rituals because of their incantatory power and sometimes by their metaphorical relationship to recognizable religious, cultural, literary, or mythic rituals; but they are self-consciously performed as theater by actors assuming roles in front of audiences. Therefore, the best approach to grasping Shepard's plays is to drop the terms *plot*, *character*, and *theme* and substitute *music*, *image*, and *ritual*.

The most obvious use of music in the plays is the direct incorporation of songs and/or instrumental music into the dramatic action or background, but even more important is the fact that Shepard generally structures his plays "musically" rather than "narratively." That is to say, he presents themes and variations which he builds, modulates, juxtaposes, and rephrases in the manner of a musical composition. Within this framework are "duets" between characters, extended "arias" (or monologues), and, in the manner of jazz, apparently "improvisational" digressions.

This musical analogy extends even more pervasively to the language itself, and no American playwright, present or past, has used language more emphatically and elaborately than Shepard. He "plays" language like a jazzman improvises on his instrument, using words not only for their meanings, but also for rhythm, color, image, and pure sound.

Although Shepard refers to a wide variety of musical styles in his plays—country and western, pop, folk, disco, blues, jazz—the most pervasive is hard rock, probably the most important single influence on his work. Richard Gilman, in his excellent Introduction to the anthology, quotes Shepard as saying in 1971: "I don't want to be a playwright; I want to be a rock and roll star. . . . I got into writing plays because I had nothing else to do. So I started writing to keep from going off the deep end," and he has, in fact, played drums for the rock band Holy Modal Rounders.

If music, especially rock, provides the underpinnings for most of the plays, it is the image, both visceral and verbal, generally combined in clusters of related, recurring images, which develop throughout the plays in powerful, surprising ways. At the same time, Shepard's imagination sometimes leads to an overload or even a clash of images that can become more confusing than provocative.

The imagery usually begins with the title, which is frequently either the primary image (*La Turista*, *Buried Child*, *Tongues*) or provides the context for the development of such image clusters (*True West*, *Curse of the Starving Class*). These suggestive title images are then made concrete with the sets. *La Turista* is a good example. The set is both "realistic" and "abstract." While obviously a motel room in Mexico, it is also an inferno of colors, even to the characters' red skins, punctuated by a few vital, suggestive objects (beds, suitcases, magazines). Immediately a harsh, even dangerous atmosphere is created.

The establishment of a special "world" for the characters is crucial to the plays, one that already contains energy, tension (and sometimes confusion) ready to explode in action. Whether elaborate or simple, there is never anything in a Shepard set that does not stimulate a visceral response and/or play a central function in the development of the action. The set of *The Tooth of Crime*, for example, consists only of "*A bare stage except for an evil-looking black chair with silver studs and a very high back, something like an Egyptian Pharaoh's throne, but simple, center stage*," quite enough for a play that consists of one long, single, elaborated action, a duel or "walkdown" between two rock stars for possession of the throne. Even in the recent "realistic" plays, with more or less representational sets, crucial images are emphasized in the setting: the set of *Curse of the Starving Class* is dominated by a refrigerator and pile of wooden debris, both of which take on profound resonances in the course of the play; in *Buried Child* a flickering television set becomes a focal point of action and theme.

The physical imagery persists throughout the plays, reinforced by the language. *La Turista*—the illness that attacks tourists—sets the "sickness" imagery of the play, which explores, in a progressively more intense, erratic, and disturbing way, the "sickness" of being American or, perhaps, simply human. Images of sickness, death, and decomposition saturate the language of the play. In Shepard's best work the musical structures and rhythms combine with such patterns of imagery into powerful, unique dramatic rituals.

Two such rituals comprise the action of *La Turista*, a play about the archetypal American tourist couple: Kent (the man) and Salem (the woman). In the first act Kent becomes sick from "la turista" and medical help arrives in the form of a costumed Mexican witch doctor and son. Kent collapses and the witch doctor performs a voodoo ceremony, which includes the decapitation of two chickens and the splashing of their blood on Kent's prostrate body. In the second act, which actually precedes Act One in time, Kent and Salem occupy an American hotel room, where Kent comes down with sleeping sickness (or perhaps a drug overdose? a bad trip?). The medical team arrives, another father and son team (played by the same actors), this team dressed in Confederate Army garb, complete with pistol. In this act the voodoo ceremony is replaced by Shepard's favorite cultural-mythic ritual, the "cowboy walkdown." When Kent refuses treatment and accuses the doctor of wanting to turn him into a "beast," the doctor draws his pistol. Kent retaliates by "drawing" and pointing his index finger. The two stalk each other, "shooting" verbally with increasing frenzy. The duet culminates with Kent swinging over the doctor's head on a rope and crashing out of the room, leaving the outline of his body in the wall in the manner of an animated cartoon character.

The "walkdown" ritual is repeated, even more elaborately, as the central action of *The Tooth of Crime*. The duel is between Hoss, the champion rock star, and Crow, his challenger. During the first act, the challenge is made, the hero prepares himself, and the "townspeople" (Hoss's coterie of followers) wait expectantly. In the second, the challenger arrives, the contenders feel each other out carefully, and finally they clash in a pure, extended, ritual shoot-out. Their weapons are costumes, words, and gestures or, more precisely, "styles," but these are as deadly as guns; Hoss, the loser, does, in fact, finally shoot himself. The contest is formalized and generalized by having a referee, dressed like an NBA official, a scoreboard, and a chorus of cheerleaders. As the men stalk each other, Hoss and Crow assume different identities, languages, styles; they copy and parody each other, probing for weaknesses. Paradoxically, the two men are very real, both as individuals and as archetypes who exemplify, in Gilman's words, "the exaltation and tragedy of fame." In *The Tooth of Crime* Shepard merges the "cowboy" and the "rock star," the two primary character types in his vision. Both are lonely, alienated, free-spirited types, ultimately doomed by lost meanings, the deadness of their culture, the falseness of its myths, and their own frustrated intensities.

These techniques and ideas carry over into Shepard's more recent works, but in a subtler, more "realistic" fashion, and this apparent turn in the direction of orthodoxy probably helps to account for his recent recognition. It is no accident that his most acclaimed play, *Buried Child*, is his most accessible. Will this new application of his talents and vision to a more conventional dramatic approach result in a full realization of Shepard's potential? Or, while this shift might give the plays more cohesion and direction, will it mute their music, energy, and originality?

*True West*, the most recent play in the anthology, is disappointing. Like *The Tooth of Crime*, *True West* invokes the Western "walkdown," but the realistic content of the play almost submerges the ritual completely. Austin, a devitalized screenwriter who has sold out to commercialism and Hollywood, is besieged by his rough older brother Lee, an "authentic" cowboy type, free-spirit, and free-lance burglar. As Lee gradually assumes the "artist" role, Austin retaliates to win back his manhood by burglarizing the neighborhood. Eventually the competition escalates to violence as Austin strangles Lee while their mother looks on. Except for a few scattered images—especially the mass of toasters Austin accumulates during the play—*True West* lacks the poetry and power of the earlier plays.

In *Curse of the Starving Class* and *Buried Child* Shepard turns his attention and new approach to the subject that has long been the staple of American theater, the family. Both plays focus on the disintegration of a lower-middle-class rural family. In *Curse of the Starving Class* the family is not exactly starving, at least not literally, but they are certainly hungry, hungry for meaning, for direction, for recognition, for love. Both the father, Weston, and the mother, Ella, think they can find those things by selling the homestead, but the children, Emma, who is just coming of age, and Wesley, the older son, know better. "It means more than losing a home," Wesley tells his mother, "it means losing a country." Of course they do lose it in the end, to gangsters, to pay the father's "old debts." This summary makes the play sound mercilessly bleak and completely conventional, but it is neither. The energy and vision of Ella and especially of Weston suggest hope, even if the story offers none, and, while the plotting is ordinary, even trite, the play contains some of Shepard's most lyrical and intense speeches, along with some extremely potent physical images, notably the empty refrigerator, which takes on symbolic importance, and the concluding visual image of the play, a bloody skinned lamb carcass.

Like *Curse of the Starving Class*, *Buried Child* ends with a powerful image. As the aged father, Dodge, lies dead on the floor and Halie, the mother, rambles on at the audience about the rain and the new crops, Tilden, the eldest son enters: "*In his hands he carries the corpse of a small child at chest level, staring down at it. The corpse mainly consists of bones wrapped in muddy, rotten cloth.*" It is a shattering conclusion to a play that, despite a number of uncharacteristic literary echoes (Henrik Ibsen's *Ghosts*, 1881; Pinter's *The Homecoming*, 1967; Albee's *The American Dream*, 1968) is a strikingly original, purely Sam Shepard version of basic American themes—family, success, loss of roots, the American dream. In *Buried Child* Shepard has tamed his imagination and lyrical flights without, as in *True West*, stifling them altogether. The conflict between the three generations, sparked by the competition between the two sons, Tilden and Bradley, and the intruding grandson, Vince, is a powerfully convincing realistic action that becomes almost mythic by the introduction of potent physical images. Although realistic in presentation, the final moments of the play achieve ritual intensity to move the audience at the deepest levels. *Buried Child* thoroughly deserved its Pulitzer Prize (the first awarded to an Off-Broadway play).

It is not possible yet to see where this new direction will take Sam Shepard. Only one thing seems certain: he will continue to experiment, to improvise, to let his talents and vision find their own directions. Certainly the recent shifts in theme and approach, whether temporary or permanent, present risks, but it has been by the taking of risks that Sam Shepard has established himself as the most exciting playwright in America today.

*Keith Neilson*

**Sources for Further Study**

*American Playwrights: A Critical Survey.* I, 1981, pp. 81-111.
*Village Voice Literary Supplement.* December, 1981, p. 7.

# SAND RIVERS

*Author:* Peter Matthiessen (1927-    )
Photographs by Hugo van Lawick
*Publisher:* The Viking Press (New York). 213 pp. $19.95; paperback $11.95
*Type of work:* Natural history
*Time:* Late 1979
*Locale:* Selous Game Reserve, Tanzania, and East Africa

*A natural history account of a safari into the unmapped, inaccessible Selous Game Reserve*

Writer and naturalist Peter Matthiessen and wildlife photographer Hugo van Lawick joined a safari in late 1979 into the Selous Game Reserve in southern Tanzania, East Africa.

The Selous is not a park and has no facilities for visitors. It is the largest wildlife sanctuary on the continent of Africa and is second in size only to the Wood Buffalo Park in Alberta, Canada. Its area of twenty-two thousand square miles makes it larger than Wales or Maryland, and it claims it to be the home of thirty-six species of large mammals. Of all the great parks and game reserves in East Africa, it remains the least accessible and the least known.

Britisher Tom Arnold, a theatrical producer and Member of Parliament, had organized the expedition. He had been traveling to Africa for several years and had spent a great deal of time with Brian Nicholson, the former warden of the Selous. In 1976, Nicholson, also a charter pilot, flew him down to the Selous. Arnold was fascinated, saying that there was an enigma about it and that it was a vast wild place that scarcely anyone knew.

Arnold found that almost nothing had been written about the Selous, and he hit upon the idea of an ultimate safari, with Peter Matthiessen writing the book, Baron van Lawick as photographer, and Brian Nicholson as leader. Lawick was working with Louis and Mary Leakey, the anthropologists, when he was commissioned by National Geographic and became their man in East Africa. Later, he became a free-lance photographer, and he readily agreed to join the safari.

The book takes the form of a journal in which Matthiessen notes not only flora and fauna but also the personalities of the people on the trek. Brian Nicholson is the leader and the leading character, a man utterly absorbed in keeping unspoiled this last outpost where no white men have ever been before. At the beginning, Nicholson is described as cross, stiff, and uneasy, scarcely ever looking anyone in the face, a tall thin man with a sardonic expression. Matthiessen calls him a bitter man, cynical about all forms of progress.

Matthiessen constantly refers to Nicholson's two idols, Frederick Courtenay Selous and Constantine John Philip Ionides. Selous was a naturalist, elephant hunter, and explorer who was once "white hunter" to Theodore Roosevelt.

The Game Reserve was named after him in 1922. Ionides, or "Iodine" as he came to be known, was born in Southern England in 1901. He became a British Army officer but early in a promising career retired from the Army, taking up solitary hunting expeditions. He was much influenced by Frederick Courtenay Selous' book *A Hunter's Wanderings in Africa* (1881). He considered Selous' death in 1917 a personal loss and became deeply interested in working for the Selous Game Reserve.

During a tenure of more than twenty years as the Selous Game Ranger, Ionides worked tirelessly to extend this wilderness with its poor soil and abundant tsetse flies. He discouraged human settlement, believing that the boundaries of the Reserve should be enlarged for the wild animals for which it was best suited.

Ionides was an early conservationist who dreamed of a great and self-perpetuating African wilderness where animals might wander in "merciful ignorance" of human beings. An outbreak of sleeping sickness from the tsetse fly in regions he wished to add to the reserve, helped with his proposals.

Brian Nicholson began working for Ionides in the early 1950's when he was nineteen, and they became fast friends. Ionides trained him as his assistant in elephant control to take over most of his duties; in turn, Nicholson considered Ionides as a foster father.

Ionides formally retired from the Game Department in 1954 to give full time to collecting uncommon creatures on commission for various clients, including the National Museum in Nairobi, which still displays Ionides' gorilla group, bongo, and addax, and an assortment of other creatures including a black mamba snake. Ionides was an avid snake collector and used to find the hospital verandas at Mtwara excellent places for snaring cobras.

With the "Africanization" of the park warden jobs in the early 1970's, the wildlife industry lost much of its international appeal, and the reduction of game wardens, engineers, and mechanics led to a revival of poaching, which previously had been brought under control. Nicholson, realizing that he was beating his head against a wall, resigned his post and returned to Kenya, where he found a job as a charter pilot. He never lost his first love for the Selous, though, and thus was easily persuaded by Tom Arnold to lead the safari, although he admitted grave doubts about the conditions they would find in the game reserve.

Among others invited on the safari as guests were Maria Eckhart, who was born at the foot of Mt. Kilimanjaro; David Paterson, a young Hong Kong businessman; Richard Bonham, director of Nomad Safaris; and Melva Nicholson, Brian's wife, and his family. All of these stayed at the base camp with Tom Arnold while Peter Matthiessen, Brian Nicholson, and the native porters proceeded on a foot safari following dry river beds ("sand rivers").

They trekked for two weeks through the wild bush, encountering no one, going through a wilderness no white man had ever seen before, not only seeing animals at close range but seeing them in minute detail. They found that, although there is less game now than there was twenty years ago, there are still herds of animals that are truly wild and without experience of fear of humans.

They had to avoid close contact with the unafraid lions, elephants, and hippopotamuses. Though they carried guns, only once were they alarmed to the point that they might have to shoot to save their lives. This was when they stumbled upon a mother rhinoceros and her sheep-sized calf at ten yards. Would she charge? Matthiessen calls her the ugliest and most beautiful creature imaginable. Luckily, the near-blind, huge creature did not attack. Matthiessen observes that the rhinoceros has been on the earth six hundred thousand years and has no enemy but man.

In the Selous, the most recent estimate of rhinoceros numbers, made during the air survey of 1976, arrived at the figure of four to five thousand, the last large, healthy population of this species in the world.

Nicholson is very fond of elephants, as is Matthiessen. In his monograph on "The African Elephant," Nicholson says that when feeding on new grass, the elephants appear to get into a very contented frame of mind and it is possible to approach to within fifteen yards without much risk of being seen. The contented elephants either close their eyes completely when grazing or else look down toward the ground at their feet. The elephants gorge themselves on the fallen fruits of the marula tree, which seem to ferment in their stomachs and make them drunk or sleepy, causing them to lie down on their sides and snore, and Nicholson says one can hear an elephant snore from a great distance.

There is no scarcity of hippopotamuses. Matthiessen describes a herd of a hundred hippos resting on their knees in the thick gray broth of mud and manure. They had stomped the water lettuce to a green mat. The banks of this large pool are packed and baked as hard as concrete. Sometimes, he says, hippos remain underwater for minutes at a time, just soaking or enjoying short strolls over the bottom. Then their heads emerge, their froggish pink eyes and round pink ears and then their large nostrils that can close tight underwater. The hippo calves are born and suckled in the water and lie so low, with only their nostrils showing, that they are hardly noticeable. Although Matthiessen and his friends had no untoward hippo experiences, Nicholson tells of a time when an angered hippo bit a man in two.

The crocodile is shunned at all times, and when one is sighted by those getting a bath, it takes the languor out of bathing. When the safari came out on the banks of the Luwegu River, they saw no elephant at all but only a large crocodile which was lying out on a bar along the bank, its jaws transfixed in the strangled gape with which these animals confront their universe.

Nicholson has great respect for the leopard, whose big, deep, tearing coughs resemble the sound of a ripsaw cutting wood. He says that the leopard is keen in eyesight and hearing as well as sense of smell and can hide so well that he is invisible even when closely approached. Following a wounded leopard is very dangerous; Nicholson's stepfather was mauled by one and had to have his leg amputated.

Matthiessen calls the impala the emblematic antelope of Africa; it seems to occupy the ecological niches filled further north by the gazelles. In the long grass of the miombo shrub, these elegant antelopes have the kongoni habit of climbing onto ruined termite mounds in order to see better. Their harsh snorts, sounding like a sneezing bark, serve as a warning of the approach of any lion.

The sable antelope with its harlequin head moves with the elegance of a horse, unlike its relatives the wildebeests, the gazelles, and the kongoni, who all bounce along with that odd gait called "pronking." The sable antelope has been given the generic name Hippotragus (horse antelope) because it lifts its hooves high, head high too, chin toward the chest, as if to accentuate the grand sweep of the curved horns.

The wildebeest has imposing horns, but Matthiessen says such horns are ill-suited to a long sad face with odd ginger eyebrows. The wildebeest has a goat's beard, a lion's mane, and a slanty back like a hyena; the head is too big and the tail too long for its rickety body, and Africans say that the wildebeest is a collection of parts that were left over after God had finished all the other creatures.

Zebras yap and whine like dogs and are not hunted by the natives because the tribesmen of the Sudan-Zaire border believe eating striped beasts—kudu, bushbuck, eland, zebra—may bring on leprosy.

Only one animal draws contempt from Matthiessen—the hyena. He says it has the most disagreeable call, which fills the night with excited whoopings that turn to high eerie giggling and laughter. Its footprints resemble those of a dog but it is really an aberrant cat.

Matthiessen describes the African animals with loving detail but he does not neglect the birds. Some that he mentions are the chinspot flycatchers, white-headed black chat, the lesser blue-eared starling sparrow weavers, brown-headed parrot, African skimmers, greenshanks, the little stint, hornbills, white-headed vultures, bee eaters, green pigeons, violet-crested turaco, golden buntings, white-breasted cuckooshrike, pied barbet, and a flock of thirty-two open-billed storks. He explains that their bills have an odd space between them through which one can see the sky.

The unusual trees and flowers encountered on the safari are described and are pictured in some of the sixty-four color photographs by Lawick. These pictures capture the mood of the safari and are works of art.

At the end of the trek Matthiessen asks Nicholson if he thought the safari was worthwhile. Nicholson admits that when the idea was proposed to him he was against bashing off into the bush with some folks he had never before seen. By the journey's end, however, he has taken a great deal of pleasure in coming back to the Selous, checking out the game and visiting the old trails. Nicholson says that the Selous is the only place on earth where he feels that he belongs, but when asked if he would want to be buried in the Selous, as Ionides had requested, he replies that he does not care what they do with him after he is dead.

Nicholson does care, however, what happens to the Selous. He thinks the Selous ought to be set up under its own authority, financing itself and administering itself, not vulnerable to people who are not really interested. If only for economic reasons, Tanzania owes it to the future of its country to see to it that this place does not disappear, because it is precious and unique.

*Ellen Devereux*

### Sources for Further Study

*The Atlantic Monthly*. CCXLVII, May, 1981, p. 84.
*Christian Science Monitor*. LXXIII, April 13, 1981, p. B1.
*Library Journal*. CVI, March 1, 1981, p. 567.
*Natural History*. XC, June, 1981, p. 76.
*The New York Times Book Review*. LXXXVI, May 27, 1981, p. 1.
*Newsweek*. XCVII, April 27, 1981, p. 92.
*Saturday Review*. VIII, April, 1981, p. 68.
*Smithsonian*. XII, April, 1981, p. 153.
*Times Literary Supplement*. October 23, 1981, p. 1227.
*The Wall Street Journal*. CXCVII, May 11, 1981, p. 26.

# SAUCE FOR THE GOOSE

*Author:* Peter De Vries (1910-    )
*Publisher:* Little, Brown and Company (Boston). 232 pp. $11.95
*Type of work:* Novel
*Time:* The 1970's
*Locale:* Terre Haute, Grand Rapids, and New York City

*A good-humored, highly verbal spoof of practically everything contemporary, including consumer advocacy and feminism, though human nature—both male and female—seems to be the major satirical butt*

> *Principal characters:*
> DAISY DOBBIN, a young writer-career woman, reasonably liberated
> EFFIE SNIFFEN, her Terre Haute contemporary and New York rival
> BOBSY DIESEL, their college classmate (perhaps unreasonably liberated) and now editor of *Femme* magazine
> JENNIE DOBBIN, Daisy's mother, a professional citizen and passionate consumer advocate
> FRANK DOBBIN, Daisy's father, a Terre Haute paving contractor
> DIRK DOLFIN, a Dutch international businessman, owner of *Metropole* magazine, one of ten best-dressed men
> DOG BOKUM, a womanizing supervisor at *Metropole* magazine

No matter what the specific content of his novels, Peter De Vries writes with wit and humor and, nearly always, of the desperate strategies with which unhappy, unmoored American men and women, chiefly of the affluent classes, attempt to disguise, if not palliate, the triviality and emptiness of their lives. More often than not, De Vries's novels imply positive values absent from his characters' aimless and frenetic experiences, and he hints that what they need to fill the void is as simple a thing as faith. It becomes increasingly clear in *Sauce for the Goose* (the prolific and trenchant humorist's twentieth novel, depending on which list you consult) that De Vries has in mind old-fashioned religious faith, though recognizing the realities of mid-century life and the difficulties of fiction, he never allows his characters to break through to a conversion. Their denials, however, sometimes indicate their dissatisfaction in the absence of belief.

Toward the end of *Sauce for the Goose*, the protagonist Daisy Dobbin, her career and personal life in shambles, passes the time in her father's hospital room by reading an "unpublishable novel." De Vries observes that the woman in the unpublishable novel "was turning to religion on page a hundred and twelve." He adds, "That was, for Daisy, a window on which intellect had forever drawn the shutter."

Daisy's sometime lover, Dirk Dolfin, an international businessman trained for the Dutch Reformed clergy, whispers to her "sweet nothings" after making love, but "his sweet nothings were among the weightiest things in Christendom." After making love the first time, he tells her the distinction between supralapsarianism and infralapsarianism. The second time, "he murmured some more church history, elucidating doctrines grimmer, if possible, than the last. . . ."

Another of De Vries's comic devices functions also to keep the reader aware of the need for belief, or the trappings of belief. When Daisy "sins" against her feminist doctrines, or otherwise lapses from the standards she sets for herself, she mentally assigns penances—sometimes ten Hail Marys, sometimes five Our Fathers, or Ten Gloria Steinems, Betty Friedans. Thus, though Daisy Dobbin is herself ironically distanced from the practice of religion or serious thought about it, De Vries suggests the substitution of feminism for Christianity—and he suggests the need for belief. Like most fine humorists, De Vries keeps a steady eye on the darker side of life; he recognizes that comedy deals with matters of life and death. The epigraph to *Tents of Wickedness* (1959) pointed up his awareness of the tradition of "serious humor," for it read: "You must not think me necessarily foolish because I am facetious, nor will I consider you necessarily wise because you are grave."

The epigraph to *Sauce for the Goose* is appropriately a poem by Elinor Wylie (1885-1928) which wryly sums up the state of being both human and woman. The poem begins with the hope not to confuse oneself with either eagle or antelope. As a human, the poet says, one is born alone; as a woman, one is hard beset and lives by squeezing nourishment from a stone. Still, though "the years go by in single file," Wylie says none "has merited my fear/ and none has quite escaped my smile." The irony of the verse and the circumstances of Wylie's unconventional life in the 1920's make the epigraph doubly significant.

De Vries's publisher rightly denies that *Sauce for the Goose* is "a satire on women's lib," though, at first, one has the uncomfortable feeling that the book is willfully setting up situations to make legitimate feminist protest appear both shabby and trivial. The bare bones of the plot support such a reading, but bare bones rarely represent a good book to advantage. De Vries's very exuberance assures that he will not single-mindedly reduce any aspect of America's makeshift culture and morality to simplistic terms. As a novelist, he makes sure that he sets up no straw men, and, if he raises a smile at the sometimes excessive ardor of feminists, he also ridicules their opponents. Enough funny things happen in this book and enough targets are sighted and hit that feminism can be said to take its proper place as *part* of the American culture of the 1970's.

Daisy Dobbin, a highly verbal and caustic child of average, nutty parents in Terre Haute, emerges from Kidderminster College, her head filled with considerable erudition imparted by various "dehydrated old parties" (dop's) and is writing for a Long Island paper. At the urging of her college classmate Bobsy Deisel (who dresses like a stevedore, smokes panatelas, and can sing in two registers at once—"a laryngeal fluke"), Daisy undertakes to infiltrate New York publishing houses to expose the widespread practice of sexual harassment. At her first job, she attracts the interest of no one but an earnest soul who inquires if she has "made a decision yet." When she asks about what, the answer is "For Christ." The humor increases as Daisy tries to attract the lechery she does not find. She works her wiles on happily married Leo Pokus, for whom the promise of a sexual adventure suggests the necessity of telling his wife all. Daisy demands of Bobsy: "Get me out of this den of rectitude."

At her next assignment, this time at *Metropole* magazine, Daisy scarcely has time to attract prurient interest before she falls in love with the magazine's publisher, Dirk Dolfin, for whose affection she finds herself competing with her girlhood chum, Effie Sniffen, whose mother Josie was Daisy's father's girl friend in his youth. Like most undercover agents and spies, Daisy suffers a conflict of heart and head, feelings and duty. She tumbles almost at once into Dirk's bed and goes to great efforts to forestall his offering her any advancement in return for her favors. Ironically, with their marriage at the end of the book, Dirk gives her the magazine. Ample reward, indeed.

In what appears to be De Vries's most blatant underselling of the woman's movement, he allows both Daisy and Effie to foreswear all principles of sisterhood in the battle for Dirk. Furthermore, he makes Bobsy Diesel a caricature of the man-hating lesbian. After unsuccessful sexual overtures to Daisy, Bobsy decides to assign the exposé of sexual harassment to another writer. Daisy tells Bobsy that the experience "shows how right you are about sexual harassment on the job. You don't exaggerate. It's everywhere."

Daisy's feminism is never quite convincing. An aphorism spoken by a dull date drives her to commit herself. He says "The female mentality is like a bar of soap—constantly eluding our grasp." De Vries assures the reader that Daisy is a feminist "as ardent as any in essentials," but he adds that she thinks the word *sexist* the movement's "crowning foolishness." He suggests almost total insensitivity when he has her wonder "who would not want to be whistled at by truck drivers?" Here and elsewhere De Vries reveals his position as an aging middle-class American man.

When Daisy expresses her estimate of the "foolish susceptibilities of middle-aged men," De Vries cannot resist editorializing, "which perhaps aren't all that foolish." The author's values come through also when Daisy recalls things that her mother's cleaning woman said, such as referring to a mannish woman as "one dem 'lezibethans" and to another as "one dem 'maciated women." Humor at Bobsy Deisel's expense slips into the stereotypical, as in her being able to sing in two registers and loving kumquats—a sexual allusion. In college she earned the nickname of "Lay miserable" and her coiled hair reminds Daisy of German pastry and of snakes. An even better comedy and satire would be a book in which the author's hand was less obvious.

De Vries ties his book together on a slender thread having to do with Daisy's acceptance of her parentage. When Daisy and Effie were growing up in Terre Haute, Effie told Daisy that she was not real—she was adopted. Daisy, delighted that her putative father (who wears socks to bed and snacks on pigs' feet) and her putative mother (a sharp-tongued woman well-suited to rearing an "ixenvay") are not her real parents, makes up glamorous parents and a distantly romantic home. When, in a fairly unlikely turn of events, Daisy, Effie, and Dirk all turn up in Terre Haute, the two women have a showdown and Effie admits that she had no basis for thinking Daisy adopted. By then, of course, Daisy is prepared to accept her parents as they are, and is even fairly proud of her mother's stealing a car from an auto agency as part of her war against Detroit. She even sees the humor when her wealthy and glamorous husband puts on weight and turns out to be addicted to snacking on pigs' feet.

*Sauce for the Goose* is not one of De Vries's better plotted books, but much that happens in the early chapters set in Terre Haute helps to enforce his larger theme. Just as Jennie Dobbin expresses something of the generalized American malaise by escaping Terre Haute to Grand Rapids and by tireless consumer advocacy (she is capable of reporting the lapses of one Better Business Bureau to another), so her husband Frank displays all the features of dispirited middle age: affairs followed by tearful confession followed by periods of boasting contrition. He muffs his suicide when the clichéd car-in-the-garage runs out of gas.

At low ebb in her own affairs, Daisy must return to Terre Haute because of her father's concern over his wife's theft of a demonstration car. While Jennie Dobbin watches from the dining room, father and daughter lie in wait to take movies of a next-door neighbor throwing stones back into the Dobbin's yard, from which Dobbin has thrown them into the neighbor's yard. The boundary dispute has gone on for years, as have various other quarrels involving the same neighbor's failure to pen his dog (Poly Esther). Engrossed in filming his irate neighbor, Dobbin is hit in the head by one of the stones. Moments before the enemy, a fabric merchant with the unlikely name of Ghookasian, appears, Dobbin extols the value of "going at things in an adult fashion, the mature outlook." He concludes, "Be grown-up, that's the ticket. Ah, here's our rat fink."

Daisy recalls the senseless violence (so-called by a policeman) of vandalism to Dirk's apartment just before she left New York. She considers life: "Violence was built into the universe, the cosmos ran on it." She decides, "It was all versus. Mother versus General Motors, Father versus Ghookasian, her versus Dirk Dolfin. . . . She versus herself."

Daisy's decision to marry Dirk involves other unlikely and amusing events, but De Vries is too wise an observer of the American scene to end things happily ever after. Daisy realizes with certain clarity that one day she will divorce Dirk, and her mother, never a respecter of blood ties in matters of consumerism, telephones regularly to announce intended suits against products Dirk manufactures. In possession of *Metropole* magazine, Daisy cleans house and begins righting salary inequities; she even gives her old friend Bobsy Deisel a job.

Like most of De Vries's work, *Sauce for the Goose* is notable primarily for its verbal wit. If Daisy were not so articulate and even erudite, one would quickly tire of her. Even when De Vries hauls humor in by the ears, one is likely to be amused. He stops the action at a crucial moment, for example, to report the failure of a long-planned pun. An Englishman, excusing himself from a Sunday brunch in Terre Haute, is horrified when no one responds to his parody of Robert Frost. He says he must cut his grass and then adds, "I have premises to keep and miles to mow before I sleep." His hostess assures him that she understands perfectly. Desperately, the man repeats his lines, which only Daisy appreciates.

The failed pun helps make De Vries's point. Americans, increasingly cut off even from their native tradition, muddle through by joining movements, marrying, and having tasteless affairs. The final word is spoken by an aging man, appropriately named Christian Crocker, who cannot understand people's saying marriage is doomed. "All five of mine worked out," he says.

*Leon V. Driskell*

## Sources for Further Study

*Best Sellers.* XLI, November, 1981, p. 282.
*Booklist.* LXXVII, July 1, 1981, p. 1387.
*Esquire.* XCVI, November, 1981, p. 22.
*Library Journal.* CVI, August, 1981, p. 1564.
*The New Republic.* CLXXXV, October 14, 1981, p. 38.
*The New York Times Book Review.* LXXXVI, September 20, 1981, p. 14.
*The New Yorker.* LVII, October 19, 1981, p. 200.
*Newsweek.* XCVIII, October 5, 1981, p. 81.
*Saturday Review.* VIII, September, 1981, p. 60.
*Time.* CXVIII, September 21, 1981, p. 81.

# THE SECOND CHANCE AND OTHER STORIES

*Author:* Alan Sillitoe (1928-     )
*Publisher:* Simon and Schuster (New York). 219 pp. $12.95
*Type of work:* Short stories

*A collection of eleven stories, predominantly psychological in nature, which deal in the main with blue-collar and middle-class English characters*

Human beings live in a world of their own perceptions, a world which they can explain or share only partially, even if they wish to do so, with those whom they come in contact. One of the virtues of fiction is that it may immerse readers in realms of thought and emotion other than their own and thus expand the limited horizons of their own consciousness. Through such imaginative constructions readers become more keenly aware of the infinite shapes of psychological reality. The concentrated effects and limited focus of short fiction lend themselves particularly to the exploration of thought processes. This is certainly true of the best stories in Alan Sillitoe's *The Second Chance and Other Stories*.

The collection of eleven pieces of short fiction presents a variety of subjects from lower-, middle-, and upper-middle-class English life, ranging in time from the mid-nineteenth century to the present. Sillitoe's style is terse, fast-moving, and hard-edged. Though it is interesting to compare the themes and effects of some of his stories with those of other authors, there is nothing derivative about his style or vision. The narrative development of the most effective and characteristic stories in this collection is based primarily on the movement of the protagonist's mind.

"The Second Chance," which is given pride of place and title in the collection, may be described as an Edward Albee-like psychodrama in the form of short fiction. A retired major who has lost his fighter-pilot son in World War II encounters in a pub an ex-convict who not only is the physical duplicate of his son but also has the same first name. The major's wife has never gotten over the loss of her son and the two have never been able to acknowledge their loss outwardly, much less to console each other in their grief. In the hope of revitalizing his wife, who has withdrawn deep into herself since the death of her son, the major makes an implicit deal with the well-born ex-convict which calls for him to pretend to be the man he resembles.

The story, which is something of a tour de force, has many fine qualities. It keeps the reader's attention through the development of a gradually increasing psychological momentum brought about by a series of revelations concerning the past experiences and relationships of the central characters. The juxtaposition of various angles of vision, predominantly those of the major and the ex-convict, whose relationship with his father turns out to be as unsuccessful as that which the major had had with his son, intensifies the impact of the final revelation. The crushing conclusion of the story says, in effect, that second chances are ultimately futile because the most appalling failures are the results of forces and feelings over which one ultimately has no control. The story is marred, however, by a weakness which the fascination of its style and theme cannot entirely obscure. Though its psychological momentum may be strong enough to create in most readers the willing suspension of disbelief necessary to accept the incredible biological and circumstantial chance that sets the story in motion, it is probably not strong enough to overcome the extent to which the gradually revealed character of the fighter-pilot son is shaped to fit into the ingenious psychological configuration of the plot.

Thematically and technically, "No Name in the Street" is a much simpler and stronger story, which might well, without the irony operative in the title story of the collection, have been called "The Second Chance." The protagonist is Albert, a former collier—a down-and-outer who has led a lonely isolated life. His only companion is a mongrel dog which he has trained to retrieve stray golf balls on the town golf course at night as a means of supplementing his welfare check. Into this slough of a life comes an opportunity for a richer, more meaningful existence in the form of a marriage to an attractive, good-natured widow. As Albert prepares to move his meager possessions from his dingy quarters to a better section of town, his dog, frightened by the prospect of change, takes refuge behind the stove. The conflict that ensues mirrors a conflict that is taking place within the protagonist. Albert is frightened by a move that is designed to shake him out of the grubby lethargy of his past, perhaps demanding more of his potential as a human being than has ever been required of him. Without sentimentality, the quality of his character is emphasized through his loyalty to the mongrel which has been the only object of communication and affection in his life since the death of his mother, and the pain which attends growth or expansion of spirit is strikingly and poignantly reflected in his inner struggle.

"The Meeting" comments on the sometimes sad perversity of human nature. A male commercial traveler picks up a female commercial traveler in a bar and, over drinks, the two begin to speak of their former mates. It gradually becomes clear that they are discussing their own marriage and that it is only through the game they are playing that they are able to maintain a relationship which, though officially ended, is sustained by an attraction they cannot define or escape. Through a ritual of pretense which they carry on once a year, they find themselves able to communicate their feelings for each other far more effectively and honestly than when they were man and wife; and each year their one night of love brings them closer to each other than they had ever been. One is, however, left with the feeling there is nothing destined for their relationship other than to meet and part as highly successful commercial travelers.

"A Scream of Toys" follows the fortunes of Edie, a sensitive, imaginative working-class girl who, during World War II in England, yearns for a release from the coarseness and the humdrum dreariness of the environment into which she has been born. She develops a friendship with a gentle, kind Italian prisoner of war who has become a collaborator and who is as much a prisoner of the circumstances of his birth as she is of hers. At the conclusion of the story they move toward a consummation of their feeling for each other that is destined in its consequences to be as cruelly illusory and ultimately as empty as a childhood experience of Edie's which is described at the outset of the story and from which the title is derived. This is a subtly constructed, strongly felt story—one of the best in the collection.

"Confrontation" is, psychologically speaking, a Chinese box of a story. A young man at a cocktail party tells an apparently gratuitous lie which results in the dissolution of his marriage. He later begins a relationship with the woman to whom he told the lie, who apparently acted as an unwitting catalyst in the breakup of the marriage. The story suggests that casual social actions and reactions may conceal far more than they reveal, but the subtle twist of ironic retribution that neatly ties up the psychological action of the story seems more clever than convincing.

"Ear to the Ground," though less subtly and artfully done, may be compared both in technique and theme to Ring Lardner's masterpiece, "Haircut." The first-person speaker in this story—a former teddy boy who has married, reared a family, and now, in middle age, is on the dole—bitterly complains about his son, whom he has driven to theft; his wife, whom he may drive to prostitution; and the welfare state, which he blames for all his country's problems. He is not aware of the extent to which his whining rationalizations expose his own monumental lack of character and morality.

"The Devil's Almanack," like Robert Browning's "Porphyria's Lover," is a chilling depiction of the thought processes of a deranged mind. A mid-nineteenth century English postmaster has murdered his daughter upon discovering that she is pregnant with the child of a young aristocrat. A stolid matter-of-fact man who spends all of his spare time taking daily measurements of the weather for his almanac, he finds himself caught up in a tangled web of emotions that include jealousy and an unnatural attraction to his daughter. He is hanged for the murders of his daughter and the lover who intended to marry her, and he encounters death with the same dispassionate, scientific cast of mind that had characterized his measurements of the surface of the earth.

"The Fiddle" traces the career of Jeff Bignal, a coal miner who entertained the lower-middle-class inhabitants of the neighborhood in which he grew up by playing the fiddle on long summer evenings. The music enriched the life of the neighborhood until Jeff, tiring of the long hours in the mines, sold his fiddle and put himself into business as a butcher. The story is not so much about Jeff as it is about the small neighborhood in which he lived, a group of run-down houses first put up during the Industrial Revolution, now resting on the edge of the city across the river from fields which represent a life of the past. The music of the fiddle becomes a symbol of the enduring human desire for beauty.

"The Gate of a Great Mansion" takes the reader into the fever-stricken mind of an Englishman on the brink of middle age who years before had set out for China to make his fortune, propelled by the hopes of his family. The success which he sought has eluded him, and as he lurches through the city to a lodging drearier than the past which he had set out to redeem, he sees it for what it is. Amoy is an illusory gateway to the riches of China. In his imagination, the inner fire of his body is projected onto the city which becomes a gate of paper, a gate destined to be consumed by the fires of ill-conceived ambition. Like "The Devil's Almanack," "The Gate of a Great Mansion" is interesting because of its inside view of the way in which a mind that has been traumatized by illness works; the illness in this story, however, is physically rather than psychologically induced. This story suggests a larger theme—the set of social circumstances brought on by the Industrial Revolution that generated the desire for escape and often led to frustration and despair. What is projected through the mind of the protagonist of "The Gate of a Great Mansion" is a darker side of the social vision reflected in "The Fiddle."

In "A Time to Keep," a fifteen-year-old-boy, one year away from entering the world of work, is fascinated by the feel and look of books—particularly exotic, out-of-the-ordinary books. As a reader he is something of a dilettante, reading here and there desultorily, more concerned with the pleasure of the books in themselves rather than in what they might do for him. He has no ambition other than to acquire the status of manhood, which will come with his entrance into the working world. By chance he witnesses an incident which in itself and in the influence which it has on an older cousin he admires provides him with an insight into the significance of what the life of a blue-collar worker adds up to, and he returns to his books with a different vision of their relationship to his life. Like "No Name in the Street," this story leaves one with the impression that one has experienced an important turning point in an individual's life.

"The Sniper" is perhaps the most extraordinary story in the collection. In one sense, it may be seen as a variation, in another social and intellectual key, on the combined themes of Fyodor Dostoevski's *Crime and Punishment* (1866) and Henry James's "The Beast in the Jungle." It is at the same time an entirely original story which makes a provocative comment about the nature of the human mind and the nature of life. In the early days of World War I, a young English tenant farmer ambushes and murders a man with whom his wife has been having an affair. He enlists in the army intending to leave his wife for good and believing that his crime will soon be discovered. This belief that God will "pay him out" haunts the remainder of his life. It turns him into an outstanding soldier and eventually leads him back to his wife after the war. He confesses his crime twice—once to a comrade on the battlefield and again as an old man when he climbs onto the counter of a pub and sings out his story. He dies of old age, taking the truth of the crime which has given shape and quality to his life to the grave. The soldier to whom he confessed was killed in action and the witnesses in the bar assume that his song and dance was an act of senility.

*William B. Toole III*

### Sources for Further Study

*America*. CXLVI, September 12, 1981, p. 126.
*Business Week*. May 11, 1981, p. 15.
*Library Journal*. CVI, April 1, 1981, p. 817.
*Listener*. CV, January 22, 1981, p. 120.
*New Statesman*. CI, January 16, 1981, p. 20.
*The New York Times Book Review*. LXXXVI, April 19, 1981, p. 6.
*Quill & Quire*. XLVII, May, 1981, p. 34.
*Spectator*. CCXLVI, February 14, 1981, p. 23.
*Times Literary Supplement*. January 23, 1981, p. 76.

# THE SECOND STAGE

*Author:* Betty Friedan (1921-    )
*Publisher:* Summit Books (New York). 344 pp. $14.95
*Type of work:* Social science
*Time:* 1970-1981
*Locale:* The United States

*A discussion of the history and future of contemporary feminism*

Contemporary feminism is sometimes said to have begun with the publication in 1963 of Betty Friedan's *The Feminine Mystique*. In that book, Friedan described for American women "the problem that has no name" and brought to popular consciousness the necessity for changes in women's roles, rights, and responsibilities. Since 1963, Friedan has been among the most visible of women activists. Founder and first president of the National Organization for Women, she also helped to form the National Women's Political Caucus, and for the last two decades she has lectured and published widely on women's issues. Friedan's stature as a feminist and her intimate acquaintance with the movement's history make her most recent book, *The Second Stage*, a highly significant and credible one. Friedan's involvement in the issues she discusses is such that her book cannot be ignored, whether one agrees with its conclusions or not.

It is no wonder that some of Friedan's sisters have attacked *The Second Stage* for its betrayal of feminist solidarity. The book's thesis is that the women's movement of the 1960's and 1970's has run its course, that feminism is inadequate for the needs of the 1980's, and that the sex-role revolution has already entered a new phase. Throughout the presentation of this important thesis, the reader cannot help wishing that some energetic editor had given Friedan's prolix sentences more force and had insisted on footnotes, or at least a bibliography. Friedan divides her argument into two parts, each five chapters long. The first part, called "End of the Beginning," is by far the more persuasive section. It is here that she discusses the replacement of the feminine mystique with a "feminist mystique," which she connects with the media-encouraged bra-burning image of such groups as SCUM (Society for Cutting Up Men) and of such individuals as Mary Daly, Kate Millet, and Shulamith Firestone. Friedan argues that the analogies constructed by these theorists—analogies between class warfare and racial oppression on the one hand, and, on the other, the oppression of women by men—were far too rigid. By insisting so fervently on the classist-racist-sexist analogies, Friedan says, the most radical feminists failed to account for the distinctiveness of female experience.

An equally serious consequence of their rigidity is the antifeminist reaction represented by such individuals as Phyllis Schlafly and by such groups as the Moral Majority. Pointing out that the issues which have most fundamentally divided feminists and antifeminists concern the family, Friedan claims, in her third chapter, that the family must be the "New Feminist Frontier." In this chapter she explicitly rejects the careerist, antimale, antifamily stance associated with radical feminism and asserts that the full personhood of women must include both work and love:

> Personal choices and political strategies of women today are distorted when they deny the reality of both sets of needs: women's need for power, identity, status and security through her own work or action in society, which the reactionary enemies of feminism deny; and the need for love and identity, status, security and generation through marriage, children, home, the family, which those feminists still locked in their own extreme reaction deny. *Both sets of needs are essential to women, and to the evolving human condition.*

Friedan recognizes that if women are to become fully human, then men must change as well; in Chapter 4 she discusses "The Quiet Movement of American Men" toward expression of those "soft," "messy" feelings and needs that have traditionally been reserved for women. The book's first section closes with a description of the effects of admitting women to the United States Military Academy. One cannot help remembering Virginia Woolf's exploration, in *Three Guineas* (1938), of the links between machismo and militarism as one reads Friedan's account of her visits to West Point, her talks with female and male cadets, and her sessions with army "warriors" and with a new generation of officers who see weaknesses in the John Wayne style of military training and authority.

The five chapters which make up "End of the Beginning" deal with the immediate past. Never forgetting for long the feminist credo that the personal is the political, Friedan supports her analysis with interviews, conversations, and personal experiences, as well as with statistics and psychological and sociological studies. When she turns to the second part of her argument, however, called "The Second Stage," she writes with less authority. In this second part, Friedan apparently intends to speculate about what is to come, but Chapter 6 concerns the role played by women in the 1980 presidential election and the international women's meetings in Mexico City and Copenhagen. Friedan then moves rather abruptly to an account of a study conducted in 1979 by researchers at the University of Michigan. Called "Juggling Contradictions: Women's Ideas About Families," the study suggests that in their personal lives most women are able to reconcile the ideological conflict between family and equality, between love and work, even though in the political arena that same conflict has led to extreme polarization between those who call themselves feminists and those who claim to be pro-family.

On the basis of the Michigan study, Friedan concludes that the antagonism between these two factions is false: "There are *not* two kinds of women in America," she says; "that ideological split is continually being resolved in real life by juggling and rationalizing of new necessities in traditional terms, and old necessities in feminist terms. . . ." This is important news indeed, but it seems badly placed in the future-oriented second section of Friedan's argument. In Chapter 7, Friedan describes two leadership styles, Alpha and Beta. Alpha leadership is analytical, rational, quantitative, abstract, direct, and aggressive; it is, in other words, stereotypically "masculine." Beta-style leadership is, by contrast, stereotypically "feminine"; it is affirming, receptive, generative, integrative, intuitive, relational, qualitative. Friedan predicts that Beta-style leadership will be more highly valued in the future than it has been in the past and observes that "evolution itself . . . seems to be moving in what might be called a 'feminine' direction." She then says that in the future both women and men will seek not only flexible work hours but also flexible definitions of career "success" so that both parents can be more fully involved in the processes and responsibilities of child care. A necessary corollary to such changes would be changes in the physical structures in which people live. Drawing heavily on Dolores Hayden's *The Grand Domestic Revolution—A History of Feminist Design for American Homes, Neighborhoods and Cities* (1981), Friedan discusses such practical arrangements of physical space as community kitchens, dining rooms, and nurseries, combined, on the Swedish model, with private living and sleeping areas.

The concluding chapter of the section and the book warns that extreme polarization of sex roles breeds an obsession with sex as "dirty" and contributes to social violence. In this part of her discussion, Friedan lapses annoyingly into the abstract jargon of psychological-metaphysical speculation. The final chapter also reiterates an earlier warning that discussions of sexual preference are best confined to the private sphere, a view that has, understandably, not endeared Friedan to those feminists who have politicized their lesbianism. These warnings are as close to practical advice as Friedan comes in her effort to shape a "human politics" that will go beyond "sexual politics."

Of course, it is never as easy to predict the future as it is to understand the mistakes of the past. Friedan is at her best when she argues that the most serious weaknesses of contemporary feminism have been its failure to articulate its clear claim to issues involving the family, and its failure to raise those issues in ways that would draw broad support. Friedan suggests, for example, that it makes better political sense to advocate the "choice to have children" than to call for "free abortion on demand." She is also persuasive when she argues that for women and men simply to reverse confining roles is an inadequate solution to the problem of sexual inequality. Another inadequate solution which Friedan deals with in painfully convincing detail is that undertaken by the "superwoman" who feels she must meet two standards of perfection: the standard set by the perfect housewife-mother who does not work outside the home, and the standard set by the successful male professional who has a wife to take care of the details of home and family. Friedan points to psychological studies which reveal that women in their twenties and thirties report a high incidence of stress; the conflicts and choices faced by such women, to whom Friedan frequently refers as "our daughters," are presented with all the urgency that characterizes these conflicts in real life. Rejecting both role reversal and feminine machismo, Friedan clearly sees that true sexual equality depends on fundamental changes in social and economic institutions.

Her optimism about the likelihood of these changes actually occurring in the Second Stage seems to arise from the fact that she herself has so thoroughly experienced the First Stage. Friedan generalizes too hastily from her own experience, putting the matter in familiar dialectical terms: Americans have lived through thesis (the feminine mystique) and antithesis (feminism); now they are ready for a synthesis forged from the polarized opposites of love and work, a polarization that rigid sex-role stereotyping has forced on women and men alike. Certainly Friedan's own efforts to contribute to the forging of such a synthesis are admirable, but what of those women who have yet to come to an understanding of their shared history as women and who have yet to experience legitimate anger about male dominance? Friedan would probably dismiss such feelings as "an acting out of rage that [doesn't] really change anything," but she cannot dismiss the failure of the Equal Rights Amendment, the wage gap between women and men, or the conservatism of a federal administration in which few women hold high positions and which has made clear that it will not enforce affirmative action guidelines. Neither can she dismiss the fact that few corporations offer the sort of flexibility in maternity and paternity leaves and in career planning that would allow the Second Stage to become a reality for families.

Because Friedan does not take sufficiently into account all these and other indications that for many Americans the First Stage has scarcely begun, one has difficulty sharing her optimism about the Second Stage, as much as one might like to do so. Perhaps in twenty years it will be possible to view *The Second Stage* as a prophetic book with the importance now assigned to *The Feminine Mystique*. In the meantime, those who support the sex-role revolution would do well to cultivate a strong feminist awareness, while at the same time working toward the sort of synthesis proposed by Friedan. After all, just as extremism makes moderation possible, and just as a perspective on the past is essential to the meaningful living of the present and to intelligent planning for the future, so antithesis and synthesis may well have to exist side by side until that glorious day when women and men can claim true equality and full humanity.

*Carolyn Wilkerson Bell*

### Sources for Further Study

*Booklist*. LXXVIII, September 15, 1981, p. 74.

*Christian Science Monitor*. LXXIII, October 28, 1981, p. 17.
*Commonweal*. CVIII, December 18, 1981, p. 726.
*Maclean's*. XCIV, December 7, 1981, p. 76.
*Ms*. X, December, 1981, p. 16.
*Library Journal*. CVI, November 1, 1981, p. 2125.
*Nation*. CCXXXIII, November 14, 1981, p. 496.
*National Review*. XXXIII, October 16, 1981, p. 1215.
*The New York Times Book Review*. LXXXVI, November 22, 1981, p. 3.
*Saturday Review*. VIII, October, 1981, p. 66.

# SELECTED LETTERS OF RAYMOND CHANDLER

*Author:* Raymond Chandler (1888-1959)
Edited by Frank MacShane
*Publisher:* Columbia University Press (New York). 501 pp. $19.95
*Type of work:* Letters

*A generous selection of letters confirming Chandler's distinction as a letter writer as well as a novelist*

The great revelation of Frank MacShane's excellent biography, *The Life of Raymond Chandler* (1976), was that Chandler the novelist was also a marvelous letter writer. MacShane used fragments of Chandler's letters to stitch his narrative together, quoting extensively from them throughout the book. Now MacShane has edited a generous selection of the letters, confirming Chandler's distinction where so many gifted writers have been disappointing.

The *Selected Letters of Raymond Chandler* has already received the highest praise. Chandler's voice in these letters is intimate, conversational. They are an invitation to a writer's world, with the talk shifting from dust jacket photos and reprint rights to brilliant, offhand analysis of writing and writers. The creator of Philip Marlowe is also quick with a one-liner. He says of Edmund Wilson—a favorite antagonist—that the *Memoirs of Hecate County* (1946) make "fornication as dull as a railroad time table." Of James Cain he says that "everything he writes smells like a billy goat." Of the pulp magazine where he went to school, Chandler observes that a " lot of *Black Mask* stories sounded alike, just as a lot of Elizabethan plays sound alike. Always when a group exploits a new technique this happens."

Reviewers of the *Selected Letters of Raymond Chandler* have rightly singled out these qualities for praise—his voice, his informal writing lessons, his wit— yet having done this, one must step back and look at the book as a whole. This collection of letters tells a story; it has a plot. Frank MacShane calls Chandler's a "sad but decent life," but that does not go far enough. Chandler's letters reveal a defensiveness bordering on paranoia and an urge to cut all "competitors" down to size. They reveal a proud man wrestling with self-contempt, a mind torn by raging contradictions.

Raymond Chandler was born in Chicago in 1888. In 1895, after his father abandoned the family, Chandler moved to England with his mother. He attended Dulwich College, one of the better English public schools, where he received a good classical education. Chandler wanted to be a writer, and after a two-year sojourn in France and Germany he worked for several years on the fringes of literary journalism in London. During this period he published, by Frank MacShane's count, twenty-seven poems (intensely romantic, "cloying and saccharine"), seven essays, and a handful of reviews and short anonymous newspaper pieces. Discouraged by his lack of literary success,

Chandler left England for America in 1912, at the age of twenty-three.

He settled in California and began a series of short-term jobs. In 1917, he enlisted in the Canadian Army and saw heavy front-line action in France in 1918. After his discharge he returned to California, where he began working in the oil business, starting in the accounting department but quickly rising to the executive level; he was vice-president of several companies. Chandler got married in 1924, when he was thirty-five and his wife, Cissy—who had to divorce her husband to marry Chandler—was a young-looking fifty-three. Within a few years he was drinking so heavily that—after repeated warnings—he was fired from his oil-company job in 1932.

Chandler began writing again, and after several unsuccessful attempts at serious "straight" fiction he discovered the "pulps" specializing in detective stories, particularly *Black Mask*, which featured Dashiell Hammett. In 1933, Chandler, at the age of forty-five, published his first story, "Blackmailers Don't Shoot," in *Black Mask*. He continued to publish stories until 1939, when he published his first novel, *The Big Sleep*, his breakthrough. From that time on he was a novelist and—for a long stint in Hollywood in the 1940's— a screenwriter.

*Selected Letters of Raymond Chandler* picks up Chandler's story in 1939 (there are only two earlier letters included, both from 1937), when he had decisively established himself as a writer. Or had he? At least ninety percent of the letters in this collection argue at some point in defense of his kind of writing or attack "literary" writing—and many letters do both. This mood of self-justification and perpetual sniping was not missing from MacShane's biography, but in the letters it is pervasive and obsessive.

Chandler had a right to be bitter and resentful. His novels are among the finest in contemporary American literature, yet during his lifetime—and even, to some extent, today—he was dismissed as a "crime-writer," never deserving serious attention. One of his most relentless critics, however, was Chandler himself. Chandler began with the ambition to be a "serious" writer; his models were Victorian, Edwardian, and—more distantly—classical. There is a telling sentence early in MacShane's biography, describing the young writer in London: "Chandler seems to have been quite unaware of the literary revolution underway in England at the time he began to write, represented by the work of Pound, Wells, Ford, Yeats, Lewis, Lawrence, Conrad, and even Hardy and James from an earlier generation."

Chandler found another route to modernism, via American detective fiction, which he came to like a Martian with a mixture of detachment and the joy of discovery. It was like learning a new language, a language he made his own to create lasting works of literature. He was never satisfied, however, with his own achievement. There is a plaintive letter to Alfred A. Knopf as early as 1943, in which Chandler says that he wants to do a Philip Marlowe novel which is not a mystery. "Is this possible," he asks Knopf, "if I use a character who is already established in mystery fiction?"

Tragically, Chandler could never convince *himself* that his novels were "literature." The *Letters* include a number of passages in which Chandler speaks of his "magic," the distinctive quality of his writing; he knew his gifts. Yet these passages have an air of bravado as well. Had Chandler been secure in his achievement, the attacks of Edmund Wilson and his ilk would hardly have troubled him. Instead, he became increasingly strident in his attacks on anything "literary" or "pretentious"—categories which seemed to include most of the serious writers of his time.

It is strange that many early reviews of Chandler's *Letters* have lavishly praised his hit-and-run literary criticism. On his own work (except when principally engaged in self-justification) and on the craft and art of writing, Chandler is wonderful—worth ten writers' workshops. On other living writers—with a few exceptions—he is completely unreliable. His judgments of his contemporaries are rarely disinterested; rather, they make an endless litany of self-justification.

That a writer should be ungenerous to other writers is not extraordinary. James Joyce, whose letters have none of the verve of Chandler's, was much worse than Chandler in this respect. Joyce's ungenerous spirit suggests a rather cold self-sufficiency; Chandler's defensive criticism can be read with greater sympathy, but it is sad, exasperating, and terribly predictable. The characteristic note of this criticism is sounded in a letter to Charles Morton of *The Atlantic Monthly*: "Thank heaven that when I tried to write fiction I had the sense to do it in a language that was not all steamed up with rhetoric." It is not enough for Chandler to assert that his "overheard democratic prose" (Ross Macdonald's apt phrase) is one valid way to write; he implies that anyone who writes differently is "steamed up with rhetoric."

This note recurs again and again in the *Letters*. After a manifestly unfair dismissal of Elizabeth Bowen's *The Heat of the Day*, 1949 ("poor dear Elizabeth is falling into the sad error of thinking that the involution of the language necessarily conceals a subtlety of thought"), he remarks: "I should be grateful that I went through the arty and intellectual phase so young and grew out of it so completely that it always seems a little juvenile in others, whatever their ages." The same tone informs Chandler's comments on James Agee and Ross Macdonald, among others.

Chandler's great achievement persists. His novels are finally receiving the recognition they deserve. They have long been recognized by the "arty and intellectual" set against whom Chandler directed so much contempt. There is a veritable Chandler cult in France; viewers of Jean-Luc Godard's *Alphaville* will remember Lemmy Caution reading in bed, holding *Le Grand Sommeil* in one hand and a pistol in the other. Peter Handke's novel *Der kurze Brief zum langen Abschied*, 1972 (mistranslated as *Short Letter, Long Farewell*, 1974) alludes to Chandler's novel, *The Long Goodbye* (1953). Indeed, Chandler may turn up anywhere: Walker Percy's Lance Lamar (in *Lancelot*, 1977) carries a briefcase containing "a fifth of Wild Turkey and a hard-cover copy of *The Big Sleep*." That is a tribute which Chandler could have appreciated. He would also have appreciated a fine job of bookmaking: the *Selected Letters*, like all clothbound books published by Columbia University Press, is Smyth-sewn and printed on acid-free paper. It is a handsome volume, fit to rest on the desk shown in the jacket-photo, where Chandler sits with his cat and his pipe.

*John Wilson*

## Sources for Further Study

*American Film*. VII, November, 1981, p. 75.
*American Spectator*. XV, January, 1982, p. 35.
*The Atlantic Monthly*. CCXLVIII, November, 1981, p. 90.
*Book World*. XI, October 25, 1981, p. 1.
*The New Republic*. CLXXXV, December 16, 1981, p. 39.
*New Statesman*. CII, November 27, 1981, p. 30.
*The New York Times Book Review*. LXXXVI, November 15, 1981, p. 7.
*Observer*. November 29, 1981, p. 26.
*Time*. CXVIII, November 9, 1981, p. 115.
*Village Voice*. XXVI, November 25, 1981, p. 42.

# SHADOW MAN
## The Life of Dashiell Hammett

*Author:* Richard Layman (1947-    )
*Publisher:* Harcourt Brace Jovanovich/Bruccoli Clark (New York). 285 pp. $14.95
*Type of work:* Literary biography
*Time:* 1894-1961
*Locale:* Baltimore, San Francisco, New York, Hollywood, and the Aleutian Islands

*A first and basic biography of America's most influential writer of detective fiction*

Principal personages:
DASHIELL HAMMETT, a novelist
RICHARD HAMMETT, his father
ANNIE BOND HAMMETT, his mother
JOSEPHINE DOLAN HAMMETT, his wife
MARY JANE HAMMETT, his first daughter
JOSEPHINE REBECCA HAMMETT, his second daughter
LILLIAN HELLMAN, a playwright
JAMES WRIGHT, a Pinkerton operative
WILLIAM FAULKNER, a novelist
ROSE EVANS, a housekeeper

This, the initial biography of Samuel Dashiell Hammett, shares an inevitable handicap with its subject: that of being first. Richard Layman essays the task with an emphasis on basic information that is certain to disappoint many readers and reviewers who will expect something much more sensational. He relies exclusively on public and private records, published statements, verifiable interviews and testimony, and Hammett's own writing. Layman gives fair warning of this in his Preface: he is interested in what actually happened, to the extent that he has been able to substantiate it. His style is deliberately pedestrian. He does not interpret, he does not speculate, and he rarely infers. He neither suppresses nor exploits. Thus the book is often a recital of facts, plot summaries, records, and transcripts.

However frustrating this approach to a first biography may be, it is the only correct one. It forms the essential base upon which any ensuing biographical studies of Hammett must be constructed. A writer of less integrity than Layman might have produced a semifictional biography replete with colorful speculation and innuendo: after all, Hammett was a colorful personality. If Layman felt any temptation to do so, he has resisted it successfully. *Shadow Man* is essentially a detailed report, notable for directness and objectivity.

A further handicap that confronted Layman was the evident reluctance of Lillian Hellman, Hammett's closest friend and intermittent lover for some thirty years, to assist those who have attempted to carry out research on his life and work. Her recorded comments vary from statements to the effect that a biography was her own intended project to a remark that she would never write one. Hellman does not consider herself a sentimentalist, and she has made this clear in her published memoirs; however, it is equally clear that the bond between herself and Hammett was a close if stormy one—and, perhaps, too personal for her to share. Layman undertook *Shadow Man* without Hellman's blessing and she did not hinder him.

Yet another handicap is Hammett's own reticence and sense of privacy, a barrier that will always be difficult to penetrate. He seldom revealed much of his inner self and he frequently obscured his own trail. Layman has followed up many leads and asked many questions; he has also been assisted by two other Hammett researchers, David Fechheimer and William Godschalk, who have shared their own findings with him. Fechheimer, appropriately enough, is a San Francisco detective who has applied the methods of his profession to Hammett.

Layman readily admits that there are gaps in this account, and he has made no attempt to conceal them. This is perhaps an understatement: the facts themselves raise a great many questions, aside from speculation in areas where the records are silent. This aspect of *Shadow Man* underscores its greatest importance to other researchers. The known is clearly defined and the paths of future inquiry are evident, although they are not belabored. That there will be more books about Hammett is a foregone conclusion; aside from his contribution to American literature, he was a complex man whose life contained enough material for several books, all of them interesting.

Layman's account of Hammett's childhood is well-drawn and circumstantial, but the area is one that deserves much further exploration. Born in 1894 to Richard and Annie (Bond) Hammett, he was christened Samuel Dashiell. The difficult middle name, pronounced with the accent on the second syllable, has doubtless baffled all of Hammett's readers and most of his friends, to whom he was known as either Dash or Sam. It was provided by Annie, who thus honored her ancestors the De Chiells. Richard was a drinker and a womanizer; Annie was tubercular. Hammett evidently inherited his mother's illness or a weakness in regard to it. He would also appear to have inherited his father's behavioral traits, for, although he swore he would never treat any woman the way his father treated his mother, he was unable to keep that promise in later life.

Hammett worked for Pinkerton's as a detective, except for a brief tour of duty with the Army, from 1915 until he was hospitalized with tuberculosis in 1920. He married his nurse, Josephine Dolan, in 1921. Unable to work full time, he tried his hand at writing—first with advertising copy, then with short fiction. His first detective story featuring the "Continental Op" appeared in the leading detective fiction pulp magazine, *Black Mask*, in 1923.

Pulp fiction has long been automatically dismissed as trash by a literary establishment that has never bothered to study it. It is true that this genre has several characteristics that militate against its acceptance as valid litera-ture, all deriving from the formula to which it was written: simple plotting, sketchy characterization, exotic and sometimes improbable settings, total exclusion of sex except for occasional implications, the requirement of a happy or triumphant ending for the protagonist and defeat for his opponent, with subordination of all other elements to action. Action and more action was demanded by editors, and the writers cheerfully supplied it.

These drawbacks aside, there is something to be said in favor of pulp literature. It provided acceptable popular entertainment; at the same time, it was an outlet for the talented storyteller or yarn-spinner, and much of it is an extension of folk and oral traditions. It is by no means alone in its adherence to a formula; the more prestigious slick-paper counterparts had a formula of their own and, indeed, what is called serious literature adheres in its turn to formulae of equal rigidity, devised by the opinion molders of its time. When due allowance is made for the constraints imposed upon them, it will be found that many of the pulp writers produced work that was surprisingly well-written and effective. Some who later achieved wide and lasting popularity served their apprenticeship in the pulps: Erle Stanley Gardner, Van Wyck Mason, Edison Marshall, and Frederick Faust (Max Brand) are examples. It is true that none of them elevated the craft to a level likely to be recognized as art, though there was genuine talent in each. They were essentially storytellers.

The step from writer of popular fiction to author of serious and highly regarded novels is an exceedingly difficult one. It is axiomatic in the literary world that popularity and greatness cannot coexist, that literature cannot be popular and serious at the same time. There are obvious exceptions but they have been made with great reluctance. An objective view would hold that if popularity endures for one or more generations, some level of validity must exist; however, the barrier remains a formidable one. Seen in this context, Hammett's achievement is especially remarkable.

Dashiell Hammett did not invent the "hard-boiled" detective story, but he was the first writer to give it authenticity: authenticity in terms of plot, situations, dialogue, material, and character. His detectives never act in a manner inconsistent with the rules of their profession. They and all other elements utilized by Hammett are inspired and illuminated by personal experience—an advantage Hammett possessed over most of his competitors. The characters are based on people he knew; his detectives are made three-dimensional by quixotic touches that apparently derive from Hammett's own personality. Above all, his unerring awareness of common speech and his ability to achieve a hard, direct perception of a world enabled him to produce powerful, compelling novels that capture a part of America's common existence and make the subtle transition between genre fiction and art. *Red Harvest* (1929), his first novel, best exemplifies the transition, betraying as it does the pulp origins from which it developed. It would be no more than a conventional blood-and-thunder action tale, were it not for the truer-than-life dialogue and the sense of complete authenticity: even the extended mayhem is made credible. *Red Harvest* was followed in rapid succession by the other novels: *The Dain Curse* (1929), *The Maltese Falcon* (1930), *The Glass Key* (1931), and, finally, *The Thin Man* (1934).

Hammett, whose tuberculosis had isolated him from his family for varying periods, finally left his wife and children permanently in 1929, moving from San Francisco to New York. By this time his second novel had been published; in 1930 the first film based on one of his books was released and he was becoming affluent; by 1934 he was finished as a writer.

The evidence, as presented by Layman, would indicate that Hammett was a man ruined by success. He drank, became irresponsible and undependable in regard to his various commitments, and spent more money than he made. Whether he ever shared any of his new affluence with his family is unclear from the record, and the degree to which he did or did not neglect them is not stated. The impression is that they were conveniently forgotten. Yet there seems to have been no animosity: he visited his wife occasionally and sometimes stayed with her for a while.

Hammett met Lillian Hellman during the winter of 1930-1931 and lived with her off and on for the rest of his life. Although they were not constant companions and not always congenial, they seemed to have complemented each other reasonably well. He provided criticism and advice in regard to many of her plays; she encouraged him to become interested in leftist politics. Prior to his acquaintance with Hellman, Hammett seems to have been apolitical. His stories would indicate a realistic awareness that no party or ideology has a monopoly on graft, corruption, or violence. Once the commitment was made, he lent his name and energies to a wide variety of leftist causes. This kind of activity has long been fashionable in intellectual circles, but there can be no doubt that Hammett was sincere. He cared little for fashion and Hellman has emphasized his integrity. The record, as presented by Layman, confirms this. It is nevertheless disquieting to find him condemning Nazi brutality and at the same time endorsing the Stalinist purges: he was evidently not altogether immune to the moral inconsistencies inherent in zealotry.

In spite of his political activities, age, and uncertain health, Hammett managed to enlist in the Army during World War II and it is amusing to note that for two years the FBI was unable to determine his whereabouts. He edited an apolitical newspaper for soldiers in the Aleutians, was liked by those who knew him there, and enjoyed the interlude thoroughly.

The postwar years were not kind to Hammett, and he eventually came to grips with investigators of the McCarthy era. Layman reprints the testimony in full, in an appendix. The impartial reader will admire Hammett's steadfast refusal to be intimidated, but may also conclude that both parties to the dispute should have been spanked and sent home. Sentenced to prison for six months, Hammett served his time without complaint and remarked later that it was like going home: the criminals had not changed at all since he had worked for Pinkerton.

He was not without a sense of humor. In 1930, while writing book reviews for the *New York Evening Post*, he included a long list of errors frequently committed by writers of mystery and detective stories. Witty and incisive, they should be required reading for every contemporary writer of best-selling thrillers. Heroes are still checking safety catches on revolvers and revealing in other ways their abysmal ignorance in regard to the tools of their trade.

All these aspects of Hammett's life and work invite speculation, raise questions that beg for answers. Layman's book is aptly named: it offers the shadow of the man but not his substance, and even the shadow has been built up only after much painstaking detective work.

As stated at the outset, Hammett had the disadvantage of being first. As the pioneer of a new art form, his work automatically became a standard by which his successors are measured. Of these it is probable that only one, Raymond Chandler, has equaled or surpassed him, and Chandler had the example of Hammett's work to build upon. Chandler freely acknowledged the indebtedness. All this may not be entirely fair to Hammett, and there may be some truth in critical statements to the effect that Hammett stopped writing because he had carried his achievement to his highest point and had no more to say on the matter. Whether this is in fact true, or whether Hammett simply allowed his talent to be destroyed by success, is one of the many questions that remain to be answered.

In addition to his narrative, Richard Layman has provided a detailed chronology, full chapter notes, the appendix already mentioned, and an index. Other works consulted are cited in the notes and there is no separate bibliography.

*Shadow Man* is an important book and one that sets desirable standards for any first step toward biography. Layman rightly deplores the current tendency to develop portraits through the use of fictitious or apocryphal material that highlights some preconceived estimate of character or personality. His work will be the starting point for all his successors; he has eliminated false leads that others would find it necessary to refute. This is encouragement of the highest order.

*John W. Evans*

**Sources for Further Study**

*Christian Science Monitor*. LXXIII, August 12, 1981, p. 17.
*Library Journal*. CVI, June 15, 1981, p. 1307.
*New Statesman*. CII, October 28, 1981, p. 23.
*The New York Times Book Review*. LXXXVI, August 23, 1981, p. 9.

*Saturday Review*. VIII, July, 1981, p. 66.
*Time*. CXVIII, July 20, 1981, p. 73.
*Times Literary Supplement*. June 5, 1981, p. 619.

# SHAKESPEARE'S DIVISION OF EXPERIENCE

*Author:* Marilyn French (1929-    )
*Publisher:* Summit Books (New York). 376 pp. $15.95
*Type of work:* Literary criticism

*A study of the dramatic works of William Shakespeare from the perspective of what the author terms "gender criticism," this work explores the depiction of issues related to sex and power in characterization and plot development to offer a general theory of male-female relationships in Western culture*

As a reading of William Shakespeare's works and as an exposition of certain themes in Western culture, this work raises a whole host of questions which can best be gotten at, perhaps, in the context of Marilyn French's work to date. The author of a highly-praised work on James Joyce's *Ulysses* (1922), *The Book as World* (1976), French is best-known for her two novels of emerging female awareness, *The Women's Room* (1977) and *The Bleeding Heart* (1980). French did her Ph.D. work at Harvard University in the late 1960's and early 1970's; her first novel *The Women's Room* draws on that experience. In that novel, the central character, a female graduate student at Harvard, comes to a profound new sense of personal awareness and maturity through renouncing her inherited stereotypes of what is appropriate behavior for a woman in favor of a strong affirmation of herself as a capable adult able to make responsible choices and to take charge of her own life.

What makes *The Women's Room* so powerful is its evocation of the conditions in which young women came of age and entered into adulthood in the United States in the 1950's. Those conditions are characterized by bondage and failure—the ties to home and husband and family and suburbia which could fulfill few and which destroyed many. Against that background, French contrasts the sense of post-divorce 1960's freedom, in this case the freedom to return to graduate school, to take charge of one's life, to start anew with a sense of self that is substantially healthier and more responsible than any the 1950's world could offer.

*The Bleeding Heart* takes the story of the professional academic woman a few years further. In this novel, the central character, now a member of the academic profession, gets a grant that takes her to England and an English university for a year of intensive research. While there, she has a tumultuous affair with a man whom she alternately clings to and struggles against as she tries to consolidate her gains in terms of self-worth and self-assurance.

What these works have in common, against the background of the women's movement, is a sense of the profound struggle necessary to overcome the crippling self-image women in America derived from their culture's expectations of them in their formative years, especially the 1950's. Clearly, women who grew up in postwar America were sold a horrible and dehumanizing bill of goods; they were told that if they essentially remained children and did not enter the adult work-world, but instead mothered their husbands and their children, they would be well taken care of. Considering much of the rhetoric of the women's movement, that is a very seductive self-image, one that is frighteningly difficult to overcome, even if the alternatives are madness or despair.

One of the ways in which women have had to fight to make room for themselves as adults in professional circles and to claim their right to a positive image of themselves is to read the condition of their formative existence backwards in time and to universalize it by making it a fundamental condition of Western society. This is not to say that former ages were not sexist, at least in our sense of the term. It is to say that the kind of criticism that French writes in *Shakespeare's Division of Experience* is understandable more in terms of what is needed now for women to lay claim to their own share of the Western cultural tradition than it is as a straightforward discussion of Shakespeare.

For what French offers in this book is, in effect, a laying-claim to a place for Shakespeare in the canon of writers helpful for women to read who are struggling to overcome their own inherited and culturally acquired self-image, substituting for it a more positive and self-affirming one. To do this, she first posits definitions of masculine and feminine "principles" as understood in Western culture. In her terms, the masculine principle is based on the ability to kill, while the feminine is based on the ability to give birth. The masculine is characterized by the desire for power and control, the need to impose order, to fix, to make permanent. It is individualistic, action-oriented, thinking, linear. The feminine, on the other hand, is characterized by a concern for feeling, for sensation, for pleasure, for the quality of life, for the cyclic permanence of nature.

French further posits that the Christian Church split the feminine gender principle into two aspects, the good and the bad. Under the good were placed benevolence, compassion, mercy, subordination, humility; under the bad were placed sexuality and the pleasure of being. The cost of this division was an identification of woman as a threat to order, to structure, to permanence, and the deprivation of the "good" image of woman of her fundamental sources of energy and power.

In effect, the male principle became the definition of what it was to be human, while women were seen as threatening unless they placed themselves under masculine domination. Women become either superhuman or subhuman, but never merely human.

French proceeds to examine Shakespeare's plays in terms of the ways in which his characters act out these principles. She sees at least two of his works as transcending the dichotomies of the principles—*King Lear* (1605) and *Antony and Cleopatra* (1606-1607)—but, for the most part, she sees him affirming the need for male control of women. Indeed, she finds in Shakespeare a "terrified loathing" of feminine sexuality, and a continued equation between male and human. His value is in his affirmation for a need to combine, at least on occasion, the two gender principles, although she argues he never could imagine a world without male-dominated power and control in which women needed to restrict their sexuality.

Such an approach to Shakespeare is so blatantly reductionistic and so much in violation of traditions of reading and thinking about his work formed by both male and female scholars that it is hard to accept. The legions of Shakespearean characters who do not act according to "gender principles" leap readily to mind; French knows this, but her response is that in such cases characters combine parts of the two principles. In spite of how well or how badly her approach deals with the reality of Shakespeare's work, however, its reading of Western culture simply will not bear the weight of historical investigation. Certainly, women have gotten a raw deal; certainly, writers of the past reflected the prevailing world-view of their age. Nevertheless, the past is always much more complicated than any reductionistic scheme, and one does violence to the past when one forces it into any scheme that denies its complexity. In this case, one denies the humanity and the validity of all the women of the past who have lived humanly and heroically in spite of whatever constrictions were placed upon them.

That is why this book needs to be seen as not really about Shakespeare at all, but about how one can function as a woman in an academic world when one must constantly struggle with one's own past. The narrator of this book is, in effect, the central character of French's novels who must constantly reassert, to herself and those around her, her right to be a woman, a human being, and a scholar. Something of that struggle involves making room in the world of scholarship for one's own ideas, one's own responses, in the terms of one's own experiences. What is more important about this book than what it says about Shakespeare is the fact that it has appeared, that it exists, that it comes from a major press with all the academic trappings of footnotes and favorable comments on the dust jacket from Harvard faculty members.

In this book, the central figure of French's novels has completed one phase of her quest. She has moved through graduate school, through apprenticeship, and now has a book with all the trappings of a major scholarly effort behind her. The novels record the cost of this progress in terms of human suffering. The question that remains is whether or not the full range of human experience of literature can be brought into the academic mainstream. Certainly, this book suggests that the struggle has had its costs in terms of breadth of response as well as its successes. Only the future can tell how much growth in a sense of common humanity will also result.

*John H. Wall, Jr.*

## Sources for Further Study

*Best Sellers.* XLI, May, 1981, p. 207.
*Book World.* XI, March 8, 1981, p. 1.
*Choice.* XVII, June, 1981, p. 1416.
*Library Journal.* CVI, June 1, 1981, p. 1223.
*The New Republic.* CLXXXIV, April 11, 1981, p. 38.
*The New York Review of Books.* XXVIII, June 11, 1981, p. 20.
*The New York Times Book Review.* LXXXVI, March 22, 1981, p. 11.

# SIX PROBLEMS FOR DON ISIDRO PARODI

*Authors:* Jorge Luis Borges (1899-    ) and Adolfo Bioy-Casares (1914-    )
Translated from the Spanish by Norman Thomas di Giovanni
*Publisher:* E. P. Dutton (New York). 160 pp. $11.50
*Type of work:* Short stories
*Time:* 1941-1942
*Locale:* Buenos Aires

   *Six detective stories in one of the classic forms of the genre—the famous sleuth—combined with satire and burlesque*

> Principal characters:
> DON ISIDRO PARODI, an armchair detective through no fault of his own
> GERVASIO MONTENEGRO, a radio actor and nitwit
> ACHILLES MOLINARI, a reporter, first "client" of Parodi

*Six Problems for Don Isidro Parodi*, as the dust jacket reveals, is part of the publisher's program to supply all of Borges' major works in English translation. Although the goal is commendable, one may doubt whether the book would ever have appeared had Borges not been its coauthor. *Six Problems for Don Isidro Parodi* was first published in Argentina in 1942 under the pseudonym "H. Bustos Domecq," and remained untranslated until now; it consists of six detective stories which are interesting and sometimes amusing, but which are neither brilliant in themselves nor essential to an understanding of Borges' development as a writer.

The choice of the detective genre deserves some explanation. Borges is well-known not only as a great fantasist but also as one of South America's leading authorities on English and American literature. The detective story is an important part of the English-language tradition, and Borges studied its origins and forms as they appeared on both sides of the Atlantic. Borges' criticism of the detective story preceded his own efforts in the genre, and he fell prey to a temptation to which others have succumbed: something about the detective story inspires its admirers to lay down rules for its execution, and Borges was no exception. In 1935, he wrote a piece entitled "Los laberintos policiales y Chesterton" for the Argentine literary magazine *Sur*. An English translation of the article is now available, in *Borges: A Reader* (1981), edited by Emir Rodriguez Monegal and Alastair Reid. In the article, entitled "Chesterton and the Labyrinths of the Detective Story," Borges describes his own idea of the "code" of the detective short story (he excludes the detective novel from some of these rules).

The detective story should possess, according to Borges, (1) a maximum of six characters, to the violation of which rule he attributes what he calls "the tedium of all detective movies" (it should be remembered that the essay was written in 1935); (2) the early inclusion of all information needed to solve the mystery (that is, no strangers are brought in at the last minute as culprits, no clues become crucial unless the reader has had the opportunity earlier to grasp their significance); (3) the strict economy of means, that is, the inclusion in the story of nothing unnecessary to the plot; (4) a recognition by the author that how the crime was committed is more important than who committed it, especially if the revelation of the criminal consists of the mere naming of a name without a personality; and (5) that the mystery must have only one possible solution and that the solution must be surprising without resorting to the supernatural. Borges says that he derived the five points from reading G. K. Chesterton's "Father Brown" mysteries, although the points apply as well as such sets usually do to any "classic" detective story, from Edgar Allan Poe's "Murders in the Rue Morgue" to something published in the latest issue of *Ellery Queen's Mystery Magazine*. The rules will furnish a useful measuring stick for examining the stories in *Six Problems for Don Isidro Parodi*.

Throughout his writings, Borges frequently mentions Chesterton—in one of the stories in this volume, "The Nights of Goliadkin," a criminal adopts the alias of "Father Brown"—but the English writer is not the only influence on *Six Problems for Don Isidro Parodi*. One of the most noticeable of these other influences affects Borges' central character, Don Isidro Parodi, and the kind of detective that he is. Two brothers created by Arthur Conan Doyle illustrate the principal types of sleuth: the first of these is, of course, Sherlock Holmes, whose ratiocination is so overpowering that it frequently obscures the fact that Holmes is primarily a man of action. His characteristic impulse is to catch a train to visit the scene of the mystery, to move with speed when the occasion warrants, even to apprehend the criminal himself, sometimes with whatever force is required. The other type, the true "armchair detective," is illustrated by Sherlock's brother, Mycroft. Portly and indolent, sequestered in his study or club, Mycroft has an absolute aversion to physical action: his only tool is his mind. He begins a formula for characters of the same build and inclinations carried on in, for example, Nero Wolfe.

Don Isidro Parodi, as his name suggests, is in fact a parody, and particularly of this second kind of detective: he is fortyish, fat, with a shaven head, and he is absolutely immobile, although through no choice of his own. In what may be the funniest touch of the book, Parodi never leaves his room, or more precisely, his cell: he is serving a life sentence for a murder someone else committed. The typical Parodi story consists of narratives delivered to him in one or two sessions by the actors in the mystery, followed by a return to his cell, at which time he delivers the solution.

Parodi is introduced in the first story, "The Twelve Figures of the World," the story in the collection that adheres most closely to Borges' own prescriptions. The story contains only four main characters: Don Isidro, Achilles Molinari (the dupe), and two Syrians, Ibn Khaldun (the victim), and Izz-al-Din (the murderer). There are a few spear-carriers, but only these four have important roles. The mystery in "The Twelve Figures of the World" resembles those in many of Conan Doyle's stories in that it is not so much a question of who killed Ibn Khaldun, but rather the solving of an associated puzzle that hints at supernatural intervention: Molinari, while believing that he is being initiated into a secret society, appears to pick four specified men from a crowd of one hundred and fifty identically robed, veiled, and hooded figures. Molinari, who approaches Parodi with the problem, yearns for an explanation of how he accomplished his initiatory feat even more than for the identification of the murderer. The second question is, after all, a police matter, but the first touches him directly.

Borges and Bioy-Casares violate the former's third rule, but permissibly: a few paragraphs of background about Parodi appear in the story. While these details do not contribute to the plot, they are nevertheless needed because this is the first story in which Parodi appears as a character, and the reader must have some information about him.

The fourth rule, however, is followed to the letter. What interests the reader as well as Molinari is not who killed Ibn Khaldun, because to the reader the killer's identity is obvious. Unless Borges plays the same trick he scolds others for—bringing in a convenient stranger solely for the purpose of being the criminal—the murderer can only have been the fourth character. Instead, the fascination for the reader lies in how the trick was played on Molinari, and the clever explication of the trick is the high point of the story.

Whether the fifth point—that the mystery should have only one possible solution—is satisfied or not depends more on the ingenuity of the reader than the skill of the author. Be that as it may, the conclusion of "The Twelve Figures of the World" is complete and pleasing.

The other five stories seem less successful, for a variety of reasons. Consider, for example, "Tai An's Long Search." Borges is the unquestioned leader in the production of pseudobiblia of all kinds: his stories are filled with mentions of, references to, even excerpts from nonexistent books, articles, poems, and so on, by nonexistent authors. *Six Problems for Don Isidro Parodi* shows this penchant from its first pages, which display an introduction written by "Gervasio Montenegro," who is a character appearing in several of the stories. Therefore, when Montenegro, in his Introduction, compares "Tai An's Long Search" to Poe's "The Purloined Letter" and other examples of "the classic problem of the hidden object," it is really Borges and Bioy-Casares making the comparison. Yet the claimed likeness is hard to see.

"Tai An's Long Search" concerns a jewel stolen from a Chinese temple, its transportation to Buenos Aires, the murder of the thief by a temple priest sent to recover the jewel, and the return of the jewel to its home. The jewel is clearly the equivalent of Poe's letter, but Poe's sought-for object lends its special flavor to the story by being in plain sight. The jewel in Borges story, by contrast, is in two different places before and after the murder of the thief. Before the killing, when the jewel is being hunted for, its hiding-place is humdrum rather than extraordinary: it is buried in the garden. After the thief's murder, the site of the jewel is much cleverer, but at that point, no one is looking for it: the thief is dead and the agent has already recovered it.

Other stories have different faults, some of them attributable to language problems rather than to the authors. For example, in "Free Will and the Commendatore," the reader is deluged with names: important characters are Carlos Anglada; his wife Mariana Anglada; Pumita Ruiz Villalba, Mariana's sister; Ricky San Giacomo, Pumita's fiancé; Commendatore San Giacomo, Ricky's father; Eliseo Requena, Ricky's half-brother and the Commendatore's illegitimate son; Giovanni Croce, the Commendatore's financial adviser; and Mario Bonfanti, a member of the Commendatore's household. These eight characters are in addition to Parodi himself and the dozen or so other names mentioned in passing. The number of principals, then, violates Borges' first rule—that the story should contain a maximum of six—and their names are a stumbling-block to the English-speaking reader. If the names were "Johnson," "Smith," "Dawkins," and so on, they might be easier to sort out, but for the British or American reader, trying to keep straight Villalba, Anglada, Requena, and Pumita, even four characters may be too many. An especially bothersome example of this problem is the name of a character in "Tai An's Long Search": the character named Fang She is a he.

Surprisingly in a work by Borges, the humor (at least in part) is often heavy-handed. The nouveau riche (particularly those with literary or artistic pretensions) are constant targets of the book's satire; to find that one is a fertilizer magnate is amusing, but when similar characters in other stories work for Dyno-Rod Pipe, Drain, and Hygiene Services, or win the Raggio Olive Oil raffle, or pioneer the importation of linoleum substitutes, the method becomes predictable.

Finally, the translation reveals that the book is at an awkward age: the speech of the characters is filled with the slang of the 1920's and 1930's. That time has not receded enough for the slang to seem quaint; it simply makes the stories sound old-fashioned. Words and phrases such as *stuffed shirt*, *ninny*, *gaga*, and *hot air* date the characters and the stories in which they appear.

*Six Problems for Don Isidro Parodi* shows Borges trying his hand at a form in which he has often declared his interest, but the book will not place him on a level with Poe or Chesterton or Conan Doyle within that genre.

*Walter E. Meyers*

### Sources for Further Study

*The Atlantic Monthly.* CCXLVII, April, 1981, p. 122.

*Christian Science Monitor.* LXXIII, August 25, 1981, p. 18.
*Harper's Magazine.* CCLXIII, July, 1981, p. 74.
*Library Journal.* CVI, January 15, 1981, p. 164.
*Listener.* CVI, August 13, 1981, p. 153.
*National Review* . XXXIII, September 18, 1981, p. 1096.
*New Statesman.* CI, June 12, 1981, p. 18.
*The New York Times Book Review.* LXXXVI, March 29, 1981, p. 3.
*The New Yorker.* LVII, May 25, 1981, p. 137.
*Quill & Quire.* XLVII, July, 1981, p. 66.

# SIXTY STORIES

*Author:* Donald Barthelme (1931-    )
*Publisher:* G. P. Putnam's Sons (New York). 457 pp. $15.95
*Type of work:* Short stories

A retrospective collection of fifty previously collected short stories, nine previously uncollected stories, and an excerpt from the novel The Dead Father

The writing and study of fiction has become increasingly metaphysical in recent years; as criticism becomes more fictional and fiction becomes more critical, both reflect on each other and on themselves, as in the surrealistic funhouse of John Barth in which mirrors reflect mirrors in infinite regress. The result is a radical brand of irrealistic fiction which self-consciously proclaims itself antimimesis, antireality, and antimeaning. Conservative critics such as Malcolm Cowley and John Gardner find this trend morally disturbing, with Cowley claiming that such fiction has no subject or theme except the difficulty the authors find in writing fiction when they know a great deal about technique and have nothing else but that knowledge to offer their readers.

Ever since Donald Barthelme's first story appeared in *The New Yorker* in 1963 and his first collection of stories (*Come Back, Dr. Caligari*) appeared in 1964, his short fiction has been both much complained about and much imitated. Critics have complained that Barthelme's work is without subject matter, without character, without plot, and without any concern for the reader's understanding. It is, of course, these very characteristics that have made Barthelme so imitated. If Barthelme is both imitated and criticized for these reasons, so also are Robert Coover, William H. Gass, Ronald Sukenick, Raymond Federman, John Hawkes, and John Barth—writers who have earned such variously defined titles as practitioners of "antifiction," "surfiction," "metafiction," and "postmodernist fiction."

The term "postmodernist" is both the most all-encompassing and the most difficult to define. Most critics, however, seem to agree that if "modernism" in the early part of the century manifested a reaction against nineteenth century bourgeois realism, and, *à la* James Joyce and T. S. Eliot, frustrated conventional expectations about the cause-and-effect nature of plot and the "as-if-real" nature of character, then postmodernism pushes this movement even further so that contemporary fiction is less and less about objective reality and more and more about its own creative processes.

According to the basic paradigm which underlies this movement—based on European phenomenology and structuralism and further developed in psychology, anthropology, and sociology—"everyday reality" itself is the result of a fiction-making process whereby new data are selectively accepted and metaphorically mutated to fit preexisting schemas and categories. One critical implication of this theory is that literary fictions constitute a highly concentrated and accessible analogue of the means by which people create

that diffuse and invisible reality which they take for granted as the "everyday."
To study fiction then is to study the processes by which reality itself is created.

The primary effect of this mode of thought on contemporary fiction is that
the story has a tendency to loosen its illusion of reality to explore the reality
of its illusion. Rather than presenting itself "as if" it were real—a mimetic
mirroring of external reality—postmodernist fiction makes its own artistic
conventions and devices the subject of the story as well as its theme. The
underlying assumption is that the forms of art are explainable by the laws of
art; literary language is not a proxy for something else, but rather an object
of study itself. William H. Gass notes that the fiction writer now better
understands his medium; he is "ceasing to pretend that his business is to
render the world; he knows, more often now, that his business is to make
one, and to make one from the only medium of which he is master—
language."

The basic problem of such experimental fiction, however, is that it is often
called unreadable, as compared to the more realistic and therefore readable
fiction of such writers as Bernard Malamud, Saul Bellow, and William Styron.
Raymond Federman, one of the advocates and practitioners of experimental
fiction, has recently commented on this problem. Readability, says Federman,
is that which orients readers within the "reality" of the world, guiding them
back from the text to the world and offering comfort. Unreadability is that
which disorients readers, cutting off the referential paths between the text
and "reality." "Reflect on language, write language," says Federman,
"examine your relations with language within the mirrors of the text, and you
are immediately denounced, accused, and found guilty of 'experimentation,'
and therefore declared unreadable."

The short story as a genre has always been more likely to lay bare its
fictionality than the novel, which has traditionally tried to cover it up. It has
probably always been one of the great "unreadable" forms of fiction for this
reason. Fictional self-consciousness in the short story does not allow the reader
to maintain the comfortable assumption that what is depicted is real; instead,
the reader is made uncomfortably aware that the only reality is the process
of depiction itself—the fiction-making process, the language act. Similarly,
and for the same reasons, Donald Barthelme has been called an artist who
is high on the list of great "unread" *New Yorker* writers. It is certainly true
that readers schooled in the realistic tradition of the nineteenth century novel
will find Donald Barthelme tough reading indeed. For Barthelme, the problem
of language *is* the problem of reality, for reality is the result of language
processes. Such a view is as old as Giambattista Vico, who insisted that when
one perceives the world one perceives the shape of the mind which one has
projected on it, and as new as Jacques Derrida, who proclaims that the desire
to find a world in which there is an essential connection between the word
and the reality is a chimera, an illusory "metaphysics of presence."

The problem of words, Barthelme realizes, is that so much contemporary language is used up, has become trash, dreck. In Barthelme's first novel *Snow White* (1967), a character notes that when the per capita production of trash reaches one hundred percent, the pressing question turns from disposing of it to appreciating its qualities: "We want to be on the leading edge of this trash phenomenon . . . and that's why we pay particular attention, too, to those aspects of language that may be seen as a model of the trash phenomenon." Barthelme takes as his primary task the recycling of language, making metaphor out of the castoffs of technological culture. For Barthelme, as for the poet always, the task is to try to reach, through metaphor and the defamiliarization that results, that ineffable realm of knowledge which Barthelme says lies somewhere between mathematics and religion "in which what may fairly be called truth exists."

It is the extreme means by which Barthelme attempts to reach this truth and by which he performs this defamiliarization that make his fiction so often unreadable, at least in the sense in which that term is usually understood. Barthelme has noted that if photography forced painters to reinvent painting, then films have forced fiction writers to reinvent fiction. Since films tell a realistic narrative so well, the fiction writer must develop a new principle. Collage, says Barthelme, is the central principle of all art in the twentieth century. The point of collage, notes Barthelme, is that "unlike things are stuck together to make, in the best case, a new reality. This new reality, in the best case, may be or imply a comment on the other realities from which it came, and may also be much else. It's an itself, if it's successful." Speaking of his favorite story, "Paraguay," which he feels most successfully achieves this status of a new creation, he says, "mixing bits of this and that from various areas of life to make something that did not exist before is an oddly hopeful endeavor." This is the most basic form of the metaphor game, and the more unlike the terms that are mixed together the more interesting and strangely mysterious they become. Take, for example, the words *mothball* and *vagina*, says Barthelme, and put them together and see if they mean anything. One of the implications of this collage process is a radical shift from the usual temporal, cause-and-effect process of fiction to the more spatial and metaphoric process of poetry.

The most basic example of Barthelme's use of this mode is "The Balloon," the premise of which is that a large balloon has encompassed the city. The persona of the story says that it is wrong to speak of "situations, implying sets of circumstances leading to some resolution, some escape of tension." In this story there are no situations, only the balloon, a concrete particular thing that people react to and try to explain. The balloon is an extended metaphor for the Barthelme story itself, to which people try to find some means of access and which creates varied critical responses and opinions. In another story, "The Dolt," the problem is further developed: the central character is preparing for the National Writers' Examination and reads his wife a story he is writing which has a beginning and end but no middle. "I sympathize," says Barthelme at the end. "I myself have these problems. Endings are elusive, middles are nowhere to be found, but worst of all is to begin, to begin, to begin." In what is perhaps Barthelme's most autobiographical story, "See the Moon," the persona cites what is often taken to be a central tenet of Barthelme's aesthetic: "Fragments are the only forms I trust." The narrator talks about the future of his child, caught between procreative playthings at one end and Educational Testing Service at the other, directed in the middle by the Minnesota Multiphastic Muzzle Map. Thinking about how he will respond to questions his son will ask, he points to a wall filled with fragments, fragments he has hopes will one day merge, blur, and cohere into something meaningful, a work of art.

In another well-known story, "The Indian Uprising," the narrator aims for "strings of language" that extend in every direction "to bind the world into a rushing, ribald whole." He asserts that the only forms of discourse of which he approves are the litany and the list. Indeed, the list is one of Barthelme's favorite devices, in which disparate items are yoked together in strings that only end arbitrarily. The ultimate list, the paradigm for all the rest, makes up the entire story, "Nothing: A Preliminary Account." At the conclusion of this list (which is a nonlist since it lists what nothing is not), the narrator exults, "What a wonderful list! How joyous the notion that, try as we may, we cannot do other than fail and fail absolutely and that the task will remain always before us, like a meaning for our lives."

Barthelme strains at the outer limits of language, but seems forever caught in the inevitable trap of temporality and the diachronic flow, even as he aims for the pure spatialization and synchronic state of simultaneity. For although one may defeat the temporality of plot and the temporality of sentence, he is still trapped in the temporality of the word itself, and meaning is restricted to time regardless of one's efforts to escape it. In a story that seems a self-conscious capitulation to this fact, even as it parodies the fundamental problem of storytelling, "The Glass Mountain" is a series of one hundred numbered statements in which the character tries to climb the glass mountain (find the Holy Grail, reach Childe Roland's Dark Tower). The narrator's lament in this story that one must climb a glass mountain at considerable personal discomfort simply to disenchant a symbol is perhaps a metaphor for Barthelme's mixed feelings about his ironic and parodic story form. For if he is on the leading edge of the trash phenomenon, if fragments are the only forms he trusts, then he truly is trapped in an artistic situation in which he is sentenced to repeat his language experiments over and over again. Albert Guerard has called Barthelme "a cheerful historian of collapse," but reading all sixty of these stories, one begins to wonder just how cheerful and assured Barthelme is. One wonders how far he can push the parodic and ironic mode in which one even parodies those points of view that buttress one's own position. For example, in an early story such as "Shower of Gold," the existential point of view that underlies much of Barthelme's fiction is ridiculed by the litany-like use of such trashed and overused words as *de trop*, *nausea*, *bad faith*, *anguish*, and *despair*. At the end of the story, the central character says, "In this kind of world, absurd if you will, possibilities nevertheless proliferate and escalate all around us and there are opportunities for beginning again." As Barthelme says in another story, however, the problem still is to begin, to begin, to begin, and one wonders if Barthelme has not exhausted all the already exhausted possibilities of his fiction.

The central problem of the use of irony and parody in which one parodies oneself and therefore asserts nothing is best summed up in the story, "Kierkegaard Unfair to Schlegel." The persona, in referring to Søren Kierkegaard's *The Concept of Irony* (translated into English in 1965), notes that the effect of irony is to deprive the object of its reality. Kierkegaard's worry that the ironist has nothing to put in the place of what he has destroyed seems often to be Barthelme's worry as well. The limitation of the ironist, says Kierkegaard, is that the actuality he creates is merely a comment on a former actuality rather than a new actuality. Even as Barthelme says that collage is not only a comment on the old object but rather, in the best case, the creation of a new object, there is the inevitable fear that few cases ever reach such a level.

The problem is further summed up in another well-known story, "Me and Miss Mandible," in which a thirty-five-year-old man is mistakenly taken to be eleven years old and placed in a school room charged with the atmosphere of repressed sexuality. The cause of his immediate problem, and indeed the original cause of all Barthelme's stories, is the narrator's realization that although people "read signs as promises," the truth is that "signs are signs and some of them are lies." In a world in which one cannot take signs as promises, all the props are kicked out and all the assumptions are destroyed. It is one thing to have a character in a fiction confront this realization, but it is another problem when the artist himself makes this his basic view. For then there is nothing but signs and therefore nothing about which to write but the play of signs; and there is no tone to take but the ironic one. Charles Newman has said that Barthelme is the master of parody, but that he himself cannot be parodied. He marks the end of the "road of interiority." Beyond Barthelme, perhaps, the trash phenomenon cannot go. The question this retrospective collection poses is: can Barthelme go beyond Barthelme? Only time and future issues of *The New Yorker* will tell.

*Charles May*

## Sources for Further Study

*Book World.* XI, October 25, 1981, p. 5.
*Booklist.* LXXVIII, September 1, 1981, p. 1.
*Harper's Magazine.* CCLXIII, October, 1981, p. 84.
*Library Journal.* CVI, October 1, 1981, p. 1943.
*Nation.* CCXXXIII, October 17, 1981, p. 381.
*The New York Times Book Review.* LXXXVI, October 4, 1981, p. 9.
*Newsweek.* XCVIII, October 12, 1981, p. 100.
*Saturday Review.* X, September, 1981, p. 59.
*Time.* CXVIII, September 21, 1981, p. 82.

# SOME SORT OF EPIC GRANDEUR
## The Life of F. Scott Fitzgerald

*Author:* Matthew J. Bruccoli (1931-    )
*Publisher:* Harcourt Brace Jovanovich (New York). 656 pp. $25.00
*Type of work:* Literary biography
*Time:* 1896-1940
*Locale:* The United States and France

*After years of preparation, a scholar offers a masterful biography of F. Scott Fitzgerald, combining the story of his development as an author with the story of his doomed marriage to Zelda Sayre*

*Principal personages:*
F. SCOTT FITZGERALD, a novelist and short-story writer
ZELDA SAYRE FITZGERALD, his wife
FRANCES SCOTT FITZGERALD, their daughter
FATHER CYRIL S. W. FAY, a priest who influenced the young Scott Fitzgerald
SHEILAH GRAHAM, Fitzgerald's Hollywood mistress
ERNEST HEMINGWAY, an author and a friend of Fitzgerald
GERALD and SARA MURPHY, friends of the Fitzgeralds
HAROLD OBER, the literary agent for Fitzgerald
MAXWELL PERKINS, Fitzgerald's editor
EDMUND "BUNNY" WILSON, a literary critic and friend of Fitzgerald

It seems unlikely that any future biography of F. Scott Fitzgerald will supersede Matthew Bruccoli's extensively researched and brilliantly written study of the most famous portrayer of America's Jazz Age.

Appropriately, Bruccoli begins at the end, December 21, 1940, since Fitzgerald's sudden death at forty-four was an end toward which he had been lurching for most of his life. He died of a heart attack at the apartment of Sheilah Graham, the Hollywood gossip columnist who had been his mistress for several years. He had anticipated his early death when he wrote in one of his notebooks: "Then I was drunk for many years, and then I died."

In Bruccoli's biography, Fitzgerald and his gifted, spoiled, erratic, schizoid wife Zelda appear vividly alive and, almost from the beginning of their love and life together—and apart—doomed to destruction. Bruccoli remarks that "it is folly to assign blame to either partner. They conspired in a dangerous game for which only they knew the rules." If they really had any rules at the start, they changed or voided them at will as the game progressed toward its disastrous end.

Bruccoli's revealing comments on both Fitzgeralds are supported by his extensive knowledge of their letters and other private manuscript materials as well as their published work. (He has edited several earlier books on the Fitzgeralds and their writings.) Because both Scott and Zelda were intelligent enough to understand some of their own and each other's weaknesses, though unwilling or unable to control them, they indulged often in self-analysis or cross-analysis, and Bruccoli quotes frequently what they wrote about themselves and about or to each other.

In February, 1920, shortly before their marriage, Zelda wrote:

> I'm so sorry for all the times I've been mean and hateful. . . . I know you can take much better care of me than I can, and I'll always be very, very happy with you—except sometimes when we engage in our weekly debates—and even then I rather enjoy myself. I like being very calm and masterful, while you become emotional and sulky.

Zelda, a Southern belle accustomed to the attentions of numerous young men who had flocked around her, would attempt after marriage to maintain the "masterful" role and would sometimes feel jealous because her husband was receiving more attention and praise than she. The longer this continued the more Fitzgerald would resent it. Only two years later he would write: "the most enormous influence on me in the four + ½ years since I met her has been the complete fine and full hearted selfishness and chillmindedness of Zelda." Trouble was obviously looming in the marriage.

The personal characteristics which brought so much pain and sorrow to the Fitzgeralds after their marriage, were present before they met. She was an "unconventional and even wild" young woman, says Bruccoli. By 1913, when Scott was still a student at St. Paul Academy, he had already advanced in his drinking from drugstore sherry to stronger liquors. As the years passed, Zelda's mental condition deteriorated and Scott's continued drinking took an increasing toll on both his body and his mind.

Fitzgerald confessed to John O'Hara in 1933 that he had developed early "a two cylinder inferiority complex." He attempted to compensate by "alternately crawling in front of the kitchen maids and insulting the great." This insecurity led also to some of his outrageous behavior when he was drinking. "All his life," says Bruccoli, "he would play the clown when he found himself in a situation that he felt he could not handle." Bruccoli reports that by 1923 to 1924 Fitzgerald had progressed from a party drinker to a steady drinker with increasingly erratic behavior. No longer was "playing the clown" in public enough for him. He was jailed several times for drunkenness or disorderly conduct.

Though Fitzgerald did not remember everything he said and did during his drinking bouts, he remembered enough to feel guilt and sometimes shame. Ironically, his guilt about his drinking, says Bruccoli, "may have generated the self-perpetuating situation whereby he sometimes drank to alleviate the feelings of guilt provoked by his drinking."

*Some Sort of Epic Grandeur* is both the story of Fitzgerald's development and his accomplishments as a writer and the story of a man and a woman whose marriage brought periods of deep happiness, particularly in the early years, and a world of misery before it ended with Scott's death twenty years later. Zelda would die at forty-seven, a little more than seven years after

Scott, in the burning of a nursing home in Asheville, North Carolina, where she was a patient.

Scott knew early that he wanted to be a writer. As a boy he made up plays, and he published a mystery story at thirteen. At Princeton University he told his friend Edmund Wilson, who would later become one of America's most distinguished literary critics, "I want to be one of the greatest writers who ever lived." Though they continued their friendship in later years and though Wilson edited a posthumous volume of Fitzgerald's miscellaneous writings entitled *The Crack-Up* (1945), Bruccoli points out that "Wilson never broke the habit of patronziing [him]. . . . He was . . . unable to believe that Fitzgerald was a major writer. . . ."

Fitzgerald's first novel, *This Side of Paradise* (1920), assembled so many bits of leftover or reworked verse and prose from his college days that one reviewer humorously called it the "collected works of F. Scott Fitzgerald." In it, says Bruccoli, the young author is "self-conscious" and "self-indulgent" and tends to show off. Though a sensation at the time because it was so much more realistic than romanticized college novels, *This Side of Paradise* now seems very naïve.

In *The Beautiful and Damned* (1922), which pictures Anthony and Gloria Patch and their doomed marriage, Fitzgerald prefigures in part what would happen to him and Zelda. In 1930 he wrote Zelda: "I wish the Beautiful and Damned had been a maturely written book because it was all true. We ruined ourselves—I have never honestly thought that we ruined each other."

Fitzgerald's third novel, *The Great Gatsby* (1925), has been considered by many critics to be his best and one of the classic American novels. From Joseph Conrad he had learned how to avoid the jarring authorial intrusions of moralizing remarks that had weakened the earlier novels.

Using Nick Carraway as his narrator, who can comment philosophically or moralistically on the other characters, Fitzgerald keeps himself out of the book. Yet much of the novel represents his transformation of material from his own life and Zelda's into fiction, including his bitter disillusionment after she had a love affair with a French officer.

In *Tender Is the Night* (1934), his longest and most complex novel, Fitzgerald continues to use himself and Zelda in his writing. Dick Diver, a psychiatrist, perversely endangers his professional career by marrying his unstable young patient Nicole. Bruccoli says the novel "became in the writing [Fitzgerald's] attempt to understand the loss of everything he had won, the loss of everything he had ever wanted."

During the fourteen years between the publication of his first novel and his fourth, Fitzgerald had been writing short stories at a furious rate in attempts to pay for his and Zelda's reckless scale of living. As early as 1928 he was borrowing against stories he had not even written. Although a few were of high quality, such as "The Rich Boy" and "The Diamond as Big as the Ritz," most were written for ready cash and sold to high-paying magazines such as *Saturday Evening Post.*

Fitzgerald was burning himself out, writing what he regarded as little better than trash in order to pay bills and supposedly to allow time for the writing of novels on which he hoped to build his lasting literary reputation. Also, his alcoholism was increasingly affecting him a he grew older.

In 1935, while living in a hotel in Hendersonville, North Carolina, he began writing the essays in which he would confess publicly in *Esquire* magazine that his waste of physical, mental, and emotional capital as well as the foolish scattering of his money had brought a "crack-up."

Bruccoli notes the "irony of a writer writing brilliantly about his inability to write because of the loss of his capacity to care about the things and people he had once responded to so completely." The young man who had wanted to be one of the greatest writers who ever lived and who had earlier believed that he could *be* one of those writers, had now suffered what Bruccoli calls "a lesion of confidence." He saw himself as only a struggling, wavering remnant of the writer he had been.

In 1937 Fitzgerald left for Hollywood, where he hoped that high-paying work on film scripts would enable him to get rid of his mountainous debts. He did make money, but much of his script work was never filmed. He even began writing a Hollywood novel, which he never finished. (*The Last Tycoon* was posthumously published in 1941 in its unfinished state.) Unfortunately, he could not control his drinking, and in three and one-half years he was dead.

Bruccoli has painted unforgettable portraits of Scott and Zelda Fitzgerald, revealed through their own writing about themselves and each other, through observations and recollections by their daughter Scottie and many friends, and through Bruccoli's penetrating analysis of their characters.

Bruccoli's final assessment of Fitzgerald is that he is "now permanently placed with the greatest writers who ever lived, where he wanted to be all along. Where he belongs." Probably most readers of Fitzgerald would regard this as a biographer's exaggeration. More would be likely perhaps to agree with a critic who wrote a dozen years after Fitzgerald's death that "those who call him a great novelist are taking a great deal on faith, perhaps describing the writer he might have been rather than the writer he actually was."

*Henderson Kincheloe*

## Sources for Further Study

*Book World.* XI, October 11, 1981, p. 3.
*Booklist.* LXXVII, July 15, 1981, p. 1419.

*Christian Science Monitor.* LXXIV, November 25, 1981, p. 21.
*Guardian Weekly.* CXXV, November 15, 1981, p. 18.
*Harper's Magazine.* CCLXIII, December, 1981, p. 58.
*Library Journal.* CVI, September 1, 1981, p. 1631.
*National Review.* XXXIV, February 19, 1982, p. 176.
*The New Yorker.* LVII, January 4, 1982, p. 90.
*Newsweek.* XCVIII, November 23, 1981, p. 110.
*Saturday Review.* VIII, November, 1981, p. 78.

# THE SOUL OF A NEW MACHINE

*Author:* Tracy Kidder
*Publisher:* Little, Brown and Company (Boston). 293 pp. $13.95
*Type of work:* History of science and contemporary culture
*Time:* 1979-1980
*Locale:* Westborough, Massachusetts

*An introduction to the world of microelectronics and the people who inhabit it through the story of the creation of a new minicomputer*

Ever since C. P. Snow defined the world of science and the world of those not conversant with scientific language as comprising two distinct cultures, many people have lamented the separation between ordinary human experience and the realms of science and technology. The products of applied science touch people at every turn, as close as the light switch and often as frustrating and aggravating as a mistake in a computer-generated bill. Much of the anger and confusion in the modern world comes from the effects of scientific knowledge, even as the blessings of technology are increasingly taken for granted. The wonders of satellite television and video arcade games delight millions, while computer-generated mass mailings clog mailboxes with pseudopersonal letters written and signed by "people" who have no existence outside of a computer program.

Many have hoped for books written by people versed in the language of science and technology who can also translate that language into more everyday terms so that the general reading public can deal with the impact of science and technology in an informed way. In recent years, a number of writers have sought to bridge the gap between the two cultures, seeking not only to provide a nontechnical account of modern technology but also to "humanize" science by revealing something of the kinds of people who actually create and understand the machines and products that are changing lives in both major and subtle ways. The most successful of these writers has been John McPhee; on the basis of this book, one now must add the name of Tracy Kidder.

Kidder's achievement in this book cannot be underestimated; the computer is the product of technology which is transforming old electronic systems such as the telephone and bringing into being new, heretofore undreamed of devices such as the hand-held calculator, the video game, and the home data processing system. Yet, to the uninitiate, the language of computers—hardware, software, REMS, RAMS, BYTES, dot-matrix printers, and the like—is forbidding and confusing. In *The Soul of a New Machine*, Kidder takes the reader within the world of the computer engineer to bring him and his work alive and make them meaningful.

Kidder begins with a distinctively literary model—the quest story, with its heroes and obstacles to overcome against great odds under constraints of time—as old as the *Odyssey* (c. 800 B.C.), and sets it in the context of the electronics firms that surround Boston. The specific focus of his tale is an actual sequence of events, the efforts of a small team of engineers at Data General Corporation to create a new minicomputer that would work faster and handle more information than competitive models. In addition, the workers in Massachusetts are trying to develop their version of this computer faster than other Data General engineers in North Carolina. The odds are great, since the Massachusetts engineers are prohibited from using one element of technology reserved for the team in North Carolina which would have made their work easier. The stakes are high; Data General needs this machine to compete with other computer firms in a field in which it is falling behind.

Kidder knows that few readers could comprehend or care much about the technical issues at stake, although one of the important things about this book is the ease with which it explains a good bit about the working of computers. Accordingly, he enlivens the book with in-depth portraits of the various members of the Data General team. One comes to know something of what computer scientists are like—how they got to be in this field, what they do in their spare time, what their home lives are like. Most important, Kidder conveys what it feels like to attempt the untried and unprecedented in electronics, and convinces his readers of the fascination of such a challenge.

There is, indeed, a profound sense in which this story is not about computers at all, but about the ways in which human beings interact under pressure. The central question throughout the book is whether the computer will get finished in the time available, before the other team gets its built, before the company goes under for want of competitive products. The challenge facing the leadership of the team is to put together a group of people willing to sacrifice their time, energies, private lives, and egos for the sake of success, and, once having put the team together, to keep them working until the job is done. A subtheme of the book, therefore, has to do with the sources of human motivation and job satisfaction; here, Kidder takes the reader inside the interpersonal interactions of the team members and shows both the strains and the exhilarations of such "cutting-edge" work.

As a result, Kidder is able to "demythologize" computers, to reveal them as products of human labor and the human mind. This is an important achievement, and one for which readers must be extremely grateful. Faced with the computer and its powers, people often project onto it human capabilities and qualities. A distinguished computer scientist once invented a program that worked like a psychotherapist to show off the computer's powers to follow instructions in response to human input and to "communicate" with the user in the user's own language. He was horrified to discover that psychologists immediately began to wonder when the computer could take their places, ignoring the fact that the computer could do nothing but follow its program's instructions and the fact that psychotherapy demands the flexibility of human response to other human beings.

Kidder reminds his readers that the computer is essentially a series of on-off switches which can be made to give out information in forms that humans can interpret. One can project human meaning onto those forms, but that is a human activity, not the activity of the computer. He takes readers to the core of programming, where human languages give way to series of zeroes and ones, to patterns of on and off switches. The power of the computer lies in the incredible speed with which it can turn its switches on and off and thus process information which the programmer has made it possible for the computer operator to translate easily into zeroes and ones, often without ever knowing that that is what is happening.

In this light, the "soul" of Data General's new machine resides not in the machine itself, but in the men and women who put it together. Their willingness to sacrifice their individual concerns for the sake of a team effort to produce a machine that had never been built before, their excitement at working on the cutting edge of electronics, their delight in their results as well as their anger and disappointment over setbacks and failures, are what this book is really about.

Kidder thus makes it possible for his readers to approach computers in a new way, as the products of human effort and ingenuity, as tools that can enable man to do some things better and faster, rather than as magical, mysterious devices that threaten to supplant human intelligence. If one takes Kidder's work seriously, one may find oneself more willing to make use of such machines and to feel in control of them.

Perhaps more important, however, Kidder shows that the age of adventure is not over. The fact that his story lends itself so readily to treatment in terms of the ancient quest motif suggests that the experiences of the scientist and engineer are not alien to broader human experience. The old struggle of humankind to triumph over adversity is still alive and well and being acted out in the labs of Data General; there is something profoundly reassuring about that.

*John N. Wall, Jr.*

## Sources for Further Study

*Christian Science Monitor.* LXXII, September 23, 1981, p. 17.
*Library Journal.* CVI, August, 1981, p. 1558.
*The New York Review of Books.* XXVIII, October 8, 1981, p. 40.
*The New York Times Book Review.* LXXXVI, August 23, 1981, p. 1.
*The New Yorker.* LVII, October 19, 1981, p. 206.
*Scientific American.* CCXLV, October, 1981, p. 48.
*The Wall Street Journal.* CXCVIII, August 25, 1981, p. 30.

# THE SOURCE OF LIGHT

*Author:* Reynolds Price (1933-    )
*Publisher:* Atheneum Publishers (New York). 318 pp. $13.95
*Type of work:* Novel
*Time:* May, 1955-March, 1956
*Locale:* North Carolina and Europe

A young man comes of age, discovering the truth about himself, about those he loves, and about love itself

> *Principal characters:*
> HUTCH MAYFIELD, a young man learning to be a writer
> ROB MAYFIELD, his father
> ANN GATLIN, Hutch's close friend
> EVA KENDAL MAYFIELD, Rob's mother, Hutch's grandmother
> POLLY DREWRY, a former housekeeper and lover of Rob's father
> ALICE MATTHEWS, a friend of Hutch's dead mother

*The Source of Light* by Reynolds Price is a sensitive and saddening exploration of the coming of age of a young writer, Hutch Mayfield. At the opening of the book, Hutch has just quit his job as a teacher in a Virginia prep school, having felt the need to see if he has the ability to become a writer, to search for self-knowledge and to explore his talents before he begins to go downhill, a decline that his grandmother assures him afflicts Mayfield men after age twenty-five. Despite his disbelief in this premature dotage, Hutch does see his nearing twenty-fifth birthday as a turning point, and he makes plans to study for a year at Oxford, England, and to combine the study with a good deal of sight-seeing.

The complication in the novel—one which affects not only its plot but its structure as well—is the terminal lung cancer which is rapidly killing Hutch's father, Rob. The novel is divided into three parts: Book One, "The Principle of Perturbations," which takes place as Hutch is preparing to leave for England in the summer of 1955 before he knows that his father is dying; Book Two, which contains the event of Rob's death in December, 1955, entitled "The Rotation of Venus"; and Book Three, "The Center of Gravity," which tells of the aftermath of the death and its effect on Hutch. This last part covers February and March of 1956. The story is told primarily through letters sent from one character to another. These letters and the surrounding sections of exposition function symbolically: the communications network by which the letters are delivered reflects a network of emotion and concern that spreads from the Southern United States to England.

The primary relationship in this network is that between Hutch and his father. Hutch's mother, Rachel, died when the boy was born, so for all of his life Hutch's main source of emotional strength has been his father. Although many other relatives and friends have loved him, his father Rob has been the one with whom he has shared his hopes and dreams: Hutch and Rob have clung together as the only surviving Mayfield men. Hutch and his father are much alike in attitudes and desires; both are very affectionate, highly-sexed men. This particular emotion is also the area of their main difference: Rob's sexual desires have been heterosexual, but Hutch has found sexual love and release not only with women but also with other men.

Despite the love of the two for each other, their relationship has not been without problems. Each sees himself as living for the other, yet each strives to achieve some sort of personal life separate from but not exclusive of the other. Rob senses that his son will give up the long-planned year in Europe if he discovers that his father is seriously ill, so he allows Hutch to go to Oxford ignorant of the severity of the disease.

Beyond this primary relationship, *The Source of Light* explores many other contacts and connections between people. Many of these subsidiary relationships are with the older generation of women who have lived with and loved the Mayfields. Grandmother Eva Kendal Mayfield, Rob's mother, is the woman with whom Rob spends his last months while he prepares to die. She hides her sorrow from long habit, knowing that the child to whom she gave life will precede her into death. She and Rob have been close all through Rob's life, yet this relationship too is not ideal. Eva is a woman who finds it hard to demonstrate physically her affection. Rob's father had deserted her many years before, when the boy was only a year old. Eva then turned her sorrow inward, and had been unable to give her son the love that he badly needed. Eva is not a cold woman, but a very self-contained one. She keeps both pain and joy within herself, not allowing others to help her bear her grief or share her gladness. It was this inwardness, this reserve, that had driven Rob's father away from her, and it is the same quality that Rob does not understand. His inability to understand Eva's reticence is ironic, because he shows much the same secretiveness in hiding his illness from Hutch.

Another older woman, one of that generation whose personalities fill the book, is Miss Polly Drewry, the woman to whom Rob's father went after he left Eva. Unlike Eva, Polly is a warm and loving woman whose strength of character and selflessness forbid her making any claim on the man whose home and love she shared for many years. Both the son and the grandson of that man find peace in her company: she gives her love as easily as she dispenses cups of coffee, and it is Polly who in the end receives the family ring which first Rob and then Hutch gave to women whom they loved and lost.

Polly's love is outgoing, but Alice Matthews soaks up love like a well-used blotter. Alice had been a friend of Hutch's mother, Rachel, before Rachel met and married Rob. Rachel, delicate and close to unbalanced, had come to the sanatorium run by Alice's father. There the two women—one nineteen, the other twenty—had met and formed an intimate union. Rachel subsequently married and shortly thereafter died, leaving Alice with a void in her life. Yet Alice has made no attempt to fill that void: she retired from teaching art and filled her apartment with sketches of those she had loved and, like so many characters in the book, lost. Hutch visits her apartment and wonders if all the people in the pictures are dead, but finds to his surprise that only his mother is dead of all those sketched. The others live only a few miles away, but Alice does not seek their company: she prefers to keep those friendships in the constancy of her memory rather than subject them to the vacillations of day-to-day living. It is with Alice that Hutch explores both the house where his father and mother lived in the months before his birth and the graveyard where Hutch's mother lies. Alice is essentially the preserver of the past, and it is proper that she be the one through whom the past is explored.

If Alice is the preserver of the past, Ann Gatlin is the hope for the future. Hutch's relationship with Ann has been a long one, beginning several years before the time of the novel, when Hutch first went to teach in a rural Episcopal boys' school in the Virginia hills. Ann is bright, capable, and much in love with Hutch. Her desire is that Hutch will eventually settle and ask her to marry him, but Ann knows that Hutch is moving away from her as surely as she knows that she loves him. He has not asked her to come to Oxford with him, nor does he commit himself to any plans for the future.

Ann accompanies Hutch to New York to see him off, and the two plan to spend Christmas together, perhaps in Rome. Ann is passive, demanding nothing; like Eva, she keeps her feelings to herself. To Hutch she has become a stopping-place, a shelter where he can go when he is unhappy or lonely; she provides food, a place to sleep, a person to give companionship. Hutch is not attracted to founding a family of his own. He sees himself as a prisoner bound by the love-ties of his relatives, and Ann suffers from his edginess and her failure to hold his affections. Both times that Hutch and Ann spend together, first in New York and later in Rome, are tarnished by frightening occurrences. In New York, Ann falls so deeply asleep in her hotel room that Hutch fears that she has taken an overdose of sleeping pills. Later, their visit to Rome is marred by the news of Rob's impending death; the vacation is cut short when Hutch flies home without Ann. Hutch's solitary return, a sign of his reluctance to have Ann share more metaphorical journeys, marks the distance they have grown apart. Ann believes that their relationship is doomed, and she aborts the baby that she and Hutch created in Rome.

Hutch's family problems are not the primary cause of his choice of a solitary life. Although he complains, even rails against the ties that have bound him to other people, the greatest difficulty he faces is his preference for homosexuality. Although Hutch loves and reveres older women, he cannot find a lasting companionship with any woman; he chooses instead to share parts of his life with several young men.

Strawson Stuart, a former student, is one of Hutch's lovers. Earlier a troubled boy and now a young man struggling with alcoholism, Straw comes to

Hutch for understanding and comfort in the same way that Hutch had turned to Rob. Now Hutch has to take the role of a father, and impart a sense of worthiness and self-respect to the young man. Hutch achieves this by having Straw be the caretaker for the house that Rob had left to him, the house where Hutch had grown up. Encouraged by Hutch's trust, Straw learns to control his drinking and finds strength to take control of his life as well.

Another man to whom Hutch gives the strength and love of a deep and caring affection is Lew Davis, an Englishman Hutch meets on the ship carrying him to England. Lew has been touring Canada with a small circus and is now returning home. He is a sensitive man who turns to Hutch to cure the psychic ills caused by his youth as a slum child, and to remove the emotional scars raised by being a singer forced to squander his talent in a Canadian backwater. Lew is a tormented character, but during a tour of Cornwall and the Arthurian centers of southern England, Hutch is able to help Lew endure his unhappiness.

Both men learn to deal with a dawning self-realization in their tour of Tintagel, the country of Tristan and Iseult. In the setting of that tragic love affair, Hutch and Lew learn and accept what they are and what their lives will have to be. Hutch sees the castle of King Mark—Castle Dore—and thinks of the woods of Morois, where the legendary lovers consummated their love. He then envisions the world as a place where love generates its own need, as "a wild hunger generating its own food, rich and nutritious, and finally fatal." He sees love as a trap that destroys those who foolishly allow themselves to be snared. This attitude arises not even halfway through the novel, however, and events from there to the end bring Hutch to a different conclusion. By the end, Hutch has begun to see love not as a ravening monster but as the source of light—the source of all humanity and all goodness. He watches his father die, and the strength and openhearted love of those close to him help Hutch to bear his grief. With the help of Eva, and that of Sylvie and Grainger, two black servants who cared for Rob in his last days, Hutch is able to understand and appreciate the purity of the love which Rob had given to his son. At the time of his father's death, Hutch at last begins to live: he learns that European travel may help him gain experience, but it will never substitute for what Hutch has already received from his family and friends.

After Rob's funeral, Hutch spends the night in his father's house. There the spirit of the father, the essence that was Rob, stands one last time over the sleeping son, and lays a hand on Hutch's hair. Then, after touching gently and for the last time all those things in the house that needed his care, the spirit is suddenly gone. The moment shows most clearly that love is the spirit of man, and a power that crosses the boundaries of time and space, making a little world of safety and of rest.

*Walter E. Meyers*

## Sources for Further Study

*America.* CXLV, October 17, 1981, p. 224.
*Library Journal.* CVI, March 1, 1981, p. 577.
*National Review.* XXXIII, September 18, 1981, p. 1084.
*The New York Times Book Review.* LXXXVI, April 26, 1981, p. 3.
*Saturday Review.* VIII, April, 1981, p. 72.

# SOVIET DISSENT IN HISTORICAL PERSPECTIVE

*Author:* Marshall S. Shatz
*Publisher:* Cambridge University Press (New York). 214 pp. $19.95
*Type of work:* History
*Time:* 1696 to the present
*Locale:* Russia

*An analysis of political dissent in the Soviet Union within a historical framework ranging from the Russia of Peter the Great to the post-Khrushchev era*

> *Principal personages:*
> ALEXANDER RADISHCHEV, a writer and liberal activist
> ALEXANDER HERZEN, a writer, publisher, and revolutionary
> LEON TROTSKY, a Communist revolutionary
> NIKITA KHRUSHCHEV, First Secretary of the Communist Party of the Soviet Union, 1953-1964
> ALEXANDER SOLZHENITSYN, a writer and leading dissident
> ANDREI SAKHAROV, a physicist and leading dissident

In 1956, Nikita Khrushchev made his famous "secret speech" to the leadership of the Communist Party of the Soviet Union, in which he condemned many of Joseph Stalin's practices. It was an action of seminal importance. The resulting political "thaw" allowed for expressions of dissent for the first time in several decades. Such a surprising and unfamiliar phenomenon might understandably be seen as a singular, isolated historical occurrence. This excellent and concise study establishes, however, that the dissident movement in the Soviet Union is not exclusive to the 1960's. Marshall S. Shatz, a history professor at the University of Massachusetts in Boston, traces the roots of Soviet dissent deep into the Russian past and draws fascinating parallels between dissent in czarist times and today.

Shatz provides a historical dimension highly conducive to a better understanding of Soviet political life. He begins by reviewing the historical and geographical conditions that led to the establishment of autocracy in Russia. The effects of the long Mongol rule, as well as the openness of the vast territory—with its human and material resources thinly spread—seemed to make autocracy inescapable. Survival was seen as being contingent on strong central rule, capable of imposing sweeping measures to advance the state's interests. Serfdom, the quasi-enslavement of the peasants, was specifically established to serve the state's military and financial needs. It is an early example of enormous state initiatives; other comparable ones are Peter the Great's Westernizing schemes, the emancipation of the serfs in 1861, and Stalin's collectivization of agriculture and massive industrialization program. Thus, expectation of state initiative is a deeply ingrained Russian political tradition. If change and progress were to be effected, the all-powerful state would have to take the lead, for no other agent could possibly provide any impetus. To do this, an up-to-date, educated elite performing in the service of the state would be required.

The nurturing and promotion of such an elite, however, has been creating a dilemma for Russian governments past and present. Because dissidents have invariably come from the ranks of the state-sponsored educated elite, the state has been concerned with preventing the achievement of too much intellectual autonomy. Thus, an examination of the relationship between the autocratic state and its educated elite is a key to understanding dissent in Russia.

The segment of Russia's educated class which has criticized, questioned, and on occasion outrightly challenged the given political and social order is commonly referred to as the "intelligentsia." Shatz notes the term's special connotation; it is not the same as "intellectuals"; rather, it refers to those intellectuals who stand in opposition to the system. The emergence of this Russian intelligentsia was the legacy of Peter the Great (1696-1725), who initiated a vigorous program of Westernization. The nobility, whose status was directly linked to state service, was ordered by the Czar to acquire Western manner and schooling. Gradually, this led to the adoption of a new set of standards and the reevaluation of the familiar Russian environment. The impact of Western culture became especially formidable during the reign of Catherine the Great (1762-1796), a monarch quite actively involved in promoting the ideas of the Enlightenment. To encourage creativity and modernization, major reforms were implemented. From the perspective of the autocracy, it was like opening a Pandora's box. The paternalistic and arbitrary system was bound to be a source of growing frustration and humiliation for many who had begun to see themselves as truly free individuals.

Alexander Radishchev (1749-1802) is the first notable dissident whose background, education, and life experience Shatz explores, in order to explain the emergence of the Russian intelligentsia. Radishchev may be considered the "father of the Russian intelligentsia." He typifies how the government contributed to the rise of the intelligentsia by advancing the education of its own officials; in Radishchev's case it was five years of state-financed law study in Leipzig. Radishchev came to loathe the paternalistic arbitrariness of the system. A series of personal indignations and humiliations led him to a heightened empathy for other victims and a rejection of serfdom as an inherently evil institution. The growing individualism of the educated elite was accompanied by a strong sense of social mission and a keener national consciousness. Following Radishchev were the Decembrists, so named for their abortive revolt in December, 1825. They tried to seize the state and turn it into a more effective instrument for progressive change. Although the Decembrists failed miserably, they inspired a new generation of dissidents, "the men of the forties." Shatz focuses on Alexander Herzen (1812-1870), a gifted writer and the most prominent member of the intelligentsia of that era. As a "gentry radical," Herzen suffered years of imprisonment and provincial exile, revealing the striking helplessness of even the higher nobility. When he finally obtained permission to travel abroad, he never returned to Russia, instead setting up the first significant Russian émigré press in London.

In time the intelligentsia included persons from varied nongentry backgrounds. The chief mentor of "the men of the sixties" was Nicholas Chernyshevsky (1828-1889), the son of an Orthodox priest. His work *What Is to Be Done* was enormously influential in the development of the Populist doctrines which dominated the emerging revolutionary movement throughout the 1860's and 1870's. Particularly noteworthy was Chernyshevsky's portrayal of the plight of women, making him a forerunner of women's liberation. Russian Marxism arose in the 1880's and 1890's. Thus, two socialist currents competed for the intelligentsia's loyalties, to be joined by a revitalized liberal movement at the turn of the century. Nevertheless, there was a common denominator for the intelligentsia's opposition to the system. According to Shatz, it was the rebellion in the name of individual autonomy against the inherently arbitrary and all-pervasive paternalistic authority. Their personal experiences placed the dissidents in a unique intellectual and moral position to criticize and to pose alternatives. The hallmark of their protest was the vision of a more humane and just order, affording individual freedom and dignity. It is this which sustained the intelligentsia from generation to generation and gave its struggle an aura of nobility.

The post-Decembrists had given up all hope of working with the state for progressive change. The reforms pushed from above did not go nearly far enough for the disaffected elements of the educated elite. Many began to perceive the state as the very enemy of progress, embracing in their acute disillusionment theories of anarchism. A development rather fateful for the intelligentsia as a whole was the emergence of Bolshevism. Its supporters reflected a subtle but important difference: they tended to reject humanist sentiment and feeling. Leon Trotsky (1879-1940) and, of course, Vladimir Ilich Lenin (1870-1924) were the most important and typical members of this group. They regarded reason as the chief weapon. Their guiding principle was "rational egoism," and the object of their admiration was the "uncommon" man, single-mindedly devoted to duty, that is, to the socialist revolution. Lenin reportedly was profoundly impressed by a certain figure in Chernyshevsky's *What Is to Be Done* who possessed such characteristics. In his own *What Is to Be Done* (1902) the prevailing theme is ideological, political, and personal discipline. The cause has priority over everything; personal needs and aspirations must be sacrificed, if necessary. Critics of the Bolsheviks were rightly concerned that such emphasis on the socialist revolution entailed a downgrading of the value of the individual. It was said of Lenin and his followers that they did not love living *people*; they only loved the *idea* of universal human happiness.

The Bolshevik Revolution and the subsequent Civil War, a desperate struggle for survival against overwhelming odds, showed little regard for the value of individual life. Perhaps that was unavoidable, but the Communist revolutionaries created a legacy that contributed to the making of Stalinism. Under Stalin the individual shrank to a mere instrument to be used in the building of socialism. Anyone standing in the way would be ruthlessly eliminated. To eradicate all independent judgment Stalin ordered the Great Purge. Members of the intelligentsia, including many old Bolsheviks, fell victim to it. The Purge snowballed to incredible dimensions; the old intelligentsia was exterminated. The Purge also taught a powerful moral lesson, as Shatz points out, for many of its victims were Party members who learned for the first time what it meant to be an innocent victim. Some of these people rediscovered human values and reaffirmed the absolute worth of individual life.

Khrushchev's de-Stalinization effort constituted a major turning point in Russian historical development, permitting an easing of tensions in Soviet life. Khrushchev attacked Stalinism while taking care not to undermine the foundations of the Soviet system. Thus, he can be compared to the autocratic reformers of the czarist past. De-Stalinization did allow for expressions of criticism in the moral sphere, well-suited for the realm of literature. Of the numerous outstanding works of literary dissent, one of the greatest was Boris Pasternak's *Doctor Zhivago* (1957). The book was not cleared for publication in the the Soviet Union and was circulated through *samizdat*, the duplication and hand-to-hand circulation of the manuscript. Another work with profound impact was Alexander Solzhenitsyn's *One Day in the Life of Ivan Denisovich* (1963). These great works were firmly within the Russian cultural tradition, which obligates literature to fight oppression and to assume a social responsiblity.

Dissent entered a new sphere in the post-Khrushchev era with the trial of writers Andrei Siniavsky and Iuly Daniel in 1966. They were charged with the vague offense of "anti-Soviet propaganda." Clearly, in the eyes of the authorities literary freedom had gotten out of hand. In turn, many of the new intelligentsia saw ominous signs of "re-Stalinization." The trial did not have the intended deterrent effect. Rather, it touched off protests and further trials, as people were facing the fact that violations of legal due process were not a thing of the past. Dissent went beyond the moral sphere of the Khrushchev era to address the broader problems of civil liberties. The late 1960's, however, saw a steady constriction of the permissible boundaries of political self-expression. The authorities came down hard on any publicly expressed dissent in the form of protest rallies and demonstrations.

The latest stage of Soviet dissent, as discussed by Shatz, involves the effort to form permanent associations which could apply steady pressure on the government to widen civil liberties. An important example of this development is the publication in *samizdat* of the journal *A Chronicle of Current Events*. Shatz suggests that it has created a nationwide information network for dissidents. Wide recognition has also been given in the West to the Human Rights Committee, having as its leading spokesman the famous physicist Andrei Sakharov, although arrests, forced emigration, and—as in the case of Sakharov—internal exile, have gradually deprived the organization of its most active members. Such autonomous associations may represent a new stage of political consciousness, but their potential appears to be very limited. Indeed, by the late 1970's the prospects for dissidents had dimmed considerably.

Shatz concludes his analysis of contemporary Soviet dissent by noting that the social sources of dissent are strikingly similar to those generating the intelligentsia at the end of the eighteenth century. Current dissent is the most recent cycle in a recurrent pattern, involving a narrow section of the educated elite, members of the privileged classes. As in earlier times, the members of the new intelligentsia seek to protect their self-esteem and gain a measure of independence of mind against an arbitrary overbearing state. Today's dissidents seek peaceful improvement, not revolution, but there is considerable disagreement regarding the kind of change to be sought. Shatz differentiates among three major categories of advocacy: (1) the return to "pure" Marxism-Leninism, (2) the revival of religious humanism, and (3) the implementation of Western-style liberal and pluralist practices. No coherent schools of thought can be discerned.

For the time being Soviet dissent is likely to be confined to a relatively few individuals and circles. Shatz shows how it continues to be the outgrowth of the relationship between a modernizing but paternalistic state and the educated elite on which modernization depends. This is a valuable, highly readable analysis of the subject. The effective use of autobiographical and literary sources to discover the personal roots of dissent will interest specialists and nonspecialists alike.

*Manfred Grote*

## Sources for Further Study

*Choice*. XVIII, June, 1981, p. 1472.
*The Economist*. CCLXXIX, April 25, 1981, p. 115.
*Library Journal*. CVI, February 1, 1981, p. 353.

# THE SPECULATOR
## Bernard M. Baruch in Washington, 1917-1965

*Author:* Jordan A. Schwarz (1937-        )
*Publisher:* The University of North Carolina Press (Chapel Hill). Illustrated. 679 pp. $27.50
*Type of work:* Biography
*Time:* 1917-1965
*Locale:* The United States

*A comprehensive examination of Bernard M. Baruch's public career, embracing his work on the War Industries Board and his role as a Democratic Party patron and spokesman for national planning and economic stabilization*

> *Principal personages:*
> BERNARD M. BARUCH, a speculator, Chairman of the War Industries Board, adviser to Democratic leaders, and spokesman for policies of economic stabilization
> HERBERT HOOVER, thirty-first President of the United States, 1929-1933
> WOODROW WILSON, twenty-eighth President of the United States, 1913-1921
> WILLIAM GIBBS MCADOO, Treasury Secretary under Wilson and Democratic presidential contender during the 1920's
> GEORGE PEEK, an Associate of Baruch and Agricultural Adjustment Administrator during the First New Deal
> FRANKLIN D. ROOSEVELT, thirty-second President of the United States, 1933-1945
> HERBERT BAYARD SWOPE, a journalist and close associate of Baruch
> JAMES F. BYRNES, Director of the Office of War Mobilization during World War II

This exhaustingly researched "life and times" ably documents Bernard Baruch's public career from the era of World War I until his death during the era of Vietnam. Never far from the limelight, Baruch was a friend, adviser, and financial patron to some of the most influential newsmakers and opinion-makers of his time. His chairmanship of the War Industries Board and the Baruch Plan for international control of atomic energy have earned him lasting praise, although a shroud of mystery has obscured the extent of his fortune, the nature of his political motives, and the historic significance of his actions.

While this book is the most definitive political biography of Baruch to date, a fuzziness about Baruch's character remains, owing in large part to the author's decision not to render a full-scale biography. Thus, the reader learns almost nothing about his family life and is told without much amplification that he was a Victorian, a gentleman, a man's man, and a womanizer who liked prize fights, the racetrack, a shapely leg, and European spas. A secular, cosmopolitan Jew who neither emphasized nor denied his religious heritage, he was called the American Disraeli and was pilloried in anti-Semitic publications. Like Joseph P. Kennedy, another maverick speculator of questionable bloodline in WASP circles, he was regarded as somewhat disreputable by many Wall Street colleagues.

Although Jordan Schwarz provides a few details concerning the amassing of Baruch's fortune and his skills as a financial investor, the reader cannot determine accurately the degree to which Baruch used his political insider's clout for his own enrichment. Schwarz himself is ambivalent on whether he was more a selfish entrepreneur or a disinterested statesman. He presents Baruch as a broad-gauged man—conservative yet innovative, a practical idealist motivated by a desire for acclaim in the press and acceptance within the circles of the governing class. While Schwarz overuses the word "speculator" throughout the text, the word applies to Baruch's instincts as a "hunch player" in people as well as stock portfolios. Not especially well read, he was an impresario more skilled in the art of public relations than in administrative management. As Schwarz summarizes Baruch's thinking, the science of government was less important to him than the conviviality of men. A "kibitzer" most of his public career, Baruch wrote letters, testified before Congressional committees, entertained politicians at his South Carolina retreat, and offered advice to governmental officials and business leaders. Most of the assignments he took on were of the short-term variety and did not require a sustained commitment.

One role which Baruch assigned to himself was as a prophet-priest for economic stabilization. A capitalist who distrusted the extremes of laissez-faire and state socialism, he advocated national planning to curb inflation and prevent destructive competition. During wartime he prescribed comprehensive, cartelistic state controls, while during peacetime he favored nonstatist cooperative arrangements by trade associations and the like that organized society. Like Herbert Hoover, another Wilsonian, he believed in a modified free-enterprise system and sought ways to preserve it in the tumultuous, ravaging twentieth century. While the nation listened to him (even if it did not always follow his advice) during wartime, Baruch failed to articulate a practical postwar alternative to the Keynsian "New Economics" that he so abhorred. After both world wars, for example, he advocated permanent boards of arbitration to settle matters of wages and prices in order to combat industrial-labor strife and destructive inflationary spirals. Little came of these proposals. Even so, his story is worth examining, because, as Schwarz points out, it is part of "America's abortive quest in the twentieth century for social justice through economic stabilization."

Baruch made his way into politics the same way he made his fortune, by cultivating "insiders." A political contribution resulted in an offer to be on the Board of Trustees of the City College of New York, and sponsoring the appointment of Woodrow Wilson adviser Edward M. House's brother-in-law as CCNY's president helped him win him a place on the Advisory Commission to the Council of National Defense. When Baruch subsequently sold steel stock short following a tip that peace talks were imminent between Great Britain and Germany, the House Rules Committee investigated charges that he profited from privileged information. Baruch vindicated his honor by convincing the committee that what prompted his action (a speech by the British Prime Minister) was public knowledge. After America became a belligerent, Baruch liquidated all his stocks except for gold, silver, and tungsten mines and bought a million dollars worth of Liberty Bonds.

Put in charge of the Raw Materials section of the War Industries Board, Baruch became its chairman in 1918, at a time when its organization was already in place. It was an ideal post which allowed him the opportunity to earn a reputation as a responsible administrator. His open mind, generalist's flexibility, and toughness in dealing with industrial leaders impressed fellow Southerner Woodrow Wilson. Bringing up the possibility of nationalizing the United States Steel Corporation to its Chairman of the Board, Elbert H. Gary, he responded to Gary's doubts about whether any governmental official was capable of running his corporation by replying that he could get a second lieutenant to do the job. In the end, Baruch got his way by threatening to deny fuel to U.S. Steel.

Offered the post of Secretary of the Treasurey (he demurred) and named to the American delegation to the Versailles Conference, Baruch was at the apex of his prestige at war's end. In 1920 he hoped that his close colleague William Gibbs McAdoo would emerge with the Democratic presidential nomination, but the would-be candidate's hopes were dashed when he failed to get the endorsement of President Wilson (his father-in-law), who clung to hopes for a third term. During the 1920's Baruch became the financial "angel" of numerous Democrats, including Senators Pat Harrison and Key Pittman, and in 1924 he supported an unsuccessful presidential boomlet on behalf of Governor Albert C. Ritchie of Maryland after his friend McAdoo was stained by being legal counsel for Teapot Dome oilman Edward L. Doheny.

Baruch's skills as a power broker were in evidence during Herbert Hoover's last two years in office, following the 1930 election, which registered public dissatisfaction with the President. Nevertheless, he had scarcely more idea than Hoover how to get the country out of the depression. Both men underestimated the situation and regarded the crisis more as one of confidence than as a result of fundamental flaws in the system. Despite their philosophical similarities, Hoover was a more systematic thinker, whereas Baruch had fewer qualms about "obligatory" cooperation between business and the government to ameliorate the effects of the slump.

Like Mark Hanna during the 1890's, Baruch was a pragmatic realist (as well as a nationalist and an elitist) who hoped to "fix his star" to a personage of presidential timber. Hanna had become "Warwick" to President William McKinley, but Baruch had to content himself with an occasional supporting role in the administrations of Franklin D. Roosevelt and Harry S Truman.

The relationship between Baruch and President Roosevelt constitutes one of the most interestng themes of Schwarz's book. Both were strong-minded egotists who distrusted each other but could not afford the other's enmity. Roosevelt needed an emissary to Democratic conservatives, especially in Congress, while Baruch desired access to the White House. Baruch joined Roosevelt's "Brain Trust" in 1932, and there were rumors that he would be offered a spot on the cabinet. Allegedly Roosevelt held back from appointing him to such a post because of a rumor that the speculator had profited from advance knowledge of a Reconstruction Finance Corporation loan (the financial transaction had caused shares of Missouri Pacific Railroad stock to skyrocket from 15 to 50). Even so, Baruch's associates George N. Peek and Hugh S. Johnson were selected to direct the two most important recovery agencies of the first New Deal, the Agricultural Adjustment Administration and the National Recovery Administration. Schwarz concludes that Roosevelt regarded Baruch as a conniver interested in his own personal aggrandizement who was unworthy of public trust but who could be a nuisance if handled tactlessly. Thus, he named him to the delegaton which attended the abortive London Economic Conference. Baruch's impact on New Deal planning, however, was minimal; neither is there much evidence to bear out Roosevelt's harsh assessment of Baruch's motives.

After 1934 Baruch believed that the New Deal was leaning too far to the left, but he refrained from public criticism and supported Roosevelt's reelection vocally and monetarily. In 1938, however, he broke with the administration over its tax bill and even supported some Congressional Democrats whom Roosevelt was attempting to purge from the party. The following year, with war clouds settling over Europe, relations between the two gradually became more amicable, but not until after a presidential snub which wounded the speculator. The issue involved the setting up of a War Resources Board. Much to Baruch's chagrin, he was not named to it; and even though it subsequently advocated policies virtually identical to his own, Baruch criticized them. As Schwarz concludes, "In Byzantine Washington, power mattered more than principle, even for Bernard Baruch."

During World War II President Roosevelt balked at suggestions that he reassemble the War Industries Board apparatus but used Baruch to educate the public about the need for federal controls. Baruch was named as chairman of a Rubber Survey Committee, for example, and his report helped pave the way for gasoline rationing. Roosevelt did not want anyone other than himself to become a wartime "czar." When he finally decided to delegate meaningful authority within an Office of War Mobilization, the position of director went to Baruch's friend (and fellow resident of South Carolina) Jimmy Byrnes. Baruch's age and questionable health dictated against his working long hours at any rate, so he cultivated an image as an elder statesman, advising bureaucrats and the press from a park bench in Lafayette Square. Wearing plain, black, high-topped "Liberty Shoes," as he had done during World War I, Baruch preached a doctrine of meaningful sacrifice by all segments of society in order to ensure the success of the war effort. He chafed at imagined slights from Byrnes and other members of the administration, however, and grumbled to friends in 1944 that a Republican victory by presidential candidate Thomas E. Dewey would not be unwelcome. In the battle for control of the Democratic party between expansionists and stabilizers he feared that the former would jeopardize postwar economic readjustment.

If Baruch never won Franklin Roosevelt's trust, ironically he had a warm admirer in Roosevelt's wife Eleanor, whose philanthropic activities benefitted from Baruch's financial largesse. One project close to the First Lady's heart was Arthurdale, a homestead community in West Virginia which was rehabilitated with the help of New Dealers as well as private donations. Baruch believed that Arthurdale could become a model experiment in cooperative capitalism, and during World War II he used his connections to bring about the building of airplane factories in Arthurdale in order to make its economy self-sufficent. Eleanor and Bernie (as close friends called him) also agreed on the need for such welfare state measures as national health insurance. Although they parted ways on some civil rights and Cold War issues, they remained defenders of each other to their disparate constituencies.

Baruch and former Secretary of Agriculture (and Vice-President) Henry Wallace also shared a mutual respect, and in the wake of World War II Baruch echoed Wallace's call for economic cooperation with the Soviet Union. By the time of Winston Churchill's "Iron Curtain" speech, however, he had become a convert to the strategy of containment. The famous Baruch Plan for control of atomic energy was couched in terms that the Russians could not possibly accept.

In his old age, Baruch became more cantankerous in his continual calls for planning, discipline, and deflationary economic policies, and he lost a bit of his touch for ingratiating himself with the political elite. He had a falling out with President Truman, partly as a result of a ludicrous request that his brother-in-law, the Ambassador to the Netherlands, be the only official American representative at a royal wedding. Truman's reply dripped with sarcasm. Baruch enjoyed the occasional flattery of an invitation to the White House from Presidents Dwight D. Eisenhower, John F. Kennedy, and Lyndon Johnson, and he cherished being included on a 1960 list of "greatest living Americans." His ghostwritten memoir *Baruch: My Own Story* (1957) sold well, although its admonishments against inflational policies went unheeded by policymakers. Proponents of the "New Economics" were singularly unimpressed: Paul A. Samuelson dismissed his ideas as lightweight; John Kenneth Galbraith labeled him a humbug—a "man of self-inflicted self-importance."

Schwarz hedges his bet concerning the accuracy of these assessments. He intimates that an aging Baruch offered little that was original in his prescription for the postwar American economy but adds that the country might well have heeded his admonishments against inflation and the lack of national planning. Paradoxically, Lyndon Johnson's Great Society and Vietnam policies, which Bauuch approved, did much to discredit the Keynsian liberals and bring back into vogue some of the very ideas held sacred by Baruch. For that reason—and for its fairness and accuracy—Schwarz's book deserves a close reading.

*James B. Lane*

## Sources for Further Study

*Choice*. XIX, September, 1981, p. 153.
*The Economist*. CCLXXXI, October 24, 1981, p. 93.
*Library Journal*. CVI, June 1, 1981, p. 1214.
*The New Republic*. CLXXXV, September 23, 1981, p. 29.
*The New York Review of Books*. XXVIII, October 8, 1981, p. 12.
*The New York Times Book Review*. LXXXVI, August 30, 1981, p. 1.

# SPRING MOON
## A Novel of China

*Author:* Bette Bao Lord (1938-    )
*Publisher:* Harper & Row, Publishers (New York). 464 pp. $14.95
*Type of work:* Historical novel
*Time:* 1892-1972
*Locale:* China

*The life of heroine Spring Moon, spanning eighty years, dramatizes the cataclysmic effects of the Chinese Revolution on traditional life in China, seen through the experiences of Spring Moon's aristocratic clan*

> *Principal characters:*
> THE HOUSE OF CHANG, IN SOOCHOW:
>> BOLD TALENT, the son of patriarch Old Venerable and his first wife, the Matriarch
>> STERLING TALENT, the son of Old Venerable and his second wife
>> NOBLE TALENT, the son of Old Venerable and his third wife, Silken Dawn
>> FRAGRANT SNOW, the wife of Sterling Talent
>> SPRING MOON, the daughter of Sterling Talent
>> GOLDEN VIRTUE, the wife of Bold Talent
>> AUGUST WINDS, a distant relative
>> RESOLUTE SPIRIT, the son of tenant farmer Lee
>> FATSO, a faithful servant
> THE HOUSE OF WOO, IN PEKING:
>> FIERCE RECTITUDE, a Hanlin Scholar
>> LOTUS DELIGHT, his wife
>> GLAD PROMISE, their son, Spring Moon's husband
>> LUSTROUS JADE, the daughter of Glad Promise and Spring Moon
>> ENDURING PROMISE, the adopted heir of Fierce Rectitude, son of Spring Moon and Bold Talent
>> DUMMY, a mute handmaiden

The author of *Spring Moon*, like Margaret Mitchell in *Gone with the Wind* (1936) and Boris Pasternak in *Doctor Zhivago* (1958), has written of civil war and social change from a uniquely informed position. Bette Bao Lord, born in Shanghai of a scholarly, aristocratic clan, came to America as a child; her father was an official in the Chinese government. The family remained in America after the Communists won the Chinese Civil War. The author first returned to China in 1973 with her husband, Winston Lord, principal adviser to Henry Kissinger for the China opening.

In her "Author's Afterword," Lord expresses satisfaction with the timing of that reunion with her Chinese past: "Only at thirty-five was I looking at life from both sides: . . . as mother and daughter, as Chinese and American, as younger and elder, as one person and a member of a clan, no longer thinking that . . . mortality [was] but a word. . . . [In China] I heard tales of the ancestors and saw the lives of my relatives—the life I might have led.

The soul of *Spring Moon* lives in that trip. . . ."

Drawing on these personal memories and a strong sense of clan tradition, Lord has nevertheless remained evenhanded in her representation of both the "feudal" society of old China and the Communist takeover, introducing a broad spectrum of societal experiences and political reactions through her many characters. In these dramatically human terms, she shows the changing face of China over the long chaotic years of the revolution. To avoid encumbering her narration with political datelines, Lord has furnished as an appendix a four-page chronology of Chinese history from 1990 B.C. to A.D. 1981. This list provides detailed historic background for history buffs; even the casual reader, having become involved in the human dimensions of this revolution, might be expected to scan the chronology with newly awakened interest in Chinese history.

Poetic titles for each section of the novel and appropriate introductory passages preceding each chapter give *Spring Moon* the effect of a traditional Chinese novel. The author's point of view becomes apparent without cant; she writes in the understated style of traditional Chinese poetry. Avoiding direct comment, Lord shows, for example, the rage and resentment aroused by the "unequal treaties." She speaks early in the novel of a time when the "Chinese still valued scholarship above silver," then shows in later chapters the success of August Winds, the family ward who has bribed his way to wealth under the new regime. In heroic tone, her Preface to the Epilogue recounts the long March by the Communists and the leadership of the Great Helmsman; in contrast, the chapter itself depicts Lustrous Jade and her husband driven to suicide by the Party they had served so faithfully and long.

Spring Moon, the central figure, endures by adapting, representing the novel's recurrent theme of the yielding nature of Confucianism bending before the confrontational spirit of both Western Protestantism and the Communist movement. She is caught between the Confucian ideals she unsuccessfully seeks to hand down to her daughter, and the scholarly doubt of her mentor and lover. To her daughter, Lustrous Jade, she insists that civilization depends on the family, and the family on yielding filial piety, but from her mentor uncle, Bold Talent, she hears:

> The revolution has put an end to yielding. . . . Do you not see what is wrong? . . . With all Chinese? With the Old Empire? With the old ways? . . . In the end, we always yield— to tradition, to foreigners, to family, to authority, to duty. . . . What no other men will tolerate, I will endure, for I am Chinese.

Bold Talent, the philosophical patriarch educated at Yale, expresses in his thoughts and personal relationships the ambiguous position of those bred in Confucianism and educated in Western culture. Faithful to his responsibilities as head of the Chang clan, obedient in his choice of a mate, he has also allowed himself a discreet, incestuous relationship with his widowed niece. Struggling for serenity amid tumult, he writes: "I fear that when change comes to ancient ways, no matter how long in the making, no matter how fervently wished for, chaos follows." As the novel progresses, these expressions of concern yield to voices of despair. "What has happened to the revolution? Have we been dragging the lake for the moon all these years?" asks Bold Talent in 1916. Still later, the clan's career revolutionary, Noble Talent, stands over the body of his brother the patriarch, shot in the street during the "White Terror" of 1927, and weeps, "Is this what revolution means?"

For the aristocracy, revolution brings an end to centuries of tradition. The endpapers of this handsomely designed volume begin the reader's intimate introduction to the customs and values of traditional China, mapping the ancient and extensive courts of the House of Chang as it appeared in 1892. In this meticulously described setting, the irrepressible Spring Moon grows to maidenhood with bound feet but unbounded intellectual curiosity. Within courtyards and rockeries, in spare but elegant rooms furnished with calligraphy sets, rosewood furniture, and Ming urns, her clan's numerous members pass serene hours in scholarly pursuits, embroidery, and ceremonial observances. The devotion to family that characterizes the Chinese is strongly evoked through these Soochow scholar-landowners whose Clan Book covers three hundred years.

On his deathbed, the clan patriarch Old Venerable admonishes Spring Moon, "We are mere mortals who must learn not to contend with life but to yield to it." As Spring Moon matures and the civilization she has known comes unbound in the firestorms of reform and revolution, Lord's imagery moves away from the caged lark sunned by the gardener, the intricately pinned coiffures of matriarchs, and schoolrooms with gates closed against females. The bride departing cloistered in a sedan chair borne by superstitious coolies returns unveiled only a few years later, by railroad train. The open fields and earthy peasants familiar to readers of Pearl Buck's best-selling novels become backdrops for aristocrats thrown back on the land for survival. Bobbed hair, blue cotton, and callused hands replace queues, brocaded silks, and bound feet. In the Epilogue, nonagenarian Spring Moon inspires the family reunion from her home in one of the dingy hovels occupying the former site of the Chang courtyards. Her surly, suspicious neighbors provide grim contrast to the loving family and valued servants that filled the compound during her childhood. Yet in 1972, five generations of Changs, including expatriates, gather with Spring Moon among the broken tombs in the clan cemetery to honor their ancestors. Lord is obviously commenting on the importance of ancestors to contemporary Chinese, both in their homeland and overseas. Spring Moon's story expresses that continuity on a personal scale.

During the course of Spring Moon's life, which provides the framework for the impressive historical depth of the novel, the Manchu Empire dissolves, the attempt to establish a republic founders, two Japanese wars are fought, and the Kuomintang's struggle is lost to the Communist seizure of China. Events in the lives of Lord's characters reflect these national cataclysms, transposing them into keenly personal experiences without the intrusion of direct interpretation by the author.

Lord controls her complex *mise en scène* with the order and harmony of Oriental art, employing narrative, dialogue, exchanges of letters, poetry, and passages of myth to advance the plot and enrich the vision. Allowing her protagonists differing political convictions, Lord shows the clan's elders, its half-Westernized students, and its youngest liberals to be equally caught up in both the collapse of ancient order and courageous struggle for personal integrity in the midst of change they cannot avoid.

Spring Moon, educated as if she were a boy by her fond and progressive uncle, enters marriage with a developed intellect uncommon to aristocratic women of her time. She nevertheless remains fully committed to the yielding nature of Confucianism and the preservation of family unity at whatever personal sacrifice. Her strength of character survives her eighty years during which Chinese aristocracy is thrown into the mainstream of the working classes.

The two men she loves, her husband and her mentor uncle, both die as victims of civil strife. Spring Moon aids in an assassination to protect her clan; forced into hiding, she is parted from her daughter, Lustrous Jade, and conceives her only son, whom she can never acknowledge without dishonoring the clan. The daughter's mission school experience alienates her from her heritage and leads her to reject the world view of her ancient clan and turn defiantly to Communism.

The love story of Spring Moon and Bold Talent is portrayed with the restraint which gives this novel much of its poignancy. Incestuous and in conflict with the deepest convictions of the lovers, the affair evokes only compassion for the couple who so resolutely renounce their only happiness on behalf of loyalties to ancestors long dead and clan members already scattered.

This strong statement of honor is one of several noticeable parallels with two other superbly researched and written novels of civil war and its effects on aristocracy, Margaret Mitchell's *Gone with the Wind*, and Boris Pasternak's *Doctor Zhivago*. These accounts share with Lord's novel a pattern—aristocrats arriving at maturity only to see revolution sweep away the societies in which their backgrounds have prepared them to live. Testing the characters' capacity to endure and the extent to which the sense of honor is preserved or compromised under such calamitous adversity, each of these authors portrays the resilience of the human spirit.

In these novels, Mitchell's Scarlett O'Hara calluses her hands saving Tara; Spring Moon earns calluses at Learned Cinders; aristocrats seek refuge on family lands at Tara, Reed Village, Varykino; the proletariat crowds into the former splendor of the courts of Chang and the halls of Russian aristocracy. The faithful and beloved servant represented by Spring Moon's Fatso and Scarlett O'Hara's Mammy is shown to be an intimate influence and integral part of aristocratic family sagas. In each case, protagonists tempered but not hardened in the fires of war are honored: "She is the kindest person I know," Spring Moon says in sincere respect for her lover's wife. "She was the only completely kind person I ever knew," Rhett Butler says of Melanie Wilkes, the character Mitchell considered the true heroine of her novel.

Lord's attention to pattern and exquisite detail emerges in symbolic acts and objects, some of which reappear as connecting threads in the rich embroidery of clan history. A pear, or "li," (the word also means "depart") symbolizes rejection of Spring Moon's unwanted suitor, but in bringing the pear in gratitude to the uncle who arranged her rescue, she is unwittingly giving him a metaphorical reminder of her inevitable departure from his life. The game of chess figures in the web of detail for both the Chang clan and the House of Woo in Peking, into which Spring Moon marries. Her husband, Glad Promise, leaving for war and unable to face a last parting, sets up his chessboard in their bedroom and moves one soldier into battle as a message of intent and farewell. After his death in the Boxer Rebellion, Spring Moon carries that chesspiece in a small box of such symbolic treasures.

The Chang chess set, by tradition presented to the original patriarch by the Emperor Wan Li at the start of the clan's three-hundred-year history, first appears in an early chapter with Bold Talent at Yale, and is eventually buried in the ancestral courtyards by the fleeing family. Finally, although remembered, the chess set is left in its resting place by reunited survivors. This motif also appears in Old Venerable's advice to his little son learning chess: "Bold Talent, do not become too enamoured of the process; remember the goal." Those words echo for Bold Talent as he dies, with the revolution—and life's questions—unresolved.

Using detail to enrich her expression of Chinese thought, Lord recites a child's counting game of the five seasons, five directions, five elements—startling to the Western mind. She narrates Spring Moon's reaction to the Western architecture of the mission school: "All unbending as if built to challenge the elements, to confront nature, to separate rather than harmonize. If she had seen it then, she could not have left Lustrous Jade."

Lustrous Jade figures in several of the ironies underlying the novel's plot; perhaps most tragic is her disillusionment with her mother when Lustrous Jade misjudges Enduring Promise's parentage. An informant from Learned Cinders precipitates Lustrous Jade's suicide by reporting her indiscretion in mailing her mother's letter to Enduring Promise in America; ironically, this represents one of Lustrous Jade's few acts supportive of clan ties.

Such ambivalences lend convincing humanity to Lord's protagonists, caught in a century of bewildering change. Lord's characterizations imply that motifs such as the clash of old and new values, the philosophy of yielding versus the spirit of confrontation, and the question of commitment to the preservation of the family are as much a part of modern China as of this extraordinarily fine novel.

*Virginia Barrett*

## Sources for Further Study

*Best Sellers*. XLI, October, 1981, p. 256.
*Book World*. XI, October 11, 1981, p. 1.
*Christian Science Monitor*. LXXIII, November 9, 1981, p. B7.
*Library Journal*. CVI, October 15, 1981, p. 2049.
*The New Republic*. CLXXXV, October 21, 1981, p. 38.
*The New York Times Book Review*. LXXXVI, October 25, 1981, p. 15.
*Saturday Review*. VIII, October, 1981, p. 75.

# STORYTELLER

*Author:* Leslie Marmon Silko (1948-    )
*Publisher:* Seaver Books (New York). Illustrated. 278 pp. $17.95; paperback $9.95
*Type of work:* Mythic and autobiographical narratives in prose and in poetry
*Time:* Contemporary present, remembered and mythic past
*Locale:* The American Southwest (especially New Mexico) and, to a lesser extent, Alaska

*A collection of old and new anecdotes, stories, and tales centering around the individual and family identity of the author and her Laguna heritage*

As a person and as an artist, Leslie Marmon Silko defies easy classification. Some might consider her a regional author in that most of her writing emphasizes place and has as its setting the towns, villages, rivers, mesas, and mountains of north central and northwestern New Mexico—in and around Albuquerque, where she was born, and the Laguna Pueblo Reservation (near Grants and Gallup) where she grew up. Alaska, too, in a lesser way figures as a setting in her work since she spent 1974 writing in Ketchikan. At present she lives in Tucson, where she is on the faculty of the University of Arizona— and that locale also finds its way into her work.

She might also be regarded as an ethnic author who, because of her own mixed ancestry (Laguna Pueblo, Mexican, and white), has as a major concern the culture of native Americans confronting that of Anglo-Americans and Mexican-Americans in the Southwest. Moreover, insofar as Silko developed as a writer against the larger background of the Vietnam War, of the Civil Rights and the Women's movements, others might view her in political or feminist terms. She might also be identified as a poet, a writer of short stories, a novelist, and a teacher. While all such classifying is to some degree useful— primarily in underscoring her versatility—it is best to consider Silko first as an artist who just happens to be a woman with Indian ancestry, someone who grew up in the West and is a member of the postwar generation. All of these biographical and aesthetic factors are in one way or another present in *Storyteller*.

After the watershed publication of N. Scott Momaday's Pulitzer Prize-winning novel *House Made of Dawn* in 1969, the one book which is most credited with beginning a renaissance in contemporary native American literature, Silko's fiction and poetry began to gain attention in numerous journals and in widely read anthologies. These works include, *The Man to Send Rain Clouds* (1974), *Voices of the Rainbow* (1975), and *The Remembered Earth* (1979). It was the appearance of Silko's novel *Ceremony* in 1977, however, which positioned her alongside Momaday's achievement. (Others, such as Silko's Acoma Pueblo friend and colleague, Simon Ortiz, and the Montana Blackfeet/Gros Ventre writer, James Welch, have achieved similar high critical acclaim for their part in the recent surge of native American literature.)

In some ways *Storyteller* is a regrouping of Silko's past works—taking many stories which shared the limelight with other native American authors in *The Man to Send Rain Clouds* and positioning them among numerous other previously published works—including excerpts from *Ceremony*. There are new works in *Storyteller* as well, however, and the entire book takes on a fresh and coherent identity of its own in the very rearrangement of materials—and in the beautiful, personally revealing photographs which appear at intervals throughout the book. Some of the photographs are professionally taken by Silko's father and some are more amateurish in nature. Both kinds complement the text.

Thus, *Storyteller* is far from a hodgepodge of random narratives and images. Rather, it affords striking proof that the storyteller's art resides not only in the tale but in the manner of telling, in rhythms, tonalities, and inflections; in emphasis and proportion; in the teller's voice.

Silko dedicates her book "to the storytellers as far back as memory goes" and suggests that it is with the help of the affirmations which stories provide, in all their forms, that life is lived at its keenest. This power of storytelling, of words, is also a major theme in *Ceremony* wherein the novel's protagonist, Tayo, is led back to spiritual and psychological wholeness through words and their ritualized enactment. Ts'its'tsi'nako, Thought-Woman, who spider-like weaves out the story of Tayo's regeneration as her thoughts become words, is equally busy in *Storyteller* as the patterns of the book are woven together.

In its outermost pattern, serving as a border of sorts, *Storyteller* is a photo album of recent generations of Silko's family. There is Aunt Susie, who, as a member of the Reyes family of Paguate, New Mexico, married Walter K. Marmon, the brother of Silko's paternal grandfather; as a woman enamored with books and words, she went far in imprinting on her niece the magic of writing and of telling stories—the magic of memory and the oral tradition whereby generations achieve continuity. What Silko remembers of Aunt Susie is her own remembering of the telling of old Laguna stories, several of which Silko, as a kind of replica of her aunt, retells. Silko goes beyond these stories, however, to her own inventions. These are offered in the loving voice of a mother speaking to her daughter, filled with implicit advice about little girls becoming women.

Then there is Marie Anaya, also from Paguate, who married Silko's great-grandfather, Robert G. Marmon, a pioneer who traveled from Ohio to settle in New Mexico. Known as Grandma A'mooh or "A'mooh" (a Laguna expression of love), she cared for Silko when she was a baby. A'mooh, living into her eighties as Silko grew up, told of the ancient ways, of the hard times, of surviving. These narratives trigger long, lyrical accounts of the Laguna from the distant past.

Silko's grandfather, Hank Marmon, and his brother, Kenneth Marmon, are also prominent in the author's family memory. Hank Marmon had no patience for racists, whether they were early Albuquerque hotel managers or merchants who would not accept his "Indian" sons. This clash of cultures also makes for anecdotal narratives which expand thematically into other of *Storyteller's* patterns—one example being the titular short story, "Storyteller," the first of many such Anglicized story forms in the collection.

Silko's great-grandfather Stagner, his wife, Helen, and their daughter, Lillie, who was Silko's grandmother, are likewise important persons in the memory album. Grandma Helen, of the Romero family near Los Lunas, is remembered for the musical sounds of her Spanish words, and Spanish, along with English and the Indian language of Laguna, still resonates in Silko's head and heart.

Lee H. Marmon, Silko's father, not only figures into the photographs as subject but also took many of the pictures himself, a skill he learned in the Army during World War II. Whether in pictures of the family—aunts, grandparents, brothers, children—of Laguna and Paguate villages, the Marmon Trading Post, Mount Taylor deer hunts, wagon and automobile travels, or the sublime vistas of the New Mexico and Arizona landscape—sandhills east of Laguna, an open pit uranium mine near Laguna, Enchanted Mesa, the Tucson Mountains—all of the photographs in *Storyteller* contribute organically to the ideas and images which the various narratives embody.

Just as it is difficult to separate the photographs from the text of the book, so it is damaging to the book's unity to separate the poetry from the prose, the short stories from the myths, tales "spoken" from those "written," but it is finally the eight short stories and tales which in alternating sequence are the imaginative center of the many-patterned *Storyteller*. In addition to "Storyteller," these stories are entitled: "Lullaby," "Yellow Woman," "Tony's Story," "Uncle Tony's Goat," "The Man to Send Rain Clouds," "A Geronimo Story," and "Coyote Holds a Full House in His Hand."

It is impossible here to give full consideration to each of these narratives. Each is filled with contrasting voices, techniques, and styles—points of view, ways of showing and telling, of dramatization, description, and exposition. Certainly they have points in common too, with one another and with the other aspects of the volume. Each reader will invariably choose his or her favorite example of Silko's talent, judge as the speaker does in one of the book's prose poems whether or not that particular story could have been told "better" than it was.

It should be said by way of emphasizing the varying modes in which Silko is capable of writing—her variety and virtuosity in storytelling (reflecting her respect for the complexity and significance of the process)—that she is effective in both natural and supernatural "styles." She is both realist and fabulist, sometimes ambiguously lacing realism with fantasy to come up with the effect of romance. In this regard her techniques are not unlike those of Nathaniel Hawthorne.

Two beautifully haunting stories tinged with the ambiguities of romance and fantasy are "Yellow Woman" and "Tony's Story." Both involve the intrusion of the supernatural into the world of everyday. Both deal with the most common of themes in contemporary storytelling: the issue of just how much of reality is illusory, just how much individual perception of fact is a function of culture, how abstract values such as truth and falsehood, beauty and ugliness, love and hate are in the end relative.

"Yellow Woman" is an archetypal Cinderella story in native American dress. Filled with sensual descriptions of river and mountain landscapes and of physical love between man and woman, it is essentially the story of how an ordinary woman lives out the myth of her forefathers, one of her culture's stories, wherein a ka'tsina spirit (a pueblo deity) takes human form and lovingly abducts and seduces Yellow Woman. The true identity of Silva, the ka'tsina counterpart, is never definitely established. As a heroic and handsome cattle rustler and nemesis of white ranchers, he finds the story's narrator alongside the river and ascends with her to his cabin high in the mountains, where she is far removed from the domestic drudgery of her life at home with her husband, commonly enough named Al, and tasks such as preparing jello for dinner. The narrator is both a willing and a reluctant "victim"; and she both believes and doubts that Silva is indeed the embodiment of the stories of her childhood, and that she has become the Yellow Woman of myth. Although she knows that Al will not believe her story of her extended absence from home, she knows that her grandfather would have—for it was her grandfather who told her the old stories in the first place. Capable of being read in many ways, "Yellow Woman" illustrates the magic of the word in transforming the world.

Probably Silko's masterwork as a storyteller in this collection is "Tony's Story." Assuming a masculine persona in this instance, Silko offers a fictive version of an actual killing of a New Mexico state patrolman in the 1950's. Certainly the "facts" of the case were known to Silko as a youngster—as they were to all New Mexicans, given the notoriety of the events. (Silko's friend Simon Ortiz tells of the same murder in an altogether different way in his story, "The Killing of a State Cop.") However, Silko tells the story from the perspective of Antonio Sousea, a "long hair" who, much to the amazement of his Americanized Indian friend, Leon, kills the patrolman—not because he seeks revenge for the racist harassments unjustifiably meted out to them, but because he recognizes in the dark glasses, face, and overall visage of the cop an evil presence which must be exorcised, killed, and burned. Only then, he believes, will drought be lifted from the land. The entire story is not so much a defense or justification of the killing as it is an alternative insight into a culturally conditioned response to continued bullying.

"Yellow Woman" and "Tony's Story" are but two instances, though representative ones, of the narrative artistry of Silko in *Storyteller*. In one sense,

Silko is simply doing again what she so often experienced in the midst of her own family, a family to which this book pays fond tribute. She is simply telling stories, repeating and embellishing old stories and inventing new ones. As such, she is passing along her personal legacy to others in the hope of rekindling the realization that tales and their telling belong to everyone.

*Robert Gish*

## Sources for Further Study

*Booklist*. LXXVII, July 15, 1981, p. 1431.
*Library Journal*. CVI, May 1, 1981, p. 987.
*Ms*. X, July, 1981, p. 89.
*The New York Times Book Review*. LXXXVI, May 24, 1981, p. 72.
*Saturday Review*. VIII, May, 1981, p. 72.

# THE STRUGGLE FOR AFGHANISTAN

*Author:* Nancy Peabody Newell and Richard S. Newell (1933-    )
*Publisher:* Cornell University Press (Ithaca, New York). Illustrated. 236 pp. $14.95
*Type of work:* Current affairs
*Time:* Predominantly 1978 to the present
*Locale:* Afghanistan

*A study of the impact of Marxist rule and Soviet invasion in Afghanistan, with an assessment of the Afghan resistance movement*

> *Principal personages:*
> MUHAMMAD ZAHIR SHAH, King of Afghanistan, 1933-1973
> MUHAMMAD DAOUD, President and Prime Minister of Afghanistan, 1973-1978
> NUR MUHAMMAD TARAKI, a Marxist leader; Prime Minister and President of Afghanistan, 1978-1979
> HAFIZULLAH AMIN, a Marxist leader; Prime Minister of Afghanistan, 1979
> ASADULLAH AMIN, the nephew of Hafizullah and chief of secret police
> SIBGHATULLAH MUJADIDI, Afghan resistance leader and religious scholar
> SAYYID AHMED GAILANI, a resistance leader and religious scholar
> BABRAK KARMAL, President and Prime Minister of Afghanistan under Soviet occupation from 1979

At one time much of the outside world regarded Afghanistan as a remote, little-known country at the periphery of international politics. Soviet military intervention in December, 1979, suddenly and brutally altered the balance of forces in the area. Almost at once Afghanistan became a focal point of worldwide concern. The Soviet invasion touched off a new phase of the Cold War in the Middle East, and many observers have regarded this crisis in the light of heightened tensions and mounting Soviet-American rivalry in the Persian Gulf region. At the same time the relatively few Western specialists on Afghanistan have been in a position to elucidate those features of its history and internal politics that have affected the nation's struggle against Soviet domination. The Newells' work is particularly concerned with the effects of the present conflict on the peoples of Afghanistan; it summarizes much of what is known of recent political developments, and discusses the social and ethnographic elements of Afghan resistance movements. Both authors have lived and traveled extensively in Afghanistan; Richard Newell has written *The Politics of Afghanistan* (1972). Their views of the impact and the possible outcome of the Soviet-Afghan war are based upon their own familiarity with the country's peoples and way of life.

Some of the basic themes in the history of Afghanistan are stated at the outset: for many centuries the tribes situated about the difficult, forbidding mountains of the Hindu Kush resisted foreign domination, and indeed it was not until the eighteenth century that Afghan rulers achieved some measure of political unity over the peoples of the area. Later, while the British and the Russians occupied neighboring lands Afghanistan remained independent. In 1839-1842, a British military expedition was defeated in the rugged terrain south of Kabul, while in 1878-1881 British armies were unable fully to establish their control of the countryside. Afghan rulers sometimes exploited great power rivalries. Some Western amenities were also introduced; paved roads were built and electric power was introduced. From the 1920's educational curricula were devised in accordance with European models. Afghanistan obtained technical assistance from several nations; moreover, after World War II it received foreign aid both from the United States and its allies and from the Soviet Union. The first modern highway across Afghanistan was built with Soviet assistance. Soviet military equipment was supplied beginning in 1954, and Afghan officers were trained in the Soviet Union. For the most part, however, Afghan leaders were able to maintain the neutrality of their country and avoid any commitments to larger military or diplomatic alignments.

Domestic politics were complicated by rapid and uneven social development, and with increased educational opportunities a new and numerous middle class arose that increasingly challenged the authority of the monarchy. While the King, Zahir Shah, granted a constitution and permitted the establishment of a parliament, he became increasingly unpopular among politically active groups. In 1973, Zahir was overthrown in a nearly bloodless coup. His brother-in-law and former prime minister, Muhammad Daoud, took power and attempted to promote rapid economic growth. As he committed the country to an ambitious program requiring increased development credits, Daoud also became increasingly high-handed and autocratic. He spurned the counsel of parliamentary leaders and governed very much in the manner of previous monarchs. Though at the outset he had accepted leftist politicians in the government, increasingly he turned against them. For their part more radical leaders carried out a coup in April, 1978, in which Daoud was overthrown and killed.

The authors discuss the origins and significance of Marxist parties at some length. They contend that serious discontent arose among many politically conscious Afghans as a result of the disparity between the aspirations of the increasingly numerous educated middle class and the relatively few government positions actually open to them. In 1965, the Marxist group Parcham ("The Banner") was formed from disaffected politicians and civil servants drawn from the ruling party; another faction, Khalq ("The Masses"), was more radical and outspoken in its opposition to the government, and at the outset was forced to operate on a more clandestine basis. Under the Daoud regime some members of Parcham were employed in the civil bureaucracy or as army officers. They were excluded from positions of leadership, however, and as differences with the government mounted, there was a *rapprochement* between the two Marxist factions. Both groups had infiltrated the armed forces and were able to control airborne and tank units in the capital. After the seizure of power from Daoud both sides arranged for powers to be shared, though it was not long before the new Marxist regime was encumbered by internal disputes and moreover encountered serious resistance to its policies from much of the rest of the nation.

The new government rather soon was dominated by radical Marxists, as Khalq leaders displaced their more moderate colleagues and embarked on sweeping programs of social reform. Nur Muhammad Taraki, one of the founders of the Khalq group, became president and prime minister, and in the autumn of 1978 a series of revolutionary decrees were promulgated. Marriage fees and credit were regulated, and mandatory education with curricula similar to the Soviet school system was introduced; Russian replaced English as the leading foreign language taught. The government also tried to implement land reform and break up large estates. As a gesture symbolic of its commitment to revolutionary change the government adopted a red flag as its standard. The new government began to align itself more closely with Soviet-bloc nations, and on December 5, 1978, Afghanistan concluded a treaty of friendship with the Soviet Union that was in fact a military, political, and economic alliance.

Such measures provoked widespread resistance, and in response, Soviet forces for the first time were committed directly to defend the Marxist regime in Kabul. Violent disturbances, in which perhaps as many as five thousand people were killed, took place in Herat; serious outbreaks also occurred in Jalalabad and other cities. All but three or four of the twenty-eight provinces in the country turned against the government, and much of the Afghan Army refused to obey Marxist officers. In April, 1979, Taraki, though remaining in the government, was replaced as prime minister by Hafizullah Amin, a stronger though ideologically more inflexible leader. By about this time some five thousand Soviet military advisers, with helicopter gunships and heavy aircraft, had been deployed to bolster the regime. Even with Soviet assistance, however, the Khalq regime was unable to control much of the countryside. In September, Taraki visited Moscow and evidently suggested that a less rigid policy might win some support for the government. Upon his return he attempted to overthrow his rival, but Taraki himself died shortly thereafter under mysterious circumstances. Hafizullah's relations with the Soviets became increasingly strained, while his government found it more difficult to maintain any semblance of order. His nephew, Asadullah Amin, who served as chief of the secret police, was assassinated in December, 1979. A senior official of the Soviet KGB was sent to Kabul, apparently to ask Hafizullah to resign. The Afghan leader was killed during an attack on his palace by Soviet parachute troops; the Soviet envoy also died, though it is not known whether during the fighting or by his own hand. By this time the Soviet Union commenced a large-scale invasion, with nearly one hundred thousand troops, to ensure its direct control over political developments within Afghanistan.

Resistance movements had arisen against the Khalq regime and such groups were active in much of the fighting against Soviet forces. In this area, while some accounts have been rather sketchy, the authors supply some information and details on political organizations of this sort, and point to religious and ethnic divisions and affinities among them. Shortly after the Khalq coup of April, 1978, the Afghan National Liberation Front was founded in Pakistan, under the leadership of Sibghatullah Mujadidi, a respected Sufi religious leader from a distinguished family of scholars; as a political moderate he attempted to unify opposition to the Marxist regime. Another important organization, the Islamic Revolutionary Front, was led by Sayyid Ahmed Gailani, a religous moderate with great influence among the Pushtun tribes that comprise the leading national group of Afghanistan. Other factions, such as the Islamic Party and the Islamic Society were more fundamentalist and conservative, and often acted on their own inspiration. Within Afghanistan the Hazara tribes of the central highlands and the Nuristanis from the area north of the Khyber Pass historically have attempted to preserve a separate ethnic identity; they took up arms against the central government soon after the Marxist coup. Other ethnic groups in the northern portions of the country, such as the Uzbeks and the Tajiks, who are closely related to peoples of Soviet Central Asia, reacted violently against efforts to impose Marxist rule in Afghanistan. Thus in many cases the resistance has been fragmented along lines that previously had divided Afghan society, although all but some scattered elements of the urban educated middle class have opposed Marxist and Soviet domination of the country.

When Soviet troops entered Afghanistan, they attempted to establish a regime beholden to them and called upon politicians from the Parcham faction to form a government. Babrak Karmal, one of the founders of this group, was made president and prime minister; as he had maintained some distance from previous Khalq leaders it was thought that he might rally public support. Most Afghans, however, recognized Karmal's dependence on the Soviet invaders, and many army units refused to obey him. In no part of Afghanistan have the Soviets been accepted as anything but an occupying force. In February, 1980, there were strikes in ten major cities, and Kabul underwent a week of anti-Soviet disturbances; serious demonstrations and other outbreaks took place periodically thereafter in several urban areas.

Even though the Soviets have been able to operate with massive technological superiority, they have not been able to bring much of the country under control. The use of tanks and aircraft has not been decisive, and antipersonnel gas has not curtailed Afghan resistance. While reliable information is difficult to obtain—both Soviet and Afghan sources have exaggerated the effectiveness of their efforts—by comparing the accounts that are available the authors have determined the character of engagements that have taken place, and they suggest that Soviet control of Afghanistan is not and need not be an established fact. In many areas the insurgents have blocked roads and disrupted communications between Soviet outposts. Resistance groups have often operated in difficult terrain, and at some distance from one another, and as a result it has been more difficult for the Soviets to isolate or contain their opponents. On both sides there have been recurrent reports of atrocities. Afghan forces have killed Soviet prisoners, while Soviet units have carried out severe reprisals against civilians. Fighting, gas attacks, and bombing raids have driven hundreds of thousands of Afghans from their homes, yet even with their outdated, primitive weapons and limited ammunition, Afghan insurgents continue to hold out in many parts of the country.

The authors conclude that the prospects for the Afghan resistance are mixed. The Soviets would probably need to multiply their numbers in Afghanistan several times in order to prevail. There are several ways that the United States and its allies could play a part in the struggle. The Newells suggest that more extensive efforts could be made to provide medical supplies and other contributions, in cooperation with Pakistan and other neighboring states. The United States and other nations could also open negotiations with an Afghan government in exile representing the resistance groups; moreover, it could furnish small arms and other sorts of military equipment suitable for guerrilla warfare. Whatever measures are taken by the United States, however, the Newells anticipate that the Afghans will seek martyrdom or victory; the struggle for their country remains in the balance. This work should indicate the extent to which the Afghans themselves still have a role to play in the decision of that struggle.

*John R. Broadus*

## Sources for Further Study

*Choice.* XIX, September, 1981, p. 141.
*Journal of Asian Studies.* XLI, November, 1981, p. 73.
*Library Journal.* CVI, April 15, 1981, p. 870.
*Middle East Journal.* XXXV, Autumn, 1981, p. 619.
*National Review.* XXXIII, June 12, 1981, p. 683.
*The New Republic.* CLXXXIV, June 20, 1981, p. 27.
*Times Literary Supplement.* July 3, 1981, p. 753.
*The Wall Street Journal.* CXCVII, April 27, 1981, p. 30.

# THE STRUGGLE FOR BLACK EQUALITY
## 1954-1980

*Author:* Harvard Sitkoff
*Publisher:* Hill and Wang (New York). 259 pp. $10.95
*Type of work:* History
*Time:* 1954-1980
*Locale:* The United States

A succinct narrative that captures the drama of the struggle for racial equality and justice waged between 1954 and 1980

Principal personages:

LYNDON BAINES JOHNSON, Senate majority leader, who helped pass the Voting Rights Act of 1957; thirty-sixth President of the United States, 1963-1969

THURGOOD MARSHALL, leading attorney for the NAACP's Legal Defense and Education Fund at the time of Brown v. Board of Education; first black to serve on the U.S. Supreme Court

RICHARD NIXON, Vice-President of the United States, 1953-1961, who urged President Eisenhower to support civil rights; thirty-seventh President of the United States, 1969-1974

ROY WILKINS, executive director of the NAACP

GEORGE WALLACE, Governor of Alabama, who threatened to defy a court order admitting two black students to the University of Alabama

A. PHILIP RANDOLPH, head of the Brotherhood of Sleeping Car Porters and organizer of a possible March-on-Washington in 1941

JAMES FARMER, national director of the Congress of Racial Equality

MARTIN LUTHER KING JR., pastor of the Dexter Avenue Baptist Church in Montgomery, Alabama; founder of the Southern Christian Leadership Conference

This is a particularly good time to examine with Harvard Sitkoff *The Struggle for Black Equality, 1954-1980*. Civil rights activists are complaining that the gains of the last quarter of a century are under assault. The current administration in Washington has proven antagonistic to Affirmative Action plans, mandatory busing as a remedy for unconstitutional school segregation, and IRS administrative rules that deny tax exemptions to schools that discriminate. Other more extreme measures are being pushed by various senators and representatives. There is a Senate bill that would virtually reverse the Supreme Court's landmark decision in *Brown* v. *Board of Education* by denying lower courts the right to issue almost any kind of desegregation order and another Senate bill that would permit the reopening of closed desegregation cases by any individual in the community even if the desegregation plan has been successful or in effect for several years. In the House there is a proposed constitutional amendment that would prohibit federal courts from issuing any remedies after a finding of constitutional violations. A similar proposed constitutional amendment was only defeated by seven votes in 1979.

In this context, it is tempting for civil rights activists to conclude that the nation is abandoning all pretense of a commitment to end discrimination and racial injustice.

The kind of historical perspective that Sitkoff provides, however, suggests that such a conclusion would be premature. As a Northern white college student, Sitkoff had been involved in the Southern black freedom struggle of the early 1960's. His early optimism and faith in the ultimate triumph of the black campaign for human rights gave way to disillusionment and disenchantment as the struggle failed to sweep away the entrenched racism of American society. As a graduate student, his initial essays minimized the accomplishments of those who had labored to reduce the pervasive racism in our society. Yet further research, focused on the 1930's and 1940's, revealed that decades of seemingly limited surface change could nevertheless entail a variety of fundamental changes in the status of race relations that would ultimately lead to significant racial reforms. That insight is clearly reflected in his first book on the subject, *A New Deal for Blacks: The Emergence of Civil Rights as a National Issue* (1978). While the book details the failures of the New Deal in the area of civil rights, it also shows that the New Deal years constitute a watershed of developments whose outgrowth was a broad-based social movement aimed at bringing about a fuller participation of blacks in American society.

The same deeper perspective informs Sitkoff's *The Struggle for Black Equality, 1954-1980*. After sketching important developments before 1954, Sitkoff provides a succinct narrative that captures the drama of the civil rights battle during the period he calls the Second Reconstruction, 1954-1965. The Second Reconstruction period begins with the Supreme Court's landmark decision in *Brown* v. *Board of Education* and ends with the passage of the Voting Rights Act of 1965.

In his final chapter, Sitkoff talks of "The Dream Deferred." Just five days after President Johnson signed the Voting Rights Act, the most destructive race riot in more than two decades began in Watts, Los Angeles' largest black ghetto. This turned out to be a mere prelude to acts of destruction and desperation in Chicago, Cleveland, Dayton, Milwaukee, San Francisco, Newark, and Detroit. The fiery riots provided a rationalization for white expressions of hostility toward blacks. In 1968 Richard Nixon campaigned against open housing and busing for racial balance. George Wallace made the fear and resentment of blacks the central thrust of his campaign, and Hubert Humphrey, long associated in the public mind with the civil rights movement, won just one out of every three white votes. Nixon then pursued a "Southern strategy" in preparing for his reelection effort, and the transformation of the Supreme Court was begun. By 1974 there was a five to four majority willing to overrule the only desegregation plan that could work in Detroit because it required interdistrict busing and the suburbs had not themselves caused Detroit's segregation. More black students attended segregated schools in 1980 than at the time of *Brown* v. *Board of Education*. The index of residential segregation rose in nearly every American city between 1960 and 1980. As one reads Sitkoff's account of the years between 1965 and 1980, it becomes clear that the retreat on civil rights did not begin with the election of 1980. There is no new assault from President Ronald Reagan and the "New Right" but a continuation and acceleration of long established trends.

Should those who would like to see black progress despair as they watch current developments? What is the ultimate significance of the current legislative initiatives for the civil rights movement?

Sitkoff's discussion does not extend to the 1980 election and its aftermath, but it is still suggestive. Sitkoff argues that the First Reconstruction foundered on the failure of the federal government to establish a viable economic base for the freed slaves. The Second Reconstruction ended the legally enforced segregation of Jim Crow laws, but only helped the black middle class economically. Towns with black mayors and other black officials still failed to provide jobs for the jobless and adequate housing and health care for the poor, even though cities with black mayors spent more per capita for education and social services and directed a higher proportion of their budgets toward the needs of the disadvantaged than those headed by whites. Sitkoff concludes that the Second Reconstruction did not result in equality because of the lack of a thorough economic transformation. Nevertheless, he also argues that blacks are today far closer to equality than they were in 1954 and are in a better position to launch a Third Reconstruction.

If there is indeed to be a Third Reconstruction, then it, like the Second Reconstruction, may also have its roots in a seemingly unfavorable period preceding it. Although the decade of the 1930's was largely one of failure for civil rights initiatives, including the defeat of the Costigan-Wagner Anti-Lynching Bill, Sitkoff sees the decade of the 1930's as the time when the civil rights coalition of black pressure groups, the radical left, organized labor, intellectuals, and concerned Northern politicians was first mobilized.

It may be that the coalition needed to address the problems of America's black and white economic underclass is in the process of being formed. All social programs are being cut back, including those that benefit the middle class. Unemployment is reaching the previously privileged sectors of unionized labor. The economy is stagnating while inflation surges on unabated. The rich have received some enormous new tax breaks that have not yet stimulated the economy or trickled down. The new economic situation and the thrust of governmment policy may be creating new allies for the most economically disadvantaged in the black community. Likewise, the moral agenda of the "New Right" may be creating new allies for the black community on desegregation issues as well. The same court-stripping measures that are being proposed as a mechanism for stopping court enforcement of the constitutional rights of blacks are also being proposed in other areas. There are now more than forty separate bills introduced in the House and Senate to curtail lower federal court jurisdiction over such controversial constitutional subjects as abortion, prayer in public schools, school desegregation, and sex discrimination in the military. Other bills would strip the Supreme Court of its appellate jurisdiction over these issues. Quite disparate groups have a mutual interest in preserving judicial independence, just as quite disparate groups have a mutual interest in dealing with the country's economic ailments, economic inequalities, and inadequate and threatened social services. Thus Sitkoff's concluding optimism may yet prove to be justified: "However dark the moment seems, a new day will surely dawn. The struggle to complete the unfinished business of American democracy will endure until its fulfillment."

Sitkoff's optimism seems justified by the changes he has chronicled here; particularly those in education and voting. While school desegregation has not been a success, the educational levels the black community attains have improved steadily in this century. The proportion of blacks aged five to nineteen enrolled in school leaped from 60 percent in 1930 to 68.4 percent in 1940, to 74.8 percent in 1950. That figure still lagged behind the 79.3 percent of whites in school, but the gap had narrowed dramatically. And the number of blacks in college had soared from about 27,000 thousand in 1930 to more than 113,000 in 1950.

That kind of continuous improvement encouraged the NAACP to emphasize integrated education as the main route to racial equality. The first major crack in the edifice of school segregation had come in 1938, when the NAACP won a Supreme Court ruling which held that an out-of-state scholarship to a black Missourian wishing to study law at the University of Missouri denied that student the equal protection of the law guaranteed by the constitution. There followed a series of Supreme Court decisions that chipped away at legally required segregation, culminating in the 1954 *Brown* v. *Board of Education* decision:

> We conclude that in the field of public education the doctrine of 'separate but equal' has no place. Separate educational facilities are inherently unequal. Therefore, we hold that the plaintiffs and others similarly situated for whom the actions have been brought are, by reason of the segregation complained of, deprived of the equal protection of the laws guaranteed by the Fourteenth Amendment.

Unfortunately, the court subsequently rejected the NAACP's plea to order instant and total school desegregation, instead requiring only that a "prompt and reasonable start toward full compliance" be made and that desegregation proceed "with all deliberate speed." There followed a decade of resistance, subterfuge, and white racial violence. By 1964, only 2 percent of the black children in the South attended integrated schools, and none at all in the two Southern counties involved in the *Brown* decision.

Despite the failure of school desegregation, the levels of black schooling continued to increase after the *Brown* v. *Board of Education* decision. Then, about 75 percent of blacks aged five to nineteen were enrolled in school. Over 95 percent were in 1980. In 1980, about 75 percent of black students were finishing high school, compared to 85 percent for whites. Two decades earlier, only some 40 percent of young blacks finished high school. By 1980 the percentage of black high school graduates going to college (31.5 percent) had nearly caught up with that of whites (32.2 percent). Only in the proportion of black college students graduating from four-year colleges did blacks continue to lag considerably behind whites.

Like education, voting is an area in which there has been significant change despite imperfections in the federal efforts to combat racially discriminatory practices. The Voting Rights Acts of 1957 and 1960 were weak and ineffective. In 1964 President Lyndon Johnson did not have a strong and effective Voting Rights Act at the top of his agenda since he feared the adverse affect a "white backlash" might have on his socioeconomic plans for a Great Society. Rather, it was Martin Luther King, Jr. and his Southern Christian Leadership Conference staff who plotted a strategy to force the federal government to act on behalf of blacks. The 1963 campaign to end segregation in Birmingham, Alabama, led President Kennedy to propose the comprehensive civil rights act that was enacted shortly after his assassination. Birmingham convinced King and his staff that white savagery against unresisting civil rights protesters could provoke the national response necessary to move the Administration and Congress. The famous march from Selma to Montgomery was designed to lead to federal legislation ending all barriers to black voting. Sheriff Clark's troopers and deputized vigilantes gave the television cameras a revolting picture of irrational white violence and black helplessness that stirred indignation and led to the 1965 Voting Rights Act.

Together with the 1957 and 1960 voting statutes, and with the Twenty-third Amendment outlawing the poll tax in federal elections (ratified in 1964) and the 1966 Supreme Court decision invalidating the poll tax in all elections, the 1965 Voting Rights Act transformed the face of Southern politics. The 24 percent of Alabama blacks registered in 1964 became 57 percent in 1968. In Mississippi, the percentage of black registrants leaped from 7 percent in 1964 to 59 percent in 1968. By 1979, Birmingham was inaugurating its first black mayor with George Wallace sitting on the podium applauding. The number of black elected officials in the South rose from fewer than a 100 in the year of the Voting Rights Act to some 500 hundred in 1970, 1,600 in 1975, and nearly 2,500 in 1980. Equally impressive, the national total jumped from 300 hundred in 1965, to 1,400 in 1970, 3,000 in 1975, and 4,700 in 1980.

Nevertheless, blacks still participate in politics less frequently than whites. Barely 42 percent of voting-age blacks went to the polls in 1970, compared to a national turnout of 55 percent of eligible voters, and even fewer sought to exercise their franchise in 1980. This failure to vote has been explained in a variety of ways: as a consequence of poverty, as a result of black alienation from the political system, or as a legacy of past conditioning. Although Sitkoff summarizes these various theories, he neither evaluates their adequacy nor deals with the continuing shortcomings in the area of voting rights. He never mentions that covered jurisdictions actively challenged or ignored the Voting Rights Act from the moment it became law. Many jurisdictions have implemented laws which have never been precleared with the Justice Department as required by Section 5 of the Act for those guilty of past discriminatory practices. A favorite way of circumventing the Voting Rights Act has been to change—without preclearance—the method of holding elections from district-by-district voting to at-large voting in jurisdictions with significant concentrations of black population. The effect of such change is to submerge black concentrations of population in individual electoral districts into countywide white majorities, depriving blacks of any opportunity to elect candidates of their choice.

Furthermore, former Assistant Attorney General Drew S. Day III, who supervised the Voting Rights Section of the Justice Department from 1977 through 1980, testified in 1981, that even during a period of vigorous enforcement of the Act, his division had neither the time nor the resources to assure full compliance. As time goes on, the Justice Department has also been finding that discriminatory content in proposed voting law changes are becoming more common. More than 400 hundred of the 815 objections lodged by the Justice Department against voting changes in the covered jurisdictions have come during the last five years. Thus, Sitkoff's account of the problems in the voting rights area is not as strong as his account of the problems in the school desegregation area.

Nevertheless, substantial improvements have been made in both levels of schooling and voting participation, justifying Sitkoff's optimism about the capacity of the black community to effectively pursue its political interests in the future. The current situation poses new problems, but Sitkoff's historical narrative suggests that black leadership has proven itself able to learn from temporary setbacks and develop new strategies that will ultimately succeed.

*Barry Faye*

### Sources for Further Study

*Best Sellers*. XLI, September, 1981, p. 227.
*Booklist*. LXXVIII, September 15, 1981, p. 78.
*Kirkus Reviews*. XLIX, August 1, 1981, p. 1000.
*Library Journal*. CVI, August, 1981, p. 1539.
*Publishers Weekly*. CCXIX, June 26, 1981, p. 55.

# TAR BABY

*Author:* Toni Morrison (1931-    )
*Publisher:* Alfred A. Knopf (New York). 306 pp. $11.95
*Type of work:* Novel
*Time:* The 1970's
*Locale:* The Caribbean and New York City

*Toni Morrison's novel deals with complicated relationships between blacks and whites, women and men*

> *Principal characters:*
> SON, an uneducated Southern black
> JADINE "JADE" CHILDS, a Sorbonne-educated black model
> SYDNEY CHILDS, a butler, Jadine's uncle
> ONDINE CHILDS, a cook, Jadine's aunt
> VALERIAN STREET, a retired candy manufacturer; the Childs's white
>     employer
> MARGARET STREET, Valerian's wife

Like the women to whom *Tar Baby* is dedicated—mother, grandmothers, aunts, great aunts—and like the blind seeress who sends the novel's protagonist lickety-split into a Caribbean briar patch, Toni Morrison has not forgotten her "true and ancient properties." Her magical vision extends not only into the past, but also into the future, as she examines the tense alliances that shape the lives of her characters. These tensions are American society's most fundamental ones: tensions between young and old, rich and poor, male and female, black and white. In Morrison's expert hands, Isle des Chevaliers, the lush Caribbean setting in which her characters play out their complicated relationships, becomes a microcosm of contemporary American life.

Isle des Chevaliers, the reader is told, "exaggerated everything." Morrison's handling of her setting, while certainly not exaggerated, is so loving that the tiniest detail is ultimately made to resonate with significance. The island's name commemorates the legend that black slaves, upon first seeing the place, were struck blind by it; the blind descendents of these slaves still ride their horses over the hills. Other spirits inhabit the island, as well; swamps, butterflies, the very trees are, at Morrison's touch, deeply infused with consciousness. She so animates the details of her setting that its primitive vitality threatens to overwhelm the luxurious winter home of Valerian Street, a Philadelphia candy manufacturer whose retirement to Isle des Chevaliers has become a voluntary exile in preparation for death. Valerian has brought with him his wife, Margaret, twenty years his junior, and his butler and cook, a married couple who have worked for him for years. The relationship between Sydney and Ondine Childs and their employer is sufficiently comfortable that Valerian has been the patron of the Childs's niece, Jadine. As *Tar Baby* opens, twenty-five-year-old Jadine, who has been living in Paris, is visiting her aunt and uncle, and the five have settled into a civilized routine that barely subdues the island's simmering vitality.

Because Morrison narrates her story from several points of view, the reader is fully exposed to the complexity of these characters and their uneasy relationships. Valerian, a decent, humane, rational man, spends most of the day in his greenhouse, where he can manipulate the natural growth that surrounds him; his flaw is his willingness to remain innocent of what he cannot control. Valerian's wife, Margaret, fills her time with shopping, exercising, and otherwise maintaining the red-haired, fair-skinned beauty that first attracted Valerian. Her creamed and polished surfaces hide a mysterious forgetfulness that Valerian attributes to alcohol but that actually masks a much darker secret. These two frequently disagree, but their quarrels, like their diets, are, in the novel's opening passages, "seasoned and regulated," the "tiffs of long-married people who alone knew the physics of their relationship."

Sydney and Ondine conform conscientiously, though sometimes grudgingly, to the expectations of their white employers. Proud and industrious, Sydney is a Philadelphia black who dreams every night of the Baltimore neighborhood where he grew up, and Ondine is a fierce matriarchal figure whose expertise in the kitchen complements Sydney's skill as a butler. The affection between these two is as steady as their attention to their duties is meticulous. Sydney rubs Ondine's feet when they are weary, but refuses to wear the soft slippers that would ease his own, because "I'm a first-rate butler and I can't be first-rate in slippers." Sydney and Ondine both adore the orphaned Jadine, whose cultivated sophistication allows her to move gracefully between her aunt's and uncle's kitchen and Valerian's dining room. Jadine has everything— beauty enough to model for *Elle*, brains enough to study art history at the Sorbonne, and, through Valerian's patronage and her own talent, money enough to go in any direction she might choose. The product of a white man's generosity to his black servants, Jadine Childs is free-spirited, upwardly mobile, and, at times, weary of her own blackness. At one point she observes of herself "that I hate ear hoops, that I don't have to straighten my hair, that Mingus puts me to sleep, that sometimes I want to get out of my skin and be only the person inside—not American—not black—just me."

The equilibrium enjoyed by the Streets and the Childses at Isle des Chevaliers is brought to an abrupt end by the symbolically timed arrival, a few days before Christmas, of Morrison's protagonist, who calls himself Son. A poor, uneducated, streetwise Southern black, Son has left the United States after killing a woman, has jumped ship because he was homesick, and has been borne by an insistent, woman-like current to Isle des Chevaliers. There he steals food from the Streets until they discover him in the house. Instead of turning Son over to the harbor police, Valerian invites him to join the Streets and Jadine for dinner. Because Son is hungry, he agrees, even though he knows, as he later tells Jadine, "'that white folks and black folks should not sit down and eat together. . . . They should work together sometimes, but they should not eat together or live together or sleep together. Do any of those personal things in life.'" Over the next several days, Son's presence changes everything. Margaret is terrified by him, Valerian charmed; Sydney remains suspicious of Son, Ondine graduallly warms toward him; and Jadine, against her better judgment, finds herself irrresistibly drawn to this man in whose dark and intelligent face she sees "spaces, mountains, savannas." Son's attraction to Jadine is equally strong. He has watched her sleeping, has tried to "manipulate her dreams, to insert his own dreams into her"; he soon realizes that "if he loved and lost this woman whose sleeping face was the limit his eyes could safely behold and whose wakened face threw him into confusion, he would surely lose the world." As Morrison develops the relationship between Jade and Son, the reader becomes aware of the significance of the novel's title: mink-eyed, honey-colored Jade (Jadine) is Son's tar baby.

Morrison recounts the early stages of their love affair with passionate intensity. At first the two fight their feelings for each other: Jade keeps leashed tightly the "dark dogs with silver feet" which symbolize her desire, and Son tries to make her hate him by frightening her with his dirtiness. As he struggles against his own appetite, Son is warned by Gideon, the Streets' occasional yardman, that "yallas" like Jade "don't come to being black natural-like. They have to choose it and most don't choose it. Be careful of the stuff they put down." Jade is irresistible, however, and Son succumbs. Morrison conveys the momentousness of their emotional collision with long, urgent sentences whose phrasing articulates both the strength of their resistance to passion and the necessity of their yielding to it. One of the most intimate and highly charged moments in the novel comes when Son ardently holds his forefinger in the "valley of [Jade's] naked foot"; the burning impression remains long after Jade has put her shoes back on. After Christmas, the two flee Isle des Chevaliers for New York, where they pass several months in mutual absorption. When they visit Son's childhood home in Florida, however, Jade begins to confront her unwillingness to assume the roles traditionally assigned to black women. Son is equally unwilling to adopt Jade's idea of "making it," and the two reach an impasse.

It is here, in Chapter 7, that the novel's most serious weakness emerges. As they struggle to resolve their differences, Morrison's lovers cease to speak and act as individuals and temporarily become allegorical abstractions representing opposed yet inextricably connected cultural forces: "Each knew the world as it was meant or ought to be. One had a past, the other a future, and each one bore the culture to save the race in his hands. Mama-spoiled black man, will you mature with me? Culture-bearing black woman, whose culture are you bearing?" While there is no denying either the difficulty or the reality of this conflict, the reader cannot help being distressed at the novel's apparent lapse into polemicism. Of course, one must also consider the possibility that Morrison's material requires demonstration of an inescapable fact: a black's attitude toward his or her blackness, like a man's or woman's attitude toward sex roles, inevitably puts pressure on a relationship. People whose values are as fundamentally different as Son's and Jade's, Morrison seems to be saying, cannot expect passion to resolve their ideological and cultural differences. Chapter 7 aside, both Jade and Son are rounded and real; on the whole, Morrison respects their complexity far too much to allow them to remain mouthpieces for long. Their conflicting values being, in fact, irreconcilable, Jade leaves New York, and Son pursues her. The novel's final pages find Son stumbling through the mist on the far side of Isle des Chevaliers, groping toward the tropical briar patch where the blind horsemen offer him freedom from this light-skinned black woman who has "forgotten her ancient properties."

Morrison is much concerned in *Tar Baby* with these "ancient properties": with female traditions, with intimacy among women, and with the ways racial tensions complicate those traditions and that intimacy. Margaret Street recalls that as a seventeen-year-old bride she had tried to form a friendship with Ondine; the two had watched soap operas and laughed together in the kitchen until Valerian let Margaret know that camaraderie with the servants was inappropriate. For many years afterwards, Ondine keeps from Valerian and even from Sydney a terrible secret about Margaret's treatment of her baby, keeps it because "it was woman stuff. I couldn't tell your husband and I couldn't tell mine. . . . Once I started keeping it, it was my secret too." At Isle des Chevaliers, Margaret forms a schoolgirlish attachment to Jade, and childless Ondine tries to instruct Jade in the responsibilities of being a daughter, saying that learning those responsibilities is necessary to being "a real woman: a woman good enough for a child; good enough for a man— good enough even for the respect of other women." Jade is haunted by her own tar babies: the egg-carrying African "woman's woman—that mother/ sister/she"; the hat-wearing white women of her dreams; the swamp women from whose "exceptional femaleness" she strives to free herself. The Streets' blind laundress, Thérése, who once made her living as a wet nurse for white infants, believes that American women claw their babies from their wombs with their fingernails; her mistake violently parodies the abusive behavior of Margaret Street toward her son. All these details suggest the tensions between female autonomy and the supportive, nurturing female roles that Morrison suggests are necessary cultural links between past and future.

Morrison uses many such accumulations of subtle details to lay stress on the interconnectedness of her characters and to heighten the emotional effect of her narrative. A fine example of this technique begins early in the novel, when Son loses his shoes in the ocean. A few pages later, Sydney and Valerian discuss Valerian's corns and Sydney's bunions, advising each other about proper footwear. Subsequently Sydney massages Ondine's tired feet, and there is the passionate scene where Son touches Jade's bare instep. Toward the novel's end, Jade appears in expensive high-heeled boots. Morrison achieves a similar cumulative effect with innumerable well-placed details involving color. Sydney, who has "mahogany hands," notices that Valerian's skin has tanned, so his liver spots seem to have faded. As Ondine mixes white milk and cocoa paste to make hot chocolate, she comments that Jade's fashion photographs "made those white girls disappear." Sydney's rust-colored dreams of Baltimore, Margaret's sunset hair and milk-white skin, Alma Estée's wig the color of blood, Valerian's dawn-colored eyes that seem to be without melanin—these clusters intersect with other significant patterns of imagery to produce a breathtaking, incantatory richness.

Morrison's use of simile and metaphor is equally rich. Here are two examples from the beginning of the novel: the lights on a ship are "scattered like teardrops from a sky pierced to weeping by the blade tip of an early star"; "as he ate a wide surgical hunger opened up in him." This brilliant use of language is supported by the book's careful construction. The climactic Christmas dinner scene occurs in the sixth of ten chapters, and the prologue and epilogue parallel each other, Son being drawn first by the woman-like current and finally by Thérése's blind wisdom to opposite sides of Isle des Chevaliers. The prologue leads him, of course, to Jade; the epilogue suggests that Son can no more survive choosing Jade than he can endure losing her. This is a painful resolution, of deeply painful conflicts. White money and privilege have rendered Jade unwilling and unfit to participate in the traditions of her own culture, but she makes a powerfully tempting tar baby, a baby for whom motherless Son would have to renounce his past, "the true him. The him that he never lied to, the one he tucked in at night and the one he did not want to die."

*Tar Baby* makes the reader experience not only the passion between these two unforgettable characters, but also the distress and the necessity of their parting. Morrison does more: she forces acknowledgment that the gulf between rich and poor, between female and male, between white and black may be so wide that even the most potent magic cannot bridge them.

*Carolyn Wilkerson Bell*

### Sources for Further Study

*The Atlantic Monthly*. CCXLVII, April, 1981, p. 119.
*Booklist*. LXXVII, January 15, 1981, p. 650.
*Kirkus Reviews*. XLIX, January 15, 1981, p. 82.
*Library Journal*. CVI, February 15, 1981, p. 472.
*Ms*. X, July, 1981, p. 26.
*Nation*. CCXXXII, May 2, 1981, p. 529.

*The New Yorker*. LVII, June 15, 1981, p. 147.
*The New York Review of Books*. XXVIII, April 30, 1981, p. 24.
*The New York Times Book Review*. LXXXVI, March 29, 1981, p. 1.
*Publishers Weekly*. CCIX, January 23, 1981. p. 120.
*Time*. CVII, March 16, 1981, p. 90.

# THE TERRIBLE SECRET
## Suppression of the Truth About Hitler's 'Final Solution'

*Author:* Walter Laqueur (1921-    )
*Publisher:* Little, Brown and Company (Boston). 262 pp. $12.95
*Type of work:* History
*Time:* 1941-1943
*Locale:* Europe

*A historical description of the availability of information about the Holocaust from 1941 to 1943, attempting to determine who knew about this tragedy and when the information became available to the nations and peoples of Europe*

The title of Walter Laqueur's book, *The Terrible Secret: Suppression of the Truth About Hitler's 'Final Solution'* is somewhat misleading. One of the points that Laqueur painstakingly documents is that much information about the Holocaust was available to those who were willing to read and having read, believe. In a few cases, especially involving the United States government and, to a much lesser extent, the British government, the information was suppressed, but such suppression did not prevent the facts of the Holocaust from getting out and from being published by the newspapers of the period. What Laqueur convincingly demonstrates in his book is that the Holocaust was really not a secret at all. What he proves is that the very ample information about the Holocaust was merely ignored both by governments and the public alike.

Laqueur's book is a part of the growing body of literature on the Holocaust. Differing from such titles as A. D. Morse's *While Six Million Died* (1968), J. Morley's *Vatican Diplomacy and the Jews During the Holocaust* (1980), H. L. Feingold's *The Politics of Rescue* (1981), and M. Gilbert's *Auschwitz and the Allies* (1981), all of which study the question of the apathy and indifference of the Allies during the Holocaust, *The Terrible Secret* focuses on a very narrow theme—knowledge of the Holocaust. The specific questions explored in this book are: (1) "When did the information about the 'final solution' first become known to Jews and non-Jews?"; (2) "Through what channels was it transmitted?"; and (3) "What was the reaction of those who received the news?" The answers to these questions lead to the much broader question of the meaning of knowing and believing. That the response of the Allied powers to the Holocaust was apathy and indifference cannot be doubted. The titles cited above and many others clearly document that indifference on the part of the governments and peoples. Laqueur provides insight into part of the reason for such indifference—namely, the inability, failure, or refusal to believe. Contained herein is the terrible psychological problem of a truth that is so horrendously tragic, so overwhelmingly disturbing, that the human psyche cannot handle it and, therefore refuses to believe. In the case of the Holocaust there really was not a terrible secret, but while the intellect knew, the judgment refused to accept, to believe, and so reality was denied—was overridden by the emotions, or so Laqueur argues.

By implication, Laqueur's thesis provides a justification and rationalization for the apathy and indifference of the Allies and their refusal to assist the suffering victims of the Holocaust. The thesis deflects responsibility from peoples and governments and logically leads to the conclusion that nothing was done to prevent the Holocaust and save its victims because belief was not possible and, hence, nothing could have been done. The Laqueur book yields a psychological interpretation that explains all, that justifies all, and that makes the question of responsibility a matter of indifference. If one is to accept the Laqueur thesis, apathy and indifference are transformed into the concept of paralysis of the will, a normal and appropriate psychological response of the Western Allies. Given such a "normal" response, the contrary response of believing and acting to assist the victims of the Holocaust almost generates, for Raoul Wallenberg, Angelo Roncalli, Gerhard Riegner, Emanuel Ringelblum, Richard Lichtheim, and others who reported information or aided the Jews, the charge of abnormality.

The Laqueur thesis binds victim and bystander together with the same psychological mechanism. It has long been argued, from the time of the publication of Raul Hilberg's *The Destruction of the European Jews* (1961) that Jews allowed themselves to be led, like sheep, to their own destruction, in part because they could not bear to believe in the likelihood of their own destruction. Hence, they practiced self-delusion, even though they were informed. They could not believe. Laqueur cites many victims on this topic, such as David Sompolinsky, a leading member of the Jewish community of Denmark: "We did not understand the situation. Despite all indications of imminent action against the Jews we continued to be skeptical . . . we could not get used to the idea that it could happen to us. Louis de Jong attributed self-delusion to: "a love of life, a fear of death, and an understandable inability to grasp the reality of the greatest crime in the history of mankind." Laqueur expands this interpretation to include bystanders, such as the Allies. In the words of François La Rochefoucauld, "Man cannot stare at the sun or at death." Holocaust victims and bystanders alike suffered paralysis of the will and could not act to prevent destruction.

Laqueur attempts to prove his thesis through a methodical analysis of sources and publication of information. Beginning with a description of Germany, Laqueur contends that in spite of the camouflage of language, the euphemisms for the Holocaust, information about the "final solution" reached large numbers of German people. Even in a totalitarian government such a secret could not be kept because thousands and thousands of Germans were involved in the extermination of the Jews. They talked about it. Not only were members of the military aware but also multitudes of civilians. Railroads were employed in transporting Jews to death camps; banks and insurance companies were told of Jewish deaths; Jews were employed as slave labor by German companies, such as I. G. Farben. While few Germans knew the entire story, Laqueur asserts that "Knowledge about the fate of the Jews . . . was widespread even in early summer of 1942" and by the end of 1942 "millions in Germany knew . . . that most or all of those who had been deported were no longer alive."

Germany's allies were also aware of the Holocaust. The Finnish ambassador to Berlin was informed in June, 1942. Mussolini was informed early in 1942. By late 1942 most significant persons in the Hungarian government knew. Adolf Hitler's Croatian allies had early knowledge because they participated in the activities of the *Einsatzgruppen* in southern Russia. Rumanian authorities certainly knew in 1942 and the Bulgarians were informed in June, 1942. In July, 1942, arrests of Jews began in Vichy France. The victims were deported to Auschwitz and news of the mass murders was broadcast in French from London as early as July, 1942. It is difficult to conclude that the French government was unaware.

Just as the German people and their allies were aware by 1942 of the destruction of the Jews, so too were the neutral nations. The neutral nations of Europe were Switzerland, Turkey, Sweden, and Spain. Switzerland was a major reporting country for the reporters and representatives of many major international organizations. From reporters, such as Richard Lichtheim and Gerhard Riegner, the rest of the world was informed of the fate of the Jews. Information about the Holocaust was readily available in Switzerland and to Swiss governmental officials. In order to maintain neutrality, Swiss officials attempted to censor press accounts of the Holocaust but generally failed, and Swiss newspapers were outspoken in their criticism of Germany, although the Swiss government remained hostile to Jewish efforts to escape to Switzerland. Sweden was also aware by 1942 of the "final solution," although the Swedish press was less outspoken until late 1942 than the Swiss press in describing the Holocaust. Officially the Spanish government did not know of the Holocaust, but it intervened on behalf of Jews of Spanish origin and extended its protection to such Jews, often risking German ill will. Spain was far more helpful to Jews than more democratic countries. There are indications that the Spanish government knew of the Holocaust and attempted to assist where possible. Both the International Red Cross and the Vatican knew by 1942 of Jewish extermination and ignored the problem. Evidently Laqueur is not familiar with John Morley's splendid book, *Vatican Diplomacy and the Jews During the Holocaust*.

Laqueur's analysis of what the Western Allies knew and when they knew it reveals that the Allies received information about the Holocaust from late 1941 and throughout 1942. The Allied governments had many sources of information and received much information about the Holocaust from these sources. For example, the Soviet Union could not avoid knowledge of the

Holocaust from the time of the German invasion in June, 1941, because of the extensive activities in Russia of the *Einsatzgruppen*. By the fall of 1941, the *Einsatzgruppen* had murdered more than half a million Jews; the Jewish Ghetto of Riga, Latvia, had been destroyed; and fifty-two thousand Jews had been killed in Kiev. The Soviet government eventually confirmed all of this. By the spring of 1942, most of Lithuania's Jews had been murdered. News of these occurrences as well as the destruction of Polish Jews was also relayed to the Polish government in exile and then to other Allied governments and the press. The Polish government in exile was a major source of information about the Holocaust. *London Daily Telegraph* accounts in June, 1942, received wide circulation and much public attention.

In July, 1942, Dr. Gerhard Riegner of the World Jewish Congress sent his famous cable to the governments in London and Washington documenting the Holocaust and asking that his cable be sent to Jewish leaders in both capitals. The British government delayed forwarding the cable but eventually sent it to Jewish leaders. The American government did not and American Jewish leaders only learned of the Riegner cable from English counterparts. The Reigner cable was accepted in England, for many similar reports of German extermination were being sent to England. In America, this information and all subsequent information was buried by the State Department and American officials attempted to avoid publicizing in any way the events of the Holocaust. The information flowed to the United States and yet, according to Laqueur, American officials did not believe that the Holocaust was taking place. Laqueur argues that, in the words of W. A. Visser't Hooft, first secretary of the World Council of Churches during World War II:

> people could find no place in their consciousness for such an unimaginable horror and they did not have the imagination, together with the courage to face it. It is possible to live in a twilight between knowing and not knowing.

Finally, Laqueur describes the knowledge of Jews, both in Europe undergoing the Holocaust and elsewhere. Laqueur documents the case that many of Europe's Jews participated in self-delusion because they could not face the Holocaust. Jews elsewhere found it difficult at first to believe the news of the Holocaust. Eventually, however, the news was accepted as increasing information and sources became available. In spite of the Holocaust, no country was willing to accept the Jews, perhaps least of all the United States. Many Western governments continued throughout the war to downplay the Holocaust and ignore information about it. England and the United States, for example, did not believe news of the destruction of Polish Jewry, insisting that reports were exaggerated; the news of massacres "was printed but widely doubted." Even in Israel, there was little inclination to believe. As a labor leader said, "The news had reached Palestine. . . . The community read it and heard it but did not absorb it. . . ." Having sifted evidence on the questions of what and when each nation or group knew about the Holocaust, Laqueur insists that information about the Holocaust was available almost from its outset and that information grew with the progress of the destruction of the Jews. The information simply was not believed and the bystanders, like the victims, participated in psychological self-delusion.

The fault of this interpretation is the same that undermines the Hilberg thesis that Jews marched, as sheep, to the slaughter of the Holocaust: it does not take account of the complex and varied nature of Jewish resistance to destruction. Similarly, by making alleged disbelief of information the result of normal psychological reactions to the tragic events, Laqueur ignores the complexity and range of response of bystanders to the Holocaust. Indeed, many accepted the information, believed it, and either acted or refused to act on it. These responses ranged from active support of the Jews, to indifference, to hostility. Moreover, Laqueur's book demonstrates a variety of approaches to the information. He makes clear that the Holocaust, in fact, was not a "terrible secret," but widely known and understood. For this reason, many of the facts of Laqueur's book undermine the thesis that those who knew the events of the Holocaust were psychologically unable to believe them, and therefore reacted with apathy and indifference. Some people were unable to believe and were indifferent, others believed and were still indifferent, and still others believed and were not indifferent—a range of response not comprehended by a monolithic conception of normality such as Laqueur advances. By making disbelief the normal response to information about the Holocaust, Laqueur justifies apathy and indifference to the fate of the Jews in the terrible years of the Holocaust. The guilt of this failure to act on behalf of the Jews cannot be absolved by the simplistic thesis that those who learned of the Holocaust could not bear to believe or comprehend it.

*Saul Lerner*

## Sources for Further Study

*Choice*. XVIII, May, 1981, p. 1328.
*Christian Science Monitor*. LXXIII, February 11, 1981, p. 17.
*The Economist*. CLXXVI, September 20, 1980, p. 110.
*Library Journal*. CV, December 15, 1980, p. 2570.
*The New York Review of Books*. XXVIII, October 22, 1981, p. 17.
*The New York Times Book Review*. LXXXVI, February 1, 1981, p. 1.
*Saturday Review*. VIII, January, 1981, p. 77.
*Time*. CXVII, March 2, 1981, p. 89.
*Times Literary Supplement*. November 14, 1981, p. 1288.
*The Wall Street Journal*. CXCVII, February 10, 1981, p. 26.

# TIME CHANGE
## An Autobiography

*Author:* Hope Cooke (1940-    )
*Publisher:* Simon and Schuster (New York). Illustrated. 285 pp. $15.95
*Type of work:* Autobiography
*Time:* Approximately 1942-1978
*Locale:* The United States, Sikkim, India, and England

*Hope Cooke's autobiography concentrates on her decade in the Orient as Queen of Sikkim*

Principal personages:
    HOPE NAMGYAL (NÉE COOKE), the author
    CHOGYAL PALDEN THONDUP NAMGYAL, the monarch of Sikkim
        and Hope's husband
    PALDEN, their son
    HOPE LEEZUM, their daughter
    TENZING, the Chogyal's oldest son by his first marriage
    WONGCHUK, the Chogyal's second son
    YANGCHEN, the Chogyal's daughter

Hope Cooke, a poor little rich girl from New York, grew up to marry in 1963 the Crown Prince of Sikkim, a tiny Himalayan country surrounded by India, China, Nepal, and Bhutan. Her autobiography, *Time Change*, chronicles the circumstances of her life in the East and the political and personal events which kept her from living out the fairy-tale bliss promised by the press coverage of her wedding. Looking back on her life from the comfortable circumstances of summer on Martha's Vineyard in 1978, she wrote, "I can't believe what I have endured, yielded in both personal and public matters." As her story demonstrates, she did endure much, but this first book, which shows the author's considerable talent, is not told with bitterness or rancor. Instead, Cooke achieves a remarkable semblance of objectivity about her transformation from a somewhat romantic, idealistic young woman into a brave and responsible person.

Cooke relates events in the present tense, a point of view which gives the reader a sense of the immediacy of recent history, a sense of experiencing the events with her. She begins with her earliest memories at age two or three, when she and her sister came to live with their maternal grandparents after their mother's death. Although the grandparents were financially well off, Cooke felt the sting of lack of nurture throughout her childhood and adolescence. As the child of her mother's second marriage, Cooke also felt her grandmother's disapproval of her Irish father, who gave up guardianship of her to the maternal grandparents with apparent willingness. The grandmother's disapproving and stern nature seemed to prevent her from providing any emotional solace to the bereaved child, nor could the series of good and bad nannies who reared the girls in an apartment across the hall from their grandparents' place fill the void in the children's lives. Even Cooke's half-sister Harriet, who was three years older and much different from Hope in temperament and personality, provided little companionship for the lonely younger child. At least Cooke escaped the knowledge until adulthood that her mother's death in a plane crash was probably more suicidal than accidental.

Summer vacations at her grandparents' summer home in Maine relieved the alienation of Cooke's childhood to some extent. In Maine she felt free and happy with access to woods and beach. In New York she felt happy in the classroom, where she enjoyed writing and social studies, but she was unhappy at the boarding school in Virginia where she started high school. The death of Cooke's grandmother when she was about halfway through high school left her homeless again as her grandfather had died several years before. Cooke's new guardian, her Aunt Mary, then lived in Iran with her diplomat husband, Selden Chapin. In Cooke's eyes her Aunt Mary, with her vivacious personality and many opportunities to travel to foreign lands, lived a charmed existence. What was to be merely a second summer visit to Iran turned into a prolonged stay for Cooke so that she could finish high school in the Community School in Tehran. Her stay in Iran, where she felt more at home than anywhere she had been, proved to be one of the happiest times of her life. Life in Iran, with the embassy parties and even invitations to one of the Shah's palaces, provided a liberating change from the bleak boarding-school existence of Cooke's last few years. Her interest in the foreign culture, however, was far deeper than a mere preoccupation with the social whirl of life associated with the diplomatic corps. Even at sixteen, she was sensitive to social issues: she loved to mix with the local people, saw the diplomatic corps as reinforcing elitist rule, and sensed inevitable revolution. The pinnacle of her stay was a trip into India, which sparked her continuing interest in the Far East even after her return to the United States and enrollment at Sarah Lawrence College, where she took up Oriental studies.

Cooke's interest in India took her back in 1959, where at the Windemere Hotel she met Maharaj Kumar, the Crown Prince of Sikkim, who was in Darjeeling to visit his two sons at boarding school. Cooke took a favorable impression of the Maharaj back to school at Sarah Lawrence. She admired his "habit of talking in the immediate" and felt the aura of his position and his sense of loss. (His wife had died two years earlier.) Two years later she returned to Darjeeling to meet the Prince again. This time Palden Thondup Namgyal, which was the Prince's real name—but used only by Westerners—brought his four-year-old daughter, who called Cooke "Mummy." It was only a matter of time until the young woman who had never been mothered herself became the stepmother of the monarch's three children.

The wedding took place in Gangtok, the capital of the tiny country with its monarchical tradition of more than five centuries. The bride's account of the elaborate and colorful Buddhist wedding celebration in Sikkimese tradition with its exchange of scarves is much less romanticized than was the extensive press coverage of the event. Cooke's account reveals incipient problems in the marriage, such as the Prince's remoteness and her jealousy, which she frankly admits, over another woman in her bridegroom's life, a woman who attended the wedding celebration. Four days into the festivities, the death of Cooke's Uncle Selden took the newlyweds back to the United States for the funeral. In the rush of getting her passport in order, she learned that she had to renounce her United States citizenship because Sikkimese law prevented dual citizenship.

On returning to Sikkim, Cooke gave herself entirely to learning the customs of the people, redecorating the palace, and, most importantly, mothering the children. She seemed to have a natural gift for all these tasks, especially for mothering. Only a few months after the marriage, she had to learn about state funeral customs when her father-in-law died. At the time of their marriage, the older man was still the official reigning monarch, although the Crown Prince had acted in that capacity for many years. As custom dictated, the dead ruler's body, embalmed in the lotus position, was displayed on the throne in its triangular coffin for a length of time set by astrologers. After the death of his father, Cooke's husband took the title *Chogyal*, meaning ruler, and her title became *Gyalmo*, or queen.

The birth of the couple's first child, a son named Palden, took place a few weeks after the funeral. Ironically, after making arrangements for the care of Yangchen, Cooke had to drive herself through the streets of Calcutta to a hospital in order to give birth. She had taken an apartment in Calcutta a few weeks earlier in order to be near medical facilities. The Chogyal had gone to Brussels, presumably to see the other woman in his life, but he did return to Cooke a few hours after the birth of the baby. She counted on the child to help her to become more accepted in Sikkim and perhaps more important to her husband, who made no secret of his continuing interest in the other woman and who put his monarchical duties ahead of everything else in his life. To a certain extent, the Chogyal looked upon his wife as an institution and saw marriage to a Westerner, the first ever in the royal family of Sikkim, as politically advantageous. From the beginning of their marriage, Cooke struggled with her loneliness, the benign neglect with which her husband seemed to treat her, and their lack of privacy. The pattern of the marriage in those early years, however, was such that Hope's feeling of alienation was erased temporarily by some domestic or political crisis or event of great importance.

Soon after Palden's birth and the end of the mourning period for her father-in-law, the coronation consumed the attention of the household. The ceremony was an elegant and elaborate occasion. Like the wedding, it was followed by a long celebration with dancing and games. There were hopes that the ceremony might bring together the opposing political factions of the long-established Bhutias and the Nepalese, comparatively recent immigrants whose numbers constituted the majority in this country of approximately 162,000 inhabitants. The Chogyal's ancestors had originally been part of a Bhutanese tribe which came from Tibet in the twelfth century. The festival brought Indira Ghandi and other famous people to Sikkim and distracted from the tension in the personal lives of the couple.

It is not surprising that Sikkim's tenuous political autonomy preoccupied the Chogyal. Since India's achievement of independence in 1947, Sikkim had been subject to annexation by that country, and in 1950, Sikkim became a protectorate of India. During Jawaharal Nehru's lifetime, Sikkim enjoyed a fairly stable relationship with India, but in 1964, on a flight to Delhi to begin talks with him about Sikkim's future, Cooke and the monarch learned of Nehru's death and attended his funeral instead. She describes the event as frightening: "At the ghat were heads as far as one could see—unimaginable."

The political situation reached crisis dimensions a year and a half later when Cooke went to London to take the older children to boarding school in England. India and Pakistan were in an undeclared state of war, and the headlines "China Set to Invade Sikkim," which jumped out at her from the newsstands, understandably caused her great alarm. She feared for the safety of Palden and the others in Sikkim, and, of course, for the sovereignty of the country. After a few tension-filled days, the crisis was averted and she was able to return to Sikkim and at least a semblance of normalcy. The delicate political situation continued throughout the 1960's, with the threatened annexation by India, which was preferable to takeover by China, preoccupying the Sikkimese. Cooke explains the complex political background to some extent as she goes along, but some readers may desire more detail.

Despite the political tumult and tension in the background, life in Gangtok was somewhat routine for Cooke in the next few years. The royal couple's second child, a daughter, was named Hope Leezum. *Leezum*, a Lepcha name meaning "home unity," was the wish for both the country and the family. The Queen kept herself occupied with duties such as entertaining and projects such as designing clothes and learning one of the native languages of Sikkim. Notably, she spent much effort on improving the schools, especially in writing a much-needed new series of textbooks, published by the Oxford University Press in India. Sometimes, however, her projects seemed a nuisance to her husband in his continuing preoccupation with Sikkim's future, and their personal relationship continued to be strained. Through it all, and despite her growing homesickness, Hope worked for awareness of and understanding about Sikkim's vulnerability through articles and interviews: "At every interview I'd given over the years," she says, "I'd tried again and again to drive the point home that no matter how small and semiexotic we might be, we were real, we existed." A family crisis—the diagnosis by a London doctor that Yangchen's kidney disease was terminal—stunned both the Chogyal and Cooke, but a frantic trip to New York brought a more hopeful prognosis, although they were aware that a transplant would probably be necessary in time.

Internal conflict in Sikkim worsened as the Nepali majority agitated for full voting rights rather than a parity system and claimed that the last election had been unfair. The Chogyal did not oppose their demands but insisted that the change be made constitutionally, not by edict. The crisis came early in April, 1973, when crowds started demonstrations at the bazaar. Eventually the demonstrators surrounded the palace in a month-long siege. Cooke's account of these days makes the best reading in the whole book. The childhood fantasy she tells of earlier must have been a premonition of this drama: "Red Indians circling outside, I nestling and reassuring a gangly brood of children in the snug safety of our covered wagon." During that month when she sought ways to keep the children occupied and all their minds off their imprisonment, their lives were literally in danger. The crisis, which ended with only minor violence, eventually led to the sad but perhaps inevitable takeover of Sikkim by India.

Always somewhat wary of press coverage, Cooke was devastated by a *Newsweek* article of July 2, 1973, which accused her of having "delusions of grandeur" and referred to her "life of imitation royalty." The further accusation of "profligate" spending must have seemed particularly unfair, since the family traveled economy class and economized in other ways. Even worse, the article claimed that Cooke had "rewritten" history and implied that she was at least part of the reason for the takeover. This article contributed to her decision to leave Sikkim because it increased her frustration over the misinterpretation of her efforts to fit into tradition and to contribute to the culture. In August (the siege had ended in May), Cooke and the children left for New York by way of London, with the stated intention of returning to Sikkim in a few months. In her heart, however, she must have known, as she participated in a bittersweet scarf ceremony at the Buddhist chapel as a farewell, that she would not return.

Essentially a woman without a country, Cooke encountered a kind of cultural shock in adapting to life in New York after a decade in the Orient. She had the responsibility of caring for her own two children as well as her step-daughter, Yangchen, who was still facing a kidney transplant. Hope shopped at second-hand stores and sales in order to furnish an apartment and even had to learn to cook. She also had to cope with the red tape involved in seeking restoration of citizenship with a special bill in Congress, which if denied could mean deportation. She did not seek her citizenship for two years because of her concern about the continuing precarious situation in Sikkim. In 1974, the situation reached another crisis in which the Chogyal and Tenzing (who was killed a few weeks later in an automobile accident) were held under house arrest while India completed the annexation of the strategically-located kingdom. Not until the Chogyal signed his acceptance of India's constitution for Sikkim could he leave the country to see Cooke and the children. By then she had made her decision to stay.

Although she is now divorced from the Chogyal, Cooke wrote the book in the loving spirit in which she began her love affair with the East, an affair about which she tells with honesty and thoroughness. Sometimes her writing is poetic, breaking into passages that seem to be free verse in prose: "The afternoon sun dappling the reeds around the lake. Feathery grasses in the water tickling my legs. Amber cool water. Floating on my back. Free." Because she is still readjusting to life in the United States, the last part of the book understandably lacks the detachment which she achieves about the events in Sikkim. The conclusion also gives the impression that Cooke is an unfinished woman, but one who has much left to give. She has already given much with this insightful book, which, as reviewer Donald Clay Johnson points out in the *Library Journal*, "will also be valuable to Asian specialists for its unique perceptions on the moth and the flame relationship between India and Sikkim." The merits of this book definitely outnumber any weaknesses.

*Roberta Sharp*

### Sources for Further Study

*Best Sellers*. XLI, May, 1981, p. 57.
*Book World*. XI, March 15, 1981, p. 3.
*Booklist*. LXXVII, January 15, 1981, p. 651.
*Library Journal*. CVI, February 1, 1981, p. 348.
*Ms*. X, July, 1981, p. 28.
*The New York Times Book Review*. LXXXVI, March 8, 1981, p. 3.
*Saturday Review*. VIII, February, 1981, p. 76.

# THE TIME OF STALIN
## Portrait of a Tyranny

*Author:* Anton Antonov-Ovseyenko (1920-    )
Translated from the Russian by George Saunders
Introduction by Stephen F. Cohen
*Publisher:* Harper & Row, Publishers (New York). Illustrated. 374 pp. $19.95
*Type of work:* Biography
*Time:* 1917-1953, with some reflections on subsequent events
*Locale:* Russia

*A study of the political career of Soviet Dictator Joseph Stalin; a chronicle and an indictment of political terrorism and repression carried out under his orders*

> *Principal personages:*
> JOSEPH STALIN, General Secretary of the Soviet Communist Party, 1922-1953; Soviet Premier, 1941-1953
> VLADIMIR ANTONOV-OVSEYENKO, a Bolshevik military commander and Soviet diplomat, executed under Stalin
> ANTON ANTONOV-OVSEYENKO, his son
> VLADIMIR ILICH LENIN, Bolshevik leader; Soviet Premier, 1918-1924
> SERGEI KIROV, Communist Party Secretary in Leningrad and Politburo member; murdered in 1934
> NIKOLAI YEZHOV, head of Soviet security organs, 1936-1938
> MATVEI SHKIRYATOV, a member of Soviet Party Control Commission
> LAVRENTII BERIA, People's Commissar for Interior, 1938-1945; Deputy Chairman of the Council of People's Commissars, 1941-1953
> NIKITA KHRUSHCHEV, a Politburo member during Stalin years; First Secretary of Soviet Communist Party, 1953-1964
> ANASTAS MIKOYAN, Trade and Food Commissar under Stalin; First Deputy Chairman of Soviet Council of Ministers, 1955-1964
> ADOLF HITLER, Chancellor and Führer of Germany, 1933-1945

Soviet Dictator Joseph Stalin directed the largest and most destructive campaign of political repression and terrorism ever mounted by any regime. Millions perished as the result of executions, systematic starvation, and from the numerous acts of wanton violence carried out by Stalin's subordinates. Millions more were detained in forced labor camps, where many died of exposure or at the hands of their guards. Those who survived were embittered by the ordeal they had suffered, and by the loss of many of those close to them in the wholesale carnage of this period. While Stalin dealt in the most severe and ruthless manner even with those whom he could only suspect of possible opposition, he and his aides devised a ubiquitous propaganda cult in which the Soviet leader was depicted as the wise and benevolent standard-bearer of Soviet Marxist ideals. In Stalin's lifetime, history was rewritten to portray him as the defender of the revolution and the master architect of the socialist state. Even though after his death some of his actions were repudiated, Soviet officials have never permitted an open investigation or assessment of the Stalin era.

Both Western historians and Soviet dissidents have attempted to provide more complete and searching accounts of the bloodshed and havoc wrought by the Soviet Dictator. Anton Antonov-Ovseyenko's work is neither the most extensive nor the best of works of this genre; it does stand, however, as testimony to his own experiences and to those around him who perished. Moreover, as the son of an Old Bolshevik he has been in a unique position to gather materials on the administration of the terror at the highest levels. Thus he has been able to furnish some new insights on the operations of Soviet secret police and the planning of the terror by Stalin and his associates.

The author's father, Vladimir Antonov-Ovseyenko, joined the Bolsheviks during the revolution and commanded troops that captured the Winter Palace in Petrograd during the Bolshevik seizure of power in 1917. He also held several important positions in the Soviet government and distinguished himself as commander of Red Army forces on several fronts during the Russian Civil War. During subsequent struggles for power within the Party, however, he did not side with Stalin, and, though still widely respected, he was sent away from the capital on diplomatic assignments. After service as Ambassador to Czechoslovakia, Lithuania, and Poland, in 1936 he was made Proconsul to the Spanish Republic. As Stalin began to eliminate the Old Bolsheviks, Vladimir Antonov-Ovseyenko was recalled to Moscow and accused of heinous crimes against the Soviet state; formally arrested late in 1937, he was not permitted to answer the charges brought against him, and when he refused to sign the confession prepared by Soviet interrogators, he was put to death at some time during the following year. His wife, the mother of the author, committed suicide after she was imprisoned by Stalin's police. Anton Antonov-Ovseyenko was arrested three times, and from 1941 to 1953 was detained in several forced labor camps. Though for quite some time after his release he was not involved with other dissidents, he resolved eventually to set forth the record of crimes of the Stalin era, as a duty to his dead father and to those who had suffered with him. His work is a chronicle of the Stalin period intermingled with personal reminiscences and reflections on the character of the Soviet Dictator and his henchmen.

Perhaps as a reflection of his father's role in the events of 1917, the author is somewhat ambivalent on the outcome and significance of the Russian Revolution. He suggests at times that some repression would have been practiced by any Soviet regime; in other places he seems to feel that only Stalin could have carried out large-scale terrorism. He does note that shortly after Stalin joined the Bolshevik Party he took part in the expropriation of a steamship, and associated with other criminals during his underground political work. Stalin did not contribute significantly to the Bolsheviks' victory in 1917, and indeed during the Civil War he mismanaged several important campaigns. His criminal instincts and background, however, served him well later on when he began to scheme against his rivals.

Repeatedly the author mentions warnings and premonitions of Lenin and other Soviet officials who feared that Stalin might abuse power or turn on his comrades. Nevertheless, other leading Bolsheviks found him unobtrusive and few suspected the extent of his ambitions. When he became General Secretary of the Party, Stalin began to act more overtly against possible opponents; he also brought the power of the state to bear against much broader segments of the population. To compel the collectivization of agriculture, Stalin launched in 1929 a campaign of terrorism and systematic starvation against peasants who refused to relinquish their property to the state. Not content with millions of deaths in the countryside, Stalin also commenced an equally costly purge of Bolshevik Party leaders and officials. Sergei Kirov, the Party Secretary in Leningrad, was very popular in many circles, and against Stalin had polled one-fourth of the vote at a congress of the Soviet Communist Party. The arrangements by which Stalin's agents hired a social misfit to assassinate Kirov are discussed in greater detail here than in previous works; the author recounts the several attempts on Kirov's life that culminated with his murder in December, 1934. To cover his tracks Stalin arrested or ordered the murder of all those involved in the plot. He also used this incident as a pretext for action against other Party members, and charged his colleagues with complicity in the Kirov assassination.

From 1935 to 1940, Stalin eliminated almost all of the remaining Party members who had played any prominent part in the Bolshevik Revolution. Men whom Stalin had praised one day were delivered to the secret police the next; many were accused of the most perfidious intrigues with foreign powers. Stalin, who had little understanding of military science, also charged his most capable commanders with espionage and conspiracy against the Soviet state. To extinguish all memory of his victims Stalin had whole families destroyed. In one of the more touching passages of his work Antonov-Ovseyenko describes orphanages that were established for children of purged officials, where boys and girls lived apart from their parents and only occasionally were visited by widows or other relatives of executed Party members.

The author is particularly harsh in his judgment of the secret police functionaries and judicial officials who served Stalin during the years of the great terror. Many of them were adventurers or petty criminals who indulged their own base instincts at the expense of the accused. Vladimir Antonov-Ovseyenko's possessions, including furniture and his personal library, were confiscated by avid security agents. The author also describes his own entrapment by a graduate student who served as an agent provocateur and who brought charges of espionage against his fellow students. Stalin's agents frequently used blackmail, extortion, forgery, or gross physical torture to obtain confessions to charges they had devised. Leading police officials such as Nikolai Yezhov and Matvei Shkiryatov were nearly as ambitious and unscrupulous as Stalin himself. Lavrentii Beria, who replaced Yezhov in 1938 and supervised state security organs, interrogated prisoners in person, often beat them himself, and settled his own vendettas against other Party members. Antonov-Ovseyenko also censures Nikita Khrushchev and Anastas Mikoyan, Party officials who acquiesced in Stalin's crimes, even though in subsequent governments they curtailed many terrorist activities.

Stalin is depicted as the most degenerate and corrupt of all; from an unhappy family, he was beaten and humiliated both at home and at school. He had limited intellectual attainments, and resented Party comrades who surpassed him in scholarship and formal education. Always something of a loner, he was invariably suspicious of those around him. He surrounded himself with sycophants, mediocrities, and intriguers like himself. Stalin was also a physical coward, afraid of sparks and lightning; during World War II he never visited his troops at the front. His cruelty and vulgarity perpetually marred his marital life and strained relations with his daughter.

In some particularly telling passages the author discusses Stalin's relations with Adolf Hitler, whom he contends was the one man the Soviet Dictator respected. Stalin adopted some of the secret police techniques employed in Nazi Germany. He was particularly enchanted with the pact he concluded with Hitler in 1939, and by the prospects of dividing Eastern Europe with the German dictator. Stalin was disillusioned only with the German invasion of Russia two years later; when he finally began to manage Russia's war effort, Stalin only complicated matters for his own generals. By interfering in military strategy he needlessly sacrificed several Soviet armies during the difficult early years of the war. In this sense victory over Nazi Germany was achieved in spite of Stalin; moreover, not satisfied with the losses his people had suffered during the war, Stalin pressed forward with more purges and political trials. Though at times weary of such grim diversions, he plotted against Soviet Jews, and yet another round of terrorism was interrupted only by the Dictator's death early in 1953.

Antonov-Ovseyenko has serious reservations on the measures of de-Stalinization taken by the immediate successors of the Soviet Dictator. He left prison camp shortly after the change of regimes; his father was one of the first to be formally rehabilitated when under Khrushchev victims of the terror were posthumously cleared of charges against them. Nevertheless, little was done to expose Stalin's accomplices or to bring them to justice. Many of the Dictator's prosecutors and secret police were allowed to live on in peaceful retirement. For that matter, increasingly in recent years Leonid Brezhnev's government has revoked even the modest measures of de-Stalinization which Khrushchev commenced. For this reason Antonov-Ovseyenko has handed down an indictment of the crimes of the Stalin years, and a warning against any recurrence.

Antonov-Ovseyenko's work is not an academic study; it is strident, often colloquial, episodic, and impressionistic. In some places it is disjointed, and there are occasional errors of fact and chronology. Other works have dealt in greater depth with the known record of the Stalin period: the most extensive and painstaking compilation of prison camp accounts is Aleksandr Solzhenitsyn's *The Gulag Archipelago* (1974-1977), which recounts in all possible detail the system of police terror, forced labor, and executions by which Stalin ruled Russia. The most systematic study of Stalin's government by a Soviet dissident is Roy Medvedev's *Let History Judge* (1971). Antonov-Ovseyenko, who is now more than sixty years old and nearly blind, has rendered his judgment of Stalin in the light of his own background and research. His work will not displace or supersede the others; on the other hand, while often intemperate and sardonic, the author has conveyed the pervasive brutality and contempt for human life, alongside the virtual deification of the Soviet leader, that permeated an entire period of Russian history.

*John R. Broadus*

## Sources for Further Study

*Best Sellers*. XLI, October, 1981, p. 263.
*Booklist*. LXXVIII, September 1, 1981, p. 22.
*Business Week*. November 9, 1981, p. 18.
*Library Journal*. CVI, August, 1981, p. 1537.
*National Review*. XXXIII, August 7, 1981, p. 911.
*New Leader*. LXIV, October 5, 1981, p. 17.

# TO WIN A WAR
## 1918, The Year of Victory

*Author:* John Terraine (1921-    )
*Publisher:* Doubleday & Company (Garden City, New York). Illustrated. 284 pp.
$14.95
*Type of work:* Military history
*Time:* 1918
*Locale:* The Western Front, which includes France and Belgium

A study of the last year of World War I on the Western Front, primarily from the vantage point of the leaders

> *Principal personages:*
> MARSHAL FERDINAND FOCH, Chief of the French General Staff and head of the Supreme War Council
> FIELD MARSHAL SIR DOUGLAS HAIG, Commander in Chief of the British Expeditionary Force
> FIELD MARSHAL PAUL VON HINDENBURG, Chief of the German General Staff
> DAVID LLOYD GEORGE, British Prime Minister, 1916-1922
> GENERAL ERICH LUDENDORF, German First Quartermaster General
> GENERAL JOHN J. PERSHING, Commander in Chief of the American Expeditionary Forces

John Terraine, in *To Win a War: 1918, The Year of Victory*, adds to his studies of World War I which he has pursued since the early 1960's. From *Mons: The Retreat to Victory* (1960) to this work on the last months before the Armistice he has dealt in detail with individual battles, campaigns, biographies (*Douglas Haig: The Educated Soldier*, 1963, and *General Jack's Diary*, 1964), and broader studies such as *The Western Front* (1965) and *The Great War I: An Illustrated History* (1965). The author's point of view, his preferences for some individuals over others and some ideas over others, emerge clearly and without apology. This is a British author writing with a distinct national, military, and historical bias.

Terraine wants to make a number of special points beyond simply retelling the glories and trials of the end of the Great War. Much of the war has remained in the common memory: the Battles of the Frontiers; the massive bloodlettings at the Somme, Verdun, and Passchendaele; the 1918 German spring offensives. The great, final victory, however, has, he believes, been nearly forgotten by those in Britain who ought to remember. The reasons which he finds for this national amnesia are not especially edifying nor completely persuasive. Primarily, he blames Britain's Prime Minister, David Lloyd George, who plainly disliked and distrusted the Commander in Chief of the British Expeditionary Force, Field Marshal Sir Douglas Haig. Lloyd George's equal dislike of the Western Front as a slaughter pen made it impossible for the Prime Minister to credit the winning of the war to the man he so despised, won in a theater he hated. Terraine believes that Lloyd George tried to pretend that victory did not happen and in this was supported by many others who for their own reasons wanted to see the Western Front and its generals as villains. Beyond that, he charges that this forgetfulness wasted the lessons learned and made it more certain that there would be another war. Since the legend in Germany, that the German Army had never been defeated by the Entente forces, strengthened Hitler's hand in coming to power and rebuilding the military, it is an argument that can be made, but a tenuous one at best. In this work the author sets out to write a defense for men whom he sees as unjustly forgotten heroes, to support his particular hero, Douglas Haig, and to lay down another barrage in that seemingly endless struggle over the Western Front and its commanders.

This is not only a history of life in the trenches, dugouts, and officers' headquarters. At the top, besides Lloyd George and Haig, Marshal Ferdinand Foch, General John J. Pershing, Marshal Henri Petain, Field Marshal Paul von Hindenburg, General Erich Ludendorf, and the Kaiser all play major roles. Terraine tends to see them and the issues surrounding them in terms that are all too often harshly delineated in black or white, sometimes dismissing them with a peremptory adjective. Granted that Lloyd George was a slippery fox and Haig a doughty, loyal soldier, the constant juxtaposition of the two with the former always wrong, petty, or foolish and the latter always wise and modest strains credibility. This same tendency frequently occurs with other men and events and weakens what is in some ways a strong, interesting, and necessary work.

It is always difficult to begin writing about a war at any place other than at the beginning, but Terraine paints an adequate background for the momentous events of 1918 before getting to the heart of the work, the last victorious "Hundred Days" from July through October. As the year began, the Americans were only just starting to make their presence felt on the Western Front; the French and Italians had suffered, perhaps mortally, in the preceding year; and Russia was out of the fighting, although the bitter treaty of Brest-Litovsk had not yet been imposed. Britain had strained its manpower to what Lloyd George and others felt to be the edge of its limits and the army was to be reinforced only grudgingly. This meant that the British armies in the north would have to face the full brunt of the German spring offensives with substantially reduced forces. According to Terraine, these assaults would not be as formidable as they might have been since Ludendorf, displaying symptoms of paranoia and delusions of grandeur, insisted on retaining a million German troops in the east. The author sees no good purpose to this diversion of strength although a case can be made for the German First Quartermaster General. The British were strong enough to withstand these attacks although the losses of ground and lives were prodigious. Their weakened state, however, meant that they were not able fully to pursue and drive back a beaten enemy later in the year. Terraine blames the Prime Minister for this lack of strength in the army but gives inadequate consideration to Lloyd George's argument that high hopes and unfulfilled promises had already bled the Empire nearly to death and that Haig's calls for yet more young bodies to ensure success must have had an increasingly hollow ring.

The author agrees with most writers that the German military commanders, Hindenburg and Ludendorf, shaken as they were by their inability to replace the losses after the spring offensives and then by the defeat on the "Black Day" of August 8th (especially the attacks by the Canadians and the Australians), saw that the balance of fighting power had shifted irretrievably against them and that Germany had to find a way to make peace. The question became not whether or not to end the war but how best to do it in order to avoid military disaster. Terraine sees Woodrow Wilson's Fourteen Points and the President's role in the negotiations as at least in part mischievous, offering the Germans an easier way out than he believes they should have had. Implicit in much of his work is the sense that only a thoroughgoing and totally recognized defeat of the German Army might have avoided the recommencing of the Great War twenty years after the armistice.

Although giving some credit to American arms the author is severely critical of General John J. Pershing, Commander of the American Expeditionary Force, for his insistence on an all-American army with its own battles and responsibililties. Terraine understands the nationalistic pressures for a separate force, but obviously feels that the Entente would have been served better by integrating American divisions into the French and British armies. He praises the tall brave Americans but in a somewhat supercilious tone that will lead most American readers to cavil at his dismissal in a page or two of the fierce labors of over half a million American soldiers in the Argonne. The French efforts in the last months of the war are also downplayed on the grounds that the French Army had given so much in 1917 that no great things could be expected of it. Victory would come in the north.

It is in describing the last months' drive by a desperately weary British Army that Terraine is at his best. Haig, as the commander, must receive his due credit, but the author is so laudatory that one wishes for a more modest assessment. The story of these last victories needs to be retold but nothing would have been lost to British glory by sharing some of it.

Terraine is sound in his insistence on the marginal value of both tanks and aircraft in the last year of the war. Ambivalent about cavalry, the author seems to believe that the Germans could have succeeded in the spring if only Ludendorf had not been so stupid as to have left all the German cavalry in the east. On the other hand, he is aware that the formal cavalry charge was dead as long as a single machine gun swept the field. His final section on the maneuvering toward peace by an increasingly desperate German government, fearful of the army in front and despair and Bolshevism at home, is handled graphically and clearly.

The reader will need a supplementary set of maps to follow both the broad strategic and tactical sections. Very little in the way of maps is available in the book. Drawing primarily on memoirs, official histories, and secondary works, the author's style is felicitous but his judgments are frequently arbitrary and, as with almost everything else written about that terrible war, bound to be controversial.

*Charles W. Johnson*

### Sources for Further Study

*Choice*. XIX, October, 1981, p. 290.
*Library Journal*. CVI, August, 1981, p. 1539.
*New Statesman*. XCVI, November 17, 1981, p. 664.
*The New York Times Book Review*. LXXXVI, August 2, 1981, p. 13.
*Publishers Weekly*. CCXIX, April 24, 1981, p. 67.

# TWELVE YEARS
## An American Boyhood in East Germany

*Author:* Joel Agee (1940-    )
*Publisher:* Farrar, Straus and Giroux (New York). 324 pp. $14.95
*Type of work:* Autobiography
*Time:* 1948-1960
*Locale:* East Germany

The spiritual memoir of the childhood of a guilt-ridden American boy reared in East Germany

Principal personages:
JOEL AGEE
ALMA MAILMAN, his mother
JAMES AGEE, his father, a legendary American writer
BODO UHSE, his stepfather, a German Communist writer
STEFAN, Joel's stepbrother

*Twelve Years: An American Boyhood in East Germany* is an autobiographical account of eight-year-old Joel Agee's move in the fall of 1948 from Mexico to Gross-Glienicke, a village bisected by the East-West border, twenty miles from Berlin, and the twelve years he spent in East Germany.

Joel Agee was the stepson of Bodo Uhse, a German Communist writer who had been living in exile for fifteen years in Mexico. During his exile he married Joel's mother, Alma, an American Jew, and they added to the family another son, Stefan. Missing his homeland, Uhse felt the political climate in Europe was right for his return.

*Twelve Years*, a first book for Joel Agee, now forty-two, is appealingly unique in its setting. Superficially this autobiography exhibits the clichés of the adolescent searching for identity, but Joel Agee's search was considerably more difficult because he was growing up in a society where the individual's growth was subordinate to that of the community and because his own needs were subjective and artistically sensitive. Historically, those years covered a period when Joseph Stalin died, Nikita Khrushchev denounced him, and Soviet tanks invaded Hungary. Many of Bodo Uhse's dissident, intellectual friends were tried and sent to jail, and Uhse, because of his political affiliations, was uneasy about his own future and that of his family.

On a personal level, *Twelve Years* details Agee's relationships with members of his family; his friendships; his problems and failures in a series of schools because of his penchant for playing hooky, neglecting his studies, and playing pranks on his teachers; his inability to function productively in the working world; and his half-hearted participation in the Young Pioneers and the Free German Youth. In contrast to the normal everyday activities of home, school, summertime soccer games, yearnings for girls and sexual fulfillment, is the sense of failure that plagues Joel. "My fourteen-year-old world was bleak indeed."

   As Joel sees his friends mature, take up careers, marry, and engage in a settled family-style life, his own situation becomes even more bleak to him: "The real disorder was in me; I had no purpose in life. The idea of suicide began to appeal to me, not just for the soothing balm of self-pity, but for the apparent logic of it." Joel's self-image was summed up in a line he found in a collection of American Indian poetry: "Above my head I can hear the terrible sound of the wings of failure."

   Adolescent autobiographies usually fall into three categories: the early years of a writer well known to the literary world (Wright Morris's *Will's Boy*, 1981); an autobiographical account written for a young audience (Frank Conroy's *Stop-Time*, 1967); or a classical fictional rendering (J. D. Salinger's *Catcher in the Rye*, 1951). *Twelve Years* is specifically none of these, although it may be read with enjoyment by young readers, and the unknown Agee says in his remarks on the book that he has "taken liberties of fiction . . . I have changed names, I have transplanted heads, bodies, attitudes." Given these particulars, one wonders what the audience might be for such a book and, more important, why Agee wrote it. With these questions in mind, the reader must look below the superficial level to experience the full impact and implications of *Twelve Years*.

   Joel Agee, named for his paternal grandfather, Joel Tyler, is the son of James Agee, the legendary author of *Let Us Now Praise Famous Men* (1941) and *A Death in the Family* (1957), and his second wife, Alma Mailman. Joel was separated from his father in his first year when his parents were divorced. He spent a short time with him in New York when he was four; although during this visit a close and loving relationship developed, Alma and James Agee thought it wise not to reveal that Agee was Joel's father. Since Alma had by then married Bodo Uhse and Joel would be living with them, they considered it best for Joel to accept Bodo as his father. Joel was eventually told about his American father, and though there was communication between them through the books and gifts which James Agee sent to his son, letters between Alma and Agee, and plans for Joel to live in the United States with his father for a time, James Agee's death put an end to any further plans and Joel never saw his father again.

   It is especially curious then that Joel displays many of his father's personal characteristics and emulates not only his talent for writing, but his choice of material as well. *Twelve Years* appears to have been written out of the same compulsion as James Agee's *The Morning Watch* (1950) and *A Death in the Family*—the compulsion to investigate a personal past through writing. Throughout Joel Agee's narration runs the same strain as is found in James Agee's life: tomorrow will be different; tomorrow my life will take a different path, a new beginning. Tomorrow, always tomorrow. *Twelve Years* is an attempt to recapture an after-the-fact, important time, but a somewhat wasted, sometimes elusive, even lost time. It is an attempt to reconstruct events that years later nag at the mind as important, to reevaluate feelings, memories, and attitudes, and above all, to assuage the compulsive guilt that plagues the son as it did the father.

James Agee's guilt and his masochistic need to punish himself was an abstract guilt, a guilt he talked about a great deal but could neither explain nor control. This guilt was hard to deal with because it never took a concrete, intelligible form. Certainly he felt the failures of his marriages, but one failure did not prevent the next. Although when he died he left four children, little can be found to establish any evidence of a personal relationship with them. On March 8, 1940, Agee, in a letter to his friend Father Flye, writes of Joel's impending birth:

> Our child will be born within a short time now—a week or two. On that I feel such complications of hope, fear, joy, sorrow, life, death, foreboding, interest, and a dozen other true emotions on which the copyright has expired, that I am not qualified to try to touch them now.

In 1941 he wrote: "Alma is in Mexico—so is Joel—nominally, presumably, perhaps very probably, that is broken forever."

Joel Agee's guilt is at least more reasonable and manageable. He displayed jealous feelings and actions toward Stefan, the younger brother pampered because of chronic illness, but who also succeeded where Joel failed, by producing actual paintings, cartoons, and writing which were circulated among the Uhses' friends as having a mark of intelligence not evident in Joel's ventures. Joel labels Stefan the creative one ("Bodo Uhse's remarkably talented son") and himself the dreamer ("the problematic and rather woozy stepson"). "It is painful for me to write about Stefan's very sad childhood in any detail because I contributed to it, both actively and by default, out of jealousy and out of a need to dominate." As Joel grew into young manhood, however, he found his feelings toward Stefan changing and he relied upon him for enlightening explanations of feelings and emotions he did not understand and with which he lacked the ability to cope.

Haunting Joel Agee's remembrances is a vague, dreamlike quality that permeates the memoir and enhances the reader's experience of *Twelve Years*; this guilt-ridden vagueness is most poignantly apparent in Joel's penitent search for his stepfather. The déjà vu that haunts Joel Agee extends to his mother Alma. Just as her marriage to James Agee ended because of another woman, so does her life with Bodo Uhse, and she finally makes the decision to leave East Germany and return with her children to America. This separation was traumatic for both Alma and Bodo, and while arrangements were being made for passports, packing, and preparations for travel, Bodo was very ill in a hospital. He had given up hope of keeping the family together, but he sent word to Joel that he wanted to see him. Alma and her friends, feeling she had been grossly wronged, persuaded Joel not to go, a decision he later regretted. "As I said, it was easy, with so much support. But ever since Bodo died, not quite two years ago, the memory of that decision grieves me; for I never saw him again."

If Joel's relationship with his stepfather was ambivalent, he enjoyed an easygoing relationship with his mother, who played the viola and included Joel in her associations and performances with other musicians. She was proud when Joel brought her some poetry he claimed to have written, but was extremely disappointed when she found the lines in a book and realized Joel was guilty of plagarism. She was uneasy thereafter whenever Joel brought any of his writing to her, but after assuring herself that another batch of poems was original, she sent them to James Agee. He "conferred the word 'talent' on me like a badge of honor."

As a Jew, Alma never felt at home in East Germany. She wore her straight, long, black hair circling her head and pinned so tightly at the temples that her eyes had a slightly slanted appearance. She differed from the East German women in dress and in her use of cosmetics and she had no intention to alter her individuality to conform to the usual unobtrusiveness of women in the society in which she was constrained to live. She looked upon the Germans with derision and remarked on more than one occasion, "Just look at them, the master race." She impressed upon Joel their heritage.

> On several conversations, Alma impressed on me her wish that I take to heart the fact that we were Jewish; and not only that; but that we were Jews in Germany. It meant something. It meant, on the most basic level, that we were different and, perhaps purely by virtue of this difference, in some way nobler, more lovably human, than Germans.

As Alma's problems with Bodo grew more extreme, her patience with Joel's lack of work and goals in his life thinned and she became openly critical of him. In the days before their departure for America, as Alma lay weak and haggard, counting the hours until the ordeal of waiting would be over, Joel and his mother regained their close communion.

Joel's reaction to the prospect of their return to his native land was typical: "To start a new life unencumbered by my long string of failures—in America, where no one would know me! This was nothing less than a complete reprieve." As Joel talked with his longtime friend, Peter, who was a member of the East German Film Institute and determined to make a name for himself, Peter assessed Joel's life-style: "The difference between you and me is that you want at all cost to go your way, even though you don't know what that way is. I want my own way too, but I'm more willing to take direction from others."

*Twelve Years* may be read as a spiritual search. Joel Agee, cut off from his writer father by divorce and distance, experienced only once a spiritual encounter with his father, when on his illegal excursions from school he sought the privacy and protection of the woods and read for the first time *The Morning Watch*.

> And it was my father's writing that had opened my eyes. What other writer could charge words with this kind of magic? None! I felt hugely proud. Was it farfetched to imagine that he had written this for me, or at least with me in mind? Why else would he write about a thirteen-year-old boy? But Alma had told me that Richard, the boy, was really a portrait of my father when he was my age. . . . But if I disregarded the incomprehensible churchy emotions—the constant guilt, the wish to suffer for Jesus, or with him—then I could imagine that I was like Richard, and therefore like my father.

At Agee's death, however, Joel did not show any particular sadness and his only visible emotion was disappointment that he would not be going to America. Upon receiving a telegram from Jack Burling announcing the posthumous award of the Pulitzer Prize to Agee, Joel's reaction was: "No, I don't feel proud. I couldn't conceive of what it meant to be proud of someone else's achievement. Glad for them, yes—but proud? Why did he call me Joel Agee and not Joel Uhse, the name he surely knew I had adopted since coming to Germany, and which was printed in my identity papers?" (Readers will note that Agee's name is on the memoir.) Joel felt that the telegram was a reproach both to Alma and to himself and the meaning he read between the lines was that his father was an American and so was Joel; that Alma should never have left Agee, but that she did not know any better; and that Alma should not have taken Joel to a Communist country. Joel was so angry and upset by the telegram and his misguided interpretation, that he did not want to answer. Persuaded by Bodo and Alma that it would be unkind not to do so, he sent the briefest possible response: "Very happy very proud my father grateful to you stop letter follows Joel." His reaction after sending the answer was to feel ashamed for betraying his own feelings. Ironically, he felt as Alma and James Agee had wished to him feel at age four, that Bodo was his father, and he was concerned that he had hurt him.

Despite their very different circumstances, a common thread runs through the lives of father and son. James Agee's poignant descriptions and recurring guilt are echoed in Joel Agee's *Twelve Years*. *A Death in the Family* ends as Rufus, after his father's funeral, walks with his uncle: "'It's time to go home,' and all the way home they walk in silence." *Twelve Years* ends: "Now the whistle blows, the station-master holds up his baton, the train jerks into motion, and a moment later the little group of waving figures is abruptly yanked around a curve and into the past."

Some readers will feel a sadness that James Agee cannot read his son's adolescent autobiography; he would certainly have identified not only with Joel Agee's intention, but also with the beautifully written story of search. Whether the similarity between his own life and that of his famous father is a joy or a burden to Joel Agee is unknown. One can only hope that *Twelve*

*Years*, delightful to read on any level of approach, has served a positive purpose for Joel Agee, that in this book he has focused his past and purged the guilt that prevented his father from performing to his full potential. The evidence in hand is that Joel Agee is a talented writer and the expectation is that he has more to contribute to the literary world.

*Peggy Bach*

### Sources for Further Study

*The Atlantic Monthly.* CCXLVII, June, 1981, p. 101.
*Christian Science Monitor.* LXXIII, July 22, 1981, p. 17.
*Library Journal.* CVI, May 1, 1981, p. 968.
*National Review.* XXXIII, November 27, 1981, p. 1435.
*The New York Review of Books.* XXVIII, July 16, 1981, p. 49.
*The New York Times Book Review.* LXXXVI, April 26, 1981, p. 12.
*The New Yorker.* LVII, May 11, 1981, p. 155.
*Saturday Review.* VIII, May, 1981, p. 74.
*Time.* CXVII, May 11, 1981, p. 90.

# 2081
## A Hopeful View of the Human Future

*Author:* Gerard K. O'Neill (1927-    )
*Publisher:* Simon and Schuster (New York). 286 pp. $13.95
*Type of work:* Futurist speculation

*A long-range forecast by a thoroughgoing technological optimist*

Gerard O'Neill's latest book is, in many ways, a panegyric on gadgetry. *2081* is cast in four parts. The first deals with the problem of forecasting the future; the second is descriptive of five drivers of change; the third is a semifictional scenario of the year 2081; and the final section, "Wild Cards," deals with some further speculations on what the far future may bring. O'Neill makes it clear from the outset that his prime values are freedom and peace; whether his imagined world of 2081 will be one such as to ensure the survival of these values is another question altogether.

O'Neill remarks in his first section that most "futurists" of the past overestimated the role of social and political change and underestimated the role of technology (Sir Francis Bacon's *The New Atlantis* of 1629 must surely stand as an exception). If O'Neill is thinking of current futurists then he may be partly correct. Still, the recent ferment caused, for example, by Islamic fundamentalism occasions second thoughts. At best one can say that science and technology are among the driving forces of the modern age. One would also have to count religion and politics among the drivers of change. If O'Neill is intending to generalize, and it is not clear whether he is, then he has surely misread history. The eminent historian of technology, Lynn White, Jr., has demonstrated conclusively that technology has certainly not always been a driving force; in fact, until the modern era, it never has been. Societies have turned away from science and technology in the past. The period of ancient Greek science was a brief couple of centuries; ancient India turned away from such science as it had; and Islam abandoned science in about the eleventh century in favor of mysticism. Societies have turned away from technology too, and some never adopted technology that was known to exist. It was only in the Christian era of the high Middle Ages that technology was vigorously encouraged, and encouraged by, of all institutions, the Church. Still, there was not a tradition of science-based technology until the nineteenth and twentieth centuries. In the Middle Ages what passed for science—largely Aristotelian science—was taught in the universities. Medieval technology was completely apart from the universities and had no connection with the "science" taught there.

O'Neill, on the other hand, is certainly right in asserting that scientific futurists tend to overestimate the chances for major technological breakthroughs. One only need recall the biomedical scientists of the 1960's forecasting the arrival of the artifical heart by 1975.

The criticism of *The Limits to Growth* (1972) in the first section adds to the reams of paper penned against that tract. Some of the criticism has been justified. It must be remembered, however, that this study was the first seriously to explore the idea of whether there are such limits. O'Neill's contention is that limits can be overcome by technology. Here, whether he knows it or not, he is living in an ideal world of microeconomics. This the technological optimists tend to do. The idea is that when a limit or scarcity approaches, a substitution or solution turns up because this has always happened in the past. Such trend extrapolations can be dangerous. Economists are inclined to think that all scarcities are relative when it is clear that some are absolute. What, for example, can be substituted for clean air? That technology can help with problems of limit is undoubtedly true; that all such problems can be solved is far from self-evident.

O'Neill believes that no existing political system is adequate to deal with the problems of the future. He argues that technological developments will alter "international confrontations in a fundamental way." Hence for him irreversible change is not effected in a political manner but is confined to a single area—that of technology. Technology for O'Neill is apolitical. Viewed solely as a social phenomenon technology *is* apolitical, but when one sees the social matrix in which technology is embedded, one cannot escape the feeling that technology is profoundly political. Karl Marx, and Thomas Hobbes before him, saw that economic power can translate into political power. The same is true of technology. In fact, one cannot talk of technology and leave economics to one side. It has been said that technology creates its own politics.

O'Neill's view of technological innovation is that of simple trend extrapolation. Technological growth, like that of a bacterial colony, follows an S-curve: slow early growth followed by rapid doubling time and eventual stabilization upon a plateau or death. Hence one can put together an "envelope curve" showing a succession of technologies evolving and replacing one another as the function that they were designed to serve is served ever more efficiently. The question, of course, once again, is whether this substitution will continue forever. For O'Neill the future is remarkably surprise-free, and all one needs to do is extrapolate his five drivers of change into the future to obtain a preview of the world of 2081. One need only look at history, however, to see that the future is rarely surprise-free. Great upheavals, discontinuities, sea-changes, or whatever one wishes to call them, certainly are part of the past history of the human species. Sometimes change has been gradual; at others it has been surprisingly swift and has occurred in spans of time much shorter than that of a human life (and life expectancy was much shorter in the past). O'Neill does speak of war and peace issues and even thinks that nuclear weapons will be used at some time in the future. He seems to brush off problems of population growth and food production, ecological problems, and climatic change. In his view, energy and material limits are just comtemporary short-range problems.

O'Neill does not sufficiently appreciate the fact that an incredibly compli-cated technological world such as he sees in 2081 would be, in the felicitous phrase of Harold and Margaret Sprout, "multiply vulnerable." Even now it is clear that the high technology systems on which the developed world depends for its affluence and security are vulnerable to accident and sabotage. The Three Mile Island nuclear incident brings this home, as do isolated incidents of individual sabotage. Transportation and communications systems and water supplies come to mind as especially vulnerable, and one could also mention computerized systems. These systems face the "fundamental problem of fortification." Those who would protect them must prepare for every pos-sible type of sabotage and every possible type of accident. Those who would deliberately disrupt a system have the advantage of setting time and place. The world of 2081 as seen by O'Neill would not be a technological paradise, for unless there was an unprecedented absence of large numbers of alienated individuals it would be necessary to have draconian security measures. This would certainly mean, as surely as the limits to growth necessitates limiting freedom in some areas, a diminution of freedom. Freedom is relative. The limits to growth would curtail some freedoms in order to enhance others. For example, the freedom to breed and the freedom to consume in a throwaway manner would be curtailed in order to enhance the quality of life. In O'Neill's 2081, people would have the comforts afforded by the technology of that time but would be restricted with respect to access to certain vulnerable areas and would have to live with the fear that the systems might "go down." O'Neill's sanguine view of life aboard space colonies seems especially naïve. In his earlier book *The High Frontier* (1977) no mention was made of the problem of security. This shortcoming is evident in *2081* as well. The L-5 people and other space colony enthusiasts never indicate where the jail is going to be. The usual number of people inhabiting a space colony is given at about ten thousand. In an environment of a few degrees above absolute zero and hard vacuum those ten thousand people are not merely going to have to be very good—they are going to have to be very good all of the time.

O'Neill's five drivers of change are computers, automation, space colonies, energy, and communications. For him, it is the combined interactions of these which will bring about the world of 2081. For some reason, biotechnology, which seems as much a driver of change as the other five, is mentioned only as an afterthought near the end of the book. O'Neill's five forces are already active, and he proceeds on the assumption that one need only engage in surprise-free trend extrapolation of each of these, singly and in combination, to get to 2081.

O'Neill is on fairly safe ground in his forecasts concerning computers. Even though there are physical limits to how fast computers can operate, there are advances yet to be made. The year 2081 will surely be shaped by such advances. The "real breakthrough" will come when persons with no special training will have access to computers through spoken commands. O'Neill recognizes that such computer networks as will exist in 2081 will provide numerous opportunities for invasion of privacy and other electronic mischief but thinks that safeguards can be built into the future systems. One does not feel so sure when one looks at the use to which computers have been put in the Soviet Union.

Artificial intelligence he holds to be very far off, and he even thinks the term should be avoided, but a technological assessment searching for the derived consequences of the computer revolution would have to deal with the very real question of artificial intelligence. Artificially intelligent machines would use "heuristic" self-programming as opposed to the deductive algorithms of today's computers. Such machines would be able to approximate human thought processes of an intuitive sort more closely than today's machines can do. O'Neill's attitude toward artificial intelligence is consistent with his surprise-free view of the future. Who can say when the breakthrough to artificial intelligence will come (if it ever does)? Here, O'Neill is guilty of what futurist Arthur C. Clarke terms a "failure of imagination," Clarke's phrase for discounting the future.

With respect to automation, *2081* sees a world of new machines with no moving parts and hence one where the devil of friction has been exorcised. Increasing use of laser will make possible the fabrication of precisely machined parts. This is an extension of present tendencies. There will occur, O'Neill thinks, a comprehensive evolution of the six levels of intelligence and versatility. These are: level one—machines which would be familiar to persons alive today such as simple punches, stamps, benders, and so on; level two—machines which attend the level one machines and which move around to perform simple "pick-and-place" operations; level three—machines which are computer-controlled and which do actual fabrication; level four—machines which tend to and repair level threes and which are due early in the twenty-first century; level five—where humans first enter the picture, using interacting computers in the design process; level six—fully human, involving judgment and creativity. The interactive six levels eventually are to produce self-replicating machines, and once this has been achieved there is the possibility that geometric growth of such machines could take place. Such machines would not be applied to every operation but would be useful in certain areas such as outer space—self-creating modules would eliminate countless man-hours in construction.

O'Neill correctly points out that much technological unemployment would result from automation. Persons thus victimized would be supported by welfare payments. O'Neill forecasts a hobby boom for 2081. Although he does not term it as such, O'Neill has described the "technocracy" so many have written about—a society where a few technicians keep the whole affair running for the vast majority who have no qualifications or desires to be involved. Once again, although he does not use the language, O'Neill has sketched out a paternalistic society where the five percent at the top provide for the ninety-five percent at the bottom.

The next of O'Neill's drivers is space colonization, the construction of large habitats in outer space which will serve as home for thousands of people and which, O'Neill believes, someday will harbor a larger percentage of humanity than the earth's surface. He believes that the movement into space will mark the movement to an economics of abundance, for it will be quite easy to expand in space without running up on somebody else's jealously-guarded boundaries and there will be a super abundance of materials for machines, self-replicating or otherwise, to use in fabrication. O'Neill holds that even before 2081 a "substantial" fraction of the human population may be calling outer space home; some will never set foot on earth. The feasibility of space colonies has been studied and O'Neill cites a study indicating that the first major leap into space, a manufacturing complex, could be achieved in ten years with a capital investment comparable to that of the Alaska Pipeline.

The longest chapter in Part II is that on energy. O'Neill deals with most of the energy technologies discussed in the popular media. He repeats the truism that energy (on earth) is likely to be more expensive in 2081 because the low-entropy sources will have been exhausted, especially petroleum. Technology, however, will come to the rescue—there will be substitutes for fossil fuels and energy-efficient devices will be delivered. In space, of course, there will be no problem, for the sun's energy will be easily captured.

The final technological driver of change is communications. A worldwide interconnected system is envisaged with personal communication possible between any two places on earth—this through the use of advanced communications satellites in space. One derived consequence of space colonization will be some decline of voice-to-voice communication because of the psychologically irritating time-lag created by great distance. The communications of 2081 will be merely an extension of existing technologies.

Some consequences of the combined effects of the drivers of change may now be considered. The century of industrialization between now and 2081 will see long-term solutions to energy problems and will lead to individual incomes that today would be associated only with wealthy persons. Population will be near-stable. Nuclear terrorism is likely to be prevalent in the next century. Nuclear war would not be a total disaster for the human race, for much of the race will be living in outer space.

Finally, O'Neill sees three possiblities for the human future: first, the destruction of civilization; second, stasis; and finally, the dispersal of humankind thoughout vast regions of space, including that space outside of the solar system. Self-contained space colonies would thus spread humanity out into the larger cosmos in the next stage of the human adventure.

What is one to make of all of this? As remarked earlier, O'Neill is a confirmed technological optimist. There are certain difficulties with this position. Certain unprovable assumptions lie at the heart of it—that the future will be like the past ("something will turn up") and that technology will solve most or all of humanity's pressing problems ("turn the engineers loose"). It is not obvious that something has always turned up, and not all problems are engineering problems. If technological optimism has certain difficulties (such as ignoring "Murphy's Law"), should one turn to technological pessimism or join the ranks of those who are opposed to science and technology? Of course not. There are not two alternatives but three. A little-used word, meliorism, should again be given the currency it enjoyed during the Enlightenment. Technological meliorism maintains that the world is neither intrinsically good nor bad but that, rather, it could go either way. The meliorist view is not guilty, as is technological optimism, of promising more than can be delivered or of creating a false sense of security. With this in mind one can say that O'Neill has properly recognized some drivers of change and also that there is much promise in them. They will not bring the utopian state, but many humans will be better off in 2081. Nevertheless, and O'Neill agrees, things are going to get worse in the short run before they get better.

*Robert L. Hoffman*

### Sources for Further Study

*Choice*. LXII, September, 1981, p. 257.
*Christian Science Monitor*. LXXIII, July 22, 1981, p. 17.
*Library Journal*. CVI, May 15, 1981, p. 1090.
*The New York Times Book Review*. LXXXVI, May 3, 1981, p. 15.
*Saturday Review*. VIII, May, 1981, p. 73.
*School Library Journal*. XXVIII, December, 1981, p. 89.
*Sky and Telescope*. LXII, September, 1981, p. 257.

# UNDERSTANDING INFLATION

*Author:* John Case (1944-    )
*Publisher:* William Morrow and Company (New York). 228 pp. $9.95
*Type of work:* Political economics
*Locale:* The United States

*Why Americans are paying more, getting less, and what they can do about it*

Which comes first—the prescription or the description? In any political argument composed well, it is impossible to answer this question with any certainty. Description of a problem, though typically presented prior to the prescription, serves to prefigure the proposed remedy, and that is how it should be, for who would want a described problem, with its implicit explanation, to be divorced from the chosen solution? A good description, in other words, narrows the choice of conclusions, and the more complete the description is, the less room is left for alternative implications, alternative courses of appropriate action.

Furthermore, political discourse requires one to use language that is not completely neutral. Issues must inevitably involve partisan positions that relate not only to judgments of value but also to judgments of fact. It is these latter assessments, or, more precisely, the words selected to express them, that distinguish one politically relevant description from another.

*Understanding Inflation* is political ecomony at its best, and is therefore a perfect example of the descriptive-prescriptive interdependence just discussed. In exploring "why we pay more, get less, and what we as Americans can do about it," John Case spends the first 175 pages on the "why," leaving only the last twenty to the "what." Although the reader must wait so long for the author's explicit statement of solution, it is all there, albeit indirectly, in the earlier chapters, or at least almost all there, for Case does at times appear to be pointing to a solution that is very different from the one finally presented.

The main thrust of the book, the author's account of inflation, involves numerous elements. To understand inflation, one must consider it as a system, a system involving the interplay of big business, "not-so-big business," labor (including unions and licensed professional associations), and government (in its roles as employer, borrower, and consumer). As the book jacket so succinctly states, Case shows exactly how and why inflation has become a built-in feature of the American economy, as various interest groups have combined to try to insure that their share of the economy's income—whether in the form of profits, wages, or fees for services—will not fall; and how government protection of these groups' prerogatives and government spending have sustained the price rises. In addition, the impact of historical events such as the Vietnam War and OPEC actions are considered as exogenous factors that are basically beyond the control of American economic policy. What

Case presents, then, is a picture of the American political economy that is quite pluralistic. A variety of fairly equal interest groups, in the context of an overly responsive government, are seen as inflation's primary cause, and impacting on this pluralistic system from the outside are those world events beyond control. All the pieces are thus in place in the so-called puzzle of inflation.

What does all this entail in terms of what should be done? Obviously the stimulus-response relationship between interest groups and government must be broken, somehow stopping either the demands being made on government or the government's responsiveness. To attempt the former is seen as unrealistic: "Everyone, given half a chance, asks for more." Besides, in practice, since the specific "voluntary" self-controls would actually be determined by those in power, the call for everyone to sacrifice is likely to lead to a situation resembling that envisioned in a 1980 letter to the editor of *The New York Times*: "The poor will give up food stamps and summer jobs; the rich will give up Federal programs to aid the poor."

Instead, Case proposes to do something that will not put "an unfair burden on those . . . who are politically weakest." He proposes to focus on the government end of the process. Responsiveness must be drastically curtailed by adopting the only practical alternative left. In order to put a freeze on the inflationary spiral, controls must be imposed on wages and prices. Then the "demands from individual groups can be refused because everyone is being asked to sacrifice." A pluralist prescription thus emerges from a pluralist description of the underlying cause of inflation.

Yet this prescription encounters the same difficulty that an attempt at *self-control* among interest groups does, namely, how to achieve equity between the rich few and the rest of the population. Case makes no attempt to deal with this problem, which is to be expected from the fact that his ability to do so would require a departure from his overall picture of the American political economy. It is a picture, remember, that is pluralist; and a pluralist framework is not at all conducive to a concern, let alone a solution, involving the unfair burden that wage controls impose on those who are politically and economically at the bottom. As suggested earlier, however, despite Case's explicit pluralist statements, one also finds some descriptions that point to an alternative prescription. It is an alternative based on a class (or radical) rather than a group (or pluralist) analysis.

These nonpluralist descriptions are found only in the last chapter, however, in the course of defending price controls against a number of familiar objections. The descriptions arise when Case turns to a consideration of *why* recession does not cure inflation as well as it once did and *who* suffers most from this increasingly ineffective remedy. The burden of recession, notes the author, usually falls on people who already were not doing too well. It is a burden borne least by those who "not coincidentally" are most likely to prescribe recession to lessen inflation. As for the reason behind recession's increasing ineffectiveness, Case turns his attention to the role of big business. He notes that in 1980 the domestic auto industry, for example, responded to drastically declining sales by raising its prices between six and nine percent, and later he observes that "only a small number of prices respond quickly and accurately to changes in supply and demand. Others are raised to protect profit margins . . . whether or not business is good." The pricing that is unresponsive to the market occurs with most goods manufactured in the "highly concentrated" industries. It is these prices that the author proposes be controlled, and the effect of such control over such industries would be to turn them into "regulated public utilities." In contrast, the prices among not-so-big businesses, operating in a relatively competitive market, would be allowed to rise even more freely than they are able to at present under the restraints of their biggest customers—big business.

The author does, therefore, show some awareness of the relevance of class factors to an understanding of inflation, but not much. Neither the full impact of recession on poorer citizens nor the full influence of giant corporations on inflation is explored. For example, no mention is made of the fact that, in the deep recession of 1973-1975, prices in the not-so-big business sector rose only 1.8 percent, but in the big business sector prices rose an astounding 27 percent! It is, in short, Case's failure to pursue the class-based, radical analysis of which he gives only glimpses that render his understanding of inflation much less realistic than, say, Howard Sherman's well-reasoned and statistically grounded account in *Stagflation* (1976).

Be that as it is, there are other problems with the author's view. Under his plan, the government is left free to set wages, prices, and benefits (though welfare payments are not mentioned) at whatever levels deemed necessary to advance particular policies, and so, as Case correctly observes, these wage and price controls would serve to remove the veil covering the struggle over who gets what. Such a policy would make the economic struggle no more political than before, but a good deal more public.

How much the struggle would result in a more equitable distribution of society's burdens and benefits depends upon how much the distribution of ecomomic power would be equalized under Case's proposal. If the governmental regulation of big business failed to change the distribution of wealth based on corporate ownership, then surely the same economic stratum that usually wins at the expense of the rest of the population would continue to do so—even if more publicly than before. Just as surely, the new battles over policy would more sharply reveal the class conflict that uncontrolled inflation now camouflages.

If, on the other hand, the author's prescription does involve a fundamental change (which seems doubtful) in the nature of corporate ownership, then one can only wonder how his pluralist account is at all useful in understanding the class struggle that would be needed to obtain public control over those corporate oligopolies that represent the primary cause of inflation today.

*E. Gene DeFelice*

## Sources for Further Study

*Book World*. XI, March 29, 1981, p. 8.
*Kirkus Reviews*. LXIX, February 15, 1981, p. 259.
*Library Journal*. CVI, February 1, 1981, p. 341.
*Progressive*. XLV, July, 1981, p. 56.
*Publishers Weekly*. CCXIX, January 30, 1981.

# UNRELIABLE MEMOIRS

*Author:* Clive James (1939-    )
*Publisher:* Alfred A. Knopf (New York). 171 pp. $10.00
*Type of work:* Autobiography
*Time:* 1939-1962
*Locale:* Sydney, Australia

*A critic's humorous account of growing up in Australia*

Clive James has been well-known in Great Britain for the past decade as a book reviewer for several publications, television columnist for the *Observer*, and television personality. (A collection of his essays about literature and television, *First Reactions*, was published in the United States in 1980.) *Unreliable Memoirs*, perhaps only the first volume of James's autobiography, does not deal with this aspect of his life, however, but with his first twenty-two years in his native Australia, ending as he leaves home to conquer England. He sees this book, in part, as an act of exorcism: "Sick of being a prisoner of my childhood, I want to get it behind me." *Unreliable Memoirs* is almost an Australian *Huckleberry Finn* (1885) as its naïve, comic hero travels about Sydney, having misadventure after misadventure, resisting most efforts to civilize him, learning about human nature and about himself, finally lighting out for new territory. James calls the book a fictional autobiography in which people's names and attributes have been changed, "a figment got up to sound like truth."

James wants to explain what growing up in Australia in the 1940's and 1950's was like, to entertain with his comic exploits, but *Unreliable Memoirs* also has its serious side. James was born in Sydney in 1939, son of a mechanic and an upholsterer. His father joined the military not long afterward and spent most of the war in a Japanese prison camp. He survived the imprisonment only to die when the plane taking him home after the war crashed in a typhoon. Except for the occasional aunt and senile grandfather, James grew up with only his mother for company. Without using his father's death to justify any of the numerous flaws in his character, James had a "tiresomely protracted adolescence" as a result. Perhaps the most important of the book's themes is its hero's search for a father, for a sense of family. Until he went to university, almost everyone he felt close to deserted him or died. He seems to think of Australia less as his fatherland than as a fatherless land.

James presents himself as a spoiled, undisciplined, careless, insensitive child, as someone who could not and still cannot deal with authority. A benefit of his loneliness was that he became a reader while quite young, reading and rereading old issues of *Collier's*, *Saturday Evening Post*, and other popular magazines. (He did no "serious" reading before he went to Sydney University.)

James writes charmingly and amusingly about what is for the most part a rather ordinary childhood. Delightful are his accounts of constructing trenches, tunnels, and dams throughout the neighborhood, destroying an old lady's cherished poppy beds when a huge train of carts he had devised whipped out of control while roaring down the hill, learning about and avoiding Australia's numerous dangerous snakes and spiders, imitating his comic-book and movie-serial heroes by becoming the Flash of Lightning and leading a gang of masked-and-caped kids, falling in love with the young woman in charge of his Cub Scout troop. Then there is the hilarious story of the "dunny man," one of those responsible for picking up a full privy tank each week and replacing it with an empty one, who tripped over James's bicycle and was completely covered by excrement.

After scoring high on an IQ test in the fourth grade, James was sent to a school for "gifted" students. During this period he blamed his loneliness on his intellect but later decided that there was "nothing extraordinary" about his mind. (James's modesty throughout the book is admirable but grows tiresome.) Because this progressive school allowed its students to devote half their school days to pursuing their special interests, James, a war and airplane buff, spent his afternoons building sand-pit battlefields full of lead soldiers and memorizing air-recognition charts. At eleven he could recognize photographs of every aircraft ever built but knew little else.

During this time he constantly fell in love with little girls he called Lacy Skirts and Pocket Venus, but until he went to the university, the painfully shy James had to worship the opposite sex from afar: "Wallflower was an insufficient word to describe me. I was a wallshadow, a wallstain." After he got to high school, his first sexual experience turned into a typical Jamesian disaster. All the boys in the neighborhood were taking turns with the local nymphomaniac; when James's turn came, he could not get an erection. In the same spirit as that of the heroes of the boys' adventure stories he loved so much, he carried on anyway, and the girl did not seem to notice his failure.

High school involved what James considers to be the biggest mistake in his life. He turned down a scholarship to Sydney Boys' High School, which people fought to get into, to go to Sydney Technical High, despite his mother's protests, because he thought he wanted to be an aeronautical engineer and because his best friend was a student there. The decision was a disastrous one, not only because the friend abandoned him and the school was mediocre but also because he discovered he had no aptitude for mathematics and the sciences. He still regrets not having received the solid academic training, especially in the humanities, that he would have received at the other school. He was not even accepted into the Air Cadets because of too much albumen in his blood. (He did not successfully join any group until after high school.)

Not only was James no longer an academic star in high school, but also he seemed to have stopped growing and went suddenly from being taller than most of his classmates to being shorter. He spent hours in front of his mirror examining himself: "Why did the back of my head stick out so far? Why did my jaw stick out so little? As all the boys around me started turning into men, I began to wonder if perhaps I was not doomed to look boyish forever." The young James was most preoccupied with the smallness of his penis and went through a "Gypsy Rose Lee routine of extraordinary subtlety" in the locker room to keep anyone from seeing it. He finally grew to normal size near the end of high school but almost ended his sex life before it started when he ran into a barbed-wire fence: "Another quarter of an inch on those barbs and my subsequent love-life would have consisted entirely of bad scenes from *The Sun Also Rises.*" He was so embarrassed by the accident that he did not have his wound treated.

James survived his last years of high school with humor, attracting crowds with elaborately exaggerated stories about his imaginary exploits. His clowning "never made me especially popular, but at least I avoided unpopularity." Humor helped James in many ways, but it has also been a drawback: "For many years I was to remain a prisoner of my own act, like a ventriloquist taken over by his dummy. Even today, unless I watch myself carefully, I take refuge in levity." A paradox about *Unreliable Memoirs* is that while the comedy makes the book entertaining and James, as both protagonist and author, likable, it also causes some of the serious moments, as when he discusses his relationship with his mother, to seem unnecessarily somber in comparison. The same is true of James as critic; most of his reviews and essays are so witty that the reader is always looking for the punch line and is sometimes disappointed when there is none.

Even though he finished high school with an academic record which might have ruined him for life, James, as a war orphan, was entitled to a free university education and went to Sydney University. It, like his high school, was mostly mediocre with the emphasis on turning out graduates, not on imaginative thinking.

James went to work for the school newspaper, staffed mostly by bohemians, and became involved in numerous cultural activities. At first he was extremely naïve about what his new friends were talking about: "What kind of a car, I wondered, was a Ford Madox Ford? What sort of conflict was an Evelyn War?" He finally started serious reading, both for his courses and on his own, and his long-delayed education was under way.

He quickly began copying the avant-garde poses of his friends. "My cocksureness must have been terrible to behold," he writes. "Night after night I reduced my mother to tears with my intellectual arrogance." He even had a girl friend, though sex was still out of the question. Most important, the campus bohemians became the family he had never had. James's need for family was so strong that he enjoyed the seventy-seven days of basic training during his compulsory national service; he even liked drill which helped him gain "my first real measure of self-sufficiency." In an episode he labels a figment of his imagination, his basic training was completed when a beautiful older woman he had worshiped from afar seduced him.

In his last years at university, James grew as a writer in his work on the newspaper and for revues, gradually imitating his friends less while finding his own voice, learning from writers he loved: William Butler Yeats, E. E. Cummings, F. Scott Fitzgerald, H. L. Mencken, Albert Camus. By his final year he wrote almost half the newspaper, including angry letters about his own articles, and was asked to review books for the *Sydney Morning Herald*. He got a full-time position on the *Herald* after graduation, spending most of his time rewriting unsolicited contributions, a task he found to be "the best practical training I ever received" because he learned that "writing is essentially a matter of saying things in the right order."

James soon realized that he was only marking time, that he knew nothing worth knowing, and decided, although he had never been out of New South Wales, to go to England. He expected to be gone for five years, but he has never returned there to live, feeling he has been gone too long, thinking that he may have made a mistake by forsaking Australia, trying unsuccessfully to forget it, his memories of Sydney growing "more numerous and powerful." James the partial orphan became James the complete exile.

James's journey into adulthood and toward fame ends in *Unreliable Memoirs* with his seeing the lights of Southampton. The remainder of his experiences, including continuing his education at Cambridge, will be described, one hopes, in future volumes. James realizes he is not that unusual as a person and as a thinker, but he is worth considerable attention for his humor and his extraordinary skills at delineating time, place, and character.

*Michael Adams*

## Sources for Further Study

*Critic*. XXXIX, May 1, 1981, p. 5.
*Library Journal*. CVI, April 15, 1981, p. 884.
*Listener*. CIII, April 24, 1980, p. 545.
*The New Republic*. CLXXXIV, March 21, 1981, p. 38.
*New Statesman*. XCIX, June 13, 1980, p. 908.
*The New York Review of Books*. XXVIII, April 2, 1981, p. 29.
*The New York Times Book Review*. LXXXVI, February 15, 1981, p. 7.
*Newsweek*. XCVII, February 23, 1981, p. 76.
*Observer*. April 27, 1980, p. 38.
*Times Literary Supplement*. April 25, 1980, p. 469.

# VAN WYCK BROOKS
## A Writer's Life

*Author:* Raymond Nelson (1938-    )
*Publisher:* E. P. Dutton (New York). 332 pp. $21.95
*Type of work:* Literary biography
*Time:* 1886-1963
*Locale:* Primarily the United States

*A definitive critical biography of the distinguished American literary historian and critic*

Since Van Wyck Brooks's death in 1963, his reputation has been well served, both as a writer and a figure influential for his time, by two essentially critical sutdies, James Vitelli's *Van Wyck Brooks* (1969) and William Wasserstrom's *The Legacy of Van Wyck Brooks* (1972); further, Gladys Brooks, the writer's second wife, has penned an affectionate memoir, *If Strangers Meet: A Memory* (1967), and James Hoopes a competent biography, *Van Wyck Brooks: In Search of American Culture* (1977). To these books may now be added the definitive biography by Raymond Nelson, a volume comprehensive and critically astute, that treats not only the writer's life but also his impact upon his generation.

A present-day reader may wonder at the extraordinary scholarly interest that Brooks still provokes among admirers. His work, although extensive and widely read between 1915 and 1932, began to lose critical support with *The Life of Emerson* (1932) and gradually, for the next two and a half decades, seemed ever more out of touch with the mainstream of American criticism. Even these years of declining critical acclaim, however, were productive for Brooks's massive research and publication. His lifework was the five-volume *Makers and Finders: A History of the Writer in America 1800-1915* (1952), a succession of major works which established for good his reputation as America's most industrious literary historian, including *The Flowering of New England* (1936), *New England: Indian Summer* (1940), *The World of Washington Irving* (1944), *The Times of Melville and Whitman* (1947), and *The Confident Years: 1885-1915* (1952). In spite of this vast literary output, Brooks's position today, according to Raymond Nelson, "is not so much resisted, attacked, or modified as it is simply ignored. Particularly in the academy, a generation of literary professionals has come of age either not knowing of Brooks's achievement or knowing it only as a sort of curious anachronism."

Reasons for this apparent neglect of the author are not difficult to assess, and Nelson treats with fairness and perception Brooks's limitations as well as his strengths. In his literary investigation, Brooks was far more interested in culture, in the total impact of an epoch upon writers, than are most modern-day scholars. Less concerned with the "spirit" of place or time, they are generally concerned with the close analysis of formal structures and, in a larger sense, with understanding the literary conventions of the time that promoted such structures.

Brooks, on the other hand, was rarely interested in structural analysis, and although his research was monumental—while preparing for *Makers and Finders*, according to Nelson, "Brooks read every work by every nineteenth-century American writer of even the slightest merit"—the historian's judgments are often idiosyncratic, favoring in some cases minor authors over major, and judging the sweep of literature as a cultural tide from which discernible streams can be isolated and defined. Contemporary literary historians, for the most part skeptical about Brooks's large generalizations and seemingly moralistic attitudes, are far more cautious about literary rankings and discrete groupings of writers. Today, as Nelson somewhat ruefully observes, an audience for Brooks's impressionistic and moralistic criticism is on the wane; but Nelson argues with considerable force that future generations are bound to profit a great deal from Brooks's heroic method of literary synthesis.

Like other students of Brooks, Nelson has the major biographical problem of treating with nearly equal attention the man's life and his work. So deeply was Brooks involved in the life of the mind, that his activities mostly revolved around assiduous literary pursuits. For good reason, Nelson subtitles his study "A Writer's Life." Whenever Brooks was not reading whole libraries of books for research purposes or writing and revising his own work, he was spending much of his remaining time thinking about projects, corresponding with other writers, or reevaluating his ideas in the light of current scholarship. In his research for *The Flowering of New England*, for example, he read some 825 books. Up to that time, according to Nelson, "no literary history of similar depth and range had yet been attempted, and the task was possible only for a man who had the rare freedom of time, and the rarer dedication, to use it." Such scholarship required a disciplined temperament, habits of intense concentration, and a willingness to sacrifice in place of the ordinary pleasures of life a great deal of time devoted to solitary study. After rising at 5:30 A.M., he would dress himself formally, with waistcoat and tie ("out of respect," Nelson says, "for the work he was to do"), generally compose with pen until midafternoon, then spend the remainder of the day reading, taking notes, or indexing on three-by-five-inch slips of paper material to be filed away for later needs. For Brooks's biographers, these admirable habits of long and painstaking scholarship are necessary to recite, but difficult to describe in any way that fires the reader's imagination. Plainly put, much of Brooks's life—by far the greater part of his laboring hours—was sedentary.

An even greater problem for Brooks's biographers is to discover episodes of excitement in his relations with others. True to his high calling as a historian, Brooks throughout most of his life was a quiet, rational, gentle man; a dutiful husband and father; a loyal and empathetic friend; even to enemies (with a few exceptions) a fair adversary who could forgive without rancor. One such exception to his usual tolerance was his curious lifelong opposition to T. S. Eliot, whom he considered weak and dangerous. Apart from this idiosyncratic animosity, Brooks was customarily a genial, even-tempered intellectual whose friendships, especially with men of such fine character as Maxwell Perkins, Lewis Mumford, John Hall Wheelock, and Newton Arvin, lasted for many years with mutual respect. Summarizing Brooks's character, Nelson is moved to write: "I would argue . . . that he was above all a good man, a man to be trusted, as well as a remarkably talented man, and that it is both the privilege and responsibility of the biographer to trust him."

Any fair-minded reader must consent to this judgment. Indeed, the picture that Nelson evokes of Brooks is somewhat affectionately nostalgic—that of an old-fashioned gentleman of honor, a Yankee cast in the old mold of good-humored skepticism, of industriousness, practicality, and decency. In his relationships with loved ones—especially his often difficult years with his first wife, Eleanor Kenyon Stimson—he seems always to have been a fastidious, earnest, principled gentleman, with his starched high collar and muted tie asserting his simple dignity, a kind of American Victorian. During his long years of courting Eleanor, he wrote her idealistic letters about life, art, and philosophy. Later, after marriage, while he struggled to earn enough money to support his wife and two sons, he was sometimes overwhelmed by feelings of guilt and inadequacy at his failure to provide for them a comfortable home or an environment of stability. Nevertheless he chose to work at odious, mind-dulling jobs simply to earn enough money to get by, rather than to abandon his grand designs as literary historian. For a number of years he worked as a hack at the editorial room of the Century Company. He preferred to keep his income as a dictionary consultant down to subsistence level in order not to compromise his ideals. Above all, he yearned to maintain his integrity as a writer free from the pressures of social conformism.

During his middle years, Brooks's bitterly won independence and his habits of self-abnegation were nearly to cost him his sanity. By 1925 he showed clear signs of the "nervous breakdown" that was to afflict him for the next six years, growing in severity to the point at which he could be described as quite insane. These signs had begun earlier, perhaps as early as the tormented dreams of his youth, but by the 1920's, as he submerged his personal life in his intensive research for *The Ordeal of Mark Twain* (1920) and, with even greater absorption, *The Pilgrimage of Henry James* (1925), he appeared, from the inspection of loved ones and close friends, increasingly out of touch with reality. According to Nelson, Brooks's mental condition—described somewhat vaguely as paranoic but certainly a classic case of depression—deteriorated as a result of the author's identification with both American writers. Brooks believed that Mark Twain's "ordeal" was psychologically induced by that novelist's unresolved conflicts between the demands of art on the one hand and society on the other. Unable to reconcile this conflict Twain—as Brooks interpreted the basic "malady" of his life—was an incomplete man and a limited artist. In arriving at this interpretation, Brooks was forced to examine critically his own aspirations as a free artist bound by the demands of his family and associates. Brooks had always modeled his ideal character on that of the Irish painter John Butler Yeats, father of the poet William Butler Yeats. In the elder Yeats, Brooks saw a liberated artist, free to make the proper choices in vocation or social interaction that would enhance life. Comparing his own disciplined existence, involving the many personal and literary obligations he had to meet, with that of Yeats, Brooks believed that he was failing to live up to the high calling he had earlier set for himself.

Turning to his research on Henry James, Brooks became still more despondent as he compared that novelist's imagined problems with his own. To Brooks, James was a writer torn by two contrary principles: to remain in America as the spokesman of his native, unrefined culture; or to travel abroad and live in England, primarily, as the setting for a sophisticated culture more hospitable to the claims of an artist. Brooks interpreted Henry James's supposed conflict in the light of his own deeply ambivalent feelings about American culture, about Protestantism as opposed to aesthetic Catholicism, and about the role of an artist thrust into a community of protest. Using an impressionistic style to approach the complexities of James's psychology, Brooks identified his own character with that of the novelist and, according to Nelson, began to believe himself also a man without national roots, moving in the direction of an effete aestheticism.

Whatever the true causes for Brooks's breakdown from 1925 to 1931, the effects were devastating. Nelson describes in harrowing detail the course of Brooks's depression. Not until he received a foundation bequest, the generous gift of his wife's family, enabling him to write without the burden of accepting jobs at literary magazines, would he slowly work his way out of the depths of despondency to regain his sense of confidence and purpose. Nevertheless, his later years, notable for the vastness of his literary enterprise and the significant recognition that he was to receive from his colleagues, seem to Nelson somewhat anticlimactic, a falling-off from Brooks's promise as the chief literary historian of his generation.

To be sure, Nelson allows his readers objective information to make their own judgments about Brooks's achievements. His treatment of Brooks is as fair and generous as the historian's own studies of American writers. Like Brooks, who was a great stylist, a master of the succinct, memorable phrase, Nelson can condense ideas to their pithy essence, and can express with pungency scenes that demand literary savor. He is especially convincing as he re-creates the flavor of student life at Harvard during Brooks's golden years; as he establishes the intellectual climate of writers and editors involved in the publication of *The Seven Arts* (1916-1917); and, perhaps most notably, as he describes the "war of the critics" raging in the literary magazines of the 1920's. Nelson not only describes with precision social-historical epochs; but he also makes them come alive. Another substantial bonus for any reader of Brooks's biography is the considerable light that Nelson throws upon the careers of important contemporary writers as well, friends and foes alike of Brooks, who helped shape a rich, exciting, intellectual world. In understanding Van Wyck Brooks's life and struggles, Nelson helps readers to understand better the world they have inherited from this great "maker and finder."

*Leslie Mittleman*

## Sources for Further Study

*Best Sellers*. XLI, January, 1982, p. 380.
*Book World*. XI, November 8, 1981, p. 10.
*Library Journal*. CVI, September 1, 1981, p. 1632.
*National Review*. XXXIII, October 16, 1981, p. 1215.
*New Leader*. LXIV, December 14, 1981, p. 18.
*The New Republic*. CLXXXV, November 18, 1981, p. 31.
*The New York Times Book Review*. LXXXVI, November 1, 1981, p. 9.
*The New Yorker*. LVII, November 23, 1981, p. 225.

# VILLAGES

*Author:* Richard Critchfield (1931-    )
*Publisher:* Anchor Press/Doubleday & Company (Garden City, New York). Illustrated. 388 pp. $17.95
*Type of work:* Anthropology

*A gifted reporter/amateur anthropologist portrays seventeen Third World villages, probes for the universal qualities of village existence, and appraises the chances for substantial material improvement in village society*

Richard Critchfield has produced a book so questionable in its conception and so flawed in its execution that the several critical establishments into whose province it ranges are bound to dismiss it out of hand. Nevertheless, it is a wonder of a book—a stupendous tour de force; a constant provocation; a richly philosophical text; a fine blend of narration, assemblage of facts, polemic, and ideation. Critchfield's subject is the true "Great Silent Majority": the sixty-one percent of the world's people who are villagers. When one reckons that villagers comprise well over seventy percent of the populations of Asia and Africa, this figure seems even more impressive. Critchfield wishes to reveal the essential contours of village existence—psychic as well as economic contours; to situate the village experience in the context of cultural history; and to discern the general outline of "the great change" that village culture is currently undergoing.

There are well over two million villages, distributed over all the continents, existing within radically different linguistic, religious, and climatological milieus, connected to diverse economic systems. How is this "subject" to be studied? More important, is this a genuine subject at all? What qualifies as a "village"? Can a movable Bedouin tent settlement, a war-ravaged south Vietnamese rice *ville*, a tourist-infested Mexican highland hamlet, and an eastern Colorado cattle town be weighed in the same scale? Peasant, rural worker, tribesmen, semiagricultural nomad, farmer—these key terms all must come into play when one discusses villages, but each presents severe definitional problems. To qualify as a "village," must the entity in question be essentially agricultural—or can commercial or industrial activities be "mixed in" without damaging its claim to village status? Further, what are the proper conditions for studying village culture? Should villages undergoing war, famine, or economic boom be regarded as out of bounds?

With the maturation of both anthropology and development economics as academic disciplines in this century, there have emerged several great debates on how these methodological problems should be treated. Critchfield, a journalist, is quite aware of the relevant arguments, but he prefers to employ provisional definitions and get on with the investigation, choosing those audaciously direct routes that only great reporters seem to know.

To learn about villages, Critchfield has spent vast quantities of time living in—and then periodically returning to—specific villages. His preoccupation with village life is ultimately traceable to his rearing in rural North Dakota, as well as early experiences as a student of folklore in Europe, soldier in the Korean War, and teacher in India. The decisive experience, however, was Vietnam, where he survived four years as a war correspondent for the *Washington Star*. There, Critchfield gradually realized that to grasp the true shape of that hideous struggle, he had to study the traditional Confucian culture of ordinary Vietnamese in their villages. (*The Long Charade*, which appeared in 1968, details Critchfield's findings.) This experience engendered a consuming interest in the nature of village culture. Critchfield devoted the next twelve years to reporting about Third World villages. His long sojourn in Indonesia gave rise to the book *The Golden Bowl Be Broken* (1974), while a year in upper Egypt provided the material for the magnificent portrait *Shahhat: An Egyptian* (1978). Readers of the *Christian Science Monitor* and *The Economist* have been the main beneficiaries of Critchfield's journalistic efforts in the last decade.

Critchfield's passion for directly encountering his subject matter knows few boundaries. The social scientific concept of the "participant observer" utterly fails to do justice to Critchfield's modus operandi, for Critchfield obviously loves village culture and the diverse agricultural practices which sustain it. Sober and sophisticated reporter though he is, he clearly is engaged in rediscovering himself and thereby a lost America as he comes to comprehend the peculiar mysteries of traditional cultures in the throes of modernization. Critchfield is also adventurous in that peculiar, restless, quasisuicidal way of many survivors of Vietnam. The German word *Tollkühnheit*, which combines in one unity the qualities of madness, exuberance, audaciousness, and fearlessness, seems most appropriate to describe Critchfield's "methodology." Thus, *Villages'* first chapter finds Critchfield in Salvador, Brazil, carried away in the insanely violent and ecstatic six-day celebration of *Carneval*.

> Once you start dancing there's no stopping. You go on and on, one night fading into the next, a few hours of exhausted sleep, your *mortalha* sodden and stiff with sweat, downing gallons of beer to slake a steady thirst, finding, losing your friends, moving to the African samba beat, caught in the compulsive power of the music and its splintered sensual universe.

A serious injury, sustained when a bandstand collapsed over him, ended the revelry of Critchfield and some fifty other people.

In Indonesia, in 1970, Critchfield spent a week in an urban brothel, interviewing the women who worked there. In Mexico, against all the odds, he searched for and found the real Jesús Sanchez, the father of the family studied by Oscar Lewis and immortalized in the classic anthropological study, *The Children of Sanchez* (1961). Wherever he is, Critchfield insists on participating fully in all essential agricultural labor; he may be the reigning expert on village harvesting techniques and harvest festivals. Intrigued by traditional religion, he has placed himself under the "care" of all manner of fortune-tellers, prophets, shamen, conjurers, sorcerers, and magicians. In eastern Nepal he once saw a ghost. He goes about with the "knowledge" that he will die on September 8, 1988, from a gastro-intestinal ailment—the prediction of an uncannily accurate Indian soothsayer.

Anthropologists are rightfully admired for their careful longitudinal studies of particular cultural groups. The great expert on village life, George M. Foster, has focused on a single Mexican village for over thirty-six years. Study periods of over four years are not uncommon, with follow-up work as time passes. Critchfield's effort is certainly unprecedented, however, for he has spent long periods of time in over a dozen villages at widely scattered places on the globe. He has also taken pains to return at regular intervals to these places. The depth and longevity of Critchfield's engagement with Third World villages, and the breadth of his speculation, place his effort in a curious twilight region between "mere" journalism and orthodox social science.

The book's first section, entitled "People," consists of seventeen village studies, some of which involve important comparisons between two villages in the same culture. The longest of these focuses on Ghungrali Village (situated on the Punjab Plain in India) and reveals in a most dramatic fashion the fundamental transformations in agricultural technique and, accordingly, social relations characteristic of many areas of India in the last decade. When Critchfield went first to Ghungrali in 1970, he found age-old subsistence agriculture existing (and sustained by) a caste-bound social order. Although all belonged to the egalitarian Sikh religion, the villagers were distributed into two rigidly separate castes—the Jats (farmer-landlords) and the untouchable Harijans (themselves subdivided into a higher and lower order). The landless Harijans exchanged their agricultural labor for a percentage of the wheat crop and the right to harvest animal fodder on Jat land. The two castes were thus bound together by economic necessity as well as religious and paternalistic traditions.

By confining his attention to the fortunes of a single Jat family and its Harijan dependents, Critchfield illustrates the socioeconomic revolution at work in the Punjab. The status of the Harijans, he discovered, was completely dependent on the region's low wheat yield. The size of the wheat crop was in turn dictated by water scarcity and the long growth period of the traditional wheat strains. Two new factors radically altered this: the electrification of the Punjab in the 1950's, thus permitting the installation of tubewells, and the introduction of the renowned dwarf high-yield, fast-maturing wheat developed in Mexico by Norman Borlaug. With more water and better seed, the Jat landlords began to get enormous crops. While they needed the Harijans more than ever, they now resented the proportionally greater return which the Harijans were enjoying. The Jats thus proposed a reduction in the percentage of the harvest owed to the Harijans. When this offer was rejected, the Jats decided to violate age-old custom and hire migrant Hindu farm labor. The Harijans responded by organizing a caste-wide boycott of all Jat projects.

For Critchfield, understanding the outcome of this local struggle is critical, for it embodies all the fundamental changes in Indian society. Ten years later, the old paternalistic order had been completely shattered. Driven to invest in mechanized harvesters and tractors, the landlords also adopted other elements of the Green Revolution (piped irrigation, triple cropping, the planting of nitrogen-fixing "pulse" crops) and began to prosper in hitherto undreamed of ways. Because these new ventures favored those with larger land holdings and more capital, however, the richer, more innovative farmers began to drive out the poorer ones—in effect a repetition of the first agricultural revolution in England in the eighteenth century. The Harijans were forced to find industrial jobs in nearby towns. Their new status as wage laborers gave them the pride and independence to confront the Jats as equals and speak freely about all the old resentments and grievances. Fraternity disappeared, replaced by a more just but far colder, contractual, and impersonal order.

The Ghungrali "story" needs to be placed alongside Critchfield's comparative treatment of two Egyptian villages, as well as his account of the Javanese village, Pilangari. These three studies, as well as his discussion of the "red and green revolutions" in China, provide the main bases for Critchfield's defense of his "conversion to optimism." No mere travelogue, *Villages* attempts to test the validity of the great "world-system" hypotheses (most of them pessimistic) which have appeared in the last fifteen years. Thus, while the book's second section, "Ideas," takes up such topics as sexual attitudes in villages, the lively existence of the demonic, the diverse relations of village and neighboring cities, these thematic discussions are finally intended to shed light on the question of whether the Third World is doomed to endure endless rounds of overpopulation, pollution, and famine, "wars of redistribution," and population "die-backs." The disturbing theses of Dennis Meadows, The Club of Rome, Lester Brown's World Watch Institute, and Robert Heilbroner were very much on Critchfield's mind as he fashioned *Villages*.

What Critchfield has seen in Egypt, post-Maoist China, the Punjab, and Java makes him enthusiastically embrace the position which some have called "technological optimism." Having begun his village investigations with "a squishy and conventional sense of apocalypse," he has come to see "that a good many of these people are going to make it and that along the way they'll have lots to tell us." Java is a decisive test case. The world's most crowded island (ninety million) with a 1970 annual population growth rate of 2.5%, Java once seemed to Critchfield to present a hopeless case. When he returned in 1978 as an AID consultant (he subsequently produced a five-hundred page report on village Java), he was astonished to find a 1.4% birth rate, with almost all wives taking the Pill; nearly universal use of the new fertilized high-yield dwarf rice; a reversal of the old, destructive pattern of urban growth; vast improvements in transportation; a huge growth in primary school attendance; a veritable boom in rural industry and handicraft; and a proportionate (if still very unequal) improvement in the lot of the landless peasant. Most encouraging for Critchfield was (1) the vastly improved sociopolitical situation of women (which he regards as a crucial index of future progress in modernization) and (2) the seeming compatibility of traditional Muslim culture with the new agricultural technologies.

For Critchfield, rural Egypt presents a twofold picture, the general outlines of which sustain hopes for the future. Shahhat's southern Egypt remains captive to its traditions of male superiority, suspicion of higher education, repressive sexual morality, small land holdings, chronic indebtedness, and deeply fatalistic attitudes. (This is also the spontaneous, emotional, free-spirited, generous Egypt that Critchfield loves.) Delta Egypt—sober, rationalistic, open to technological innovation and female emancipation—idealizes frugality and education. Critchfield, with some regret, sees the Delta's cultural practices moving to Upper Egypt. The latter, he predicts, will survive the ordeal of change caused by the Aswan dam, partly by observing the ways of the northerners. It will, Critchfield believes, be "a long and leisurely process," and much will depend on whether Egypt can control Muslim extremism and educate many more women, while rationalizing what is surely one of the world's most burdensome governmental bureaucracies.

"Science and technology are keys to the kingdom," concludes Critchfield. The ongoing de-Maoization of China is only the most dramatic recent proof of this central fact. Critchfield is therefore particularly alarmed at the emergence of American-educated Third World bureaucrats who have imbibed the limits-to-growth gospel. These pessimists, often oblivious to the progressive changes going on around them, constitute a major threat to "The Great Change." If these types (along with Marxist "dependency theory" advocates) are Critchfield's chief antagonists, then the hero of *Villages* is Norman Borlaug. This exceptional Iowa villager, with his earthy directness and practical science, embodies for Critchfield what is best in America. Borlaug responds to the crisis not with global theories but with unimaginably productive wheat fields. No utopian, well aware of the complexity of the new agriculture, a patient student of the cultural side of agricultural development, Borlaug shows us what we Americans must become in order to insure a just future for the Third World. Predictably, Critchfield concludes his book with a plea for a new appreciation of American foreign aid, so frequently the object of attack by both the political right and left.

*Villages* is clearly an ambitious, wide-ranging work. Its major problem stems from this very fact. Critchfield has tried to discuss effectively these weighty issues *and* communicate the texture and quality of contemporary village life *and* do "amateur" peasant anthropology—all in 380 large-print pages. As a result, the book's anchor—the specific village studies—simply cannot hold the conceptual ship in place. Many of these "studies" are not that at all, but merely ten-page snapshots of particular episodes and persons in exotic places. Such "portraits" are (as Critchfield knows) no substitute for thorough background analysis. Deeply critical of the commercialization of American life, Critchfield seems himself to have succumbed to it. *Villages* has a careless, rush-it-to-press feel that comports badly with its subject matter. Critchfield is a gifted writer, but *Villages* is obviously the product of many hours of dictation. The result is a seriously flawed, very self-indulgent literary effort. That Critchfield did not permit himself the leisure and philosophic distance to produce a longer, more considered book is surprising. For these are, he tells the reader, the very qualities that one rediscovers and comes to admire by living in villages.

*Leslie E. Gerber*

### Sources for Further Study

*Book World*. XI, June 28, 1981, p. 13.
*Booklist*. LXXVII, June 1, 1981, p. 1281.
*Christian Science Monitor*. LXXIII, July 13, 1981, p. B5.
*The Economist*. CCLXXX, July 4, 1981, p. 91.
*Library Journal*. CVI, May 15, 1981, p. 1092.
*The New York Times Book Review*. LXXXVI, June 14, 1981, p. 7.
*Quill & Quire*. XLVII, August, 1981, p. 31.
*The Wall Street Journal*. CXCVIII, July 13, 1981, p. 18.

# VOLTAIRE

*Author:* Haydn Mason
*Publisher:* The Johns Hopkins University Press (Baltimore, Maryland). Illustrated.
194 pp. $14.95
*Type of work:* Literary biography
*Time:* 1694-1778
*Locale:* France, Switzerland, England, Holland, and Prussia

A chronologically selective biography of the most influential thinker of the Enlightenment, concentrating on the relationship of Voltaire's ideas to the circumstances in which they took form

Principal personages:
> FRANÇOIS-MARIE AROUET DE VOLTAIRE, philosopher, playwright, and polemicist
> FREDERICK II (THE GREAT), King of Prussia, 1740-1786; and patron and friend of Voltaire
> GABRIELLE, EMILIE DE TONNELIER DE BRETEUIL, MARQUISE DE CHÂTELET (MME DU CHÂTELET), mistress, companion, and collaborator of Voltaire from 1733 to her death in 1749
> MADAME MARIE LOUISE MIGNOT DENIS, niece and mistress of Voltaire and his companion during the later years of his life

Voltaire is possibly the best-known figure in the history of Western thought. Although he wrote at a time and a place distinguished by a wealth of literary contributions from such figures as Denis Diderot, Jean Jacques Rousseau, and the Marquis de Condorcet, Voltaire has far outlasted them all as a writer whose works are still read and enjoyed by a wide academic and lay audience. There are several factors which help to explain this continued popularity. First, Voltaire enjoyed an exceedingly long life, especially for the eighteenth century, and a very productive one. Born in 1694, he lived until 1778, remaining active to the end, and his literary production extended over sixty years, with that which is extant exceeding fifteen million words. Second, he was a man who was appreciated by his contemporaries. In 1778, only months before his death, he returned to Paris in triumph, enjoying the popular adulation accorded him at his coronation at the Comédie Française. Aware of his significance to his time and to posterity, his secretaries, Sébastien Longchamp and Jean-Louis Wagnière, chronicled Voltaire's life in their *Mémoires sur Voltaire* (1826). Ultimately he was accorded burial by the French Revolutionaries in the Pantheon, the neoclassical Parisian shrine to France's illustrious dead. Third, and most important, Voltaire wrote constantly and exceedingly well. He produced a corpus of work in a variety of literary forms, much of which remains meaningful and entertaining more than two centuries after its initial appearance. While such works as Rousseau's *Émile* (1762) and Diderot's collaborative masterpiece, the *Encyclopédie* (1751-1772), collect dust on library shelves, Voltaire's works, especially *Candide* (1759), continue to be published in many editions and, most important, to be read and enjoyed by successive generations. Voltaire, after all, attacked problems circumscribed by neither time nor place and he did this with the caustic but passionate wit of the satirist. His continued popularity is testimony to the timelessness of his writings.

Understandably, Voltaire has been the subject of a plethora of biographies, beginning with that of Longchamp and Wagnière, first published over a century and a half ago. The most comprehensive is the eight-volume account of Gustave Desnoireterres, *Voltaire et la société au XVIII<sup>e</sup> siècle*, published in Paris between 1867 and 1876. At present a team of scholars, under the direction of Professor René Pomeau, is producing an updated ten-volume comprehensive study of the eighteenth century literary giant. The most widely read biography is that of Gustave Lanson, first published in 1910, and several times after, including an English translation. In 1965, the noted historian of the Enlightenment, Peter Gay, published what has become a deservedly popular analysis of Voltaire's thought, *Voltaire's Politics: The Poet as Realist* (1959). Unfortunately, with the exception of the study by Lanson and those such as Gay's which treat only features of Voltaire's thought, most biographies of Voltaire are too long to command the interest of any but the most dedicated Voltaire scholar. In chronicling Voltaire's long and productive life in a comprehensive fashion, there is, as the late Voltaire scholar A. Delattre has observed, "'too much to say,'" and the biographer who is to be read must attempt to avoid "'the rut of compiling a true-to-life inventory.'" Lanson escaped this pitfall by approaching Voltaire in a primarily topical and secondarily chronological fashion. Haydn Mason takes a somewhat different, but effective, approach. His objective is to concentrate "on certain periods of the *philosophe*'s life, when we may hope to find the essence of the man revealed under the pressure of circumstances." He thus attempts to avoid the trap of compiling still another chronological compendium of all of Voltaire's activities.

Mason approaches his subject with impressive credentials. Professor of European studies at the University of East Anglia, he is the author of *Pierre Bayle and Voltaire* (1963) and a critical study of Voltaire's works. He has also served as editor of the works of Voltaire and Pierre Marivaux and is the general editor of *Studies on Voltaire and the Eighteenth Century* (1947). He is thus intimately acquainted with the available sources on Voltaire's life and works, and he has utilized this background to produce a brief but perceptive analysis of the maturation of Voltaire's ideas within the context of the times during which he lived.

Mason has divided his book into seven chapters of roughly equal length. In them he analyzes the seven periods of Voltaire's life which he believes were the most important in molding his attitudes. Since each is relatively isolated in time and place, he has also provided brief transitional passages and a separate Chronology to assist the reader in bridging the movement from one period to another. Thorough documentation is provided by a section of notes following the text which will satisfy the scholar but which, because of their location, will not discourage the general reader.

Mason begins with a brief description of Voltaire's youth, taking note of the early death of his mother which probably resulted in the emotional deprivation in Voltaire's makeup which manifested itself later in his life. His relations with his conservative father were volatile and resulted in the young Arouet's symbolic separation from him when he gave up his family name and adopted the name Voltaire. His relations with his siblings differed dramatically. Those with his sister, Mme Mignot, and his nieces, one of whom, Mme Denis, later became his mistress, were close and demonstrated that although Voltaire revolted against the authoritarian figure of his father, he "never revolted against the family as a whole nor against the notion of a family."

His relations with his brother, Armand, were vastly different. The latter was an ascetic and fanatical Jansenist who represented the religious closed-mindedness and intolerance that Voltaire always detested and attacked in almost all his writings. The most important formative influence of his youth, however, were his extensive travels. He made two journeys to Holland, where he observed and appreciated the "bourgeois prosperity achieved by hard work not rank; sectarian diversity revealed without fear or constraint; and the whole controlled by the spirit of modesty." His sojourn in England, necessitated by his sometimes ridiculous squabble with the chevalier de Rohan, was without question the most significant period of his youth. There not only did he observe a nobility of merit with a social consciousness, a toleration not only of religious differences but also of personal eccentricities, a respect for the rule of law, but also a freedom of thought and expression unknown in his native country. There he also became acquainted with the ideas of John Locke and Isaac Newton, who, more than any others, were to provide the philosophical and scientific framework upon which Voltaire was later to build. On the basis of his experiences in England, Voltaire composed one of his most significant early works, the *Lettres philosophiques*, published in France in 1734, and a year earlier in England as *Letters Concerning the English Nation*.

Upon his return to France, Voltaire, whose source of income from his father's estate had been unreliable, found himself in potentially dangerous straits that might have necessitated his abandonment of his career as a man of letters. In 1728, the city of Paris instituted a monthly lottery to raise funds for the repayment of municipal bonds. Voltaire became a member of a syndicate which cornered the tickets in a lottery and thereby won fortunes for its members. The gamble made Voltaire financially secure, and one cannot overestimate its importance in assuring him the opportunity to continue his literary career. Following this Voltaire entered into a love affair and literary collaboration with Mme du Châtelet, which continued from 1733 to her death in 1749. The period of this attachment is the second Mason analyzes. During the 1730's Voltaire spent most of his time at her chateau of Cirey, thus beginning "the oscillation between attraction and repulsion for Paris" which characterized the remainder of his life. The years at Cirey were important in affording him the months of isolation during which he read constantly in the fields of metaphysical and moral philosophy, science, and history. This resulted in the writing of three important treatises: the *Traité de métaphysique* (written in 1734), an inquiry into human nature; the beginning of *Le Siècle de Louis XIV* (1756), his first undertaking of the history of a civilization; and the *Éléments de philosophie de Newton* (1736), a popularization of the concept of an orderly universe derived from the writings of the English mathematician.

The third significant phase began in 1750, when Voltaire entered one of the best-known and most tumultuous periods of his life, a three-year sojourn at the court of the dynamic Frederick II of Prussia, in Berlin. The two men had corresponded for more than a decade and had met previously before Voltaire decided to accept Frederick's offer of patronage. Berlin, however, could not hold two men of such overpowering egos. Their relationship was characterized by mutual rancor and jealousy, exacerbated perhaps by a bisexual affair. Eventually Voltaire left Berlin and settled in Geneva. The two men continued to correspond, however, and maintained a high esteem for each other, although Voltaire was troubled by Frederick's enlightened excesses during the Seven Years War. Frederick's activities forced Voltaire to question his earlier conviction that Frederick ideally represented the best qualities of enlightened absolutism, which Voltaire continued to regard as the ideal political system. Voltaire's years in Berlin were not, however, without reward. While there he completed the *Siècle de Louis XIV* and derived from Frederick many of the ideas later expressed in the *Essai sur les moeurs* (1754) and the *Dictionnaire philosophique* (1764).

The fourth phase of Voltaire's life treated by Mason is the period of residence at the *philosophe*'s fine new house of Les Délices in Geneva, which began in 1755 and lasted until 1758. Although Voltaire stated that he intended to spend the remainder of his days tilling his garden at this retreat, circumstances were to dictate otherwise. Indeed, he had intitially been welcomed by the Swiss Protestant pastors to this Calvinist haven, but their support vanished when he came to the defense of Joseph Saurin, a former Protestant minister who had abjured his faith and fled to France, under the additional cloud of accusations of participation in criminal activites. By 1758, Voltaire concluded that he would never enjoy the freedom he had anticipated in a place where clerical authority remained strong. Nevertheless, his brief tenure in Geneva is of great importance. It was here that Voltaire and Rousseau entered into their famous philosophical quarrel which created an irreparable split. More important, it was during Voltaire's stay at Les Délices that he composed his most famous satire, *Candide*, a work that continues to retain its popularity. Although Mason makes no attempt to analyze *Candide*, he nevertheless performs the critical task of relating incidents in *Candide* to contemporary events witnessed by the author, such as the Lisbon earthquake of 1755 and Frederick II's victory over the French at the Battle of Rossbach in 1757.

The remaining two decades of Voltaire's life, with the exception of the final four months, were spent at Ferney, the estate community which Voltaire developed after its purchase in 1758. Located in France but near the Swiss border and Geneva, it offered to Voltaire the best of imaginable worlds to pursue his writing free of the interference of both Genevan clerics and French authorities. In his treatment of Voltaire at Ferney, Mason concentrates on two periods. The first, comprising the years 1762 to 1766, was that of Voltaire's great humanitarian activities and marked the apex of his lifelong struggle against *l'infâme*, the intolerance of organized religion. In this connection, the "greatest of all Voltaire's individual triumphs" was his rehabilitation of the memory of Jean Calas, the Protestant tradesman in cloth goods from Toulouse wrongfully executed for the murder of a son, a convert to Catholicism who probably committed suicide. This event also inspired Voltaire's penning of his *Traité sur la tolérance* (1763). Voltaire succeeded in saving from execution several members of the Sirven family who had been condemned *in absentia* on a charge similar to that against Calas. During this comparatively brief period Voltaire was also active in the La Barre case. The nineteen-year-old chevalier de La Barre had been convicted of certain acts of sacrilege in Abbeville and sentenced to death. To the surprise of many this excessively cruel sentence was upheld by the Parlement of Paris, and La Barre was executed. Here the question was not only of guilt as in the Calas and Sirven cases but also of the grotesque disproportion between the punishment and the crime. This affair in particular brought Voltaire into close contact with the Italian penal reformer Cesare Beccaria, whose ideas inspired Voltaire in his composition of the *Commentiare sur le livre des délits et des peines* (1764).

The sixth phase treated by Mason covers approximately the last five years of Voltaire's life, during which he continued to reside at Ferney. During this period he enjoyed his role as the *patriarche philosophe*, a celebrity who received guests and developed his estate into a thriving and prosperous community. While still active in opposing the forces of intolerance, Voltaire increasingly fell victim to a lifelong hypochondria which placed limitations on his everyday activities. His declining health, however, did not prevent him from enjoying a final trip to Paris, where he died on May 30, 1778. This Paris visit is the final phase discussed by the author, culminating in Voltaire's apotheosis at the Comédie Française during the opening performance of one of Voltaire's few mediocre plays, *Irène* (1778). Voltaire found himself the subject of adulation everywhere in the French capital except at the court of Louis XVI. This disappointed Voltaire greatly, for he remained firmly wedded to his conviction that the government of an enlightened prince was the best hope for progress. Voltaire's death was followed by a carefully planned clandestine removal of his body from the city, for Voltaire remained forever fearful that his remains might suffer the same fate as those of his friend, the actress Adrienne Lecouvreur: desecration and burial in unconsecrated ground. Indeed, Voltaire made elaborate and deceptive preparations for his death, fearing that his lifelong enemy, the Church, would have its final revenge on him.

Haydn Mason must be commended for his success. He has chosen those periods in Voltaire's long life which are most revealing of his character and ideas. At the same time Mason retains a chronological narrative thread which maintains continuity. While concentrating, rightly so, on the impact of circumstances on the development of ideas, Mason also provides valuable insight into the eccentricities of Voltaire's character in his discussion of such matters as the *philosophe*'s obsession with money, his hypochondria, his emotional deprivations, his possible bisexuality, and his surprisingly sincere veneration of monarchical authority. Finally, he has attempted with success to conclude with an analysis of Voltaire's influence on the world in which he lived and on posterity. This is a feature too infrequently found in biographies and general histories of major events and demonstrates the broadness of Mason's knowledge of his subject. In conclusion, this is a book which will appeal more to the student of intellectual history, especially of the Enlightenment, than to the scholar of French literature, for Mason's emphasis is on events rather than on analyses of Voltaire's many literary works. To the general reader Lanson's biography will probably continue to have the greatest appeal because of its more traditional structure. All students of Voltaire, the Enlightenment, and eighteenth century Europe in general, however, would profit from exposure to Mason's literate and balanced study.

*J. Stewart Alverson*

### Sources for Further Study

*America*. CXLV, October 17, 1981, p. 225.
*Choice*. XIX, September, 1981, p. 86.
*The Economist*. CCLXXX, August 15, 1981, p. 74.
*Library Journal*. CVI, July, 1981, p. 1410.
*The New Republic*. CLXXXV, August 15, 1981, p. 37.
*Sewanee Review*. LXXXIX, July, 1981, p. R90.
*Spectator*. CCXLVI, June 20, 1981, p. 21.
*Times Literary Supplement*. October 16, 1981, p. 1216.

# THE VOYAGE OF THE ARMADA
## The Spanish Story

*Author:* David Howarth (1912-    )
*Publisher:* The Viking Press (New York). Illustrated. 256 pp. $13.95
*Type of work:* History
*Time:* May-September, 1588, with brief reference to the periods immediately preceding and following
*Locale:* Spain and Portugal, England, Ireland, Scotland, and the Low Countries

*An account of the planning, voyage, defeat, and return of the Spanish Armada, primarily from the Spanish perspective*

>*Principal personages:*
>PHILIP II, King of Spain, 1556-1598; and the creator of the Armada
>DUKE OF MEDINA SIDONIA, Commander of the Armada
>DUKE OF PARMA, Commander of the Spanish Army in the Low Countries
>JUAN MARTINEZ DE RECALDE, a major Spanish participant in the voyage of the Armada
>ELIZABETH II, Queen of England, 1558-1603
>CHARLES HOWARD, BARON OF EFFINGHAM, LORD HIGH ADMIRAL, Commander of the English fleet
>SIR FRANCIS DRAKE, a leading English participant in the defeat of the Armada who established the principle of command of English ships by sailors instead of soldiers
>SIR JOHN HAWKYNS, a leading English participant in the defeat of the Armada who pioneered important innovations in ship construction

The defeat of the Spanish Armada in 1588 by the English under the leadership of those noteworthy English seamen, Lord Howard, Sir Francis Drake, and Sir John Hawkyns, has become, at least in Britain and Protestant America, the stuff of legend and allegory. As legend, the achievements of the English seamen have been exaggerated, as have the results of the Armada's defeat in regard to English world seapower and the security of Protestantism. As allegory the defeat has often been portrayed by British historians as a David-Goliath encounter between a new, youthful, and vigorous nation on the ascendancy and an old, senile, and lethargic nation in decline. The Armada's defeat has been ascribed to divine intervention, because the Armada was driven northward through the English Channel around Scotland and along the Irish coast, where it incurred its heaviest losses. This popular image of the event certainly was important in engendering English patriotism and in spurring the imperialist desire, and it has also helped to create the popular image of the halcyon days of "Good Queen Bess." Historians, however, have increasingly questioned its accuracy. The late Tudor historian, Garrett Mattingly, in his superb account of the event, *The Armada* (1959), while recognizing the psychological importance of the defeat, questions its immediate impact in regard to Spanish seapower and the European struggle between Catholics and Protestants. He concludes that the defeat of the Armada "raised men's hearts in dark hours, and led them to say to one another, 'What we have done once, we can do again.' In so far as it did this the legend of the Spanish Armada became as important as the actual event— perhaps even more important."

The main reason for the endurance of the Armada legend is that historians, as men in general are wont to do, have viewed the event from the perspective of the victors, the English. Older historians, such as J. A. Froude, Leopold Ranke, and Jules Michelet, have usually been either British, Protestant, or anticlerical and have thus been attracted to Protestant England and its victory over the Spain of the leader of the Counter-Reformation, Philip II. Spanish historians have tended to be understandably embarrassed and shamed by the poor showing of their sixteenth century countrymen. As a result the event has been traditionally viewed from the English perspective, with the Spanish leader of the Armada, the Duke of Medina Sidonia, portrayed as an incompetent fool and Howard, Drake, Hawkyns, and their aides as omniscient naval experts.

The objective of David Howarth, in his *The Voyage of the Armada: The Spanish Story*, is to view the event from the Spanish perspective, correcting some of the previously held misconceptions about what happened in the fall of 1588 and about the individual participants. Howarth approaches his task with impressive credentials. A British citizen, he has previously established a commendable reputation among historians through his works on historical turning points, such as the Norman Conquest and the battles of Trafalgar and Waterloo. Howarth's major area of interest is military, and especially naval, history. He is thus able to evaluate the Armada and the English fleet more objectively and thoroughly than historians with less knowledge of these subjects. Fortunately Howarth's encyclopedic knowledge of complex naval matters and terminology does not prevent him from conveying to his readers an adequate understanding of terms and issues that, in the hands of a less expert writer, could have been incomprehensible.

Undoubtedly, the ignominious rout of the Armada was hailed at the time as a miraculous achievement because it came as such a surprise, indeed a shock, not only to England but also to all of Europe and the Europeanized world. This is a theme that Howarth fails to develop at any length, and as a result he fails to convey the significance of the English response to victory at that time. Indeed, in 1588, Spain was at its apogee as a world power. As the nineteenth century belonged to Britain so the sixteenth was that of Spain. Since the completion of the *reconquista* with the Spanish conquest of Granada from the Moors in 1492, Spain had speedily emerged as the greatest imperial power the world had yet seen. Through marriage, inheritance, and conquest— all under the aegis of the Roman Catholic Church—the Hapsburgs had created an empire that comprised not only Spain and Portugal, the Netherlands,

Milan, Naples, Sicily, and other holdings in Europe but also a world empire that stretched from North and South America eastward to the Philippines. Indeed, before the division of the Holy Roman Empire by Charles V (Charles I of Spain) in 1555, the Hapsburg Empire had included Austria, Bohemia, and what remained of Turkish-overrun Hungary, as well as titular headship of the other German states. Army commanders under the Spanish flag, including Don Juan of Austria, the Duke of Alba, and the Duke of Parma enjoyed victories on land while Spanish fleets traversed the seas from the Americas to the Philippines, establishing settlements on the coasts of Africa and Asia. For five years Philip (later Philip II) of Spain had been titular king of England because of his marriage to the Catholic queen, Mary Tudor.

Riding the crest of a resurgent Spanish Catholicism, Philip II, upon becoming king of Spain in 1556, sought to undo the Protestant gains that had driven his father, Charles V, to abdication and retirement to a monastery. Acutely aware of his position as an international figure, Philip became the self-anointed champion of the military arm of the Counter-Reformation, and in so doing unleashed a personal and national obsession that eventually contributed to Spain's imperial decline. To carry out his self-ordained task of bringing his wayward Protestant sheep back into the Catholic fold, Philip, much like his father, withdrew from the active court life of Madrid to the monastic surroundings of a newly built palace, the Escorial, that imposing granite structure which still stands in isolation over twenty-five miles from the Spanish capital. In an office in this massive, cold, barren structure, Philip II, the world's most powerful ruler, attempted to run an empire as a clerk would a large corporation. Suffering from swollen knees which produced insomnia Philip "could hardly hobble the yards from his bed to the desk where . . . until dawn . . . [he worked] his ponderous, industrious way through the mountains of papers that never grew any less."

The Catholic crusade which Philip undertook upon his accession to the throne did not uniformly prosper, however. The Turks who had been defeated by the Spanish at the naval battle of Lepanto in 1571 succeeded in reestablishing themselves in the Mediterranean within two years. France was engulfed in civil war between Catholics and Huguenots. Philip, though crushing a rebellion of the Moriscoes (Muslims forcibly converted to Catholicism), never succeeded in assimilating them into the Spanish population. After 1566, the Netherlands became a major thorn in Philip's side. Indeed, the revolt of Philip's Calvinist subjects in the Low Countries was to become inextricably entwined with his growing distrust and hatred of England and its queen, Elizabeth I.

The evolution of Philip's conception of a great armada dates to Elizabeth's accession to the English throne. With the death of his wife and Elizabeth's predecessor, Mary I, Philip's hope of returning England to the Catholic

Church was endangered. Elizabeth, ever the religious moderate and astute politician, was cognizant of the fact that Mary's persecution of English Protestants, with the encouragement of her husband, had driven the English irrevocably toward Protestantism. Initially Philip offered himself as a husband to Elizabeth, hoping in so doing to maintain his control over affairs in England. He was rebuffed. Then he attempted to facilitate a marriage of his son, Don Carlos, to Mary Stuart, Queen of Scots, Elizabeth's Catholic cousin, who was considered by Catholics to be the legitimate heiress to the English throne. Nothing came of this either. Another planned marriage, that of Mary Stuart to Philip's illegitimate brother, Don Juan, collapsed with the latter's death. English piracy exacerbated Philip's hatred of Elizabeth, and for the next decade he was party to several plots to overthrow the English queen and replace her with her Scottish Catholic cousin. This idea, of course, had to be abandoned when Mary was beheaded in 1587. By this point, however, Philip had decided that he wanted the English crown for himself, and, in 1584, having acquired Portugal three years earlier and thus provided with a large Atlantic port, he began to assemble the ships which, by 1588, would form the Glorious Armada.

Convinced of the rightness of his holy crusade in the eyes of God, Philip planned to use the Armada, which numbered approximately 130 ships, as support at sea for the Spanish army in the Netherlands, under the command of the Duke of Parma, to launch an invasion of England. Planned totally in the isolation of the Escorial by a man who was convinced that God would provide a miracle, the Armada was doomed before it ever sailed. Indeed, a miracle was its only hope for success. Most of the ships themselves were ill-suited to the enterprise. Bound to the chivalric ideal, abandoned in England, that sailors sailed ships and soldiers fought, the Spanish subscribed to the soldierly concept of sea-fighting. Disdaining the use of artillery, the soldiers who sailed on the ships of the Armada favored hand-to-hand combat, preferably on land. Their goal at sea was to lie alongside the enemy ship, board it, and then engage the enemy soldiers in direct combat. These galleons with castles afore and aft looked imposing and afforded the soldiers some protection, but they, along with the merchant ships which had been poorly converted by the addition of castles, were large, bulky, and essentially unsailable. It was difficult to keep these ships in any semblance of formation because of many of the ships' inability to sail windward, and "it must have been evident to anyone . . . that the English Channel would be a one-way ride. The fleet could not sail up it except with a westerly wind, and unless the wind changed it could not sail out again. Nor could it stop and anchor. If it did, it would not be able to defend itself." Since the Spanish disdained artillery, their cannon and shot were poorly cast and markedly inferior to those of the English. Most of the ships of the Armada, then, were simply no match for the faster, better armed, more maneuverable English ships.

To virtually all Spanish leaders but Philip this was evident. The Duke of Parma, who had been unable to subdue England's Dutch allies in the Low Countries, realized that Philip's plan was totally unworkable. So did the man whom Philip placed in command of the Armada, Don Alonzo Perez de Guzman el Bueno, Duke of Medina Sidonia. Scion of a family that had attained its status by fighting the Moors, the seventh "duke was a most unusual man" among Spanish and European aristocracy and within his own family. Unlike most of his peers, Medina Sidonia "was peaceful and gentle by nature, polite, considerate and not often angry . . . [and] disliked violence and high intrigue and military life." Totally unsuited to the enormous task arbitrarily assigned him by the king, "he had never pretended to be a good soldier, nor ever wanted to be; and much less a sailor." Aware of his limitations and foreseeing that the Armada had no hope of success under his leadership Medina Sidonia demonstrated tremendous moral courage in writing discreetly to Philip and imploring him with carefully reasoned arguments to withdraw his appointment. As he had to others, the king turned a deaf ear to the Duke. Resigned to his fate, Medina Sidonia fulfilled an unwanted and impossible task with great moral and physical courage. Unfortunately history has made Medina Sidonia the scapegoat for Philip's failure. He has often been portrayed as inept and cowardly. Howarth has gone far in correcting this misinterpretation of Medina Sidonia and has transformed him into one of the heroes of the fiasco, albeit a tragic one.

Quite rightly the author saddles Philip with full responsibility for the unnecessary tragedy that resulted in the loss of some twenty thousand lives out of the original thirty thousand who sailed from Lisbon, over half of them by starvation and disease. In his closing paragraph Howarth passes severe judgment on the hermitic king: "There is no evidence that it ever entered [his] muddled mind . . . that he might be wrong in his interpretation of God's will, or that he changed his least opinion, or felt the slightest remorse at having sent twenty thousand men each to his private agony. . . . His creed left no place for pity."

David Howarth, in *The Voyage of the Armada*, has made an important contribution to an understanding of the Armada's failure by presenting the tragedy from the Spanish perspective. Through his primary use of Spanish sources he has rehabilitated the maligned character of Medina Sidonia and engendered sympathy for sailors and soldiers who endured unspeakable shipboard conditions during this unnecessary ordeal. In clear, economical prose Howarth has succeeded in clarifying technical naval jargon for the lay reader. Perhaps most important, he has ennobled those nameless Spaniards (and other nationalities who sailed for Spain) who endured unimaginable terrors, especially on their return along the Irish coast. The only major disappointment is that Howarth has made little attempt to present the story of the Armada in the context of other events in Europe during this period, an achievement admirably accomplished by Garrett Mattingly. This was not Howarth's goal, however, and he should not be criticized for what is a disappointment rather than a failure. This is a book that will be informative to the scholar and entertaining to the general reader.

*J. Stewart Alverson*

### Sources for Further Study

*The Atlantic Monthly*. CCXLVIII, November, 1981, p. 89.
*Kirkus Reviews*. XLIX, August 1, 1981, p. 988.
*Library Journal*. CVI, September 27, 1981, p. 1629.
*The New York Times Book Review*. LXXXVI, September 27, 1981, p. 16.
*Publishers Weekly*. CCXX, July 24, 1981, p. 142.
*Times Literary Supplement*. December 18, 1981, p. 1473.

# WAITING FOR MY LIFE

*Author:* Linda Pastan (1932-    )
*Publisher:* W. W. Norton and Company (New York). 72 pp. $14.95; paperback $4.95
*Type of work:* Poetry

*A collection of poems that reveal the marvelous in the ordinary*

In *Waiting for My Life*, her fourth volume of poems, Linda Pastan demonstrates with uncommon artistry the rich literary possibilities of the commonplace—ordinary situations, everyday experiences. Although much of her life is already gone, as are the children she has reared, the speaker in these poems is still waiting for her life to happen. Pastan renders the different aspects of this experience superbly. She writes about sorting through one's dreams and speculating on their nature, their feel ("Dreams"); about reading to a child ("McGuffey's First Eclectic Reader"); about the experience, as an adult, of being taught something by a child ("The Vanishing Point"). There are poems about seeing a child off to school, or to a job ("Helen Bids Farewell to Her Daughter Hermione"); about the fear that a child will come to harm; about resentment felt when departed children do not write or call. She writes about returning to familiar surroundings after an absence ("Returning"); about imagining the rest of one's life ("Widow's Walk, Somewhere Inland"). The titles of many poems suggest the everyday experiences and situations that occasioned them: "Letter to a Son at Exam Time," "By the Mailbox," "Meditation by the Stove," "Weather Forecast."

The titles alone do not suggest what Pastan makes of these ordinary occasions: poems of exceptionally sharp and vivid imagery, concise and telling. "We take from nature/ what we can," Pastan writes in "By the Mailbox." What she takes is apparently simple and familiar: tree, leaf, star, fire, bread, moon, snow, water. What she makes of these is profound.

The imagery of these poems is local in a double sense. Drawn for the most part from the speaker's immediate surroundings, the images also function locally in the poems, lighting up the meaning of a particular verse paragraph or line, as this one found in the title poem: "Sometimes my life coughed and coughed:/ a stalled car about to catch." That is the beginning and the end of the car image; it functions immediately and locally, and that is enough. In "Letter to a Son at Exam Time," poems in a college textbook (in contrast to those that "leaf out" from her typewriter) are "so many leaves pressed to death/ in a heavy book." The leaf image is elaborated no further. In "Meditation by the Stove" the scene is a kitchen where dough is "breathing under its damp cloth/ like a sleeping child." The extremely effective image is local in that it is derived from the immediate scene and from the speaker's situation as a mother and a homemaker. Rendered concisely, it is elaborated no further.

Pastan's method is not to elaborate a single metaphor to the length of a conceit which dominates the entire poem. Instead, elaboration is achieved by economical movement from statement to image, and by allowing a locally functioning image to be quickly superseded by another, as in "Dreams." Dreams are "the only afterlife we know;/ the place where the children/ we were/ rock in the arms of the children/ we have become." The remainder of the poem consists of a number of images which explore various aspects of dreams. Dreams are

> . . . as many as leaves
> in their migrations,
> as birds whose deaths we learn of
> by the single feather
> left behind: a clue,
> a particle of sleep
>
> caught in the eye.
> They are as irretrievable as sand.

Thus the poem moves, statement alternating with image. The theme generates the image, the image reveals the theme.

The success of this alternation, elaboration, and variation is attributable to the wonderful control of theme and to the aptness of the concrete details in revealing the theme. Thus, in "The Vanishing Point" the notion of perspective is vividly rendered by images succinctly stated and quickly following one another. Perspective is "a penciled dot/ drawn on a picture plane/ where parallel lines/ converge." The lines converging are like "holding two kite strings/ in one hand." The penciled dot is then seen as

> . . . that point
> the eye drifts towards
> on any horizon, the place
> where all things lost
> converge: the hairpins
> your father took slowly
> from my piled up hair
> the night we met;
> your face at five or seven;
> and someone else—a voice
> I almost listened to once—
> who never asked again.

These diverse elements are perfectly controlled by the theme.

The beautiful organization of details in individual poems has its parallel in the overall movement of this beautifully arranged collection. The three sections—"Friday's Child," "The War Between Desire and Dailiness," and "The Verdict of Snow"—are thematically and imagistically seamless, as intricately interwoven as a bird's nest. The poems in their progression create a trajectory, an arc of imagery. The book opens with an "Epilogue"— the speaker of the poems has died—in which the surface of a lake is described as "equivocal/ as the pages of a book/ on which everything remains/ to be written." A "Prologue" follows, in which "Nothing has happened yet," but just as in the "Epilogue" things are equivocal. An elk drinks from the lake, "or in the confusion of dusk/ perhaps it is simply/ an old tree/ leaning over the water."

Between the "Nothing has happened yet" of the "Prologue" and "Nothing is left to happen" of "My Achilles Son" there are wonderful repetitions and variations of theme and image. Placement of the "Epilogue" at the outset— with the speaker already dead—is exactly right in this book of poems about someone who is "Friday's Child" (loving and giving) and who, like Cassandra, anticipates everything, who knows "that every flower awaited/ its proper place/ on our funeral wreaths." Such a reversal is a way of expressing, in the book's structure, the two-sidedness of things. In the poem "In Back Of," a reverse image achieves this essential ambivalence. The poem moves, in characteristic fashion, from statement to image: "In back of 'I love you'/ stands 'goodbye.'" Words are like mirror images: "When you raise/ your right hand/ in greeting,/ they raise their left/ in farewell."

A number of the reversals in these poems involve role reversals of parent and child. In "The One-Way Mirror Back," the father's mustache "bobbed/ in the distance/ like the old rowboat/ across the lake." In "Widow's Walk, Somewhere Inland," it is the speaker's grown-up sons who are like boats that "tie up here for a while." In "The Vanishing Point," the child becomes parent, and the parent becomes a child learning about perspective.

There is hardly a poem in *Waiting for My Life* that does not deal in some way with children. From the opening "Epilogue," in which the speaker has died "no longer a girl," and which speaks of two children, Katerina and Robert, to the last poem, "Ethics," which concludes with the realization that children can save neither art nor nature nor an old woman, children are a thematic concern and a source of imagery. In "Elegy," the speaker searches for a poem "the child I was hides/ in the ear of the woman/ I have become." An image of childhood vividly describes lovemaking, which lights the body "the way as children we press a flashlight/ into our own flesh/ making each limb seem to smolder" ("When the Moment Is Over"). As an adult, the speaker watches "the trees like gnarled magicians/ produce handkerchiefs/ of leaves/ out of empty branches" and is like a child "at this spectacle/ of leaves."

In the same way that leaves are produced magically from branches, Pastan's themes leaf out into many images. The weather imagery of "Friday's Child" ("regiments of clouds/ were being formed/ that could bombard us soon/ with snow, could bury us") adumbrates the weather of "Cold Front," "Weather Forecast," and "At My Window,"—as well as the martial imagery of the entire second section, "The War Between Desire and Dailiness," and the anticipation of death in the final section, "The Verdict of Snow." The concern with aging and dying, concentrated in the third section, is prefigured in "Secrets," from part one:

> The secrets I keep
> from myself
> are the same secrets
> the leaves keep
> from the old trunk
> of the tree
> even as they turn
> color.

The curving road of "Prologue" anticipates the journey image of "after minor surgery": "the body/ like a passenger of a long journey/ hears the conductor call out/ the name/ of the first stop." The curving road of "Prologue" appears in "On the Road to Delphi," in "Presbyopia" ("Those blurred numerals/ on the page/ are tracks/ to be followed/ the rest of the way/ alone.") The road is implicit in the "mute pilgrimage" of snow "falling in silence/ toward silence" in "At My Window."

The many references to silence are, along with the noted reversals, a way of rendering an aspect of the equivocalness or ambiguity of experience. There is the "nearly perfect" silence of "Epilogue" and "Prologue." In "Secrets," the trumpet flower ironically sings "only silence." The whippoorwill's song is "never tell/ never tell/ never tell." Silence is the only message sent in "By the Mailbox." In "blizzard," an "alphabet/ of silence/ falls out of the/ sky."

Nature and experience, being equivocal, must be interpreted. Everything, even silence, is a message that must be deciphered. This circumstance accounts—if not logically, then in terms of experience—for the speaker's sense of being "someone else" ("Excursion") forever waiting for life to begin; of coming into familiar surroundings after an absence, feeling as if she were a stranger who had parachuted out of the sky ("Returning"). Experience is only half of experience, according to Johann Wolfgang von Goethe. The other half is perhaps its interpretation.

For Linda Pastan, writing is the other half of experience. Her persistent sense of being a tourist in her own life ("On the Road to Delphi") engenders a desire for "the fully lived life" ("Meditation by the Stove"), but what she remembers, she feels, "hardly happened," and "what they say happened/ I hardly remember" ("The One-Way Mirror Back"). Thus she must go "prospecting" for her life ("Waiting for My Life"). Writing is her way of reading the secrets she keeps from herself ("Secrets"); of understanding what she did not know she knew ("Letter to a Son at Exam Time"); of sending a letter "the way the tree sends messages/ in leaves" ("Eyes Only"). Writing is "the coin of metaphor spinning,/ coming up Fact" ("On Hearing the Testimony of Those Revived After Cardiac Arrest"). Entered into for this reason,

Pastan's writing—and this is rare—results in a poetry which makes clear its own necessity.

Writing about life becomes the means to the more fully realized life, as is suggested by: "Therefore I write/ in this blue/ ink, color/ of secret veins/ and arteries" ("Eyes Only"). This is the view of many poets, who have no life in the way nonartists can be said to have a life. With this volume, Linda Pastan provides an instructive illustration of the distinction Lawrence Lipking makes in *The Life of the Poet* (1981) between the ordinary biography of the poet (which, as far as the poet is concerned, "hardly happened") and the biography "that gets into poems: the life that has passed through a refining poetic fire." This is the life poets are always waiting for. Here Linda Pastan has rendered that life exquisitely.

*Jim W. Miller*


### Sources for Further Study

*Book World*. XI, July 5, 1981, p. 7.
*Booklist*. LXXVII, April 1, 1981, p. 1074.
*Library Journal*. CVI, March 15, 1981, p. 664.
*Publishers Weekly*. CCXIX, February 27, 1981, p. 147.

# WALDO EMERSON

*Author:* Gay Wilson Allen (1903-    )
*Publisher:* The Viking Press (New York). Illustrated. 751 pp. $25.00
*Type of work:* Literary biography
*Time:* 1803-1882
*Locale:* The United States, primarily New England; Europe, and Egypt

*A portrait of the life and times of American writer and thinker Ralph Waldo Emerson, thoroughly examining the impact upon him of the books he read and the people he knew*

> *Principal personages:*
> RALPH WALDO EMERSON, a minister, essayist, poet, and lecturer
> ELLEN TUCKER EMERSON, his first wife
> LYDIA (LIDIAN) JACKSON EMERSON, his second wife
> AMOS BRONSON ALCOTT, his close friend, a schoolteacher and philosopher
> MARGARET FULLER, his close friend, a writer and intellectual

Ralph Waldo Emerson once wrote that "all public facts are to be individualized, all private facts are to be generalized. Then at once History becomes fluid and true, and Biography deep and sublime." Emerson spent much of his life generalizing from private facts to discover the deepest, sublimest truth, most universally to be applied. A modern biographer, however, could hardly get an advance worth the cost of a photocopy unless he or she promised plenty of specific individualizing details about the biography's subject.

Gay Wilson Allen has certainly not failed in this promise, although this biography remains worthily "deep and sublime" as well. If not strictly a Freudian, and if generally more interested in intellectual conditions than psychological ones, he nevertheless gives a clear and detailed portrait of Ralph Waldo Emerson from earliest years to death, filling in all the corners with fascinating and valuable background material. Thus he richly explains the development of Emerson's personality, thought, and work, and characterizes not only Emerson but also his times and the life and people around him.

This is the first Emerson biography since Ralph L. Rusk's *The Life of Ralph Waldo Emerson* in 1949, and the change in title is significant. It may herald a new popular ranking of Emerson with the more revolutionary, two-name American writers such as Walt Whitman, Emily Dickinson, Herman Melville, and Mark Twain rather than with the stuffy traditionalists whose first and middle names were always prominently displayed—Henry Wadsworth Longfellow, James Russell Lowell, and so on. More important, "Waldo" was the name Emerson chose to be known by during adolescence and ever after, much as Walter Whitman became Walt and David Henry Thoreau reversed his first and middle names.

Emerson's childhood and youth were typical for the son of an early nineteenth century New England Unitarian minister. He received a thorough and early education; in fact, his father urged his mother to be diligent in drilling their young son—then only three. The drilling presumably paid off, for he went on to graduate from Harvard, writing occasional poems, and then to teach school sporadically to secure an income before embarking on the inevitable course of becoming a minister himself at the Harvard Divinity School. Oddly for one whose significance to American thought and literature has been so original and far-reaching, and yet not unlike one of his foremost admirers, Whitman, he showed no special promise either as a boy or as a young man, being outshone by his older and younger brothers.

He lacked a driving ambition, but he was far from lazy. He preferred to absorb, from books or nature, like the "transparent eyeball" he termed himself in his first book, *Nature* (1836). This preference proved wise, for he did not burn himself out early, spouting ideas before they were hardly formed; rather, once he decided to write, he was able to do so from the wisdom of years lived as well as books digested over a long period of time.

As a writer, he was driven not so much by a need to express himself as by the impulse to teach—fittingly for a minister, which he became briefly. This impulse he fulfilled initially through his sermons, and later in lectures and the essays he developed from them after he had left the church to follow his conscience.

For so strong an advocate of the virtues of nonconformity, the outer shape of Emerson's life was amazingly orthodox and bound to other people, in contrast to those of such fellow individualists as his friends Thoreau, Whitman, and Bronson Alcott. He managed to sustain basically untroubled relations with his religiously oriented mother, first and second wives, and daughters, often attended church, and was even believed in his later years to have backslid into orthodox Unitarianism, although his son denied such rumors.

One of the most interesting aspects of Allen's book is his portrayal and analysis of Emerson's many relationships. He vividly describes the emotional tightropes Emerson walked, in this Victorian age of suppressed but intense emotions, from a late adolescent crush on a younger fellow student at Harvard through suppressed sibling rivalries through his widely divergent attitudes toward his two wives to his relations with his many admirers and fellow thinkers. His stability, serenity, and agreeable temperament attracted many people to him. In fact, he came into contact with many of the great figures of his century, from the aging John Adams to an adolescent Teddy Roosevelt; he also met or enjoyed personal acquaintance with Abraham Lincoln, Nathaniel Hawthorne, Samuel Taylor Coleridge, William Wordsworth, Thomas Carlyle, John Muir, John Brown, and a brilliant father and son each named Henry James, among many others.

One of his longest lasting friendships, because of their proximity as neighbors in Concord, Massachusetts, and because of their mutual longevity, was with Bronson Alcott. At times he was too much of a dreamer for the more worldly Emerson, and their friendship was filled with disagreements, with occasional patronizing by one or the other, and with Emerson's repeated actions, heartwarming and often comical, to save the impractical Alcott and his family when a wild-eyed scheme landed them in financial straits. Emerson became such a savior to the Alcotts that the twenty-eight-year-old Louisa May, after her sister's marriage, wrote that being kissed as a bride by their friend and neighbor Mr. Emerson, "the god of my idolatry," would "make even matrimony endurable."

Emerson was a favorite with a number of women, the most prominent being the brilliant Margaret Fuller; the details of her life which Allen includes are one of the book's welcome extras. She recovered from her early infatuation with Emerson to become a frequent guest in his household and cherished companion to his wife. She was only one of several prominent intellectual women in New England, and Emerson was involved with many of them, perhaps most persistently Caroline Sturgis, whose correspondence with him contains many hints of an undercurrent of passion that Emerson knew all too well could come to naught.

After all, he was married. His second wife, born Lydia Jackson but redubbed Lidian by Emerson so that her first name and new last name would join more euphoniously, was amazingly tolerant of her husband's friendships with other women. Theirs was not, however, a marriage made in heaven, at least in the way Lidian had conceived it when she had an image shortly after making his acquaintance of coming downstairs in a wedding dress and meeting him there. This picture would come true on their wedding day, but this couple, past the prime of youth when they married at age thirty-two (she a few months older than he), would never know the passion and intensity that Emerson put into his first marriage.

Ellen Tucker was only a teenager when she met Emerson, a guest preacher at her family's church in Concord, New Hampshire, and still in her teens when she married him two years later. They shared poetic souls; indeed, Emerson would posthumously publish some of her poetry in *The Dial* and his own books of poems. At that time he was still safely within the bosom of the Unitarian Church, so Ellen's faith did not provide any source of potential friction between them. Unfortunately, she had consumption (tuberculosis), and not only was weak throughout most of Emerson's acquaintance with her but also lasted only through sixteen months of marriage. He was so heartbroken that he took to visiting her tomb daily and once even recorded in his journal that he opened her coffin.

Lidian was certainly a second choice, but she made the best of a less than perfect bargain and even named their first daughter Ellen. Unfortunately Emerson remained somewhat aloof even from his own wife, wrapped up in his lofty thoughts. When he traveled, Lidian hoped in vain for letters which would express his love for her, as perhaps he himself could not do in person. She might have predicted as much from his very letter of proposal, however;

quoted here in full, this revealingly high-minded document is a splendid coup on Allen's part, for no part of it has ever been published; Rusk, as biographer and editor of Emerson's letters, did not know of its existence.

Although Lidian became increasingly orthodox in her religion as her husband became less so, she was originally a fairly satisfactory intellectual companion to him; presumably her strong-mindedness gave Emerson greater confidence to follow his own path than Ellen's physical and spiritual fragility did.

She even joined her husband at many of the meetings that a number of New England intellectuals began holding which questioned the received wisdom of the day. The label this group came to bear, the transcendentalists, implied a shared set of beliefs, but the group was considerably varied, including reformers of various stripe: active ones such as Theodore Parker in contrast to individualistic ones such as Emerson; experimenters in new lifestyles such as Alcott and Fuller in contrast to those, again such as Emerson, whose experiments remained in the realm of thought and spirit. Of course his intellectual avant-gardism inevitably inspired all forms of nonconformity, such as the communes at Brook Farm and Fruitlands, in which Emerson declined to participate. He could hardly reject as erroneous the wild-eyed visionaries he attracted at home and abroad, having advised all to follow their own inner voices. Allen gives a fascinating account of a dinner Emerson held in Manchester during his second trip to England, after completing a series of lectures there in 1848; it was attended by assorted oddballs and misfits, united by their admiration of Emerson. Here as elsewhere Allen is most generous in describing the people around Emerson, so that the reader may experience the full flavor of his milieu.

Allen also painstakingly but interestingly traces the four-year history of *The Dial*, one of America's foremost literary periodicals, which Emerson and Fuller founded and which provided a forum for the leading radical thought of the early 1840's; though its circulation was small, it gave Thoreau and assorted lesser literary lights entrée into the literary world and featured the first appearance in print of many of Emerson's poems.

Allen has truly done a superb job of re-creating a multifaceted environment for Emerson, a fulcrum figure for nineteenth century American literature. His contribution to Emerson biography lies not in actual addition of facts so much as in placing Emerson and his work more fully in context than earlier biographers have done. The writers whom Emerson read and who influenced him, from Plato and the Orientals up to his contemporaries Coleridge and Carlyle, are thoroughly explained as important sources for his thought. In addition, Allen's frequent summaries or quotations of passages from Emerson's letters and journals and those of his family and friends give a rich sense of the man and his connections with those around him. Moreover, Allen provides a helpful chronology and genealogy, and twenty-five useful illlustrations.

Minor quibbles include some errors in the index and the desirability of clearer dating within chapters (perhaps by a running head or at least the inclusion of dates in each chapter's title).

What many may consider the truly distinctive value of this biography is the care Allen takes to summarize and analyze Emerson's works, believing that a biography of a writer is incomplete when only the external and psychological aspects of that writer's life are dealt with and not the work which has made that life significant. Some of the analyses are over-obvious or, conversely, overextensive in the context of a biography rather than a critical study, but generally readers will be grateful for Allen's putting all of Emerson's works at their fingertips, including overviews of each book Emerson published, with summaries of all the significant essays and poems contained therein, including explanations of these works' sources, whether in Emerson's experiences or readings.

Of course reading Allen on *Nature*, "Self-Reliance," "Experience," "The Poet," or "Fate," "The Sphinx," "Days," "Woodnotes," or "Uriel," is no substitute for reading the essay or poem itself, and a reader of the biography should come prepared with knowledge of some of these major works, to know the flavor of Emerson's distinctive style: his poetry's often rough rhythms but sweeping involvement in the beauty of nature and the joy of life; his tightly packed prose paragraphs overflowing with aphorisms—homespun images which capture a spiritual truth, memorable sentences which reverberte with meaning for each reader, with the purpose of getting all individuals to be themselves and think for themselves, without relying on the ideas of others. For the full flavor and occasionally knotty thought, the uplift and personal inspiration, in Emerson's work, read the various essays, enjoy the poems; Allen's book is a valuable supplement, explaining the appealing, often enigmatic figure behind the works and their various sources—from Plato to contemporary events and personal experiences—but certainly not taking the place of actually exploring them for oneself.

*Scott Giantvalley*

## Sources for Further Study

*Book World.* XI, October 18, 1981, p. 1.
*Booklist.* LXXVIII, September 1, 1981, p. 18.
*Business Week.* November 9, 1981, p. 22.
*Christian Science Monitor.* LXXIII, October 13, 1981, p. B2.
*Library Journal.* CVI, September 1, 1981, p. 1626.
*The New Republic.* CLXXXV, October 21, 1981, p. 21.
*The New York Times Book Review.* LXXXVI, November 1, 1981, p. 9.

*The New Yorker*. LVII, November 16, 1981, p. 237.
*Saturday Review*. VIII, October, 1981, p. 73.

# THE WAR WITH SPAIN IN 1898

*Author:* David F. Trask (1929-    )
*Publisher:* Macmillan Publishing Company (New York). Illustrated. 654 pp. $29.95
*Type of work:* History
*Time:* 1898
*Locale:* The United States, Spain, and Cuba

*A comprehensive history of the causes, conduct, and consequences of the Spanish-American War*

*Principal personages:*
WILLIAM MCKINLEY, twenty-fifth President of the United States, 1897-1901
MAXIMO GOMEZ, Commander of the Cuban revolutionary army
PRAXEDES MATEO SAGASTA, Prime Minister of Spain
COMMODORE GEORGE DEWEY, Commander of the American Pacific fleet
GENERAL WILLIAM R. SHAFTER, Commander of the American forces in Cuba

This latest addition to the acclaimed *The Macmillan Wars of the United States* is a scholarly tour de force. Based on a prodigious exploration of primary and secondary sources, *The War with Spain in 1898* vividly recounts the causes, battles, strategies, and consequences of a conflict the nation was reluctant to fight but steadfastly determined to win. The book also examines every dimension of the complex political and diplomatic background of the war in both America and Spain. The frenzied diplomacy that failed to avert the conflict is chronicled, as well as the rapid mobilization of regular and volunteer forces. Furthermore, in addition to describing carefully the clash of arms in Cuba, Puerto Rico, and the Philippines, Trask offers fresh insights on how the struggle transformed the United States into a major world power.

The book fills a major void in American military history. Prior to its publication, French Ensor Chadwick's *The Spanish-American War* (1911) and Walter Millis' *The Martial Spirit* (1931) were the standard accounts of the conflict. Scholars who studied the war usually focused on its causes and consequences rather than the military campaigns. A host of articles and books explore whether war could have been avoided, what groups and individuals in American society were responsible for the nation's involvement, if imperialistic motives brought it on, and how the outcome shaped the nation's new standing in international affairs. Trask's study, however, is the first definitive modern sythesis of the subject.

The author correctly defines the book as a "military-political history." He accepts as a truism that war is an extension of politics, an effort to arrive at a desired political settlement by armed force rather than diplomatic pressure, negotiations, and other means. The central focus of the book is the relationship between force and diplomacy during the War with Spain. The military strategies, tactics, and logistics are portrayed in remarkable detail. Every contour of the diplomatic and political landscape is also revealed in order to illustrate how domestic and foreign factors affected the decisions of the contending governments.

Trask breaks a great deal of new ground and challenges many long-accepted views about the war. The author, for example, contradicts the conclusion that the United States Army was badly led and fought poorly in 1898. He smashes the thesis that America crushed the Spanish in the Philippines as an imperialistic adventure, a point of view fostered in recent years by a number of scholars. He also sheds new light on the role of the American president during this period. Rather than treating President William McKinley as a blatant imperialist, Trask portrays him as a serious, talented leader who initially sought to avoid war but later skillfully used force to achieve strategic national goals. McKinley clearly labored to seek a diplomatic solution with Spain and was not at first in favor of annexing the Philippine Islands. Trask also devotes considerable attention to the war at sea, and brings to light heretofore ignored aspects of this subject, such as the voyage of Admiral Camara in relief of Manila after Commodore Dewey's victory.

Trask captures the great irony of the struggle—neither McKinley nor Praxedes Mateo Sagasta, the Spanish Prime Minister, wanted war. The American chief executive had a personal aversion to violence and feared an armed conflict would undermine his domestic priorities—a sound currency and improved tariff legislation. He was dedicated to completing the recovery from the 1893 depression and guarding the future of private enterprise. Nevertheless, the sinking of the American battleship *Maine* at Havana in February, 1898, unleashed a tide of pressures that were too severe for McKinley to withstand. A massive public demand arose for direct United States intervention to liberate Cuba, and McKinley believed that his power and effectiveness as a president would collapse if he resisted these pressures. McKinley pursued a pacific diplomatic course to a point, but by April, 1898, the ungovernable burst of public emotion forced the president to issue to Spain an ultimatum it could not accept—Cuban independence. When the European nation refused, McKinley reluctantly asked Congress to intervene militarily on behalf of the insurrectionist government.

Trask notes that on several past occasions Cuba was the target of American jingoists, and he describes the desire by some for an overseas empire or at least greater national presence in the Caribbean and Central America. Yet, none of these factors account for the decision to go to war. What was viewed as a selfless struggle for freedom provided an outlet for pent-up national feelings that had been building for a generation. Fundmental social and economic changes had occurred that fostered dichotomous feelings of confidence and insecurity. Thus, irrational impulses rather than calculated strategic, economic, ideological, or religious considerations transformed Cuban independence into a national frenzy. Ironically, the Spanish decision to fight was not based on conventional strategic considerations. Despite little chance of victory, Madrid battled to retain its possessions in order to preclude revolution at home and keep its monarch on the throne.

The decision for war surprised statesmen in both countries. Thus, each failed to make comprehensive plans and preparations. The main reason for restraint was that almost everyone had anticipated a political settlement. Spain could ready its decrepit fleet only to protect and supply the remnants of its empire in the Caribbean and Pacific. Despite its strong navy, the United States was virtually without an army; no land operations could be undertaken until a large volunteer force was mobilized.

Trask carefully adumbrates the strategic plan developed by the United States. This "indirect approach" involved attacking on the periphery of the enemy's sphere of influence, conducting operations that would result in the greatest cost to Spain and the least to the United States. The key was to attain victory at sea. The United States had naval superiority, and its first effort would be to engage the enemy in Caribbean and Philippine waters. Once control of the oceans was assured, the Army could then attack Spain's insular possessions. Ideally this strategy would force an early resolution and preclude the need to extend the scene of battle to the Iberian peninsula. Clearly, Spain was in a desperate position; it had to protect its far-flung possessions while facing insurrections in Cuba and the Philippines. Consequently, McKinley could realistically seek a quick victory that would be largely obtained by sea power. The president had only one aim at the beginning of the conflict— Cuban independence. Once the island was free, peace would be sought immediately.

The humanitarian adventure attained is principal objective, Cuban independence, but it also whetted expansionist appetites. McKinley again made careful soundings of public opinion and became convinced that the nation wanted the Philippine archipelago and other possessions. Thus, the peace conference turned into an American territorial grab, something unanticipated when the conflict began. Having been thrust into the arena of great powers, the United States, though more modestly, imitated the behavior of European nations. The subsequent necessity of maintaining an empire forced America on a path for which there were few precedents in the national experience.

Trask firmly establishes that "whatever the failings of William McKinley, he was neither a fool nor a knave." Perhaps he lacked the will to oppose war and overseas expansion. Nevertheless, he exhibited laudatory strategic insight during the struggle and a grasp of the need to relate the use of force to basic political objectives. Despite the judgments of earlier historical accounts, the armed forces performed admirably. The inexperienced force rescued its reputation after initial problems at Tampa and Santiago de Cuba, and the navy vanquished its foe in virtually every engagement.

Trask places emphasis on one of the war's consequences that has needed thorough examination. The Spanish-American War exhibited weaknesses in the organization of the country's armed forces and resulted in a broad spectrum of international responsibilities that required improvements in national defense. The Dodge Commission and other investigations resulted in War Department reforms that improved the plans and preparations for war. The creation of a general staff, improvements in the training of state militias, and other measures disposed of factors that inhibited mobilization in 1898.

The most serious negative consequence of the war was the protracted, dubious, and costly effort to suppress the Philippine Insurrection. This stain on the nation's past might have been averted if the antiimperialist movement which materialized in 1898 had gained momentum. Virtually as the Senate was ratifying the Treaty of Paris in January, 1899, the insurgents led by Amelio Aguinaldo clashed with forces under the command of General Elwell S. Otis. Aguinaldo's decision to resist American sovereignty might have been averted had the Filipinos been more skillfully dealt with.

The acquisition of an empire, while justifiable to many Americans in 1898, seemed foolish to later generations. The drawbacks of becoming more deeply entangled in Latin American and Asian affairs became apparent and dreams of expanded trade and security failed to occur. The "imperialist adventure" also ran counter to cherished national ideals, leading to concern that the subjugation of foreign peoples violated national commitments to democratic principles and the peaceful resolution of disputes. The territories acquired in no way enhanced national security, and in retrospect the overseas adventure, with the exception of achieving Cuban independence, may be seen as a national aberration.

The author concludes that the "most important consequence of the war with Spain was that it hastened the nation's acceptance of international responsibilities commensurate with its power." Thus, it was through this conflict that the United States internationally established its place in the modern world.

*Michael C. Robinson*

### Sources for Further Study

*Booklist*. LXXVIII, September 1, 1981, p. 24.
*Choice*. XIX, November, 1981, p. 437.
*History: Reviews of New Books*. X, November, 1981, p. 34.
*Library Journal*. CVI, May 1, 1981, p. 973.

# WATERLOO
## The Hundred Days

*Author:* David Chandler (1934-      )
*Publisher:* Macmillan Publishing Company (New York). Illustrated. 223 pp. $18.95
*Type of work:* History
*Time:* 1815
*Locale:* France and Belgium

A study of the campaign and the battles which brought about the final downfall of
Napoleon Bonaparte

*Principal personages:*
>NAPOLEON I, Emperor of France, King of Italy, Commander in
>Chief of the French Army
>FIELD MARSHAL GEBHARD LEBERECHT VON BLÜCHER, Prince of
>Wahlstadt, Commander of the Prussian forces
>MARSHAL EMMANUEL, Marquis de Grouchy, Commander of the
>right wing of the French Armee du Nord
>GENERAL AUGUSTUS WILHELM, Graf Neithard von Gneisenau,
>Chief of Staff to Field Marshal Blücher
>MARSHAL MICHEL NEY, Prince of the Moskowa, Duke of Elchingen,
>Commander of the left wing of the French Armee du Nord
>MARSHAL NICOLAS DE DIEU SOULT, Duke of Dalmatia, Chief of
>Staff of the Armee du Nord
>FIELD MARSHAL SIR ARTHUR WELLESLEY, first Duke of Wel-
>lington, British and allied Commander in Chief

The French writer Victor Hugo once grandiosely declared: "the battle of
Waterloo was a change of front for the universe." While it is doubtful that
such an assertion should be made for the entire universe, the remark does
reflect the profound impact that Waterloo had on Europe in the nineteenth
century. Few battles have changed the course of world history as did the one
fought near a small Belgian town in June, 1815, and "Waterloo" is still used
as a synonym for irrevocable defeat.

While the story of the battle and the events leading up to it has been told
many times before, those accounts have often been colored and distorted by
nationalist bias or individual self-defense. In this book, David Chandler, a
British military historian, seeks to explore and explain the Napoleonic catas-
trophe in a balanced way, giving credit and blame equal voice. The result is
a dispassionate, analytical study, typical of the best sort of military history.

The book opens with the escape of Napoleon from forced exile on the
island of Elba in February, 1815. Landing on the French Riviera on March 1,
the Emperor, with about one thousand companions, advanced toward Paris
and recovery of his throne. So commenced the famous Hundred Days of
Napoleonic revival.

Napoleon's successor on the French throne, the Bourbon King Louis XVIII,
dispatched a regiment of troops to confront Bonaparte. At Grenoble, Napo-

leon walked out to meet the royal troops, saying "if there is one among you who wishes to kill his Emperor, here I am." With that, instead of arresting him, the King's men cheered, fell to their knees, or embraced the man who had brought so much glory to France. As he continued northward, more and more Frenchmen hastened to join Napoleon; so many shifted their allegiance that Napoleon is said to have written to King Louis: "there is no need to send any more troops; I already have enough." Within only twenty-three days after his escape from Elba, Napoleon was back in command at the Tuileries Palace in Paris, and King Louis had fled to find sanctuary in England.

Meanwhile, news of the restoration of the "ogre" Napoleon reached Vienna, where a Congress was being held to arrange peace settlements following the earlier defeat and exile of Bonaparte. Among those present at Vienna was Czar Alexander I of Russia, who, when he heard the news, turned to another delegate, the British general, Lord Wellington, saying: "it is time for you to save the world again." The Vienna Congress then declared Napoleon an outlaw, and vowed that Europe would never make peace with him. The delegates hurried away from Vienna to bring their armies together in the Seventh Coalition against Napoleon and France. Austria, Prussia, and Russia promised to supply a total of 700,000 men for the Coalition armies. The British said they would furnish a subsidy of five million pounds, and, although the best British forces happened to be fighting in America at the time, Britain promised to send as many men as could be spared. As matters turned out, the armies of the Coalition did not exceed 500,000 men, and a considerable number of those never saw any battle action. The Duke of Wellington went immediately to Belgium to command the British, Belgian, and Dutch forces being collected there. It was decided that he and the Prussian Commander, Field Marshal Gebhard Leberecht von Blücher, would assemble a force of about 150,000 in Belgium with more to be brought in later, if necessary.

On his side, Napoleon sent out peace feelers to the Coalition leaders, which were ignored or unanswered: they were determined to extinguish the troublemaker once and for all. Realizing that he would have to fight to survive, Napoleon then ordered the renewal of conscription in France. The earlier wars had so decimated French manpower, however, that adding the conscripts to his surviving veterans and the troops from the Bourbon army, Napoleon could raise only about 300,000 men. This necessitated a strategic decision; should he take a defensive position around Paris, try to raise more troops, and wait for the Coalition armies to arrive; or should he take the offensive and strike into Belgium before Wellington's and Blücher's forces had coalesced? He decided on the latter course, and created the Armee de Nord as the strike force. By mid-May, Napoleon had gathered some 232,000 frontline troops; about half of those he assigned to the Armee du Nord, the remainder he divided into smaller groupings and placed them at points along the French frontiers to confront the Austrian and Russian armies of the Coalition, should they arrive. At this point, it should be noted that *Waterloo: The Hundred Days* contains numerous excellent maps showing the dispositions of the different armies by Napoleon and his opponents during the whole campaign.

Another strong point of Chandler's book is his chapter on the rival commanders. As to Napoleon, Chandler says that the Emperor's accomplishments rested on two groups of personal attributes. First was his complete understanding and mastery of the military profession. Not an innovator himself, Napoleon borrowed the ideas of others and used them to great effect; "he contributed little to the armies of France—except victory." Second there was Bonaparte's dominating personality, to which was added a tremendous capacity for hard work, an almost photographic memory, and an ability to "speak to the souls of his men." Napoleon's weaknesses, on the other hand, were his predictability and a tendency to underrate his opponents. Napoleon's enemies by 1815 knew pretty well in advance how he would act in a given situation. As Wellington remarked after the Waterloo battle: "The French came in the same old way, and were repulsed in the same old way." Napoleon's lack of respect for his opponents is illustrated by remarks to Marshal Soult on the eve of the battle: "Because you have been beaten by Wellington [in Spain] you consider him a good general. But I tell you that Wellington is a bad general and the English are bad troops. This whole affair will be no more serious than swallowing one's breakfast."

Chandler characterizes the Duke of Wellington as a stern, patrician taskmaster, very hard on his officers and men; constantly criticizing their efforts, and pointing out their failings and shortcomings. At the same time, Wellington proved to be excellent in strategy and logistics, and fearless in a crisis.

The Prussian Commander, Field Marshal Blücher, is seen as a rough, illeducated man, but endowed with common sense, energy, and courage. He was intensely loyal to his men, and they to him, calling him "Papa" Blücher. Blücher was especially motivated by an intense personal hatred for Napoleon; he had once declared that if he ever had the chance he would see the French Emperor hanged.

Blücher's Chief of Staff, General Gneisenau, is regarded as having been responsible for one of the most critical decisions made at Waterloo. At a point when Blücher was temporarily out of action, Gneisenau directed the Prussians to link up with the English. This ended the Napoleonic hope of driving between the two armies, and was probably the fundamental reason for the ultimate French defeat.

As to the commanders under Napoleon, Chandler finds that they were of mixed qualities. Marshal Ney, Commander of the left wing of the Armee du Nord, was extremely courageous but hotheaded and reckless; he would make several errors of judgment which contributed to the French defeat. Marshal Grouchy, a veteran cavalryman, acquitted himself well as Commander of the right wing of the Armee du Nord, despite a lack of experience in overall strategy. Likewise, Marshal Soult, the French Chief of Staff, was probably not the best man for his job, but he too did reasonably well, given his limited capacities.

By early June, 1815, the rival armies were drawing into their positions. The French Armee du Nord was by then composed of 128,000 men and 366 artillery pieces. It was divided into five corps, with each corps composed of three or four divisions of infantry, one of cavalry, and several artillery batteries. The weapons of the French were generally of inferior quality, especially their muskets, and their supply organization would prove to be defective and inadequate.

The Prussian forces were about the same size as the French. Unlike the French, however, most of the Prussians were inexperienced in battle, although deeply devoted to Prussia and to Blücher. By early June, the Prussians were divided into four corps, placed south and east of Brussels.

Wellington's army was a mixture: some thirty-four thousand British, with the rest Dutch, Belgian, and German, for a total of just under 106,000 troops. These made up 133 infantry battalions, and 109 cavalry squadrons. Wellington also had a field artillery of 216 guns, both cannons and howitzers. His forces were placed to the west of the Prussians, around the roads to Brussels.

On June 14, Napoleon consolidated the Armee du Nord in the vicinity of Beaumont near the Belgian frontier, and prepared to strike. His intention was to drive between Wellington and Blücher, and destroy them each in detail before they could link up. Very early on the morning of June 15, the French regiments crossed the Belgian border and deployed along the Sambre and Meuse rivers. By evening, the left wing under Ney was sent to take the town of Charleroi and push beyond it toward Brussels. At that moment, Wellington was attending a gala party in Brussels, where he received the word that Blucher was moving to counter the French near Charleroi. Wellington was asked, "What do you intend doing?" He answered, "I have ordered the army to concentrate at Quatre Bras (a village about half way between Charleroi and Brussels), but we shall not stop him there. We must fight him here," and he indicated another village on the map of Belgium: Waterloo.

Meanwhile Blücher's Prussians had reached another village, Ligny, a few miles northeast of Charleroi. Napoleon sent his right wing (thirty-five thousand men) under Grouchy to confront Blücher at Ligny, and hard fighting in the streets and houses of Ligny ensued. Blücher's horse was shot from under him and he was so badly bruised that he was pulled from the field. It was then that Gneisenau made a crucial decision. He ordered the Prussians to pull back to Wavre (near Waterloo) so as to be in closer contact with the British. The French pursued the Prussians northward out of Ligny, but Grouchy split his forces, sending some toward Wavre and others toward Liege and Namur, the major Prussian bases; that split would reduce the numbers of French troops available for the climactic battle to come.

Marshal Ney, meanwhile, assaulted the Dutch-Belgian-British positions around Quatre Bras. The fighting was extremely intense and Ney almost overwhelmed the Coalition forces, but Wellington sent reinforcements to slow Ney's momentum at the Quatre Bras crossroads, and, at the climax of the Quatre Bras fighting, Ney was ordered to detach twenty thousand of his troops to assist Grouchy at Ligny. This may have been the most serious blunder of the whole campaign. Had those twenty thousand not been detached, they might have made the difference between victory and stalemate for Ney at Quatre Bras. At it was, Wellington was able to withdraw his forces from Quatre Bras in good order, pulling them back to a ridge called Mont St. Jean, just south of Waterloo.

By Saturday, June 17, Wellington had deployed his men and guns along the Mont St. Jean and in the nearby stone and brick farm buildings on the estates called La Haye Sainte and Hougomont. There, in an area measuring about three miles east to west, and about a mile and a half north to south, the Battle of Waterloo was fought. Napoleon arrived on the morning of June 18, surveyed Wellington's positions, and remarked "I have them then, these English!" Just before noon of the 18th Napoleon attacked. The first French thrust was at the chateau of Hougomont. Led by Napoleon's younger brother, Prince Jerome, the French infantry partially forced their way into the chateau, but the British defenders fought back with great ferocity and ultimately were able to drive Jerome's men out of Hougomont. Meanwhile, Napoleon had directed Ney to take La Haye Sainte, the other allied stronghold. There Ney was successful. Under heavy French artillery bombardment, Wellington was forced to withdraw his men from the chateau. They were pulled back to the Mont St. Jean ridge where they formed the customary British squares of five hundred to one thousand troops each, to await the French attack on the ridge. Up the road between Hougomont and La Haye Sainte Napoleon then sent Ney and ten thousand cavalry. They charged up the ridge and into the British squares and artillery. Time after time, Ney's cavalry charged, but the squares did not break. Ney requested that Napoleon send additional forces to take the ridge. Napoleon could not spare any reinforcements, however, because in the meantime the Prussians had begun to arrive from Wavre and were breaking into the rear of Napoleon's army. The Emperor called on his Old Guard to repulse the Prussians and they responded. Blücher's men were pushed back and Napoleon's rear and flank were temporarily relieved.

Napoleon then decided to throw the Old Guard against Wellington on the ridge, who was now reinforced by more of Blücher's Prussians. It would be the Emperor's last hope of seizing victory. With Ney again in the lead, the French once more ascended the blood-soaked ridge. The British, lying hidden, waited until the French were nearly upon them before they opened fire with artillery and muskets to mow down the French columns. Within the first minute of this final charge, three hundred of the Old Guard fell. Wellington then sent in his infantry to hit the French columns on their flanks. This was too much for even the Old Guard; they either fell back or they died. The surviving French troops broke and ran for their lives, including Napoleon, who hastened back to Paris.

By June 19, more than forty-seven thousand men lay dead or wounded within the three square miles of the Waterloo battlefield. The allies and the local country folk did what they could to relieve the wounded and dying. Field hospitals were set up in farm houses and cottages, while scavengers were busy, robbing, stripping, and leaving to die many wounded men. Said Wellington: "I have never fought such a battle and I trust I shall never fight such another." Chandler calculates that the losses sustained by both sides since the campaign opened on June 15th came to sixty thousand French and fifty-five thousand allies.

Napoleon had been finally and totally defeated. In his second exile on St. Helena, Bonaparte tried to lay most of the blame for Waterloo on Grouchy and Ney. Chandler finds some justification for this, particulary in the case of Ney, who was personally brave, but lacked the ability for chief battle command. Yet Napoleon appointed those men, so the ultimate responsibility for victory or failure must be his. Furthermore, Napoleon's deprecation of Wellington and Blücher indirectly contributed to his own failure, causing him to commit errors of judgment and exercise poor control of the flow of the battle. Possibly he was also unwell; he certainly was indecisive at critical points, and so he lost the battle, his rule over France, and his liberty.

In addition to providing an interesting detailed account of the last Napoleonic battles, Chandler gives his readers a bonus: a guide for a two-day tour of the battlesites and points of interest around Waterloo today, all of which makes *Waterloo: The Hundred Days* a fine book for students of the Napoleonic era.

*James W. Pringle*

## Sources for Further Study

*Best Sellers*. XLI, September, 1981, p. 224.
*Library Journal*. CVI, June 1, 1981, p. 1218.

# WAYS OF ESCAPE

*Author:* Graham Greene (1904-    )
*Publisher:* Simon and Schuster (New York). 320 pp. $13.95
*Type of work:* Autobiography
*Time:* 1927-1980
*Locale:* England, Europe, West Africa, Latin America, and Southeast Asia

*Greene's second autobiographical work, which begins shortly after the publication of his first novel*

One of the chief appeals of Graham Greene's fiction is that it combines adventure and intellectuality, blending the thriller with the psychological and theological novel and thus providing both suspense and substance. Greene's narratives are fast-paced, his style sharp and clear, but the characters and situations have complex ambiguities. The residents of "Greeneland" usually combat a spiritual malaise in exotic, dangerous settings—West Africa, revolutionary Mexico and Uraguay, Cuba, Vietnam, Haiti, or somewhere en route along the Orient Express. The author himself is the chief resident of "Greeneland," and in flight from a deadly boredom has sought out danger zones of body and spirit, quite as much as Ernest Hemingway did, as if he were heeding Gerard Manley Hopkins' injunction that it is dullness, not danger that is to be avoided in the spiritual life. Yet Greene's novels, while drawing upon his travels and experience, are by no means autobiographical. Thus one turns with keen anticipation to Greene's two volumes of autobiography, only to find them frustrating as well as rewarding, for Greene is as reticent as he is revealing, telling much but also withholding much.

The first book of autobiography, *A Sort of Life* (1971), ends with Greene at about twenty-seven, shortly after he has had his first novel published. The reader wonders why Greene took a decade to publish the second autobiographical book, but perhaps his reticence got in the way. He did, however, write introductions to the Bodley Head edition of his collected works, and they may have prompted him to continue his life story, for with some revision, they are incorporated into *Ways of Escape*. In them, Greene does not so much interpret his writings as explain the conditions under which they were created. For more than forty years, he has been one of the most popular as well as esteemed modern writers, but despite the moderate success of *The Man Within* (1929), he was off to a shaky start as a free lance. His second and third novels were so unsuccessful artistically as well as financially that the author suppressed them; most readers are unaware of them, and they have become collectors' items. His fourth novel, *Orient Express*, or *Stamboul Train* (1932) was a success, but its two successors, *It's a Battlefield* (1934) and *England Made Me* (1935, *The Shipwrecked*), while containing some of Greene's best writing, were and are still very little read. Not until *This Gun for Hire* (1936) did he start his long string of popular as well as critical successes. Shortly thereafter, he began screenwriting, and film versions of his work (adapted both by himself and others) have helped make him one of the most widely known serious writers of the century.

Greene's life has all the ingredients of his own novels. He observes that his was a generation "brought up on adventure stories who had missed the enormous disillusionment of the First World War, so we went looking for adventure. . . ." One of his favorite boyhood authors had been H. Rider Haggard, so it is no surprise to find that Greene initially sought adventure in Africa, when in 1935 he made a walking tour of the interior of Liberia that resulted in the travel book *Journey Without Maps* (1936). There, he found no lost cities, immortal princesses, or King Solomon's mines; instead, there were cockroaches, mud villages, fever, and near death. In *Ways of Escape*, he adds details omitted from his travel book, including an account by his cousin Barbara, who accompanied him and wrote her own book of the trip, of how he almost died. His own travel book omits her presence, for he was seeking certain effects, one of which was solitude. His near death in Liberia was like a conversion, for Greene "discovered in myself a passionate interest in living. I had always assumed before, as a matter of course, that death was desirable."

Why, he does not say, except to confess that he has always been a manic-depressive. As a boy, he played Russian roulette. Before writing *The Heart of the Matter* (1948), he contemplated suicide, from which he was saved by returning to his craft as a writer; it is Scobie in the novel who commits suicide instead. After writing *The End of the Affair* (1951), Greene tried to have electric-shock treatment. "I hadn't the courage for suicide, but it became a habit with me to visit troubled places, not to seek material for novels but to regain the sense of insecurity which I had enjoyed in the three blitzes on London." Danger was a way of combating terminal ennui. As a young man, Greene once had a perfectly good tooth extracted just to save himself from boredom. Later, he enjoyed "that feeling of exhilaration which a measure of danger brings to the visitor with a return ticket." It is this exhilaration that Greene conveys to his readers that in part accounts for his popularity, but the physical dangers are usually matched by spiritual perils and mental stimulation as well.

For a long time, Greene divided his books into "entertainments" (supposedly lightweight escapist fare) and novels, but in recent years, he has dropped the distinction. He admits that he has always enjoyed reading and writing melodrama, but his is not the melodrama of his boyhood idol John Buchan, for Greene observes that the moral climate has changed and the world become more treacherous and sinister. This melodramatic intrigue becomes a symbol for the tortured times. Greene's answer to the question of why he sometimes wrote thrillers is that a writer does not choose his subject; it chooses him, and "Our whole planet since the war has swung into the fog-belt of melodrama. . . ."

Greene himself has been involved in that melodrama, for moved by "a restlessness . . . to be a spectator of history," he got into most of the hot spots of the world during the past forty-five years. A visit to revolutionary Mexico in the late 1930's resulted in a travel book, *Another Mexico* (1939, *The Lawless Roads*) and possibly his finest novel, *The Power and the Glory* (1940). Greene was in London during the blitz, and *Ways of Escape* includes a fragment of a journal he kept during that time. He spent several years of World War II with the Secret Service in Sierra Leone and reprints excerpts from his West African notebook, together with the beginning of a novel that he replaced with *The Heart of the Matter*; later, he served with the Secret Service in Portugal. He was in Prague during the revolution and Communist takeover in 1948; he was a correspondent in Malaya during the Emergency in 1951 and in Kenya during the Mau Mau uprising of 1953; he spent four winters in Vietnam between 1951 and 1955 (and reprints excerpts from his Indochina journal); was under fire in Israel during the Six-Day War; and his other journeys include visits to Stalinist Poland, a leper colony in the Congo, François Duvalier's Haiti, and Fulgencio Batista's Cuba when it was about to fall to Castro.

Moreover, he was not an idle observer but got into the thick of the action. In Malaya, he accompanied a Gurkha patrol; in Vietnam, he was on patrol with the Foreign Legion outside Phat Diem and was in a dive bomber that attacked a Viet Minh post; he also had tea with Ho Chi Minh.

Yet Greene is reticent about his own life, and instead of giving much autobiographical detail, provides brilliant analyses of such situations as the guerrilla war in Malaya, the fall of Dien Bien Phu, the tensions and terrors in Kenya during the Mau Mau uprising. Thus one learns more of what Greene has thought about these places and events than of what he did there.

Greene has been called a Catholic novelist (a label to which he objects) not because he is a Catholic convert but because a number of his works dramatize issues of Catholic faith, discipline, and dogma, and deal with what he calls "the appalling strangeness of the mercy of God." Yet one looks in vain for any detailed account of Greene's personal religious views. In *A Sort of Life*, all he says about his conversion is that since he was engaged to marry a Catholic, he thought he should take instruction; he did so and became a Catholic. Clearly, matters could not have been so cut and dried for the author of *The Power and the Glory*, *The Heart of the Matter*, and *The End of the Affair*; but unlike Thomas Merton, Greene reserves matters of faith for the confessional. In *Ways of Escape*, he reveals just a bit, saying that for more than ten years after being received into the Church, he "ad not been emotionally moved, but only intellectually convinced," that he "read a good deal of theology—sometimes with fascination, sometimes with repulsion, nearly always with interest," and that his professional life and religion "were contained in quite separate compartments" until 1937, when the persecution of the Church in Mexico and Franco's attack on republican Spain caused him to "examine more closely the effect of faith on action." In Mexico, he "discovered some emotional belief." Yet *The Power and the Glory*, one of the most eloquent testaments to the power of the sacraments, was on the Index. Pope Paul VI, however, advised him, "Some parts of your books are certain to offend some Catholics, but you should pay no attention to that." Much later, Greene confesses himself "used and exhausted by the victims of religion. The vision of faith as an untroubled sea was lost forever, faith was more like a tempest in which the lucky were engulfed and lost, and the fortunate survived to be flung battered and bleeding on the shore." Yet Greene was not the model for Querry, the protagonist of *A Burnt-Out Case* (1961), and had not abandoned the Church. To a Communist paper, he wrote that "as a Catholic I considered myself able to treat loss of faith just as freely as discovery of faith. . . ." At the same time, he found "nothing unsympathetic in atheism." Elsewhere he says that he increasingly sympathizes with the agnostic reader. Beyond that, Greene discloses very little of his spiritual journeys.

He is even more discreet about his private life, observing, "Those parts of a life most beloved of columnists remain outside the scope of this book." Thus one learns that he had a wife and two children and that his wife showed "courage and understanding" during his early years of artistic and financial struggle, but one does not even learn her name and no mention is made of her again. Instead, in passing, Greene mentions infidelities but never says with whom or under what circumstances; he says nothing about the fate of his marriage or the nature of his affairs, let alone how adultery related to his religion.

He mentions matter-of-factly that in Havana he enjoyed the brothel life, pornography, and got cheated on a sale of cocaine, but again gives no explanations or details. On the other hand, he does not hesitate to describe in detail his smoking opium in Vietnam, though he does not say why or how long he smoked it or how, aside from the external symptoms, it affected him. Perhaps he wished to experience another variety of the seediness that constitutes much of "Greeneland."

Sometimes discretion may have been dictated by necessity; as a Secret Service agent, Greene was not free to disclose classified matters. It suffices that his experiences provided authenticity for such novels as *The Confidential Agent* (1939) and *The Human Factor* (1978), which show an insider's intimacy with intelligence operations and international intrigue.

According to Greene, "Writing is a form of therapy; sometimes I wonder how all those who do not write, compose or paint can manage to escape the madness, the melancholia, the panic fear which is inherent in the human situation." In any event, Greene is nearly the complete man of letters— novelist, essayist, playwright, biographer, screenwriter, travel writer, short-story writer; the only genre missing is poetry. For four and a half years in the

1930's, he was even a film reviewer, who was once sued for libeling Shirley Temple. *Ways of Escape* is an artistic autobiography, providing indispensable insights into the writing of his books, as Greene takes the reader behind the scenes to explain problems of construction, characterization, and ambiguity. In addition, he provides affectionate portraits of fellow authors Nordahl Grieg, Evelyn Waugh, Herbert Read, and filmmaker Alexander Korda. Thus *Ways of Escape* is valuable for the literary critic and historian as much as for the reader interested in knowing the life of one of his favorite authors.

Greene himself may have spent a lifetime trying to escape from ennui, but he is incapable of boring the reader.

*Robert E. Morsberger*

**Sources for Further Study**

*America*. CXLIV, March 21, 1981, p. 233.
*Christian Science Monitor*. LXXIII, February 9, 1981, p. B2.
*Critic*. XXXIX, March 1, 1981, p. 2.
*Library Journal*. CVI, February 15, 1981, p. 453.
*The New Republic*. CLXXXIII, December 27, 1980, p. 33.
*The New York Review of Books*. XXVIII, February 19, 1981, p. 15.
*The New York Times Book Review*. LXXXVI, January 18, 1981, p. 1.
*The New Yorker*. LVI, February 16, 1981, p. 130.
*Newsweek*. XCVII, January 5, 1981, p. 56.
*Saturday Review*. VIII, January, 1981, p. 64.

# W. H. AUDEN
## A Biography

*Author:* Humphrey Carpenter
*Publisher:* Houghton Mifflin Company (Boston). Illustrated. 495 pp. $15.95
*Type of work:* Literary biography
*Time:* 1907-1973
*Locale:* England, Germany, America, and Austria

*The first major biography of W. H. Auden, and the first to make extensive use of letters and manuscripts, this extremely well-written and helpful work recounts in detail the chronology of Auden's life and locates the generation of his work within it*

> *Principal personages:*
> WYSTAN HUGH AUDEN, a poet
> GEORGE AUGUSTUS AUDEN, his father
> CONSTANCE ROSALIE BICKNELL AUDEN, his mother
> CHRISTOPHER ISHERWOOD, a writer and a close friend
> CHESTER KALLMAN, Auden's companion
> STEPHEN SPENDER,
> CECIL DAY-LEWIS, and
> T. S. ELIOT, poets

The period of the 1920's, 1930's, and 1940's is now beginning to be seen as extremely significant for the shaping of Western culture in the postwar era. Certain moments and places in those years have come to stand for decisive changes in human consciousness. The sexual openness of Weimar Berlin in the 1920's, the political conflict of the Spanish Civil War of the 1930's in the context of economic crisis, and the shifting of political relationships in the conduct of World War II have all had their profound impact on the contemporary world. W. H. Auden, who participated in all these events, has for that reason, along with his ability to respond imaginatively to his experience of these events, become, after T. S. Eliot, the major poet of the twentieth century. A frequent visitor to Germany in the 1920's, an observer of the Spanish fighting, and an immigrant to America just before the outbreak of World War II, Auden was able to chronicle his age, and give it its appropriate name—the Age of Anxiety.

It is therefore especially important for an understanding of Auden to have a work such as Humphrey Carpenter's biography, a work that locates the writing of his poetry and other works in the context of Auden's life. Carpenter, soundly, does not try to offer detailed explications of the writing; instead, he allows generous quotation from the work to illuminate Auden's response to the events he observed or in which he participated. As a result, Carpenter's biography of Auden is a splendid companion to Auden's works themselves, an account of the life that is both pleasurable to read and destined to become a constant point of reference for serious study of the works.

This is not to say that the historical context out of which Auden wrote will "explain" his poetry; it is merely a claim that, especially for a poet such as Auden, given to deliberate obscurity in much of his writing, knowing the context and at least some of the more personal references will enable fuller and more informed response. Carpenter is able to orient readers to the kinds of personal and cultural issues and situations in which Auden was involved as he composed his work. Such knowledge will not take the place of his works themselves, but it will enable readers to approach them more intelligently.

Especially in some areas of Auden's life, Carpenter is able to combine a directness that clarifies with a sense of decorum that avoids the sensationalistic. Many modern biographers delight in the candor with which they can relate the intimate lives of their subjects, and Auden might easily have received such lurid treatment. Except for a brief heterosexual relationship in middle life, Auden was openly and often aggressively homosexual and had a long series of both "one-night-stand" encounters and more enduring relationships with a wide variety of male lovers. This fact was well-known to all who had more than the most superficial acquaintance with him, yet in the manner of a more circumspect age, it was never openly proclaimed. Carpenter, in his treatment of this aspect of Auden's life, avoids the pitfalls of lurid revelation by being specific and candid without trying to explain or explain away something he had to deal with if he were to write Auden's life.

Carpenter offers the sweep of Auden's life, from its beginnings in Yorkshire, through the early years of education, the years at Oxford, the Berlin experiences, the years as a schoolmaster in rural boys' schools, the Spanish experiences, and then the years Auden spent in America and Austria, moving to a close with Auden's return to live at Oxford, and his death in Austria in 1973. The text is augmented with a splendid selection of photographs and a haunting reproduction of a group of sketches of Auden made by an Austrian artist at a poetry reading given the night Auden died. Carpenter divides the life into two large sections, the period 1907-1939, in which England was Auden's home, and the period 1939-1973, in which Auden lived chiefly in America and, after the war, in Europe. What binds the life together, at least in Carpenter's reading, is poetry; Carpenter's Auden developed a strong sense of literary vocation early in life and, in effect, lived to write for much of the rest of it. Carpenter traces Auden's developing sense of literary form through a variety of experimentations, and then traces through the mature work Auden's shifting concerns with theme and subject.

Carpenter describes Auden's early interest in politics leading up to his trip to Spain and his progressive disenchantment with the quality of modern life after his experiences in the Spanish Civil War. Through this period Auden was reaching out for the larger schemes of meaning, a process which ultimately culminated in a reawakening of interest in the High Church Anglicanism of his boyhood experience. Along the way Carpenter chronicles Auden's long-standing friendship with Christopher Isherwood and his often painful but enduring relationship with Chester Kallman.

Throughout, Carpenter sustains interest through the effective use of quotations from letters to and from Auden, as well as the recorded memories of participants in these events who are still living. In fact, if one were to make any criticism of this book at all, it would be that Caprenter provides so much information that one sometimes loses sight of larger, more long-term developments in Auden's life. Perhaps at some point in the preparation of this biography Carpenter made a conscious decision to avoid speculative discussion about Auden's interior development in favor of the safer ground of external, chronological detail. While one must be grateful for all that Carpenter provides, there are times in which a bit more risky venturing into psychological analysis could have been both appropriate and effective.

In any case, Auden's poetic and literary achievement is securely fixed at the top of the modern literary ladder. Thanks to Carpenter's book, and other recent editorial recoveries of different versions of Auden's poems, one can look forward to a long and rewarding series of studies which will examine more closely Auden's development as an artist. Until they appear, one can, with Carpenter's guidance, enjoy Auden himself. Carpenter's life will surely be one of the foundations of Auden study for many years to come.

*John N. Wall, Jr.*

### Sources for Further Study

*Christian Science Monitor.* LXXIII, November 9, 1981, p. B9.
*Commonweal.* CVIII, November 6, 1981, p. 633.
*Library Journal.* CVI, September 15, 1981, p. 1735.
*New Statesman.* CII, July 3, 1981, p. 20.
*The New York Review of Books.* XXVIII, December 17, 1981, p. 53.
*The New York Times Book Review.* LXXXVI, October 4, 1981, p. 1.
*Newsweek.* XCVIII, September 28, 1981, p. 92.
*Saturday Review.* VIII, September, 1981, p. 54.
*Spectator.* CCXLVII, July 4, 1981, p. 19.
*Times Literary Supplement.* July 3, 1981, p. 745.

# WHAT WE TALK ABOUT WHEN WE TALK ABOUT LOVE

*Author:* Raymond Carver (1939-    )
*Publisher:* Alfred A. Knopf (New York). 159 pp. $9.95
*Type of work:* Short stories

*A collection of seventeen stories published originally in various American literary quarterlies during the late 1970's*

From its beginnings in the nineteenth century, the American short story has always been more closely associated with lyric poetry than with its overgrown narrative neighbor, the novel. Regardless of whether short fiction clung to the legendary tale form of its ancestry (as in Nathaniel Hawthorne) or whether it moved toward the presentation of the single event (as in James Joyce) the form has always been a "much in little" proposition which conceals more than it reveals and leaves much unsaid.

There are two basic means by which the short story has pursued its movement away from the linearity of prose toward the spatiality of poetry—either by using the metaphoric and plurasignificative language of the poem or by radically limiting its selection of the presented event. The result has been two completely different textures in short fiction—the former characterized by such writers as Eudora Welty in the 1940's and 1950's and Bernard Malamud in the 1960's and 1970's, whose styles are thick with metaphor and myth, and the latter characterized by such writers as Ernest Hemingway in the 1920's and 1930's and Raymond Carver in the 1970's and 1980's, whose styles are thin to the point of disappearing.

Carver's first collection of stories, *Will You Please Be Quiet, Please?*, published in 1976 and nominated for a National Book Award, was, although drained of imagery and other language devices usually associated with prose lyricism, at least characterized by a play with the plenitude of language, exploiting talk as a means of understanding in the colloquial fashion of Sherwood Anderson. In *What We Talk About When We Talk About Love*, however, language is used so sparingly and the plots are so minimal that the stories seem pallidly drained patterns with no flesh and life in them. The stories fulfill the by-now familiar expectations of modern antifiction, associated with such writers as Julio Cortazar, Heinrich Böll, Jorge Luis Borges, Donald Barthelme, Eugène Ionesco, and others: they are antiplot, anticharacter, antitheme, and antianalysis. The stories are so short and lean that they seem to have plot only as one reconstructs them in memory. Whatever theme they may have is embodied in the bare outlines of the event and in the spare dialogue of characters who are so overcome by events and so lacking in language that the theme is unsayable. Characters often have no names or only first names and are so briefly described that they seem to have no physical presence at all; certainly they have no distinct identity but rather seem to be shadowy presences trapped in their own inarticulateness.

The charge that is often lodged against such fiction is that it is dehumanized and therefore cold and unfeeling. Such a charge ignores the nature of art that has characterized Western culture since the nineteenth century and which José Ortega y Gasset so clearly delineated thirty-five years ago in *The Dehumanization of Art*. In their nostalgia for the bourgeois security of nineteenth century realism, critics of so-called antifiction forget that the royal road to art, as Ortega delineates it, is the "will to style," and to stylize "means to deform reality, to derealize: style involves dehumanization." Given this definition of art, it is easy to see that Raymond Carver's stories do emphatically embody "the will to style." Carver realizes that the artist must not confuse reality with idea, that he must inevitably turn his back on alleged reality and, as Ortega insists, "take the ideas for what they are—mere subjective patterns—and make them live as such, lean and angular, but pure and transparent."

The lyricism of Carver's stories lies in this will to style in which reality is derealized and ideas live solely as ideas. Carver's stories are more "poetic," that is, more "artistic" than one usually expects fiction to be and thus help define the difference between the loose and baggy monstrous novel and the taut, gemlike short story. Georg Lukacs, in his *Theory of the Novel* (1972), describes the short story in a way that perfectly delineates Carver's stories, for they select events that "pin-point the strangeness and ambiguity of life," events that suggest the arbitrary nature of experiences whose workings are always without cause or reason. In Carver's stories, as in the short story form generally, according to Lukacs, the focus is on "absurdity in all its undisguised and unadorned nakedness," and the lyricism is concealed behind the "hard outlines of the event." Absurdity, says Lukacs, "is given the consecration of form; meaninglessness *as* meaninglessness becomes form; it becomes eternal because it is affirmed, transcended and redeemed by form."

The first story in the collection, "Why Don't You Dance?," is one of many examples of this particular kind of lyricism in Carver's fiction. Plot is minimal, event is mysterious, character is negligible. A man puts all his furniture out in his front yard and runs an extension cord out so that things work just as they did when they were inside. A young couple stop by, look at the furniture, try out the bed, have a drink, and the girl dances with the owner. The conversation is functional, devoted primarily toward making purchases in a perfectly banal garage-sale way. At the conclusion, the young wife is telling someone about the event. "She kept talking. She told everyone. There was more to it, and she was trying to get it talked out. After a time, she quit trying." The problem is, the event cannot be talked out; it is completely objectified in the spare description of the event itself. Although there is no exposition in the story, the reader knows that a marriage is over, that the secret life of the house has been externalized on the front lawn, that the owner has made a desperate metaphor of his marriage, that the hopeful young couple play out a mock scenario of that marriage which presages their own, that the event itself is a parody of events not told, but kept hidden, like the seven-eighths of the iceberg that Hemingway said could be left beneath the surface of prose if one knew one's subject well enough.

Things not said because they are unsayable also underlie "Gazebo," a story of a shadowy couple named simply Holly and Duane who have taken over as managers of a motel. As Duane says, everything was just fine, that is, until he began a purely sexual relationship with a Mexican maid. The story recounts the break-up of the marriage as the couple withdraw from their work and spend the time drinking and talking in one of the motel suites. They stop registering guests, stop cleaning the pool, and stop answering the phone, until the management people write that they are coming to close things down. Duane, who speaks in the clichés of modern youth, faces it all helplessly. "We knew our days were numbered. We had fouled up our lives and we were getting ready for a shake-up." As in other Carver stories, the event is more than can be articulated or escaped, and the couple in the upstairs motel room serve as a stark metaphor for marriage, infidelity, nostalgia for lost dreams, and divorce in the modern American landscape.

In "Tell the Women We're Going" and "So Much Water So Close to Home," perhaps the most shocking stories in the collection, sexuality and violence combine in extreme ways that remind one of the mystery of the inextricable relationship between these two primal emotions. "Tell the Women We're Going," is only a summary account of the marriage of two friends, filled with banality and backyard barbecues, until Bill and Jerry go for a ride during one of these barbecues and start following a couple of girls. Bill, who is the protagonist of the story, merely wants sex or even to see the girls naked; if nothing works out he will not be too disappointed. The piece is no story at all until the final paragraph, when abruptly the slackness tightens in a brutal epiphany for the reader: "He never knew what Jerry wanted. But it started and ended with a rock. Jerry used the same rock on both girls, first on the girl called Sharon and then on the one that was supposed to be Bill's." Although the shock has not been explicitly prepared for in the story, it has been prepared for tacitly. There is no particular aberration in Jerry that makes him kill the girls. It is only that he has reached a point of helplessness, or disappointment, or boredom, or frustrated need, or resentment, or a combination of all these that makes the murder inevitable. Whatever cultural or psychological significance the story suggests is left to the reader, but any attempt to explain the event away would be to reduce it.

Whereas "Tell the Women We're Going" *ends* with violence and sex, a conclusion toward which the entire story inevitably moves, "So Much Water So Close to Home" *begins* with a scene of sexual violence of which the story then works out the implications. The event is related by the wife of a man who goes on a fishing trip in the back country with some friends. When they reach their camp site, they see the nude body of a young girl, wedged in some branches that stick out over the water. The men make various excuses for not doing anything; they set up camp, fish, play cards, and drink for two days before hiking out and calling someone about the dead body. After hearing about the incident, the wife becomes alienated from her husband and obsessed with the event, even going to the young girl's funeral. When she comes back home, however, her husband looks at her and says, "I think I know what you need," and begins to unbutton her blouse. Her distracted, yet urgent response, which ends the story is: "That's right. . . . Hurry." Again the stark event is sufficient, for one knows that the wife has seen herself in the dead girl, has seen herself violated and dehumanized, reduced to body and made a thing to be ignored by a group of men playing their men-only escape games. At the same time, after having seen the dead girl, the wife sees sex as the means of a desperate effort to hang on to life. The dilemma of woman in its most primal sense, apart from social considerations, is most vividly embodied here. The problem faced in the story is not one that the ERA can eradicate, nor one that social issues can touch.

All the stories in Carver's collection have more the ambience of dream than of reality. They are unconcerned with social issues and values, yet the stories are not parables in the usual sense, for even as the characters are representative rather than real, they are still feeling figments of Carver's imagination. They give the feel of emotional reality which reaches the level of myth, even as they refuse to give the feel of physical or simple psychological reality. The characters inhabit a real, albeit sketchily delineated world, a world that seems primarily oneiric even when it is concretely described. In this way, Carver's stories are representative examples of the tendency of the short story to focus on dreams and subconscious awareness. Recent studies of dreams indicate that people seldom, if ever, dream of social issues and events; similarly, the short story form has never had the social consciousness of the novel. The short story is a primal rather than a derivative form, focusing on experiences that deal with primitive hopes, dreams, anxieties, and fears.

The central theme of Carver's stories is the tenuous union between men and women and the mysterious separations that always seem inevitable. In the title story, two couples having a drink before going out to dinner talk about their previous marriages. One woman says her ex-husband loved her so much that he dragged her around the room, saying, "I love you, you bitch." When she finally left him, he drank rat poison and later finished the job by shooting himself in the mouth. Her present husband, Mel, says, "If you call that love, you can have it," but Mel does most of the talking as he ponders aloud about the transient and elusive nature of love. He tells about an old couple who are in the hospital after an auto accident. The old man becomes depressed because his bandages and casts will not permit him to turn around and see his wife in the bed next to him. Mel is insistent about the significance of this: "Do you see what I'm saying? . . . I mean, it was killing the old fart just because he couldn't *look* at the fucking woman." After this, the conversation dies down and the liquor is gone, but no one moves, not even when the room goes dark.

The need for love, the fear of love, the futility of finding it and keeping it, and the inability to say anything meaningful about it are all treated in the story "One More Thing" in a most economical way. As a man gathers up his things to leave the house after an argument with his wife, he stops at the door and says, "I just want to say one more thing," but the last line of the story is, "But then he could not think what it could possibly be." In "A Serious Talk," a similarly abbreviated story, a man vainly struggles to get back with his wife and once more she drives him out of the house; he picks up an ashtray to throw it, but leaves instead. "The thing was," he thinks as he walks out, "they had to have a serious talk soon." Even as he gets in and starts the car, he holds on to the ashtray, a solid yet meaningless emblem of his frustration.

In two completely absurd satires, "The Viewfinder" and "Popular Mechanics," a man without hands takes photos of the house of a man deserted by his wife and family as the man sits on his roof and throws rocks, and a couple engage in a literal tug-of-war with their baby, pulling very hard until, as the last line of the story ambiguously reveals, "In this manner, the issue was decided." In "Sacks," a young man realizes the bleakness of his own marriage as he listens to his father tell of his affair with a saleswoman, and in "The Calm" another man decides to leave his wife after witnessing an argument in a barber shop about a hunting trip in which a man allowed a wounded animal to die slowly without finishing it off.

The stories are all bleak black-and-white snapshots of the American marital scene, but told in such a way that the universally human mystery of union and separation is exposed, if not revealed. The stories may be related in a terse, laconic voice that refuses to become involved, but it is not a voice that suggests heartlessness and dehumanization. Rather it is a voice that makes one care because one recognizes, although perhaps in a vague inchoate way, the same mysterious sources of fear within oneself. The so-called dehumanization of modern American fiction actually reveals a humanity that goes deeper than the ordinary everyday understanding of that term. The kind of humanity that Raymond Carver's stories reveal can neither be understood nor cured by the supermarket psychology that tries to pass for human understanding today; it can only be captured in the pure and painful experience of human beings who come together and come apart.

*Charles May*

## Sources for Further Study

*The Atlantic Monthly*. CCXLVII, June, 1981, p. 96.
*Hudson Review*. XXXIV, Autumn, 1981, p. 459.
*Library Journal*. CVI, March 15, 1981, p. 678.
*The Nation*. CCXXXIII, July 4, 1981, p. 23.
*The New Republic*. CLXXXIV, April 25, 1981, p. 38.
*The New York Review of Books*. XXVIII, May 14, 1981, p. 37.
*The New York Times Book Review*. LXXXVI, April 26, 1981, p. 1.
*Newsweek*. XCVII, April 27, 1981, p. 96.
*Saturday Review*. VIII, April, 1981, p. 77.
*Time*. CXVII, April 6, 1981, p. 82.

# THE WHITE HOTEL

*Author:* D. M. Thomas (1935-    )
*Publisher:* The Viking Press (New York). 256 pp. $12.95
*Type of work:* Novel
*Time:* The first half of the twentieth century
*Locale:* Europe

*A historical-fictional account of European consciousness during the first half of the twentieth century as experienced and witnessed by Lisa Erdman-Berenstein*

> Principal characters:
> SIGMUND FREUD, Austrian neurologist and founder of psychoanalysis
> LISA ERDMAN-BERENSTEIN, his patient and heroine of the novel

All human beings are survivors. They love and they work, as Sigmund Freud said. They also march toward their deaths from the moment they are born. Wanting to return to the womb is a flight from death toward oblivion. *The White Hotel* is a poetic/dramatic expression of this dialectic. It moves relentlessly toward a paradoxical conclusion: that living and dying, loving and hating, despair and hope are complex unities.

*The White Hotel* creates its context through the character of Lisa Erdman-Berenstein. Through her life, a dispassionate yet penetrating portrayal is presented of a European culture in the process of change and crisis. Lisa's inner struggles echo those in the outside world. Her consciousness becomes a metaphor for social and political reality. Throughout the novel, her visionary inner life finds expression in the *real* outer world. She even foresees her own death at Babi Yar. As the novel progresses, "reality" becomes too complicated to unravel. It becomes thoroughly mixed with fantasy, hope, and denial. The dead come to life at the end of *The White Hotel*, and one must ask: in what ways do they live on? In what ways have they perished? How do human beings survive the experience/recognition of their own mortality?

Freud would have enjoyed *The White Hotel*. D. M. Thomas skillfully weaves in some actual events in Freud's life along with his (fictional) psychoanalytic work with Lisa Erdman. Freud becomes a character in a story which concerns him. He is historically real; artistically fictional. He goes on being Freud, even with an imaginary patient. Using a Freudian framework for the novel, Thomas is able to set out his portrayal of Lisa on many levels. Lisa is a real person (within the novel), and she is a fictive person in her own writings. She is the object of a case study by Sigmund Freud and therefore also becomes a combination of her own life and Freud's imaginative re-creation. The novel peels away the layers of her life, exposing the lies, distortions, and half-remembered incidents, yet her story ends with a reality which is beyond belief (Babi Yar) and a conclusion that is clearly a fantasy. Freud's work, of course, uncovered and called attention to these paradoxes in human experience. He changed the way people view themselves and their society. In the face of death, people continue, and beyond their deaths, others continue for them.

*The White Hotel* uses the Freudian theory of the repetition compulsion as a structural device. Events are repeated, twisted, repeated. The novel opens several times. There is an author's Note and a Prologue, a poem, a recapitulation and expansion of the poem and then the case study, *Frau Anna G.* Almost a third of the book is used to set the scene and to preview the rest of the book. One begins and begins again, and as one begins one learns about ending. The slaughter and the sweet redemption are both foreseen by Lisa. She contains within her psyche the essence of humanity. She sees destruction and love, hatred and replenishment. She has been there before and will return again.

Lisa Erdman is introduced by Freud in the third chapter, entitled *Frau Anna G.* Although the reader has already met her via her journal and sexually provocative poetry, the case-study approach serves to combine a view of Lisa as both a real person and as a figment of another's literary imagination. She is simultaneously a universal, vital consciousness and an individual subject for study. Freud says that Lisa was the second child of moderately well-to-do parents. Her father was a Russian Jewish merchant and her mother, a cultivated Polish Catholic. Throughout her life, the burden of religious choice weighed on her. Although she marries in her twenties a young anti-Semitic lawyer and wears a cross around her neck, her interest in Judaism and her ambivalent wish to be Jewish and be close to her father remain. Her second marriage at age forty to Victor Berenstein, a Jew, almost reverses her position. When she dies at Babi Yar, she at first tries to escape by showing papers that prove her non-Jewishness, yet she cannot free Victor's ten-year-old son because he has papers that attest to his Jewishness. Her ambivalent commitment to a religious ideal is solved. She dies with the Jews and awakens as a Jewish refugee in Palestine.

A central conflict for Lisa is her sexual life, both real and fantasied. In true Freudian fashion, the story of Lisa's childhood unravels through dreams, associations, transferences, screen memories, and workings through. When she is five, her mother dies in a hotel fire, and soon afterward her uncle, who is married to her mother's twin sister, dies. Lisa's father becomes morose and withdrawn, and although Lisa grows into a multilingual, well-educated teenager, she suffers from a deep unhappiness and loneliness. At seventeen, she leaves Odessa, where she has lived most of her life, and goes to St. Petersburg to make her way as a singer. There, she falls in love with a zealous but sadistic political revolutionary, becomes pregnant, has a miscarriage, and eventually moves to Vienna to live with her mother's sister. Within three years, she is engaged to be married and is developing a promising career in the opera. When the war breaks out, her husband is drafted. Although a little lonely, she is happily enlarging her career. Just before her husband is scheduled for his first home leave, she develops terrible pains in her left breast and ovary as well as an incapacitating breathlessness. Deciding that she can never make her husband happy, she eventually convinces him to have their marriage annulled. That break occurs four years before she comes to Freud. During that period, she has lived with her aunt, now a devout Catholic, and continually visits physicians to try to find an organic cause for her pains.

Although outwardly demure and subdued, Lisa presents a poem and then a journal to Freud which race with sexual energy and scatalogical vision. The story concerns her and Freud's son, whom she meets on a train while returning to her four-year-old son. The young man seduces her, then invites her to spend some time with him at a lakeside resort, the White Hotel. The poem and the journal recount nights and days of intense, endless sexual activity which occurs in their room, in the restaurant, in a boat, in a forest. The sexual hunger and pleasure is all-consuming and self-focused. As a backdrop to this scene, however, four major catastrophes occur. First, there is a flood which drowns many of the inhabitants; then, when they take a boat ride, there is a hotel fire in which many perish while they, on the lake, witness the conflagration. The third disaster is a landslide which buries the mourners who have been burying those killed in the fire. Finally there is a cable car accident. People float through the air to their deaths. Lisa "sees" all this as she moves in endless sexual rhythm.

Working with Freud, Lisa gradually unravels some of the meanings of the White Hotel. The storm that occurred on the night Lisa was told about her mother's death in a hotel fire connects the White Hotel (with its nourishing yet consuming character) to a wish to be reunited with her mother and return to her mother's womb. In the White Hotel, there is no division between self and other. The two bodies cling together despite outer tragedy; they are united in nurturing death. The sexual fantasies suggest not only libidinous connections between a mother and child but also other incestuous relationships. Here are revealed the love affairs between Lisa's mother and her uncle, between Lisa's mother, aunt, and uncle, between Lisa's father and the housekeepers. Lisa has witnessed some of these couplings and learns that her mother and her uncle perished together in a hotel fire. Lisa's wish that she might be the real daughter of her uncle and therefore not be part-Jewish influences her decision to end her marriage to Willi. Because he wants children, Lisa fears his discovery of her mixed ancestry. Additionally, she does not want to pass on the burden of this mixed allegiance. Her pains and breathlessness begin as she decides she cannot remain married.

Eventually, Lisa's pains abate, and she continues with her life without Freud. She is not an outstanding singer, but she is good enough to be asked to stand in at La Scala for a major opera star, Serebryakova. She goes to Milan and is warmly received by Serebryakova and her husband, Victor. Vera (her real name) is not singing because she has broken her arm and plans to return to Kiev. A warm friendship develops among the three and when Vera leaves, she confides to Lisa that she is pregnant. Victor and Lisa work together and continue to develop their friendship. Tragedy strikes when Vera dies in childbirth. Four years later, Victor writes to Lisa and offers her a part in an opera he is directing as well as a proposal of marriage. His son Kolya needs a mother, and Victor's mother, who has been caring for the child, wishes to return to her village as she is very old and ready to die.

After many weeks of deliberation, Lisa accepts the marriage proposal and moves back to Russia. On her honeymoon, she visits her beloved Odessa, walks by her father's old business location, and discovers that the old white house which had been her home is now converted into a health resort (a white hotel). It is here that she makes the connection with the past, the present, and the future beyond her life. She smells the pine trees near her old home and suddenly

> as she stood close against a pine tree and breathed in its sharp, bitter scent, a clear space opened to her childhood, as though a wind had sprung up from the sea, clearing a mist. It was not a memory from the past but the past itself, as alive, as real; and she knew that she and the child of forty years ago were the same person. . . . And when she looked in the opposite direction, towards the unknown future, death, the endless extent beyond death, she was there still. It all came from the scent of a pine tree.

The last two chapters of the book recapitulate in eerie ways the visions, impressions, and accounts in Lisa's poem and journal. The war is on, and Victor, as a Jew, has been taken away. Lisa and Victor's ten-year-old son are fleeing from the Germans, who have invaded Russia, but they do not escape. They are trapped at Babi Yar and watch as babies are thrown into the air and bodies fall into a large coffin already containing thousands of corpses. The incestuous embraces analytically explored with Freud here take on a sardonic turn as Lisa and Kolya, naked and doomed, embrace in the death pits of Babi Yar.

The final chapter moves beyond the life of Lisa Erdman-Berenstein to a new/old Lisa, alive and hopeful with Kolya, her parents and family in Palestine. Lisa visits her mother, makes peace with her father, and begins work with a new but scarred British soldier named Richard Lyons. Lisa watches the thousands of immigrants coming to Palestine and wonders why life is like this. Not surprisingly, there are echoes of the old question asked at the White Hotel: "'Is this all there is?' she asked, apologetically. 'It's all we know about,' said the young woman, in thoughtful tones."

The final sentences of the novel again repeat the old in the presence of the new. Human beings survive even as they perish: it's all they know. "She smelt the scent of a pine tree. She couldn't place it. . . . It troubled her in some mysterious way, yet also made her happy."

*Faith Gabelnick*

## Sources for Further Study

*Encounter.* LVII, August, 1981, p. 56.
*Library Journal.* CVI, February 1, 1981, p. 370.
*Nation.* CCXXXII, May 2, 1981, p. 537.
*The New Republic.* CLXXXIV, March 28, 1981, p. 35.
*New Statesman.* CI, January 16, 1981, p. 21.
*The New York Times Book Review.* LXXXVI, March 15, 1981, p. 1.
*Newsweek.* XCVII, March 10, 1981, p. 89.
*Saturday Review.* VIII, March, 1981, p. 72.
*Time.* CXVII, March 16, 1981, p. 88.
*Times Literary Supplement.* January 16, 1981, p. 50.

# WHITE SUPREMACY
## A Comparative Study in American and South African History

*Author:* George M. Fredrickson (1934-    )
*Publisher:* Oxford University Press (New York). 356 pp. $19.95
*Type of work:* History
*Time:* The 1600's to the present
*Locale:* The American South and South Africa

*A comparative history of South African and American race relations*

The most important subject for comparative study in American history is the rise and fall of that "peculiar institution," Afro-American slavery. In the last thirty-five years, a significant body of literature has appeared that has compared the slave system in the United States with slavery in Latin America. These works have sparked a lively and continuous debate.

The first of these works was Frank Tannenbaum's *Slave and Citizen: The Negro in the Americas*, published in 1946. This book presented the thesis that the treatment of slaves was milder in Latin America than in the United States, a difference attributed by Tannenbaum to the strength of the Roman Catholic Church in Latin America, which encouraged better treatment for and more frequent manumission of slaves.

Also important to Tannenbaum was how the freedmen fared after they were released. Again he argued that the freedmen were treated better in the Latin American nations than in the United States. The work of Stanley Elkins and Herbert Klein confirmed this view of important differences between the slave systems of British America and Latin America.

In 1966, David Brion Davis in *The Problem of Slavery in Western Cultures* offered the first important critique of the Tannenbaum-Elkins-Klein thesis. Davis maintained that Tannenbaum stressed the differences in the slave systems to the neglect of the many similarities. He further felt that, if there were differences, they were caused not so much by the legal and cultural heritage but by economic differences, the number of slaves involved, the type of slave employment, and the ratio of slaves to whites. Carl Degler and H. Hoetink have strengthened the thesis that it was the economic situation that shaped the slave system and not the Catholic Church or the King of Spain.

George M. Fredrickson in *White Supremacy: A Comparative Study in American and South African History* not only continues the comparative approach regarding slave and citizen but expands the historical purview to include another area of the world for a frame of reference—South Africa. Fredrickson is not the first to compare South Africa with the American South; William Wilson in his analysis of racism in *Power, Racism and Privileges* (1976) and Kenneth P. Vickery in an article in 1974, "Herrenvolk Democracy and Egalitarianism in South Africa and the U.S. South," have produced interesting works comparing South Africa with the United States South, but

Fredrickson is the first to break new historical ground by his careful analysis and superb scholarship.

This work is a model study in the growing field of comparative history. Using a large number of sources in American and African history, Fredrickson has also used significant works in the social sciences. He has given his readers the perspective needed to understand the complex field of race relations, covering two continents and three hundred years of history with a sensible organization and clear approach.

Six general topics are presented in the work: (1) the opening of these two frontiers to white settlement and the awakening of the settlers to new conditions and native dangers; (2) the development of slavery and the working out of a slave culture; (3) race mixing and the drawing of a color line; (4) sectional conflict with central authorities and the results of these disagreements; (5) the emergence of industrialization and the growth of class and racial conflict; (6) the appearance of Jim Crow in the South and apartheid in South Africa. What gives this work its unity is the author's focus on the white man's policies and beliefs and the understanding that this "emphasis provides . . . the causes, character, and consequences of white supremacy in the two societies."

In both South Africa and the American South there were long, bloody wars between whites and natives for control of the land. To rationalize the taking of the land and the destruction of native culture, the whites used the religious and social differences between themselves and the natives: conquest was idealized as a struggle between heathen savages and civilized Christian whites. When religious fervor and the issue of racial inferiority sparked confrontations, the end result was usually death and the removal of the natives.

Fredrickson points out the interesting fact that the removal of southern Indian tribes to the trans-Mississippi West occurred at the same time, the 1830's, as the Great Trek of the Voortrekkers from the Cape Colony to the area north of the Great Fish River. There were, however, crucial differences in these removals. In the United States, the natives were forcibly removed by the American government to make way for white farmers; in South Africa, the Boers trekked northward because of the refusal of the British government to provide them with land to increase the size of their farms. Unlike the American farmers, the Boers often felt like a persecuted minority. Thus the Great Trek was as much a reaction against unpopular governmental policies as it was a search for new lands.

One of the most important problems that the early settlers in South Africa and the American South faced was how to develop a labor force that would meet the special needs of the growing colonies. Both finally decided to rely on imported nonwhite slaves. Those who were shipped to the American South came from West Africa, while the slaves sent to South Africa came from East Africa and Southwest Asia.

It was believed that the white workers were more likely to be difficult than black slaves, and thus, economics aside, nonwhite slaves promised more stability and order for the white owners. Indeed, changes within the white community, such as the advancement of whites politically and socially, often had detrimental effects on blacks. For example, during the age of Andrew Jackson, there was a liberalization of laws allowing white males the right to vote, but at the same time more severe restrictions were being placed on slaves in the South. One cannot understand the history of white supremacy in South Africa and America without recognizing the tensions and divisions within the white community. The enslavement of blacks served to bind the white community closer together.

Racism was not what initially caused the enslavement of the Africans; indeed, racism as a so-called scientific concept did not appear until the eighteenth and nineteenth centuries. It was their heathenism and the fact of their captivity that allowed for their enslavement. The author points out that historians have made much over the question of what position American blacks held before the slave codes began to appear in the 1660's. In fact, they had already been considered slaves because they were thought to be heathens. The most significant change coming out of the codes of the 1660's was the declaration that even slaves that had converted to Christianity were to remain slaves.

This emphasis on ancestry was in effect a shift to race from religion as a reason for enslaving the blacks. Because of the fact that more blacks were becoming Christians, it was necessary for the whites to shift the focus from heathenism to skin color. This change happened more quickly in the South than it did in the multiracial South African society, but by the late eighteenth century both societies had developed social orders based on caste-like differences between blacks and whites. As it was normal for whites to be free, so it was normal for black-skinned persons to be slaves. In the nineteenth century, South Africa was less rigid than the American South in its racial policy; free blacks there had many of the same rights as whites. For example, there was no ban on interracial marriage in South Africa, as there was in the South.

Nevertheless, the effects on whites of the enslaving of blacks had a similar impact; it set up a way of viewing blacks as inferior beings. To whites, black Africans were not only uncivilized but without any redeeming virtues. They even murdered their sick and aged. They were believed to be warlike, lawless, and sexually promiscuous, and were considered by some to be related to the anthropoid apes, after reports appeared of African women cohabiting with orangutans. Thomas Jefferson claimed that the orangutan lusted after black women in the same manner that black men desired white women. These racist views held by whites prevailed long after slavery was abolished in the nineteenth century.

Two of the most important ideologies affecting slave societies were the growth of free labor and capitalism. These ideas produced a critical view of the slave system, which clearly differed from the popular ideologies in Britain and America. Once slavery was considered anticapitalistic and an impediment to economic progress, the time was ripe for its overthrow. This economic liberalism plus a growing humanitarian impulse merged to initiate the final attack on slavery in the early nineteenth century.

The abolition of slavery was imposed on the United States South and South Africa from the outside. In the United States, it was the North that forced Emancipation and Reconstruction of the South in the 1860's and 1870's. In the British Empire, it was England that passed the laws that freed the slaves throughout the empire, including South Africa. Another similarity was that in these former slave societies the freedmen were for some years allowed to vote and even hold political office. These noble experiments in freedom were ended by the early twentieth century as white supremacists passed laws that severely restricted the rights of blacks.

The failure to continue to extend basic rights to the blacks was caused by the weakening of humanitarianism and the emergence of Social Darwinism and scientific racism. In the South, white racists used violence, economic coercion, and political disenfranchisement. By 1910, the result was the establishment of an all-encompassing caste system. In the South there developed a deep and sometimes violent response to social change, based on racial fears inherited from the antebellum period. This Herrenvolk ideology had enabled the planters to gain the support of nonslaveholding whites for the slave system. So, too, after slavery was abolished, racist politicians were able to use racial fears to gain the support of poor whites for the system of segregation. Racial pride, more than economic or political reasons, bound the white South together. Anything that maintained this Solid South and its racist assumptions was acceptable—Klan violence, corrupt elections, and lynchings.

The white response to change in South Africa was different and more complex. There were no laws establishing segregation, or outlawing miscegenation, or forbidding blacks from voting as there were in the South. Yet racism existed, even though many of the extreme racists had moved northward during the Great Trek, in effect segregating themselves, and by their migration ceasing to have much influence on the drafting of the laws. Though legally blacks could vote, only whites were elected to political office in South Africa. The white man controlled the economic system and allowed blacks to hold only menial jobs as farmers and laborers in the gold and diamond mines.

As in most comparative studies, there are weaknesses in this work. The basic problem that Fredrickson confronts is to convince the reader that there are sufficient reasons to attempt this comparative work. Although there are significant similarities between South Africa and the American South, there are basic differences. One of these is the difference in population. In the

South, the whites are a clear majority, in South Africa the black population predominates.

It would have been helpful had the author discussed the individual relationship between white master and black slave, comparing the relationship between masters and slaves in South Africa with that in the South.

It would also have been appropriate for the author to have devoted more time to the period from the 1940's to the present. In this part of the work he could have shown how the most racist segment of the civilized world, the South, was finally surpassed in that honor by South Africa in the 1940's and 1950's.

Two of the most interesting racial stories of the twentieth century have been how the South was pulled out of the morass of race hatred and how the policy of apartheid has pushed South Africa farther down the road toward possible race war. While Fredrickson believes there is little hope for the accommodation of the races in South Africa and the establishment of a multiracial society there, he believes, perhaps too optimistically, that there might be a change in policy by the South African whites. If they cannot transcend their racist past, race war is probable, resulting in the ultimate victory of the blacks and the removal of the whites from their homeland.

*Richard A. Van Orman*

## Sources for Further Study

*America*. CXLV, August 15, 1981, p. 76.
*Choice*. XXVIII, May, 1981, p. 1320.
*Commentary*. LXXI, April, 1981, p. 84.
*Journal of Southern History*. XLVII, November, 1981, p. 593.
*Library Journal*. CV, December 15, 1980, p. 2568.
*National Review*. XXXIII, May 29, 1981, p. 617.
*The New Republic*. CLXXXIV, February 21, 1981, p. 31.
*The New York Review of Books*. XXVIII, March 5, 1981, p. 26.
*The New York Times Book Review*. LXXXVI, January 25, 1981, p. 1.
*Newsweek*. XCVII, February 23, 1981, p. 73.

# A WILD PATIENCE HAS TAKEN ME THIS FAR
## Poems 1978-1981

*Author:* Adrienne Rich (1929-    )
*Publisher:* W. W. Norton and Company (New York). 61 pp. $12.95
*Type of work:* Poetry

*A series of poems of anger and love from a perspective of fierce survival*

For more than thirty years, Adrienne Rich has charted the emotional, political, social transformations of her time. Using her own life as the image of the deeply particular and impressively universal, Rich has carved into the American awareness a consciouness of change. Beginning as a finely controlled craftswoman writing in the style of Robert Lowell in the early 1950's, Rich in *A Change of World* (1951) spoke to the constraints of womanhood, the limits of the female environment. Late in the 1950's, *Snapshots of a Daughter-In-Law* marked her bursting forward to chart a new sensibility. The poetic line was less rigorous; language and rhythm began to work together in the by-now familiar Rich tapestry. *The Will to Change* (1971) and *Diving into the Wreck* (1973) most clearly connected Rich to political changes—to the Civil Rights movement, the war in Vietnam, the women's movement. Her marriage, which ended during this period in the late 1960's and early 1970's, had produced three sons, and, as Rich sharpened her feminist sensibility, she also pondered her role as the mother of males. *Diving into the Wreck* poignantly works through male/female relationships: the pain of her lost idealizations, the harsh reality of her husband's suicide, the motherly fear for her sons' involvement in the war.

Since the mid-1970's, however, Rich has moved more and more toward an examination of women's relationships to one another, to their foremothers, heroines, and to inner psychic processes. Rich, now in her fifties, and a lesbian living and working in Massachusetts, writes from a feminist-lesbian perspective. Most of her poems are about women, addressed to women, and/or concern women's lives in different kinds of environments. From New York City to New England, the South, Midwest and Southwest, Rich gathers portraits, retells historical anecdotes, quotes her foremothers. This is women's poetry, developing new images, thirsting for original contact in an old, familiar context.

The tone of *A Wild Patience Has Taken Me This Far* is firm, open, unflinching. In the past, Rich has written more poignantly, even masochistically, about the way women suffer out their lives. Underneath her despair has been an enduring idealism and optimism. In these poems, the effect is more flat, matter-of-fact. In "For Julia in Nebraska," Rich describes the world of a sister/writer, Willa Cather. She calls upon Julia to listen to this story, for "history/ is neither your script nor mine/ it is the pictograph/ from which the young must learn." Rich wants to state the unstated, the feelings, issues, yearnings, and facts which women before her have harbored. Willa Cather was silent about her love for women; her society would not permit her to write on this topic. Thus, in these poems Rich speaks what has been unspeakable: "THE HISTORY OF HUMAN SUFFERING/ like bound back issues of a periodical/ stretching for miles" ("Culture and Anarchy").

These poems scour history, not to cleanse and erase the suffering of women, but to erode the veneer of silence and distortion, romance and self-sacrifice. In "Culture and Anarchy," the voices of nineteenth century women such as Susan B. Anthony, Elizabeth Barrett Browning, Ida Husted Harper, and Elizabeth Cady Stanton are a chorus to a poem about a stormy August afternoon. The forces of outer natural turbulence remind the poet about the history of revolution. The pages fluttering on the table, the torrent of typing upstairs, connect the storm to the ferocity of a writer's creativity and to the inevitable bursting forth of contained energy. As she writes, she weaves through a litany of women who lived through historic storms of their own making and connects herself with them. Rich's "dream of a common language" as well as titles of many of her other books of poetry are mentioned in this poem. She thereby uses her own poetry as a way of connecting herself to her work and her work to the work of other women. She relates women's history, sees herself as part of that history, and knows that the history she wants to write must arise from the minutiae of daily living—not through glamorous upheavals and glorious tales of victory: "freedom is daily, prose-bound, routine/ remembering. Putting together, inch by inch/ the starry worlds. From all the lost collections" ("For Memory").

Rich's book *Snapshots of a Daughter-In-Law* illustrated her departure, ideologically and poetically, from a male-dominated, restricted world. In *A Wild Patience Has Taken Me This Far*, Rich goes back to many of these early, enduring topics to record openly the new facts and to state the conditions of the silences. In poems such as "Mother-In-Law," "Grandmothers," "Frame," "Turning the Wheel," and "Ethel Rosenberg," Rich intensely tries to remember or project onto the unknown what could possibly be known or understood. "Tell Me Something," says the Mother-In-Law, and the Daughter-In-Law replies at the end of the poem: "Your son is dead/ ten years, I am a lesbian,/ my children are themselves" ("Mother-In-Law"). The poetic line is abrupt, shocking, unadorned. Flattering adjectives are avoided. Rich has had secrets, too, and she is bent on uncovering them, in particular and universal senses. She writes to Ethel Rosenberg, executed on the day Rich was married. Rich wonders whose execution this was. "I gave myself in marriage/ then slowly severing   drifting apart/ a separate death   a life unto itself" ("Ethel Rosenberg"). Rich tries to connect through a date in history, but she is decades removed. Ethel is dead, Rich's husband is dead; if they had been alive, there would be different, unimaginable stories. She struggles with her nostalgia, her yearning for similarity, sisterhood. ("Ethel Greenglass Rosenberg would you/ have marched to take back the night/ collected signatures/ for battered women who kill. . . .”). She confronts this guilt in the execution of Ethel Rosenberg and perhaps, implicitly, her womanly guilt in the suicide of her husband. She acknowledges that Rosenberg might have had very different political views: she might not have been a feminist, might not have left her husband, might not have identified herself with women in the way Rich has done. She might, in fact, have chosen to live out her life, quietly and alone, keeping her secrets intact.

These poems thus separate and join women together. In disclosing her secrets, Rich uncovers others, enforced through death, beyond imagining or reconciliation. There is a finality embedded in these discoveries and an enduring challenge: How to confront and understand the female experience “as it is not as we wish it/ as it is not as we work for it/ to be . . . ourselves as we are in these painful motions/ of staying cognizant” (“The Spirit of Place”).

This book of poetry seems aptly named. There *is* a wild patience contained in each poem. Disclosing more openly than she has done before the facts of her past, Rich nevertheless does not dive into the wreck of these disappointments. Her grandmothers, widows, Southern women “impotent and brilliant” who thought the lesson in life to be learned was “amnesia,” are presented as human beings whose stories are only partly told by their poet-granddaughter. “Yes, I was like that; but I was something more,” they might have responded to Rich. Ironically, that “something more” is forever lost. The wild enthusiasm of the poet, the almost frantic joy Rich displays as she uncovers her family portraits, is contained in an awesome, patient acceptance of her own shortcomings and ignorance.

In the final set of poems, “Turning the Wheel,” Rich once again confronts history without nostalgia. The “set” for her poetry is the Southwest. “It’s all been done,” she writes; yet she writes about it again—like the “Ghazals” of 7/14/68:ii in which she acknowledges: “For us the work undoes itself over and over:/ the grass grows back, the dust collects, the scar breaks open.” She returns to the past to uncover the present. “False history gets made all day, any day,/ the truth of the new is never on the news” (“Burden Baskets”). Women, to, falsify history; they collude with oppressors, they draw back, conceal their power. The women were colonized, their art made into rituals of slavery; they stumbled, failed themselves. “Nostalgia,” writes Rich, “is only amnesia turned around.” These women, as are all human beings, were imperfect. The white women, anthropologists, architects, writers, historians, were involved in covering up stories of exploitation. The sharing is a sharing of fallibility, of multiple selves living out lives. “Turning the Wheel” ends without ending. A series of eight poems, it restates the themes within the collection, generalizing the particular (“the road to the Grand Canyon always feels/ like that road and no other”) and particularizing the general (“as I talk to you all day whatever day"). It confronts the partly told history of the experience of being a woman and ends with memory and missing. The past is always recalled imperfectly and so is the present, for it relies on the human imagination. "After so long, this answer/ As if I had always known/ I steer the boat in, simply" ("Integrity").

*Faith Gabelnick*

### Sources for Further Study

*Best Sellers*. XLI, January, 1982, p. 394.
*Library Journal*. CVI, October 15, 1981, p. 2033.
*Ms*. X, December, 1981, p. 21.
*The New York Review of Books*. XXVIII, December 17, 1981, p. 32.
*The New York Times Book Review*. LXXXVI, December 20, 1981, p. 7.
*Village Voice Literary Supplement*. December, 1981, p. 20.

# WILLIAM CARLOS WILLIAMS
## A New World Naked

*Author:* Paul Mariani (1940-    )
*Publisher:* McGraw-Hill Book Company (New York). 874 pp. $24.95
*Type of work:* Literary biography
*Time:* 1883-1963
*Locale:* The eastern United States

*A massive literary biography which demonstrates the growth of one of America's best poets in the context of historical and personal change*

Principal personages:
WILLIAM CARLOS WILLIAMS
FLORENCE "FLOSS" HERMAN, his wife
EZRA POUND, his sometimes literary friend
T. S. ELIOT, his perennial poetic antogonist

New Jersey's reputation does not create confidence in the state's ability to inspire poetry. Its image hangs, like those of Detroit and Brownsville, in the national mind as a place to be avoided altogether or, in cases of grim necessity, to be passed through as rapidly as possible. Sandwiched between urban centers with better public relations—Philadelphia, New York, and Washington—New Jersey is disliked by those who have never explored its varieties. Such is unrequited love.

In fact, this state has been a source of one of the strongest American poetic traditions, flowing through the nation's literary heritage as clearly as the waters of its Pine Barrens. From Walt Whitman's Camden to the Paterson of William Carlos Williams and Allen Ginsberg, New Jersey's special mixture of urbanity and rural backwardness has been a microcosm of the nation's physical and moral character. From the old industrialism of its overpopulated Northeast to its usually forgotten South, this state has offered a condensed imaginative opportunity for those poets, old and new, who wished to sing of the American enterprise.

William Carlos Williams was very much a poet of New Jersey, as his *Paterson* (1946-1951) made so clear. Like Hart Crane's *The Bridge* (1930), which Williams both admired and feared, this long poem found the material of poetry in the complex relations of the city setting. In his growth from early romantic effusions, through Imagism, to this epic, Williams more and more placed his verse in its social, cultural, political, and physical context. This sense of context is also the achievement of Paul Mariani's massive biography.

While Mariani's work may be a bit too long and too crammed with details of Williams' literary and personal life, it nevertheless produces a sense of living time and place. By varying the nature of his exposition—sometimes objective, sometimes critical, sometimes humorous—Mariani delivers a cornucopia of facts without becoming boring. He avoids the terse, lifeless style of Reed Whittemore's biography of 1975 without surrendering to the mawkishness of hero worship.

While Mariani's admiration and love for Williams are evident, he maintains his objectivity. He draws heavily on Williams' own entertaining but loosely structured autobiography, *The Autobiography of William Carlos Williams* (1951), but he does not take it at face value. In telling his own life's story, Williams had relied heavily on anecdote and remembered conversations. The book was self-consciously limited, sporadic, and discontinuous. The reader feels intimately engaged with the quirks of Williams' personality but also somewhat trapped by this same "I." Mariani tries instead to balance the claims of personal immediacy, historical accuracy, and critical distance.

Mariani demonstrates that Williams' growth as a poet stemmed from his family situation, the tremendous technical, political, and economic changes of his epoch, and the envy, competitiveness, and jealousy that constituted the interpersonal foundation of that apparently theoretical and impersonal movement known as Modernism. Williams is seen with all his hats as son and father, husband and friend, doctor and poet, critic and dreamer.

Many of Williams' continuing interests seem to have been born with him. Both of his parents contributed to his creativity: his father was dramatic, philosophical, and literary while his mother had talents in music and painting. Both parents may also have contributed to his demand for "American poetry": his father never gave up his English citizenship, and his mother constantly remembered her Caribbean-French background. Perhaps this explains why William Carlos Williams, in an age filled with expatriates, did not feel the need to locate his sensibility abroad. Williams himself enjoyed that which he had discovered in Edgar Allan Poe, the "genius of place." He grew up with New Jersey, watched his Rutherford change from the three thousand of 1913 into a fair-sized city. He was educated at two great Eastern establishments: The Horace Mann School and the University of Pennsylvania, where he went to medical school and met Ezra Pound. Despite his very human occupation and despite his love for his wife and his family, his colorful friends Pound and Hilda Doolittle, Williams chose to write more about places and things than about people.

Williams' concentration on an immediacy of perception is not strange: it is a standard of American literature. From the Puritans' typology to the oceanic affirmations of Whitman that Williams loved so well, American writing has been based upon sensation more than reflection, phenomena more than noumenal concepts. It is easy to see why Williams favored Pound's personal eccentricities over T. S. Eliot's "extinction of the personality" and veneration of the classics. Williams' poetry was a self-conscious turning away from previous models, a revolution toward the United States. As his growing reputation and influence indicate, his path toward the present, toward the moment of the poem's making rather than the past of poetry itself, is an enduring contribution.

Williams' growth into freedom did not, however, come easy. By the 1940's he had twenty-three books in print but was still not a very well-known poet. It was not until 1951, when the fourth volume of *Paterson* was published, that he began to gain any real attention. That he had any time at all for poetry or the public is surprising, given the great demands of both his family and his medical practice.

This division of Williams' interests was not, however, as great as it seemed. His work kept him in touch with vitality and desire, not the fragmentation and *Angst* of *The Waste Land* (1922). Rather than seeing the world flying apart in a centrifugal motion of accelerating history, he saw poetry, like medicine, pulling things together. His poetry binds and heals. Through his sense of humor he could see similarities, not breaks, between the disparate facts of life and the urban setting. Thus, when his first pamphlet of poems was published in 1908, two years before he received his medical license, containing numerous mistakes, he joked that the book was "about half errors—like the Passaic River in its relationship to the sewage of that time." The same elements, the same midden heap of city waste, are present here as in T. S. Eliot's "The Love Song of J. Alfred Prufrock," but this mix forms a constructive opportunity for Williams' mind, a place of humor, not neurosis.

This ability to affirm differences, to join objects together, did not stem from a loose character, not even to the degree that structural slack is found in Whitman. Williams was exceedingly hard on himself in his pursuit of an American "free verse." He recognized very early that traditional free verse was itself binding, that it did not allow him to follow the dictates of his poetic populism. Just as he struggled with the case of Nicola Sacco and Bartolomeo Vanzetti, just as he struggled with immoral hospital administrators, and just as he struggled with economic theory during the great depression, he also struggled for a poetry and poetic theory which was bound by the rigors of necessity and causality rather than the injustices created by the arbitrary imposition of rules.

By 1913, Williams no longer saw a poem in strict lines or feet but, again borrowing from Whitman's imagery, as a sea, "an assembly of tides, waves, ripples." While the stress here may seem to fall on an unbridled freedom, the word "assembly" demonstrates that this complexity is synthetic, made according to rules generated by the poetic occasion and the poetic subject and not traditional structures. This is the responsibility of choice, a bound freedom.

Some of this notion of poetry came from other twentieth century masters. Especially from 1912 and on Williams was helped by Pound, who, as usual, was an even better advocate and productive critic for his friend than for himself. Williams also benefited from the prose experiments of James Joyce: as Williams' poems were appearing in *The Little Review* so was *Ulysses*. Here, as in Whitman, he saw the power and rhythm of oral inflections.

All of this background ultimately contributed to his modern epic of the city, *Paterson*. Here he was able to put together what Eliot's early poetry had torn apart. He saw urban life, as Joyce did in Dublin, an incarnate memory of the past playing against the developments of the present. Whitman had said a hundred years before that "the United States themselves are essentially the greatest poem"; Williams found this same poetry in the city which microcosmically reflects, as does its state, the union from which it sprang.

In *Paterson*, Williams moves beyond Imagism's limited pictorialism and past the previous limits of his own poetic personality: he becomes more eclectic and complex. Gleaning from his background in both science and the humanities, economics and sexuality, he plays pieces of borrowed prose and bits of real letters against his own multifoliate poetic lines. The effect is of many voices, a dialectic of a community and not the shards of a previous age. That Williams died before completing this expression of his age is appropriate, for *Paterson* is a poem about the flow of time, history, and community, not an individual; it could be whole only in its interest and not its form.

Because Williams found so much of his art in his life and environment, this literary biography is especially useful and relevant. Mariani makes lucid the degree of relation between the man and his words: biography and literary criticism are not separate issues for this poet. If during a first reading of this massive work some of the extensive detailing of facts seems unnecessary, the reader is grateful in retrospect. Like the landscape of New Jersey and the verse Williams drew from it, Mariani's book is full, but, to the attentive reader, none of its parts are wasted or without consequence.

*Daniel D. Fineman*

### Sources for Further Study

*The Atlantic Monthly.* CCXLVIII, December, 1981, p. 92.
*Booklist.* LXXVIII, October 1, 1981, p. 175.
*Harper's Magazine.* CCLXIII, December, 1981, p. 55.
*Library Journal.* CVI, October 1, 1981, p. 1928.
*The New Republic.* CLXXXV, November 25, 1981, p. 36.
*The New York Times Book Review.* LXXXVI, November 22, 1981, p. 1.
*Saturday Review.* VIII, November, 1981, p. 83.

# WILL'S BOY

*Author:* Wright Morris (1910-     )
*Publisher:* Harper & Row, Publishers (New York). 200 pp. $11.95
*Type of work:* Memoir
*Time:* 1910-1930
*Locale:* Nebraska, Virginia, Chicago, California, and Texas

*A memoir of the first twenty years of a writer*

Principal personages:
WRIGHT MORRIS
WILLIAM HENRY MORRIS
GERTRUDE
THE MULLIGAN FAMILY
UNCLE HARRY
UNCLE VERNE
UNCLE DWIGHT

Whether the question "Who am I?" is answered before one writes an autobiography or after the fact, the answer is as important to the writer as to the reader. Wright Morris, found crying at a carnival because he had lost fifteen cents in the sawdust, was comforted by a voice, "You're Will's Boy, aren't you?" And seventy-year-old Wright Morris answers, "And so I proved to be." After reading *Will's Boy*, one wonders whether it has taken Morris more than six decades to realize fully the implications of that answer or whether he has always known intuitively what he expresses in "To the Reader."

Each drop that falls is the center of a circle that is soon overlapped by other circles. The apparent obliteration of the circle does not eliminate the radiating vibrations. This image of endlessly renewed and expanding circles is my own ponderable cosmos.

Wright Morris began his career in 1942 with the publication of *My Uncle Dudley* and for forty years he has continued to write novels of consistently high quality, photo-texts, short stories, and collections of critical essays. In his style and in his subject matter, Morris may be considered a modern, sophisticated Mark Twain—an authority on Americana and the American Dream. In technique, both in his photographs and in his writing, he surpasses Ernest Hemingway, who said he exposed one tenth of the iceberg; often, Morris exposes nothing, but by a deliberate focus on what is not there, he evokes with an illuminating flash what was once there.

Most literary biographers would say that the work is the life, with the suggestion that the work proceeds in chronological order as the life proceeds. Wright Morris' life and work however, are proof that, at least for him, the work is grounded in the early formative years of childhood and that his works, though they come throughout the life, are formed out of impressions and beliefs of those early years. "If growing up meant to abandon these sentiments," he says at the end, "Will's boy would be slow to grow up."

Morris has said that in his early years, he "led and was led by, half a dozen separate lives." The thread running through those different lives was Morris' imagination. To attain some sense of distance and objectivity and to develop the conceptual vision he held of his work, Morris processed the raw material of his early life and the circumstances surrounding the various events in fragments. Morris wants to "use a minimum of words for a maximum effect," and this intention, especially in *Will's Boy*, allows him to create what David Madden calls "a fiction of moments," densely charged with implications. This stylistic device gives passages, like photographs, a stop time effect. These moments are like lost objects that Morris retrieves in memory's fiction in "lampglow and shadow," a repeated phrase. Significant in *Will's Boy* is the number of lost articles: Joey Mulligan's St. Christopher medal, Wright's two chameleons (they turn up in *One Day*, (1965), the foul ball that Babe Ruth hit and Wright caught and, more important, the pocket he tore from the champ's uniform (these turn up in *The Field of Vision* (1956), and many more. These lost objects are retained in the memory and imagination of the author as literary artifacts, focal images in his fiction. Concrete things may get lost, but memories never do. They always coexist in future times and places. Morris'obsession with these fragments, moments, artifacts make each seem equally important.

An evolving pattern gives unity to Morris' work. *Will's Boy* is evidence that Morris has finally reached the point where he can relate the events of those first twenty, formative years in a straightforward, chronological fashion.

To show how his imagination over the following fifty years has transformed those episodes, all those people, and those separate Morris selves, Morris weaves into the narrative of his memoir more than twenty-five passages from his novels, short stories, and personal essays. For example, as Morris talks of his father's attempt to run a chicken farm, he works into the flow of the narrative a long passage from *The Works of Love* (1952), his fictional rendition of his father's life. The many facets of this technique enrich the reader's response. Genres are juxtaposed, memoir to fiction; point-of-view techniques are juxtaposed, Morris' first person to Morris' omniscient voice.

In another instance, Morris, recalling his school days with Joey Mulligan, juxtaposes his own first person point of view with a passage from *The Man Who Was There* (1945) in which one of Morris' fictional selves speaks in the first person. This technique literally demonstrates that the center of Morris' "cosmos" and thus of each of his novels is his childhood.

*Will's Boy* supports Morris' claim that most of his fiction evolves out of the first twenty years of his life and that each new fiction evolves out of previous works. To some extent all writers draw on their early years, but *Will's Boy* is a unique and intriguing literary phenomenon in the way Morris mingles his memoir of those years with key images from the fiction those years produced.

Why does he end the story of his life at twenty? The technique of weaving passages of his fiction into his memoir *in itself* seems to declare that once a person becomes a writer, the major events in the life thereafter are acts of imagination in the daily process of writing—"the ceaseless, commonplace, bewildering interlacing of memory, emotion and imagination."

> First we make these images to see clearly; then we see clearly only what we have made. In my own case, over forty years of writing what I have observed and imagined has replaced and overlapped what I once remembered. The fictions have become the facts of my life. (*Earthly Delights, Unearthly Adornments*, 1978)

Morris begins his memoir with his birth to Grace and William Henry Morris on January 6, 1910, in the Platte Valley of Nebraska. From a farm near Zanesville, Ohio, Will Morris went to Chapman, Nebraska, to work for the Union Pacific Railroad; Grace Osborn, born on the bluffs south of the Platte, met Will in a barber shop in Chapman. Six days after Morris' birth, his mother died. At her death, members of the family debated as to who should rear infant Wright; it was decided that, with the help of Anna, his mother's friend, he would remain with his father.

Morris did not realize what it meant to lose a mother until years later. He calls *Will's Boy* an "abiding chronicle of real losses and imaginary gains."

> Much of my life would be spent in an effort to recover the losses I never knew, realized or felt, the past that shaped yet continued to elude me. Had Grace Osborn lived, my compass would have been set on a different course, and my sails full of more than the winds of fiction. Am I to register that as a child's loss, or a man's gain?

In the opening section (there are no chapter numbers), which covers eight years of Morris' life, the style is complex and rich in description and epiphanies; the vision of childhood is one of a somewhat fairy-tale existence: "The voice the child attends to is the one that speaks without the need of an answer—the voice of fire, of thunder, of wind, rain and silence." Morris inserts a passage from *Earthly Delights* relating the child to all small creatures who "are only at their ease under something"—a culvert, a table, a piano box, seats of wagons and buggies, low bridges, dark hiding places under front porches. He uses the technique of calling up a living image by describing what is left after the departure of the physical: "but I preferred the shimmering fragment of suspended time that I saw through the porch slats where the train had just been, but was no more." He enforces the image of his busy father: "the bicycle he rode to and from his work often lay on its side, the front wheel still spinning."

In another passage from *Earthly Delights*, Morris emphasizes an important point about his work, and one which should be important to all writers, especially those who claim that only what is real is valid.

One reason I see it all so clearly is that I have so often put it into writing. Perhaps it is the writing I remember, the vibrant image I have made of the memory impression. A memory for just such details is thought to be characteristic of the writer, but the fiction is already at work in what he remembers. No deception is intended, but he wants to see clearly what is invariably, intrinsically vague. This gives rise to the image. Image-making is indivisibly part of remembering.

The first phase of Morris' life ends when his father brings home a new wife, Gertrude, who is closer in age to Wright than to his father: "with her arrival my childhood world expands." Indelible images from *Inhabitants* (1946) and *The Field of Vision* illuminate this first phase.

In the next two sections, the Morrises move "with great expectations," after Will has hit on the idea for furnishing the customers of the railroad with fresh eggs and starting a chicken farm, to Kearney and then to Schuyler, Nebraska. After disastrous episodes that are comic in some cases, Gertrude is fed up with country life and the chicken business. She and Wright have become close allies and the separation that Will illustrates when he refers to them as "them" becomes "us against him." "They" persuade Will to move to Omaha, where he begins his chicken and egg business on a larger scale. From the Maxwell Hotel in which they live before they find a house and where Wright and Gertrude spend many happy hours in the lobby, they move at last to a house. Gertrude finally can stand no more of this life, and she leaves behind her the results of her frustration and anger, a kitchen and bedroom in which she has broken windows, slashed bedsheets, thrown pots into the yard, spilled talcum over the rugs, and stuffed rags and towels into the bowl of the toilet.

"All by myself I was learning about life. . . . I became a listener." Of his relationship with his father, Morris says, he "was a ponderable presence, more than a voice, more than a father." Throughout the memoir, passages from *The Works of Love* (1952) suggest what Morris' imagination made of his father. Wright and his father move back to the hotel and then into a small apartment that is close to Farnam School. It is here that Morris first learns that he is "half an orphan" and meets Joey Mulligan.

Wright is invited to visit Joey Mulligan's home. Mrs. Mulligan, feeling sorry that he is "half an orphan," approaches Will Morris about keeping the child in her home. For two sections, Morris describes his life with the Mulligans. As he depicts the relationship between Mr. and Mrs. Mulligan, he includes passages from *One Day*. He describes the neighbors, his teachers, his enemies, his childhood friends, among them Davy Goodman, whose vocabulary of "fluent, venomous, wonderful curses" held a special fascination. The child Morris experienced very little mental or physical discomfort from his unstable life; in fact, every day and every new situation was a new adventure to be savored. "I renewed my daily great expectations." Out of that great enjoyment—and out of even greater acts of imagination—grew Morris' fictional works.

When Will Morris tells Wright he has found a woman who will in time become his new mother, he also decides that the slight, seventy-eight-and-a-half pound, thirteen-year-old needs a vacation from the city. So it is to Uncle Harry, Will's brother, "a heavy, dour, silent man with his family, but given to deadpan joshing with his neighbors," and his wife Clara, "a tall lath-flat woman with a high-pitched voice, who likes to work," and their farm in Norfolk that Wright travels for the summer, intending with "great expectations" to perform whatever chores he can. Out of that experience thirty years later came parts of *The Man Who Was There, Inhabitants,* and *The Home Place* (1948), including photographs of objects described in the memoir. In a departure from the simple style that he uses in most of his first person narrations, Morris achieves perhaps one of the best long descriptive passages in the memoir in relating his arrival at the farm. When Uncle Harry takes him to the station at the end of the summer, Morris, again evoking an image of what is not there by describing what is there, says, "He didn't ask me to come again, or wait to see if the train came and stopped for me, but got his Ford turned around, bucking it forward, then drove off in a cloud of dust. There was no wind at all to move it. When it finally settled there was nothing to see."

The return to Omaha at first seems to hold some hope of a more stable life, as Will Morris meets him at the station with the news that his Uncle Verne has come to live with them and help with the business. "What he liked most of all was a roller-coaster road with the wind in his face, and then he liked me."

Wright is introduced to his prospective new mother, Mrs. Van Meer, and her children. Gertrude reappears, and his father, after increasingly irregular appearances, disappears. After giving Wright some suspicious gold money, Uncle Verne also leaves. Wright, afraid to spend the money Uncle Verne has given him, steals some money; he is referred to a juvenile officer who feels sorry for him because he is "half an orphan." Because he will not reveal who his father is, she is forced to send him to a reformatory. Here he lives with about thirty boys, some of whom threaten him and try to make him fight. He worries that no one will come for him since no one knows where he is. Miraculously, his father appears in a Big Six Studie to take him away. "When I asked him where we were going he replied, 'Chicago, kid.' I don't know why, but the older and bigger I got the more he called me kid." Omaha had failed to live up to their "expectations."

Half way through the book, Morris begins "a new life" with his father in Chicago. At first, Will is elated to be in the big city and he gets a position with the Northwestern Railroad. Wright goes to school (sometimes), later gets a job with Montgomery Ward, accidentally discovers a victim of organized crime, and when he is told he has talent, begins a correspondence course in drawing. Wright's relationship with his father deteriorates; feeling repulsion at his father's living habits and his constant involvement with women, he finally takes a room at the Larrabee Y. "Kid, it's your own life." Because of the way he handles the difficult boys, Wright is told he has a future at the YMCA, that he has been "chosen." In one of his strangest acts of transformation, Morris invests the Christ-like transvestite Paula Kahler in *The Field of Vision* with his own Y experiences, extending them wildly in his imagination. Oddly, Morris includes no passages from that novel in this section. This is one of those experiences Morris seems to have needed to write about in a way far removed from himself, before he could, as now, write about it more intimately.

Wright's father, like a bad penny, appears in the lobby of the Y. "What I want, kid, is a new start for us in California." The "new life," the "new start," is a major motif in the book. Planning to buy a car, Will advertises in the newspaper for riders to share expenses and interviews those who answer the ad. Unable to find suitable traveling companions, they decide to get a car and set out and worry about the passengers later. They buy an Essex coach. Wright is seventeen: "Coming back to a place you like can be nice, as I had felt coming back to Omaha from the farm, but taking off for California, with the first snow falling, is like nothing else." Near Kansas City, the Essex breaks down and they buy a 1921 Big Six Studebaker. When this car also breaks down, they buy a 1919 Buick touring car and with some acquired passengers they start out again. After passing through Albuquerque, Wright drives the car off the road into the soft sand and they are stuck. A motorcycle friend from Albuquerque comes along and, with Wright on the rear of the cycle and his father in the sidecar, they arrive in San Bernardino.

They settle in Los Angeles for a time but it fails to live up to their "expectations" and they decide once more to find some passengers and a car and head for Chicago. On this trip, they arrive in Lake Village, Arkansas, just as the levee breaks. In the panic that follows, Wright is separated from his father, but continues the trip hitchhiking and finally arrives "in Chicago, my hometown" where he is reunited with his father who has arrived two days before him. As an inserted passage suggests, it is out of these automobile adventures that *My Uncle Dudley*, Morris' first novel, evolved.

Wright goes back to school and meets Dorothy, who falls in love with him and has matrimony in mind. Eventually, through communication with his mother's sister Winona in Boise, Idaho, he gets the chance to go to college. What most raises his "expectations" is that even though it is a Seventh-Day Adventist College, with which he is unfamiliar, it is in California, his concept of Eden. Wright shares a tearful good-bye with Dorothy: "Later she cried, and we clung together in the dark stairwell smelling of wet galoshes, but fifty years would pass before I could measure my real loss against my imaginary gain."

The eleventh section is the longest and one of the most memorable. Because of his voiced opinions and beliefs, contrary to the beliefs set forth by the members of the college, Wright was asked to leave, and he decides to go to work for his Uncle Dwight in Texas. Wright likes his Uncle Dwight and grows to tolerate the neutral treatment by Agnes, his wife, but after some traumatic experiences he turns to thoughts of his future and returns to Chicago. Morris uses fragments of this experience in very different ways in several different works. Some of Wright's experiences with the Gudgers becomes those of Mrs. Ormsby as a girl in *Man and Boy* (1952); the incident in which Wright lures the hog with a corn cob in his fly becomes a central experience in the life of Walter McKee, who is very unlike Morris himself, in *The Field of Vision*. The hog butchering episode figures again in "The Rites of Spring" (1952), a short story, and in *Cause for Wonder* (1963), with a more Morris-like boy.

Back in Chicago, Wright meets fourteen-year-old Lois Baker, who stirs feelings of young manhood. He meets Laurie Lusk, a boy at the Y, and together they decide to drive Laurie's Model A Ford to Pomona College in California. Once more Wright is on the road, having again left a girl he cares about. Places are important to Morris because a new place means a new life and to revisit means resurrection. As they approach Pomona College, engraved on the college gates is "Incipit Vita Nova" which translates "Here begins a new life." Pomona College "far exceeded my expectations." Morris is twenty years old; his next "new life" will be as a writer.

The relatives and friends that Morris encountered in those twenty years seem to have been almost inhabited by Morris; there is a sense that he passed through them, soaked up their characteristics and not only used them as they were in novels, but merged and mixed their varied characteristics and personalities and circumstances to form new and different characters. Morris himself becomes a character in his fiction, transforming himself to many different characters, from Agee in *The Man Who Was There* to the very different Paula Kahler and Mrs. Ormsby.

As Morris tells the story of his first twenty years, one sees vividly the child grown into young manhood, but the effectively placed passages from the fiction also make one feel the hovering presence of the seventy-year-old Morris. One feels no separation between man and boy.

*Will's Boy* continues the tradition of literary excellence in the forty-year career of Wright Morris. Whether events are reported as they happened or whether they have become in time something entirely different through Morris' imagination does not matter to Morris: "What is 'real' is a matter of imagination. It is the image that matters. Does it enchant us, move us or mysteriously stir us?" (*Earthly Delights*). It is only when reality has been transformed through imagination that it becomes important, and to those who indulge themselves *only* in facts, Morris says:

Wanting no nonsense, only facts, we make a curious discovery. Facts are like faces. There are millions of them. They are disturbingly alike. It is the imagination that looks behind the face, as well as looks out of it. (*Earthly Delights*)

With this credo, Morris diminishes the earthly, increases the delights.

*Peggy Bach*

## Sources for Further Study

*The Atlantic Monthly*. CCXLVIII, August, 1981, p. 87.
*Christian Century*. XCVIII, October 7, 1981, p. 1004.
*Christian Science Monitor*. LXXIII, July 29, 1981, p. 17.
*Library Journal*. CVI, June 1, 1981, p. 1224.
*The New York Times Book Review*. LXXXVI, August 16, 1981, p. 12.
*The New Yorker*. LVII, August 10, 1981, p. 107.
*Newsweek*. XCVIII, July 13, 1981, p. 77.
*Saturday Review*. VIII, June, 1981, p. 58.

# WINTER GARDEN

*Author:* Beryl Bainbridge (1934-    )
*Publisher:* George Braziller (New York). 157 pp. $8.95
*Type of work:* Novel
*Time:* The present
*Locale:* England and Russia

*As official visitors in Russia, three English artists and an admiralty lawyer discover a world that is both commonplace and bizarre: a world that is very similar to—and very different from—their own*

> *Principal characters:*
> DOUGLAS ASHBURNER, an English admiralty lawyer
> BERNARD DOUGLAS and ENID DWYER, English artists
> OLGA FIODOROVNA, a Russian interpreter
> MR. KARLOVITCH, Secretary of the Russian Artists' Union
> NINA ST. CLAIR, another English artist
> BORIS SHABELSKY and TATIANA, Russian artists

Beryl Bainbridge's ninth novel, *Winter Garden*, is set in Russia, but the principal characters are English, and the novel's concerns transcend nationality. Douglas Ashburner, an admiralty lawyer, accompanies three English artists, including his lover Nina St. Clair, on a tour of Russia, sponsored by the Russian Artists' Union. In the course of the tour, the rather ordinary, middle-aged Ashburner is confronted with the contradictions—the lack of certainty—that seem to characterize modern existence everywhere. Throughout the novel, the ordinary and the bizarre intermingle to a dizzying degree. Contradiction infuses every aspect of the novel: plot, characterization, and theme. Even Bainbridge's style, which is characterized by a deft balancing of the humorous and the sinister, contributes to the message that life is never quite what it seems.

Reinforcing this particular message, the plot revolves around the tension between expectation and realization. For each of the visitors, Russia is not quite what he or she expected; but the problem is particularly acute for Douglas, whose expectations of golden moments with Nina are dashed almost from the start. Arriving at the airport, he is greeted offhandedly by Nina, who is feeling slightly ill and will make no promises about their sleeping arrangements during the tour. To make matters worse, the balding, conventional Ashburner is uncomfortable with the other artists: Bernard Douglas, a loud, outspoken man; and Enid Dwyer, a rather neutral woman, who is somewhat enamored of Bernard. Once the group is on the plane, Bernard takes the seat beside Nina, and Douglas must sit with Enid, who clearly wishes to be elsewhere. Later, when the group arrives at the airport in Moscow, Douglas' unhappiness is compounded by the fact that his luggage is missing. Feeling increasingly uncomfortable with his unconventional compatriots, Ashburner wonders why he has left his home and his wife to come to Mother

Russia, which appears cold, uncomfortable, and dull.

Although Bainbridge tends to keep the traditional British distance between herself and her character, her sympathies clearly lie with Ashburner, and much of the action is presented from his point of view. Manipulated in his marriage, Douglas is equally inept in his love affair, and this journey seems to offer the first hope for a comfortable liaison with Nina. Since Nina constantly stresses the need for keeping their relationship secret from her husband, a famous brain surgeon, Douglas has had to make love to her in awkward places and positions—often standing up. Once Nina even hides her lover in a closet to keep his whereabouts secret from her husband—who never appears. With the dampening of his hopes for golden evenings with Nina, Ashburner's spirit sink; he thinks of his wife whom he cares about, although he knows she sees him in much the same light as the family dog—dependable, but incapable of independent action.

From Douglas' point of view, matters go increasingly awry. Met at the airport by the official interpreter, Olga Fiodorovna, the group quickly becomes aware that their stay will be much too well-organized. An attractive, stylishly dressed woman, the interpreter is also domineering, high-handed, and officious. Finding in Olga Fiodorovna an unpleasant tendency to lecture on the glories of Russian history and landscape, her charges often long to be left to fend for themselves in this alien land. Within the group, only Douglas questions the careful shepherding she provides for her charges. His earlier suspicions that the little entourage of English artists will not be entirely free on their two-week tour of Russia is heightened by the absence of Nina on the first day of the tour. Olga explains Nina's absence as a response to an impromptu luncheon invitation from Boris Shabelsky, a Russian artist and an acquaintance of Nina. Later that day, Olga attributes Nina's continued absence to ill health; according to Olga, Nina is resting in a sanatorium and will join the group later in Leningrad.

Bernard and Enid readily accept these explanations, even when Nina's stay in the sanatorium lengthens into days, and she fails to join her friends in Leningrad. For Douglas, however, Nina's continued absence and his inability to get in touch with her become concrete proof of the contradictions between what their official interpreter says and the reality of how things are. Torn by longing for Nina and distressed at the strangeness of his surroundings, Douglas begins to see the events of each day in a sinister light.

For Douglas at least, contradiction and confusion seem to abound. Douglas questions a mysterious and inconclusive phone call from an unknown "Boris"—was it simply a mistake, a caller who had the wrong number, or was the caller Shabelsky with a message from or about Nina? There are other confusing events. Apparently mistaken by his Russian hosts for Nina's husband, the brain surgeon, Douglas is taken to a hospital to view an operation. As he surveys the scene in the operating chamber, Douglas fantasizes—or actually sees?—that the patient possesses the same star-shaped scar that Nina has on her forehead. Collapsing at the hospital, Douglas is taken to his hotel to recover. That evening he is relieved to learn that Nina telephoned the hotel the night before—although he later learns that only Olga talked to the caller. In a disquieting episode the following day, Douglas thinks that he catches a glimpse of Nina at a cemetery he and Enid are visiting. Later, at the Kirov Theatre in Leningrad, Douglas again thinks he sees Nina, only to have her disappear, almost before his eyes.

As these incidents reveal, Bainbridge relies strongly on mystery and possible coincidence to form the plot of the novel and to promote the sense of contradiction and confusion that mark the world of *Winter Garden*. It is no doubt a credit to Bainbridge's skill as a creator of suspense that the reader is never quite sure if Douglas is the only person who suspects the truth; if he has constructed a fantasy world; of if he is, in fact, physically ill. Rather amusingly, there is some reason to suspect the latter since the unworldly Douglas learns from Bernard that certain unpleasant physical symptoms Douglas has been experiencing can be attributed to a venereal disease contracted from his beloved Nina, who had not gotten around to informing her lover about the problem—although she had told Bernard.

There are times, however, when the reader may find the clues overly subtle and the humor disconcerting. The star-shaped scar, for example, is mentioned only once before the crucial scene in the operating room—and only briefly then. Thus, the reader may not make the same connection between Nina and the scar that Douglas does. While Douglas' naïveté about venereal disease— and about Nina—is both touching and amusing, the reader is left in a quandary: is Douglas a serious witness or a fool? The latter seems likely since Douglas' credibility as a witness is already under attack; no one else sees the events he does. On the other hand, much that happens in the novel remains confusing and unexplained. Even at the end of the novel, there are no explanations concerning the disappearance of the luggage or the disappearance of Nina. The luggage at least is returned, although it obviously has been searched, but Nina's whereabouts remain shrouded.

Although the use of contradiction in the plot of *Winter Garden* is sometimes disconcerting, the use of contradiction in characterization generally works well. Bainbridge shows her characters from varying perspectives, and each view presents a slightly different picture. In the portrayal of her characters, Bainbridge clearly means to say that people are not always what they appear to be or, more accurately, that they may appear in different guises to different people. The author's main concern is with the tendency of observers to bring certain preconceived illusions or desires to the act of perception. To the hapless Douglas, who longs to bring excitement to his routine existence, Nina represents an ideal of the unconventional, liberated artist. In sharp contrast, Nina seems second-rate to Enid and a lightweight to Bernard—both of whom have their idiosyncratic reasons for viewing their colleague as they do.

This diversity of view could be simply amusing, or pathetic, but since Bainbridge places the problem of how the characters are to be perceived in a larger framework than the purely social one, the problem becomes a very serious one indeed. Since the four English tourists are in a foreign country where they may or may not be embroiled in sinister events, it does matter whether the group can trust one another's accounts—or, perhaps even more important, whether anyone is able to see the truth and to communicate it to the others.

For the reader, the problem is compounded by the characters' unpredictability; an individual's responses often seem precisely the opposite of what one would expect them to be, given the public identity the individual projects. Douglas, ostensibly a staid representative of the establishment, becomes an irrational alarmist or a visionary observer—depending on one's interpretation of events—when he is faced with the mishaps of the trip. On the other hand, Bernard, the flamboyant, unpredictable artist, tends to take a maddeningly prosaic approach to these same events. According to Bernard, everything that goes wrong is the result of a computer foul-up. Obviously, these characters will not trust one another's interpretations of events, and Bainbridge gives just enough credibility to each view to leave the reader also slightly uncertain.

Uncertainty is no doubt the response the author wishes to elicit. Beware of people, Beryl Bainbridge seems to say; they are just as unpredictable, as quirky and contradictory as events. The "beware" is uttered sadly, despite the cool distance Bainbridge maintains between herself and her characters. These characters are all rather pathetic in their way, even the flamboyant Bernard and the self-possessed Olga. All seem to suffer from a failure to connect—with others, the landscape, the world. Indeed, the major thematic issues of the novel grow out of the author's concern for her characters' inability to thrive in the sterile "winter garden" of the modern world.

Bainbridge's use of contradiction in the depiction of her characters and in the working out of plot carries through to thematic issues and is central to the two major thematic concerns of the novel, the difficulty of communication and the problem of separating illusion and reality. These two themes are closely related: the person who cannot separate illusion and reality will have a problem communicating any valid ideas—or perhaps even emotions—to someone else. In a modern, peripatetic existence, the problem has both individual and bureaucratic implications. At the end of the novel, Douglas is caught up in a bureaucratic nightmare; held in custody because he is suspected of being a spy, Douglas has no idea what punishment the future may hold. From the reader's point of view, his hosts' response is not altogether surprising since Douglas has been behaving erratically; on the other hand, strange events have been going on. The problem for both Douglas and his hosts may simply be a problem of communication; however, both parties must be able to distinguish between illusion and reality if they are going to communicate.

The likelihood of that happening is remote. Even on an individual basis, Douglas has not been able to communicate with others—not even with Nina, the woman he loves. Love without communication no doubt deserves the name of fantasy, not passion, but Bainbridge treats this lover sympathetically, though humorously. To be able to love at all requires real gifts, as Bernard notes. At the end of the novel, Douglas sees himself and Nina as two people "in a bleak landscape, frozen in their tracks." The difficulties of communication, much less love, seem almost insurmountable in such a framework. One can hardly blame Douglas.

Bainbridge has the particular gift of being able to create a novel that succeeds both as a suspense narrative and as a thematic work. While the reader may desire more clues about both the plot and the theme, Bainbridge leaves only slender clues because she wishes to make the point that explanations about the complexities of modern existence do not come easily. Left at the end of the novel on the verge of understanding, the reader—like Douglas—can only bow to life's contradictions.

*Alice Drum*

## Sources for Further Study

*Best Sellers*. XLI, May, 1981, p. 43.
*Booklist*. LXXII, February 15, 1981, p. 774.
*Encounter*. LVI, May, 1981, p. 90.
*Guardian Weekly*. CXXIII, December 21, 1980, p. 22.
*Kirkus Reviews*. XLIX, January 15, 1981, p. 86.
*Library Journal*. CVI, March 15, 1981, p. 677.
*Listener*. CIV, November 20, 1980, p. 699.
*The New York Times Book Review*. LXXXVI, March 1, 1981, p. 9.
*Observer*. November 2, 1980, p. 29.
*Times Literary Supplement*. October 31, 1980, p. 1221.

# WITHIN THE WHIRLWIND

*Author:* Eugenia Semenovna Ginzburg (1906-1977)
Translated from the Russian by Ian Boland
Introduction by Heinrich Böll
*Publisher:* Harcourt Brace Jovanovich (New York). 423 pp. $17.50
*Type of work:* Memoir
*Time:* 1937-1967
*Locale:* Primarily the Kolyma region of Soviet Siberia, also Moscow

*In this sequel to* Journey into the Whirlwind *(1967), Eugenia Ginzburg completes the powerful narrative of her eighteen years of detention at prison camps and her sentence of internal exile in Soviet Siberia*

> *Principal personages:*
> EUGENIA SEMENOVNA GINZBURG, the narrator
> ANTON WALTER, a doctor of homeopathic medicine; Eugenia's second husband
> JULIA KAREPOVA, formerly a prisoner; Eugenia's friend
> VASYA AKSYONOV, Eugenia's younger son
> ALYOSHA AKSYONOV, her older son, who died of starvation in Leningrad
> VALENTINA ZIMMERMAN, the Elgen camp commandant

Thumb through the pages of Eugenia Ginzburg's memoir and discover, instead of the expected clutch of photographs that usually record episodes from a writer's life—snapshots of relatives, lovers, friends—a single gray-and-white illustration. It is a map of northeastern Siberia, a landscape of permafrost and rock outcroppings that resembles a chart of the moon's surface, or perhaps a map of hell. In this region of Kolyma, the permanent site of prison camps and settlements with names such as Mylga, Elgen, Shturmovoi, and Belichye, the author spent eighteen years of her life, from February, 1937 to March, 1955.

In the first volume of her memoirs, *Journey into the Whirlwind* (1967)—published in England under the title *Into the Whirlwind*—Ginzburg chronicled the years 1934 to 1939, from the time of S. M. Kirov's assassination in Leningrad, through the Stalinist purge of suspected or imagined anti-Party traitors that followed, and culminating in 1937 with her own arrest and expulsion from the Party on the grounds of "participation in a Trotskyist terrorist counter-revolutionary group." Far from threatening the Stalinist regime as a terrorist, Ginzburg—at that time the wife of Pavel Aksyonov, an important Party functionary in Kazan—had been a loyal Communist. As a journalist and teacher, she had dutifully followed the Party line concerning Kirov's murder; but she had not joined the chorus of denunciation of Professor Elvov, a former colleague who had come under fire as a Trotskyite. Nor had she extenuated her presumed guilt by denouncing friends or associates in the Party for similar counterrevolutionary activity. Instead of following the jackals in their purge of innocents, she demanded justice and forced the bureaucrats to make a conspicuous example of her intransigence.

In 1935, she lost her license to teach; in the summer of 1937, after a brutal interrogation, she was sentenced to ten years of imprisonment; then she languished for the first year of her punishment in the harshest of Soviet prisons: Yaroslavl. Placed in solitary confinement in a damp cell, she suffered indignities almost too terrible to describe, but managed somehow to survive in prison until July, 1938, when her sentence was "commuted" to ten years of forced labor in Siberia. From Vladivostok, she and other "counter-revolutionary terrorists" were shuttled from camp to camp, until they took up their miserable residence in the Kolyma region of permafrost and desolation. By 1939, when *Journey into the Whirlwind* concludes, Ginzburg, nearly dead from exhaustion, malnutrition, and exposure from working as a tree-cutter, had through good fortune been saved by a Leningrad surgeon to work at a less exhausting task. Employed in the Elgen camp as a nurse for children born of prison inmates, she had little cause for optimism.

The second volume of Ginzburg's reminiscences begins at this point. At first she is content working under the kindly supervision of Dr. Petukhov, but her position in the camp worsens some time after German armies invade the Soviet Union. Because of her German-sounding name, Ginzburg is interrogated by authorities of the Registration and Distribution Section, who release her for the ironical reason that her name indicates Jewish origin as well. "This must have been the first time in the history of the world," she comments wryly, "that being Jewish was an advantage." In time, however, her security is endangered by the Elgen commandant, Valentina Mikhailovna Zimmerman, a ruthless and fanatical puritan who persecutes with zeal any miserable inmate who violates the slightest deviation from camp regulations. Ginzburg runs afoul of Zimmerman for committing the petty "crime" of destroying a piece of paper from her pocket and is punished, losing her post for a sentence at Izvestkovaya, the "isle of the damned."

Even at this camp, the "punishment center to end all punishment centers," Ginzburg manages, almost miraculously, to survive; and after working at a lime quarry to the limit of exhaustion, she meets at the Taskan food processing plant another savior, Anton Yakovlevich Walter. This "jolly saint," a doctor of homeopathic medicine, eventually is to become Ginzburg's second husband, the man who will share her life through many of the grim years of her Siberian captivity. Dr. Walter, a German-born Catholic—and therefore twice suspect—is as guiltless of crime as she, but is also broken in health as a result of his imprisonment at the Dzhelgala gold mines. Nevertheless, his cheerful nature, his faith in God, and his inviolate human decency always strengthen Ginzburg, even when her will to survive seems to ebb, for always her position as a condemned political criminal threatens her very existence. Against this threat and suffering, she has the sole option of ending her life, of committing suicide to conclude at once her anguish. She rejects this option, survives torments that most people could never endure, and at last is redeemed from her captivity. No doubt the love and wisdom of Dr. Walter greatly sustained her through these years; without him she probably would not have lived to write a testament to truth. Dr. Walter's noble character shines through this testament (he died in 1959, eight years before *Journey into the Whirlwind* was published in the West), a memoir of two shared lives.

Yet to designate *Within the Whirlwind*, like the previously published book, simply as a memoir is to reduce its scope. In his perceptive, moving Introduction to the volume, Nobel Prize-winning novelist Heinrich Böll chooses to describe the work instead as "a *narrative* book in the category of 'autobiographical novel.'" Böll makes the point that he does not regard this book as a novel in which material is invented, for "not the smallest detail is invented: 'novel' stands for structure, for the arrangement of an immensely copious amount of direct experience." Certainly, *Within the Whirlwind* is a work of great artistry, whether a reader chooses to call the book a narrative, an autobiographical novel, or—what is the most nearly satisfactory description— a memoir. Without fictionalizing any of the parts of her experience, Ginzburg selects the commonplace as well as meaningful details of her life and infuses them with extraordinary power. The reader discovers not only the particular story of Eugenia Ginzburg, but also—as is true of all art—the play of universal passions.

As an artist, Ginzburg treats her experiences as a mythic narrative involving the three movements of a cycle: a time of comparative ease and security, during which she is able to function as a competent human being; this is followed by a time of betrayal, in which an authority-figure such as Zimmerman or a false friend such as Krivoshei delivers her to destruction; then a countermovement of release or restoration with the help of a redeemer; only to begin again a new cycle of terror. By 1947, Ginzburg has completed the terms of her sentence as a "known terrorist," and briefly she tastes of what she calls "the chalice of freedom," but she is not truly free. Though at liberty to depart the Siberian concentration camps, she is not yet rehabilitated as a loyal Soviet citizen.

Perhaps the most ironical section of her reminiscences—for most Western readers a section difficult to comprehend as a political reality—is the final portion dealing with her years at Magadan. Here she lives with Dr. Walter, whose prison sentence has several years to run, and with an adopted daughter, an orphan rescued from destruction. They are content, or reasonably so, working long hours for very little money—Dr. Walter in his profession and Ginzburg as a music teacher—but they are constantly on guard. Their words, their gestures, their expressions might betray them as enemies of the state. Once more they might be divided as a family, or sentenced again to the Siberian camps. Indeed, their worst fears materialize. Innocently reading a child's story, Chukovsky's "The Little Cockroach," Ginzburg mentions to a supposed friend, the engineer Krivoshei, that the tale seems to have a second level of meaning, one satirical of Stalin. Without realizing her lapse, she has committed the serious error of expressing a political statement (even though the language was Chukovsky's and not hers) and she suffers the consequences. Yet once more, before she can be condemned again to a prison term and almost certain death, she is saved—this time by the demise of Stalin. During a brief political thaw that follows this cataclysm within the Party bureaucracy, she is able to strike out on her own, a free citizen emboldened to regain her full rights. For the time being, her mythic struggle seems to come successfully to an end.

In turning her life into myth, Ginzburg allows the reader to participate in her experiences, not simply as an onlooker or a judge but as an active force. One cannot react as a spectator to her story; a reader is gripped by her moral struggle and is forced to struggle along with her. Indeed, the major quality of Ginzburg's art is a moral imagination that penetrates into the essence of things. Unlike Alexsander Solzhenitsyn, whose message is as earnest as a Hebrew prophet's, Ginzburg writes as a thoughtful, educated woman, neither a titan nor a saint.

Before her captivity a wife and mother of two children (one who died of starvation during the Nazi seige of Leningrad), she tells her story because she must unburden herself of the weight of anguish. Hers is not a cautionary tale, nor a call to battle. She understands the full horror of Stalinism—and behind that epoch the Communist ideology that continues to permit tyranny to flourish—but she limits her political theme to the particular world that she has experienced. In fact, a reader anxious to discover in Ginzburg a fiery denunciation of Marxist-Leninism will probably be disappointed; she deals with the facts and substance of her life, and that life is luminous for her generosity of spirit. She forgives freely, saving her anger for those wholly wicked. For example, after describing a scene at the school graduation exercise in Magadan, at which the officers' wives are dressed in furs and fine garments but her clothes are shabby, she remarks parenthetically: "I am really being dreadfully ungrateful. These tastelessly overdressed matrons had shown their humanity and provided Vasya with free lunches at the expense of the parents' committee all the time I had been in Vaskov's house." Typically, Ginzburg can understand and allow for the fallibility of those who had slighted her.

The supreme measure of the writer's art, as well as the finest test of her moral imagination, is the reunion scene when Ginzburg, after years of waiting to visit her younger son Vasya Aksyonov, finally approaches him with trembling eagerness. She has not seen him since he was a child of four, and now as a lad of sixteen he comes to her almost as a stranger. In the company of other people, some indifferent to her deepest feelings, some watching to enjoy a sentimental spectacle, Vasya whispers to her, "Don't cry in front of them." With these simple words, the son identifies himself as a true child of his mother. In their solidarity, they oppose the vulgar crowd and stand together emotionally. At once and for the rest of their time together, understanding leaps between them, and the reader, who lives in the experience as well, is nearly ashamed to intrude upon the scene. Yet in appreciation of Eugenia Ginzburg's life, of her sufferings and few triumphs, it is necessary to be a witness to *Within the Whirlwind*. Ginzburg's own words call the reader to be such a witness: "It is this cruel journey of the soul and not just the chronology of my sufferings that I want to bring home to the reader."

*Leslie Mittleman*

## Sources for Further Study

*The Economist*. CCLXXX, August 29, 1981, p. 79.
*Library Journal*. CVI, November 1, 1981, p. 2133.
*The New Republic*. CXXXV, August 1, 1981.
*New Statesman*. CII, October 9, 1981, p. 24.
*The New York Times Book Review*. LXXXVI, July 12, 1981, p. 10.
*The New Yorker*. LVII, August 31, 1981, p. 104.
*Saturday Review*. VIII, June, 1981, p. 58.
*Time*. CXVII, June 22, 1981, p. 77.
*Times Literary Supplement*. September 4, 1981, p. 1009.
*The Wall Street Journal*. CXCVIII, August 27, 1981, p. 18.

# WORK, FOR THE NIGHT IS COMING

*Author:* Jared Carter (1939-    )
*Publisher:* Macmillan Publishing Company (New York). 47 pp. $10.95; paperback
   $5.95
*Type of work:* Poetry

*This collection, winner of the Walt Whitman Award for a first book of poems, is composed with unusual calmness and authority*

Jared Carter has taken his time producing his first full-length collection, and the result is a performance of remarkable maturity. A glance at the acknowledgments shows that most of the poems had their previous publications only a year or two before the book appeared, but that a few go back to 1969. Nevertheless, this book does not contain the experiments, the tried-on voices and forms, that characterize many first books. Carter has decided what he is doing, and he sets about doing it knowledgeably.

Most of the poems have a kind of geographical setting or background in the Middle West; the place is identified in some of the poems as Mississinewa County, which Carter says is "east of Spoon River, west of Winesburg, and slightly north of Raintree County." It is a place where the past is remembered, talked over by men in trucks on their way to construction sites, by loafers on the porches of village stores. The pace of life, and of the poems, is steady and patient; the details of both are seen as something to be treasured.

The first poem in the book, while not explicitly placed in this setting, provides something like an epigraph for the poet's concerns; it is called "Geodes," and is ostensibly about the rock-hound's pleasure in these hollow stones lined with crystals. Without strain or insistence, the end of the poem becomes metaphorical:

> I take each one up like a safecracker listening
>
> For the lapse within, the moment crystal turns
> On crystal. It is all waiting there in darkness.
>
> I want to know only that things gather themselves
> With great patience, that they do this forever.

So it is with the events and people of these poems; one has the feeling that Carter has carried them around in his head for most of his life, not as "ideas for poems," but as matters that have gathered meaning with the same patience with which the poet seems to have developed his craft.

For this reason, many of these poems, agreeable as they are on first reading, often require an immediate second reading, because Carter has a pronounced tendency not to force a meaning upon an event. Many of these poems are brief narratives of past events, but they end almost abruptly, without proffering the kind of self-conscious "closure" that might have given the reader too easily a sense that he had come to what the whole poem was driving at. "Turning the Brick," for example, is a short poem about the Depression years, when men were given work which had to be invented; on their hands and knees, they came up the brick-paved street, giving each brick a quarter-turn. The bricks themselves are decorated on the bottom, with emblems or a date; one is held out for the children to look at, and then replaced, and the man goes on with his job. It is a fully realized moment, like an unusually informative old photograph; no single detail in the poem has been put there to advertise what is "poetic" about this scene, or to insist on a "meaning." Yet at the end of the poem, one thinks, "Yes, that is how it was; I should know, because I have just been there."

Occasionally, Carter will create more conclusive effects at the end of a poem. "The Undertaker" is a carefully detailed narrative of the trials of one Sefe Graybill, the only bidder on the task of moving three hundred graves from a cemetery about to be flooded by a new reservoir. Because no one in the immediate area will work for him, Graybill drives northward to small crossroads cafes, finding aging men who need the money he will pay, by the grave, for this task. Two stanzas describe the men's slow discovery of continuity, of the fact that they are older than the men who once dug these graves and are now dead; and of various artifacts buried with a few of the older citizens. The end of the poem, then, uses the word "last" in a way that has earned a rich burden:

> Fell overcome with heat, one did, the first day;
> Another struck by the sun; two more threw down their tools
> And walked away. The few who stayed till the job was done
> Rode together in the back of Sefe's pickup each quitting time
> To a tavern on the highway, near where they parked.
> No one else would go there then. Sat there drinking,
> Cursing Sefe, buying him drinks, swearing they could not last.

In the presence of a representative passage from Carter's poetry, it is useful to notice not only the easy, conversational style, but also the ways in which that style keeps poetic compression from being excessively obtrusive. In the first three lines, careful sound patterns are established, in which the long and short "u" sounds and the long "a" sound create, or reinforce, the pace and tone; and the tightness of the last line is partly achieved by the unobtrusive use of "Cursing" and "swearing." In the strictest sense of the term, this poem is cast in free verse: one connot tell from the first ten lines what the meter of the eleventh is likely to be. On the other hand, the line-lengths are all roughly the same, and the poem falls into seven-line stanzas. The difficulty with working in this way is to avoid creating the impression that the poem is not quite finished; a certain amount of symmetry sometimes makes the reader fret over the asymmetrical aspects of the poem. One of Carter's strengths is that he can write in this almost prosy way without seeming prosy.

One further proof of Carter's mastery of his usual form is that it takes some effort to discover that there is only one rhymed poem in this collection. Many of the poems are arranged in uniform-looking stanzas which do not rhyme; the one rhymed poem, "The Measuring," is only a few poems from the end of the book, and does come as a slight but pleasant surprise, just enough to send the reader back through the collection in a search for rhymes that he might have failed to notice.

Still, "The Measuring" seems just right, not a piece of attitudinizing. It is a bit of folklore, a tale about a spell cast by the sexton's wife, for the benefit of one who seeks "one last remedy" for an unnamed illness. In the sexton's house, the wife undresses the subject and measures him with brightly colored bits of string, crown to toes, muttering incantations the while. Everything in this poem relating to the subject and his companion is vague and uncertain. The first line gives most of the subject's symptoms: "You're sickly pale—a crooked root." This is highly suggestive of some sort of conjuration, as if the subject had been hexed by what is known as "root work," or at least believed himself to have been so cursed. The measuring is a recurring motif in folk medicine, and constitutes here a kind of exorcism. All this may be fairly obvious; a significant fact about the poem, however, is that it does not depend for its effect on a knowledge of these beliefs. Instead, the form of the poem, and its diction, create a context in which these beliefs come to be quite clearly operative, whatever their original source. The poet's imagination, in other words, is equal to the task of handling folk beliefs with respect for their power.

This respect for a community and its beliefs, and tales of residents now dead or past their prime, is one of the chief sources of this book's strength. In poems such as "Watching the Stream" and "At the Sign-Painter's," a love of ordinary men and their extraordinary lives and work is splendidly expressed. "Watching the Stream" is a slightly elusive title, not becoming clearly appropriate until near the end of the poem. In it, the speaker remembers listening to the old wall-eyed men who sit in town on Saturday afternoon, telling stories. The poem retells, or merely hints at, a total of nine such stories in two and a half pages, using names and other carefully chosen details. On the occasion with which this poem begins, the men are talking about cripples and how they got that way; the central anecdote involves a man who had to have his hands amputated, then spent months perfecting his technique with a harness, a pistol, and a length of twine, in order to shoot the doctor; but he misses, and never tries it again. By the end of the poem, the reader is fully absorbed into the world these men are bringing back, and understands the almost Homeric way in which the names are used.

The tie of place, the knowledge that gathers and reinforces itself as one grows more deeply into knowledge of his family's traditions, is increasingly rare; fewer people live where their parents did than was the case fifty years ago. Carter, however, does not seem to be writing out of any troubled sense that he must preserve something that is vanishing, true as that might be; he is, instead, working with what he knows best.

An acknowledgment of his having come early to a literary love of his place is made, glancingly, in "At the Sign-Painter's," where once again a few anecdotes are recalled before the speaker settles down to a loving description of the sign-painter's shop, and his love for the sight of words "Forming out of all that darkness, that huge disorder."

This is one of the clearest and strongest first books to have appeared in recent decades. Such an utterance, typical as it is of reviewers' conclusions, does not say enough, though it is true. *Work, for the Night Is Coming* is a beautiful, enriching book.

*Henry Taylor*

### Sources for Further Study

*America*. CXLV, July 18, 1981, p. 36.
*Book World*. XI, June 7, 1981, p. 5.
*Booklist*. LXXVII, February 15, 1981, p. 790.
*Changing Times*. XXXV, August, 1981, p. 66.
*Hudson Review*. XXXIV, Autumn, 1981, p. 423.
*Library Journal*. CVI, February 1, 1981, p. 357.
*The New York Review of Books*. XXVIII, December 17, 1981, p. 32.
*The New York Times Book Review*. LXXXVI, May 10, 1981, p. 12.
*Virginia Quarterly Review*. LVII, Summer, 1981, p. 94.

# THE XYZ AFFAIR

*Author:* William Stinchcombe (1937-    )
*Publisher:* Greenwood Press (Westport, Connecticut). 157 pp. $23.95
*Type of work:* History
*Time:* 1797-1798
*Locale:* The United States and France

*A detailed description of a diplomatic incident in 1798 which almost drove the United States and France to war, a conflict which neither wanted*

> *Principal personages:*
> JOHN ADAMS, second President of the United States, 1797-1801
> CHARLES M. DE TALLEYRAND-PERIGORD, the French Minister of Foreign Affairs
> CHARLES COTESWORTH PINCKNEY,
> ELBRIDGE GERRY, and
> JOHN MARSHALL, the three-man American commission
> NICHOLAS HUBBARD (W),
> JEAN HOTTINGUER (X),
> PIERRE BELLAMY (Y), and
> LUCIEN HAUTEVAL (Z), Talleyrand's intermediaries

In 1797, President John Adams, in an effort to mend deteriorating relations with France and block what some believed was the road toward war with America's "sister republic," dispatched a three-man commission to France to negotiate outstanding differences. The commission (manned by John Marshall, Elbridge Gerry, and Charles Cotesworth Pinckney, the latter already in Paris as the unreceived United States minister to France) was never formally received but rather was subjected to a long and drawn-out series of conversations with intermediaries of Charles M. de Talleyrand-Perigord, the French Minister of Foreign Affairs. During those conversations it was suggested to the American envoys that a combination of loans and bribes would expedite proceedings considerably. Outraged, Marshall and Pinckney ultimately returned to the United States while Gerry, led to believe that he could preserve peace, stayed on. Eventually he was ordered home under a cloud.

The XYZ Affair (named for three of the four intermediaries who approached the American delegation seeking loans and bribes) has been used by historians to illustrate a number of things. Some have seen the affair as an example of French perfidy, which made an alliance with Britain not only wise but necessary. Others have viewed the incident in domestic political terms, seeing it as a temporary setback in the Jeffersonians' rise to power. Still others use the affair as an introduction to the Federalists' efforts to deprive their opposition of its civil rights in the form of the Alien and Sedition Acts and the repressive measures carried out under those laws.

The XYZ Affair itself, however, has not been the central focus of any study by modern historians. In *The XYZ Affair*, William Stinchcombe seeks to fill that important void by concentrating on the affair itself and not its political, diplomatic, or constitutional implications. In doing so, Stinchcombe has provided a clear portrait of two republics (the United States and France) who wanted peace with each other but whose pride, diplomatic language, internal politics, and diplomatic procedures seemed to thwart the efforts for peace of both nations.

Stinchcombe portrays President John Adams as a man who was more moderate and accommodating toward France than toward his own party. As Adams said prior to his inauguration, "I am more their [France's] Friend than they are aware of." Adams's own vanity and lack of managerial style, however, made it almost inevitable that his own policies would fail. By trying to put together a bipartisan commission to go to France without consulting his own cabinet, the haughty President made a political blunder of the first order. The result was that the three-man delegation that was eventually appointed was neither as bipartisan nor as talented as Adams had wanted. For all their abilities, Marshall, Pinckney, and Gerry were seen by France as an unfriendly commission and were far less popular than the earlier ministership of James Monroe, a man both sympathetic to and popular with the French Republic. Moreover, Adams's utterances for public consumption revealed little of his real feelings (moderate and accommodating toward France) and these statements both confused and angered the French Republic.

For the French, Talleyrand, like Adams, desired peace. Also like Adams, however, Talleyrand was obliged to be more prideful and bellicose in public than he was in private. Hence, the two nations were not really very far apart. Both wanted peace, yet each believed that the other had insulted it and drifted away from the alliance of 1778. Neither Adams nor Talleyrand was severe enough politically to conduct real diplomatic negotiations. Both sides were willing to give a good deal to maintain peace between the two republics. In seeing the two nations as basically pacific, Stinchcombe has drawn from the earlier work of Albert H. Bowman (*The Struggle for Neutrality*, 1974).

As Stinchcombe ably shows, however, the timing of the proposed negotiations made it almost inevitable that they would fail. Adams needed a quick diplomatic triumph to head off critics at home and maintain his shaky leadership of the Federalist party. On the other hand, Talleyrand needed to play for time in an effort to solidify his own position in the rapidly changing French Republic. A coup in France in September, 1797, removed from power a number of pro-American moderates, leaving men more belligerent in their language and more conscious of French pride. For this reason, Talleyrand believed that he had to stall the talks with the Americans until his own power base was more secure.

For this reason, according to Stinchcombe, Talleyrand sent intermediaries to the still-unreceived American delegation, requesting both an explanation of Adams's bellicose remarks and a loan and/or bribe to the French government. Apparently the French diplomat was using the demands for money to play for time but was in deadly earnest about seeking an explanation of Adams's remarks. The Americans, not used to the European style of diplomacy, confused the two requests and hence made a breakdown of talks nearly inevitable.

Stinchcombe has clarified this complex problem by examining in some detail the four go-betweens (actually *W*, X, Y, and Z) who approached the American envoys. All had economic interests in the United States, interests which in some cases they hoped would revive their economic fortunes. One would suppose, then, that they were familiar enough with American ways and the American character to foresee the outcome. Yet the envoys' apparent stubbornness seemed to surprise them, for none of them wanted to alienate the nation in which so much of their hopes were contained.

Moreover, Stinchcombe makes a real contribution by analyzing the American community in Paris, which numbered more than two hundred by 1797. These men and women, mostly mercantile, knew enough about the intricacies of French customs to advise the three-man commission. They desperately tried to translate French diplomatic language and customs for the envoys, but they too met with failure, owing in no small part to the apparent blindness of Marshall and Pinckney, two men who returned home heroes because it was believed they (and American honor) had been insulted.

In Stinchcombe's view, the whole unpleasant experience (which very nearly brought the two nations to war) seemed to show Americans that it was necessary for them to "separate their own experiment from European practices," that European diplomacy was inherently corrupt, pulpy, and rotten, and that the new nation must isolate itself from these lower political forms. As Marshall said, "It is in America and America only that human liberty has found an asylum." Surely a gross overstatement, but one which Americans continued to believe.

John Adams comes off less well in Stinchcombe's book than the vain New Englander would have liked. Though his instincts for peace were correct, his public belligerence and his use of the war fever for political gain clearly make him a less admirable character than the one which other historians have portrayed. Similarly, the three-man delegation comes off less well.

Some will object that Stinchcombe has not delved deeply enough into domestic political considerations and subsequent constitutional questions (the Alien and Sedition Acts are never mentioned), but those subjects have been examined adequately elsewhere, and such criticism unfairly expects the author to do something he never intended to do in the first place. What Stinchcombe *has* written is a concise examination of an incident in American history which has rarely been seen on its own terms. Given the temptations to wander onto oft-tread paths, it is a commendable achievement.

*William Bruce Wheeler*

## Sources for Further Study

*American Historical Review*. LXXXVI, October, 1981, p. 918.
*Choice*. XVIII, July, 1981, p. 1603.
*History: Reviews of New Books*. IX, July, 1981, p. 180.
*Journal of American History*. LXVIII, September, 1981, p. 371.
*Journal of Southern History*. XLVII, November, 1981, p. 599.
*Library Journal*. CVI, March 1, 1981, p. 557.

# YOU CAN'T KEEP A GOOD WOMAN DOWN

*Author:* Alice Walker (1944-    )
*Publisher:* Harcourt Brace Jovanovich (New York). 167 pp. $10.95
*Type of work:* Short stories

*The survival of women in a racist, male-dominated society*

In an age of racism and sexism, a writer cannot remain uncommitted, unless he or she is satisfied with the status quo. During the recent past, the emergence of a plethora of literature about sociopolitical conditions in the United States and elsewhere has provided a certain degree of euphoria for the many who could not translate fervent ambitions into reality. Alice Walker's book of stories, *You Can't Keep a Good Woman Down*, is a hybridization of fiction and nonfiction to whet the appetites of those who need such emotional upliftment.

Prior to writing the book under review, Walker had published the novel, *Meridian* (1976), and two other fine books of poems (*In Love and Trouble*, 1973, and *Revolutionary Petunias and Other Poems*, 1973), among a few others. In *You Can't Keep a Good Woman Down*, on the other hand, she sacrifices coherence and sense of purpose for her racist-feminist megalomania. Apart from a few interesting stories, interspersed with chapters on pornography, the book is a collection of spit-fire materials in which Walker lashes out against American racism and male chauvinism, particularly white-male domination. For analytical convenience, the selections could be rearranged and divided into three groups: political essays, love stories, and general short stories.

The first of the "general stories" is "Nineteen Fifty-Five." In this story, a middle-aged white director signs a contract with a black singer to record her song. He also buys up the rest of the copies of the record from the stores, to enable his very young, inexperienced, white male singer to record it. The song becomes a hit and its new singer, Traynor, is transformed into a fabulously rich, world-acclaimed "Emperor of Rock and Roll." Despite his smashing success, however, Traynor feels guilty about using Gracie Mae Still's song, which, ironically, he does not understand. In appreciation for the song and, perhaps, to tone down his remorse, he showers money and very expensive gifts, including a farm, a Cadillac, and a replica of his luxurious mansion, on his benefactress. Finally, Traynor dies tragically, leaving his millions of fans crying on the rampage.

The story is built on the life of Elvis Presley. Gracie Mae Still is reminiscent of Big Mama Thornton, and the song, of Mama Thornton's "Hound Dog." The story is one of the many powerful arrows Walker draws upon from her political armory. The theme is the commerical exploitation of black artists by their white counterparts. Also, the story exemplifies the general theme of the book: the power of women. Gracie Mae Still's energies, transmitted through her song, transform a whole generation of people; she outlives four husbands and bears no grudge against Traynor.

The main character in "How Did I Get Away with Killing One of the Biggest Lawyers in the State? . . . ," on the other hand, is understandably remorseless. A fourteen-year-old school girl is raped by her mother's employer, Bubba, a lawyer who is the son of a rich, racist, ingratiating bigot. The rape develops into consensual sexual intimacy, and the lawyer plies the girl with gifts and money. Bubba makes the girl sign papers for her (sane) mother, who becomes hysterical about the goings-on, to be committed to an asylum. An attempt to release the woman from the asylum is stifled by Bubba's father, and, later, the poor woman dies. In revenge, the girl kills Bubba in his own office and takes away his money.

"How Did I Get Away with Killing One of the Biggest Lawyers in the State?" is a story of evil and deceit, an example of misused power, particularly adult abuse of childhood innocence. Despite her having acquiesced to Bubba's wily acts, the girl is still the stronger character in the story. Her reawakening to the lawyer's machinations symbolizes a renaissance of the oppressed—all the people who are raped by swift, uncontrollable currents in the stream of life. Her strength is further shown in the clever way in which she kills Bubba and takes his money, and in her fortitude in babysitting Bubba's children to enable his wife to attend his funeral. The story symbolizes the triumph of blacks over whites, of women over men, of childhood innocence over adult machinations. It also contrasts life in the stinking ghetto to that in the affluent environs.

Another successful revenge story is "Elethia," an account of how a black school girl, Elethia, steals the effigy of "Uncle Albert" from the restaurant where she works, with the help of her friends. The group burns the effigy and keeps the ashes in a jar to commemorate the event. The difference between the two is that, whereas the anonymous girl's success is a pyrrhic victory (because of her mother's insanity and her eventual death), Elethia's is a carefully planned and well-executed plot.

In real life, "Uncle Albert" was Albert Porter, the son of a slave couple whose wealthy, domineering, and greedy owners kept them ignorant of the Emancipation Proclamation for ten years, in order to exploit them. Again, in real life, Albert worked in this "Whites-Only" restaurant as a foolish, gullible, over-zealous, and unquestionably happy waiter. The story is full of symbolic irony. Albert epitomizes a high degree of enslavement. Besides being an over-dutiful worker, he enjoyed seeing blacks prevented from eating at that restaurant. His boot-licking gullibility makes him a prototype Uncle Tom. Elethia, the girl who organizes the plot to burn the effigy, is contrasted to Uncle Albert. She is young, visionary, revolutionary, and forward-looking. As a careful schemer, Elethia is dedicated to the annihilation of all the Uncle Alberts and Aunt Albertas who contribute to the economic and social enslavement of her race.

One of the better stories in the collection is "Fame." It is a beautiful description of a rubber chicken banquet to honor an old black college instructor, on the occasion of her 111th literary award. The purpose of the story is to highlight the enduring success of a woman in a male-dominated world of college professors and administrators. Mrs. Andrea Clement White's unusual success allows her to scorn her colleagues at the college.

So does Sarah Davis look down her nose on black men in the story, "A Sudden Trip Home in the Spring." Sarah, a pretty black girl in a white college in New York, feels unable to draw or paint black men because she cannot bear to trace defeat onto blank pages. The author's feminism rings clear when, at the end of the story, she makes Sarah reflect on the recent funeral of her father. Sarah acclaims complacently that she is a woman of the world, who has buried her father and would soon know how to sculpt a likeness of her grandfather in stone.

Walker's feminism is evident in her love stories, too. As usual, her prop is race. Her view is that writers can make a contribution to their medium and to a necessary fight by writing stories in which pornography is confronted openly and explicitly. She also thinks that the black woman has served as the primary outlet for the Euro-American man's pornography. All four of the stories in this group—"Porn," "The Lover," "Laurel," and "The Abortion"— illustrate her views.

Politically speaking, "Porn" is the mildest of the love stories. It is an explicit account of two divorcees' exploration of sex and pornography. In "The Lover," on the other hand, there is no visual aid but inspiration from nature. Here, a black woman and an astute Jew meet at an artists' colony in New England to complete their writing. The story departs from the stereotype of the abused black woman, for here the woman is the seducer.

In "Laurel," the man is a super-aggressive pursuer. Six weeks after a passionate meeting with Annie, Laurel is involved in a near-fatal accident which leaves him mentally paralyzed forever. After a long convalescence, Laurel begins to seek Annie, who has since married and has a child. Laurel's unexpected visit to Annie's family is as embarrassing as his half-witted letters are nauseating. The story illustrates the profound effects of a woman on a man.

The last of the "love stories," "Abortion," is a description of a black couple's struggles to terminate a fetus. The woman, Imani, is portrayed as strong-willed and persevering, while her husband, Clarence, appears as simple and nonchalant. While Imani agonizes from an illegal operation, her workaholic husband assiduously tries to help improve the administration of his boss, a black mayor. Toward the end of the story, Imani equates her abortion with the politics of the day, particularly with the trial of the suspects in the murder of a high school graduate.

In order to obtain a reduced sentence, the white defense attorneys plead that Holly Monroe's death was victim-provoked. Imani thinks that her problems during her abortion symbolize the lawyers attempts to blur the truth. In the end, Imani is separated from Clarence. Her strength lies in her perseverance during the abortion, and her prevalence over Clarence to undergo a vasectomy. Finally, Imani exhibits her maturity by not indulging in sexual politics during the break-up.

Unfortunately, sexual politics seems to undo the couple in "Coming Apart," the first of the few stories which assert the political power of women. Walker uses this story to lash out against men, particularly white males. Dismayed at her middle-aged husband's interest in pornography, the chief character begins to fear that she is growing old and losing her sex appeal. She begins looking at lesbian pictures and reading and commenting on feminist literature (aloud).

Among other subjects, the woman reads about the Black Panther movement, the portrayal of black women in violence, the ubiquitous presence of racism, and the denial of humanity through slavery, lynching, and rape. Walker preaches that a multitude of causes prevalent within a white-male dominated American society have not merely stripped away the black man's role as protector and provider for his famly, but have made him lose his self-identity.

The black woman has similarly been pushed to a passive role in society. Walker is bitter about the treatment of women in pornography. She complains that, while white women are regarded as "objects," black women are treated as "animals." Consequently, both black and white women are now threatening white male masculinity and power.

In the next story, "Advancing Luna," a black man rapes a white woman, Luna. Strangely enough, Luna informs only her black friend and confidante, in order not to precipitate the lynching of Freddy, the criminal. A year later, however, Luna foolishly shares her bed with the poor, desolate, and hungry Freddy. Walker's characterization of Luna is fictitious and confusing.

Walker appears at her best in her emotional apologia to Ida B. Wells. Having shared Ida B. Wells's conviction that black men are not as rape-conscious as stereotyped, the writer has come to realize that, after all, not all black men are undeserving of the accusation. Her dilemma is that, as a writer, she cannot write contrary to the truth, but her assertion of the truth might perpetrate lynching and similar crimes against black men and, to a considerble extent, their women, too. Therefore, Walker prays to Ida B. Wells's spirit for forgiveness and guidance in deciding about interracial rape.

The author soon slips back into her usual obnoxious, racist, antisocial rampage. She claims that America is a sick society whose people are not committed to social justice through the provision of equal housing and educational and employment opportunities. It is only when such basic needs are satisfied that black men and white women will be able to live together as *compañeros* (brothers and sisters), struggling together to find the true meaning of "rape."

Walker's final contribution to womanhood is expressed in a letter to a friend she has snubbed. "A Letter of the Times" is not an apology for her behavior, but an explanation of how women, particularly black women, have been mutilated through marriage and other social institutions, and an attack on the media's effrontery in exploiting their suffering. She calls on all women, especially the learned ones, to unite as twin sisters to help the suffering.

Several of the stories in *You Can't Keep a Good Woman Down*, particularly those discussed under "general stories," are interesting. Apart from, perhaps, "Nineteen Fifty-Five," however, whose beauty is marred by its incessant nonstandard English, all the "stories" in the collection are humorless. The book is written in a belligerent, racist language which, coupled with its confused welter of thoughts and actions, hampers the understanding and enjoyment of the reading. The tone is too political, and the repeated references to the assassinations of the Kennedys, Martin Luther King, Jr., and Malcolm X, are unnecessary.

Walker's attitude to sexual politics is equally pugilistic. Worst of all, her description of sexual acts and her bold preference for sexual and excremental imagery impair the beauty of her language and weakens her message. The plots are confusing, undeveloped, and incoherent. "Petunias," for example, is a half-page of historical information which is unrelated to the themes in the collection. Despite its philosophy, "Coming Apart" similarly fails as a story. The characters are odd, flat, and superficial. Finally, the reader is haunted by the omnipresent voice of the author. It is a voice which echoes the sarcasm of Claude McKay and the fiery fury of James Baldwin; it is the breath which fans the fire of social discord, but does nothing to ameliorate it.

*Edward Twum-Akwaboah*

### Sources for Further Study

*Book World*. XI, May 31, 1981, p. 11.
*Booklist*. LXXVII, April 1, 1981, p. 1080.
*Library Journal*. CVI, April 15, 1981, p. 905.
*The New York Times Book Review*. LXXXVI, May 24, 1981, p. 9.
*Publishers Weekly*. CCXIX, March 20, 1981, p. 56.

# ZUCKERMAN UNBOUND

*Author:* Philip Roth (1933-    )
*Publisher:* Farrar, Straus and Giroux (New York). 225 pp. $10.95
*Type of work:* Novel
*Time:* 1969
*Locale:* The eastern United States

*Nathan Zuckerman, thirteen years after his visit to a famous author in* The Ghost Writer, *copes with the ambiguous implications of his own fame following publication of his first successful novel*

> *Principal characters:*
> NATHAN ZUCKERMAN, a novelist
> LURA ZUCKERMAN, his wife
> ALVIN PEPLER, an ex-marine, nonstop talker, expert in trivia, and
>     Zuckerman's secret sharer
> ANDRE, Zuckerman's literary agent

In 1960, Philip Roth was the boy wonder of American letters; by age twenty-seven, he had four stories in *O. Henry*, and *Best Stories* anthologies, he had won the National Book Award for his first book, *Goodbye, Columbus* (1959), and he had been appointed to the faculty of the prestigious Iowa Writers Workshop. In the following decade he published two very earnest novels, *Letting Go* (1962) and *When She Was Good* (1967), neither of which created the kind of critical or popular attention that marked his entry into the literary world. Then in 1969, he made an instant name for himself as the bad boy of American letters with a book that made masturbation a subject and obscenity an art, *Portnoy's Complaint*. A new tone was set which was followed in the next three years with the satiric *Our Gang*, the Kafkaesque *The Breast*, and the farcical *The Great American Novel*. Since then, with *My Life as a Man* (1974), *Reading Myself and Others* (1975), *The Professor of Desire* (1977), *The Ghost Writer* (1979), and now *Zuckerman Unbound*, Roth's work has been primarily concerned with self-justification and stock-taking.

In his Introduction to *Reading Myself and Others*, an anthology of essays and interviews, Roth pointed out that he was involved with the writer's "seemingly interminable task of self-justification." Although he felt in that collection, with so many words already written in its service, that this task would no longer be so pressing, he concluded his introductory notes with the reservation that "it may not be within my power, or for that matter, in my own best interest, ever to consider that particular job done." Four books later, the job still goes on. However, *Zuckerman Unbound*, which continues the adventures of that ficitional creation Nathan Zuckerman, introduced during Roth's first stock-taking novel, *My Life as a Man*, and taken up again in *The Ghost Writer*, may indeed signal that Roth's particular job of self-justification is finally finished. At least, *Zuckerman Unbound* attempts to lay several of Roth's ghosts to rest: notably the dominant father figure that has always preoccupied him and the frequent public accusation that he is anti-Semitic and self-hating in his writing. The book also makes one more (hopefully the last) effort to answer the question posed so often to Roth after the publication of *Portnoy's Complaint*: "How did you write that book?"

*Zuckerman Unbound* focuses primarily on Zuckerman's reaction to the publication of his successful novel *Carnovsky* in 1969 (the same year that Roth published *Portnoy's Complaint*). He has made a million dollars, has been on the cover of *Life* magazine, is stopped by strangers on the street, is gossiped about by starlets on television talk shows, is criticized for depicting Jews in a "peep-show atmosphere of total perversion," and has his "sex credentials under scrutiny by the press." His anxiety about this response, especially given the restrained kind of writing he has published previously, is best perceived by his agent, Andre, who reminds him how stultified he felt writing "proper, responsible" novels and being a model of "Mature Adult Behavior." Andre tells him he purposely set out to sabotage his own "dignified, high-minded gravity" and now that he has done it, he is humiliated that no one sees it as a "profoundly moral and high-minded act."

In addition to coping with fame, primarily in a farcical manner (which has him briefly dating Caesara O'Shea, a sex symbol who reads Søren Kierkegaard and who leaves him for an affair with Fidel Castro), Zuckerman must deal with his recent separation from his third wife, a saintly lawyer and do-gooder; with Alvin Pepler, an ex-quiz show contestant with a photographic memory who dogs his steps; an anonymous caller (whom he suspects is Pepler) threatening to kidnap his mother; and the death of his father, which Zuckerman's brother blames on the book *Carnovsky* with its humiliating picture of the Zuckerman family in particular and Jews in general. This is indeed a great deal to cope with in a short book with only four chapters, and this is perhaps the reason that *Zuckerman Unbound* seems vaguely unsatisfying. Rather than a unified novel, it reads more like a fragmented effort to tie up various artistic and psychological loose ends.

The most interesting aspect of *Zuckerman Unbound* is its treatment of the relationship between the written world and the unwritten world. A brief background of Zuckerman's earlier fictional life in this novel and in *The Ghost Writer* may help put the issue in perspective. Zuckerman begins his existence as the fictional creation of Peter Tarnopol in two "useful fictions" in *My Life as a Man*. Tarnopol writes the stories to try to exorcise the effects of his disastrous first marriage and to help to define himself as a man and an artist. Thus, Nathan Zuckerman is the persona of Peter Tarnopol in "Salad Days" and "Courting Disaster" in the first half of *My Life as a Man*, and Tarnopol is in turn the persona of Philip Roth in Tarnopol's "True Story" in the second half of the novel. Even as Roth purposely makes the reader confuse and blend the three figures in *My Life as a Man*, mixing autobiography with fiction on several levels at once, he also attempts to clarify the distinction between them. In an interview with Joyce Carol Oates after publication of *My Life as a Man*, Roth said that the "legend of the self" is a "useful fiction" that readers frequently mistake for veiled autobiography; these "useful fictions" constitute a "kind of idealized architect's drawing for what one may have constructed—or is yet to construct—out of the materials actuality makes available."

Thus when the reader meets Zuckerman again in 1979 in *The Ghost Writer*, the nature of his "actuality" is not so clear. Should one respond to him still as Tarnopol's persona, which then places Roth himself at two steps removed from Zuckerman? Is Zuckerman always to remain a fictional creation of a fictional creation? In *The Ghost Writer*, Zuckerman, at age twenty-three, makes an artistic pilgrimage to his spiritual father, E. I. Lonoff, a reclusive writer, in order to receive confirmation for his own art and perhaps for himself as a man and a son. Zuckerman yearns to follow Gustave Flaubert's advice and what he perceives to be Lonoff's model—to live his life in serenity and to save his flamboyance for his writing. This ideal is complicated for Zuckerman, however, by the complaint of Lonoff's wife that "not living is what he makes his beautiful fiction out of." At the end of the novel, when Zuckerman does get permission to write the kind of novel that he in fact finally writes in *Zuckerman Unbound*, he has not yet clarified for himself the kind of life he should lead.

The title, *Zuckerman Unbound*, suggests several possibilities. It may be that Zuckerman is unbound at the novel's very beginning; that is, that he has already been released from writing with the dignified restraint that characterizes his former idol Lonoff, or that characterizes his own creator Tarnopol in "Courting Disaster," or that characterizes his ultimate creator Roth before *Portnoy's Complaint*. It also may suggest that the book itself, like Percy Bysshe Shelley's *Prometheus Unbound* (1820), has been written to perform the process of Roth's unbinding—a release from the reader's mistake that Roth's "useful fictions" are veiled autobiography and a release from the authoritarian father figure that has hounded Roth's characters since a Rabbi named Binder tried to bind one of his earlier "useful fictions" in "The Conversion of the Jews." The first effort to unbind Zuckerman is made farcically with the help of the stereotype schlemiel figure Alvin Pepler; the second effort involves the seriocomic death of Zuckerman's father as Zuckerman tells him current theories about the creation of the universe on his deathbed.

Alvin Pepler, who calls Zuckerman the Proust of Newark, is an ex-television quiz-show winner from a 1950's show called "Smart Money." He was caught up in the scandal that resulted when the show's producers convinced him to lose so that a goy, Hewlett Lincoln (who has been given the answers), could win. The producers' justifications for this deception parodies, yet accurately reflects, the ironic relationship between art and reality that so concerns Roth. The producers tell Pepler that they cannot ask random questions of the contestants, because then nobody would know the answers twice in a row. "You have to have a plot," they say, "like in *Hamlet* or anything else first class." To the producers, Pepler is not a contestant, but a performer, and they are making art just as William Shakespeare did,

> with a plot, and conflict, and suspense, and a resolution. . . . Does Hamlet get up from the stage and say I don't want to die at the end of the play? No, his part is over and he lies there. That is the difference, in point of fact, between schlock and art. Schlock goes every which way and couldn't care less about anything but the buck, and art is *controlled*, art is *managed*, art is always *rigged*. That is how it takes hold of the human heart.

As hypocritical as this sounds coming from the mouths of television producers, it still rings true for Roth and perhaps for the reader in an inevitable, although aesthetically troublesome, way. For it is the rigged, arranged, controlled nature of art that makes Zuckerman see himself as the "cutthroat caricaturist" of his own parents who gives graphic reports of encounters with women to whom he has been "deeply bound by trust, by sex, by love." Moreover, it is this essential characteristic of art that makes Zuckerman (and therefore Tarnopol and Roth) create novels "disguising themselves as actuality itself, as nothing less than real. . . . A book, a piece of fiction bound between two covers, breeding living fiction exempt from all the subjugations of the page, breeding fiction unwritten, unreadable, unaccountable and uncontained."

At the end of *Zuckerman Unbound*, Zuckerman is indeed unbound from those people he has been bound to by trust, sex, and love, and he stands alone, unbound even to his own past. The illusion is created that Zuckerman, the original fictional persona of Tarnopol, has escaped the limitations of the page and, even as his actions are rigged by Roth, is unbound from the very book that binds him.

Moreover, Pepler takes on the role of a new persona created by Zuckerman, as Roth's novels become peopled more and more by fictional creations of fictional creations of fictional creations. Pepler accuses Zuckerman of basing his novel *Carnovsky*, not on his own life, but on "what my Aunt Lottie told your cousin Essie that she told to your mother that she told to you. About me. About my past." In this way, Pepler, who, like Jorge Luis Borges' Funes the Memorious can forget nothing, inserts himself in Zuckerman's place, becomes his "pop self" and perhaps the subject of Zuckerman's next novel, *The Vrai's Revenge*. When Pepler reads the first paragraph of his proposed review of *Carnovsky* to Zuckerman (a review that belabors the relationship between fiction and autobiography), Zuckerman feels the way Ernest Hemingway might have felt if the lion came up to him with his review of "The Short Happy Life of Francis Macomber."

*Zuckerman Unbound* deals more explicitly with the nature of Roth's art than any other work he has written with the exception of *My Life as a Man*. Because it seems more like tying up loose ends and exorcising old ghosts, it achieves this self-reflexive nature less successfully than that earlier book. At the end of *Zuckerman Unbound*, with all ghosts (except Alvin Pepler) exorcised, Zuckerman ponders the problem of his own identity, asking: Who are you supposed to be? "No one," he answers, "and that was the end of that. You are no longer any man's son, you are no longer some good woman's husband, you are no longer your brother's brother, and you don't come from anywhere anymore, either."

The question now, for those who have followed Roths career, is: Is Roth also similarly stripped and therefore ready to begin in a new nonautobiographical key in his new novel? Or will Alvin Pepler, the creation of Zuckerman, who is the creation of Tarnopol, who is the creation of Roth, reappear, now at four removes from the author, to continue to haunt the pages of Roth's written world?

The issue of novels about novels or novels that take their own novelistic status as their subject matter is, of course, not limited to Roth. Although fictional self-reflexivity has an ancestry that dates back to the birth of the novel itself, most emphatically in *Don Quixote* (1605, 1615) and *Tristram Shandy* (1759-1767), it has only been in the last thirty years with the work of Borges, John Barth, William H. Gass, Robert Coover, John Fowles, and other practitioners of the "literature of exhaustion" that the mode has come to be a dominant one in literature. In works by these writers, technique, or the process of fiction itself, becomes the primary subject matter; and antifiction (which Gass has called simply another name for metafiction) becomes a means of exploring reality itself as a fictional creation. This shift is related to the influence that European phenomenology and structuralism has had on Anglo-American literature and criticism in its challenge to the previously dominant empiricist tradition.

Roth may be an interesting example of this trend to watch, for now that self-reflexivity and the exposing of the nature of illusion has moved into the popular media of film, for example in *Pennies from Heaven*, *The French Lieutenant's Woman*, *The Stunt Man*, and *One from the Heart*, literature may be searching for another departure. The question is: Can art's intense examination of its own artifice be pushed to even further extremes, or is the time now ripe for a reaction to such self-analysis? Philip Roth's next novel may provide some clues about the nature of such things to come.

*Charles May*

### Sources for Further Study

*America*. CXLV, November 7, 1981, p. 287.
*Christian Science Monitor*. LXXIII, June 10, 1981, p. 17.

*Library Journal*. CVI, May 1, 1981, p. 993.
*Nation*. CCXXXII, June 13, 1981, p. 736.
*The New Republic*. CLXXXIV, May 23, 1981, p. 36.
*The New York Review of Books*. XXVIII, June 25, 1981, p. 21.
*The New York Times Book Review*. LXXXVI, May 24, 1981, p. 1.
*The New Yorker*. LVII, May 25, 1981, p. 140.
*Newsweek*. XCVII, June 8, 1981, p. 89.
*Time*. CXVII, May 25, 1981, p. 90.

# CUMULATIVE AUTHOR INDEX
## 1977-1982

I

BARTLETT, IRVING H.
Daniel Webster, (79) 143
BARUK, HENRI
Patients Are People Like Us: The
Experiences of Half a Century in
Neuropsychiatry, (79) 532
BASKIR, LAWRENCE M. and
WILLIAM A. STRAUSS
Chance and Circumstance: The Draft,
the War and the Vietnam Generation,
(79) 88
BASS, JACK and WALTER DEVRIES
Transformation of Southern Politics, The,
(77) 832
BATE, W. JACKSON
Samuel Johnson, (78) 735
BATESON, GREGORY
Mind and Nature: A Necessary Unity,
(80) 536
BAUMER, FRANKLIN L.
Modern European Thought: Continuity
and Change in Ideas, 1660-1950, (78)
581
BAUMONT, MAURICE
Origins of the Second World War, The,
(79) 516
BEATTIE, ANN
Chilly Scenes of Winter, (77) 154
Falling in Place, (81) 304
BECKETT, SAMUEL
Company, (81) 184
BELITT, BEN
Double Witness, The, (78) 276
BELL, DANIEL
Cultural Contradictions of Capitalism,
The, (77) 184
BELL, MILLICENT
Marquand: An American Life, (80) 517
BELLOW, SAUL
To Jerusalem and Back, (77) 828
BENJAMIN, WALTER
Reflections: Essays, Aphorisms,
Autobiographical Writings, (79) 575
BENNETT, EDWARD W.
German Rearmament and the West, 1932-
1933, (80) 344
BERG, A. SCOTT
Max Perkins: Editor of Genius, (79) 428
BERGER, THOMAS
Neighbors, (81) 606
Reinhart's Women, (82) 671
Who Is Teddy Villanova?, (78) 899
BERGERON, LOUIS
France Under Napoleon, (82) 296
BERKHOFER, ROBERT F., JR.
White Man's Indian: Images of the
American Indian from Columbus to the
Present, The, (79) 847
BERLIN, ISAIAH
Against the Current: Essays in the
History of Ideas, (81) 9
Personal Impressions, (82) 632
Russian Thinkers, (79) 627
BERRY, WENDELL
Unsettling of America: Culture and
Agriculture, The, (79) 795

BERRYMAN, JOHN
Freedom of the Poet, The, (77) 299
Henry's Fate & Other Poems, 1967-1972,
(78) 384
BESCHLOSS, MICHAEL R.
Kennedy and Roosevelt: The Uneasy
Alliance, (81) 467
BETHELL, NICHOLAS
Palestine Triangle: The Struggle for the
Holy Land, 1935-48, The, (80) 634
BETTELHEIM, BRUNO
Uses of Enchantment, The, (77) 876
BEYERCHEN, ALAN D.
Scientists Under Hitler: Politics and the
Physics Community in the Third Reich,
(78) 743
BIDART, FRANK
Book of the Body, The, (78) 136
BILLINGTON, JAMES H.
Fire in the Minds of Men: Origins of the
Revolutionary Faith, (81) 340
BILLINGTON, RAY ALLEN
Land of Savagery/Land of Promise: The
European Image of the American
Frontier in the Nineteenth Century,
(82) 421
BINION, RUDOLPH
Hitler Among the Germans, (77) 357
BISHOP, ELIZABETH
Geography III, (77) 326
BLANCHARD, PAULA
Margaret Fuller: From Transcendentalism
to Revolution, (79) 422
BLANKFORT, MICHAEL
Take the A Train, (79) 737
BLOOM, HAROLD
Poetry and Repression, (77) 627
BLUM, JEROME
End of the Old Order in Rural Europe,
The, (79) 188
BLUM, JOHN MORTON
Progressive Presidents: Roosevelt,
Wilson, Roosevelt, Johnson, The, (81)
665
V Was for Victory, (77) 880
BLY, CAROL
Letters from the Country, (82) 444
BODE, CARL, Editor
New Mencken Letters, The, (78) 603
BÖLL, HEINRICH
And Never Said a Word, (79) 29
Bread of Those Early Years, The, (77)
119
Missing Persons and Other Essays, (78)
577
BONKOVSKY, FREDERICK O.
International Norms and National Policy,
(81) 445
BONNIFIELD, PAUL
Dust Bowl: Men, Dirt, and Depression,
The, (80) 244
BONTEMPS, ARNA and LANGSTON
HUGHES
Arna Bontemps-Langston Hughes
Letters: 1925-1967, (81) 57
BOOTH, PHILIP
Before Sleep, (81) 71

II

III

IV

V

VI

VII

VIII

IX

X

XI

XII

XIII

XIV

XV

XVIII

XXI